Contract and Commercial Manag
The Operational Guide

CW01024101

This book is dedicated to the memory of Margaret Carey who inspires us all by planting small seeds of partnerships and friendships worldwide.

CONTRACT AND COMMERCIAL MANAGEMENT
THE OPERATIONAL GUIDE

Van Haren
PUBLISHING

Colophon

Title:	Contract & Commercial Management - The Operational Guide
Lead Authors:	Tim Cummins, Mark David and Katherine Kawamoto
Contributory Authors:	IACCM
Copy Editor:	Jane Chittenden
Publisher:	Van Haren Publishing, Zaltbommel, www.vanharen.net
ISBN Hard copy:	978 90 8753 627 5
ISBN eBook:	978 90 8753 628 2
ISBN ePub:	978 90 8753 972 6
Print:	First edition, first impression, October 2011
	First edition, second impression, February 2012
	First edition, third impression, January 2014
Design and Layout:	CO2 Premedia bv, Amersfoort – NL
Copyright:	© Bmanagement 2011

For any further enquiries about Van Haren Publishing, please send an e-mail to: info@vanharen.net

Foreword: By the Board Members of IACCM

As executives and senior managers in some of the world's major corporations, each of us has had direct oversight for aspects of contract and commercial management within our business. Individually, we have observed the growing role and complexity associated with contracting and this has been reinforced through our experience as elected members of the IACCM Board of Directors.

It is clear that contract management is an increasingly diverse and important organizational competence and this demands greater consistency and efficiency in its management. It also requires more creativity and the tools and techniques that are necessary to improve the quality of judgment and decision-making. Each of us is aware of the difficult balance between control and compliance on the one hand, and agility and flexibility on the other.

While such tools and techniques are fundamental building blocks, the skills, competence and professionalism of the people who work in and around the contract management space are also key. This book represents an important contribution to that heightened competence, offering as it does the first comprehensive view of contract and commercial operations from a cross-industry, bi-partisan, worldwide perspective. It is an ambitious work that seeks to rise to the challenge of managing business relationships in today's complex global markets and equipping the practitioner with a robust 'body of knowledge' that reflects leading practices.

Dave Barton	Director of Contracts	Agilent Technologies
Adrian Furner	Commercial Director	BAE Systems
Diane Homolak	Global Legal Operations Quality and Strategy Manager	Hewlett-Packard
Monu Iyappa	Executive Vice President Legal	GMR Infrastructure Ltd
M.C. McBain	Vice-President Global Alliances & Contract Development	IBM
Steve Murphy	Vice President, Contracts	Raytheon Integrated Defense Systems
Nancy Nelson	Global Contracts Director	CSC
Gianmaria Riccardi	Director, Commercial Business Management Europe	Cisco Systems
Alan Schenk	VP Common Process, Contracting & Compliance	BP

Craig Silliman	Senior Vice President & General Counsel	Verizon
Margaret Smith	Executive Director Contract Management	Accenture
Peter Woon	VP, Procurement and Supply Chain	Marina Bay Sands Pte Ltd

Preface

About this book

All around us is rapid change and growing complexity. The demands on contract negotiation and management have never been greater. There is an urgent need for sustainable practices that support flexibility and dynamic change.

Those who are responsible for contract management must heed the calls for greater collaboration, more innovation, greater readiness to simplify the rules and procedures that will allow management to address turbulent market conditions. At the same time, we must achieve increased rigor, greater compliance and improved controls in our contracts and relationships.

Making sense of these conflicting issues demands a more consistent view of contracts – their purpose, their structure and the terms we use within them. It demands the use of common methods and techniques, common terminology and attitudes to risk and opportunity.

To add to these pressures, we are witnessing a steady increase in the influence of emerging markets and newly powerful economies that cause us to question some of the well-established traditions of contract management and the law. This means we must engage in dialog between different business, legal and social cultures to establish clear and mutually acceptable first principles.

It is in this environment that we offer this Operational Guide, to equip those who must manage the complex contracting requirements demanded by today's global markets.

About the authors

The International Association for Contract & Commercial Management (IACCM) is a non-profit organization that owes its origins to the growing complexity of world trade and the consequent need for increased and more consistent skills, knowledge and procedures in the field of contract and commercial management.

The Association was founded in 1999 to fill the gap in international understanding and competence in contracting. Its purpose is to explore and disseminate 'best practice' in the formation and management of trading relationships, as well as equipping business managers and negotiators with the knowledge required to navigate within today's environment.

Through ongoing research, IACCM provides many of today's top corporations and government agencies with the knowledge they require to develop the process and skills that ensure the integrity and success of their contracts and commercial practices. IACCM is unique in representing both buyers and sellers, ensuring a consistent body of knowledge and reducing the risk of unsuccessful outcomes through the promotion of mutual understanding and more collaborative working.

This book is an operational guide to those practices and methods. It has been compiled and reviewed by a wide variety of professionals and academics, representing multiple industries, countries and commercial disciplines. The book is therefore a practical resource for anyone involved in contracts, their negotiation or management.

Tim Cummins,
CEO, International Association for Contract & Commercial Management
www.iaccm.com

Acknowledgements

We would like to thank the team of experts who contributed in such a major way to this ground-breaking publication. They have spent much time and kindly given their expertise to encourage better practices and understanding worldwide.

First of all we thank the Lead Authors: Tim Cummins, Mark David and Katherine Kawamoto for pulling together the structure, the approach and much of the text. They inspired the most professional approaches from the supporting teams as well as dedicating much time to drafting, refining and re-refining the final work. Their persistence, patience and humor is greatly appreciated.

We also wish to thank the international team of experts who contributed to and reviewed the manuscript. Respected experts world-wide have been kind enough to spend hours supporting other team members, reviewing text and also sharing invaluable experience. Always positive and professional, these experts demonstrate the true strengths that can be found in this area.

Team

Ravindra Abhyankar	Purwa
Natarajan Balachandar	TECHNIP INDIA LIMITED
Gerlinde Berger-Walliser	ICN Business School
Guillaume Bernard	Schneider Electric
Alexander Beyer	complon
Chris Caro	IBM
Arthur Cohen	Praxis Consulting, LLC
Jacqui Crawford	BP
Arvind Dang	Central Park Estates Private Limited
Xavier Darmstaedter	DACOTA Consulting
Alvaro de Leon	Transcom
Vivek Durai	tman Law Partners
Eric Esperne	Dell Healthcare & Life Sciences
Jesús Álava Fernández	INITEC TR Group
Jean-Marc Fraisse	NNEPharmaplan
Ernest Gabbard	Allegheny Technologies
Claudia Gerlach	Nokia Siemens Networks
Max Gutbrod	Baker & McKenzie – CIS, Limited
Margo Lynn Hablutzel	CSC
Roselle Harde	Accenture
Robert J Hatfield	Improvement Advisory Services

Phoebe He	Avnet
Jan Heidemann	Consultant
Paul Carter Hemlin	Contract Management Direct
René Franz Henschel	Aarhus University
Christof Höfner	Nokia Siemens Networks
Diane Homolak	Hewlett-Packard Company
Linda Hopkins	Accenture
Doug Hudgeon	Operating Efficiency
Monu Iyappa	GMR Group
Agustín Garzón Jordán	Agilent Technologies
Amit Kapoor	Mahindra Satyam
Tiffany Kemp	Devant Limited
Anton Klauser	Nokia Siemens Networks
Ingo Köhler-Bartels	Dimension Data Germany
Mireille Lafleur	Alstom (China Investment Ltd.)
Tom Larkin	Solathair Management Consulting, LLC
Ashif Mawji	Upside Software Inc.
Tim McCarthy	Rockwell Automation
Peter McNair	SEA Business Management Pty Ltd
Stefan Moecking	Unisys Outsourcing Services GmbH
Daniel Nagel	BRP Renaud & Partner
Jamie Napper	Best Buy Europe / Carphone Warehouse
George Neid	Raytheon Company
Nancy Nelson	CSC
Viv Nissanka	BBC
Jeanette Nyden	J. Nyden & Co
Thomas Oswald	Booz & Company
Makarand Parkhi	Aquatech Systems
Elekanyani Phundulu	Transnet Freight Rail
Carlos Pistone	Alcatel-Lucent
Philippe Poisson	BT Global Services
Ramakrishna Potluri	SAP
Gianmaria Riccardi	Cisco Systems
Ignacio Romera	INNOKEY
David Ross	BT
Greg Russell	Project Advice Services Limited
Ronnie Sefoka	Sasol
Satender Sharma	Petrofac International
Jan Ole Similä	Nord-Trondelag University College
Abhishek Singh	Adhani Institute of Infrastructure Management
Nigel Spink	Thales Rail Signalling Solutions Inc

Kokkula Srinivas	Bharat Biotech International
Mark Swarthout	CSC
Anita Thussu	Infosys Technology
Rajeev Thykatt	Infosys BPO Ltd
Mike Tremblay	HP
Amina Valley	SAIC
Daniel Vohrer	The Linde Group
John Weiss	The Highland Group
Lyndon White	Dial Before You Dispute Pty Ltd
Joginder Yadav	Nokia Siemens Networks
Alexander Yavorchuk	Oracle Inc.
Edwin T Y Yeo	

The views expressed in this title by the contributors are personal and it should not be assumed that they represent the formal views of their employers or organizations.

We would also like to thank Jane Chittenden, Copy Editor, for her work in finalizing the manuscript.

Contents

Foreword: By the Board Members of IACCM   V

Preface   VII

Acknowledgements   IX

1   Introduction: contract management – a global context   1

1.1   The challenge of choice   2

1.2   Impacts upon contracting   2

INITIATE PHASE

2   Understanding markets and industry   13

2.1   Identifying potential markets   15

2.2   Market segmentation   19

2.3   Competitive analysis   23

2.4   Product definition   24

2.5   Contracts role in PLM   25

2.6   Identifying risks   26

2.7   Matching the agreement to the market   26

2.8   Summary   27

3   Understanding requirements   29

3.1   Why requirements matter   29

3.2   Early involvement   30

3.3   Defining the role of requirements   31

3.4   Factors driving improved specifications   33

3.5   Increased frequency of volatility and change   34

3.6   Managing inevitable change   34

3.7   Strategic and cultural fit   34

3.8   What goes wrong   35

3.9   Five key milestones   36

3.10   Tools and techniques for ensuring milestones are met   40

3.11   Common causes for delay or failure   46

3.12   Summary   52

**4   Financial considerations – understanding cost and
      setting charges   53**
    4.1   Introduction   53
    4.2   Bid strategy: why does cost matter?   53
    4.3   The role of the contracts professional   54
    4.4   Bid strategy: the importance of cost analysis   55
    4.5   Contract standards as cost management tools   57
    4.6   Contract terms as a cost management tool   58
    4.7   Contract terms that can potentially reduce cost   60
    4.8   Dependencies   63
    4.9   Bid strategy – how to set your charges   63
    4.10   Contract terms – differences that may have financial impact   65
    4.11   Bid strategy – differences that may have financial impact   66
    4.12   Pre-bid phase: cost-benefit analysis   68
    4.13   Summary   76

5   Aligning risk through financial modeling   77
    5.1   Introduction   77
    5.2   The importance of economic alignment   77
    5.3   The basics of financial modeling   78
    5.4   The MediaCity case study   78
    5.5   Making judgments   80
    5.6   Financial model elements   80
    5.7   Some basic principles and terms   81
    5.8   Pricing mechanisms   82
    5.9   Gainshare and shared benefits   83
    5.10   Other factors   84
    5.11   Summary   84

**6   Routes to market – partnerships, alliances, and distribution and
      sourcing options   85**
    6.1   Primary types of contracts used in large businesses   85
    6.2   Use of agents and representatives   86
    6.3   Local, national and international laws   97
    6.4   Identifying potential suppliers and relationships   100
    6.5   Evaluating project scope   103
    6.6   Options for contracting   105
    6.7   Summary   106

7	**Request for Information**	**107**
7.1	Request for Information – Pre-Bid phase	107
7.2	Selecting and assembling the RFI team	108
7.3	Beginning the RFI	110
7.4	RFI content	110
7.5	Change control and support	115
7.6	Experience and stability	115
7.7	Functional, technical and business requirements	115
7.8	Software and hardware requirements	116
7.9	Budgetary pricing	117
7.10	Support	117
7.11	Security requirements and considerations	117
7.12	Review, validation and distribution	118
7.13	RFI conclusion	118
7.14	Alternatives to an RFI	119
7.15	Supplier's perspective	120

8	**Undertaking a Terms Audit**	**121**
8.1	Reasons for undertaking a Terms Audit	121
8.2	Purpose of a Terms Audit	123
8.3	Consequences of inappropriate terms	123
8.4	When to audit	124
8.5	The warning signs	126
8.6	Understanding impacts	128
8.7	Undertaking a Terms Audit	128
8.8	Sample audit	130
8.9	Summary	131

BID PHASE

9	**Bid process and rules**	**135**
9.1	Introduction	135
9.2	Bidding process preliminaries	136
9.3	Bidding vehicles and when to use them	136
9.4	Supplier's requirements response	139
9.5	Scoring and ranking the suppliers	139
9.6	Managing the RFx process	141
9.7	Evaluating responses – overall score	144
9.8	Supplier notification and the BAFO process	145
9.9	BAFO process and final contract	146
9.10	Supplier award notification	146

9.11   Supplier post-award issues   146
9.12   Summary   147

10   Request for Proposal preparation and content   149
10.1   Introduction   149
10.2   Defining, managing content and drafting bid requirements 150
10.3   Pricing information (seller only)   159
10.4   Security, health and safety requirements and consideration 160
10.5   Managing the evaluation process (buyers)   160
10.6   Summary   163

**11   Responding to a Request for Information or Request
       for Proposal   165**
11.1   Introduction   165
11.2   Background: the procurement process   165
11.3   Identifying an opportunity   167
11.4   Execution of non-disclosure agreements   167
11.5   Contracts professional involvement   168
11.6   Why have a bid process?   168
11.7   Key elements of a bid process   169
11.8   The role of the contracts organization   172
11.9   Contract management – adding commercial value   173
11.10   The bid goes on   174
11.11   Approvals   175

12   Request for Proposal management   177
12.1   Introduction   177
12.2   Role of the contracts professional   178
12.3   The RFP document   178
12.4   Supplier selection and RFP distribution   182
12.5   Contract negotiations   187
12.6   Notifying unsuccessful suppliers   188

13   The influence of laws on the bid process   189
13.1   Introduction   189
13.2   Basic principles   189
13.3   The influence of laws: international summary   190
13.4   The influence of laws: UNCISG   195
13.5   Offer and acceptance   201
13.6   Conditional offers and revocation of offers   203
13.7   Problems with preliminary arrangements   205

13.8	Closing the deal	207
13.9	Pre-contractual negotiations	208
13.10	Arbitration and alternative dispute resolution	211
13.11	Local law: civil code versus common law	218

14 Costs identification **221**

14.1	Cost overview	221
14.2	Activity-Based Costing	222
14.3	Tax consequences	222
14.4	Allocations	223
14.5	Opportunity costs	224
14.6	Cost of poor quality	224
14.7	IT systems costs	224
14.8	Hardware costs	225
14.9	Software costs	225
14.10	Infrastructure costs	225
14.11	Personnel costs	226
14.12	Other costs	226
14.13	Consensus on approach	226
14.14	Credibility of assumptions	226
14.15	Risk assessment	227

15 Opportunity evaluation **229**

15.1	Introduction	229
15.2	Involvement	230
15.3	Preparation	231
15.4	Evaluating the scope	235
15.5	Assessing the risk	239
15.6	Avoiding reference pitfalls	245
15.7	Evaluating the relationship	246
15.8	Judging customer sophistication	248
15.9	Evaluating future opportunity	250

16 Proposal preparation **253**

16.1	Introduction	253
16.2	Is it worth bidding? The four critical questions	253
16.3	Understanding the customer	256
16.4	Understanding the customer – buying criteria	257
16.5	Understanding the competition	258
16.6	Reviewing and assessing risks	259
16.7	Working with the pursuit team	260

16.8   Responding to the RFP documents   261
16.9   Responding to the RFP documents   262
16.10 Characteristics of successful bidders   263
16.11 Customer contact   263
16.12 Green Team review   265
16.13 Red Team review   266
16.14 The Executive Summary   266
16.15 Bid submission   268
16.16 Negotiations and pricing   269
16.17 Relationship selling   271

17   Evaluating the proposal   273
17.1   Overview   273
17.2   The evaluation framework   273
17.3   Primary categories   277
17.4   Product evaluation criteria   278
17.5   Intangible criteria   282
17.6   Other evaluation components   284
17.7   Implementing the evaluation framework   285
17.8   Alternative approaches   288
17.9   Factors for success   289
17.10 Summary   290

DEVELOPMENT PHASE

18   Contract and relationship types   293
18.1   Introduction   293
18.2   The importance of relationships   293
18.3   Primary types of contracts used   295
18.4   Product and services contracts   295
18.5   Contracts for services   301
18.6   Solutions contracts   306
18.7   Outsourcing   308
18.8   Turnkey contracts   313
18.9   Summary   316

19   Contract terms and conditions overview   317
19.1   Overview   317
19.2   Start right   317
19.3   Purchase contracts and why they matter   318
19.4   Areas that the contract should address   319

19.5	Types of contract and some issues	321
19.6	Separating business and legal terms	322
19.7	Key elements in contracts	323
19.8	Summary	334

20   **Technology contract terms and conditions**   **335**

20.1	Introduction	335
20.2	A specialized discipline	335
20.3	Definitions	339
20.4	Scope of Use	343
20.5	License types	344
20.6	Assignment and rights to use	346
20.7	License versus ownership	347
20.8	Audits and compliance	349
20.9	Software maintenance services	349
20.10	Hardware contracts: overview	351
20.11	Performance	352
20.12	Support and maintenance services	353
20.13	Upgrades	356
20.14	Compatibility	357
20.15	Services contracts: overview	357
20.16	Statements of Work (SOWs) and milestones	358
20.17	Termination	359
20.18	Summary	361

21   **Term linkages, managing cost and risk**   **363**

21.1	Overview	363
21.2	The challenges of term linkages, managing cost and risk	363
21.3	Contract structure	364
21.4	Negotiated terms	365
21.5	Active versus passive terms	366
21.6	Terms Audit	366
21.7	Term analysis	367
21.8	Shifts have impact	369
21.9	Paradigm shifts	369
21.10	Legitimate terms that miss the point	371
21.11	Performance cost of the deal	372
21.12	Acceptance provisions	373
21.13	Preferences – supplier versus buyer	373
21.14	Multi-country projects	373
21.15	Contract pricing arrangements	374
21.16	Summary	380

22 Statement of Work and Service Level Agreement production   381

22.1   Introduction   381

22.2   What is an SOW?   381

22.3   Why is an SOW required?   382

22.4   Basic process for developing an SOW   383

22.5   How do SOWs and SLAs relate?   386

22.6   Service Level Agreement (SLA)   387

22.7   IACCM outsourcing survey   388

22.8   What is included in an SLA?   388

22.9   Other SLA considerations   393

22.10   Summary   394

23 Drafting guidelines   395

23.1   Introduction   395

23.2   Clarity   395

23.3   Contracting transformation   396

23.4   The contract document   397

23.5   Why a written contract?   398

23.6   What form should be used?   400

23.7   Rules of contract interpretation   400

23.8   Other contract interpretation guidelines   401

23.9   Background to contract drafting   402

23.10   Drafting best practice   403

23.11   Before you start   403

23.12   Drafting a complete agreement   404

23.13   Amendments and attachments   404

23.14   Drafting techniques   406

23.15   Contract terminology   406

23.16   Writing style   409

23.17   Tools   412

23.18   Summary   413

NEGOTIATION PHASE

24 Approaches to negotiations – framing, strategy and goals   417

24.1   Negotiations overview   417

24.2   Introduction to framing, strategy and goals   420

24.3   Framing   420

24.4   Goals   423

24.5   Strategy   424

24.6   Stages of negotiation   427

24.7 Leveraging your experience 434
24.8 Planning and tactics 434
24.9 Tools for establishing a negotiation foundation 438
24.10 Summary 440

25 Negotiation styles – positional versus principled negotiations 443
25.1 Introduction 443
25.2 Perspective and precedent 443
25.3 Negotiation options: positional versus principled 444
25.4 Factors that influence your choice 445
25.5 Positional versus principled negotiation 446
25.6 Characteristics of positional negotiating 446
25.7 Characteristics of principled negotiation 447
25.8 Recognizing positional negotiation 447
25.9 Advantages and disadvantages of positional negotiating 448
25.10 Advantages and disadvantages of principled negotiating 450
25.11 Non-negotiable issues 452
25.12 Countering the positional negotiator 453
25.13 Is principled negotiation worthwhile? 455
25.14 Summary 457

26 Negotiating techniques 459
26.1 Introduction 459
26.2 Preparation 459
26.3 Negotiation power 463
26.4 Abuse of power 465
26.5 Opening offers 466
26.6 Physical/logistical considerations 468
26.7 Connecting with the other side 469
26.8 What happens if there is no agreement? 472
26.9 Technological challenges 475

27 Tactics, tricks and lessons learned 479
27.1 Introduction 479
27.2 The last gap 479
27.3 How to cross the last gap in negotiations 484
27.4 Competitive tricks and ploys 488
27.5 Another perspective 493
27.6 Summary 494

MANAGE PHASE

28 Manage phase overview   **497**

28.1   Introduction   497

28.2   Manage phase overview   498

28.3   Contract management activities   504

28.4   Contract management software   506

28.5   Contract management resource planning   508

28.6   Communication   512

28.7   Summary   516

29 Transition   **519**

29.1   Introduction   519

29.2   Contract management after signature   519

29.3   Contract analysis   520

29.4   What is 'the contract'?   522

29.5   Analyzing and understanding terms and conditions   523

29.6   Core contract elements analysis   525

29.7   Setting priorities   526

29.8   Transition meeting   527

29.9   Transition and organization   528

29.10   Transition - meeting goals   529

29.11   Summary   530

30 Risk and opportunity   **531**

30.1   Introduction   531

30.2   Understanding risk and opportunity   531

30.3   Understanding and managing opportunity in contracts   535

31 Monitoring performance, tools and techniques   **539**

31.1   Introduction   539

31.2   The contract management role   540

31.3   Post award contract management activities   542

31.4   Status reviews: internal   557

31.5   Status reviews: external   558

31.6   Typical issues and problems   558

31.7   Summary   559

32   **Change control and management**   **561**

32.1   Introduction   561

32.2   The realities of change   561

32.3   Designing a change control procedure   565

32.4   Contract claim   572

32.5   When parties do not want a change control and management process   574

32.6   Case studies   575

32.7   Summary   577

33   **Dispute handling and resolution**   **579**

33.1   Introduction   579

33.2   What is a dispute and what causes a dispute?   580

33.3   Common operational disputes causing ongoing problems   584

33.4   What does the contract say about dispute resolution?   586

33.5   Possible consequences of a formal dispute   588

33.6   How to avoid a dispute   590

33.7   Dispute handling and resolution: recovery   591

33.8   Resolution steps: from least to most complex   594

33.9   Solutions to disputes: negotiation   595

33.10   Solutions to disputes: mediation   596

33.11   Solutions to disputes: arbitration   597

33.12   Solutions to disputes: litigation   598

33.13   Case study: an actual dispute and how it was resolved   599

33.14   Summary   601

34   **Contract close-out and lessons learned**   **603**

34.1   Introduction   603

34.2   Types of termination or close-out   604

34.3   Final acceptance   604

34.4   Final acceptance: actions   606

34.5   Expiry of term   607

34.6   Termination   607

34.7   Expiry of term or termination: actions   608

34.8   Close-out - key risks after the delivery of the contract   610

34.9   Continuing obligations   611

34.10   Lessons learned   613

34.11   Summary   614

Annex A Glossary   **615**

Annex B IACCM training   **625**

CHAPTER 1

Introduction: contract management – a global context

The concept of trade is a characteristic unique to the human species. With each advance in human communications, the complexity of trade has increased[1].

It is this growth in complexity that drove the need for contracts, as a written record to 'memorialize' the negotiation that had taken place and which committed the parties to some future exchange of value.

Over time, the knowledge gained from past transactions led to a body of experience which became enshrined in laws or customs, influencing the process by which trading relationships were formed, the parties involved in their formation and the means by which they were recorded.

Today, we are at the beginnings of a new era for communications – a world connected via electronic networks that allow unparalleled speed, enabling relationships to be formed and managed in ways that were never previously envisaged. It is the unknown nature of this networked world that represents a new level of complexity for society as a whole, but especially for the politicians who are charged with its regulation and the business leaders who must navigate through the risks and opportunities that it represents.

A survey by IBM Corporation[2] revealed that 79 percent of Chief Executive Officers (CEOs) see 'increased global complexity' as a major challenge over the coming years. Of course, mastering complexity has been a key trait of humanity over the centuries, but at this time it has taken on a new intensity. At its heart, according to these CEOs, is the difficulty created by 'the growth of interconnections and interdependencies'. What do they mean by this – and how does it relate to the world of contract management?

---

1 'Before the Dawn': Nicholas Wade
2 IBM Corporation '2010 IBM Global CEO Study' May 2010

1.1   The challenge of choice

Globalization has driven a massive expansion of choice, in particular in the world of trade. Whether as a buyer of goods and services or as a seller, there are few corners of the world where it is no longer possible to find a trading partner. For some, this means new markets; for others, it may mean access to new resources, improved skills, or lower cost supplies. The problems that come with this explosion of choice are many. For example, how do you assess which options are best? How long will that assessment take you? What risks may be associated with your choice – and how do you find out about them? And at the same time as one business is on this journey of discovery, so are its competitors – are they moving faster, or smarter? Will they innovate before me? Do you any longer know who your competitors are – who may emerge from parts of the world where you did not previously play?

Businesses face dramatic and exciting new opportunities, but also very real threats. Many of the CEOs were concerned about issues such as customer loyalty and reputation risk. Why? Because networked technologies mean there are no secrets any more and customers can be accessed by competitors, new and old, at far lower cost. It has become much easier for a customer to undertake regular re-bids using e-procurement technology. It has become inevitable that the media, or bloggers, or disgruntled members of the public will highlight any slip in quality, governance standards or organizational integrity. Misjudgments, mistakes and ethical lapses take only minutes to appear on the worldwide web.

1.2   Impacts upon contracting

Many of these issues touch upon the contracting and commercial capabilities and practices of the organization. The CEO survey offered more detailed insight. Executives are hoping for greater creative leadership from within their organizations. They highlighted three particular areas for focus. They want staff who are:

- Better at managing risk
- Better at eliminating rules and bureaucracy
- Better at forming and managing customer relationships

In the opinion of many executives today, those charged with contracting would certainly be found wanting on at least one of these focus areas – and in some cases, all three. The question for many professionals is whether they wish to have change imposed upon them by others, or to be drivers of that change – the 'creative leaders' who are being sought by the CEO community.

The contracting process can operate at two very distinct levels. In some organizations, it is seen as the discipline through which corporate or organizational policies and practices are implemented. Those charged with the role of contract negotiation or management are essentially compliance managers or administrators, either preventing or limiting the scale of deviation from 'the rules'. Their discretion may be limited or non-existent and they typically rely on others to make operational decisions. They have no meaningful role in the strategy that underlies the standard policies or practices – and feel no sense of responsibility for ensuring that these standards enhance competitiveness or economic performance.

At the other end of the scale, the contracting process is seen as a key instrument for quality control and brand management. It is understood to be not only the instrument through which policy and practice are implemented, but also the closed-loop system through which they are maintained or challenged. Contract and relationship structures, individual terms and conditions and contract governance procedures are constantly under review to ensure they support market advantage and reinforce brand image and reputation.

In either case, operational management of contracts is a critical discipline. This book focuses on the operational aspects, with limited reference to the over-arching strategies and policies that determine the quality of the contracts themselves. These will be addressed in a separate Contracting Strategy volume.

This book is about contracting. But of course there are multiple forms of contract and therefore it is important to define the scope of the types of agreements or relationships that are covered.

First and foremost, the book is about business contracts and it is predominantly about business-to-business relationships. Within this there is some discussion and distinction between public and private sector and passing reference to issues associated with consumer contracting. While the primary focus is on the provision of goods and services (including intangibles such as software), there is also reference to distribution, alliances, teaming arrangements and joint ventures. Finally, it is written with a global perspective, acknowledging the variations created by different cultures and jurisdictions.

Philosophy

It may appear strange to start a book on contracting with a statement of philosophy, but it is important to state that this work has the aim of increasing the probability of successful trading relationships. We present the view that contracting must become a core business competence to assist in understanding, evaluating and overcoming the complexity and challenges of today's global markets.

This position is reflected in the work of a growing number of academics who show particular interest in the connection between contract management and relationship management. Specific examples include Nobel prize winner Professor Oliver Williamson, author and educator Kate Vitasek, outsourcing guru Professor Leslie Willcocks and a host of thought-leaders who collectively belong to 'the school of pro-active law' (Professors Tom Barton, Kaisa Sorsa, Henrik Lando, Rene Henschel and Gerlinde Berger-Walliser being notable examples).

To achieve that end, it seeks to be inclusive of a wide range of viewpoints and to encourage balancing of interests and needs, in a way that is appropriate to the extent and duration of the contract that is being formed. It encourages openness and honesty, but of course we cannot prevent our readers from using the information in whatever way they deem appropriate. In general, we suggest that adversarial or confrontational relationships do not tend to work; but as with all things, this is not always true. Suppliers in particular may choose to stick with domineering customers and learn how to leverage their relationship. But we see limits in how much such a relationship will achieve.

This philosophy leads us in general to warn against unbalanced or inappropriate allocations of risk. It also encourages the parties to question transactional, as opposed to relational, behaviors, recognizing that all choices carry a cost. A good example of this readiness to question is contained in an article by British economist John Kay, entitled 'It's time to rip up your unwritten contracts'. In it, Kay suggests that the shift from performance based on long-term relationships to performance based on transactional contracts has reduced input prices, but damaged longer-term profitability.

We seek to explain and bring those costs to the surface, in ways that will assist good business judgment and support sustained business success.

The role of law

The role of law is acknowledged as fundamental to contracting practice and process. Any contracts expert must appreciate the impacts of different legal traditions – for example, statute law versus common law. These differences will impact the attitudes of the contracting parties; they will affect the length and content of the contract; they are likely to influence the language and will certainly determine the choice of words.

This book briefly describes different legal systems and how these may impact certain aspects of the contracting process. However, it is not a legal textbook and takes the position that contracts are first and foremost economic, rather than legal, instruments. The earliest contracts were to record business and economic principles; the legal aspects came later and in many cases appear to have overwhelmed or obscured the original purpose, often undermining the economic value or rewards. In attempting to redress this issue, there is no suggestion that the law – and the role of lawyers in contracting – is not important. It is simply to remind readers that the law is just one of many interested parties – or 'stakeholders' – in this process and by allowing it (or any other stakeholder) to dominate, we will frequently end up with a poor or failed outcome.

The conflict between rules and good outcomes is perhaps most apparent (or at least most widely reported) in government and public sector contracting. There, rigid application of acquisition procedures can often work against the interests of those they are designed to protect.

Understanding the other side

Human relationships cover a spectrum, from the mere acquaintance to the deeply committed. As they cross this spectrum, the extent and depth of communication, mutuality of interests and cooperation shifts. The importance of considering the needs and interests of the other party grows and indeed becomes a determinant of the relationship's success and a dependency for its increased depth.

Thus it is with business relationships and that is why this book presents the perspectives of both customers and suppliers. In some areas, their interests converge; in others, they may appear polar opposites. But in every case, the parties form a relationship because each believes it will be better off with it than without it. The contracting process is a voyage of discovery – first in establishing the potential for a match, then in attempting to shape and define it, finally in overseeing its implementation and – perhaps – termination.

It is in fact ironic that many of those who lead today's contracting process or contract preparation come from professional backgrounds that encourage adversarialism and 'winning'. Lawyers, procurement specialists and even CEOs tend to be highly competitive individuals and their training promotes a 'them and us' attitude, often bereft of trust. Yet today's business philosophy is more and more about 'collaboration' and 'partnering' in ways that are entirely alien to many established contracting models and procedures. The old world was about 'winning the deal' on terms that were to your innate advantage; the new world is about 'winning the outcome' – that is, ensuring that each side is motivated to optimize the final results by a sense of shared benefits.

All good contracts and successful relationships require some level of collaboration and they tend to flourish if there is an appreciation – and respect – for the needs of the other side. Hence this book seeks to offer its readers an appreciation of alternative values and points of view. This does not imply weakness or compromise; such understanding in fact strengthens any deal-maker or negotiator, or anyone preparing a draft contract or managing a trading relationship. Through understanding, we can consider a range of possible 'value trades'; we can reduce cycle times; we can encourage all stakeholders to develop consensus and to work towards common goals and targets. Ultimately, a failure of understanding leads to weakened communication and heightened probability that the contract will fail.

This is reflected in research such as IACCM's annual 'most frequently negotiated terms' study, which also explores the most common sources of claim and dispute. Unclear requirements, mismatched measurements and selection criteria and inadequate communication and governance standards are the drivers of disagreement and potential failure.

Traditional contracting does not always reflect this view. Indeed, many procurement processes or standard forms of contract appear deliberately adversarial. Large corporations tend to a 'take it or leave it' approach – they see limited need or purpose in efforts to understand the other side. Such an approach is of course legitimate and supports internally driven views of managing risk and efficiency. However, this book may lead many to question the extent to which such an attitude is beneficial and it will provide the counter-party with suggestions on how to deal with 'the non-negotiator'.

Overall, our purpose is to increase the probability that contracts will succeed and will underpin healthy, mutually rewarding relationships. And that is why we consider it essential that the book covers the point of view of both sellers and buyers.

Who does contracting?

It is inevitable that many readers will want to know what skills are needed or what organizational model will work best to ensure successful contracting. This book does not seek to answer those questions in any depth because the answer is 'It depends'. A companion work on 'Contracting Strategy' will address these topics in depth and offer detailed guidance on how to develop the skills and resources needed to ensure successful contract procedures.

Therefore this book endeavors to focus on the operational aspects of contracting, remaining neutral on who it is that performs the relevant tasks. In truth, the scope of work that is covered will rarely be performed by just one individual, function or department. Contracting is by its nature a diverse activity, drawing on many areas of skill and knowledge.

However, it is inevitable that certain terms are used in the book that may imply certain job roles or organizational alignments, so it is important to briefly describe or define what these terms mean.

Commercial: in general, commercial management or the commercial process tends to be broader than the role or activities implied by the term 'contract management'. However, we find that gap is narrowing (see the definition of contract management below). 'Commercial' is often used to describe activities that are non-technical and can therefore embrace areas such as sales, marketing and business operations. Our definition is not so wide and embraces only those areas that are of direct relevance to the structuring, content and performance of the contract. We see the role of a 'commercial manager' or of the 'commercial process' to ensure that all relevant stakeholder views have been incorporated and evaluated, to ensure that the needs (of the customer) and capabilities (of the supplier) have been aligned. In this sense, we view the contract as a tool to undertake and oversee 'commercial assurance' of a deal or relationship and this may be from either a customer or supplier perspective.

Contract management: historically this has been viewed as a more administrative – and therefore much narrower and more reactive – activity than commercial management. It has often been a role that safeguards the rules or practices of others, rather than changing or questioning those rules. However, this book challenges that narrow definition and positions contract management as an activity equivalent to commercial management.

Procurement: as with other terms in this section, today we face a wide variety of job titles for those in the procurement function and indeed, in many organizations, procurement activities may be conducted by people who are not procurement professionals or within a procurement organization. Unless the context is clearly otherwise, the word must be seen as a broad description of an activity, rather than a formal job role or functional definition.

Contract or Commercial Manager: as stated above, we have in general sought to avoid the implication of specific job roles. These terms should be taken as indicating the performance of particular tasks, irrespective of who is actually performing them. We recognize, for instance, that 'the contract manager' in many cases might actually be a project manager, or a lawyer, or an engineer or a sales representative – and indeed, during the lifecycle of a specific contract, all of these individuals may be involved in performing contract-related tasks. However, we also recognize that many of our readers will be dedicated contracts or commercial professionals who see these terms as job titles – even though they too will acknowledge that the process we lay out in this book probably goes beyond the average scope of a contract professional's job. This breadth of content may lead some to question whether the book goes too far in its claims to be about contracting operations. Our perspective here is that if we are to produce successful contracts and trading relationships, we must understand the overall process by which they are produced and take steps, as professionals, to ensure the quality of that process and our eventual work product.

Contracting process: as the previous definitions explain, this book seeks to describe a high-performing business process through which successful contracts and trading relationships are formed and managed. To the extent that it is practical, we try to describe differences that will result from the types of contract or relationship that a business wishes to enable. For example, high volume commodities demand a fundamentally different model from complex services or major, long-term projects. However, while the complexity of the task to be performed is dramatically different, the list of tasks remains highly consistent; the big difference is over who performs those tasks, how they are performed, and the time it takes to reach completion. It is these factors, of course, that lead us back to the opening statement about variations in job roles, skills and organization.

The structure of this book

The aim of this book is to provide an operational guide to contracting that is independent of variations in organization or role. It is structured to reflect a process-based view, broken into the following phases:

Initiate: this phase is devoted to ensuring understanding of markets and their interaction with business needs and goals. It explains the importance of aligning these factors with contract structures, terms, policies and practices, to increase the probability of successful trading relationships and the overall efficiency of the contracting process. Without such alignment, contracts rapidly become viewed as an impediment to doing business.

Bid: this phase explores the bidding and proposal activities undertaken by each party to determine the extent of the 'fit' between needs and capabilities. It examines the financial aspects of the proposed relationship and highlights the legal and regulatory issues surrounding bid and proposal activity.

Development: this phase is dedicated to the development of an appropriate form of contract and the considerations and issues that most frequently require attention. It provides a framework that should enable better understanding of the risks associated with the specific relationship that is being evaluated and also provides a base for negotiation planning.

Negotiation: this phase provides an in-depth guide to negotiation of a contract. It recognizes that a growing number of negotiations are today 'virtual', using technology as an alternative to face-to-face meetings. It also highlights many of the issues and challenges that contract negotiators tend to encounter, both within their own organization and with the behavior or attitudes of the other side.

Manage: this phase examines the approaches needed to ensure successful implementation and management of the signed agreement. Many contracts span multiple years and it is frequently the case that they undergo major changes and, potentially, fundamental renegotiations. It is this phase that determines whether or not the results or outcomes envisaged at the time of contract signature are in fact achieved – or perhaps even exceeded.

Moving forward

This book is based on content that was developed for IACCM on-line training modules. It has been developed in response to the wishes of many contracts practitioners to have a formal operational guide that supports their day-to-day activities, and can also be used by others who have a periodic need for guidance on contract management.

As with most disciplines, contract management is not static. Indeed, today's global business environment suggests that we face a period of dramatic and rapid change in the way we create and evaluate terms, conditions and contracts. It is envisaged that 'best practice' will demand regular updates. These will be achieved in part through the on-going interactive nature of IACCM on-line training materials, where students form active discussion groups and where message boards offer a forum for new issues and approaches.

Readers are invited to use these forums, accessible at www.iaccm.com, to share their experiences and raise questions that are not adequately answered by this book. The Lead Authors also welcome direct communication and undertake to ensure that all contributions are taken into account for future editions of this work.

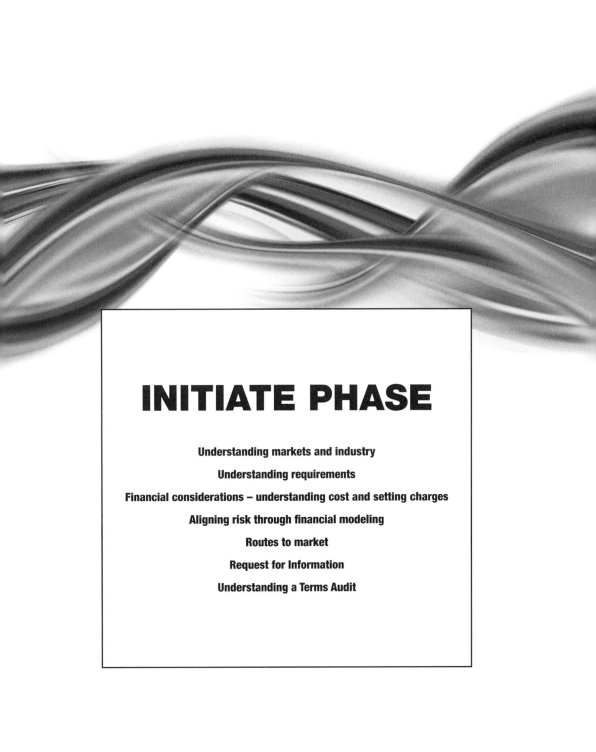

INITIATE PHASE

Understanding markets and industry

Understanding requirements

Financial considerations – understanding cost and setting charges

Aligning risk through financial modeling

Routes to market

Request for Information

Understanding a Terms Audit

CHAPTER 2

Understanding markets and industry

This chapter provides best practice perspectives in understanding the markets within which you offer or procure your products and services. A comprehensive understanding of the marketplace enables effective alignment of commercial contract activities, such as the contract and its terms and conditions, the sourcing/sales strategy, negotiations and the management of the agreement.

The concerns for the supplier are in understanding how to go to market, understanding competitive forces and managing the inherent risks with a potential customer . The buyer's concerns focus on how to achieve 'the best deal' , how to maintain leverage over the supplier and how to cope with changing needs and demands, as well as broader supply risk issues. The extent to which these concerns are fully understood and analyzed will determine the success or failure of the sales or purchasing strategy.

Defining products or services with appropriate terms and conditions is a critical element of product development and marketing, and this is not just a one-time activity. Throughout the product lifecycle, terms and conditions must undergo regular audit and update to reflect changing market conditions, new technologies or functions, business capabilities and customer demands. This chapter describes and explores this alignment and how it is managed in best practice corporations.

The real issue is that terms and conditions should at the very least support successful business – and at their best, represent a source of competitive advantage. Too often, that is not the case. A study conducted by IACCM in 2011 revealed that only 10 percent of business managers believe that their organization's terms and conditions provide a source of competitive advantage, with 40 percent stating that they represent a source of disadvantage. This is significant, because a misalignment between contract terms and other aspects of the sales and marketing cycle or business strategy will damage brand image, create delayed or lost sales, increase the volume of disputes or dissatisfied customers, or result in missed opportunities to develop value or innovate.

It is worth considering how close your company is to best practice in this aspect of terms and conditions management. Some aspects to explore are:

- How closely linked is your contracts group with product or service development marketing?
- Can you describe the differences in product or service packaging for each major customer or market segment and the impact that this has had on the associated terms and conditions?
- How frequently do deals have to be handled as special bids?
- What are the primary areas that need negotiation, or where your company policies cause a 'no bid' or rejection of customer requests?
- What business-related issues do customers and suppliers identify as sources of frustration or difficulty in dealing with your company?
- How many contracts result in post-award disputes?
- What documented process is there for regular re-evaluation of terms and conditions for each product or service?
- What are the typical bid and contract cycle times for each market segment?
- Are these longer or shorter than they were a year ago?

If you don't have the answers to these questions, or if some of them show negative results, it means you don't have the right linkages in place. So what should you do about it?

Best practice companies have clearly identified contract resources aligned with each product and service area and embedded at an early phase of development, to ensure the terms and all related business practices, policies and procedures have been considered before the product reaches the market. And they remain in place to oversee ongoing trends, special bids, shifts in product features, upgrades, new solutions packaging, changing markets, or regulatory and competitive conditions.

While even this is not foolproof, it certainly helps the company provide a consistent approach and avoid extensive internal confusion and case-by-case exceptions. Best practice companies have thought through the role of contracts in their marketing and business policies.

For example, Microsoft once had a reputation for inflexibility in its terms and conditions. But that reputation – whether or not it was deserved was in many ways a direct consequence of its success. Given its product dominance, there was no reason for Microsoft to spend time and effort negotiating contract terms. Indeed, a hallmark of successful brands is that they don't negotiate and, in general, they don't accept significant risks. As markets mature and competition grows, the attitude to contracting shifts. Today, for example, Microsoft is one of the leaders in evaluating new and improved contract terms and contracting strategies that can drive faster, simpler and more balanced contract negotiation.

So if you have unique or dominant products or services, you set the terms and conditions. Only as the desirability or unique characteristics of your brand and its products decline or become challenged by competition is there a need to show real flexibility in terms.

There are six key elements that the contract management professional, whether buy-side or sell-side, needs to understand:
- Identifying potential markets
- Market segmentation
- Competitive analysis
- Product definition
- Identifying risks
- Matching the agreement to the market

2.1 Identifying potential markets

For most companies, the contract management process (buy-side or sell-side) is not as well integrated with product lifecycle management (PLM) as it could be. The results of this are missed opportunities for incremental revenues or customers and potential loss of competitiveness. It may also mean chasing after inappropriate markets or customers – those who demand commitments you are not equipped to meet. At its worst, inappropriate contract terms can build or reinforce negative market image for your brand and create an opening for your competitors.

Understanding potential markets is the first necessity for both the supplying and buying organizations. In today's global economy, the complexities of the marketplace have grown exponentially from the basic local offerings of the last century. For potential suppliers, it is not just about finding the right location that matters, but also finding the right mix of product/offering, value-added services, competitive pricing and innovation that will help make your organization a dominant player in the market. For the buying organization, piece-price costing is a small concern compared to the impacts of transportation and regulatory fees, intellectual property concerns, supplier viability risks, and the ecological and sociological impacts from the suppliers you choose, or the subcontractors your supplier chooses. Let's take a look at five practical examples that illustrate these points in more detail.

First, let's take the example of aluminum casings for power-tools. The product itself is a forged metal casting that will require minimal milling / grinding / polishing before being assembled into a complete power-tool. As a supplier wanting to enter the market, you would need to first understand the basic requirements to manufacture this product. Availability of bauxite, a strip-mining operation to gather the ore, a foundry to process the ore into aluminum, and a reliable transportation system to ship your customer's product are just a few of the core requirements. Since the availability of bauxite in the world is a known factor, and since it is easier to ship the finished product rather than the processed ore, locating your business near the processing foundry is probably the best idea. For the buying organization, however, production and assembly facilities could be located anywhere in the world, therefore access to transportation by rail and ocean need to be considered due to the weight of the finished product. Also for the buyer, the lead-time from the foundry to the production floor is a major concern.

Understanding the market dynamics leads both buyer and supplier to some major questions such as:
- Who should own the inventory in the case of damage during shipment?
- How long would it take the buyer to find a new supplier if necessary?
- How much business does the buyer represent versus the return on the investment to supply their goods?
- Are the dies, or molds, for the casings owned by the buyer or the supplier?
- Who retains the intellectual property rights (that is, dimensions, weights, milling points, air/fluid ports, etc) to the casing?
- And what risks do the buyer and supplier take if a competitor can produce a more durable and lighter version?

Second, let's consider a similar product produced from more common raw materials, corrugated paper packaging. For the supplier, the concerns in production are relatively similar: access to lumber, a mill that transforms wood to paper, machinery that transforms paper to corrugated board and transportation to the customer. But for the buyer, the location of the supplier is much more critical. Corrugated paper is not as durable on the high seas as aluminum castings. High moisture in the air can damage product faster and more thoroughly so it is necessary to turn away from a global market and look more regionally or locally to the production facility. Also, packaging lines are notorious for not being 100 percent to the specifications of their design. This means that having a local representative of the supplier nearby to adjust the sizing on the cut corrugated board is necessary to ensure an efficient packaging operation. The questions asked previously are still of importance to both the buyer and supplier, but new questions can also arise, such as:
- Who carries the cost of the local representative that makes sure the corrugated production works with the packaging lines?
- Since lead-times for delivery are shorter than ocean voyages, how frequently will shipments be made?
- Can the supplier adopt Just-in-Time Inventory practices to accommodate the buyer's new production requirements?

Third, let's consider the example of a large multi-national bank contracting with a supplier to produce footballs as part of a marketing campaign in the Euro 2008 football competition. A condition of the bank's contract signed with the supplier of the footballs was a ban on the use of child labor. However, the supplier was not certified by the Pakistani government and some of the footballs produced were being sewn by men, women and children in a Pakistani village at a half the regular cost or approximately 39 centimes per football. Both buyers and suppliers of products need to understand the reputational impact of their business dealings and ask questions such as:

- What are the environmental impacts from the production of the goods being purchased / sold?
- What are the sociological impacts of the production of the goods being purchased / sold?
- What are the intended uses of the goods being bought?
- How can association with Company X affect my company's reputation?

Fourth, let's take a look at an example of an abundant resource found around the world with minimal transportation requirements and (potentially) 24/7 availability: computer programming. In almost every corner of the world there can be found a software programming house that will help companies on the other side of the world meet their programming needs for a fraction of the cost it would require to hire programmers in their home regions. Companies from every major industrialized nation are scouring the world for the next low-cost country to invest their programming funds for more efficient software programs produced faster and for less money. Entry into the market is fluid from the perspective of suppliers as long as they are able to keep up with the ever-growing changes.

The key questions from the supplier focus on the intellectual property rights of the developed material. But in some parts of the world, the lines defining intellectual property rights are blurred or sometimes completely ignored. Buyers need to be careful in placing their trust in areas that might sell or steal information in order to make a profit. Another great risk in this arena is turnover of the core resource, people. Basic economic theory dictates that when demand is high, suppliers can charge higher and higher prices until the supply and demand curves equal out. In the case of outsourced or offshore programming, this translates into large turnover of programmers due to their ability to go to competitive suppliers for a higher salary. Quarterly labor turnover of 20 percent is not unheard of in this sector, which translates into a loss of efficiency for the supplier and the buyer. Before entering into this potential market, both the buyer and the supplier need to understand the total cost of doing business and how to maintain a steady supply of reliable services to ensure success.

Finally, the 1990s and 2000s have ushered in remarkable changes and growths of new markets. Both buyers and suppliers are trying to compete in an ever-expanding global economy and therefore need to understand how to create a market – possibly by using a concept from another industry or through innovation.

The contract management field has experienced this growth of a new market in the past 10 years through the expansion of the internet. In the late 1990s and early 2000s several new e-sourcing or e-contracting portals were developed at the height of the 'dot-com' era. Before the development of these e-tools, contracting and Requests for Proposals (RFPs) were manually intensive processes that went on for weeks on end. Auctions were conducted with hammers at real-estate sales or high-end auction houses. The concept of using the internet, itself an unproven technology, to reach a globally diverse marketplace seems today like a natural progression. But during the development of these tools, a huge concern was whether the contract management profession would embrace this untried technology-finding financial backers to support development, and beta-test customers to help test-drive the software bugs. Finally, getting suppliers to comply with electronic Requests for Information (RFIs) and e-auctions was a daunting task to open up this new marketplace. Contract management professionals in major organizations were wary of the information being sent through an untried and (potentially) unsecured medium. Today, only a few of the original developers still survive. Most have been absorbed by large software houses after breaking ground on software development and beta-testing 'bug fixes.'

Despite all this technology and the apparent simplification that it has introduced, as a supplier with an innovation or a buyer trying to find a supplier for a new product line, key questions remain:

- Is the new product under development something that the customer is asking for?
- If not, then where will I find customers? How will this product generate its own demand for future growth?
- As a buyer with a new product line, how will I find a supplier who can work in the new material / process design that will help transform my product offering?
- Who owns the development risk, the buyer or the supplier? Who owns the development cost?
- What happens if the supplier (developer) goes out of business due to lack of funds? Who owns the intellectual property rights or source-code for software?
- What happens if the developing company (buyer) wants to have more than one supplier in the future? How long can I (the supplier) protect the revenue stream for the new product / process design?

From a contract manager's perspective, the understanding of markets and their inherent risks is vital information when it comes to constructing an agreement and defining terms and conditions specific to the market. This aspect is addressed in the penultimate section of this chapter.

2.2   Market segmentation

Companies have traditionally tended to segment their markets either on customer lines or on product lines or on geographic boundaries.

For example:
- Consumer versus small business versus large enterprises
- Corporate users versus departmental users
- Country variations or looking at buyer groups and extended enterprises
- Hardware versus software versus services

Companies often segment their organization and marketing plans by these product lines and/or geography. This is entirely understandable – the products may have unique characteristics in those different markets – and of course it is important to monitor the profitability of each of them. But such segmentation can also complicate sales. For example, if customers or markets require a mix of products and services, or if customers cross your geographic boundaries, then a product-based or geography-based view is likely to create internal contention and battles over revenues and resources.

So best practice companies have to look at markets and customer sets in a holistic way. They need to ensure that their internal organization and capabilities reflect and remain in line with a market-based view, not an internally driven perspective.

This needs-based segmentation may cut across many of the traditional lines and sources of information. For example, ways you might look at your customers include distinguishing new from incumbent; exploring the proportion of incumbents who are terminating or switching to alternative suppliers; distinguishing those who buy locally from those demanding global or multi-country agreements. Such analyses enable investigation of more detailed requirements or reasons for lost loyalty. This enables exploration of terms that might better address specific needs, or capabilities that you may need to seek from your supply network.

An example of the type of action that such analysis can generate comes from the aerospace industry, where one major contractor was determined to remain at the forefront of innovation. This proved successful at winning new business, but the contracts staff noted that they were experiencing increased incidence of liquidated damages claims from many of their new customers. Investigation revealed that the claims mostly related to late delivery and the cause of these late deliveries was tracked to the suppliers of the 'innovative' products and services. Further analysis showed that the worst offenders were small companies that were full of bright engineers and developers, but lacked embedded project management skills. Rather than threaten them with harsh penalties or termination, the contract manager proposed that her company should place project management staff within these companies to eliminate short-term exposures and to develop longer-term capability. This proved highly successful, not only eliminating the delays and the costs of liquidated damages, but also generating a high level of loyalty from these fast-growing and innovative suppliers.

If you segment successfully it will lead to higher margins and limit the need to negotiate. This is a subject that is not solely of interest or the preserve of marketing or sales organizations. It is a matter of importance to contracts professionals to ensure that we are both aware and involved in market segmentation and related research to optimize our contribution to business success.

In judging markets, one tool that can be used to identify and evaluate the external forces affecting a particular market, industry or country is to evaluate the Sociological, Technological, Economic, Environmental and Political factors (STEEP) that impinge on the market, industry or country in which you are buying or selling your product. Some analysts have added 'Legal' to these factors and rearranged the mnemonic to PESTEL[3], or PESTLE. For convenience in this chapter, we will include legal issues under the Political segment, as most legal requirements stem from the political implications of the host and/ or source countries. STEEP provides an added level of depth to later risk analysis by highlighting the need for appropriate contingency plans.

This is one tool to help understand the marketplace and can be used in conjunction with SWOT (Strengths, Weaknesses, Opportunities and Threats) analysis and Porter's Five Forces in order to:
- Identify the relative strength of each factor and consider how it will shape the strategic approach in the future
- Identify likely changes to the STEEP landscape
- Draw conclusions as they relate to the potential sourcing strategy

As discussed previously, you first need a clear definition of the scope of the market. Then, using the STEEP analysis grid above (Figure 2.1), generate a checklist to brainstorm all of the known or unknown forces that could exist. This allows you to classify the forces and ask probing questions to quantify each force and the effects on the business and contracting strategy. Each force has specific questions that will help break down the element into more manageable subsets.

---

3   Gillespi (2007) Gillespie: Foundations of Economics – Additional chapter on Business Strategy, Oxford University Press

STEEP Analysis Template

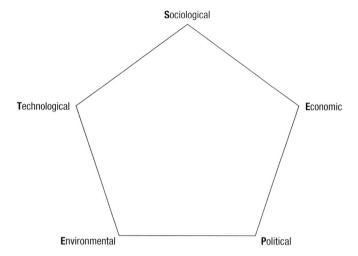

Figure 2.1:   STEEP analysis matrix

Sociological:

- What is the standard of education locally?
- What is the local government's attitude towards minimum wages and minimum working age?
- What relevant work ethics or practices apply and what are the legal requirements? Do we know what future legislation may bring?
- Is a skilled workforce available and in what quantity?
- What is the culture with regard to training the workforce?
- What is the propensity to labor disputes or industrial disruption?
- What local cultures/religious aspects are there to deal with? (E.g. work on Sundays/ Saturdays; observance of deadlines or commitments etc)
- To what extent may local standards be in conflict with the standards expected in other markets and be a potential source of reputation risk (e.g. attitudes to bribery, health and safety, the rights of children or minorities)?

Technological

- To what extent is modern technology available – power supplies, computer use, internet, telecommunications? Does the local government promote awareness of e-commerce and support its adoption and use?
- What is the average company investment in enterprise solutions?
- How willing are local suppliers to accommodate new technologies/embrace change?
- What is the technological rate of change?

- How quickly do new technologies come to market? How does this affect our depreciation policies for capital expenditure?
- What level of obsolescence is there?
- How technologically complex is the product/service we are purchasing/selling?

Economic

- What is the economic growth in the relevant countries?
- What are the trends in turnover, profit and growth in the countries we use?
- What are the current infrastructure levels?
- What are the investment levels in the infrastructure in the countries that we currently and potentially source from?
- What are the export/import duties/quotas? Are they likely to change over the next three to five years? (These can add dramatic cost increases to moving goods around.)
- What are the economic conditions of the market – monopoly, competition etc?
- How stable is the currency? What provisions are necessary to cover fluctuations?
- Are there any favorable loans/grants available from government for existing or new factories?
- Is there a history of shortages of key commodities or disruption to supply?

Environmental

- What is the local government's attitude to the environment? How does this fit with our ethical stance?
- What are the attitudes of our customers to the environmental impacts of our products? How does this fit with our ethical stance?
- What are the supply market's current environmental issues / concerns?
- What is the cost (financial) of seeking a solution with a high environmental impact? How does this fit with our ethical stance? How could this affect our reputation in the industry?
- What quality / acceptance / import or export requirements may be relevant?

Political

- How well does the government support exports?
- How stable/what is the likelihood of political change?
- How could such changes affect our business?
- What legislation affects the local business environment – taxation, incentives etc?
- How stable is the political climate of the country concerned?
- How effective is the judiciary if we have a claim to make within this country? What is the likelihood of getting compensation for stolen goods or damage to company property?

- What is the judiciary system based on, precedent or legislation? Does the legislation tend to protect the buyer) or the seller when it comes to disputes?
- What, if any, trade barriers exist? What is the current trading relationship like between countries?

From a contract manager's perspective, market segments have a direct influence on the minimum number of 'boilerplate' contracts that will need to be thought through. Indeed, in some markets. It may be that contracts are almost irrelevant, because of the challenges of enforcement and the culture that dismisses their relevance. A contracts professional must explore whether further sub-categorization is necessary before standard boilerplate contracts are drafted for each segment, or some alternative approach to managing risks is devised.

2.3 Competitive analysis

An important input to contract management strategy is an understanding of the competitive positioning of individual companies within the market. The first step in taking this approach is to score the companies on the axis of negotiating power ranging from low to high. Typically, companies closer to the low end will be customers who depend on the service or products the supplier provides or suppliers who provide commodity products with many competitors. Companies at the other end of the axis will tend to have more options available to them than to source these services or products from the supplier or a dominant market position. Alternatively, these will be customers who the supplier thinks can generate a high degree of repeat business or can help the supplier enter new markets via referrals. Whatever the reason, the supplier must aim to retain these customers, albeit at the cost of providing relatively higher contractual flexibility. However, rather than providing contractual flexibility to all such customers, the supplier should consider an alternative dimension typifying the varying strength of its products or services. Suppliers very rarely have only one product or service. Often, the suite of services or products on offer can be categorized as dominant or non-dominant. Based on the two dimensions of buyer power and product / service dominance, four different contract management strategies can be considered.

	'High power' suppliers	**'Low power' suppliers**
'High power' customers	Attempt standard contracts.' Battle of forms' likely.	Customer likely to impose standard contracts
'Low power' customers	Supplier may impose standard contracts.	Attempt standard contracts

Table 2.1 Contract management strategies

A company must be careful in determining for which products or services it wishes to enforce standard contracts. If customers or suppliers have suitable alternatives available to them, there is a high likelihood that a non-negotiable approach will deter prospective buyers or suppliers and may even preclude an initial exploratory approach or discussions that lead to increased value.

IACCM's recent benchmark studies show that 92 percent of organizations maintain standard contracts for their business-to-business trading, but only 11 percent succeed in imposing them 'all the time'. At present, the buyer is far more likely to succeed in applying their standards.

2.4 Product definition

Providing products or services with appropriate terms and conditions is a critical element of product development and marketing, and this is not a one-time activity. Throughout the product lifecycle, terms and conditions must undergo regular audit and update to reflect changing market conditions, new technologies or functions, business capabilities and customer demands. For most companies, the terms and conditions process is not well integrated with product lifecycle management. The results of this include missed opportunities for incremental revenues, customers, additional value, alternative suppliers and potential loss of competitiveness. It may also mean chasing after inappropriate markets, suppliers or customers – those who demand commitments you are not equipped to meet. At its worst, inappropriate contract terms can build or reinforce negative market image for your brand and create an opening for your competitors.

Best practice corporations view PLM as a key discipline. A phase of PLM covers commercialization. Some companies operate with comparable rigor in developing service offerings. In general, the linkages between PLM and procurement are well defined. But often, similar connections with the contracts process or organization are either ignored or are non-existent. As a result, many products come to the market with ill-considered terms and conditions, often highly standardized and poorly aligned with market conditions. This weakness is often sustained throughout the product lifecycle.

Consider these examples from the technology sector.

- Stratos Communications Technology – where one major vendor licensed it only for use within the US – for a customer set wanting global communications.
- RISC systems with embedded code licensed from ATT and containing pass through terms that prevented customers from making modifications – even to their own software.

- A much-heralded video and music on demand service by two major international corporations – but overlooked the need to gain agreement from the owners of the copyright.
- In the scramble to move from commodities to solutions, many computer manufacturers raced to acquire relationships with software and service providers. Deals were struck in the thousands – typically without any thought to the resources or the process needed to create marketable offerings. Subsequent research revealed that more than 90 percent of these relationships never generated any revenue for either party.

All of these are examples of product or service developments that lacked commercial discipline. Each of them failed to draw on the sort of analysis and questioning that any experienced contracts professional should have provided.

2.5 Contracts role in PLM

In some companies, there are dedicated contracts professionals within each product or services group, involved from the outset and throughout the product lifecycle. This works well so long as they remain up-to-date with external events and pressures, thereby proactively identifying the need for, or validity of, proposed term or offering updates. Secondly, they must have a method and incentive to work with other groups of contracts professionals to develop integrated solutions, to share ideas, to ensure that changes do not create major exposures to policies or practices in other parts of the business.

In many industries, the role may be driven by regulatory conditions and the need to ensure compliance. But this fails to address the specific needs of the market. How individual contracts professionals work will vary, but those in PLM need to have greater awareness of marketing, creativity and strong analytical skills. For example, one major corporation had its commercial contracts staff trained to lead market-planning workshops. These sessions focused on the value propositions needed to achieve market success, translating them into the commitments and capabilities that would be expected by each major market segment. These commitments and capabilities were then tested against corporate policies, processes and resources to ensure that they could be undertaken – and the risks that would result if there was failure. Often these sessions created awareness of a whole range of performance undertakings or guarantees that the product management team had not even considered in their design – and which the procurement team had certainly not enabled through contracts they put in place with key suppliers.

Such planning remains necessary throughout the product life-cycle – for example, in creating periodic promotions or in determining end-of-life withdrawal or continuing obligations.

2.6   Identifying risks

The issue of performance commitments is perhaps the most difficult area. We all want to make ambitious claims for our products, especially if they face hurdles to entry such as significant innovation, or because we are searching for competitive differentiation. But if we claim capabilities that will deliver substantial savings, or dynamic cycle time reduction, or opportunities to establish market leadership, then the potential customers are likely to want guarantees of success and compensation for failure. These may take the form of onerous liabilities, or liquidated damages. They may take the form of guarantees of specific performance. They may take the form of demands for exclusivity or protected rights. The terms related to a product have to be commensurate with the perceived risks associated with their acquisition or use. They must address those concerns at least as well as the competition – and potentially better – but it is a fine balance. Differentiation through terms and conditions must be seen as positive, and not because they mask a performance flaw. Products and services are acquired to do a job, not because they offer better compensation when they fail.

A frequent weakness in product marketing is the inability to support performance or value claims with either formal guarantees or clear financial benefits ('return on investment'). This has made many buyers cynical towards their suppliers' assertions of 'value-add' or 'competitive differentiation'. If such benefits are genuine, it is important for the contracting process to ensure that they are quantified and result in tangible differentiated commitments.

2.7   Matching the agreement to the market

Contracts professionals need, therefore, to ensure that the contractual 'wrapper' they provide to the sale or purchase supports, re-enforces and adds value to the relevant sales or business strategy as demonstrated by the following examples.

In the first case, we'll look at a situation involving data storage systems. These are certainly commodity products – and that is how they were treated by product managers at one major computer manufacturer. They came to market packaged with standard purchase prices, volume discounts and standard terms on warranty and warranty service. Performance commitments were based on the standard specifications and a standard 4-hour call-out time. Now, let's look at this from the perspective of two customers, both requiring 18 units. One customer was the New York Stock Exchange, which planned to use the systems to support and record real-time trading. This was a mission-critical application and the customer needed close to 100 percent availability during trading hours. That meant a comprehensive back-up plan and onerous performance terms, with significant liquidated damages for failure. The 4-hour call-out time was unacceptable.

The second customer was a global oil and gas company requiring the systems for monthly financial reporting by its international operating divisions. While important, this application meant that there was greater tolerance for reduced support levels and the customer was more interested in a discount.

In an ideal world, by product marketing staff and their colleagues in Contracts should have recognized market or customer segmentations and the need for different term-based offerings. In a contracts department, we pride ourselves on our risk management skills. In this case, risk had not been understood or managed. The customers faced significantly different levels of risk; a smart supplier would have taken advantage of this and created distinctive approaches with prices based on service levels. This would have made them easier to do business with, potentially differentiated them from the competition and removed an uphill battle over justifying their prices.

The second situation similarly reflected a standard 'one size fits all' approach, based on rigid internal policies that made life simple for the staff functions, but showed no understanding of market trends. A licensed program with use limited to enterprise members just didn't fit a market where there was increasing networking across companies. For Sales, trying to sell to a joint venture consortium, there was no way to breach the internal rulebooks. Even worse, because each situation was handled by separate staff groups or lawyers with no central recording system, the company was not even aware of the increasing frequency of such demands. It had also failed to act on its own revised public strategy, which talked to the digital networked economy but continued to offer terms and conditions reflecting a traditional country and enterprise based business model. That left frustrated customers and sales representatives battling a bureaucracy that simply quoted rulebooks and would not take ownership to develop new terms and contract offerings.

2.8 Summary

On the sell-side, grasping market needs and understanding how these vary by industry or other form of segment (c.g. customer size, geography) will drive the creation of appropriate forms of offering and terms to package a product or service. On the buy-side, these needs must be enabled with appropriate supply contracts and relationships. Having said that, the understanding of markets and industries has wider ramifications than just product definition and positioning. It can also influence negotiation strategies. Often the buy-side negotiations are driven by the standard procurement metrics of price, delivery, and quality, without apparent understanding of the sell-side commitments. This often leads to post signature problems that could have been prevented if both the buyer and the supplier understood their respective markets better.

CHAPTER 3

Understanding requirements

It is of great importance that requirements and contracting strategy are aligned at the outset. Indeed, there is growing evidence that failure to clarify requirements and the associated contracting structure is the biggest single cause of poor performance. This chapter looks at the issues relating to the requirements that will be included in a contract, whether emanating from the buyer, the supplier, the wider marketplace, industry standards, law, regulations, or custom and practice. It provides the reader with:

- An understanding of why requirements matter
- Knowledge of techniques for establishing and validating requirements
- The ability to distinguish requirements from solutions
- Awareness of common causes of failure or delay
- The ability to allow for and manage change

3.1 Why requirements matter

It may come as no surprise that the quality of the Statement of Requirements weighs greatly on the success of the project. The requirements definition activities will result in a document that is the functional cornerstone of the contract, as well as the authoritative guide for solution design.

The benefits of robust, detailed requirements include achieving a better solution, lower costs, and improved implementation and adoption. Deficient requirements can lead to wasted time, high levels of frustration, a decision to proceed with the wrong solution, or ultimate failure of the project altogether.

In many cases, achieving exact alignment is impossible. So some deviation from requirements is to be expected, and the best possible outcome will be achieved by choosing the closest fit. In this case, the purchasing team needs to prioritize requirements so that key criteria are met; and the selling team must do likewise. Indeed, in situations where innovation is a goal, the contract may need to be based on very general requirements that envisage 'what' is to be achieved without either side knowing 'how' to achieve it. These situations demand a distinctive approach, often known as 'agile contracting', which assumes frequent change as a fundamental element of the relationship and accepts that success may not be achieved.

The requirements do, of course, include the functional and technical aspects of the particular solution being purchased. There will also be a host of other matters to be taken into account in determining the best fit, such as:
- Timescales for implementation
- Cost of solution (external – paid to suppliers)
- Cost of solution (internal – purchaser's resources required to make it a success)
- Legal and contractual risks
- Technical and implementation risks

An analysis of requirements that takes all of these elements into account may produce a very different outcome from one that assesses functional requirements in isolation. In reality, businesses need to be comfortable with the overall cost-benefit/risk ratio of a new solution and should not allow this broader picture to be dictated by the technology alone.

There also needs to be a recognition that requirements change. Often contracts professionals act as if this never happens or should not happen when the reality is that change is a fact of life – particularly in contracts for non-commodity products or that are medium to long term in duration. There is a risk that Procurement's aversion to 'scope creep' can result in levels of inflexibility that frustrate desirable and necessary change.

3.2   Early involvement

One of the most common complaints from those responsible for contracts is that they were 'involved too late'. By this they mean that they were not engaged in the process of requirement setting (buy-side) or evaluation (sell-side). The problems that result from this are several:
- Requirements are often not clear or well documented, causing back-tracking and delays when drafting the contract or associated documents.
- Risks and consequences are often poorly assessed, resulting in complex, perhaps adversarial, contract negotiations.
- Requirements should drive the contract and relationship structure and these elements therefore must be considered in parallel or they will generate some level of conflict.

If those who perform the contracts role are frequently involved too late, they must question why it is that other functions are failing to understand their value. Might it be because they are associated with highlighting problems, rather than offering creative solutions to the identified requirements?

3.3 Defining the role of requirements

Requirements definition applies to all contracting activities, including acquisition of property, plant and equipment, software development, parts and sub-assembly manufacturing, and in some cases, complete outsourcing arrangements. Requirements are the:

- Basis for the Request for Proposal (RFP) and responses
- Framework for guiding appropriate solutions
- Basis for pricing the project
- Foundation for negotiating the contract
- Key component for communicating the solution details among stakeholders
- Critical contract component or reference
- Basis for determining acceptance of the project
- Basis for change control later in the implementation phase of the project.

Strategic alignment and business value

Development of the solution should be done against performance expectations, such as return on investment (ROI), process improvement, cost reduction, or risk mitigation. Strategic direction will be likely to influence the priority of functionality, features, terms and conditions. For example, companies pursuing an aggressive acquisition strategy will value a solution's market position and integration capabilities, whereas a company that has wide internal adoption of a particular solution will value leveraging the existing investment in installation, training and support. The key strategic requirements are often expressed in terms of:

- Can the product, service or solution be configured to align with current infrastructure or strategies
- Will it achieve the target ROI?
- How will it perform against scorecard metrics?
- Will usability and effectiveness translate into easy and thorough implementation or adoption?
- Is the supplier capable of supporting customer strategies – for example, innovation, flexibility, required levels of cultural fit?

In assessing value, it is also important to consider acquisition alternatives that may differ from the way you have traditionally acquired or evaluated a product or service. For example:

- While 'green IT' may be more expensive to purchase, it may diminish costs in another budgetary area, such as energy use.
- Are there alternatives to traditional payment or commitment methods – perhaps lease or rental, versus outright purchase?
- Has a service-based offering emerged in a category where historically the main options were product based? This might allow a switch to use-based or performance-based charges.

Continuous innovation by suppliers results in the need for fundamental re=appraisal of acquisition strategies, budgeting and value assessment. It may also create a need to explore several requirement alternatives.

Ease and efficiency

In many cases, the detailed functional requirements may drive to a limited number of options based upon technology capabilities and supply constraints. The internal governance structure may limit possibilities to a few options in order to:

- Align solutions across divisions
- Leverage current investments
- Keep maintenance costs low
- Facilitate integration with existing systems, suppliers or business process
- Facilitate centralized support
- Enhance corporate data flow
- Reduce users' learning curve
- Minimize disruption associated with change

Balancing standards with 'best of breed'

At some point, the functional requirements for a particular solution may be at odds with company policies and standards, or the conflicting demands of different stakeholders. At this point, the debate between 'best of breed' and corporate standards begins – with governance requiring substantial justification for deviating from those standards.

The increased costs of implementation, maintenance, support and training need to be offset by enhanced functionality and ultimately, ROI. In some cases, corporate governance may preclude any consideration outside corporate standards.

Risk and cost avoidance

Accurate and complete requirements are critical in terms of risk mitigation. More thorough requirements mean:

- A greater understanding among stakeholders
- The ability to anticipate cultural and technical issues
- Clearer communication with between customer and supplier
- Reduced cost of poor quality and rework
- An agreed platform for the management of future change

To the extent that the requirements fail to clearly define the outcome, the costs for both parties can explode. This may be in the form of , pricing that includes unnecessarily high contingency factoring, costly change procedures, low satisfaction and adoption rates, contention throughout the implementation and delivery phase and potentially, failure or rejection of the product or service. Involving suppliers in proposing alternative ideas or approaches can help manage this by identifying options from which the best approach can be followed.

Increasingly, it is recognized that 'good practice' includes the facilitation of direct and managed interaction between user groups and suppliers to ensure that end user needs are understood. In this case, the role of Procurement is to support and manage such discussions so that there is proper control and to oversee requirement prioritization.

3.4 Factors driving improved specifications

The key factors driving improved specifications are:
- Growing user sophistication
- Greater complexity of technical environments.

Growing user sophistication
The need for more complete requirements is driven by the increased sophistication of users and customers, including increased expectations for productivity and flexibility, and a need to implement strategic programs.

Greater complexity of technical environments
The need for increased quality of requirements statements also reflects a complexity of the environment, including interdependencies among and within systems and networks. As an example, an insurance company was looking to improve financial reporting by consolidating applications, going from four applications to two. Initial requirements identified 13 application interfaces that needed to be developed and tested. During the course of development, the number of data 'handoffs' shot to 57, dramatically increasing the time and cost to build the application, migrate and reconcile data, and test all the systems in the integrated environment. Better quality initial requirements would have flagged up the high number of interfaces, resulting in more realistic cost and time budgeting, and a more successful project outcome.

3.5 Increased frequency of volatility and change

The growth of interconnections and interdependencies in today's globally networked business environment has multiplied the sources from which uncertainty and change may emanate. Floods in Pakistan, ash clouds over Iceland and earthquakes in Japan are examples of the disruptive events that would be difficult and highly inefficient to predict. We know that recurrent economic upheavals are also outside the skills of risk managers to anticipate, either in terms of severity or timing (if they were predictable, we would have only wealthy risk managers).

We must distinguish risk *forecasting* from risk *management.* The levels of forecasting accuracy are highly variable; our ability to manage risk events should be embedded. But certainty over requirements, 'cumulative' changes can become impossible to manage. The issues we face may be regulatory, environmental, political, economic, social or technical in nature. For example, the defense industry has undergone wrenching shifts in recent years, as conventional threats gave way to terrorism, long-running attempts at 'nation building' and unpredictable theaters of conflict. Given the long duration of programs in this industry (often 30 years or more), the ability to manage requirements has become a major source of competitive difference and 'agility' is a critical competency for all participants in the supply chain.

3.6 Managing inevitable change

While requirements should be as definitive as possible to eliminate poor interpretation of design and functional elements, they must allow for flexibility. Some change is inevitable, and the requirements document must be considered from the outset as the foundation for change control – or even the document that establishes as a key requirement the supplier's competence at managing change. Some contracts today are awarded in order to reach a firm definition of requirement or to establish feasibility. In complex situations, such an approach is often a fundamental aspect of good risk management.

Exact changes are impossible to predict, but trends can identify areas that are subject to change. These may include business processes as well as regulatory and technical environments. The requirements should specify where flexibility will be important, allowing suppliers to anticipate where technical design should accommodate change.

3.7 Strategic and cultural fit

Good practice demands consideration of the importance of broader factors than price or product quality and looks also at the value of the relationship. In any long-term agreement, the outcome will depend to a large extent on the synergy between the key participants. If they cannot operate in harmony, they are likely to fail, or to deliver below potential. Time is absorbed in managing disagreement or papering over cracks.

If innovation is important, or if flexibility or collaboration are going to be required, these factors must be included in the evaluation and selection process. Such factors are often difficult to accommodate within a rules-driven acquisition process. They have proved especially difficult in government and public sector projects, because they often appear to be 'subjective' or 'qualitative' factors, which do not lend themselves readily to objective analysis. Yet of course they can be handled objectively, by seeking references, or having suppliers present the approaches they would take, or by analyzing the supplier's organization and skills model. Similarly, suppliers should explore the extent to which they see cultural fit in the customer; it makes little sense to embark on a project that you can see will be fraught with risk or disagreement.

3.8 What goes wrong

Requirements often miss the mark. 88 percent of respondents to an IACCM survey indicated that improving the quality of requirements was the number one factor, critical to improving contract performance in their organizations.

The issues that arise most commonly in requirements definition are:
- They are often incomplete.
- They may represent someone's view of the solution, rather than reflecting true requirements.
- There is frequently a failure to understand the range of stakeholders who should be included in requirements development.
- There may be ignorance of corporate policies and standards, particularly in companies with multiple divisions.
- There is a tendency to rush to a solution and specify answers to a problem, rather than describe the need or issue for which a solution or fix is being sought.

Finally, during the lifetime of a deal or relationship, requirements will evolve and conditions will change. To the extent possible, requirements need to take these into account.

Lessons learned – case study
A global bank was developing an application to process trades of fixed income financial instruments. The users were those in the branch and at the call center who were licensed to sell securities. The company was rushing to development after having developed initial requirements.

The requirements were developed in a Joint Application Development (JAD) session that included senior division managers. One of the approved suppliers was selected to develop the interface. The bank had insisted upon a fixed price contract. However, the requirements were vague, and the supplier insisted upon a large contingency to cover the uncertainty of the requirements. This contingency was unacceptable to the bank.

The bank and the supplier agreed to an additional series of requirements sessions to narrow the specifications. The supplier insisted that all stakeholder groups be represented in the sessions, at both management and line levels. During the first of those sessions, it was revealed that the branch account representatives (thought to be the primary users) would need a screen design and reporting capability that would allow easy customer validation of the desired trade before execution. This drove an immediate process and interface redesign, as well as additional reporting capability.

A subsequent session revealed that the 'primary' branch users actually represented only 8 to 10 percent of the trades. The majority of trades were executed through the call centers, a group of users that were never adequately represented in the original JAD sessions.

The redefined range and priority of stakeholders, and the recognition of the regulatory practice of validation with the consumer before execution of the trade in the original requirements, resulted in a final Statement of Work (SOW) that was 33 percent greater than the original budget, but 20 percent less than the figure that included the contingency.

The UK's National Audit Office recently reported on a similar failure to engage stakeholders in a government project to centralize the operation of fire and rescue services. In his commentary, the head of the National Audit Office said: "This is yet another example of a government IT project taking on a life of its own, absorbing ever-increasing resources without reaching its objectives. The rationale and benefits ... were unclear and badly communicated to local stakeholders .... Essential checks and balances in the early stages of the project were ineffective. It was approved on the basis of unrealistic estimates of costs and under-appreciation of the complexity of the IT involved and the project was hurriedly implemented and poorly managed. Its legacy is a chain of expensive centers whose future is uncertain".

3.9 Five key milestones

For major projects, requirements definition is a process rather than an activity. This means that it should be managed with key milestones to enable those involved to determine whether they are making progress, and how close to a 'good' set of requirements they are.

Know your stakeholders

The first step in gathering requirements is identifying the stakeholders. If you get to the end of a project and you discover that a key stakeholder has been left out of the process, the project is in danger of failing. Even if, by good fortune, the needs of this stakeholder have been catered for, they will often present a continuing challenge during deployment of the solution because they will not have been part of the process from the beginning.

Do not continue to the next milestone unless you have a high degree of confidence that you understand who the stakeholders are and what perspectives they bring (see the National Audit Office example above to understand the consequences of ignoring this phase)

Know your business objectives

Once you know the stakeholders, the next milestone to be achieved should be understanding the business objectives for the project. What does the business want to get out of this acquisition? For example, Is it about streamlining processes, increasing productivity or increasing margin?

To meet this milestone you must have a clear understanding of the business objectives. At this stage, your business objectives should be:
- Unambiguously documented
- Widely reviewed
- Signed off by all the stakeholders

A green light at this stage ensures that all stakeholders know why they are engaging in this project and that their objectives are aligned.

Understand the specification

The third milestone requires you to be clear about the functional and technical requirements for the project. There are many tools to assist in this process, which are discussed below. At all stages during the functional and technical requirements definition, the team should be checking back against the business objectives to ensure things are heading in the right direction. And each set of stakeholders should be involved in this review to ensure that one party's view is not having a disproportionate effect on the requirements definition. If it is not possible to understand the functional and technical requirements in sufficient detail to give confidence that you know what you are buying, stop, re-assess and, as necessary, re-do this phase until the confidence level is sufficiently high to enable moving forward.

Agree the acceptance procedure and criteria

It is essential to have a mechanism for determining whether the business requirements, the functional requirements and the technical requirements have been met.

Many projects fail on this single point: nobody has thought about how to determine whether or not they have succeeded.

During this stage you will:
- Define measurable criteria for business success, to focus the project team on outcomes rather than activities
- Refine and improve requirements, to replace vague objectives with measurable ones
- Ensure every participant in the project is clear about what 'success' looks like
- Understand the procedure for acceptance.

It may be necessary to revisit previous phases as you consider how to test whether business, functional or technical requirements have been met. Doing this work now, before the deal is done and the contract is signed, greatly increases the likelihood of a successful project outcome.

Acceptance criteria should be aligned and integrated with corporate measures, as well as with prioritization factors. The same criteria used to justify the investment in the first place should be used to measure success. These measures and expectations should be defined upfront and included as baseline performance expectations in the original requirements documentation. Ongoing monitoring will inform ongoing improvement and hold the supplier accountable.

Measures can be qualitative or quantitative. In one example a pharmaceutical company had created a knowledge portal expecting scientists to publish their work to the benefit of the entire research and development community. The community had high membership, but there was little knowledge sharing. By measuring how the portal was used, and sending out a survey the company was able to understand the degree to which the community was reluctant to publish findings for fear of losing credit for their work. They realigned the program allowing in-depth research and analysis of previously published studies. Use of the portal and the benefit to the community have grown steadily since.

Put in place a robust change management process
The world does not stand still, particularly during the course of a long and complex project. Technology moves on; business goals change; financial markets soar or dive; personnel change.

'Scope creep', the process by which one set of requirements evolves into another, is often cited as the cause of failed, over-budget, over-time, under-performing projects.

There are three ways to manage change during a project:
1. Ignore it and put the cost and time overruns down to experience

2. Forbid it, and insist on continuing with the original plan, even if it no longer does what is needed

3. Identify changes clearly, analyze their impact on cost and timescales, and seek approval from the key stakeholders before proceeding.

For most large projects, particularly those with a long duration, option three is the most appropriate. However, it is not without its challenges. Identifying changes requires a clear initial specification. Managing the process means being prepared to hold up the project until the appropriate analysis has been done, and stakeholder sign-off has been attained. Both of these can cause difficulties and stresses during the project. A robust, practical, pragmatic change management process that enables changes to be assessed and approved quickly will contribute greatly to a successful project outcome.

Although option one appears to be impractical, there may be some projects (generally those of limited complexity and duration) where this is the most practical approach. Changes can be paid for with a 'bucket' of extra cash, days or other resources that is dipped into as required.

Provided that changes are continuously tied back to business objectives and acceptance criteria, this can be a fast and effective way to complete a project in a changing environment. It does, however, require a certain amount of trust and co-operation between buyer and seller. Both parties must be committed to achieving the best outcome for the best price, if this option is not to deteriorate into perpetual scope creep. Identifying appropriate incentives for the seller, which reward timely and cost-effective project completion, can be very effective in offsetting the desire to simply 'spend the bucket'.

Of all of these options, option two is the most rarely implemented. When it is, it may be as a result of a prolonged period of scope creep that has prompted the organization to conclude that any system, however out of date, is better than no system. It tends to be a response to poor experiences in the past, rather than an active choice. If project and contract management resources are strained or under-skilled, this option can be the safest route through a risky project. Although adding changes after the project is completed will inevitably increase cost, the benefits in terms of simplicity of project management and certainty of budget and timescales may be sufficient for this to become the most appropriate option.

It is common for customers and suppliers to battle long and hard over the precise definition of what constitutes a 'change or amendment' and what consequences it will have (e.g. on timing or price). This difficulty often leads to a compromise or 'shelving' of the issue, but by so doing the parties are likely to be creating the seeds for future contention and disagreement.

3.10 Tools and techniques for ensuring milestones are met

There is no one right way to achieve the five key milestones outlined in section 3.6 above. The most suitable approach will vary depending on the type of product or service, the risk associated with the project, the time available for selection and implementation and the preferences of your stakeholders. Nevertheless, there are some common tools that are useful in achieving these milestones (Table 3.1).

Milestone	Tools
Know your stakeholders	Stakeholder identification process Project management templates
Know your business objectives	Business objectives questionnaire Structured business objectives interviews
Understand the specification	Requirements checklist Requirements gathering questionnaires Structured requirements interviews Joint Application Development sessions Research and benchmarking
Agree the acceptance criteria	Acceptance criteria derived from requirements and business objectives.
Put in place a robust change management process	Prototyping Change control documentation and sign off process

Table 3.1   Requirements milestones tools

Stakeholder identification process

The process for identifying stakeholders varies greatly depending on the type of product or service. A good starting point might be to query your accounts payable systems to determine who has bought products or services of this type before and to check who approved these purchases from a financial or technical level. Involving your Corporate Risk team early in the process is often useful in identifying stakeholders. See also Chapter 6 for a more detailed analysis of possible stakeholders and their roles.

You may find that part of the requirements analysis process involves a 'walkthrough' of the route that each piece of information, product or equipment will take as it passes through the new solution. In taking a physical or theoretical 'walk' in the steps of that same piece of information, product or equipment, you will identify the various parties who have a part to play in moving it through the business. Some of these will be minor players, while others will be major stakeholders – until you have 'walked the walk', it may not be clear who is who, and some stakeholders may slip through your net completely.

The larger and more complicated the product, system, service or project you are looking to implement, the higher the probability that some stakeholders will fail to be identified. But similarly, there is a risk that some in the business will make assumptions about who is using what, and would need access to the equivalent facility in the new solution.

When re-negotiating contracts for various of its telecommunications facilities, a cable network provider identified a number of leased lines that it had been paying for over many years. The IT department, considered to be the major stakeholder, was asked who was actually using the lines. The response – "We don't know, but someone must be…" – did not provide much confidence to the commercial team conducting the review. The CFO supported a decision to switch the lines off and 'see who shouts'. Nobody shouted, and the company saved several hundred thousand British pounds in one swift move. It is reasonably safe to assume that any unidentified stakeholders would have made themselves public fairly quickly.

As with all stages of the requirements development process, validating assumptions is essential. Assuming that something is important to stakeholders who do not exist is as expensive and dangerous as missing out a key stakeholder with a real requirement.

Project management processes

Most companies have established robust project management processes that include checklists, analysis tools and workflow, but these approaches are not always applied to scoping requirements. By formalizing the requirements definition process as a project, companies are able to assure that all stakeholders have an opportunity to weigh-in early in the requirements development.

One company that had five divisions instituted Ringi, a Japanese process for reaching decisions by consensus. This required broad review of all major projects in an effort to eliminate redundancy, increase purchasing power and leverage institutional experience.

Business objectives questionnaire

Identifying business objectives at the outset serves two purposes. First, it ensures that your requirements are focused on the end goal, and second, it is a good way to engage stakeholders at the start of the project. Stakeholders are usually more interested in the benefits they will see from this project than they are in the tedious detail that has to be gathered and understood during the course of the project. A good way of engaging your stakeholders and gathering useful information for the business objective is to ask them to rank, in order of importance, a list of five to ten potential business functions that may be positively affected by the project.

Questionnaires are an invaluable tool for reaching broad stakeholder populations. They are essential for global or other geographically dispersed organizations. Questionnaires represent a low-cost alternative to face-to-face sessions. They also broaden reach as appropriate, serving as much to communicate as to gather information.

Ensure that your questionnaire provides a mechanism for stakeholders to contribute their own suggestions. There are certain to be improvements to current functions that will have been obvious to those within the business unit, but which have not previously had a voice. A well-designed questionnaire can stimulate discussion and creative thinking, offering potential benefits in excess of those initially envisaged by the project. A strategic and organizational-level filter will be required at some stage, but it is generally better to work from a long-list to a prioritized short-list than to pre-determine the short-list before all stakeholders have had their say.

Business objectives structured interview

Once you have the survey results, you have a good format to use in a structured interview with the most important key users. Structured interviews assure one-on-one focus for requirements questions. They also help to ensure understanding of the nuances in the responses provided in the survey. The downside is that they are time-consuming, both to conduct the interviews and to perform the follow-up aggregation, analysis and reporting.

Requirements checklist

It is critical that the requirements gathering process encompasses the full range of requirements that may affect the project. These involve spanning dimensions such as

- Investment strategy (such as time to market, quality differentiation, etc.)
- Corporate governance – including regulatory requirements, reputation risk
- Corporate policies and standards (such as security standards, support for ISO certification or audit requirements, health and safety)
- IT policies and standards (e.g. technology platforms, supplier status, etc.)
- Financial performance (such as payback period or ROI)
- Functional performance
- Strategic partnership requirements
- Human impact evaluation
- Cross-border interoperability
- Quality standards
- Service Level standards
- Terms and conditions
- Warranty and maintenance
- Supplier relationship
- Integration or homologation requirements
- Export / import and logistics considerations

Requirements questionnaire

Questionnaires are also a useful tool in identifying the more detailed requirements. They can be implemented in paper form or electronically, depending on the resources and culture of the organization. There is a skill and a craft in designing questionnaires to ensure they derive the right answers rather than driving them through directed and slanted questions.

A positive example of effective use of a requirements questionnaire is that of a children's charity, operating in 63 countries, which was planning to implement a new system to capture field information about children and their communities. Local privacy sensitivities, as well as unique infrastructure capabilities, made specific information about each location essential. In some instances, children were raised by extended families, so addresses were irrelevant. In other cases, power was available only four hours per day, and phone services were non-existent. The requirements had to detail unique issues for each location. A requirements questionnaire was met with appreciation and achieved a 100 percent response rate, albeit with some encouragement.

Structured requirements interviews

Structured requirements interviews can be critical in the development of detailed, process-rich systems or projects. One approach is Usability analysis, where experts will interview relevant managers and users, then observe them in their work environment, recording details of process and workflow that is then incorporated into the requirements.

Requirements definition workshop

There are various approaches to reaching agreement on requirements, but one is to hold a requirements definition workshop. All major project management methodologies include the framework for such workshops, which may be internal or collaborative between two or more participants in the supply chain. Many times, there will be several such workshops, for example one to grain consensus between internal stakeholders and then a joint workshop between customer and supplier.

The requirements definition workshop is a good practice. It enables disciplined discussion and positive approaches to solving differences or uncertainties. Such workshops can also be used to develop plans for the best contract or relationship model, or to develop a negotiation strategy. 'Best practice' companies ensure that their contracts staff are familiar with such methods and that more advanced practitioners have the training to run a workshop, either internal or joint.

Sample frameworks and workshop outlines can easily be found on the internet.

Research and benchmarking

Requirements are often enhanced through benchmarking similar projects. These can be enabled through relationships with partners, benchmarking tours, and blind benchmarking studies referencing competitors, as well as by relevant references provided by suppliers. Typically, benchmarking delegates define a range of issues in which they are interested and look to identify best practice that may apply to their project. Benchmarked factors may include:

- Technical standards
- Service level requirements for Service Level Agreements (SLAs)

- Training and support programs
- Levels of innovation or flexibility.

Acceptance criteria

Once the stakeholders have been identified, business objectives confirmed and requirements defined, it is time to prepare the acceptance criteria. These are essentially the way to determine that the business objectives have been met, and that the requirements have been delivered. Preparing them at this stage is extremely useful in ensuring that the requirements have been defined thoroughly and unambiguously.

Begin with the business objectives, and consider each in turn. How will you know that this objective is not currently being met? What are the metrics and tools that have prompted the new requirements? And how will you know that your solution has delivered what was needed to meet this objective?

Only by examining each objective with a critical eye will you be able to identify appropriate acceptance criteria. As you work through this process, you may choose to discard some objectives as being not measurable or sufficiently objective, or you may be comfortable using a 'softer' measurement.

Consider the example of an organization implementing a contract automation system. Along with straightforward objectives such as reducing legal costs, or reducing negotiation cycle time, there may be less easily measured objectives like 'making our organization easier to deal with'. How do you determine how easy you are to deal with? And what tells you that your clients currently find you difficult to deal with?

If there has been consistent feedback from customer satisfaction surveys indicating that your organization is difficult to negotiate with, or slow to prepare contracts, this will give you a good basis for comparison once the new system is in place. The acceptance criterion for this business objective could be a certain percentage improvement in the scores for 'speed to prepare contracts' in a post-implementation customer satisfaction survey.

A similar approach, repeated for each business objective, will result in a measurable and usable set of acceptance criteria at the business level.

Be aware that it may be some months (or in some cases, years) post-implementation, before it will be possible to assess whether these criteria have been met. The original supplier may be long gone by the time you are in a position to determine whether the project was actually worthwhile, and met its original ROI and other objectives. And certainly, you will not be able to use many of these acceptance criteria to reject the solution presented to you – timeframes and dependencies upon your own organization will mitigate against you here.

However, this does not mean that there is no benefit in investing time and effort in determining, and measuring success against, the business criteria. Only by doing so will lessons be learned and the real value of the solution determined. A positive outcome will reinforce the benefits of a structured approach; a negative one may suggest further work is required. Either way, good acceptance criteria will enable performance to be measured in a way that contributes to the future self-knowledge and effectiveness of the buying organization.

Determining functional acceptance criteria is an altogether more straightforward affair. Beginning with each high-level functional group, ask how you will know whether this function has been delivered successfully or not. Is it a question of technical accuracy? Speed? Usability? Flexibility? Then, drill down to each individual requirement – some will be self-evident, while others will require further clarification to determine success. You will inevitably find, during this process, that your functional requirements become more finely tuned and clearer. You may need to go back to your stakeholders, to clarify exactly what they were aiming for. You may question whether a particular functional requirement is in line with the business objectives.

The acceptance definition process should act as a verification and validation process for both business and functional requirements, helping to tie them together, ensure consistency, and inject some realism into the proceedings.

Prototypes and pilots

Requirements are usually detailed descriptions of functionality, design and other attributes. Most stakeholders will be hard-pressed to devote the time to fully understand technical requirements. One way to support understanding is to develop a prototype or model and present it to users as a self-guided tour, or in the context of a presentation or roadshow. Such visualizations communicate design and process quickly and effectively, reducing project changes due to misunderstandings. Occasionally, this might even extend to a limited pilot program in order to ensure full testing and validation. This can be especially valuable in testing services, where there is no tangible product and user acceptance and use is key to success.

Software prototypes can run from crude wire-frames to detailed design studies. Manufacturing prototypes are usually done in terms of physical samples. Equipment prototypes are usually handled as demonstrations.

Scoping studies

A variation on the requirements workshop and the prototyping approaches is the scoping study. This can be particularly useful when you want a fixed price for a project that does not currently have a fixed scope. You appoint a selected contractor (ideally your preferred bidder for the project, but not necessarily) on a fixed-price, fixed-term scoping project. They work with your team to determine the requirements, investigate alternatives, and clarify specifications. The deliverable from this scoping study is a comprehensive set of requirements that could be used as part of your Request For Proposals (RFP) process with a number of potential suppliers.

Be aware that if the contractor has their own proprietary solution, the temptation will be for them to develop requirements that reflect their own capabilities. It is your responsibility to ensure that the resulting deliverable meets your needs, and not simply their aspirations.

A further variant is the 'agile contract'. This is an approach first used in software development, but increasingly applied to projects where there is a high degree of uncertainty and a need for close collaboration and teamwork between the parties. Such agreements have a series of on-going milestones or 'gateway reviews' and at each of these there may be further negotiation and funding releases, or a decision to terminate or try a new direction.

Change control documentation and sign-off process

Once the acceptance criteria have been defined, and the project started, you should communicate with stakeholders regularly as the project progresses. Tie the communication to the benefits they will realize.

Project changes can be a source of frustration for the project managers and confusion for the stakeholders. If changes are required to the project, these are often best discussed in terms of risk to achieving the benefits, and agreement should be sought from stakeholders that these risks are real and change is required. Once the stakeholders agree there is a need for change, the change control documentation can be presented and signed.

3.11   Common causes for delay or failure

The common causes for delay or failure are:
- Failure to prioritize
- Solution-driven answer (defining 'how' when it should have been 'what')
- Forced solutions
- Outsourced solutions
- Ignorance of the range of stakeholders
- Ignorance of the internal economy
- Failure to understand complexity
- Ignorance of standards
- Ignorance of human impact
- Aggressive use of competition to drive lowest price
- Complex and poorly defined supply chain relationships.

Failure to prioritize

When multiple stakeholders are clamoring for conflicting standards or processes, or when the scope of the requirements exceeds the time or budget allocated to a project, it becomes necessary to prioritize. The first step is to identify the primary decision criteria, which often align with the key business objectives for the project. Depending on the scope and nature of the solution being procured, these may be high-level objectives (increasing value in the business) or very localized ones (reduce production errors requiring costly re-work). Regardless of the naming or number of key criteria, the approach remains consistent. Stakeholders then identify the 20 or so factors that define each of the primary criteria. Scoring the options against each factor then identifies the optimal priority of requirements to support the broad stakeholder community in an initial release. Future releases can then add capability in the order prescribed by the prioritization results.

Solution-driven answer

There is often a propensity to gravitate to 'commoditized' solutions for reasons of cost and ease of implementation. This is often a result of someone having seen the solution demonstrated or implemented somewhere else, and it is easy to assume that it will be a correct fit. Adopting an existing solution can also be seen as the cheapest, fastest path to resolving a problem.

In the case of a global insurance company, its property and casualty division was looking for a global software solution to handle its underwriting, claims and accounting functions. Its European management chose to implement a 'shrink-wrapped' solution for global implementation, only to find that it lacked the capability to conform to the US's regulatory-driven processes. The company is currently developing an in-house solution that will replace the purchased product globally, requiring an additional, costly and disruptive technical migration in other parts of the world.

Another example of the solution-driving-the-requirements is when a company chooses to implement a product that, while robust, may be inflexible. Certain core capabilities may align with the need, but design, or lack of features, may force significant process reengineering or costly and inefficient workarounds. This was the case with a major European telecom operator who contracted for an industry leading standard Human Resources (HR) solution and then found the cost of adapting the solution to accommodate the large number of different types of allowances paid to employees delayed the implementation and inflated the cost by orders of magnitude.

The purchasing process then becomes a balancing act that requires careful analysis. Should the company develop or customize a solution to meet its many specific requirements, or should it adopt a readily available solution and deal with any gaps and inconsistencies? That analysis is only available after having performed detailed requirements definition.

Glossing over the detailed requirements before supplier selection and expecting to add details during implementation will undoubtedly lead to unexpected challenges and costly supplier claims to address extensive change to the contract.

Forced solutions

Even large corporations have faced having solutions forced upon them, and have struggled with the resulting process changes. This sort of solution coercion happens when:

- A powerful customer demands that a supplier interfaces directly with its systems
- A supplier offers favorable pricing that is contingent on adoption of its solutions
- An acquiring corporation forces its subsidiaries to adopt its systems
- An established supplier redesigns its product, forcing updates or upgrades

Even in these cases, requirements definition is essential in order to define the impact and required adjustments to practice or processes. For example, in one company, the management team assumed that adoption of a customer-mandated software solution would have relatively little impact.

The true impact became apparent only after implementation, forcing minimal process change, yet significant time and expense associated with employee retraining. In some cases, such changes may have an impact on trade union agreements. Detailing and communicating requirements before such a decision will reduce the likelihood of costly pushback after the decision.

Outsourced solutions

Companies that rely on outsourced information technology, professional services or manufacturing processes, may result in the use of the providers' standard solutions. This may or may not be problematic and scoping the requirements will help determine the level and cost of adaptation required before selecting a supplier. Once a solution is implemented, solution providers may change technologies or processes as part of ongoing modernization, resulting in some impact to customers.

Outsourcing requirements are often output or outcome-based. This approach is frequently ideal for driving the efficiencies envisaged. They need, however, to be fully considered to understand what, if any, impact may result in relying on the supplier rather than having detailed requirements in place.

Further factors to consider are the off-set between lower prices versus more customized services and the discipline of product or service refresh. Customers often want the latest updates or versions – but how frequently and with what level of disruption?

Case study: inability to visualize impact

Perhaps the biggest risk to a solution-driven implementation is the failure to visualize the process and cultural impact of the solution. One company has calculated the cost of poor requirements definition in tens of millions of dollars over the course of one year, a significant percentage of its budget for such services. This resulted from a failure to understand

- Regulatory requirements in some of the countries in which it operates
- Push-back from users due to language inflexibility and process constraints
- Conflicting internal economies that disincentivized adoption
- Unanticipated support and maintenance requirements

The result has been adoption of a mandate for a human impact study as part of the requirements for any proposed solution.

To control the risks of imposing a solution, perform a gap analysis between the detailed requirements of the stakeholders and the specifications of the solution. The more detailed the requirements, the greater the ability to understand the impact of gaps or conflicts. It may be a good idea to consult with third parties to help anticipate shortcomings in other, similar implementations and assess the impact of those gaps.

Solution-driven answer

As discussed above, there is a propensity to gravitate to 'commodity' solutions for reasons of cost and ease of implementation, the perceived path of least resistance. When insufficient requirements definition and analysis has resulted in unexpected process variation or pushback, the costs can skyrocket, the delivery timetable destroyed, and the ultimate implementation of the solution put in doubt. Forcing a solution is just one reason for delay or failure.

Ignorance of range of stakeholders

Many companies fail to address or even identify the full universe of stakeholders. The results range from resentment on the part of those who were ignored to delays by late-coming changes to the requirements, to the complete abandonment of the project due to missed milestones and budget overruns.

Ignorance of internal economy

Internal economy describes the forces within a division or a company that drive decisions and behaviors. At a macro level, internal economy can include cost allocation practices that drive short-term cost cutting at the expense of planning for growth, or force managers to look outside the company's internal suppliers to external sources that represent a savings to the division but are more costly to the corporation. At a micro level, internal economy is reflected in personal incentives or disincentives surrounding activities such as sharing knowledge and data among peers or workgroups. Requirements rarely anticipate the impact of internal economy. However, when they do, relatively simple economic realignment can have a profound impact on project success.

As an example, a manufacturing company with five divisions realized that there was millions of dollars of redundant spending each year. The holding company's hands-off culture provided no incentive for standards. However, by reengineering the internal economy, the chief financial officer was able to reduce licensing fees for common software applications. Also, divisions were encouraged to collaborate and develop joint requirements; divisions could recover costs by leasing back to other divisions. And if three or more divisions participated, the expense for the project would become a corporate investment, removing the project from the individual division's balance sheet.

Failure to understand complexity

All projects have hidden complexity, and not just in the technical environment. Requirements documentation must address the hidden factors of culture, support and governance in addition to the more obvious functionality, migration and infrastructure components. It is also important to understand – and manage – the difference between things that are complicated, versus those that are truly complex. Managing the implementation of a new phone system is complicated, because there are many interacting elements and dependencies, but a proficient project manager will make this appear simple. Complex environments are those where there are many uncertainties and there is likely to be ambiguity and regular change. This unpredictability means that the quality of communications and the extent of systems thinking must be far greater.

Ignorance of standards

Many divisions or functional groups have gone a long way down a development or acquisition path only to find out, and in some cases after extensive expenditure, that the solution will not comply with corporate standards. In some cases, the deviation can be justified. In all cases there is cost associated with the deviation. In a few cases the project has been scrapped altogether, with huge financial and personal costs.

Ignorance of human impact

Most project teams are unable to accurately assess human impact, and yet virtually all projects have some human impact – at the very least, a training requirement, or an impact on productivity. Look for changes in personal incentives, including compensation. Will new systems force changes to trade union agreements? Will usability issues reduce productivity? One approach is to benchmark other companies' efforts to articulate human impact.

Allowing for and managing changes and updates

Change is inevitable and the requirements documentation is the foundation for change control throughout the project. Vague requirements require guesswork. Increased requirements specificity reduces avoidable changes and delays due to misunderstandings. Change also comes from forces outside the control of the project team and the requirements must be updated to reflect these. These forces include changing technologies or new product introductions. In some cases these changes have flow-through effects to other areas of the business. Such changes must be reflected in updates to the requirements documentation, even if the project is well into production. Failure to incorporate them results in potential dispute at the time of final acceptance or delivery.

Market forces also drive change. Regardless of the product or service, companies must be responsive to customer preferences and competitive challenges. While speed is important, carefully managing change while carefully updating the requirements documentation is critical.

All industries are affected by regulatory mandate. Laws such as Sarbanes-Oxley, Gramm-Leach-Bliley, and the EU Data Protection Directive drive process and system changes. Compliance is to some degree dependent upon change control and requirements documentation.

Dealing with incumbent suppliers

Most contracts are renewing or replacing an existing product or service supply and therefore the requirements phase must take account of any incumbent supplier. This factor affects both the customer and the prospective bidders.

The fact that the process is addressing a renewal or replacement should not affect its rigor. Business objectives, requirements and acceptance / selection criteria remain important – though there is danger that objectivity could be lost. For example, incumbents may have generated powerful friends or enemies within your organization and they may seek to influence requirements accordingly. In one recent example from the oil and gas industry, a procurement specialist complained that ' the business unit has inserted a requirement that services are provided without use of sub-contractors. They have no reason for this, except that the incumbent does not have certain internal capabilities and therefore cannot comply. But there are no performance issues and no one can explain a good reason for this added requirement'.

Transition to a new supplier may have significant economic or performance implications that must be taken into account. A recent bid in the defense industry included the need to establish considerable infrastructure in a remote location – giving the incumbent an obvious price advantage. The bid manager needed to think through how to separate the bid elements to allow a true comparison of price quotes – and also to consider ways to deal with the implications of a supplier switch.

It is not unusual for the requirements team to find they are being driven by senior management motives that might include:

- A bid process designed solely to put pressure on incumbents to lower their prices
- A bid process where requirements are weighted towards the incumbent, to ensure contract renewal
- A bid process where requirements are weighted against the incumbent, to ensure their exclusion

These factors can lead to a lack of honesty and integrity in the bid process, resulting in potential damage to organizational reputation in the market (yes, suppliers do research and have ears as well!). Such a reputation will be damaging to the quality of bids received and the extent to which the winning supplier feels obliged to demonstrate on-going honesty and integrity in the way they behave (eg future price increases, early warning of problems etc). It is important that the bid team considers such factors and alerts management to the dangers of such behaviors.

3.12 Summary

Understanding requirements is the essential first step in a successful project or procurement. These requirements are not limited to technology or functionality – they embody the business objectives for the project, the needs of all of the stakeholders, and the financial and timescale needs of the organization.

There are a number of tools available to help you identify and validate your requirements. More time spent on this phase of the process will reduce errors and costs further down the line, and will increase the likelihood of a successful outcome. Ensure that you have completed all stages of requirements definition to a level that gives you and the organization confidence, before giving the go-ahead to a project; this puts your project on a sound footing for future progress.

CHAPTER 4

Financial considerations – understanding cost and setting charges

4.1 Introduction

Once you've read this chapter you are able, as a buyer or a seller, to understand the importance of sound understanding of how your cost is determined, how cost may affect your bid strategy and how contract standards and contract terms may contribute to reducing cost and optimizing profitability. At the same time you will be ensuring products and services are beneficial to your sellers, your buyers and your own company, securing long term and mutually satisfactory value-chain relationships. The key message of this chapter is for you to realize that a thorough understanding of the complete cost picture – your own and that of your trading partners – is key to achieving profitability.

In this chapter we will explore the most important financial considerations that influence bid strategy, contractual standards and contract terms. We will touch upon the principles behind costing and setting charges; identify the various charging methodologies and structures that could apply and in what situations they are most appropriate; evaluate the links between charges and risk management; and provide examples of the contractual term variables that are likely to have most impact on costs and charges. We will also illustrate the links between contractual terms, cost and charges with examples that highlight best practice – and also how failure to make the right connections will damage profitability.

4.2 Bid strategy: why does cost matter?

Businesses aim to make profits and without a clear understanding of their internal and external costs they cannot set charges that will drive profitable outcomes. For sellers, the charge must be set at a level that your customer is prepared to pay and which, at the same time, is still profitable for your company; buyers must set their expectations of charges at a level that the seller is willing to provide the product, program or service for. This means you have to understand issues that determine value and be able to explain those values to potential customers and sellers. You must also be aware of alternatives – either from competitors, alternative solutions, or from doing nothing. Your contracts must represent good business value for both parties, e.g. the benefit to the buyer must exceed the costs to the seller and the charge the buyer pays will, in most circumstances, be somewhere between the seller's cost and the buyer's benefit.

Often, contracts involve standard products or services, with standard charges or charges that are not negotiable. Sometimes, they involve non-standard or 'customized' products, programs or services, where costs are less predictable and charges may be highly negotiable. In all cases, whether standard or non-standard, judgments have to be made about the correct allocation of costs. For example, most companies offer a range of products, programs and services that are offered to different segments/buyers. The approach to costs within the sell- or buy chain may vary accordingly. Depending on which costing methodology is applied, these differences may either be taken into account – resulting in significant variations in allocation, based on actual costs; or they may be averaged – leading to potentially inefficient pricing decisions. Also, your go-to-market model may affect your cost model (or, more specifically, your profit margin).

Today's competitive markets have forced suppliers to innovate in their charging and pricing models. In some cases, these are superficial (for example, product bundling masquerading as a 'solution') but in many there are alternative value propositions. For example:
- Increased responsibility for outcomes
- Greater commitment to performance levels
- Alternative payment or charging schemes

Outsourcing, software as a service, cloud computing and 'power by the hour' are all examples of the transitions from traditional product supply to the world of services and solutions. These transform the economic model and risk characteristics for both suppliers and their customers and therefore have fundamental impact on contract terms and structures.

4.3   The role of the contracts professional

In our experience, financial considerations are too often overlooked or ignored by contracts professionals. This is mostly because they have little authority and frequently no visibility to key data – for example, the underlying cost information and structure. This means major opportunities to have an impact on profit or to increase win rates can be lost. It also means that many commercial contracts staff lack confidence in challenging or questioning their colleagues in Finance; this means valid discussion is stifled – and opportunities are missed. Most terms and conditions have direct cost impacts – for both the buyer and the seller – and of course therefore affect the price and value of the proposed contract. Best practice corporations ensure that terms are not negotiated in isolation from the price. They do this either through totally integrated cross-functional teams, or by ensuring financial visibility and competence in their commercial contracts staff. The latter approach is increasingly common and, in IACCM's view, the right path to follow.

A top-performing professional will ensure not only that they understand the make-up of their own proposal, but also that they focus on questions that will reveal the customer's sense of value. This may lead either to the inclusion or exclusion of offering elements, or to creative approaches to price or the overall cost of ownership. The purpose of this chapter is to explore these options and to encourage awareness and understanding. We will not spend significant time on costing or pricing from a formal accounting or financial analysis perspective.

4.4   Bid strategy: the importance of cost analysis

There are various ways to distinguish cost types; some legislation requires you to apply 'open cost calculation' models, especially in business-to-consumer selling. The most commonly used distinctions between cost types are:
- Fixed or variable: your fixed costs are those you cannot change (e.g. Long term lease or rental arrangements, inventory depreciation, etc.), while variable cost can be managed (e.g. use of subcontractors etc.)
- Cost allocation types: some costs can be directly allocated to the product, program or service (e.g. code development, building a solution, etc.), while others (e.g. Staff- or real estate cost) can only be allocated indirectly

Some contracts contain charges in addition to the initial charge based on additional cost, e.g. cost for overtime or off-shift work, cost of living adjustments, etc.

Although most costs are related to production or to effort (as shown above), some costs have no such link and are merely applied to cover (financial) risks, e.g. to cover for debt collection, insurance, increased liability amounts.

Risk based costing requires a sound understanding of the applicable type of risk, as described in Carnegie Mellon University's Continuous Risk Management Guidebook:
- External risks: dangers from outside your organization which may lead to damage or loss, e.g. terrorist attacks, natural disasters, wars, but also recession or government regulations
- Internal risks: dangers from within your organization which may result in damage or loss, e.g. erroneous strategies, mismanagement, errors, fraud or theft
- Non-controllable risks: situations that may lead to damage or loss that your organization can exert no influence on but that can usually be insured against, accrued or hedged

- Controllable risks: scenarios that may result in damage or loss that your organization can usually anticipate, or react adequately to.

Given the above, you need a broad picture of the overall value chain of your company. Michael Porter identifies such a value chain as a means of analyzing an organization's strategically relevant activities to understand the behavior of costs. Competitive advantage comes from carrying out those activities more cost-effectively than your competitors. In his book *Competitive Advantage*, Porter breaks the value chain model into five primary stages:

- Inbound logistics
- Operations
- Outbound logistics
- Marketing and sales
- Service

These stages are supported by the infrastructure of the company (human resource management, technology development, and purchasing/procurement), are inter-linked and depend on efficient processes. For example, the relationship between sales, operations and procurement can determine how much stock is to be carried and therefore reflected in the cost of inventory held.

In their book *Competing For The Future* Hamel and Prahalad go a step further and anticipate today's more virtual business structures, where companies depend on a mix of alliances and outsourced relationships, stating: "...Companies should cease to be preoccupied with their degree of vertical integration and their own 'value chain' – their various value-creating activities, such as production, marketing and service. Instead they should pay more attention to their ability to create 'virtual integration' by allying with, and purchasing from, competitors. Rather than analyzing competitiveness purely on the basis of individual companies, people should realize that the most relevant unit is formed by 'open clusters' – the networks that form relationships of supply..."

It is in this complex environment that most of us operate. And with complexity comes opportunity – the chance to ask new questions or see things from a new perspective. It is this aspect of innovation that enables creativity and added value. The key message here is to think laterally, beyond the obvious, beyond the established rules and procedural boundaries.

To analyze the value chain of your company it is necessary to first identify its activities. For example, a manufacturing company producing computers and a services company, such as a consulting or accountancy firm, would operate with different structures and these differences would affect the relative importance of each cost element. The relevance of operations within the manufacturing company will usually be higher than that of operations within an accountancy firm. As an example: with over 60 percent of its costs being allocated to operations, a manufacturing company should initially concentrate on this area to maximize savings (= reducing cost), while for an accountancy firm the main cost drivers are operations at 26 percent and marketing at 21 percent, suggesting an almost equal savings potential.

Porter identifies 10 'cost drivers', the most quantifiable of these being economies and diseconomies of scale, learning or experience effects, and capacity utilization. The big difference between traditional accounting methods and the value chain approach is that the latter focuses on the customer, rather than purely internal perspectives. The value chain examines producer costs but also considers the consumer costs involved (cost of ownership).

For example, for the end-user, the cost of a vehicle includes not only the purchase price or lease payments, but also such factors such as devaluation/depreciation, fuel cost, insurance and maintenance service costs. A value chain approach looks at how the seller can influence these costs through value creating activities and product attributes.

4.5   Contract standards as cost management tools

Contracts professionals should contribute at two levels: **strategic** (any activity that affects the entire business or a market segment) and **operational** (any activity that influences a specific customer, supplier or opportunity).

At the strategic level, you need to consider not only contract terms, but also issues such as contract standards. These can significantly affect your internal costs and also those of your trading partners. They fall into a broad category of 'ease of doing business'. For example, many companies operate with a standard relationship agreement which then requires signed supplements or purchase orders to bring them into effect. These 'umbrella' terms were traditionally thought to be far more cost-effective than creating a new agreement with each transaction. However, the drawback to this approach is that the agreement is often very long – it attempts to cover the full range of products, programs or services that might potentially be required – and it may prove complex to change and update. Historically, it seemed worthwhile to follow this approach because of the need to obtain signatures and keep physical, paper copies of every agreement. It was also agreed that 'contentious' terms (such as limitations of liability, indemnities and other 'boilerplate' clauses) could be negotiated once and then avoided.

Today, that situation has changed. Electronic contracts and signatures mean that there are new possibilities. Contracting structures can be more dynamic, more readily segmented around relationship types and, consequently, more cost effective. However, while this certainly streamlines the way contracting is done, the debate remains over whether certain terms are best handled through a Master Agreement – and the answer is that this probably makes sense in many long-term relationships.

At a strategic level shifts in technology, business practice and legislation must constantly be reviewed to ensure your company's approach to contracting is competitive, cost effective and facilitates the ease of doing business. One major company, by adopting e-commerce contract solutions for its smaller customers, reduced its costs of contracting by nearly $15 million; it also increased the integrity and enforceability of its contracts and raised customer satisfaction in this segment by three percentage points.

But be careful, the following example shows it is easy to get things wrong.

Under pressure from a powerful executive in Sales, the contracts staff at Company X launched a project to eliminate the need for customer signatures on order forms. They moved to a position where they could accept electronic forms. It was estimated that the new approach would shorten lead-times and reduce administrative costs. In fact, it did enable an immediate reduction by taking out the equivalent of seven employees and this, in combination with accelerated cash flow, reduced paperwork and storage, plus other minor benefits, was forecast to lead to year one savings of more than $2 million. The contracts group was proud of its achievement.

Several weeks later, the Director of Contracts received an irate telephone call from another Sales executive, complaining about the complexity of the new order process. Unfortunately, no one had tested with their customers to ensure the signature-less, electronic approach would work. On further investigation, it was discovered that more than 80 percent of customers had in fact rejected the new system. Far from simplifying transactions and reducing costs, the changes were having the opposite effect. And the headcount reductions meant that the burden was falling on the Sales representatives.
In this situation, those responsible for the project had failed to consider the value chain. They had taken a good idea and identified some tremendous benefits, but these were based only on internal analysis and they had failed to explore whether this could be implemented successfully.

The strategic role also applies to those who support product or service development, or perhaps industry groups, where the analysis and offering development need to be based on understanding of market segments. We are going to look at this activity in conjunction with the operational work of supporting specific bids or customer requirements.

4.6 Contract terms as a cost management tool

Moving beyond contract structure and delivery methods, there is a massive opportunity hidden in many individual terms and of course in the nature of the relationship offering itself.

Most terms and conditions rely in part on business processes, not just our own, but those of the other party. It is tempting to simplify those processes – or even eliminate them – through changed terms. However, each time you change the terms you will probably have affected complexity and consequently impacted costs, so you must analyze the impact. A simple example of reducing complexity while maintaining your business processes is in an area like software licensing. Historically, software vendors created complex procedures to monitor license use. They wanted their customers to maintain a physical count of the number of users, or the size of processors. Such complexity created a high probability of non-compliance and led to a great deal of time and resource being expended on monitoring and control. Those vendors who identified improved methods of charging and monitoring – for example, through electronic methods – established a competitive advantage.

Often costs are relatively fixed and your decision will focus on how they are apportioned. For example, shipping or delivery costs cannot be avoided, and the debate is mostly to do with which party will cover them. As discussed in other chapters, terms can be viewed as 'active' (requiring processes or resources, e.g. payment terms) or 'passive' (terms that require no processes and only come into effect if something else happens or fails to happen, such as a natural disaster – *force majeure*). You need to think about both types of terms from a financial perspective, but in quite different ways. Active terms have a direct impact on actual process costs. Passive terms could have a catastrophic effect, but in most cases have no bearing on day to day processcosts (also refer to the types of risks outlined above).

This is an important consideration. A change in active terms – e.g. payment provisions, physical delivery, warranty performance, training obligations – has a direct and measurable cost; this can be assessed in determining margin and can fairly easily be tracked during the contract lifecycle. This is not the case with passive terms; they are mostly covering the degree of liability if something goes wrong. So while the consequence can be measured in financial terms, the probability often cannot. And this is where many organizations struggle. They attempt to 'price for risk' – but what price increase should apply to a $5 million increase in the limit of liability? What price increase should apply to a change in the causes of force majeure? How much should the price reduce if your customer does not require third party indemnity? Battles over these passive terms are complex and often situational judgments.

Some risk experts make the following distinctions::
- Qualitative risk estimates: the probability and the impact of risks are indicated in descriptive terms, for example high, average or low risk
- Quantitative risk estimates: these estimates give mathematical interpretations of the probability and express the impact of the risk in numbers.

Within quantitative risk estimates, the following is further defined:

- Variability: the impact of an event that cannot be influenced by further research or calculation. As with the chance on tossing heads or coins, the chance is 50 percent, cannot be influenced and does not change
- Uncertainty: this has to do with a lack of knowledge and/or experience concerning the probability and the impact of risk.

It is easier to estimate the impact of the risk than it is to estimate its probability, both in qualitative and quantitative risk assessments.

When assessing risks most organizations tend to be too optimistic. Certain powers in the organization have an interest in estimating the risk as low as possible; for example, the sales team has an interest in doing business rapidly and will be inclined to assess business risks to be low. Research by the International Centre for Complex Project Management (ICCPM) revealed a similar tendency among business executives – it termed this 'the culture of optimism' – and their findings have been cited by a number of leading politicians, including the UK's Minister of Defence. In addition, optimism is fed by, for example, severe competition or social pressure. This means you should have a clear understanding of all risks involved, qualify those risks and be subsequently able to financially quantify (= cost) those risks.

4.7   Contract terms that can potentially reduce cost

Warranty conditions and service costs are among the areas where contract terms have the potential to reduce costs or limit uncertainty. If a product, program or service has high reliability, the price impact of embedding 'free' warranty or service may be small, but the customer value – relative to competition – may be high. By extending warranty or including service costs for a specified period, the customer has essentially reduced the cost of ownership relative to the competition. However, you need to be sure that this is an offering that the customer values. If, for example, your customer has its own service center, or views products that fail as disposable, they will see no value in an extended warranty or inclusive service package – and in fact, will make your life more difficult by requiring this element to be withdrawn and a compensating price reduction.

Sometimes there are elements of an offer that could perhaps be handled more cheaply or at a higher quality by a subcontractor or third party 'outsourced' provider Alternatively, you may spot activities that the customer has assumed they will perform, but which can actually be added to your proposal at a lower cost, thereby enhancing the attractiveness of your offer. Without a good understanding of costs and a readiness to explore financial aspects of the deal, opportunities like this will not even be considered.

Taking further examples, other areas where terms have direct impact on user costs may be in areas like shipping or distribution charges, or even in a field such as taxes. While many think of these as areas outside their control, you may very well be able to devise schemes where you can structure deals and prices to the customer's advantage. The timing of title transfer, or the use of intermediaries, or disaggregation of product elements into separate pricing and invoicing are the sort of opportunities that can be explored. This is particularly the case with international trade.

Much negotiation time is spent on terms that are 'owned' by your Finance department – but unfortunately, most of them are about containing the consequences of things going wrong – the 'passive' terms we discussed earlier. They are about the financial limits of liability, or the extent of indemnities, or the percentage of liquidated damages. These terms leave little room for creativity – they are essentially confrontational in nature. However, best practice companies address these contentious areas by active terms or measurements that reduce the risk of failure. They seek to offer terms or processes that give customers confidence that the product or service will work, or that the identification and fixing of problems will be superior to that of the competition. This can be through something as simple as dispute identification and resolution policies and approaches, or the method for recording and reporting service level performance, including service level penalties (in case you do not meet the agreed service level) and service level credits (in case you –consistently meet or exceed agreed service levels).

On this last point, IACCM reviewed many examples of the high cost that poor service level management represents for many companies. In one case, an automotive manufacturer expended more than 800 man-years of effort on disputes over service level performance and service credits – an annual cost of more than $80 million. In another case, a telecoms provider had almost 400 staff extracting nearly $200 million a year from its suppliers in service credits – but at what cost to the provider's performance to its customers? In both cases, smart suppliers spotted an opportunity to offer dynamic web-based reporting and a collaborative resolution / fault elimination process. Not surprisingly, they became a preferred supplier.

The contracts professional should always consider those areas of their offering that may either bring extra value to the customer – reducing their costs and risks – or which should be eliminated because they offer little value, for example because the customer can do these things at lower cost. One word of warning – creativity must be undertaken with a good understanding of the applicable legal and regulatory frameworks. For example, in the past, customer concerns were sometimes addressed with generous and penalty-free rights of return, or deferred payment. Since the introduction of new accounting standards (e.g. Sarbanes-Oxley) and revenue recognition rules, such provisions are unlikely to be acceptable. The same caution must be applied to customer rights of product or service acceptance; ignorance can lead to severe penalties – for example, you need to be aware of competition law, laws relating to intermediaries, the growing body of environmental law and your own company's structure for tax and accounting. 'Creative contracting' in these areas may result in significant exposures.

Let's look at two case studies – one that led to a significant competitive advantage and the other that resulted in an embarrassing customer situation and potential litigation.

Furniture companies represented a major market segment for a composite board manufacturer, but its principal customers were in the construction industry. Product specifications were based on the dominant influence of the construction sector. The market was highly competitive and Sales constantly demanded lower prices as their only significant means of differentiation. An enterprising commercial manager wondered whether there might be other terms that could create differentiation. She explored some obvious areas like quality and warranty, payment and delivery lead-times. While minor changes could be made, none seemed to offer meaningful added value to the customer. However, while exploring delivery, she noticed that several customers had the products shipped to a third party – and she asked why. Her inquiries led to the discovery that the board was too thin for use in most furniture manufacture. Therefore it was shipped to mills, where it was cut and glued to create double thickness board. She contacted Manufacturing to establish whether it was possible to produce board to the required thickness. While the answer to this question was no, it became evident that internal facilities were available to undertake the cutting and gluing. The result would be cost savings for the customer of more than 12 percent and also a shortening of more than 50 percent on product lead-time. Through this initiative, Sales was able to win several new customers and drive increased satisfaction in existing customers, while also raising the margin on sales.

In another situation, Sales was similarly pressing for lower prices and had been losing business to the competition. Finance and Contracts felt that their demands were unreasonable. A major account salesman was working on a large opportunity that included the provision of phone systems to several of his customer's overseas subsidiaries. Prices in those markets were very high. He decided that if he could find a way to reduce those prices, he would be able to offer a competitive package price to the customer and avoid the need to fight for discounts in the home market. He identified several used systems that had been repossessed or taken back as part of a recent upgrade campaign. He included these in his customer proposal, including the need for minor modifications to comply with local technical requirements. As a result of this packaging, his company won the business. Contracts now became involved – and immediately demanded that the sale be halted. They alerted top management to the fact that exclusive dealer relationships in several of the markets precluded direct supply of the equipment. They cited this as another example of the 'lack of controls' over Sales and the need for much tighter discipline, including the review by Contracts of all proposals before they were submitted.

During the subsequent investigation, it became evident that Contracts and Finance had extensive review rights, but these added little value except in terms of control and compliance. They also introduced extensive delays. As a result, Sales tried to avoid these departments.

The customer deal was honored, although the compensation that had to be paid to the local dealers eroded any margin on the products. If these negotiations had occurred in advance of the commitment, the margin could have been safeguarded through considerable reductions in cost (shipping, duties and services). The lack of internal integration and failure to offer a creative 'can do' service had resulted in significant profit erosion and damaged the image of the Contracts group.

4.8 Dependencies

A key challenge when using the value chain method for cost analysis is that this forces you to study cost impacts outside your own organization and potentially extends over the lifecycle of a product or service. This creates additional uncertainties and risk. For example, continuing with the car analogy mentioned earlier, costs of ownership may be dramatically affected by shifts in fuel costs, taxes or insurance charges. This might lead to revision of purchasing decisions – or even, in extreme circumstances, cause users to reverse past decisions. Such an effect might flood the market with used vehicles, driving down the price for new models.

Any form of cost analysis requires choices to be made and some level of estimating. The more the analysis depends on future events, the greater the risk of inaccuracies. Therefore costing is not an activity that can be undertaken once and then forgotten. And the value chain approach, even more than others, introduces areas of unpredictability and change that require regular monitoring. However, its advocates would point out that these factors should always be taken into account in any comprehensive risk analysis – the value chain method simply ensures these critical elements cannot be ignored.

4.9 Bid strategy – how to set your charges

We stated earlier that one of the attractions of a value chain approach to cost analysis is that it causes a focus on the end-user's cost of ownership or cost of doing business, and therefore assists in determining the affordability of acquisition by different types of buyer or different market segments.

Of course, affordability is not just an issue of capital expenditure; it is also a matter of cash flow and timing. Hence the commercial contracts professional must always be open to creative financing solutions. The options in this regard have reduced due to international rules over revenue recognition. Schemes like deferred payment are no longer allowed in most corporations, at least not without top executive authorization. But there are many price or charge options that companies use to address the differing needs of their customers. You need to discover what price or charge customers are willing to pay, which may not be a uniform story.

To determine what to charge for products or services, ask the questions below (Table 4.1).

What are your **costs** of production? (Direct and indirect)
What is the customer prepared to **pay**? (The urgency of market demand)
Are there distinctive market **segments** (Industry, type, geography)?
What are your **competitors** charging – and what charging formulas are typical to each market? (Market research data)
What **margin** do we need – what is the underlying **strategy**?

Table 4.1:   Questions to ask about pricing and charging strategy

The level of need and perception of value may differ between segments – for example, a large corporation may gain substantially greater benefit than a small company; the value in a services business may be much greater than that in manufacturing. You need to have answers to these points because it is fundamental in setting your charges and understanding your profit margin. For each customer set or segment, you also need to understand competitive pricing – and be sure to check whether the product, program or service is like-for-like in terms of specifications, quality, features and functionality. Your company executives or marketing groups may have set principles in terms of market positioning. It is key for you to understand these principles and strategies.

You must also understand and assess ways to manage different approaches between customer segments. How will you 'fence' and justify variations between offerings, especially if the price differences are substantial?

Your role in setting the charges is to protect or expand profit margins. You may run into conflict with the Sales drivers, whose target is often based on revenue rather than profit. To reconcile positions, you must focus on value to the customer. Determining this requires understanding of product positioning and the options for re-positioning. For example, are there business terms you can add, delete or complete to make your offering more attractive, without adversely affecting profit margins? Alternatively, are there ways to differentiate within the product, program or service itself – perhaps by adding or subtracting certain features or clothing it with a different set of services?

In competitive markets, charges are always under pressure. Your role is to find ways that you can selectively differentiate without compromising future negotiations. You can be sure that customers talk with each other. No deal is confidential. If you give a special price to one customer, others will soon know about it. You must be able to explain the differentials in terms of costs or other elements that are specific to that deal or that market segment.

4.10 Contract terms – differences that may have financial impact

Terms attach to the products, programs and/or services you market. Products, programs and services differ in fundamental attributes; with products, there is a tangible good and title generally transfers from the seller to the customer (or perhaps a third party, such as a financing company). Title to programs seldom passes; programs are licensed for use by your customer and the charge may differ (e.g. user based, usage based, 'on demand'. Title to services cannot pass although intellectual property is an intangible item and represents an exception. Services are mostly consumed entirely and their charges are often based on the volume or amount consumed – for example, an hourly rate (e.g. for legal services), or an amount per unit (for utilities). Sometimes, customer can pre-buy services at a fixed rate (e.g. commodity services), either for a pre-set volume or based on a mutually agreed usage estimate.

Intellectual property is a hybrid. Increasingly, it may not be tangible (it is often simply code, such as software, though it may be in written form, such as a business process). Title to intellectual property may change hands – for example, if it is a 'work for hire', commissioned by a specific customer. But often title remains with the developer or inventor, since this is the know-how from which they make a living. In that case, the charge is often for a license or a right to use and the seller will define restrictions on the scope of use and the rights, if any, to transfer those rights.

Whereas with products the end user may have a right to resell (not in competition with your channel), with services there is rarely anything to resell. Intellectual property is something that needs to be protected. By sharing intellectual property or exceeding the rights of use, a customer threatens the seller's income potential. So in determining charges and the terms associated with them, you need to understand the degree to which your product, program or service must be protected and the extent to which user rights must be limited. You also need to consider the cost and effectiveness of monitoring and enforcement – and the impact this may have on competitiveness.

Another key factor that varies significantly between industries (and within industries, depending on the geography in which sales occur) is the choice of distribution channels (the 'sell through' and 'sell with' examples in the above schedule). Is this a direct sale, or through a third party? Are sales agreed through physical or electronic methods? The issue of customer proximity significantly affects perceptions of value and expectations over the degree of negotiability.

As discussed earlier in this chapter, many sales today are what we call 'solutions'. That is, they are packages of products an/or programs and/or services designed to address specific customer needs. This has led to more creative approaches to pricing and financing. As a buyer, you may be faced with a range of options, e.g. an outright purchase price, or a use-based service charge, or a lease. There are even options such as shared benefit or shared risk schemes where charges depend on agreed results; and in offerings like outsourcing, there may be tiers of charging, with basic charges raised or lowered depending on whether or not you achieve agreed service levels (service level credits or penalties, see above). Where performance is key to the customer's profitability or reputation, they will often wish to use financial incentives to encourage good performance. These must be considered in setting charges and gauging profits. For example, liquidated damages for delay or failure to reach agreed targets may eliminate margins; on the other hand, bonuses for early delivery or exceeding targets may enable improved profitability.

All these potential variables lead to complex discussions and calculations to ensure appropriate business terms that align company policies and goals while protecting revenue, margins and competitiveness. The need for your expert involvement is evident; you must understand the principles of costing and setting charges and be ready to ask leading questions about marketing and financial assumptions. Also, you must recognize the linkage with contract terms and be ready to adjust these in a way that helps achieve desired business results.

4.11   Bid strategy – differences that may have financial impact

The most common formula for a product is to set a selling price per unit. This may then be negotiated in terms of a discount or the addition of incremental benefits at no additional charge. However, if a customer cannot afford the purchase price, there may be other options, either through the supplier or by introduction of a third party. This could include a lease or a loan.

Certain products may be suited to a charging formula based on the level or type of use. This has been typical for software and other forms of license (the 'user based' and 'usage based' charging described above). One difficulty in this approach is how to monitor the chargeable event and payment compliance. Ideally it requires some form of metering.

Services are frequently charged on the basis of use, e.g. most utilities and professional services. However, they may also be undertaken on a fixed rate. For example, your customer wants a new process to be defined and documented. You estimate this will take 50 hours to complete, but there are several dependencies. Your preference is therefore to bill at an hourly rate of $150. The customer is reluctant to enter into an open-ended agreement; they suggest a fixed price of $6,000. How might such a situation be reconciled? One key element will be to document the deliverables in detail and to include dependencies and assumptions. You must protect yourself against 'scope creep' or other uncertainties if you are undertaking to work at a fixed fee. You may also want to include a 'performance bonus' and you may want to ensure that stage payments are made, so you do not have all your income waiting until the work has been completed. Make sure that you are always in the driver's seat in any fixed price services contract – you are the decisive party, not your customer.

Another option is for charging to be based on performance. 'Performance-based contracts' set charges based on outcomes – for example, achieving 98 percent availability of an aircraft or meeting specific standards for a cleaning service. Often such agreements include a level of 'risk and reward' based on the performance level (or 'outcome') that is achieved. This will result in some form of liquidated damages or withholding payment in the event of sub-standard performance; and may result in some level of bonus for out-performing the targets (however this will depend on over-achievement having value).

Finally, consider carefully who will be the greatest beneficiary of your product, program or service; it is often not the immediate buyer, especially in the case of services and solutions. The end user is the point of greatest influence; if they deem your product a 'must-have', it will substantially increase your power in any price negotiation. This is the real meaning of the value-chain that we have been discussing above. Price and charge options have a range of derivatives, including shared risk pricing, the introduction of the 'private finance initiative' in the public sector, and the complex models used in areas like outsourcing. Two case studies illustrate these points for your consideration. Each situation reflects changed conditions that create the need or opportunity for a revised assessment of charges and terms.

The first situation arose in a software company. Their primary offering was an enterprise application that assisted inter-operability between other software programs. Traditionally it had operated within a single enterprise location. It was offered under a license that limited use to within the enterprise. There were various charging options, based on the number of locations to be covered. The license was also specific to a particular geography – so a company with locations in several countries would take local licenses to cover their operations in each country. As markets and technology changed, enterprise applications became increasingly international and networked. The company's marketing message started to emphasize that it offered 'global networked solutions'. Consider the implications that this may have had for the company's licensing terms and charging methods.

In the second situation, an aerospace company sold mechanical components to an airframe manufacturer that assembled and sold aircraft to airlines. The company redesigned the component to include embedded software. This resulted in a substantial reduction in routine maintenance costs and aircraft downtime. The contracts department was asked to advise on potential changes to the business terms and charging strategy. You should consider this situation initially in terms of the value chain impact (reducing cost of ownership) and how different stakeholders might perceive this innovation. Then consider likely additions or changes to terms and conditions and how this change might affect charges or charging methods.

4.12   Pre-bid phase: cost/benefit analysis

Cost/benefit overview

A cost / benefit analysis is a component of the business case developed for consideration of procurement for goods or services. Understanding how to prepare a compelling cost / benefit analysis is a critical business skill as it is a required component of any material investment. While a well prepared cost / benefit analysis alone will not get a project approved – the project must also be aligned to strategic direction and trump competing projects in the competition for limited resources – a poorly prepared cost / benefit analysis alone can certainly kill a project.

Distinguishing a full cost / benefit analysis from total cost of ownership calculation

In its most simple form, a cost / benefit analysis can merely consider the total cost of ownership (or TCO) over the useful life of the asset. The TCO calculations can include the obvious: purchase cost, implementation costs, maintenance and support costs. Thorough cost of ownership analysis embodies a cradle-to-grave view of costs: from resources required to develop the business case, draft the Request For Proposals (RFP) and manage the bid process, through to decommissioning and disposal of the asset. The other half of the cost-benefit equation, the benefit (steps 2 and 3), can be left largely unquantified. This approach may be appropriate for small investments or when making comparisons – that is, once the business case for an investment has been established – to enable you to distinguish among multiple options. This chapter focuses on the steps involved in preparing a full cost / benefit analysis.

A full cost / benefit analysis is typically required for all larger investments. Fortunately, this can be completed relatively quickly provided you keep in mind that a cost / benefit analysis is merely a projection and that your projections will always remain ... projections. Your cost / benefit analysis will hinge on assumptions and, when those assumptions are changed, your cost / benefit analysis will change. There is no point in spending hours quantifying non-material factors in a cost / benefit analysis. Focus on the material factors, get them as close to correct as you can, and highlight to your stakeholders your view of the magnitude of the potential variance in the material factors and what can be done to reduce the magnitude of this variance.

The key to building a compelling cost / benefit analysis is:
- Identifying the material factors
- Gaining consensus across your stakeholders that you have correctly identified the material factors

Once you have accomplished this, the next step of getting your stakeholders to agree a range of likely values for those assumptions becomes easier, and once those ranges are established, the rest of the analysis can be performed easily and without generating significant disagreement across your stakeholder group.

The remainder of this chapter details the three steps required for a cost / benefit analysis:
1. Calculate the investment cost
2. Project the savings or additional revenue
3. Determine return on investment (ROI) from the cash flows

The first and the third steps are often uncontroversial provided you can, in step 2, prepare a convincing projection of expense savings. Step 1, investment costs, can be thought of as the costs associated with completing the project. Step 2, expense savings, can be thought of as the day-to-day operational costs of the business function that is affected by the project. Expense savings are the benefit side of a cost / benefit analysis. Step 3, the ROI, shows whether the project is worthwhile given the projected expense savings.

This chapter briefly discusses calculating the investment cost (step 1), introduces Monte Carlo simulations as a mechanism to project savings in a compelling manner (step 2) and then shows you three ways to derive the ROI from the first two inputs (step 3).

1. Calculating the investment cost

The complexity involved in calculating the investment cost varies directly with the complexity of the project. Calculating the investment cost when replacing equipment in a plant is easier when the project does not involve any changes in process. If all you are doing is decommissioning one piece of machinery and dropping another piece of machinery in its place, the costs are typically easily quantified – the cost of decommissioning, the cost of the machinery, and the cost of installation. If, however, you are engaged in re-engineering the workflow of the entire operation then several other factors need to be taken into account such as re-designing the processes and retraining staff, as well as any changes required to supporting systems, applications and services.

Many projects such as replacing an enterprise resource planning (ERP) system span a period of years and the investment cost will often include a significant investment in year 1 with lesser amounts payable in years 2 through 5. The calculation of the initial investment must include the costs over the entire life of the project. In the example below, the initial investment is $1.485M against anticipated expense savings of $2.489M. Note that the initial investment is not broken down into expenses and capitalized items. When preparing an ROI calculation consider all payments to be cash payments. Note also that when preparing your initial investment calculation, you must provide sufficient detail to allow the stakeholders to understand what is being purchased, but not so much detail that the overall understanding of the project is compromised.

In the investment cost analysis below, you can see that the year 1 cost are expected to be $1.045M dropping to $200K in year 2 and down to $60K by year 5. The difference between the investment cost and the expense savings is $1.004M.

	Year 1	Year 2	Year 3	Year 4	Year 5	Total
Expense savings		622	622	622	622	2,489
Expenses						
Resources	800	100	50	30	25	990
Training	150	100	50	50	50	400
Contingency	95					95
Total	1,045	200	100	80	60	1,485
Total	−1,045	422	522	542	562	1,004

Figure 4.1   Initial investment analysis of a project over five years

The initial capital outlay and project related expenses are often quantifiable with a reasonable amount of certainty. Commonly, as in the table above, variance is managed by including a line item named 'contingency' which can be agreed amongst the stakeholders as appropriate, given the perceived uncertainty of the investment costs.

The expense savings are far more difficult to quantify and often are the source of significant disagreement amongst stakeholders. One method of quantifying the expense savings is the Monte Carlo simulation, which is described in more detail below.

2. Project future cash flow

Once you have identified the initial investment, you need to project the future cash flow from this investment. This amount is more difficult to determine and it is often very difficult to gain consensus amongst stakeholders. One method of presenting future cash flow is using a Monte Carlo simulation.

The simulation below is used to generate the expense savings shown in the table above. A Monte Carlo simulation has a number of required inputs. First, you need to define the factors that will affect the benefits that will be generated by your project. In the example below (A) the factors are listed as Transactions, Help desk calls, Development and Support and Servers.

For each of these factors, enter the range of volumes that you will typically see in your current operations. In the example below (B) the range is set at 10-13,000 transactions per month, with a cost per transaction of $10. In (E), you can see the anticipated costs of these transactions. The Monte Carlo simulation runs through hundred of scenarios and calculates that, with a high degree of certainty, you should expect them the cost of these transactions to fall between $1.3M and $1.45M per annum with an average at $1.37M.

In (C), you can see that after the investment is made, you still expect to see 10-13,000 transactions but you expect the costs to drop from $10 per transaction to between $8 and $9 per transaction. In (D), you can see the range of anticipated costs of the transactions drops to $1.08M to $1.26M with an average of $1.17M. (F) shows that on average, the investment should see a net savings of $207,398 from the reduction in transaction costs.

The same process is followed for the other three factors until you arrive at the result (G) that your current costs are about $1.908M and your expected costs after investment should drop to $1.286 for a net savings of $622K.

One of the primary advantages of the Monte Carlo simulation is that it allows any number of variables that cannot be precisely defined and generates a range of expected results. Table (E) above is an example, showing that current costs can range from $1.7M to $2.1M and costs post-investment (D) to be somewhere between $1.17M and $1.4M.

Another advantage is that the method allows insight to the factors that drive the savings. In the screenshot below, the cells with the greatest impact on the result are highlighted in (F). You can see from this that Transactions and Development and Support factors are driving this result and particular focus should be directed at ensuring the cost and volume assumptions for those factors are as accurate as possible.

3. Calculate Return on Investment

1. Break-even cash flow analysis
Break-even analysis explores the return in terms of that point in time when revenues from the investment equal the amount of the investment. This is the break-even point. Calculating the break-even point requires considering the cash flows, comparing outflows, or costs, with inflows, or revenues, on a periodic basis over the life of the investment.

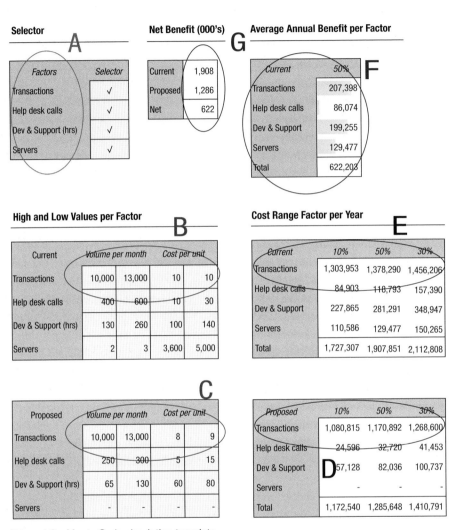

Figure 4.2   Monte Carlo simulation template

If we look at the table above we see that in year 1 of the investment, outflows greatly exceeded inflows. In years 2 to 5, inflows exceeded outflows and the investment became net positive early in year four.

To calculate the break-even point of the investment, look at the number of years the investment remains in the red. In the table below, the last year in the red is year 3 so the break-even point will be sometime in year four. To calculate exactly when in year 4 you will break even, divide the year four running total by the year four net savings. In the table below, you would divide $442K by $542K for a result of 81percent. Subtract this from 1 to obtain 19 percent. Your break-even point for this investment is 3.19 years. The shorter the payback period, the better the investment.

2. Net Present Value

Up to this point, we have not addressed the issue of the cost of capital. Borrowing money for an investment costs money, how much is dependent upon interest rates, or money that you have now could be invested to generate interest income. So money that you have now is generally worth more than having that same amount at some time in the future. The concept is known as the Time Value of Money and the formula for its calculation is:

$$NPV=\sum_{t-1}^{T}\frac{C_t}{(1+r)^t}-C_0$$

The good news is that calculation tables are freely available via the internet – but for those who wish to understand more, here is an explanation and worked example.

Present Value represents the current value of a given amount of money in the future. The greater the interest rate, or the longer into the future we base our calculations, the lower the Present Value of the money. Present Value equals the investment value (or return), divided by one plus the annual interest rate, to the nth power, where 'n' equals the number of years before the money is received. So for an expected one million dollars in revenue due to materialize in three years with annual interest rates at 12 percent, the Present Value of that money is one million divided by 1.1 cubed, which is one million dollars divided by 1.404, or $711,780.

To put this into the example above assuming a 12 percent rate of return, in year 1, the present value of our expenditure is the actual expenditure of -$1.045M. In year 2, we expect to receive $422K net. This number divided by 1 plus our minimum rate of return (1.12) results in a discounted rate of $377K. In years 3, 4 and 5, despite an increase in net savings to over $500K, because they are further away in time the discount increases, resulting in a discounted return of $416K, $386K, and $357K respectively.

In the above scenario, the discounted return on the investment is $491K, which is less than the non-discounted return of $1.004 but still represents a 33 percent return on investment.

3. Internal Rate of Return

Most organizations operate with an Internal Rate of Return (IRR) which is set by their Finance Department and used to evaluate investment decisions. It is often necessary for the contracts expert to understand the specific IRR requirements – and of course it is helpful to know this in respect of your trading partner, since it may assist you in positioning your bid or requirements.

An IRR calculation forecasts the rate of return offered by an investment project over its useful life and is sometimes called the *yield on project*. It is estimated by finding the discount rate that equates the present value of a project's cash outflow with the present value of its cash inflow. The calculation results in finding the discount rate that will cause the net present value of a project to be equal to zero.

Critical Success Factors

The key to a successful cost/benefit analysis is:
- Understanding the most material factors that influence the numbers
- Ensuring that the assumptions underlying those factors are as accurate as possible.

The business is best served by achieving realistic cost/benefit analysis. To achieve this, be sure to incorporate risk analysis to identify potential barriers that will derail cash inflows or other expected benefits. Identify hidden costs to assure realistic financial projections.

Finally, extend the business case to be the foundation for ongoing performance measurement. The criteria that are used to justify an investment should then be used to judge its ultimate success and provide insight into areas needing corrections in order to achieve success.

Aligning investment with strategy

If all financial analysis methodologies contain such high levels of uncertainty, why do business cases rely so heavily on them? There are two responses – first, they are the tools that most directly predict the company's ability to make money. Those companies that have pursued detailed costing methodologies, enforce strict budgetary controls, and incorporate robust forecasting technologies are able to evaluate investments with a fair degree of confidence. The other response is that companies are turning to non-financial analysis capabilities to be used in addition to, or sometimes instead of, their traditional financial counterparts.

Alternative approaches look to mitigate the speculative nature of pure financial analysis by introducing strategic or process considerations. They include development of multiple criteria decision models as the basis for investment decisions. These models consider opportunity analysis, alignment with strategy, risk analysis and responsiveness to customer demand and competitive trends.

Consensus on approach

When developing a business case, it is essential to use approaches generally accepted within the company. This eliminates having to educate your audience on a new approach. If standard approaches won't adequately make the case, it will require a compelling reason for an alternative approach. Make sure the audience understands why you are deviating from the norm. Even when using a unique approach, use terms and criteria that everyone will understand. If the company standard is Internal Rate of Return, be sure to evaluate the investment in those terms.

Use alternative approaches such as Balanced Scorecard or Constraint analysis in addition to, not instead of, the norm. Address risk scenarios and other non-financial elements in terms that all stakeholders can understand.

Neutralizing bias

Most business cases are approached as justification for an investment. So there is usually a strong bias to inflate benefits and minimize costs. Politics, influence and simple precedent also work to create a bias. So in one sense, the role of quality cost/benefit analysis is to neutralize bias.

Credibility of assumptions

Bias also exists in the assumptions expressed in the business case, especially non-financial assumptions. A strong business case will clearly state the assumptions on which it is based. These may be increasing competition, rising interest rates, new regulatory pressures. Be sure all parties agree on the overriding assumption before addressing the details of the analysis.

Provide evidence on which assumptions are based. If some of the assumptions are weak or otherwise open to debate, address alternate cost/benefit scenarios that could play out if specific assumptions prove unrealized. Where wrong assumptions might undermine the business case altogether, be sure to provide anticipated remedies and projected costs if specific assumptions were to prove unrealized.

Risk assessment

Risk can be expressed in terms of the likelihood that assumptions are true, and that processes will run as planned. All elements of a cost/benefit analysis should be challenged and validated from a risk perspective. What if trends don't continue, what if interest rates go in the opposite direction?

Cost/benefit analysis must assess identify the areas of greatest risk, and articulate the remedies to manage those risks.

Incorporating key indicators in supplier evaluation

The business case, and its integrated cost-benefit analysis, lives long beyond the initial project approval. Some elements should be incorporated in to the RFP so that potential suppliers understand the underlying goals for the investment and can make sure that their response aligns with expectations. This understanding allows suppliers to consider alternatives in their proposals that can better achieve the desired results.

Fulfillment of the business case is also the foundation for supplier evaluation criteria. Suppliers should be selected in part on the basis of their ability to deliver on the business objectives outlined in the business case, and in part on their ability to address the risks identified in the business case.

Linking metrics with requirements

As we have mentioned, fulfillment of the business case is the primary project or purchase objective. The detailed requirements created after initial project approval should be developed to optimize cost/benefit scenarios. One approach is to cascade requirements from the high-level objectives in the business case. For example, if the cost/benefit analysis identifies cost considerations such as allocations or implementation support, make sure that those responsible for those elements are aware of the assumptions, buy in to them, and are capable of delivering them.

You may want to ask those responsible to sign off the figures in the business case. These metrics then become part of the requirements and the contract as a whole. The requirements should identify "sensors" to report on business financial and non-financial performance metrics, and inform when any component of the cost/benefit analysis deviates from expectations. This serves two functions – it will allow contract managers to identify issues and make corrections during the course of implementation, and it will provide a more robust basis for future cost/benefit analyzes.

4.13 **Summary**

This chapter has addressed a wide range of cost and pricing issues from both a customer and supplier or market perspective. As explained at the beginning, many contracts experts are not closely involved in financial analysis and this frequently results in missed value opportunities.

In considering this chapter, we encourage those involved in contracting to think not only about their internal cost and value calculations, but to understand and evaluate those of their trading partners. It is through this alignment that we can often spot opportunities for creative or innovative commercial solutions that deliver enhanced economic value. It is also through this alignment that we can respond to executive demands for greater value-add.

Good contracting focuses on the contract as an economic instrument. This can only be achieved through clear understanding of costs, pricing and financial assessment techniques and their inclusion in both internal and external negotiations.

CHAPTER 5

Aligning risk through financial modeling

5.1 Introduction

This chapter builds on earlier chapters related to cost identification and financial considerations and explains in greater depth some of the more complex situations a contracts team may encounter. Its purpose is to create awareness of financial modeling, rather than to develop specific expertise, and it relates only to modeling for the sale or provision of a product or service.

Whereas previous chapters have discussed some of the tools typically used by the customer organization to assess costs and evaluate their acquisition alternatives, this chapter is more applicable to the supplier. However, as with the previous chapters, we believe that those who work on the buy-side should study and understand the concepts we set out in this section, since it will make them better-informed negotiators and business partners.

5.2 The importance of economic alignment

How often have you heard about business relationships that fell apart because the supplier was not making money, or because the buyer felt that they were not receiving value, or were being 'nickel and dimed' (charged for every little extra service) for every change? Or perhaps there has been a major change in market or competitive conditions and the relationship was unable to adjust far enough or fast enough to survive.

If you dig into the fundamental cause of most contract failures or disappointed outcomes, you will find that one or both parties felt that there was inflexibility, unfairness or bad faith. And the underlying catalyst for that feeling is almost always economic.

Business contracts are about money. In the end, the driver behind every contract is economic. They are created because the parties anticipate there is potential for *mutual* economic gain.

The word 'mutual' is highlighted because it seems that contracts professionals and negotiators often forget about this fundamental driver for the transaction or relationship. They become so obsessed with details of risk allocation or internal measurements that they forget that success depends on both parties feeling motivated to perform – and that the motivation must be maintained throughout the contract lifecycle.

Sometimes, the problem may be that the contracts specialists have limited visibility of the financial implications of the deal. In that case, they are designing the contract or negotiating the terms in a vacuum. They cannot possibly understand the value or the economic impacts of their trading position – and the probability of failure is thereby dramatically increased.

5.3   The basics of financial modeling

The issues outlined above explain why financial modeling is such an important element of the contracts toolkit. Discussions of contract structure, terms, risk allocation and negotiating strategy should *never* be undertaken without full understanding of the underlying economics.

There are many categories of financial model, depending on the nature of the product or service to be sold or acquired and the pricing or charging formula that will be used. The chapter on financial considerations set out many of the basic considerations in understanding cost and value and supports a standard transactional view of costing and pricing. However, many contracts extend over a prolonged time period and are subject to a range of uncertainties – perhaps even initial uncertainty over precise requirements or the methods that will be used to achieve objectives. Financial modeling in this case will be used to analyze the consequences of that uncertainty and may in turn influence the structuring of the contract or the terms and conditions to be applied.

As the following case study illustrates, we must sometimes be courageous in our approach, we must sometimes challenge or change the standard rules, because there are occasions when those rules, rather than protecting us from risk, will actually be the source of risk.

5.4   The MediaCity case study

Most contracting processes are highly rules-driven. The terms are dictated by a range of stakeholders from Legal, Finance, Operations, Product Management and various other functions. Contracts or commercial staff may have limited authority to make changes; their role is to impose standards or to reconcile and manage differences between stakeholder perspectives and market needs, negotiating within permitted boundaries. On occasion, they may develop creative commercial solutions to intractable problems. But as this story illustrates, they must use their analysis of the economic factors underlying the deal to drive an appropriate contract strategy.

The MediaCity development in Manchester, UK was a $500m project at the leading edge of technology and included a complex mix of suppliers, operating under both public and private sector procurement rules. Unlike most major construction projects, it came in on time and within budget.

In common with a growing number of today's complex projects, MediaCity involved major uncertainties. The specifications were in many areas imprecise or highly generalized – for example, that the buildings must comply with the environmental and regulatory standards applicable in five years' time. The key certainties were the date for completion and the reputational damage that would occur in the event of failure. In such circumstances, no one could even be sure whether the anticipated budget was realistic.

At the outset, a strategic risk decision was made. It was estimated that traditional contract negotiation would take a minimum of six to eight months, and that this would make the completion date unachievable. The negotiation team would also face so much uncertainty that there was a high probability they would never reach agreement. Because of this uncertainty work started under a Memorandum of Understanding that released an initial $8m to enable start-up. Once this funding was exhausted, further top-up funds were released. More formal contracts were negotiated in the background while work continued – and this work was of course providing the contracts teams with real-time data that was steadily validating many of the underlying assumptions over achievability.

Another strategic decision related to the criteria for supplier selection. Given the many uncertainties, it was obvious that individual price estimates would have limited meaning and that the key to delivering within budget would be the combination of experience and attitude. In appointing suppliers, the contractor was looking for evidence of collaborative working and a sense of shared ownership for problems.

This spirit also influenced the approach to risk management. There was no formal risk register. The integrated project team operated on principles of openness and transparency. When issues arose, they were immediately communicated across the team to enable resolution or mitigation and to allow updated cost and budget estimates.

In combination, these approaches add up to a contracting and financial strategy. They broke many of the rules associated with traditional contracting, yet they led to a successful outcome. They do not represent a model for every project or relationship, but they illustrate the need for contracts and commercial professionals to exercise judgment and to develop flexible approaches to their work. Importantly, this 'agile' approach meant that the risks of the parties were contained. By working within specific funding releases, the budget-holders gained continuous visibility into progress and could determine at each step the 'riskiness' of releasing more money.

It is the ability to understand when the rules do not apply that is the essence of good judgment in every profession. In the world of contracts and commercial, we need more people who exhibit this courage and understanding.

5.5   Making judgments

The point of this example is not, of course, to suggest that 'breaking the rules' should be business as usual. But it causes us to focus on a dual aspect of risk.

First, we must ask whether this is a business deal we want to win or engage in. If yes, can it be achieved within the current rules, or will they in fact increase the chances of failure? (In the case above, it was clear that the rules would indeed cause failure to meet the prescribed requirements. They would make project overruns inevitable.)

Second, if the standard rules are getting in the way, specifically which ones need to be changed and are we capable of managing the consequences of that change? In other words, can we handle the risks associated with deviating from our normal risk control procedures?

As a final point, before we get into aspects of financial modeling, it is important to think of risk in terms of failure to maximize potential. When we think of it this way, we no longer bind ourselves only to the deal that is currently on the table, but we recognize that this deal may change over time and that our procedures must therefore be adaptive to that change – perhaps new market conditions change the underlying requirement, or market demand results in significant increases (or declines) in the value of the contract. Good risk – and financial – management enables us to deal smoothly with these changes in potential, to ensure we maximize the value from the contract, rather than move into claims, disputes or arguments over who was to blame for sub-standard performance.

5.6   Financial model elements

Previous chapters have outlined the importance of stakeholder analysis and that is also true with financial modeling. An understanding of who is affected and in what ways will be critical to our ability to understand and evaluate costs and budgets.

The following elements must be considered in order to fully and accurately evaluate the nature, timing and extent of cash flows from proposed sales contracts.

Measures
Measures include:
- Revenues
- Cost of goods sold / cost of sales
- Overheads and allocations
- Cash flows

Time

Time elements include:
- Overall timeframe (life of contract)
- Intervals (months, quarters, years)

Drivers

Drivers such as volume, price, availability of product/ service, specific contract terms that dictate production, delivery, quality, transfer of ownership, etc will have an influence on:
- Termination clauses and their impacts
- Penalty clauses and their impacts

Risk

Risk elements are closely related to drivers, but these elements focus on the uncertainty of cash flows – such as SLA terms that introduce or fail to reduce uncertainty; material adverse change (MAC) clauses that allow the buyer to walk away from the deal, on-demand delivery availability, quality, etc.

Metrics

Standard financial metrics that integrate the effects of measures, time, drivers and risk include:
- Net present value (NPV)
- Internal rate of return (IRR)
- Payback

Many of these areas have been described in previous chapters. Reference back to the case study above will illustrate that sometimes a number of the key factors needed to build a financial model are either highly uncertain or not known. These areas of questionable or missing information clearly represent risks – and will therefore influence how you proceed and specifically how you advise management. Sometimes, your recommendation may be that the levels of uncertainty represent a barrier that is simply too great – and that the deal should not proceed. In other cases, as in the case study, it may be that you suggest the deal should not proceed in the proposed or standard business form – in other words, that you need a creative approach that will allow management of the uncertain elements and will ensure that the blanks are filled in as the project progresses.

5.7   Some basic principles and terms

In most long-term projects, the seller faces substantial start-up costs. It is normal for many of these costs to reduce or disappear over time. Examples might be the need to acquire buildings or tooling, create a new call center, hire new or specialist staff, undertake extensive research or engineering and design plans or prototypes. Costs that are specifically related to the project must be recovered and it is unusual for the customer to fund them up-front. They will therefore be recovered over the life of the project.

Some of the early costs and various areas of on-going activity are likely to reduce over time. However, others may increase – for example, labor or raw material costs tend to escalate. Conversely, others – such as the costs of IT – may reduce, and as full volume is reached, the supplier can normally achieve greater efficiencies – for example, it may be possible to reduce staffing, or to employ cheaper and less skilled labor.

In many contracts – especially in areas such as outsourcing – there is an assumption that costs will reduce over time and therefore many contracts today include terms where charges will also fall. Buyers have come to expect price decreases year-on-year; this is not an unreasonable assumption, but may prove dangerous if the parties do not work collaboratively in achieving those reductions. For example, there could be a tendency for suppliers to achieve cost cutting through measures that compromise quality or health and safety.

When making financial assessments – and gauging the economic riskiness of the proposed contract – the parties must be clear about whether this is an acquisition based on **inputs** (that is, what is used – time and materials) or **outputs** (outcomes or results achieved, such as number of successful sales, percentage of satisfied callers, achievement of flight hours) or **transactions** (numbers of calls) or **resource units** (number of users, number of desktops). Sometimes, the method of payment may also be material to the method chosen – for example, does the customer expect a cost-plus approach, or open-book accounting (principles that are common in government contracts).

Different approaches to charging have very different risk profiles, especially if the demand levels are unpredictable or subject to change. And as the list of elements (above) indicates, that riskiness is also increased or diminished depending on what other terms the customer expects. For example, a right of early termination or on-demand flexibility will have major impact on the possibilities of cost under-recovery or unplanned extra expense.

All financial models must make assumptions. Clearly, the more factors that have to be assumed, the greater the chance that something could go wrong.

5.8 Pricing mechanisms

In practice, the pricing mechanism that the parties agree will generally be reflective of the overall risks that the deal represents. For example, a contract with a fixed scope is more likely to be managed through a fixed price. Those with a variable or uncertain scope increasingly result in the use of an up-front 'design and build' contract to verify the price.

Output pricing has become increasingly popular in circumstances where the product or service is more commoditized – which means of course that this tends to apply in situations where the product or service is relatively mature. It also tends to be used extensively in areas such as telecommunications. Input pricing is again used in contracts with greater uncertainty and the absence of reliable 'baselines'. These may not have the level of uncertainty that requires a design-and-build approach; for example, the parties may be very clear about what they want to achieve and that it is achievable – but there may be a series of factors that cause some cost uncertainty. An example would be in first-generation business process outsourcing, or where a customer is demanding significant customization to an otherwise relatively standard offering.

When input pricing is used, the customer is more likely to demand more detailed insights to the cost base and is also more likely to demand regular cost benchmarks.

5.9 Gainshare and shared benefits

There is often discussion over whether suppliers should be incentivized to 'out-perform' or be rewarded for excellence or innovation. Some view this as unnecessary, arguing that suppliers should be motivated by wishing to retain their customer's business and by the forces of competition. Others suggest that financial incentives motivate increased attention and a commitment to continuous improvement – and that if the benefits are shared, this is fundamental to a win-win relationship.

In general, shared benefit agreements have proven popular in concept, but relatively rare in practice. Many times, this is because it can be hard to associate any specific economic benefit with the improvement. However, this is not always the case; for example, it may make sense to offer an incentive for early completion of a new building or early implementation of a new IT system. Even here, the customer will want to be sure that this really does represent a stretch target for the supplier and that they are not simply paying more for 'business as usual'.

If you are considering a 'gainshare' provision, some particular points to consider include:
- Setting a baseline on which both parties can agree
- Defining what is the expected level of service and what represents 'exceptional' standards (and perhaps demonstrating this through benchmarks)
- Having a reliable method for demonstrating benefit – such as sustained savings or process improvements

- How events outside the supplier's control – such as customer behavior – will be handled
- Deciding how the risk or reward will be allocated and what the duration should be
- Whether the supplier is entitled to protect any unique intellectual property or method that led to the superior performance

5.10   Other factors

In conclusion, there are a number of other factors that often arise in the delivery of longer term, performance based contracts. For example, in outsourcing agreements it may be necessary to build provisions relating to cost of living adjustments or the handling of foreign exchange movements. Since the drive for much outsourcing is labor arbitrage, but in many low cost countries these salary and exchange movements are extremely volatile, both parties will be anxious to build in protections.

Service credits or liquidated damages are another area of growing importance in any outcome or performance based agreement. The parties should be cautious not to use these provisions in a way that disincentivizes openness and sharing of risk mitigation. A sliding scale based on the level of openness can be a good idea, to ensure the parties are motivated to work together to fix problems early. But even then, the amount 'at risk' is likely to be a major area of contention. It is also important to ensure that these provisions link closely to the true Key Performance Indicators (KPIs) – of which there should be relatively few.

Business change is another area that is hard to manage. Customers increasingly want flexibility, yet suppliers have often made major investments to generate capability. There is no easy answer, though in some cases there can be agreement over the compensation due for early termination.

5.11   Summary

Financial modeling and its alignment with risk identification and management are increasingly important because of the growing trend to outcome and performance based contracts. Both suppliers and customers need to ensure a maturity in their understanding and discussion of the financial impacts of their agreement and to establish a fair and reasonable balance of risk, including terms which support open discussion and high quality governance of the relationship they have established.

CHAPTER 6

Routes to market – partnerships, alliances, and distribution and sourcing options

Business relationships take many forms. Before appropriate terms can be established, it is critical to determine the type of relationship that will best fit the capabilities and goals of the parties. This chapter investigates partnerships, alliances and distribution, and the related competition rules and laws to be aware of when entering into a relationship.

6.1 Primary types of contracts used in large businesses

As discussed in previous chapters, contracts assume great significance in business-to-business relationships. In the supply of services, the contract frequently represents the only tangible definition of what will be delivered and establishes important procedures. Contracts also answer the questions who, what, when and where, as well as 'what if'.

In this chapter, we will examine the common contractual partnering and aligning relationships and laws controlling them:
- Agency or sales representative
- Teaming, joint venture and sales consortium
- Prime contractor, subcontractor, distribution
- Partnership arrangements

Responsibility and ownership for these contract and relationship types varies significantly between, and often within, companies, especially in areas like subcontracting, distribution or 'alliances'. However, organization matters far less than procedural clarity and accountability; weaknesses in these are among the most frequent causes of relationship or opportunity failure.

6.2 Use of agents and representatives

Many companies use agents, representatives and distributors to help in generating sales or performing services in market segments or countries. Some of the reasons for their use are:

- A company may be unfamiliar with business practices, cultural customs and ways of conducting business in a particular market.
- Third party channels may be a more cost-effective way to reach customers, especially in consumer or small business markets.
- Agents/distributors may have previously established relationships with customers to help open up sales opportunities.
- Third party channels may be able to offer incremental value, such as specialized services, that adds to the core product.
- Customers may prefer to buy from locally owned and known entities rather than from a foreign company.
- A company may not have a subsidiary, joint venture or other direct means of marketing and supplying products and services within a particular country or territory.
- There may be special relationships required or helpful to do business in a particular market, such as some Middle Eastern countries require that business is handled through a local agent or distributor.

Establishing third party channels of this type is not a straightforward decision and results in significant business consequences. Although at one level it may expand and complement your marketing efforts, at another it places severe restraints on your freedom of action in the market. For example, you may no longer be able to make direct sales to customers in that territory; you lose some flexibility in negotiating prices; you may be obliged to use the channel, even when your customer wants a different approach.

As a buyer, it is important to understand the distribution methods used by your suppliers and how they plan to ensure your contract requirements are handled effectively. This section discusses some of the selection procedures and their implications. Both buyers and sellers should be familiar with these principles because:

- They place restrictions on the supplier's actions – and, depending on business objectives, these may affect the choice of supplier .
- Increasingly, buyers control or influence elements of their company's third party relationships – for example, through placing subcontracts or managing certain types of supplier programs. Often subcontracts may be placed with organizations that are also agents or distributors of your company; this requires special care and understanding of the legal implications.
- Unless you understand agency / distribution principles and laws, you cannot make effective decisions or ensure proper controls or safeguards in your contracts.

The legislative environment governing these relationships is complex and varied. It is, of course, essential to ensure that the decisions you make are informed by the latest updates on competition and agency law. It is also critical to understand whether there are potential issues under relevant bribery and corruption laws (e.g. Foreign Corrupt Practices Act – FCPA, Anti-Bribery Act etc.). Traditionally, local third party agreements were used to pay 'commissions' or 'facilitation payments' to key decision-makers, especially in government contracts. In some markets, pressure for such activity remains strong and must be avoided. There are occasions when the contract manager may become aware of such pressures and it is their duty to ensure senior management is made aware.

The market

Product distribution methods have changed dramatically in recent years and continue to evolve. Some companies now sell their products directly through the internet, but have services and support provided by distributors. Others may sell through distributors and handle support via telephone and the internet. Some companies sell directly in their home territories, but use distributors in areas where they do not employ a resident sales force. Some questions to answer when deciding whether to employ an agent or distributor:

- Is the use of an agent or distributor justified by market demand for your products and/ or services?
- What competition laws will apply and what effect will they have on your freedom of action (for example, in selecting third parties, in establishing market terms, in setting prices, in managing customer relationships)?
- Is there sufficient demand in the region to justify a separate agent or distributor or could the territory be covered by a representative in an adjacent territory?
- Is the market too large to give exclusivity to a single agent or distributor (and will the law allow this)?
- Is it reasonable to expect an agent or distributor not to handle competing goods in the market (and can you prevent it)?
- Will this require a long-term strategy that can be pursued only by someone with significant financial resources?
- Should you go with a well-established third party who can immediately provide access to the market even though this may require more sharing of profits?

The customers

Agents or representatives may provide a better service to the local customer base than a direct sales force. For example:

- The product is going to be sold exclusively to government agencies.
- The representative has access to government officials involved in procurement decisions.
- The product is part of a larger or turnkey project, requiring access to project coordinators and the ability to work with project engineers.
- If a long-term sales effort focused on a particular customer is required, the situation will probably be better suited to an agent than a distributor.

- If the sales are to a broader base of ordinary commercial customers, a distributor with an existing network of sales outlets may be more appropriate.
- If the customers prefer to purchase local products, you may choose to use a distributor that will sell your company's products under its own label.

The product

A third party may better represent the product or service itself, for example:

- The marketing of the product requires advanced consulting, engineering and technical personnel to effectively sell the product and your company alone cannot supply the talent needed. A major ERP system or construction project might be examples.
- The product is complementary to another line of products, making it desirable to 'piggyback' on the distribution of other products. Examples are Disney products such as the Shrek character toys being distributed through Burger King children's meals, or the on-board service and assistance systems sold in conjunction with many new cars.
- It is essential for servicing or supply of the product to have sufficient resources and spare parts available locally, and your company cannot efficiently achieve this through its own resources. A product like bearings is a good example; aircraft support and maintenance services represent another.
- Strategically, your company may wish to avoid the costs, risks or complexity of physical presence in particular markets (either geographic, or specific market segments).

Agent versus distributor

In determining whether an agent or distributor should be selected, it is best to look at the situation from each perspective. Consider the following:

- Factors favoring an agent:
  - When it is important to exercise a high level of control over the marketing and sales activities of the representative, including price and terms and conditions.
  - Preference for selling directly to the customer in order to build goodwill in the market.

- Factors favoring a distributor:
  - When you are not willing to assume risks of non-payment by the customer.
  - If you don't want a commission-based compensation structure.
  - You want someone else to carry inventory of the products and parts and provide repair and warranty services.

The key distinction between agents and distributors is that the agent is a representative of its principal and owes a duty of 'good faith'; in most instances customer recourse remains directly to the principal. A distributor (may also be termed reseller, remarketer, dealer) is an independent entity, operating at arm's length and over which the 'principal' has limited rights of influence or control; customers are the distributor's customers and their primary recourse is to the distributor.

So a fundamental question in determining which is appropriate in a particular market situation is the degree of control that you wish to exercise over your channel and the extent to which you wish to maintain customer relationships with your company. A distributor not only possesses, but takes title to the goods being sold, unlike a sales representative or agent, who may hold the goods temporarily (or who may take orders that are then fulfilled directly by the manufacturer), but does not own them. The distributor is acting on its own behalf, usually by purchasing the goods from the manufacturer, adding a profit margin and reselling the goods. Attempts to set or influence distributor sales prices are in many cases illegal and breach competition laws in most major jurisdictions.

Choosing a representative

Now that you have determined what type of representative to choose, what are typical criteria to choose the right representative?

The agent or distributor should be asked to provide references, financial information, and affiliations, as well as a certification that the candidate has read and agreed to relevant policies and laws, such as the US FCPA and Export Control or equivalents.

A contracts professional should review all potential agreements and negotiation strategies before negotiating with a distributor or agent. Aside from the certifications of compliance with the company's policies, national and local laws and other standard legal protections, all agent and distributor contracts should be very specific as to what action is required on their part, what goals are to be met and what restrictions apply.

There is no single template for every agent/distributor agreement as there will need to be consideration of the business objectives and the market circumstances. The following provisions are usually ingredients in formulating most agreements:

- Consider the distributor's distribution channels and capabilities to move products.
- Authorized territory – may be geographic or based on market segment (e.g.; the country of France, the State of Maryland, any company with less than 100 employees, pharmaceutical companies only – but remember that in many situations – especially Europe – you may be unable to impose restrictions. In those cases, you may instead have to look at creating incentives, such as bonuses, that encourage compliance with your goals).
- Minimum amounts of sales or purchases required from the agent / distributor to be able to continue and have their agreement renewed. (Again, such provisions are not acceptable in all countries, so you may once more have to look at bonus schemes or similar. If you have concerns in this regard, it may be wise to carefully consider a) the

term of the agreement and b) your overall channel strategy and structure – for example, whether you should have multiple tiers of distribution).

- Performance terms, such as training personnel reporting to you and marketing budgets. Link non-performance by the agent/distributor to cause for termination.
- For distributors, price provisions. What they will pay for goods, or the discount(s) they receive from your standard prices. Suggested sales prices to end-users (companies cannot determine firm end-user prices for distributors). In the case of agents, prices at which equipment can be offered (if known at the time of agreement).
- For agents, basis of commission structure, expense limitations.
- For agents and distributors outside your country, currency fluctuation. This should cover the percentage of fluctuation between your national currency and foreign currency that is acceptable before prices or commission rates must be renegotiated.
- Start and end dates. Avoid 'evergreen' renewal clauses, which allow the agreement to renew automatically unless terminated in writing. The agreement should terminate at the end of the period stated. Your company's lawyer can advise you on local laws affecting termination, OECD anti-corruption convention, US FCPA and Export Control clauses, and for agents and distributors operating outside your country. Consider the administrative implications of managing renewal / terminations and ensure you are capable of handling them.
- Stock holding / inventory obligations and handling of returns. What happens to 'old' product, for example when you discontinue or introduce a revised product line? What happens on termination?
- Obligations to provide services, such as customer support, warranty.
- Quality obligations – type of premises required, staff training etc.
- Confidentiality policies, handling of confidential information and trade secrets.

Business consortia

A customer who wishes to purchase separate systems, items of equipment, parts of a network which are to be integrated and installed as an operating unit has three options:

- Purchase the system by contracts with separate suppliers
- One supplier acting as a prime contractor
- Establish a sales consortium

When the customer contracts with separate suppliers, elements of the system are purchased from different suppliers and installed. Project management and responsibility for inter-operability etc. reside with the customer, either through their own staff or perhaps with an appointed consultant. If construction work is needed, a construction contractor provides it. A consulting engineer or other party may be responsible for integration on behalf of the customer.

If the customer contracts with one firm, this single supplier serves as the prime contractor and accepts responsibility / risk for eventual performance. The prime contractor normally supplies its own goods and services, sources other items, obtains or provides required construction services, and integrates the project.

The size and complexity of certain projects has led to the development of the sales consortium as an alternative response. Under the consortium mode, the suppliers and the construction contractor assume responsibility to the customer and share responsibility with one another. This is a method of bidding that has become increasing popular for turnkey or other large contracts or where risk is too great to reasonably be assumed by a single entity.

What is a consortium?

A consortium is defined as: *An alliance between companies by which, in tendering for a project, they make clear to the customer that it is their desire to work together, and that their tenders have been coordinated on that basis.* The companies usually exercise a great deal of care to make sure that their individual offers are such that they dovetail together and collectively comprise a complete scheme. Customers will generally require that the companies involved give a joint undertaking that the project will be complete and will operate satisfactorily. In most cases there is a statement that the members of the consortium are jointly and severally liable to the customer. This means that each member of the consortium is legally responsible to the customer for its scope and the scope of each of the other members of the consortium. The consortium agreement is entered into to apportion this responsibility and set out the other rules that will govern the members of the consortium.

Given its complexity, development and drafting of such agreements is a lengthy process, requiring extensive cooperation between the affected parties. Leadership of contract development may be with either the buyer or a leading supplier; in some cases, it is outsourced to a law firm with extensive experience in similar situations, or a drafting committee is formed with representatives from all the major participants.

Clauses in a consortium agreement

The clauses in a consortium agreement listed below will typically require particular focus in drafting and development.

- Identification of consortium members
- Scope of work
- Responsibility for claims
- Proportionate value
- Limitation of liability
- Nature of the relationship
- Material breach /default

- Managing the consortium
- Resolution of disputes
- Contract performance
- Governing law
- Contract negotiation
- Definition of terms
- Engineering services
- Bid preparation
- General conditions

Consortium issues to consider

Once you have decided to participate in a consortium, there are other issues to consider and resolve.

- Will this be an association of equals or should some companies participate as subcontractors? Who will serve as members versus subcontractors?
- Are there tax issues that will influence the manner in which the consortium is structured?
- Are there other financial incentives available; for example, can a US company benefit from reduced interest rates or other subsidies if the company bids in consortium with another company? A local company? With local content guarantees?
- Has the significance of joint and several liability been evaluated by a suitable level of management?
- Has there been an adequate evaluation of the financial strength of each prospective member? Is special protection needed?
- Should members be permitted to assign responsibilities? To subsidiaries? With or without guarantees? Should the parties have the right to approve subcontracts? Are parent company guarantees being sought? Should they be?
- What technical, financial or business data will the members supply to each other?
- Must such data be held in confidence?
- Will the arrangement be exclusive or are the parties free to bid on the project with other companies?
- Who will bear the expenses associated with preparation of the proposal? Who will coordinate the proposal? Are the responsibilities of the bid bond understood and assigned as appropriate?
- Will the price to the customer be in one currency or in several currencies? Has the impact of exchange variations been considered in the risk-sharing agreement?
- Will one member serve as liaison with the customer to arrange meetings for negotiations? Will all members be present at such meetings?
- Will a member have the right to withdraw without penalties in the event the customer insists on terms that are not acceptable to that party?
- How will responsibilities be assigned? Equipment, engineering, field services, training?

- How will the consortium be managed? Will one member provide overall management? Will the project be managed by a committee?
- How will decisions be made? Unanimous agreement? Majority of members? Majority of interest? Will there be a lead firm?
- Which company will provide the field project manager? What scope of authority will they have?
- Will each member have a representative in the field? Will an outside consultant or sales agent be retained? How will consultant or agent costs be allocated?
- Will members provide services to other members? Work and residence permits? Office facilities?
- Who will be responsible for providing the necessary insurance and bonds?
- How will the parties allocate costs associated with local taxes and duties?
- What happens if one member becomes overextended or bankrupt? Can the parties evict a member who fails in performance of duties?
- What procedures should be followed for omitted work or changes?
- How will liquidated damages be allocated? Who will be responsible for performance guarantees?
- Will extra costs resulting from defects or delays be attributed entirely to the responsible member? How will liability be allocated?
- Will all members be bound to each other to the end of the warranty period?
- What events will cause a prior termination?
- How will disputes be resolved? Technical questions? Other issues?
- Will the consortium agreement be governed by the same law and jurisdiction as the contract with the customer?
- Does the customer's country have any special laws on consortia?
- Are there other regulatory issues that must be considered? Antitrust? Business practices? Export Control?

Consortium versus prime contract or subcontract

A **consortium** has limited and entire scope, stands behind its own work and participants' work, has direct control of its own scope, and has less control over participants' scope.

A **prime contractor** has entire scope, stands behind its own work and subcontractors' work, has direct control of its own scope, and has contract control over subcontractors' scope.

A **subcontractor** has limited scope, stands behind its own work, and has direct control of its own scope.

The proportional share of each participant is an important factor to consider in determining which bid mode is warranted. A consortium of three members, each with approximately one third of the work is more viable than a project divided 70 percent, 25 percent and 5 percent.

Joint ventures, alliances and teaming agreements

A joint venture is a cooperative business activity between two or more separate organizations for strategic purposes. These organizations can be privately owned companies, government agencies or other existing joint ventures. The joint venture may be implemented solely through contractual agreements to engage in cooperative or joint activities. In the marketing context, these are usually called 'Teaming Agreements' while in the development context they are more commonly termed 'Joint or Cooperative Development Agreements'. A true joint venture is implemented through a new entity in which a company and other parties make an equity (ownership right) investment.

A company usually enters into joint ventures to gain or improve access to markets. Although most joint ventures are manufacturing ventures, some involve product development and others involve joint marketing activities.

The major reasons/advantages of manufacturing joint ventures are:
- Some countries have a legal requirement for local ownership in order to do business
- Tax and duty advantages. To secure these advantages, normally a minimum participation is required (example: in China, incentives apply once participation reaches 25 percent)
- Lower labor and shipping costs
- Established customer contacts, knowledge and infrastructure for local marketing
- Need to have the customer as a strategic partner (in some cases, customers for some product offers may be a joint venture partner for other products or markets)
- Need to respond to a tender-preference for local value added
- Gaining access to capital or other resources
- Unwillingness by the parties to accept a subsidiary role in the venture, or inability to exploit the perceived opportunities with existing business structure

Governments of many less developed countries have reasons for encouraging joint ventures:
- Encourages local self-sufficiency
- Helps to create local jobs and boost employment
- Stimulates national pride and intellectual capital
- Gains local control over technology, know-how
- Reduces foreign exchange costs and improves balance of trade
- Encourages local suppliers to grow and prosper
- Reduces cost of infrastructure development
- Some governments require Joint Venture arrangements as a condition of market entry

A government may want capital infusion, technology and risk sharing, with some control over product manufacture. Your company may want to establish a strategic position in a very large market.

Teaming agreements and alliances

Typically, a teaming agreement is a simple contract under which a company prepares a bid with one or more companies in order to respond to a Request for Proposal (RFP). A company and its team members have complementary capabilities (each adds something the other lacks), and by working together, seek to increase their chances of winning the bid.

Teaming may also take the form of joint advertising or promotion. That is, when the parties have not targeted specific RFPs or customers, they may still want to promote their respective products jointly (for example, at trade shows or at customer presentations). Often, at the request of customers, teaming may also lead to complex technical cooperation and joint product development and/or joint ventures.

In any form of teaming, the roles and responsibilities of the parties must be clearly defined. This is as much in the interests of the buyer as that of the sellers. Usually, one company acts as the prime contractor for the customer, with the team member as a subcontractor. In these cases, the prime contractor has overall responsibility for preparing the proposal to the customer and carrying out the commitments made. It is important for each party to be responsible to the other for its share of the proposal. In addition, the parties may agree not to participate in competitive bids against each other during the teaming agreement. The precise scope and duration of such non-compete provisions will obviously vary. They may simply cover this particular sales opportunity, or the duration of the bid process. The provision will normally lapse as soon as the parties have been eliminated from the bidding.

Teaming agreement commitments

With joint ventures, and especially in joint development agreements, protection of each company's proprietary and intellectual property is a significant concern. The teaming contract should specify the type of technology, training and other information to be received from each party and how confidential information will be handled. Often, it may be necessary to specify that information will not be deemed confidential because you may wish to avoid the potential for subsequent lawsuits.

It is important to gain commitments upfront with teaming partners. Entering into obligations without 'back-to-back' commitments from subcontractors is a common source of weakness and contract failure. Appropriate non-disclosure agreements should be in place before sharing any information with a prospective teaming partner.

What are sometimes called back-to-back agreements are actually a version of teaming where your company is acting as the subcontractor and another party (Value Added Reseller – VAR, Joint Venture, or even a competitor) is acting as the prime contractor. These agreements should also be in place before submitting a bid to a customer. Any terms and conditions negotiated by the prime contractor that will put your company under obligations should be in accordance with your company's interests and should not expose your company to unacceptable risks. The same types of issues addressed in teaming agreements must be addressed in back-to-back agreements.

Teaming agreement issues

Issues to be covered in any teaming agreement include at a minimum the following:

- Proposal preparation – division of responsibilities. The prime contractor coordinates the total response; teaming partners submit their input to the prime contractor and have direct customer contact only if requested by the prime contractor.
- Relationship of the parties – they are independent contractors. Neither should commit the other to any action without the prior approval of the other party. The prime contractor should handle communication with the customer. The team members will often agree not to participate in competitive bids against each other during the teaming agreement (see above). Approach an agreement not to compete with great care, especially if your company has many divisions who may be affected by such an agreement.
- Statement of Work (SOW) – who will provide what types of products, services, technical information.
- Costs and expenses- each party should be responsible for its own expenses. Work out responsibility for reimbursement of taxes and administration expenses.
- Limitation of liability and 'hold harmless' agreements
- Bid or performance bonds required. The teaming partner should take out a performance bond in favor of your company for its portion of products and services.
- Confidentiality
- Termination
- Publicity
- Dispute resolution
- Entire agreement
- Limitation of claims

The result of successful teaming should be a winning bid or a good marketing plan, depending on the strategy for the teaming arrangement. If your company is the prime contractor you should then prepare a sales and/or licensing agreement with the customer and a subcontract or sublicense with your team members.

Equity Joint Ventures

Equity Joint Ventures are becoming very common for IT companies as business is expanded globally. The Equity Joint Venture entity has a separate identity and autonomy in pursuing strategic business opportunities. The investors typically have allocated degrees of:

- Ownership (this can vary from under 50 per cent – non-controlling – to 70 percent or more – complete control)
- Operational responsibilities
- Financial risks and rewards

There are some potential negatives to a Joint Venture that need to be addressed. The primary dangers are that partner interests typically diverge over time, or that there were hidden agendas or objectives from the outset that lead to inevitable conflict. Other dangers include:

- Potential for eventual competition with the parent company or other joint ventures of the same company
- Lack of control over quality and service
- The markets for the venture change or disappear
- One partner's technical contribution does not live up to the other's expectations
- Risk of sharing proprietary information with actual or potential competitors
- Uneven costs or benefits, leading to reluctance to continue investment / support

These are among many problems that can arise and which should be anticipated and dealt with in the Joint Venture agreement. In particular, it is critical that the venture partners agree how dissolution will occur, including disposition of assets / liabilities at that time. As recent examples have shown (e.g. the Concert Joint Venture between AT&T and British Telecom.), failure to plan dissolution of the venture can lead to significant delays, cost and uncertainty – destroying much of the intrinsic value of the Joint Venture company in the process.

6.3 Local, national and international laws

Individual countries as well as states within the US have special laws to protect agents, representatives and/ or dealers. It is very important that these are analyzed before entering into a relationship with a third party because they impose very real limitations on the supplier's future freedom of action.

There are many laws that determine the number of distributors that a company may use as well as the relationship between the manufacturer and their distributors. One example is the European Union (EU), which regulates the anti-competitive aspects of distributor use, or what they call vertical restraints. There are regulations regarding price fixing agreements, which are prohibited. Other prohibited practices, under certain circumstances, include direct or indirect non-compete obligations where the duration is indefinite or exceeds five years.

One type of restriction covered by these laws is that companies may not be allowed to terminate an agreement with an agent or dealer, even if their written contract is only for a specified period.

If they terminate such an agreement, without proof that the agent or distributor was in breach of its obligations, they might have to pay the third party significant damages, typically based on its expected future earnings. In some jurisdictions, damages could also be assessed if the company decides to use a second agent or distributor, thereby limiting the potential sales or profit of the first one. In others, it may be illegal to appoint a sole or exclusive distributor.

Countries and states have these laws to protect their own people from exploitation. Sometimes a company hires an agent or distributor just to get their 'foot in the door' in a new market. Once the business becomes established, they may no longer feel that the agent or distributor is needed. The agent or distributor may have incurred expenses to establish the new business, or to generate goodwill or may have given up other opportunities. An example is given below.

> The Dominican Republic passed a law in 1966 designed to protect representatives or agents of foreign companies as well as distributors of foreign products. The law requires that all such agreements are registered and provides penalties for foreign companies who terminate such agreements without 'just cause'. If the court determines that an agent or distributor agreement has been improperly terminated, the penalties will include reimbursement of the following:
> - All the agent/distributor's expenses and losses arising from the termination
> - The value of the agent/distributor's investment in the business
> - The value of the promotional efforts of the agent/distributor
> - An amount equal to the agent/distributor's gross profit for the last five years

Many states in the US also have laws pertaining to termination or non-renewal of distributor contracts.

Other examples are discussed briefly below.

In Belgium, you can't terminate a distributor agreement without paying a significant amount for the 'goodwill' the distributor has established on your behalf. The termination payment may amount to two or three years of the distributor's income. In many other European countries, protection exists for agents, but not distributors. In Belgium, two renewals of a distributorship contract constitute a contract for an indefinite duration. In Ecuador, only the representative has the right to terminate. In Thailand, you are obliged to continue commission payments to your local representative for several years after termination.

Whether the termination laws apply may depend on whether the third party is considered an agent or a distributor. This distinction can be very technical and varies from country to country. If you don't properly make this distinction in the contract, it could be very costly.

You may also be limited in your ability to grant distribution rights. Algeria prohibits the use of any representative. Both Indonesia and Bahrain allow a foreign company to appoint only one agent to represent a particular type of business. In many of the Middle Eastern countries, the agent or representative must be a local citizen (and the term 'agent' is in truth a misnomer; they will frequently be much more assiduous in the protection of their local contacts and customers). Saudi Arabia prohibits direct sales and requires that a local representative is used to make all sales.

If your distributor is to have an exclusive territory within the EU, you need to check the antitrust laws. Depending upon how this is handled in the contract, companies may be found in violation of them if they grant a distributor the rights to sell in one EU country and prohibit it from selling in another.

Check applicable tax laws. Are payments to companies subject to a local withholding tax? Can you credit local taxes paid against foreign sales for domestic tax purposes? The manner in which local tax law may define 'permanent establishments' may make it difficult to use agents without becoming subject to local taxation. In some cases taxation can be avoided or minimized with the proper contractual structure.

Consider the impact of local labor laws. If these laws affect only individual agents, you may want the agent to be a corporate entity. If the protective legislation extends only to distributors, you may decide to consider only agents. The risk that local labor laws will apply is much greater in an agency relationship. And those laws can be extremely onerous and protective of the local party's rights; they may also commit you to handling extensive reporting and other 'bureaucracy'.

Factors to consider when selecting an agent or representative:
- Does local law permit, require, restrict or forbid use of sales representatives?
- If permitted or required, must the sales representative be a local national? Must the agreement be registered? Are there restrictions on the rate or amount of commissions?
- Are there local laws that restrict or penalize termination of agency or distributor agreements?

Termination

At least 32 countries and 14 states in the US have laws affecting relationships with agents, representatives and distributors. It is important to be aware of the conditions under which you are operating and include appropriate language in agreements, to lessen the impact of restrictions in the law. The best time to think about the dealer relationship is before it begins, because the objectives and circumstances of the parties usually change over time. All agreements need to cover adequately the potential for termination.

There are many European statutes that offer severance indemnities to agents terminated without 'just cause'. These can range from two or three months' worth of commissions the agent would have received to two or three years' worth. In Belgium, distributors may also be entitled to severance indemnities. Many Central American and Caribbean statutes have provisions to protect distributors or agents from termination of their agreements.

For example, Honduras provides for five years of gross profit or five times average gross profit if the contract is less than five years, and some Asian countries are now following similar models (e.g. Thailand).

If the local law does not define 'just cause', be sure to define it in your agreement. If the local law defines 'just cause' as failure to perform essential obligations, be sure to use the phrase 'essential obligations' when referring to such obligations in your agreement.

6.4   Identifying potential suppliers and relationships

When searching for the right relationship, either as the buyer searching for suppliers or the agent/distributor searching for a business relationship, it is advisable to consider looking at the commodity/category in a fresh way. Before entering an agreement, you must review the inherent market realities of the commodity from both the supplier's and the customer's point of view in order to determine appropriate business requirements and their impact on criteria and specifications. The market route matrix shown below will enable:

* Appropriate ways of looking at price
* Clear views of the role of business requirements
* An understanding of supplier behaviors and motivations (and a flag for any that are inappropriate to the quadrant the commodity is in)

As shown in Table 6.1 below, market route analysis involves a 2 by 2 matrix with coordinates that correspond to customers and suppliers. All potential commodities and categories can be related to this matrix.

Multiple suppliers	Tailored Service focus Qualify process Cost plus pricing	Generic Price focus Qualify parts/materials Market pricing
One supplier	Custom designed Innovation focus Qualify design capability Target pricing	Proprietary Vulnerability focus Qualify specification Value pricing
	One customer	Multiple customers

Table 6.1:   Market route matrix

From a buyer's point of view, suppliers tend to have fundamentally different mindsets and perspectives depending on the market route quadrant they operate in. By understanding the suppliers' mindsets, buyers can negotiate more effectively. Being mindful of behaviors from a different quadrant is a way that buyers use market route analysis to develop and implement commodity strategies. For suppliers, understanding the motivations of the buyers will allow the supplier to gear their proposals and agreements to match the business requirements of their customers. Table 6.2 helps to outline some, but not all, of the possible mindsets and their corresponding attitudes between suppliers and buyers.

Quadrant	Supplier mindset	Buyer mindset
Tailored	"I am selling my process" • Open shop, show off facility and employees • Flexible • Quality and service oriented adaptable (unless they target the low end in which case you get a cheap "garage operation")	Excellent candidates for: • Alliance • Pre-sourced relationships • Friendly Purchase Price Cost Analysis • Open book pricing • Continuous improvement • Value engineering • Joint teams • Jointly driving out cost
Custom	"I provide unique creative value" • Will show off creative staff • Likes close working relationships • Dislikes price discussion, would rather focus on value • Image conscious • Technical orientation • Personal relationships are important in selling	Excellent candidates for: • Target price/design competition • Preferred Supplier List • Innovation sourcing • Manage value up (rather than cost down) • Involvement of supplier in new product development (NPD) • Complacency (watch for cycles)

Quadrant	Supplier mindset	Buyer mindset
Generic	"I've got to beat the competition" • Ready to deal, negotiate • Comfortable with competition/leverage • Would like to reposition on value • Closed shop, jealous, guarded, combative • Less trustworthy, less trusting • Used to having fair weather friends • Cost conscious • Price conscious	• Watch for repositioning on value • Brand names • Incursion into Research and Development (R&D) • Use leverage, then use more • Be market savvy • Look to logistics costs for breakthrough savings • Understand and manage supply demand issues/opportunity • Be very careful before going strategic
Proprietary	"I'm in control" • "I'll charge as much as they can afford" • "I own this technology/idea" • Very closed shop • Arrogant • Very slow to recognize competition • Matter-of-fact • Limited value added (unless that is what creates the proprietary status)	• Look for substitutes • Challenge the specification • Find leverage items to bundle with • Risk and Vulnerability Analysis
Quadrant	Supplier mindset	Buyer mindset
Tailored	"I am selling my process" • Open shop, show off facility and employees • Flexible • Quality and service oriented adaptable (unless they target the low end in which case you get a cheap "garage operation")	Excellent candidates for: • Alliance • Pre-sourced relationships • Friendly Purchase Price Cost Analysis • Open book pricing • Continuous improvement • Value engineering • Joint teams • Jointly driving out cost
Custom	"I provide unique creative value" • Will show off creative staff • Likes close working relationships • Dislikes price discussion, would rather focus on value • Image conscious • Technical orientation • Personal relationships are important in selling	Excellent candidates for: • Target price/design competition • Preferred Supplier List • Innovation sourcing • Manage value up (rather than cost down) • Involvement of supplier in NPD • Complacency (watch for cycles)

Quadrant	Supplier mindset	Buyer mindset
Generic	"I've got to beat the competition"	• Watch for repositioning on value
	• Ready to deal, negotiate	• Brand names
	• Comfortable with competition/ leverage	• Incursion into R&D
	• Would like to reposition on value	• Use leverage, then use more
	• Closed shop, jealous, guarded, combative	• Be market savvy
	• Less trustworthy, less trusting	• Look to logistics costs for breakthrough savings
	• Used to having fair weather friends	• Understand and manage supply demand issues/opportunity
	• Cost conscious	• Be very careful before going strategic
	• Price conscious	
Proprietary	"I'm in control"	• Look for substitutes
	• "I'll charge as much as they can afford"	• Challenge the specification
	• "I own this technology/idea"	• Find leverage items to bundle with
	• Very closed shop	• Risk and Vulnerability Analysis
	• Arrogant	
	• Very slow to recognize competition	
	• Matter-of-fact	
	• Limited value added (unless that is what creates the proprietary status)	

Table 6.2   Buyer and seller mindsets and attitudes

6.5   Evaluating project scope

Proper project scope management is critical to the success of any project or business relationship. The amount of care in developing a proper project scope upfront will show enormous rewards later in both the time and money spent by both parties. Later in the book we will discuss more in depth the Statements of Work (SOWs) and Service Level Agreements (SLAs) that will document, describe and evaluate the essential and technical requirements for any work being performed. For now we will review how to evaluate and align our potential relationships with the potential project scope.

It is necessary at the beginning of the contract management lifecycle to start outlining a written scope document. The scope document will then form the foundation upon which the agreement between the supplier and customer will be built. The written scope document defines both the project deliverables and project objectives. Scope statements define and confirm the understanding of the product or project scope among stakeholders. A good scope statement will be read by all stakeholders and mean the same thing to each. If you review a scope statement with a variety of stakeholders and receive a variety of interpretations, it is a sign that the scope statement is not clear enough.

There are two distinct but related scope statements that you will deal with:

- Product scope – defines the features and functions that characterize a product or service.
- Project scope – defines the work that must be done in order to deliver the product(s) according to the product scope.

Before anyone can begin drafting a scope statement it is necessary to have a clear understanding of both the product and the project scopes. It is highly recommended that:

- All parties involved will have reviewed the business requirements of both the supplier and the customer
- All parties will have clarified the responsibilities between customer and supplier.
- All parties will have identified and agreed upon any constraints and work that is specifically excluded from the scope.
- All parties have had discussions with their relative sponsor and other major stakeholders to incorporate any last minute updates or changes.

A properly formatted scope statement should include these essential elements:

- Business case – which justifies the project and goals, in order to evaluate future options.
- Product description – a summary of what the product is or is supposed to do.
- Project deliverables – a summary level list of items whose completion is required to complete the project.
- Project objectives – measurable criteria such as cost, schedule, quality measures, etc., that are to be met in order for the project to be successful. Objectives should follow the SMART system: Specific, Measurable, Actionable, Relevant and Time bound
- Supporting detail – a description of any assumptions or constraints considered during the development of the scope statement.
- Change control process – while typically, a separate document, each scope statement should briefly outline how the project scope will be managed and how agreed changes will be incorporated into the project deliverables.

The following is an example of how to generate a successful scope statement. This seven-step procedure is just one example to help in the development of basic scope statements. For more complex projects, it is recommended to use senior, experienced project management personnel during the scooping of the work to be performed.

1. Review the business requirements for the project as well as the product specifications and requirements. The only way to prepare an accurate scope of work is to know exactly what tasks are involved in the project. Make notes of any unusual items or conditions that may have been overlooked or misunderstood.
2. Find an appropriate template for your scope. If your company doesn't have its own scope template, use a simple word processing document to list each scope item individually in a numbered list. Include your company's name and the company the scope is being issued to, as well as the name of the project and the date.

3. Create a general scope that is applicable to all participants. For example, there are certain tasks on a construction job that every subcontractor must complete. These may include cleanup, safety issues, project meetings, wage reports, schedules or permits.
4. Prepare a detailed scope for each party. For example, in co-developing software with an outsourced provider, outline the developing, testing, and implementation procedures separately and identify the personnel responsible for each phase.
5. Look for areas that are potentially overlapping between two areas and be sure to clarify in the scope who is responsible for what task.
6. Include any ancillary tasks that are specific to one party. In the case of a construction agreement, one party might be responsible for filing of all drawings, wiring diagrams and attaining all legal permits.
7. Review the scope with each stakeholder to ensure all items are understood, and that both parties are in agreement with the scope. This action is usually done at a scope review meeting, which is held before a formal contract is awarded.

As the project progresses the scope statements may need to be revisited and revised to reflect approved changes to the scope of the project. The scope of the project will also be subject to the type of relationship and ultimate contract being employed.

6.6   Options for contracting

There are three popular types of relationship-based contracts:
- Partnering – sharing the project management responsibilities through open communication and shared objectives. This only works effectively when both parties have the same level of commitment. Having to define the commitment level in more detail can reduce this to a more classic contract.
- Project alliances – is a time-based approach for a particular project and ends after the project is completed. The alliance is based on a mutually shared risk-and-reward scenario for both parties. This requires open book costing from both parties and an agreement to put at risk profit and most often overhead.
- Strategic alliances – similar to project alliances but for a much longer commitment, usually a number of years. A classic example would be a long-term outsourcing relationship that provides goods or services in exchange for a guaranteed cash flow. The inherent benefit of a strategic alliance is that both parties will begin to understand each other's requirements and can institute continuous improvements to increase profitable returns in the future.

Specific industries have also generated standard contracting models that may be adjustable for different risk / relationship types.. For example, in engineering and construction there is widespread use of standards such as FIDIC or the NEC model contracts. The US industry has also developed model terms and practices, including some specialist approaches to dispute resolution. In the UK, the oil and gas industry has models and worldwide has adopted certain common practices, such as a 'knock for knock' approach to insuring certain areas of risk. The advertising and media industry, and to some extent the world of real estate, also tends to operate on a variety of standard forms. However, none of these models has succeeded in gaining universal appeal or acceptance and the 'not invented here' syndrome is alive and well in the world of contracting, especially among the legal community.

6.7 Summary

Classic contracting methods employed in the past are shifting to accommodate the four types of relationships reviewed in this chapter. While relationship-based contracts are merely variations of existing structures, the main goal is to create a more collaborative relationship where the needs of the supplier and the customer are more equitably balanced. As shown earlier in Table 6.1, disconnects between the business needs of the supplier and customer can reduce the opportunities for innovation and efficiency improvement. Classic contracting will typically focus heavily on pricing as the controlling factor while passing risks off to each party in an inequitable manner.

Relationship-based contracts, conversely, help to strengthen the supplier / customer relationship by developing a shared vision and commitment to the objectives. By balancing the relationship versus project management aspects of the contract, both parties are able to remain flexible in order to optimize their respective project deliverables.

CHAPTER 7

Request for Information

This chapter describes when and how to use a Request For Information (RFI) as part of the selection process. It also addresses the extent to which the RFI process includes or affects contracts and terms and conditions. Increasingly, RFIs need to assess supplier offering variations and commitment and performance capabilities. They may also address aspects of organizational or cultural 'fit'.

7.1 Request for Information – Pre-Bid phase

The Pre-Bid phase includes various types of preparation activities including communication to your suppliers/customers/ prospects. An RFI is very similar to a Request for Proposal (RFP) except that it is used at an earlier stage when the intent to purchase has not yet been established and is therefore more exploratory in nature and will generally be less precise in specific requirements. An RFI may be issued to inform a 'make or buy' decision or it may be issued to gather information to assist business and associated procurement strategy, for instance in an emerging field or in relation to suppliers new to the market or from geographies not considered previously.

It is worth noting that the terms and conditions associated with an RFI should not be so restrictive that it limits either the information a supplier is prepared to provide or how a prospective customer may use information received to a degree that frustrates the intent of the information gathering process.

As a buyer, even if your company has the capability to produce a product or service itself, you may still want to know what it would cost to have an outside supplier provide it, or what additional benefits could be achieved from an external source. In other cases, you may need to develop a new capability and wish to establish 'make or buy' options.

Usually, an RFI is used to decide if a new project will be beneficial to your company. The RFI will help you determine the feasibility of producing the product or service internally, procuring it from an outside supplier, or doing nothing at all.

7.2   Selecting and assembling the RFI team

The contracts or procurement professional in their dialogue with the relevant business unit will identify that an RFI will be valuable and necessary to pursue and, with the business unit, will initiate a Requirements Gathering Session (RGS).

At this stage it is important to identify all relevant stakeholders and to select team members who are needed to provide information and obtain approval for any project (see also Chapter 3). The level of involvement of each will depend on what is required from them to complete the RFI. In most RFI efforts, the following representatives are required:

- The executive sponsor
- The program or project manager
- Technical representatives, including those from IT, engineering, quality, or other relevant functions
- Finance
- Business development/Marketing
- A legal representative
- A contracts professional
- Any others whose input will have bearing on the product or solution, such as Human Resources (HR), change management or corporate performance measurement.

Defining and managing roles: executive sponsor

An executive sponsor is a high level executive who has the authority to fund and approve the project and also accepts responsibility for the RFI from the beginning to the end of the process. The executive sponsor is an integral part of the make/buy decision, serves as an envoy to all higher levels of management that may be needed during the process and clears roadblocks. The executive sponsor is not involved in the day-to-day RFI process. Other team members make presentations about the progress or direction of the project to the executive sponsor at various phases of the RFI process. The project manager is responsible for keeping the executive sponsor updated on all milestones.

Defining and managing roles: project management

The project manager may be the contracts professional or someone from the business unit. They serve as the main facilitators for the RGS, control the overall RFI project and assist in the preparation of the RFI. They schedule and call all the meetings and invite the team members who are needed for any subject to be discussed in the meetings. They also research and identify, through interaction with the team members, all dependencies within the project, which may include facilities, hardware, software and systems.

Defining and managing roles: technical representation

The technical representative plays a critical role by supplying the technical information needed to create the RFI. They define, in technical terms, the quality standards that apply to the project as well as any system or hardware parameters. Examples of information they supply are internal company technical guidelines, system architecture definitions, database identification, service levels, capacity requirements and performance requirements, just to name a few. The technical representatives are responsible for translating the functional requirements of a project into technical language that can be understood and used by suppliers to complete their response to the RFI.

Defining and managing roles: finance

The finance representative will ensure that all necessary business case and financial approvals are addressed and in place and work with the RFI team on financial analysis, payment and funding options.

Defining and managing roles: business development/marketing

Depending on the subject of the RFI, it may be appropriate for business development or marketing specialists to be involved to provide the external marketplace objectives and challenges, to help the RFI team translate that into requirements or questions for the potential suppliers.

Defining and managing roles: legal representation

The legal department is not involved in the day-to-day writing of the RFI, but provides advise and counsel for terms and conditions or language that may be required within the RFI. The contracts professional will work closely with the legal representative during the writing of the RFI to ensure proper terminology has been used. The legal department will provide the final approval before releasing the RFI to the potential suppliers.

Defining and managing roles: contracts professional

The contracts professional acts as the central control point for the creation and writing of the RFI document. They provide the list of approved suppliers that have been qualified to participate in the RFI process, and if there are requests to use suppliers that are not already on the approved supplier list, they serve as the focal point to request, receive and distribute any information from the new potential supplier. In all instances the contracts professional serves as the communication interface between any supplier or potential supplier and the user community. If any meetings are required with the suppliers in the RFI process, the contracts professional coordinates the scheduling and format of the meetings and will take the lead role in the dissemination of any information to the suppliers. The contracts professional has complete preparation and distribution control of all verbal and written communications with the suppliers in the RFI process.

7.3 Beginning the RFI

Requirements gathering sessions (RGSs) provide the vehicle for the necessary business areas, such as finance, technical, operations, marketing to meet to discuss the proposed project or service and establish the RFI content – the functional and technical requirements as a business requirement. Chapter 3 addresses approaches to gathering requirements. The key point for the requirements associated with an RFI is that they need to be kept at a level that enables the requirement elements to be categorized into 'nice to have' and 'need to have' and at a level that avoids the customer and the suppliers having to produce huge amounts of detail – that can wait for subsequent interactions.

The RFI coordinator must work with all the interested functions until a complete and comprehensive RFI is developed and distributed to potential suppliers. The following sections explain the complete RFI process.

Executive overview presentation

Upon completion of the RGS session, depending on the corporate governance in your organization, an overview is presented to the executive sponsor or approval forum to obtain approval to send the RFI to prospective suppliers. It should include the details of the project and the reasons that this project should be sent to suppliers as an RFI. You should remember that the executive sponsor is often involved in a variety of projects from a high level perspective and will need to be re-introduced to your project in the overview. Next you should state the basic objectives of the project, emphasizing the benefits to the executive sponsor's mission. You should then state the proposed scope of the project and finish with a summary of the project that, once again, emphasizes the positives of the project in relation to the overall mission of the sponsor.

7.4 RFI content

Every RFI should contain a range of basic items, including the covering letter, and an executive overview if applicable. Some RFIs are, however, self-explanatory and do not need an introduction by the overall project business executive. The RFI should include a recommended or required response format, required supplier information, as well as any high-level functional and technical requirements.

Since this is not a detailed RFP, only high-level budgetary pricing information needs to be returned. Finally, the RFI should include any legal terms and conditions as well as security requirements.

Covering letter

This section of the RFI contains the critical information needed to have a successful bid process. The contents should identify the purpose and objective of the RFI along with the timeline for response. If a suppliers' conference is planned, the date, time and agenda of the conference should be communicated in this section.

The covering letter of the RFI should contain specific instructions, including contact information, dates, and times and mailing addresses to be used for the response. Detailed instructions should be provided for changes to the RFI for questions/responses, for budgetary cost boundaries, currency standards, contractual obligations and affiliation disclosure requirements.

The covering letter expresses the company's intent to gather information that will allow it to make business decisions relative to future procurement needs for a particular product and/ or service enabling decisions to be made whether to proceed to an RFP, who to invite and the content of the RFI. Make it clear that the company intends to evaluate all responses on the basis of the technical, functional and business requirements. These criteria may include budgetary program cost, completeness of the supplier's response, supplier's warranties, management support, product support, future evolution path together with the quality and service expected by the company.

The supplier's response should be complete and explain any variations from the requirements of the RFI. Your covering letter should explain that any deviations or assumptions used in the development of the proposal must be explained within the proposal.

You should also make it clear that suppliers have the obligation to ask questions and to clarify any issues they do not fully understand or that may be ambiguous. You should answer all questions from each supplier; however you are not required to answer any questions. If a question cannot be answered, contact the supplier and explain why the question cannot be answered. It may be that the question is somewhat vague or totally unrelated to the RFI. You may require the supplier to resubmit the question. It should be made clear that any questions answered by the company would typically be communicated to all the suppliers to ensure fairness (and this may be a mandatory requirement in government / public sector activity). Exceptions to this rule require careful consideration – in some highly innovative areas it may prove damaging to the input you receive if answers are shared.

The covering letter should express the company's understanding regarding the legal status of the responses. The nature and short timescales for an RFI mean that it is not appropriate to seek the same legal enforceability required with a full-scale RFP. Suppliers should, however, be advised that RFI responses will be used to make business decisions and should, therefore, be able to be relied upon for such purposes.

The covering letter should also state that the company reserves the right to withdraw the RFI and discontinue the process at the company's discretion. In case the supplier decides not to respond to the RFI, the company should state in writing that the supplier is responsible for returning all documents to the company and that the confidentiality of such documents must be maintained.

Along with the suppliers' instructions, the covering letter should specify exactly when the response to the RFI is due and in what format it must be submitted. The instructions should contain an email address as well as a geographical address for submission.

Executive overview

The executive overview section of the RFI explains, at a very high level, what is expected of the supplier's product or service and generally how it functions in the overall process. Explain that if this project becomes a 'buy' situation, the suppliers must understand the context for their product and/or service and the over-arching business objective.

General information

It should be communicated to the suppliers that they may be required to execute a non-disclosure agreement (NDA) between the companies. If a prospective supplier refuses to sign one, that supplier will be excluded from the RFI process. However, while requiring NDAs has become common practice, there is a need for caution. Firstly, the supplier may request that such protection is mutual – by no means an unreasonable request, but you must ensure that the potential implications have been assessed. Second, if you have internal development teams who may be working on similar of overlapping products or ideas, you must consider whether your company could be exposed to future claims that you 'stole' the supplier's intellectual property. In those cases, you may in fact require an agreement that covers the potential for such claims and in fact specifically denies any obligation to confidentiality.

If for any reason during the RFI process there is a requirement to work within your company's facility, there should be a statement requiring the supplier to adhere to the company's work/safety rule policies regarding such issues as access restrictions and security rules and regulations.

The RFI should, if applicable, include specific information for any expenses incurred in the preparation of the RFI that may qualify for reimbursement. The explanation should be sufficiently detailed so that no misunderstanding about what expenses are reimbursable will occur. An RFI should be a normal cost of doing business to the supplier and the supplier should not be asking for expense reimbursement.

Last, the guidelines for the RFI should describe the process to be used to evaluate each supplier's response and to assess the supplier's relative competitive position with the understanding that the technical requirements outlined in the RFI must be met in order to qualify for consideration.

Other considerations for evaluation will include at a minimum:
- Budgetary costs, including one-time implementation and continuing operations and update costs
- The supplier's Security Plan, ownership information, details of operations
- Acceptance of key terms and conditions
- The supplier's financial condition
- The supplier's experience and quality control processes
- Submission of creative approaches/ideas.

Proposal (response) format

It is important that all the suppliers to an RFI understand the format requirements for their responses. These must be consistent in order to be fairly evaluated – one against the other. The suppliers' RFI response format detail should contain:
- A covering letter including the supplier's name, address, and contact information for the person who is authorized to make representations for the supplier.
- Conceptual alternatives and explanations on how they will meet the requirements.
- Feasibility assessment of each proposed alternative.
- Assumptions the supplier made while preparing the proposal.
- Additional information relative to the RFI; other materials, suggestions, discussions that are appropriate, etc.
- Any material and data not specifically requested for evaluation, but which the supplier wishes to submit. Also, you may want the suppliers to include references to those pages that are relevant to the response that may include standard sales brochures, pictorial material and alternative proposals the supplier may want to present.
- Cost and schedule estimates.

Terms and conditions

Terms and conditions of the RFI need to reflect the specific business circumstances. Particular consideration should be given to:
- Confidentiality provisions – these might be very restrictive if the project associated with the RFI is of a highly sensitive nature
- Intellectual property – both to protect the customer's intellectual property and also to address the ability to use content from prospective suppliers' responses in any subsequent RFP

- The level of commitment expected to avoid circumstances where suppliers' responses to a subsequent RFP are orders of magnitude different from their RFI responses, possibly invalidating the RFI outcome, RFP process and associated activities or expenditure
- Mapping out the key contractual provisions anticipated to be part of any subsequent contract,

Required supplier information

This section contains information relevant to the way the suppliers operate their businesses. In it you should request detailed technical, financial, quality and management information. This information becomes an important part of the final evaluation process and plays a substantial role in selecting the successful supplier.

Corporate information obtained from the suppliers should include, but not be limited to, financial statements, corporate structure, legal or material restrictions that would preclude the suppliers ability to deliver on a project, any previous work performed for your company or any of your company's subsidiaries, and any similar work done for other corporations relative to the proposed RFI.

You should instruct the suppliers to provide at least five references who can be contacted during the RFI evaluation process. The information for each reference should include company name and individual contact names – with complete mailing addresses, email addresses and telephone numbers.

Depending on the type of proposal, the management of the relationship is crucial to the success of any potential engagement. The suppliers should identify their management processes and practices for project management and general management.

It is important that suppliers have sufficient resources to support the RFI. Request information containing the size of the organization and total number of employees. The suppliers should describe their in-house expertise with respect to the proposal.

If this RFI involves software you will need to have the suppliers recommend standards and methodologies for performing software maintenance, enhancements, convergence, system upgrades and development. They should know what tools are needed to implement the proposal and whether these are commercially available of if they are proprietary.

If any of the supplier's physical facilities are to be used to perform or demonstrate options, each supplier should describe the size and location of that facility, security procedures for safeguarding confidential and proprietary information, the physical structure and location of the facility, and their disaster recovery plans. If applicable, have each supplier describe its current infrastructure, equipment and communication facilities and capacities, and how communication between the two companies will take place.

7.5 Change control and support

Change happens. You may find as you explore options and get further into the RFI process that the business, functional or technical requirements change. Ensure that a methodology for tracking these changes is in place and a communication plan accompanies it and is executed. All changes to the RFI must be communicated to all the bidding parties in order to preserve a fair bid.

7.6 Experience and stability

Require the suppliers to supply any information on previous experience with any of the systems or processes described in the RFI, either with your company or within the industry. Also request the suppliers to supply any information of previous experience with any of the hardware or systems described in the RFI.

Require the suppliers to provide their organizational statistics, number of years they have been in business, their total number of employees, and level of employees to work on the proposal process.

Ask if they do any business with your company or any its subsidiaries. What is their history with your company? If they have dealt with your company, find out whom they dealt with and make sure you talk to others in your company who have used them in the past.

7.7 Functional, technical and business requirements

Supplier proposals should contain all the functional technical and business requirements and specifications for the proposed product or service, including information related to integration or compatibility with your existing or planned process, systems, architecture or infrastructure, including engineering or construction designs. This may include a need for them to work with existing or proposed suppliers or sub-contractors – which in some circumstances may include their direct competitors. Testing their readiness to comply with such requirements as early as possible is important and may save a lot of wasted effort.

Proposed solutions should outline the needs for any dedicated or specifically skilled project team members necessary to execute the plan. Ask the supplier to provide examples of skill sets and training activities that will be required to execute the proposal.

Establish the need for any dedicated communication links between the supplier and the company, and the type of communication links required. Suppliers must explain how the protocols adhere to your company's existing standards or enhance them.

Instruct the suppliers that they must define progress reviews and inspections required for the proposed deliverables, using a repeatable methodology.

Your company's support team responsibilities need to be defined. These may represent changes to how the company's internal work requests are usually handled – such as obtaining internal customer requirements, defining and managing the project schedules, participation in the testing of all deliverables. Depending upon the nature of the RFI, other responsibilities may be required.

7.8   Software and hardware requirements

If software development is required, suppliers must outline the company's software methodology. This should include impact analysis, systems analysis, and detailed design; build code processes and the various testing scenarios – unit, string, systems, and integration, load and user acceptance tests.

If maintenance of the product (production support) is required, suppliers must explain who will have level 1, 2 and 3 responsibilities during maintenance. Also, any version management or variances should be indicated and explained.

If hardware is required, include the hardware and software configuration, systems performance – batch and online, the ability to interface with other hardware and software, the company's power requirements, systems support requirements, spare parts availability, space requirements and future upgrades.

This is only a shortened list of software and hardware requirements.

The company's technical representative will include in the RGS the acceptance criteria and the severity level failure parameters for all the measurable objectives. This is needed whatever the product may be.

Your technical representative may allow the suppliers to recommend a deliverable with a certain level of failure. In that case a complete risk analysis and risk management plans must be included.

7.9 Budgetary pricing

At a minimum, the suppliers will provide rough price levels or estimates in the overview of expected information, pricing requirements and fee schedules.

You should request each supplier to provide budgetary pricing and fee schedules for the proposed project. Projected pricing must be fully comprehensive and complete. The projected pricing will be used in part to select suppliers for a subsequent RFP and revise the budget for the project. All one-time and recurring costs for hardware, software, installation, training, and support must be fully addressed. Projected pricing should be based upon the proposed project. If a supplier introduces 'hidden costs' in an RFP, that supplier shall be disqualified.

Suppliers should provide projected pricing based on the technical, functional and business requirements.

If applicable, suppliers should also submit a maintenance proposal for the first year that will be in effect for one year from the date of the end of the warranty period and an option of four subsequent years. The suppliers will include proposed rates for the additional four years. Suppliers should also supply 'help desk' processes to assist the implementation team in resolving questions and achieving the proposed installation schedule.

7.10 Support

The support requirements and support capabilities of the suppliers should be identified and explored. Understanding the cost sensitivities of different support options can have a material impact on the total cost of ownership.

7.11 Security requirements and considerations

Your security department will provide all the security requirements for the RFI. These requirements must be included within the RFI and you should instruct the suppliers that they must adhere to all security requirements.

Requirements are likely to include data security and guidelines at your company's locations and supplier's locations, as well as your security requirements for transmitting confidential information or personal data. In situations where any data transmission may be across national or regional boundaries, you must ensure your understanding of the implications. For example, different regulatory regimes impose very different standards around aspects of personal data and cross- border transmission can have unintended consequences. As examples, the EU is rigorous in protecting its citizens' personal data and does not accept the standards applied in the US. If you plan to have European data coming to the US, you must ensure you are in compliance with 'safe harbor' provisions and registrations. On the other hand, if you are dealing with US-based data management, the release of this data to an overseas location will result in it coming under the provisions of US anti-terrorism laws and may subject your customers' data to scrutiny by the US Federal Agencies.

7.12   Review, validation and distribution

During the writing of the RFI, you may require various checkpoint meetings with the team members to validate and approve what is written.

When the RFI is completely written and ready for distribution to the suppliers, all bid team members should review it. Once all the team members have validated and approved the RFI, contract management will release the RFI to the suppliers.

The RFI is issued solely for information and planning purposes and does not constitute a solicitation for further services. Responses to the RFI are not offers and are not generally accepted to be binding contracts.

7.13   RFI conclusion

The team will review the RFI responses and present their findings and conclusions to the project executive. The conclusions and RFI bid evaluation may be a 'make' decision or a 'buy' decision.

If it's a 'make' decision, the project will be concluded within your company. There are many reasons this may happen. The primary reasons are:
- Suppliers' prices are too high
- The suppliers' timelines are not in line with your project timeline.

If the decision is to buy, there are two options (which should have been identified in the RFI itself):

- Choose the best supplier from the RFI and have that supplier be the supplier of choice for the project.
- Send out the project under an RFP. The team may decide not to include all the suppliers who responded to the RFI. The reason for this decision may be that some suppliers' projected costs may be prohibitive, their technical conclusions not in line with the project or they may have 'no bid' the RFI.

It may happen that the project executive will make a decision to 'kill the project'. The direction of the business may indicate that this project is no longer needed or based on the responses from the suppliers and in-house evaluations the project may be too costly or technically unfeasible.

The company executives may 'kill the project' or have the team re-evaluate the project and go through the RFI process again.

Whatever the outcome, make sure you respond to all the suppliers and let them know your company's decision, then document the process for your 'lessons learned' files.

7.14 Alternatives to an RFI

Occasionally it may be appropriate to explore development alternatives with one or several suppliers and avoid the constraints imposed by an RFI process. This could be due to the innovative nature of the proposed development, he limited number of viable suppliers, or the costs or competitive sensitivities inherent to gathering the necessary information.

In such circumstances, it may be necessary to handle the process through joint confidentiality undertakings or even to contract with one or more suppliers on a chargeable basis to develop prototypes or proof of concept analysis.

Such arrangements are unusual, but may be necessary for particularly complex projects where there is a high level of importance, uncertainty or risk. In such circumstances, particular care must be taken regarding issues such as intellectual property rights, and safeguarding the potential at some point to progress to a competitive bid, or cease activity altogether.

7.15 Supplier's perspective

The RFI provides opportunities for:

- Existing suppliers to re-enforce their established position, highlight how existing investments, including the commercial relationship, can be exploited, and beat off the competition from new entrants
- Peripheral suppliers to become more embedded with the customer or move into a more strategic relationship
- New suppliers to engage with a prospective customer in a more formal manner than previously with the possibility of being involved in a subsequent RFP and ultimately a contract
- All suppliers to influence the decision-making process and RFP content providing increased chances to win a contract.

CHAPTER 8

Undertaking a Terms Audit

Once you have read this chapter you are able, as a buyer or a seller, to understand the need and importance of a Terms Audit, how to initiate such an audit and with what frequency. The key message of this chapter is that you realize that your terms are not only important internal management tools, but may also give clear indications on the position of your company relative to competitors.

8.1 Reasons for undertaking a Terms Audit

Dependent on your company's size, position or trade you may have developed your own terms or have adopted a set of terms established by your trade organization. This chapter aims at companies that have developed their own terms that can be divided in 'buyer' and 'seller' terms subject to the following schedules (Table 8.1).

BUY FROM:	BUY THROUGH:	BUY WITH:
Supplier(s) or supplier Group(s)	Procurement agencies Co-ops Trade organizations	Trading group(s)

SELL TO:	SELL THROUGH:	SELL WITH:
Local or international and commercial or Public end users	Distributor(s) Remarketer(s) Reseller(s)	Agent(s) Associate(s)

Table 8.1   'Buyer' and 'seller' schedules

Why would you want to undertake a Terms Audit? Essentially, it is a matter of competitiveness. Terms and conditions may seriously affect your attractiveness as a flexible trading partner; they may affect your costs of doing business or expose your compliance with regulatory requirements. How do you ensure your cost and ease of dong business is constantly optimized while maintaining effective compliance? Have you taken an outsider's look at your terms lately to ensure that they meet the business needs and objectives? Have you had a closer look at the terms used by your main competitors? If you think that your terms are not in line with business objectives, are hampering -or even preventing- the execution of business deals, or don't fit the products, services or strategies your company has recently announced, then it is time for a review and tune up.

Most 'buy from' and 'sell to' companies have a base set of terms which they tend to label 'General Terms'; such terms usually apply to any and all procurement or sales transactions and contain standard sections such as payment terms, late payment fees, intellectual property rights, limitation of liability, etc.; usually such terms are 'powers reserved' by other functions. For example, the intellectual property rights section is usually owned by the company's legal department, which has the sole discretion (that is, powers reserved) to change the wording of this section in any given situation. Other terms are owned by other functions in the organization (payment terms will have financial impact, increasing the limitation of liability cap will affect pricing and insurance, etc.). Tuning up General Terms will require serious preparatory work because you will need a sound business case when trying to convince the 'experts' in Legal, Pricing, Security, Treasury or Accounting functions. Usually, General Terms are non-negotiable, especially in smaller transactions; many jurisdictions have stringent rules for drafting and applying General Terms and the weaker party in any transaction is likely to receive more protection than their stronger counterpart, certainly when that counterpart imposes their General Terms on the weaker party.

All 'buy from' and 'sell to' companies tend to have a huge variety of transaction documents (e.g. Statements of Work, Program License Agreements, Software Acquisition Agreements, etc.) which will all reference the General Terms of that company. Also, when announcing new products, programs or services, a company may introduce specific terms in support of those products, programs or services. These specific terms tend to be flexible upon announcement date to promote and facilitate their smooth introduction. In addition, when introducing such new products, programs or services, companies may introduce flexible terms for replacement products or programs to reduce stock. Evidently, the most important term here is the price, linked to discount offerings, special payment- or financing terms, etc.; consequently, the terms of one company may exist in a huge variety. However, the terms for certain 'off the shelf' products or programs (and some 'commodity' services) are non-negotiable, both in business-to-business and especially in business-to-consumer marketing. When you sell a low value operating program you will not negotiate terms, and when buying a coffee machine your seller will not allow you to negotiate the terms (other than, in some instances, the price).

In this chapter our focus will be on the terms of any 'buy from' and 'sell to' contract. We will look at 'contract boilerplate' (e.g. General Terms), and also at transaction documents – that is, attachments, schedules, Service Level Agreements (SLAs) and miscellaneous other documents that together make up the defined term 'contract'.

8.2 Purpose of a Terms Audit

Contract terms fall roughly into two categories: active clauses and passive clauses. Active clauses are those that demand underlying resources or business processes for their management, execution or control, such as payment terms, contract or project changes, warranty service or product delivery. Passive terms are those that do not require any underlying process – they only come into effect as a result of some specific action or omissions that affect performance of the overall contract; examples of passive terms include force majeure, limitation of liability and indemnities.

Active clauses are those that usually have the greatest impact on business efficiency, operational cost and profit. Failure to comply with active terms may result in passive terms being invoked; they are primarily about the containment or extent of consequences when failure occurs. Passive clauses are generally perceived in most businesses as the terms that deal with risk – although in truth, all terms deal with risk – while passive terms merely describe, contain and ring-fence the consequences of these risks.

8.3 Consequences of inappropriate terms

Overall, if your terms are uncompetitive or inappropriate to trading conditions, this may have negative consequences:
- Other companies may be unwilling to do business with you because your terms are too demanding in relation to their risk or margins, or your competition may be offering greater partnership or collaboration
- You may be inducing unnecessary levels and frequency of negotiation, delaying deal closure and incurring avoidable costs
- You may be containing consequences of failure, but missing opportunities for enhanced profit, innovative solutions or stronger relationships
- You may be missing opportunities to drive greater business efficiency through standardization or planned term options (rather than multiple and customized exceptions)
- You may have missed new areas of risk that are not adequately addressed by your current terms – for example, electronic incident reporting, changes to competition law or new data protection regulations

- Your terms may induce high risk behavior in your trading partner (or by internal functions, trying to avoid partner conflict) and result in extensive exposure – for example, in health and safety, regulatory compliance and reputational risk.

Individual stakeholders in your company will often take firm positions regarding terms policies; these positions can make your company sometimes very hard to do business with. Examples are policies over ownership of intellectual property (one major corporation tried to take the position that it wanted ownership rights to all of its suppliers' intellectual property); liabilities – this is the number one area for contention since buyers and sellers take polar opposite positions (this is even true inside our own company – and one challenge to Legal is to explain how they can reconcile their own divergent positions); others look for indemnities or liquidated damages at draconian levels that would potentially put their supplier out of business; and even areas like policy over Women Owned or Minority Businesses, where stringent rules and procedures can eliminate many of the potential suppliers and create a highly uncompetitive environment.

Other examples are in fields like inter-company tax rules, where rigid positions within Finance can effectively eliminate the company from entire market segments. On the other hand, we have also seen US companies operating with 'illegal' terms in Europe, because they simply transferred their US contracts to the European markets without adequate review or understanding in areas like competition law, data protection or intellectual property rights resulting in severe financial risk, for instance, by the limitation of liability provision being invalid.

Corporate governance regulations and topics like local legislation on revenue recognition or bribery and corruption have set many companies scrambling to review their terms and the procedures by which they can be negotiated and changed – in itself, this is one aspect of an audit, although more easily achieved and accepted internally because of being imposed from the outside.

8.4   When to audit

For most companies, the tricky thing is to recognize when it is time to undertake an audit, to read the warning signs that perhaps your terms are no longer competitive or that maybe you are missing a trick somewhere. Should terms be audited every six months, every year, every two years? Should all terms be audited with the same frequency, or does the need vary? These are the types of questions people ask – so what are the answers?

One clear reason for undertaking a thorough audit is if there is a conscious shift in market strategy, or segmentation – for example, a 'sell to' company may need to move towards a more service- oriented offering because of commoditization; or a 'buy from' company may wish to drive more coherent segmentation of supplier types and relationship models. Or perhaps, a 'sell to' company may now have gained dominance for some of the products and the services it provides. It can therefore now afford to tighten the terms and conditions and still continue to grow its sales at the desired pace.

Another common driver is because of adopting new internal software applications or more general process re-engineering. Such opportunities clearly should not be missed – it would certainly be a pity to embed old and inappropriate terms into your contracts repository or templates – but you shouldn't wait for such infrequent occurrences. The real answer is that you should undertake an audit whenever your monitoring mechanisms tell you that there is a need; so the key is to decide what are those monitoring mechanisms and how do you implement them?

We have already touched upon the difference between General Terms and terms in transaction documents. The first set of terms tends to be fairly stable over time, while the latter may change very frequently, such as with any new program release or version announcement.

'Best practice' companies are those with a closed-loop system, whereby there is continuous feedback based on market experience and changing business needs and conditions, ensuring demand-driven review of specific contract terms or commercial policies and practices on a regular basis. Most of these companies draw from IACCM's annual research of 'the most frequently negotiated terms and conditions' and compare the results with their experience. For example, if the terms that result in most frequent push-back by trading partners are related to payment, or acceptance and delivery, or service levels or indemnities, it makes sense to focus on possible changes to these terms to facilitate negotiations and closing business. On the other hand, these areas may represent an opportunity for negotiation and value-trades – if they matter to the market, don't necessarily give them away, but train negotiators to offer fall-back terms in exchange for some item that you value.

Similar research should be applied to the areas of contract where you are most frequently observing claims or disputes – whether you are the buyer or the seller. These represent opportunities to improve internal process or practice, often in the way that terms are negotiated or managed. For example, if there are frequent disagreements over the agreed scope, or whether a change is chargeable or non-chargeable, it makes sense to understand why these problems arise and how they might be reduced in frequency.

Large organizations often fall into the trap of designing one-size-fits-all contracts for both their purchasing and sales operations that display fundamental misunderstanding of the relative costs, risks or norms of different industry segments. There are limits to the standardization that can be achieved. If you wish to maximize efficiency and hold constructive negotiations, your audit must include proper analysis of the various product and service types, to ensure proposed terms are appropriate to the industry and geography, and represent a fair balance of risk and reward. For example, the terms for a mechanical part will not be identical to those for a personal computer with embedded software. The terms regarding maintenance services will not be the same in Chicago as they are in Harare, or on an offshore oil platform. But terms audits also need to take place at a more mundane level, whether or not there have been significant changes in products or services or in the regulatory environment. That is because competitive standards change and business processes change. Your terms may have become misaligned on either count, leaving you either hard to do business with, or incurring avoidable internal costs and conflicts.

As already explained, there is no universal specific period within which such audits should take place, but there are some good indicators that an audit may be overdue. Best practice organizations consider the indicators and the pace of change in their marketplace to:

- Regularly re-read the general terms in order to make sure they are still fit for the current contracting needs
- Obtain legal alerts to advise on forthcoming changes to law or jurisdictional issues
- Set a recurring date for a general review and sign-off
- Cross-check any translations of the terms to validate that any changes have been properly incorporated

One telecommunication company instigated such a schedule of review and was amazed to discover that all its suppliers were being requested to sign up to provisions relevant to nineteenth century Strowger mechanical technology that had no application in the electronic digital era. All suppliers complied with this request but it was unclear whether this was done consciously as a provision that would and could never be enforced or because they had always agreed to it.

8.5   The warning signs

A number of organizations develop key performance indicators (KPIs) for individual business units including the Contracts Group. A gradual or sudden degradation in KPI performance or perhaps even a prolonged period of inconsistency is reason enough to warrant a Terms Audit.

Although an organization may have a KPI monitoring process in place, there are a number of warning signs that can suggest if a Terms Audit is due. Ironically, the most obvious is when your contracts group feels overwhelmed by demand for its services. This can often lead to growing misunderstanding – with such heavy workloads, the contracts staff cannot understand why sales or executive management question their value-add. They don't see that this leads others to perceive them as a roadblock, a barrier to simplification. And often they are right. An increased volume of special bids, exception requests, non-compliance or pressure for concessions is a sure sign that things are not synchronized with the market. Of course, this may be a product or service issue – problems with quality, functionality or even brand image – in which case there are limits to how much term changes can help. But even then, a Terms Audit may identify changes to offering structures or specific term revisions that will assist competitiveness.

The easiest indicator of where to start auditing is the frequency with which specific exceptions are occurring. Some companies now have accurate data – for example, through their contract management software or other data capture systems. Some use services like the IACCM annual study of most frequently negotiated terms to gain insights. But many have no data. They should start by undertaking an internal questionnaire – overall, it is possible to gain a relatively accurate impression. The assessment needs to go beyond specific terms and understand the degree to which exceptions tie in to specific offering types or markets. Obviously you want to prioritize your efforts into the areas that have most strategic and revenue impact.

As you become more sophisticated in techniques, you will want to include benchmarking. That is, undertaking specific comparative studies versus key competitors or equivalent contract types. This data will often be difficult to acquire – few customers are going to reveal exactly what your competition is offering. But you do have options. You can commission a study through a third party; you can turn to the various IACCM studies and reports; you can conduct interviews with new recruits to your company; you can talk with your own Purchasing organization who may actually be working with some of those competitors. And you can look on the internet – you will be surprised how much information is in the public domain.

It is important to build links to your trading partners to create relationships that go beyond just negotiation. If the only time you speak to your contracts counterparts is when you are in the heat of a negotiation, you are missing a great opportunity. Sales will often try to keep you apart – they may fear that you might develop a relationship that could somehow threaten their control. What control? They represent your company, which is far bigger than Sales. Of course you must be sensitive to overall strategy and you must avoid jeopardizing specific opportunities. But it is entirely legitimate and worthwhile for you to discuss commercial terms with your opposite number and to build understanding of their drivers and business needs, so you can tune your offerings accordingly. Finally, look for venues where buyers and sellers have open discussions, or seek advice from external experts.

8.6   Understanding impacts

Many organizations – especially when buying goods or services – introduce terms that are designed to meet specific functional goals, without understanding or assessing their wider impact on performance. This is true of many risk allocations and especially in 'penal' terms (liabilities, liquidated damages) or situations where imbalanced power results in a feeling of 'unfairness' (price, termination rights, IP ownership). However, the issue extends even to areas such as performance measurements, obligations regarding on-going price reductions, or requirements to 'innovate'. Such terms raise the levels of risk for the supplier and may drive counter-productive behaviors designed to defend them from harm, rather than to meet expected outcomes.

Unbalanced terms tend to create an adversarial or blame-based relationship. They frequently constrain flows of information and encourage dishonest and mistrust on both sides. This results in heightened levels of risk, extended lead times, unproductive workload and lost opportunities. Relationships flourish when both parties are committed to mutual success; they struggle to survive if each party is looking after its own interests.

At its worst, poor contracting and relationship management will lead to a loss of loyalty between the parties. Given that customers depend on their suppliers to deliver core business capability, this is a major risk to take. In certain industries – automotive and telecommunications are perhaps the most obvious – draconian contract terms have in the past caused suppliers to switch focus to customers who they feel are more fair and more ethical. This means they switch their marketing and development budgets and the focus of innovation to your competitors.

This loss of loyalty is often not visible until it is too late; but there are warning signs, such as adversarial relationships, loss of comparative innovation regular switching of resources and an unwillingness to cooperate.

8.7   Undertaking a Terms Audit

It is important you list the main steps you need to undertake. These are to ensure you are both identifying the major opportunities and prioritizing them. Remember, your audit is in part to address the things your trading partners are telling you need to be changed, and in part to drive your own performance improvements. The connection between the problem and the solution may not initially be obvious. For example, we recently encountered a company that was offering an automatic escrow clause to reduce customer risk; in return, it would not negotiate any flexibility on its standard limitation of liability. They had identified a strategic opportunity – and the value of the risk they were accepting outweighed the benefit to the customer of pursuing more onerous liability terms. To make sure that such strategic opportunities are identified in the Terms Audit, it is important to have the right representation in a Terms Audit exercise. It is likely that the contracts group might want to run a Terms Audit as an internal team activity, but the most value can be derived by engaging representatives from as many customer-facing units as possible (if you are a 'sell to' company).

At other times, changes in the law or in technology may be driving changes that are primarily about simplification or efficiency. Electronic contracting is a good example of this. Or you may need an update because of regulatory shifts or new standards.

Whatever you might do, you will need a good understanding of the portfolio of relationships and contract types currently in use and you need some data related to the importance of that term to the relevant market. As previously mentioned, you might use the data provided by IACCM's study of negotiated terms as a backdrop to your work. Does this reflect typical experiences in your company? Is your list of terms that suppliers or customers dislike the same as your industry generally? If different, are the differences positive or negative? Can you see trends that might represent opportunities for differentiation – for example, if payment terms are generally lengthening, might you gain competitive edge by reducing your payment period and obtaining some other benefit in return? Or might you introduce a factoring service so that your suppliers could get paid earlier – making you a more attractive customer and protecting their cash flow?

You need to brainstorm each term for strategic opportunities, including how it is linked with other terms in the contract. From these steps, you will identify your 'heavy hitters' – the terms that are top of the list. You will evaluate the issues your trading partners may have – be realistic on this, neither too pessimistic nor too optimistic. Sales will probably tell you that any change is dangerous; don't believe them – often customers and suppliers are surprisingly accepting of changes, so long as they can understand the business rationale. And of course, the pain here only really applies if your contracting model is one of umbrella or relationship terms. In transactional agreements, you don't have anyone to notify.

Finally, document the expected benefits – savings, reduced negotiation, heightened competitiveness, greater compliance – and identify the means by which you will measure and report on results. Then move ahead and get the executive support you need to drive these changes. As with any audit you must ensure adequate audit trail, mainly to avoid inconsistencies between the various contractual documents. It makes sense to maintain a corporate contracts traceability matrix, something like the following (Table 8.2).

Documents Terms	Boilerplate – US	Boilerplate – UK	Statement of Work (SOW) – Customer A	Change control – Customer A
Limitation of liability	Clause 2.3	Clause 2.3	-	-
Notice period	Clause 3.1	Clause 3.1	Clause 6.7 (overrides)	
Warranty	Clause 2.4	Clause 2.6	-	CCN031 (overrides)

Table 8.2   Contracts traceability matrix

If, for example, the outcome of a Terms Audit is to reduce the notice period from 45 days to 30 days, the contracts traceability matrix can suggest the different documents that will have to be altered or considered (Boilerplate – US, Boilerplate – UK and Statement of Work (SoW) – Customer A), for this change to be truly effective.

8.8   Sample audit

Company A was under pressure on a wide range of risk terms. Each negotiation seemed to focus on aggressive price cuts, accompanied by demands to negotiate liabilities, indemnities and warranties. This was most pronounced in major accounts and was affecting over 40 percent of revenue opportunities. The legal and contract management staff felt they were entering every negotiation on the defensive and with no real opportunity for trades or offsets; it seemed it was just a matter of how to contain the level of confrontation and limit the extent of concessions. Company A operated off standard terms and contracts. There were no pre-approved term options and no published guidance that would assist evaluation of relative deal risk (in other words, standard terms were accompanied by an attitude of standard deal and relationship types).

An audit revealed these shortcomings, but more importantly the background research highlighted reasons behind customer concerns and broader market trends. It was evident that:

- The company needed a method to evaluate the relative risk behind different deals
- Risk term alternatives (fall-back options) had to be introduced to reflect the differing levels of probability
- Discussion of risk terms should have occurred much earlier in each negotiation, rather than being left to the end and the absence of real trade-off opportunities
- New 'bargaining chips' would be introduced to discourage such strong focus on the major risk terms. These would tackle other areas of customer risk and therefore represent attractive alternatives. For example, creative positions were developed on topics like price guarantees (most favored customer clauses), termination for convenience and service level undertakings, including liquidated damages.

Over the next twelve months, the contracts group monitored market experience. They saw an average reduction of more than 10 percent in typical negotiation cycle times and they achieved close to 70 percent reduction in the incidence of non-standard risk terms (that is, those that were not satisfied by the range of options now available) in their contracts with major accounts. This was a direct contrast to the experiences of their main competitors.

8.9 Summary

Terms Audits are important for both sell-side and buy-side operations, including distribution and teaming agreements. They elevate contracting to a strategic position in the company and ensure competitiveness and value. They safeguard you from having terms and conditions that may undercut executive goals and strategies. As one executive recently commented, "Our negotiations typically represent functional positions – and these often undermine business objectives".

A Terms Audit prevents this from being the case within your organization and will help you avoid the inefficient or inappropriate terms that negatively impact profitability and performance..

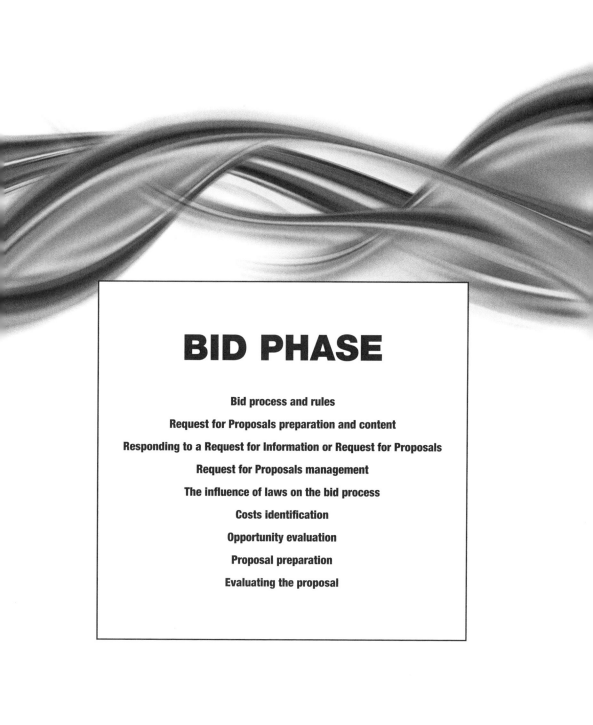

BID PHASE

Bid process and rules

Request for Proposals preparation and content

Responding to a Request for Information or Request for Proposals

Request for Proposals management

The influence of laws on the bid process

Costs identification

Opportunity evaluation

Proposal preparation

Evaluating the proposal

CHAPTER 9

Bid process and rules

9.1 Introduction

This chapter provides the high-level procedures and considerations necessary for running a competitive procurement and will consider when other forms of procurement may be appropriate. From a sell-side perspective it is useful to understand what conditions make an effective bid process and the buy-side's motivation. This insight enables a better understanding of how to make an effective response.

As indicated in previous chapters, the buyer needs information to support their purchasing decision. They may request this information from potential suppliers in three different ways – an RFP / RFI/ or RFQ. The first two letters mean 'Request For' whereas the last letters of 'P', 'Q', and 'I' stand for 'Proposal, 'Quotation or 'Information'. When the three of these are jointly referred to, a term RFx is used.

An RFQ is used when a buyer simply wants to know how much the supplier will charge for an item or service. This describes the item or service as required and requests a supplier response, which should cover the rate, payment terms and delivery period.

As covered in Chapter 6, an RFI is appropriate when the buyer asks for more details about the product/ service, supplier and the response should provide price, product literature, strength of the supplier and answers to the buyer's query key features of product, and other conditions. It may also enable the supplier to set out alternative offerings or commercial models that may affect how you formally approach the market.

An RFP is the most complicated and provides complete and detailed information about the requirement and goals of the buyer in formal documentation; it also contains instructions for preparing the proposal, the draft of a standard contract and standard response form, and criteria for proposal evaluation.

Whereas ownership may vary from company to company and organization to organization, it is clear that the contracts professional has a critical role either in managing the whole bid process or as a key contributor.

9.2 Bidding process preliminaries

As set out in previous chapters, preparation is the key to a good procurement. Try to gather as much relevant information about what you're procuring, the individuals involved, the business need and timing, and any cost/budgetary/comparisons with previous procurements. Be aware of your internal process and who needs to be involved in the procurement at various levels. Early on, try to locate the managerial sponsor who will eventually approve the procurement.

Research the potential suppliers. Check trade groups/ periodicals/ advertisements/ word-of-mouth. Gather research on the supply and demand for the product. You may need to consult an industry expert. Stay close to your end-users to find out what business need they are trying to solve and what constitutes success for them.

9.3 Bidding vehicles and when to use them

RFI, RFQ, and RFPs communicate your needs to the supplier and the level of your confidence in the solution. The boundary lines for RFI, RFQ and RFP may overlap, but the descriptions given reveal the main purpose of the documents.

RFI: you have little information about the solution and need to explore an idea or get information from suppliers about how they would solve your needs.

RFQ: you have precise information about purchase (usually a commodity item), there is little variation in the product and you are primarily interested in the best price on the best terms.

RFP: used to solicit proposals from suppliers where you have strong and well thought out business requirements.

Table 8.1   RFx definitions

The RFP takes the most time to prepare and manage. If you can use an RFQ, it will be easier than an RFP. The RFI is usually a preliminary step before issuing an RFP. The RFI helps to gather information to be used in the eventual RFP (or helps you decide not to issue an RFP).

Sometimes a mini-RFP (an RFP with few requirements and few price components) is more appropriate for smaller or less complex procurements.

The RFI/RFQ/RFP may not be appropriate in all cases, especially if time is of the essence or if only one supplier offers the product you want. In a sole-source environment, you may want to consider a longer-term commitment with the supplier to lower the price or investigate developing alternative sources of the product or building it/supplying it yourself.

Pre-existing relationships with suppliers take precedence for pricing. You may have better (and faster) options than using RFQs: electronic business exchanges and reverse auction sites may give you faster and lower bids for RFQ-type procurements.

Definition and contents

Some organizations have well-developed libraries of RFxs. If yours does not, then you might develop a standard to use in the future.

Don't overburden the RFx with superfluous information or with questions or requests that would make more sense for only the finalist suppliers to answer. You don't want to discourage companies from bidding by setting the bar too high – that is, forcing all suppliers to commit to a large amount of upfront work. It is important to remember that the bidding process can result in substantial costs for the suppliers; show the same respect for them as you hope they will show to you.

You may include your company's standard or amended contractual terms and conditions in an appendix, but should not require the initial set of suppliers to reply directly to those terms and conditions in the first round of bidding, unless there are elements that are so critical or unusual that you consider the ability to comply absolutely critical. You are putting the suppliers 'on notice' concerning the language you expect to apply to the transaction and this should assist them in assessing risk and pricing. Suppliers should tell you if they can't accept your required language and you should encourage them to indicate the price impact (benefit) associated with their variation.. The interaction between buyer and supplier on terms and conditions is one of the key aspects of the role of the contracts professional and there should be a clear process to map out the route to achieving resolution.

Your research should have included gaining insight to industry norms on contract terms, so you avoid proposing redundant or inappropriate terms (e.g. a standard services agreement when you are seeking a software license).

Purpose and timeframe

Watch for 'tunnel vision' in crafting the RFx– you may become so familiar with the procurement that you leave out key aspects in the description. In particular, ensure clarity over what you are trying to achieve through this procurement. For especially significant projects it is worth engaging a person in your company (with no exposure to the procurement) to read the RFx introduction: If that person can articulate the procurement's basic value proposition, then you've done a good job. Understand that the supplier will feel pressure to respond to your RFx and not ask too many 'dumb' questions

Setting the dates is important, but the most important date is the Response and Bid Due Date when the suppliers must return their response to your RFx. We suggest using an 'Intent to Bid' Due Date to canvass how many suppliers intend to respond. That will give an early indication whether your RFx has hit its target audience properly or whether you need to send it to additional suppliers.

Administrative information

Try putting yourself in the supplier's position and ask what kinds of questions and directions the supplier needs in order to respond adequately. Note that most large suppliers have specialized RFP response teams that are used to getting standardized RFPs and will expect you to supply this kind of information upfront.

The choice of primary point of contact(s) should be made before issuing the RFP since the suppliers' questions can start arriving shortly after they have looked at the RFP. You can also have the overall RFP project manager as the main point of contact, with a secondary technical contact.

In that case, the technical questions are logged and forwarded to the technical contact and then sent back through the main contact. This process is slower, but ensures better control and flow of information.

Business and technical requirements

The hardest RFP work will be to create a good set of requirements. For more information on requirements, see Chapter 3: *Understanding requirements*.

Your requirements team needs to understand the business proposition for the procurement – the problem you're trying to solve. Remember, if the procurement is simply getting a particular item because you must have that item, then an RFQ is more appropriate. That is, you issue an RFP because there are multiple solutions to the procurement or because the supplier's solutions differ from each other but could all be satisfactory.

Technical requirements in an RFP, therefore, should be those that are absolutely necessary for compatibility, performance, or future enhancement. Always question technical requirements that specify a particular supplier's standard or appear arbitrary in terms of specification. Ask why such particular technical requirements are needed. Sometimes a more general way of specifying a technical requirement will be fairer to all suppliers and provide you with a better solution.

Your company may have particular standards for a system, often industry standard specifications, which many manufacturers meet. Those company standards should be referenced if applicable.

Case studies

A Belgian bank issued an RFP for new electronic entrance doors to replace traditional wooden doors at its branch network. This was in part to improve security, though additional benefits were to reduce heating costs and to enhance the bank's image as a 'modern' institution. It forgot to include a requirement for post-award support and maintenance; such a need had not featured in the past. The contract was awarded and the new doors were installed at its major branches. Several weeks later, an incident occurred and three customers were trapped inside the doors when the mechanism failed. It took several hours to find support and release the customers. When it came to negotiating the maintenance contract, the bank had no power – but far more important, its reputation had been severely damaged by the incident, which featured on the main pages of all the major news media.

In another case, a Spanish company entered into a two year 'partnership' agreement, as a way to ensure committed supply and obtain lower prices. The award was made to a new specialist supplier because they offered lower prices than an incumbent who offered similar services, but also had a wider range of capabilities. However, after six months, business priorities changed and the service was no longer required. The agreement did not contain any early termination clause and the 'lowest bid' supplier had no other service capabilities, so there was no possibility of offering alternative business as an offset. The only option was to pay substantial compensation fees.

9.4 Supplier's requirements response

It is recommended that you send two spreadsheets along with the RFP. On one, have a list of requirements in a gridded format allowing suppliers to check-the-box for an answer with an explanation. On the other, have a cost format listing the kinds of cost details you need (initial purchase price, future maintenance price, price of requested near-term upgrades and/or future upgrades). Spend some time practicing filling out the spreadsheets yourself before you send them; this will eliminate most oversights.

Ensure that your requirements team understands the limitation of the answers so that they phrase the requirements clearly in order to be answered that way.

9.5 Scoring and ranking the suppliers

Think through and establish the proposal scoring process and overall weightings before you send out the RFP. This helps validate the RFP contents and ensures you ask for everything you need for the initial bidding round. You can always ask for additional information in your best-and-final-offers round.

The requirements must be prioritized. Not all requirements can or should be mission-critical; otherwise it will be difficult to differentiate among the suppliers. You will use the developed scoring matrix to make preliminary supplier selections and the final supplier selections.

The detail of the scoring matrix can be developed after the RFP is issued and before proposals are received, to avoid the possibility or perception that the scorings will be influenced by a particular proposal or supplier. It is important to have clarity about the elements that go into the scoring and their relative weighting. This not only assists the decision-making process but also should be appropriately communicated to the suppliers so they can understand the priorities when they formulate their proposals.

Suppliers' cost response

You will simplify RFx management by clearly separating the requirements evaluation from the cost evaluation. Spending time developing the cost spreadsheet will help you focus on the kind of pricing you want back from the supplier. It will facilitate comparison and reduce confusion when making comparisons.

Resist efforts by the suppliers to supply their own formatted cost responses. It will just complicate your internal evaluation process and make it harder to compare prices. However, if a supplier has identified a cost category that has not been included in your cost matrix, be sure to explore how other suppliers have addressed those costs. It may be common to all suppliers, but was overlooked since it wasn't spelled out in the spreadsheet.

Evaluation criteria for the decision

The RFx is a natural progression from high-level description, to requirements, to cost elements then to the overall evaluation process. The suppliers should have some idea of how you are going to grade them, but allow enough flexibility so you are not locked into a particular method or weighting scheme. The suppliers should not know the specific weights of your ranking (otherwise they may contest your evaluation)

Don't disclose unnecessary or competitive information to the suppliers. This is a fine line, but you want to protect your internal team members from being inundated with direct supplier questions or having to deal with the suppliers' complaint if they lose. It is part of your job, as the RFx lead, to be the buffer between the supplier and the internal team managing the balance between ensuring information is treated appropriately and a useful dialogue with the prospective suppliers.

9.6   Managing the RFx process

We cannot emphasize strongly enough that you must establish an overall single point of contact (POC) for the RFx and broadcast this internally and externally. Also, the supplier should have a single POC on their side.

The RFx should note very clearly that attempts by the supplier to go around the POC will result in disqualification. Remember that as RFx team lead/POC, you are managing two processes: (1) supplier-company interactions and (2) intra-company communications. Both are equally important to a successful RFx process.

Key management topics

As the supplier-company interface, you take many perspectives as the gatekeeper. Remember that one of your goals is to encourage competition and keep good suppliers interested in bidding on your business – now and in the future.

Assembling your internal team

You may not have much choice concerning who joins your RFx team and the role of the contracts professional varies from company to company. It is nevertheless important to educate your team members on the RFx process and pitfalls. If you do have some choice in selecting team members, especially those involved in creating requirements or the cost spreadsheet, try favoring those who have a good grasp on efficient and precise language with a business/technical background. Even in an ideal situation, you can help by educating the team on good practices.

If your internal team already has experience in responding to RFxs, there is still value in refreshing the appropriate approach to build on previous successes and address any old bad habits. Don't forget that senior management should approve the team at some level.

Managing the project

The RFP process is generally only used for a large procurement (whatever your company considers large). Thus you should treat the RFP process with the same consideration your company uses for managing other large internal projects. In most companies, that includes a project plan with staffing expectations, milestones, and PERT and/or GANTT charting (or at least some sense of critical sub-project components). At a minimum, the due dates referenced in your RFx should be mapped into your project plan to ensure they are reasonable and that you have adequate staffing to support those dates.

Managing the supplier

Expect suppliers to ask questions about your RFx. Ensure you have a question/answer process referenced in the RFP for the suppliers. Be aware that suppliers will try to extract information from you, your company, or members of your team (if the suppliers know who they are) in order to gain a competitive edge. This may be done in a friendly way or in a deliberate attempt to slant the procurement in their direction. Your job is to maintain a 'level playing field'.

The role of the POC should be re-enforced within the RFx team and the wider organization. Depending on the scale of the project, it may be appropriate to ensure that upper management is aware of the POC for the procurement. You should encourage upper management to refer all RFP questions to the POC. Management will have plenty of opportunity to ask questions either during the oral presentations or through the POC. Convince management it is in their best interests to let the POC do his or her job.

Managing the supplier – handling questions

Typical questions you may receive from the suppliers include:
- Clarification on requirements, especially requirements marked as 'must-have'.
- Questions about technical specifications that appear to be linked to a particular vendor.
- Whether there really is a budget for the project.
- Whether management has already internally selected the winner (and that the RFP is just a formality).
- Whether the supplier can propose its own solution (one not contemplated by the RFP).

Since all suppliers must comply with the must-have requirements, those will receive the most scrutiny. You should understand why those requirements are must-have from your company's perspective: If you don't understand, meet with the requirements team before you issue the RFP to ensure that you do.

Suppliers will also try to assess your financial assumptions (such as your budget) and may ask leading questions. Don't encourage suppliers to continue to ask inappropriate questions – politely but firmly deflect them.

If a supplier has a 'brainstorm' approach to solving your RFP issue, hear the solution and discuss with other team members; but remember that the supplier's ability to meet your requirements has not gone away.

As part of the project management discipline, capture and log the questions you receive from the suppliers. You will want to send your responses quickly, but not immediately. Try to wait until all the suppliers have had a chance to look at the RFP and send questions to you – the only exception is if you find you have made a significant error in the RFP, which should be corrected and broadcast immediately.

Treat the questions confidentially and don't reveal in your responses who asked the questions. A format would be "A Company asked the following question "......." and the answer is "........". The questions do not have to be verbatim quotes; modify the questions to ensure they sound generic or to answer questions from multiple suppliers at the same time.

Changing the RFx timeline

Always monitor your internal timeline against your project plan, looking for critical path issues. When the timeline becomes extended (it rarely contracts), suppliers will like to have more time to complete their bid responses, but internally, you may lose key project members to competing tasks.

Companies tend to underestimate the time required to respond to an RFx. The response time, however, is shortened when you do an excellent job in preparing the RFx, especially the spreadsheets for responding to your requirements and cost parameters. Three weeks (from the date received) is a typical response time for a small RFx effort, but each industry has standard practices for what it considers a reasonable time to respond. Note that response times are highly dependent on the time of year (intervening holidays lengthen the process) and the type of procurement.

Managing the supplier – presentations

Schedule oral presentations in your RFP timeline. The oral presentations will generally be used only for final suppliers.

Try not to schedule more than one presentation per day; it is usually better not to wear out your evaluation team. Scheduling the presentations back-to-back will maximize the possibility of suppliers bumping into each other if that will enhance your competitive position (however, the suppliers usually have a good idea of who's bidding and usually don't need this kind of 'encouragement'.)

If the supplier is bringing a senior executive to the presentation, ensure that you have a senior representative from your company there at least to greet the supplier. Often the supplier will want to continue the oral presentation discussions over lunch/dinner 'as our treat'. Find out your company's policy on this kind of gratuity. Generally, it is better to politely decline such offers unless all suppliers have or will extend such offers. Note that this gives the supplier an excellent opportunity to gain information through multiple channels beyond the control of the POC/RFP lead... another good reason to decline.

Evaluating the suppliers' responses

After receiving the RFx responses, you will need to first check them for completeness. Any key missing components (e.g. a spreadsheet) should be reported immediately to the supplier with no more than 24 hours to correct.

You will need to schedule your team to review the responses and distribute the materials and the scoring sheets. It is often better to have a quick organizational meeting to discuss the procedures rather than just sending out the materials. Ensure you specify the deadlines for completion and broadcast that to management (such deadlines should already be on your project timeline).

Pricing considerations

The cost proposal should receive extra scrutiny to ensure that the supplier has complied with your format and that the bids are complete.

If a supplier's bid is out-of-bounds, give that response further analysis to determine the origin of the discrepancy. Be careful when speaking with suppliers about their cost assumptions, so not to give away any negotiating leverage. Sometimes you can contact that supplier and ask careful questions to confirm your intuition (e.g., "Have you broken out all the components of your bid (usually the key question)?"; "You understand we requested 10 units just for our headquarters building and not for all offices, yes?").

Be sure to discuss any major pricing discrepancies with your management.

9.7   Evaluating responses – overall score

Preparing the overall evaluations is the most difficult part of the task. Procurements vary too much to give specific guidance on how to combine the requirements score and the cost scores.

Some companies like to use formulas such as ranking the suppliers best to worst on each category then use a percent factor – for example, requirements score = 45 percent; supplier quality/reputation = 30 percent; cost score = 25 percent – and combine the scores that way. However, simple ordinal rankings ignore percentage differences between the suppliers, so you may want to use more sophisticated weighing schemes.

Some companies employ 'hurdle' functions where suppliers must do better than some satisfactory level on each ranking criterion in order to be considered. For example, a company may have submitted the best requirements answers and have the best (lowest) costs, but have a very bad reputation and be in bankruptcy. Even if their overall score is best, you might use a hurdle function to eliminate them because they received too low a score in an important evaluation category.

Consideration should be given to having a Best and Final Offer (BAFO) bidding round. This provides the suppliers with a solid base from which to make their final offer. This ensures that any requirements that changed during the bidding process are properly addressed and provides the suppliers with the opportunity to provide a more compelling solution. This is more appropriate for large scale complex requirements and care needs to be taken that by adopting this approach on every opportunity you're not training your supply base to initially submit non-competitive bids in the knowledge that there will be another opportunity to submit an offer.

9.8 Supplier notification and the BAFO process

Generally, it is better to have two or three suppliers in your Best and Final Offer bidding round. However, it is easier to manage two suppliers than three (or more) and easier to pick a clear winner.

How many suppliers you should allow to continue to the BAFO round depends upon the number initially bidding, the competitive nature of the environment, and perhaps some political factors as well as the practicalities of managing a parallel dialogue.

Be sure to remind the final suppliers what is required of them next, especially if you plan to have supplier presentations of their solution. Not all RFP bidding processes need a final round; that is, you can make your selection from just the initial bids, but generally speaking, you will get the supplier's best terms by holding a BAFO round. Weigh the time or the staff needed to conduct a BAFO round with possible improvements in price or terms/conditions.

Ensure you have the approvals to proceed with the procurement at this time. You can report to management a not-to-exceed price for the procurement, so the approximate price of the final purchase should not be a mystery. Obtaining this approval will also make it easier to negotiate with the suppliers.

Proceeding without reasonable budgetary assurances from senior management could lead to damaging your relationship with key suppliers and being accused of negotiating in bad faith. That is, you should not hold a final round unless you have reasonable expectations of following through with the purchase.

The final round is aimed at lowering the cost of the suppliers' proposal and ensuring that your company has a good understanding of their solution and their commitment to deliver as specified. Few modifications in requirements, if any, should occur at this time. If the suppliers' pricing comes in below expectations, you might consider expanding your procurement. If so, submit your new quantities or scope to the remaining final suppliers and have them reply using your standard pricing spreadsheet.

9.9   BAFO process and final contract

The BAFO suppliers should receive your company's standard procurement contract or should respond to the standard contract you included as an appendix in the RFP.

The suppliers will resist spending time on your contract in advance of getting the bid; however, you lose leverage unless you negotiate at the same time. Some contract terms may be critical to a successful supplier selection (warranty and liability, for example) and some of the requirements may need to be translated/reinforced by paragraphs in the contract.

Any representations made by the suppliers in their response to the RFP should be referenced and included in the final contract.

9.10   Supplier award notification

The process for choosing the supplier is similar to the one used to select the preliminary suppliers, except you may add criteria based on the suppliers' presentations and how the supplier has responded to any new requirements. Otherwise, you will use the same overall scoring matrix and adjust for the suppliers' new cost proposals.

The contracts professional needs to ensure that the decision or recommendation is supported by a structured, documented final approval process and the final decision is discussed with key members of the RFP team. In parallel the contracts professional should communicate with their management, alerting them to the final decision and include written summaries of the decision-making criteria and analysis.

It is possible that new issues arise at this late stage. They should only be contemplated if failure to do so would invalidate or jeopardize the decision and consequent implementation. The winning supplier(s) should be contacted to finalize any outstanding contractual issues and once they have been finalized satisfactorily advised that they have been awarded the contract.

9.11   Supplier post-award issues

You should alert the losing suppliers soon after you alert the winning supplier.

Be prepared to assist the losing suppliers to understand why they were not selected. This process should be fairly short and must avoid information that may be contentious, or subjective, that could potentially give rise to complaints or challenge. If you have done a good job preparing the RFP, it will be easier to explain to a particular supplier why they were not successful, to assist them in improving for the future..

Never disclose the confidential information of any supplier in your explanation. You can tell a supplier their pricing was too high and give some reasonable indication of whether they were close or not, but you should not give the losing suppliers enough information to pinpoint the winning bid.

If a supplier failed to impress the team owing to a particular interaction or failure to adequately address a key requirement, you should mention that to the supplier's representative. It is typically best to communicate information verbally, rather than in writing, and to have more than one member of staff involved.

9.12 Summary

A thorough bid process takes a good deal of preparation and forethought. This yields rewards many times over by having a relatively stress- free procurement. Tailor the size of your RFx efforts to the complexity of the procurement and the associated risks to your company of not having the requirements met. And embark on the RFx process with a view to the end result of a partnership/ relationship with your supplier(s) of choice by treating the prospective suppliers as potential partners rather than future enemies as you go through the bidding process.

CHAPTER 10

Request for Proposal preparation and content

Once you have read this chapter you are able as a buyer to prepare a Request For Proposal (RFP) and assess the feedback you receive in response from your bidders. Alternatively, as a seller you will be able to respond to an RFP you have received from your customer. Although the buyer and seller approach have some differences, there are a lot of commonalities that we have highlighted in this chapter. The key message is that, as a buyer, you should always be specific in your requirements to your bidders. As a seller, you should respect the limits the buyer requests when completing your response to the RFP. However, as a supplier, you may indeed know the market better than your buyer counterparts. Be prepared to discuss leading edge innovations, alternatives to the requested specifications, or further value-added services that can offer a greater Return on Investment (ROI) to the buying organization.

This chapter should be read in conjunction with the chapter on RFI preparation since there are significant overlaps in the process.

10.1 Introduction

The RFP (or 'tender') is issued by the buyer to two or more suppliers asking them to prepare and submit their proposal based on the parameters in the RFP.

There are five key elements that the contract management professional, whether buy-side or sell-side, needs to understand:

- Selecting and assembling the RFP (buyer) or proposal (seller) team
- Defining, managing content and drafting associated documents
- Managing the evaluation process
- Obtaining validation/review and executive approval

This chapter provides the reader with the ability to:
- Assure strong representation in creating the RFP or proposal
- Create a robust RFP or proposal
- Identify appropriate terms and conditions
- Define distribution of the RFP or proposal
- Selecting and assembling the appropriate team

On completion of the make/buy analysis and the project/product definition, the business owner makes a decision to buy or respond and the contract management group is contacted to select a team to define, write, or respond to the RFP. It is important to select all the team members who are needed to provide information and/or approval for any project. The level of involvement of each will depend on what is needed from them to complete the RFP or proposal. In most RFP efforts the following roles are required:
- The executive sponsor or business owner
- The bid or project manager, sales manager (seller) or procurement manager (buyer)
- Technical representatives, including those from IT, engineering, quality, or other relevant disciplines
- Finance and legal representatives
- Someone from the security department
- A contract management representative, and any others whose input may support the product or solution (e.g. Human Resources – HR, Treasury, Manufacturing, product management, change management or corporate performance measurement).

It is typically necessary to determine a 'core' team, versus contributors. This will vary by the nature of the acquisition or proposal and the review and approval procedures. For details of likely roles, see the chapter on RFI preparation.

10.2 Defining, managing content and drafting bid requirements

Every RFP should contain the following basic items:
- Covering letter
- Executive overview
- Guidelines for the RFP (buyer only)
- Recommended (buyer) or required (seller) proposal format
- Required bidder information (buyer) or clear customer information (seller)
- Functional and technical requirements
- Pricing information (seller only)
- Legal terms and conditions, and
- Security requirements.

Covering letter

As a buyer, your covering letter expresses your company's intent to gather information that will allow it to make business decisions relative to procurement needs for a particular product or service. It should be made clear that the company intends to evaluate all responses on the basis of net program cost, completeness of the bidder's response, bidder's warranties, management support, product support and related business functions together with the quality and service expected by the company. As seller, your covering letter should always reference your customer's RFP (e.g. date, contact, specific references) and the date of your covering letter must always be within the deadline set by your customer.

The bidder's response should be complete and explain any variations. You should explain that any deviations or assumptions used in the development of the proposal must be explained within the proposal. Likewise, your response to your customer as a seller should contain the same; of course, you will aim to have as few deviations or assumptions as possible, but it is hardly possible to respond to a customer RFP without any such deviations or assumptions.

You should also make it clear that each bidder has an obligation to ask questions and / or to clarify any issues that they do not fully understand or that, in their view, may be interpreted in more than one way. Your company should attempt to answer all questions from each bidder; however it is not required to answer all questions. To ensure fairness and equal treatment and to avoid preferred supplier challenges, any questions you answered to one bidder should be communicated to all the bidders. In the covering letter to your customer you should apply the same approach: never guess or assume when in doubt but ask questions to your customer and have them answer those. If the customer's response does not answer your question or does not fully answer it, you should leave the applicable issue blank rather than filling out "an" answer.

The covering letter should express your company's understanding of the legal status of the responses. Procurement typically seeks to have proposals considered as a contract component or to be contractually binding if accepted. Suppliers typically seek to exclude the response as part of the contractual agreement. How this is ultimately handled may be affected by negotiations or jurisdictional issues. The same applies on the seller side. Some jurisdictions consider a proposal to be a contract once the proposal is accepted by the other party, which might have significant implications. It is even more complex to issue (buyer) or respond to (seller) an RFP in international transactions with multiple countries involved.

The covering letter should also state that your company reserves the right to withdraw the RFP and discontinue the process at your company's discretion. If the bidder decides not to respond to the RFP, your company should state in writing that the bidder is responsible for returning all documents to the company and the confidentiality of such documents shall be maintained for a period of at least two years from the date of the covering letter. As a seller it does not always make sense to put in disclaimers as those weaken your commercial position (your customer wants to receive a response that they can work with).

Along with the bidders' instructions the covering letter should contain instructions for the bidders who choose to respond. The company should specify exactly when (date and time) the response to the RFP is due and exactly what format is acceptable. The instructions should contain an email as well as physical address for submission. Any margin for confusion should be eliminated.

As a supplier, responding with a covering letter acknowledges your understanding of the buying organization's requirements. This is also a further opportunity to quickly summarize the salient points within your response and to offer the opportunity to explain and clarify any questions in a formal one-on-one meeting. While the response to the RFP should be the major component and the focus of the letter, it would also be a good idea to highlight any positive relationships existing with the buying organization or new awards / recognitions your organization may have that can strengthen your case. A word of caution though: most buyers will see too much 'sales speak' in a negative light. Keep the letter focused and concise.

Executive overview

Following the covering letter, the executive overview section of the RFP details the products or services that you are requesting from the bidders or that your customer is requesting from you. The overview explains, at a very high level, what is expected of the bidder's products or services (or what your customer expects from yours) and, in high-level descriptive terms, how these products or services will be used. It is important that bidders understand how their product or service is intended to be used in your company's process and to be certain the global objective is understood by both parties. Both parties must agree that the proposed bidder solution will accomplish the intended results. Similarly, you should be clear to your customer and be specific in your executive overview on the intended use or application of the products or services. Please note: don't make statements that may imply implicit warranties, e.g. stating the service aim at achieving a specific result; such statements are dangerous, as under some jurisdictions your proposal, once accepted by the customer, establishes an agreement.

General information

This section of the (response to the) RFP contains all information in support of a successful bid process. Its contents must be explicit and detailed and should, as a minimum, contain the purpose and objective of the (response to the) RFP, clear references to the customer RFP (seller) and, dependent on the complexity of the RFP, a reasonable timeline for response (buyer). If a bidders' conference is planned, the date and time of the conference should be communicated in this section. The General Information section of the RFP should also contain contact information and mailing addresses to be used for the response (buyer). In addition, the buyer should give clear instructions on how to ask questions (format, reference, etc.), details for a complete response, the level of detail in the bidder's cost overviews, currency standards, treatment of tax (e.g. VAT) and import/export implications, the bidder's expiry date for the bid price, any contractual obligations potentially affecting the response, and affiliation disclosure requirements.

The buyer's RFP should also include exact details of how the bidder should supply an economically sound and straightforward proposal that clearly addresses the required product/services. Normally marketing or promotional materials should not be included in the RFP unless your company has a specific need for such materials. In your response to an RFP as buyer, you should keep your response to your customer as factual as possible, addressing the questions as instructed by your customer. Usually customers are not interested in receiving brochures or promotional material, so providing such things will not necessarily help you to get on the customer's shortlist.

Communicate to the bidders if the proposal contains your company's proprietary information. If there is a requirement to work within your company's facility, there should be a statement requiring the bidder to adhere to the company's policies on such issues as access restrictions, security and safety rules and regulations. The same principle applies when responding to a customer's RFP: if you believe certain issues in the RFP are in conflict with your company's policies and practices then you must address those issues clearly in your response.

The RFP should, if applicable, include specific information for any expenses incurred by bidders in the preparation of the RFP that may qualify for reimbursement. The explanation should be sufficiently detailed so that that there will be no misunderstanding of what expenses are and are not reimbursable. When responding to a customer RFP you may indicate that certain activities will be provided at a charge (which you should mention in your response); it makes sense to be transparent about the reason(s) why you have to impose such charges.

Lastly, the guidelines for the RFP should describe the process to be used to evaluate each bidder's response and to assess the bidder's relative competitive position with the understanding that the technical requirements as outlined in the RFP must be met in order to qualify for consideration.

Other considerations for evaluation will include at a minimum:
- Costs, including one-time implementation and continuing operations and update costs
- The bidder's Security Plan and/or IT Security Compliance Policies (e.g. ITCS104, ISeC)

- Acceptance of your company's key terms and conditions
- The bidder's financial situation/position
- The bidder's experience with the requested products/services and related quality control processes
- Submission of creative approaches/ideas

Proposal format

It is important that all bidders you invite to respond to your RFP understand the format requirements for their responses. These responses must be consistent in order to fairly evaluate one against the other. The bidders' RFP response format detail should contain:

- A covering letter including the bidder's name, address, and telephone number of the contact person who will be authorized to make representations for the bidder. The covering letter must include the signature and title of the person authorized to sign on behalf of the bidder to bind the bidder to the proposal, subject to jurisdictional authority and final acceptance. It is unlikely that a proposal will be accepted without clarification, negotiation or adjustment. However, as stated above, some jurisdictions consider accepting a proposal will constitute an agreement. Although this may be beneficial to your company in some instances, it is common that bidders will include business conduct in their response to your RFP
- A table of contents containing a comprehensive overview of all proposal materials, identified by sequential page numbers and by section reference numbers
- A section containing all bidders' assumptions made while preparing their proposal
- The required bidder information requested in any attachment to the RFP, such as Statement of Work (SOW) templates, company's contractual documents, etc
- A description of the functional/technical solution proposed to meet any specific request submitted to the bidder as an attachment to the RFP
- Any material and data not specifically requested for evaluation, but which the bidder wishes to submit. Also, you may want the bidders to include references to those pages that are relevant to the response that may include standard sales brochures, pictorial material and alternative proposals the bidder may want to present. You may also want to ask the bidders for any reference accounts you may subsequently check
- A pricing schedule and accompanying information
- The financial model of the bidder's proposal.

Terms and conditions

It may be appropriate to state that the terms and conditions of any existing agreement between the bidders (buyer) or customer (seller) and your company shall govern and control the transactions under this (response to the) RFP, and that the bidder/customer concurs with these terms and conditions unless they specifically object in writing and provide alternative terms and conditions. Be sure that each bidder knows that they are required to make any such changes in writing in their response to the RFP and that any such exceptions will be part of the evaluation criteria.

Required bidder information

This section contains information relevant to the way the bidders operate their business. In it you should request detailed technical, financial, quality and management information. This information becomes an important part of the final evaluation process and plays a substantial role in selecting the successful bidder. Corporate information provided by the bidders should include, but not be limited to, financial statements, corporate structure, legal or material restrictions that would preclude the bidders ability to deliver on a project, any previous work they performed for your company or any of your company's subsidiaries, and any similar work done for other corporations relative to the proposed RFP, e.g. ask the bidders to provide relevant reference accounts that you may contact during the RFP evaluation process. The information for each reference should include company name, individual contact names with complete mailing addresses, email addresses and telephone numbers.

Depending on the type of proposal, the management of the relationship is crucial to the success of the engagement. The bidder should specify how they have set up their management process and associated practices for both project- and general management.

It is important that bidders have sufficient resources to support the project being bid. You should request information containing the size of their organization and total number of employees, identifying how many are administrative and support employees versus the number available for project assignment relative to the RFP. The bidder should also indicate the number of employees by location and describe their in-house expertise with respect to the proposal, categorizing technical expertise by platform. They should further describe their training strategy for staff assigned to the project detailing their experience, career development and training programs. Bidders should also describe to you their employee hiring profile over the past three years and indicate the number of hires and percentage of experienced to inexperienced hires. Also ask for their attrition/retention strategy describing how they manage staff turnover.

If the RFP involves software you will need to have the bidders describe their standards and methodologies for performing software maintenance, enhancements, convergence, system upgrades, version- and release management, any escrow arrangements, third party intellectual property rights (and the bidder's authority to sub-license) and any software development. They should also describe the tools they use within their methodologies and identify if these tools are commercially available of if they are proprietary.

If any of the bidder's physical facilities are contemplated for use in performing under the engagement, each bidder should describe the size and location of the facility, security procedures for safeguarding confidential and proprietary information, the physical structure and location of the facility, and disaster recovery plans and preparedness. If applicable, have each bidder describe their current infrastructure, equipment and communication facilities and capacities, growth capacities and ramp-up time expectations. If your company requires a dedicated off-site facility, have the bidders submit a full description of the facility that would be dedicated to your company.

When responding to a customer RFP, all of the above information should be carefully considered in preparing your proposal. Also address the intellectual ownership of any materials developed under the transaction (owned by customer, owned by you, or jointly owned) and propose any (re)marketing rights of such materials.

Exploring the bidder's flexibility

If applicable, ask if the bidder would be willing to transfer the facility over to your company if its strategy warrants this on a later date. Would the bidder be willing to provide your company with staff as consultants to another third party facility? Would the bidder be willing to augment staff in their facility with third party consultants hired by your company? What maximum ratio of third party staff to bidder's staff will the bidder accommodate? Would the bidder be willing to use company personnel as all or part of the team? Would the bidder acquire tools and methodologies preferred by the company at no additional cost? Would the bidder train your company's staff in preferred tools and methodologies, at no additional cost? And, lastly, would the bidder be willing to train your company staff if emerging technologies were required by new development projects?

Quality and quality processes

The quality of the bidder's work and products delivered under this engagement must improve over current levels and continue to improve year after year; this is not a specific requirement you ask of them but is (or at least should be) their standard way of doing business. The bidder must explain to you in detail how they have implemented their quality management processes and how these will be applied to your company's project. You must ask the bidders how they assure quality. Are there any formal procedures used within their organization? If so, how will quality flaws be minimized by their quality assurance plan, and what are the quality metrics from the bidder's prior or existing application maintenance or development projects? What strategic initiatives to improve customer focus and process orientation are in place? Ask the bidders if they are ISO certified and, if so, ask them to provide the name of the authorized evaluator that last certified their organization along with the date of certification. Certain markets apply their own quality standards and associated certifications; make yourself familiar with these standards and have bidders submit all associated information.

If applicable, ask if the bidder has been appraised on the SEI's[3] Capability Maturity Model (CMM) by an independent appraiser. If yes, they should indicate the scope of the appraisal,

---

3   SEI: Software Engineering Institute at Carnegie Mellon University

provide the name of the appraiser, the results and the date of the appraisal. Ask for a description of best practice used in the bidder's facilities and ask them to describe any proprietary process/methodologies used in their facilities. Lastly, (and if applicable under the RFP) ask the bidders to describe their productivity metrics for software development and maintenance work and quantify the productivity improvements they have measured in their facilities and the level of improvement they expect in future.

Project change control

Ask the bidders to describe their change management process and submit in the proposal your change management process for comparison. Ask if the bidder understands and agrees with your company's process. It is extremely important that both parties agree on a change management process before signing the agreement. If the RFP requires hardware or software development and your company requires the bidder to maintain the product, include your company's process for production support, including all Service Level Agreements (SLAs). Ask the bidder if they concur with the company's processes and if not, ask the bidder to provide comments and most importantly, require each bidder to provide pricing for production support.

Ask the bidders if they agree with the terms and conditions in your SLAs attached to the RFP. You may want to indicate in the RFP that SLAs are a major evaluation point and if any bidder has a major exception to SLAs, you will assess that accordingly. Ask the bidders what tools and processes they use for testing and indicate what metrics must be achieved before an application change is considered acceptable to you and ask them to describe their methodology for testing and associated audit procedures. Emphasize that high quality, clear and concise documentation is important to your company and ask the bidders to describe how their documentation is produced and will be delivered (e.g. on-line manuals), how often this documentation is updated and what type of specialized personnel they assign for preparing documentation.

Outsourcing experience

If this is a service or outsourcing RFP, ask the bidders if they have any experience in outsourcing and have them provide the number of customers, type of applications, (for example financial, call center, data center, etc.,), the number and type of full-time resources engaged, whether their support was provided on-site or off-site, the term of the average and longest contract, contract dates and the total contract value of the average maintenance projects. Ask what, in their view, distinguished their organization from other providers in those transactions. Require the bidders to describe their step-by-step procedure to transfer the overall responsibilities to their staff.

Identify the activities that will be managed by your company's staff, jointly with the bidder, or by the bidder's staff, before transition, during transition, during transformation and during 'steady state'. Ask the bidders to provide a brief narrative of their approach for the time frame, how many and what type of company resources will be needed and for what period of time, and how they plan to manage the transition of specific tasks from your company to their staff.

Experience and stability

Require the bidders to supply any information on previous experience with any of the systems, programs, materials or processes described in the RFP, either with your company or within the industry. If such experience is available, the bidders should clearly describe the type of experience they have and elaborate on the results they have achieved in the past. Be sure to require the bidders to provide their organizational statistics and ask them to supply the number of years they have been in business, their total number of employees, total billing for the past three years and if they do or have done any business with any of your company subsidiaries, either locally or internationally.

Statement of Work or functional/technical requirements

The RFP should contain a specimen Statement of Work (SOW) or all functional and technical requirements and specifications required for the proposed product, program or service. (Please refer to the Statements of Work or Requirements Definition chapters for more information on those topics.) The bidder should dedicate a skilled, experienced and skilled project team to support the project. Make clear that bidders are responsible for all training activities necessary to keep the skills of their personnel up-to-date. Require bidders to establish and maintain communication links with your company and any specific methods or standards you require – for example, capabilities for electronic communication or connections into your ERP systems.

Instruct bidders that they must complete the requested deliverables, initiate reviews and hold inspections as required in this RFP section and to comply with requirements for periodic status reports which should, as a minimum, contain project status, resource utilization (if a services proposal), variance/deviation reports and metrics.

Under this section of the RFP, your company's support team responsibilities should be defined. These responsibilities may include how your company's work requests from internal customers are handled, obtaining internal customer requirements, defining and managing project schedules, participating in the testing of all deliverables and participating in project conference calls. Depending upon the nature of the RFP, other responsibilities may be required.

If maintenance of the product (production support) is requested, it should be made clear to the bidders who has level 1, 2 and 3 support responsibilities during maintenance. Detail exactly what you expect, e.g. maintenance on a 24/7 basis, spare parts distribution,

SLAs, off site/on site maintenance or how revisions to the product, service, equipment or program are handled. Work with your technical representatives and your procurement manager to include all aspects of production support. They will include within the RFP all applicable technical requirements and specifications for the products, programs or services. If integration or compatibility with existing or future products, services, system or process infrastructures, or other suppliers, is required, this must be specified.

.

Have an in-depth discussion with your technical and procurement colleagues to ensure all technical requirements, functionality and specifications are sent to the bidders. If you do not send a complete set of requirements to the bidders, it will make it difficult when negotiations are complete and you still need to fine-tune these specifications. Remember, the key words in an RFP are *clarity of requirements*!

Your company's technical and procurement specialists will provide the applicable language for topics like acceptance criteria and severity level failure parameters for all the measurable objectives. This language may allow bidders to provide a deliverable with a certain level of failure. As an example, severity levels may define a failure, where severity 1 may be worst case and severity 3 may be a minor failure. Instruct the bidders that your company requires acceptance testing for all deliverables.

10.3 Pricing information (seller only)

The buyer should request each bidder to provide pricing and fee schedules for all items requested in the RFP. As a seller, the pricing must be fully comprehensive, detailed as requested and complete. The pricing will be used in part to select the bidder and revise the budget for the project. All one-time and recurring costs for hardware, software, installation, training, and support must be fully addressed. Pricing should be based upon the proposed project only. If a selected bidder introduces 'hidden costs' during negotiations, that bidder should be disqualified and, based on your bid evaluations, the next best bidder should be selected. Bidders should provide pricing based on the requirements, nothing more and nothing less. If applicable, they should also submit a maintenance proposal for the first year and an option of four subsequent years with rates, which will be in effect for one year from the date of the end of the warranty. Options to renew after the initial years must be clear and fully explained for all products, licenses and services proposed. Bidders should also supply 'help desk' processes to assist the implementation team in resolving questions and achieving the proposed installation schedule. Instruct the bidders that price information must remain firm for a minimum period (e.g. 180 days) from the issue date of the RFP.

Each product, program or service under the RFP may be unique. If this is the case, and the RFP is released to all approved suppliers who are currently under an existing company agreement you may require that unique terms and conditions be included in the RFP. Advise the bidders that acceptance of these product-, program- or service- unique terms and conditions will be part of the overall bidder evaluation process. If you are including bidders who are not on the approved list or not under an existing company agreement, include your company's contract within the RFP, along with any unique terms and conditions that may apply.

10.4 Security, health and safety requirements and consideration

Ensure that any necessary security or health and safety requirements are included in the RFP and instruct the bidders they must adhere to these at all times, including where applicable during the RFP process. Requirements may include data security and guidelines – at your company's locations and the bidder's locations, the company's security requirements for the bidder's personnel at the company's locations and security requirements for transmitting confidential information or for on-going operations. For the seller, it is critical to establish whether the buyer's requirements are achievable (either too tight or too loose, based on your own corporate guidelines) before initiating the response to the RFP.

10.5 Managing the evaluation process (buyers)

Strategies can sometimes be created without giving full consideration to all of the options available or the risks involved. They can also be based upon highly subjective criteria such as past relationships or may fail to meet the business requirements set by the stakeholders. None of these possibilities is likely to meet the objectives of the business; therefore an alternative method of assessing options is required. This method needs to be based on a structured, rigorous approach that clearly evaluates options against a defined set of requirements. Before the RFP is issued, the buying team needs to agree on the criteria to measure a successful response.

There are two types of answers to an RFP that are possible and need to be considered at the time of RFP creation, the 'quick win' and the 'long-term strategic option'. In some cases, it may be that the requirement is for both a quick win and a long-term strategy. In that case, the RFP should require the supplier to explain how they would manage the migration between these phases.

A quick win is a cost reduction opportunity that can be fully implemented within twelve months and has no detrimental impact upon the medium and long-term strategies within the Commodity/Category plans. Quick wins are needed to deliver immediate first-year benefits to ensure business profitability over following years. Specifically, quick wins can:

- Contribute significantly to the achievement of Year One cost reduction objectives.
- Immediately improve cash flow.
- Help to obtain senior management commitment as they see the Commodity Management process delivering the objectives, providing the team with a 'pass' to deliver medium and long-term strategies.
- Condition the supply base, showing that the buying organization is serious about changing the status quo and current business practices.
- Enhance team morale, as the team sees the process helping them to meet and exceed objectives
- Secure support for the Commodity Management process from functional management (outside of procurement) who see early, tangible evidence of delivery that meets or exceeds their business requirements.
- Promote process thinking within the team.

While quick wins will develop throughout the bidding process, most organizations will seek to focus on the mid- and long-term strategic options that will deliver continued benefits throughout the buyer-supplier relationship. An options evaluation tool needs to be agreed to by all parties to provide an objective, consensus-based process whereby each option can be evaluated against key criteria. These criteria are weighted according to their importance such that the option scoring the highest against them can be defined as the option that is most likely to meet the business objectives. The risks against each option are also assessed, with the final option selected having the greatest possibility of meeting the business requirements and also having a high probability of gaining approval from the key stakeholders.

Options evaluation is a method whereby the possible options generated by the team can be assessed to identify the option or group of options most likely to meet the business requirements. The process provides:

- A method of identifying the criteria to be used
- A method to make sure the criteria are Specific, Measurable, Achievable, Realistic, and Time-bound (SMART)
- A method of weighting the criteria to identify the most critical
- An overall score against the weighted set of criteria
- A method of assessing risk associated with each option
- An output in the form of a preferred option that can be explained to key stakeholders

Evaluation of the available options on closure of the RFP enables the buying team to generate consensus around the strategy to be followed and reduces the risk of subjective views dictating the direction that the business will take. The options evaluation matrix shown below (Table 10.1) puts a structure around what can often be a vague, subjective options selection process. This table ensures that each option is measured against the key business criteria it is to meet and assesses the risks associated with each option. The level of objectivity created and the focus on business requirements generates a high degree of consensus and this, combined with a well-structured output, significantly increases the buy-in from key stakeholders.

Criteria	Weighting	Option 1		Option 2		Option x	
		Rate	Score	Rate	Score	Rate	Score
The benefit must be greater than $XX USD	Go/No go	Go		No go		Go	
The resources should be restricted to manufacturing	Go/No go	Go				Go	
The benefit must be delivered in a 12 month time scale	10	3	30			10	100
No specification changes	8	8	64			0	0
Existing suppliers should be used	6	0	0			6	36
The difficulties should be no greater than medium	4	4	16			0	0
Total			110				136

Table 10.1   Options evaluation matrix example

To ensure success, there are several key questions that should be asked in the preparation of the options evaluation criteria:

- Business requirements
  - Are all or most criteria linked to business requirements?
  - Are all or most business requirements included in the criteria?
  - Are all key business requirements covered by the criteria?
- Clarity of criteria
  - Does everyone have a shared understanding of the criteria to be used?
  - Are the criteria as SMART as possible?
- Weighting
  - Are the weightings representing a fair view as to what is important to the business?
  - Have any weighting been given too high or too low a priority in relation to others for reasons other than business reasons (e.g. office politics)?
  Are the weightings likely to skew the result towards a pre-determined option?
- Risks
  - Have all significant risks got an action plan against them that will mitigate the concerns of those involved?

Suppliers should also use this same type of options evaluation in preparation for an upcoming negotiation upon successful awarding of a bid response. By preparing different scenarios upfront a supplier can be poised to respond to challenges or negotiation tactics employed by the buyer. This does not mean that the best offer is not presented at time of RFP response, but that each business criterion that is offered is understood and an appropriate 'cost' (either quantitative or qualitative) can be applied. This concept is expanded further in Chapter 15: *Opportunity evaluation*.

10.6 Summary

When preparing the RFP you may require various checkpoint meetings with the team members to validate and approve what is required at that stage. When the RFP is complete and ready for distribution to the bidders, it must be reviewed by all bid team members and approved by the executive sponsor. Once all the team members have validated the RFP and executive approval is obtained, contract management will release the RFP to the bidders on the same date and time. If this is a major RFP, most bidders, if not all, will be aware of the impending RFP. The next chapter will address managing the process after the RFP is distributed to potential suppliers.

For the supplier, receipt of the RFP triggers action by the proposal team to evaluate the requirement and formulate a response. This must include evaluation of win-rate probability and the levels of risk, based on the extent to which business capabilities meet or exceed customer requirements.

CHAPTER 11

Responding to a Request for Information or Request for Proposal

11.1 Introduction

Once you have read this chapter you are able as a seller to respond to a Request for Information (RFI) or Request for Proposal (RFP) that you have received from your customer. Your aim is to become the chosen supplier in providing the response that best meets the customer's needs. Companies today are spending more time planning and conducting source selection than ever before. The trend from purchasers is towards more comprehensive screening and fewer supplier relationships with longer duration contracts. Clearly, selecting the right supplier is one of the most critical decisions a purchaser will have to make. To that end suppliers need to be well versed in the best practices for ensuring they become the chosen supplier.

In this chapter we will cover:
- An overview of the procurement process from both a purchaser's and a supplier's perspective
- Information on executing non-disclosure agreements
- The rationale for a bid process
- The bid process itself
- The role of contract management in the bid process

11.2 Background: the procurement process

Before discussing this aspect of the Bid phase in detail it is useful to understand something of the process that the purchasing organization has undergone before requesting a bid from a supplier. Purchasers need to obtain goods or services to run their business. Obtaining goods or services involves uncertainty and risk because it involves dealing with an outside organization not completely within the purchaser's control. Contracts with suppliers relating to the goods or services being obtained are the means of managing that specific uncertainty and risk; procurement organizations have, of course, to address other associated risks whether internal or external. These contracts also provide the vehicle for delivering the value envisaged and planned for resulting from the procurement and sales processes.

As discussed in earlier chapters, in the course of deciding who to purchase from, the customer will go through a process of analyzing the risks that purchasing from a third party will create, identifying potential suppliers, defining and specifying requirements, drafting the contractual terms and conditions and deciding on the key factors upon which a supplier will be chosen (the evaluation criteria).

If a purchasing organization has uncertainty in relation to any of the areas raised above it will often issue an RFI as a method of gathering information from targeted potential suppliers in preparation for a follow-on interaction with those suppliers. An RFI does not indicate a purchaser is seeking a specific contractual relationship, but instead asks potential suppliers to submit information on their capabilities and expertise. Potential suppliers will do so because the RFI indicates that there will in almost all cases be a follow-on interaction leading to an award of contract.

It is important for suppliers to understand that an RFI is typically used by a customer to engage specific potential suppliers to:
- Obtain up-to-date technical information on available products
- Identify consultants and experts
- Develop consortia, alliances and partnerships
- Build a supplier network
- Obtain information to support decision making
- Prepare for an effective RFP

Assuming an RFI is unnecessary or has already been undertaken, then purchasers will normally request tenders, quotes or bids in writing through procurement documents generally known as 'solicitations'. Solicitations generally take one of the following forms:
- Request for Proposal (RFP)
- Request for Quotation (RFQ)
- Invitation to Tender (ITT)

Solicitations should set out the purchaser's needs clearly and in sufficient detail to ensure certainty during the contractual relationship with the ultimate supplier. A high quality solicitation is crucial for the success of the purchasing activity. What all these documents have in common is that – except in the most unusual circumstances – they are a request for a supplier to make an offer, which is capable of acceptance by the purchaser. The purchaser is seeking a specific contractual relationship with the supplier it deems best meets the evaluation criteria. This critical point is addressed in more detail later in this chapter.

11.3   Identifying an opportunity

Let's look further into the sales process from the supplier's perspective. To be successful in business requires the ability to identify potential contract opportunities and to win and perform such contracts profitably. When a piece of prospective business is identified it is critical that the supplier can recognize whether that opportunity is one they want to win. In so doing they prevent valuable time and resource being wasted on opportunities they couldn't, or wouldn't want, to win. A potential contract must be appropriate – that is, it fits within the strengths of the supplier, and commercially sound – that is, it enables the supplier to earn a profit or gain another benefit such as increased market presence or the opportunity of future business. Suppliers need to explore the market place by engaging in pre-sales activity to be able to define existing and potential customers, and to create a sales plan (or business plan) based on customer needs and understanding the competition.

This information will additionally form a key part of the bid process. With all sales opportunities, time is of the essence. Suppliers need to do what they can to influence a purchaser's decision making process in their favor as early and as quickly as possible so as to improve their chances of success and reduce the opportunities available to their competitors. Timeliness is made more critical with RFIs and RFPs, as they will contain a date by which a response must be submitted. In such situations a supplier bid process is vital to the decision making process.

11.4   Execution of non-disclosure agreements

In all but the rarest of cases, both RFIs and RFPs contain information that is commercially sensitive to the purchaser. In some cultures, the purchaser will wish to protect such information by requiring all intended recipients to sign a non-disclosure agreement (NDA) before issuing the RFI or RFP. From the supplier's perspective, the information provided in response will also be commercially sensitive in that it will detail some or all of the following areas:

- Current strategy and possibly future direction
- Current and possibly future technology
- Service capabilities
- Operational methodology
- Pricing
- Existing customers or market potential

It is therefore often of importance to both parties to have an NDA in place before sensitive information is released.

A purchaser's NDA should be reviewed and approved by the supplier's contract management organization before signature.

11.5 Contracts professional involvement

Why is the contracts professional involved? The precise role of the contracts expert varies. At its simplest, the role is about compliance. In a rules-driven organization, the contracts group has primary focus on risk avoidance, so is looking to avoid specific high-risk contractual terms. If its purpose is to review and perhaps negotiate a particular set of terms (typically areas like liabilities, indemnities, and other legally oriented provisions), the opportunities to shape the deal and add value may be limited. In general, the more restricted the role and the more it is rules-driven, the later the contracts group becomes involved. It is in danger of being perceived as a 'business prevention department' – and in such circumstances, other groups (especially sales) will seek to avoid its involvement.

A typical indicator of this rules-driven approach is when the contracts group frequently complains that it was involved too late. At the other end of the spectrum, there are contracts organizations that are fully engaged throughout the bid process and may even take prime responsibility for it. In many companies the bid management facilities and resources are owned by the contracts group. In such environments, the organization is looking to the contracts professionals to take a lead role in shaping the deal and overseeing the cross-business coordination necessary for its success.

There are of course many variants between these two positions. And those are often likely to be variations even within the same company if it handles multiple contract and relationship types. As already mentioned, the key to best practice is to have clarity throughout the organization of the scope of the contracts organization's role and how this varies by type of deal or relationship and how it adds value and increases the chance of successfully wining and delivering profitable business.

11.6 Why have a bid process?

The bid process is a critical activity in any company. It represents the key decision-making phase in turning an opportunity into profitable business. Not only is bidding a critical part of winning new business but it is also resource-hungry and stressful. There is never enough time to prepare the perfect bid response and invariably there are never enough resources due to competing business demands. To ensure that everyone involved in preparing the bid is working in the same way towards the same goal is vitally important. It is essential to understand that there is no one process that will work for all companies and for all bids, no matter what the size. What works for a complex, high value bid may very well prevent a low value bid going out on time. In the same way, responding to an RFI is likely to be less taxing on resources than responding to an RFP if only because a response to an RFI usually does not constitute an offer, which can be contractually binding. The critical thing is to have a process and to follow that process where practical.

An effective bid process is built upon:
- Clear and mutual understanding of its goals and the values different participants bring to it
- Service level commitments and performance measurements
- A 'front-end' that operates intelligently to segment and prioritize opportunities
- A defined workflow that distinguishes review and approval roles, and when they are required
- Information/data gathering that collects what is needed and also captures history and precedent

Some key indicators of best practice include:
- The percentage of business requiring review/approval (both as a percentage of total business and as improvement over time)
- Average cycle times (how long the process takes by major deal type and improvement over time)
- Internal satisfaction measurements and improvement over time
- Win/loss rates and cause analysis
- Project reviews, identifying change dispute levels and linkages to bid process
- Levels of disputes and liability claims
- Success rate in delivering business plan profits through implementation

11.7 Key elements of a bid process

Bid/no bid decision

Deciding whether to respond to an RFI or RFP should be a conscious decision involving those individuals who have the expertise and authority within the company. Bidding is an expensive, resource-hungry business and the bid/no-bid decision is critical, as heavy investment of time (and therefore money) is about to start.

The bid/no-bid decision requires analyzing the risks versus the opportunities of a potential business deal and then deciding whether to proceed. A bid/no-bid meeting is the recommended forum for decision making of this importance.

It is worth bearing in mind, however, that even if a decision is made to proceed with a bid, circumstances change and the flexibility to revise an earlier decision is vital. Those involved with the bid should continue to question the bid decision at all stages of the bid process.

The following inputs are needed for a bid/no-bid decision:
- The solicitation – this should be circulated to those individuals who are to make the bid/no-bid decision as soon as possible after receipt to enable a full and detailed study of all relevant issues
- Purchaser-specific information – the primary needs of the purchaser and any information that exists around budget and strategic plans
- Competitive analysis – strengths that will need to be exploited and weaknesses that need to be resolved
- Supplier specific information – market strategy and where appropriate bid costs and available funding.
- Understanding whether this is part of the business plan and if not, why not?
- Status of relationship with customer
- Understanding of customer's goals, issues, impacts
- Do the products and/or services fit?
- What, if any, are the differentiators?
- Is there an understanding of the price level required to win and, if so, is this achievable?
- Is there a supported risk mitigation plan?
- Are the resources to deliver known and available?
- What are the customer's options?

This information (if analyzed honestly) will provide the supplier with:
- Understanding of the risks associated with the project
- Analysis of supplier's ability to respond successfully and pricing analysis
- Make/buy strategy
- Timeline for bid activity
- Plans to influence purchaser at high levels
- Key proposal features (critical success factors, resources required and a strategy to win)
- Key themes that need to be reflected throughout the bid

The role of the contracts organization is fundamental to this process. However, the contracting organization does not operate in a vacuum and the bid process needs to ensure all relevant decision makers are involved as appropriate.

The outputs of the bid/no-bid meeting are:
- Continue with the preparation of the proposal … or not
- Approval of the funding required to bid (where appropriate)
- Identification of whether teaming partners and/or subcontractors are required

The bid team

The structure of the bid team will depend on the size and complexity of the proposal. One thing is certain: the ability to co-operate, communicate (including the ability to receive and deliver constructive criticism) and put the task of preparing the bid first is vital if the bid is to be successful.

In general a bid team should include people to handle the following roles:
- Bid manager – manages the preparation of the bid and is responsible for ensuring the bid is submitted on schedule and (where appropriate) within budget
- Project manager – will be responsible for managing the project post contract award, therefore needs to satisfy himself/herself that what is being proposed is achievable
- Business development or sales manager – provides information on the customer, the market place, and the competition (including what price should be bid)
- Product management / marketing
- Business operations / manufacturing
- Services representatives – provide information on all services related issues
- Finance manager – ensures that all elements of the project are costed and validates pricing models reflecting the effect of differing profit margins
- Contract or commercial manager – (as a minimum) provides input on the contractual terms
- Purchasing manager – ensures that all issues relating to third party suppliers are covered
- Legal – provides specialist legal advice where needed
- Writers – experts on the technical response, management and company background, who will draft the response (it is normally the case that those individuals listed above will also perform the writing task)

Proposal preparation

Now the real work activity begins. The bid manager needs to allocate each section of the solicitation to the individual responsible for providing the response, while at the same time making clear the key win themes that each writer must strive to include as well as guidance as to how much detail is expected and rules about the terminology that must be used. It is critical that from the start the themes, strategy and solution are clear to all involved. This will ensure that the writers know exactly what they are selling and how to go about selling it before they put a word to paper. It is recommended that an outline of the intended proposal is prepared and circulated as set out below.

A well-prepared outline is the foundation for a clear, consistent and logical proposal, a proposal that can be easily understood by the purchaser.
- Using the RFP as your framework, assign each purchaser requirement to a place in the outline. Break the outline into sections and subsections to ensure the different requirements are covered. This ensures that each requirement is addressed in the final proposal.

- Assign each of the purchaser's evaluation criteria as stated in the RFP) to each section of the outline (cross-referencing the RFP section number).
- Review the intended outline to ensure it flows logically, that the purchaser will be able to review it easily, that the emphases are where you wish them to be and that it conforms with the requirements of the RFP.
- Assign each of the sections within the outline to an individual (the writer) who will be responsible for drafting the response. State clearly where each response will fit within the final proposal.
- Provide specific instructions to each writer as to the themes, terminology, style and number of pages they should be providing.

The outline should be circulated promptly and a meeting held to ensure that everyone fully understands and is in agreement with the outline of the proposal. The longer this first bid meeting is delayed the greater the chance that someone has gone ahead and done their own (very different!) thing.

11.8 The role of the contracts organization

For the purpose of this chapter, the following assumptions are made about the contracts organization role in the bid process:
- It limits involvement to those situations where it can add greatest business value.
- While this will sometimes be unavoidably focused on limiting risk, the organization's aim should be to expend its time on adding value through creative solutions.
- By creative solutions, we mean contract elements and commercial ideas that expand the value of the deal, exploit the opportunities represented by risk and create sources of competitive advantage, while remaining within an overall acceptable risk profile.

To perform this role, the contracts organization needs a broad array of business skills and knowledge. For example, they must be able to interpret business direction and strategies and turn these into supporting commitments. They must be able to analyze and evaluate purchaser requirements and translate these into business capabilities. They must be able to access available capabilities and determine ways in which they can meet or exceed the stated purchaser's needs. They must be able to identify and creatively mitigate risk in a manner that satisfies purchaser and internal needs.

It is never too early for the contracts professional to get involved. They should be part of the bid team from the very start of sales strategy and planning and form part of the team that makes the bid/no-bid decision.

11.9 Contract management – adding commercial value

As mentioned earlier, responding to an RFP involves, in all but exceptional circumstances, the making of an offer capable of acceptance by the purchaser. Even if (as is normal) the purchaser chooses not to accept the response (offer) without clarification or negotiation, it has contractual implications, since the customer will rely on statements and documents provided at this time and will seek to incorporate them as part of the final agreement.

The days when a response to a solicitation could simply attach the supplier's standard terms and conditions are largely gone. It is increasingly a requirement that the supplier provides a 'point-by-point' response to each and every term within the purchaser's contract. This takes time and should not be left to the last minute, especially as it may be necessary to take a non-standard approach to some of the purchaser's contractual requirements and such an approach invariably involves gaining the approval of senior management (including the legal department).

It should be made clear at this stage that the bid process should not be confused with the non-standard contractual terms approval process. While both are clearly linked they should exist as separate processes.

How far a supplier needs to go in agreeing to a purchaser's contractual terms will be influenced by a number of factors, including:
- The competitive landscape
- Knowledge of the purchaser's key commercial concerns
- Previous contracts with the purchaser
- The performance of previous projects for the purchaser
- The experience of the purchaser with other suppliers
- The importance of the proposed solution to the operation of the purchaser's business
- The supplier's approach to risk

As discussed in the chapters on developing standards, it is clearly a major benefit to have pre- established standard contract terms that can be used where a point-by-point response is not required and that will alleviate the need for active intervention or support from the contracts organization. Nevertheless it is relevant to bear in mind that the whole bid response document will be relied on by the purchaser who will seek to incorporate documents provided at this time as part of the final agreement.

A commercially astute contract manager can add real value in reviewing the proposed bid to ensure that it is contractually sound. Such activity includes reviewing Statements of Work (SOWs) and making clear to writers of technical responses that their language should be free from overblown marketing rhetoric. Similarly an astute contract manager can ensure that if there are any cost implications in what has been offered (e.g. an extended warranty period), these have been covered in the pricing model.

11.10 **The bid goes on**

We highlighted earlier the need for a meeting of the bid team as soon as possible after the bid manager has prepared an outline of the intended proposal. This meeting is critical to ensure that everyone understands the strategy to be used for winning the bid plus their roles and responsibilities in achieving that strategy.

A detailed milestone schedule is essential if the bid is to be kept on track. This should be distributed amongst the bid team; during the subsequent regular bid meetings any slippages should be highlighted and an action plan agreed to bring the schedule back on track.

A solution review meeting should be included within the milestone schedule. The solution review should be a thorough examination by the bid team of the proposed answer to the purchaser's requirements. The review needs to address whether the solution goes far enough in meeting those requirements, or even perhaps too far!

Once the solution has been finally agreed the design should be 'frozen' so that the task of writing the response can begin in earnest. It is normal for the design to be frozen no later than half way between receipt of the RFP and date of proposal delivery. It is critical that the date for freezing the design is adhered to if all other tasks relating to the preparation of the proposal are to be completed in a professional manner.

Once the design has been frozen the task of ensuring that the right subcontractors are involved can be finalized. It is vitally important to put in place draft agreements with subcontractors so as to minimize the risks associated with dealing with third parties for whom the sole method of control is via a subcontract. If agreements with subcontractors are not in place then the only way of managing this risk is to include a contingency in the costs, which will have the effect of raising the price.

It is clearly essential that the purchasing department is involved in the subcontracting activity as early as possible. The third parties must agree to all terms and conditions which the purchaser requires of the supplier (e.g. extended warranty). Negotiating such 'back-to-back' agreements is extremely difficult after award of the main contract as the third party will know that the supplier has little alternative but to accept the position the third party adopts.

Finally comes the Red Team review. The task of the Red Team is to read the proposal from the purchaser's standpoint, so the version of the proposal that is provided to them should be as close to the final version as possible. The Red Team comprises senior departmental managers who read the entire proposal or specific sections with the aim of ensuring the proposal complies with the requirements of the RFP, is clear and consistent and addresses the key win themes throughout, whilst identifying any risks to the supplier or the purchaser.

The result of the Red Team review is an assessment of the acceptability of the proposal to the purchaser. The Red Team should identify strengths and weaknesses and make recommendations on how to improve the proposal. It is for the bid team to then address those recommendations.

11.11 Approvals

Approvals are an integral part of the contracting process for all companies. It is normally the case that all responses (or offers) that are capable of acceptance are subject to receiving formal internal approvals. Such approvals may be granted as part of a lengthy process or via a quick meeting with the managing director and finance director. This normally means that responses to RFIs which contain no pricing (other than list prices) and which are clearly expressed to be non-binding are not subject to the approval process. The milestone schedule must allow time for the approval process to take place and for the information required by the approvers to be made available in good time. Best practice organizations perform a bid preview providing the key decision makers and approvers with early visibility of the opportunity and the particular challenges that will need to be overcome to win the business.

CHAPTER 12

Request for Proposal management

After reading this chapter, you will be able to provide integrity to the Request for Proposal (RFP) process. You will understand how to identify appropriate bid team participants, assure an objective and thorough evaluation and complete a supplier selection that will stand up to queries and challenges.

This chapter includes:
- Supporting bids and RFPs
- Updating / changing requirements
- Responding to supplier contacts, term and condition variations, 'value-add' initiatives
- Communication – internal, supplier and third party
- Links to documents/websites for extended guidance

12.1 Introduction

Once the make/buy decision has been made and you have decided to go outside the company to purchase the product or service you need, a Request for Proposal (RFP) is used to obtain the best solution. Generally RFPs are used when the purchase is very complex and you are releasing a large amount of information to suppliers.

RFP management requires managing a range of processes during the course of selecting a supplier. The RFP management process can be time-consuming and require a great deal of work. Writing the RFP is only a small part of the total process, which starts with selecting and assembling the bidding team, and runs all the way through supplier selection and notifying and debriefing unsuccessful suppliers.

12.2 Role of the contracts professional

The contracts professional often acts as the central control point for the creation and writing of the RFP document. This role encompasses a number of aspects:

- Managing the list of approved suppliers who have been qualified to participate in the RFP process. If there are requests to use suppliers who are not already on the approved supplier list they are the focal point to request, receive and distribute any information from the new potential supplier
- Being the communication interface between any supplier or potential supplier and the customer's internal user community
- Coordinating, scheduling and managing any meetings with the suppliers during the RFP process, contract management coordinates the scheduling and format of the meetings
- Taking the lead role in the receipt or dissemination of any information to the suppliers
- Choreographing the decision-making and negotiations with the prospective suppliers
- Ensuring the RFP process is managed with discipline and in an ethical manner

The cross-functional team

The contracts professionals, in their dialogue with internal business teams, identify the need to proceed with an RFP either as a result of an earlier RFI process or an internal decision to buy. They will then move to lead or be a major contributor in selecting a team to define and write the RFP. It is important to identify all team members who are needed to provide information or approval for any project. The level of involvement of each team member will depend on what is needed from them to complete the RFP.

Team members should include the executive sponsor and project manager, as well as representatives from technology, operations, finance, legal, security, support, business development or marketing, if appropriate, and the contracts professional.

12.3 The RFP document

The RFP should include everything a potential supplier needs to scope and price the project or product and detail full instructions for responding to the RFP. Chapter 10: *RFP preparation and content* provides a detailed description on the necessary elements of an RFP .

Functional/technical requirements

If a Statement of Work (SOW) is not included within the RFP, this section contains all the functional and technical requirements and specifications required for the proposed product or service. Chapter 22: *Statement of Work and Service Level Agreement* provides more information on this topic.

Your technical representatives will include within the RFP those technical requirements and specifications for the products and services. If software development is required, outline the company's software methodology. This should include impact analysis, systems analysis, detailed design, build code process and the various testing scenarios – unit, string, systems, integration, load and user acceptance tests. If hardware is required, include the hardware and software configuration, systems performance – batch and online, the ability to interface with other hardware and software, the company's power requirements, systems support requirements, spare parts availability, space requirements and future upgrades.

This is only a shortened list of software and hardware requirements. Have an in-depth discussion with your technical representative to ensure all technical requirements, functionality and specifications are sent to the suppliers. If you do not send a complete set of requirements to the suppliers, it will make it much more difficult when negotiations are complete and you are into an ongoing relationship with the supplier.

Remember, the key word in an RFP is **requirements**. The company's technical representative will include the acceptance criteria and the severity level failure parameters for all the measurable objectives. This is needed whether it is hardware or software or any other product. Your technical representative may allow the suppliers to provide a deliverable with a certain level of failure. As an example, severity levels may define a failure, where severity 1 may be 'worse case' such as a fault impacting on the end user, severity 2 a fault affecting the use of the deliverable but such a fault is not visible to the end user, and severity 3 may be a minor failure either of a cosmetic nature or where there is a straightforward workaround with no impact on the end user. If your technical representative allows the supplier to ship a deliverable with a severity level 3 failure; include this within the RFP.

Acceptance

Instruct the suppliers that your company requires acceptance testing for all deliverables and a successful test will have no outstanding level 1 or level 2 failures. However, all failures, including level 3 failures will be fixed on a priority basis.

Maintenance and support

If maintenance of the product (production support) is required, explain to the suppliers the requirements for level 1, 2 and 3 support, for example:

- Level 1: Basic first-line support for handling straightforward problems such as installing software and resetting passwords. The goal for this group is usually to resolve 70-80 percent of customer issues without having to escalate them.
- Level 2: More experienced and knowledgeable technical support for a specific product or service, handling advanced technical troubleshooting.
- Level 3: Highest level of technical support in resolving the most complex problems as technical experts.

Identify whether the responsibilities during maintenance are to be discharged by the customer or the supplier and, where the customer is to perform any maintenance, what support is required from the supplier to facilitate this.

Ensure that requirements are fully detailed. There can, for instance, be naïve assumptions as to what is covered by warranty and no-one wants to have to explain why the newly acquired computer system needs to be dismantled and shipped back to the supplier to have a fault fixed. Consideration should be given to maintenance on a 24 × 7 basis, spare parts distribution, Service Level Agreements (SLAs), off-site/on-site maintenance or how new revisions to the code or hardware are handled. Work with your technical representatives to include all aspects of production support.

Supplier project team and communication

Require the supplier to dedicate a skilled project team with the necessary experience and expertise to support the project, and to provide the names and resumes of the proposed team members along with plans to manage staff attrition and ensure staff continuity. Suppliers should be responsible for all training activities necessary to keep the skills of the supplier's personnel current.

Require the suppliers to establish and maintain communication links between the supplier and your company. These support ad hoc discussion as well as structured communications and periodic meetings. The protocols must adhere to company standards.

Instruct the suppliers that they must complete the required deliverables, initiate reviews and hold inspections as required, using a repeatable methodology. The project manager shall instruct the suppliers regarding periodic status reports. These reports should contain as a minimum: project status, resource utilization (if a service proposal), variance reports and metrics.

Customer's team and responsibilities

Under this section of the proposal, your company's support team responsibilities will be defined. These responsibilities may include how the company's internal work requests from internal customers are handled, obtaining internal customer requirements, defining and managing the project schedules, participating in the testing of all deliverables and participating in project conference calls. Depending upon the nature of the RFP, other responsibilities may be required.

Pricing

At a minimum the suppliers will provide pricing information on the overview of expected information, pricing requirements and fee schedules.

The range of price and contract types is largely determined by two factors:

1. The extent to which the requirements can be precisely defined (standard to developmental)
2. The associated degree of performance risk/financial liability that either party is willing to accept.

The factor relationship typically follows this model:

A. Standard/precisely defined requirements = firm fixed prices
B. Less firmly defined requirements = cost plus fixed fee (profit)
C. Purely a purchase of labor resources (sometimes called staff augmentation) = time and materials or labor hour

You should request each supplier to provide pricing and fee schedules for the proposed RFP. Pricing must be fully comprehensive and complete. The pricing will be used in part to select the supplier and revise the budget for the project. All one-time and recurring costs for hardware, software, installation, training, and support must be fully addressed. Pricing should be based upon the proposed project. If a selected supplier introduces 'hidden costs' during negotiations, that supplier shall be disqualified and, based on your bid evaluations, the next best supplier would be chosen.

Suppliers should provide pricing based on the requirements. If applicable, they should also submit a maintenance proposal for the first year and an option of four subsequent years with rates that will be in effect for one year from the date of the end of the warranty. Options to renew after the first years must be fully explained for all products proposed. Suppliers should also supply 'help desk' processes to assist the implementation team in resolving questions and achieving the proposed installation schedule.

Instruct the suppliers that price information must remain firm for a defined time period (e.g. 180 days) from the due date of the RFP.

Legal terms and conditions

The product or service requested under the RFP may be unique. If this is the case, and the RFP is released to all approved suppliers who are currently under an existing company agreement, the legal department may require that unique terms and conditions are included within the RFP. Advise the suppliers that acceptance of these unique terms and conditions is part of the overall supplier evaluation.

If you are including suppliers who are not on the approved list, include your company's contract for the type of project required within the RFP, along with any unique terms and conditions that may apply.

While acceptance of company terms of contract is the requested and preferred response, there will often be some objections along with the accepted terms. Many companies will anticipate this situation and ask that any objections are clearly defined along with the supplier's suggested alternative terms.

Security requirements and considerations

Your security department will provide all the details for security requirements, which must be included within the RFP. You should instruct the suppliers that they must adhere to the all security requirements.

Requirements may include data security and guidelines (at the company's locations and the supplier's locations), the company's security requirements for the supplier's personnel at the company's locations and security requirements for transmitting confidential information.

12.4 Supplier selection and RFP distribution

The bid team determines how many suppliers they want to participate in the RFP. As discussed in section 12.2 the suppliers are chosen from the list of approved suppliers and new suppliers once the capabilities of the supplier have been reviewed and it has been determined that a new supplier is capable of performing the work needed to produce the product or project required in the RFP.

If this is a major RFP, most suppliers, if not all, will be aware of the impending RFP.

When the RFP is completely written and ready for distribution to the suppliers, it is reviewed one final time by all bid team members. When all the team members have validated and approved the RFP, Contract Management issues the RFP to the supplier. It should be understood that Contract Management has complete distribution control of all verbal and written communications in the RFP process with the suppliers. Distribution of the RFP may be done via surface mail, courier, collection by the suppliers, email or through an automated RFx system.

An RFx system is an RFP software package used to generate the proposal electronically, assign the proposal tracking number, send the proposal to the selected suppliers, and receive the proposal from the suppliers. Such systems may work as a portal which suppliers access, as an automated electronic RFP distribution and bid receipt tool or as an integrated on-line bidding tool.

Bid evaluation committee

The evaluation process is typically handled in two dimensions – technical/operational and pricing/commercial. To ensure objective technical evaluations, the standard protocol is to require suppliers to completely remove pricing data from the technical/management proposal sections; then the evaluators only initially receive the sections they are assigned to evaluate, and the technical evaluators' judgment is not biased by undue emphasis on pricing variations. Following initial scoring, the team committees converge for joint determinations.

The evaluation process should be performed in accordance with an Evaluation Plan so that objectivity and fairness can be maintained and substantiated. The Evaluation Plan is prepared and approved before receipt of the proposals and should identify the Evaluation Chairperson, together with the overall review process detailing the technical/operational and pricing/commercial elements.

The plan should include evaluation scoring sheets, a guide for consistent scoring regardless of who is performing the evaluation, and a template for the proposed scoring summary. The plan should also include the Evaluation Schedule.

In addition, the chairperson is responsible for assigning committee members' specific assignments and for assuring that required presentations and reports are completed as necessary.

The evaluation process is covered in more detail in Chapter 17: *Evaluating the proposal.*

Supplier interface during bid

No matter how well the RFP is written, suppliers may misinterpret certain items within the bid or request clarification of some points. This will lead to questions from the suppliers during this RFP process. If this happens, the suppliers should be instructed to send all questions to a specific individual in the Contract Management department.

Contract Management sends these questions to the appropriate person from the cross-functional team. For example, if only one supplier sends in a question, the question and your response is sent to all suppliers. You must never disclose the identity of the originator of the question to the other suppliers. The answers may be emailed to each supplier or otherwise electronically distributed, such as via the RFx system.

If this is a very complex RFP and you expect questions from the suppliers, you may include within the checkpoint section of the RFP a date for a suppliers' conference. This will include the date and time of the conference, location, when and who to submit questions to, and the number of suppliers' personnel who may attend. It would be advantageous to have all the questions and answers in a printed format and ready for distribution to each supplier who attends. Make sure you inform each supplier not to include any confidential information in their questions as other suppliers will be seeing or hearing their questions and your answers. Contract Management normally leads the suppliers' conference. Make sure that all cross-functional team members are present.

If questions come up during the conference that can't be answered, inform the suppliers when you will send the answers to them and how the answers will be sent.

You may receive a request from a supplier or suppliers for an extension of the due date. Discuss this with other members of the cross-functional team, and if all agree to the extension, inform *all* suppliers that the response due date is extended.

RFP response

All responses to the bid must be submitted through an RFx system, courier, hand delivery by the supplier or surface mail on or before the due date. Email submissions may be considered but care needs to be taken to ensure the submissions are received securely and the time of delivery can be assured.

Any proposals received early must be kept securely and not opened until the due date and time to avoid giving the perception of giving an unfair advantage to one supplier over another or risking accusations that information leaked to suppliers who had not yet submitted their offer. You may also be informed by a supplier or suppliers, before the RFP due date, that they will not be responding to your bid. Ask the supplier why they won't be responding to the bid and also instruct them to return all the bid information to you.

If a bid response is received after the due date, it should be rejected unless the delay was demonstrably outside the control of the supplier, advised prior to the closing date and time for bids, the security and integrity of the bidding process is maintained and the other prospective suppliers informed. Make sure each supplier is aware that if a bid is received by you after the due date it will be rejected unless there are truly exceptional circumstances. You want to avoid even the appearance of any possible collusion. Every supplier must be assured that they are all treated in the same manner to avoid potential ethical and legal problems.

Bid evaluation and scoring

Proposals should be scored using a combination of rankings and weights. The proposal evaluation sheet is a numerical tally sheet for entering the proposal rankings and applying the weights for each of the evaluation criteria. The scores for the questions are then totaled. The evaluators will also be required to supply a rationale for the scoring of each question. A standard approach is to segment requirements into Mandatory (must have) and Optional (nice to have), with several gradations in the latter category. Mandatory requirements are assessed on a simple Pass- Fail scoring, with any Fails eliminating that offer from further consideration.

If any showstopper problems are found, they should be brought immediately to the attention of the chairperson. This type of problem might be caused by matters like the inclusion of a supplier's proprietary information in the proposal, missing required exhibits, and obvious gross misinterpretation.

Other issues, such as alternative approaches to the project, may force a different approach to the evaluation or revised evaluation criteria. In such a case, the chairperson will need to decide how to handle the exception: whether to re-evaluate all proposals, or simply continue and present the alternative approach to the business sponsor for further consideration.

It is usual for an RFP to ask suppliers submit descriptions of past performance, and customer references. Your team should include a 'Due Diligence' interviewing of selected references – usually over the telephone, having pre-arranged timing with the past customers. Unusually complex projects may require site visits to those prior customer installations. For the more typical telephone interview, it is recommended that they are conducted with two people: the contracts lead (who should be able to handle the business aspects), and a technical representative. Prepare a standard script of key questions, and try to frame these so they elicit more content than a 'Yes-No' response. Whichever person is not engaged in a dialogue with the past customer's representative should be taking notes.

If the project is especially important or complex, or initial evaluation of the proposals fails to produce a clear winner, the chairperson must determines if face-to-face reviews are necessary and schedules them accordingly. If face-to-face reviews are not necessary, the chairperson contacts the suppliers to obtain answers to any questions.

It is common practice to have all suppliers attend face-to-face reviews individually. You may elect to invite only those suppliers whose proposals merit further consideration. In the latter case, be careful because excluding some suppliers may expose the process to downstream challenges. Also, note that face-to-face reviews are in addition to a suppliers' conference, and are used only after receipt and evaluation of the RFP response.

A more detailed approach to applying evaluation criteria is provided in Chapter 17: *Evaluating the proposal.*

Face-to-face presentations

RFP responses may be sufficiently complete that so the evaluation process can proceed without face-to-face reviews. Minor questions may need to be asked on a conference phone call in order to clarify pieces of information. However, the evaluation team may need to gain additional insight by meeting the proposed technical and management personnel and discussing their approach, rationale and response to questions. This is particularly important in a complex or highly significant project where it is vital to ensure there is a full understanding and meeting of minds with the chosen supplier.

Face-to-face presentations give suppliers an opportunity to explain their proposal. The evaluation team can gain clarification of issues and gather data to support or re-evaluate their tentative conclusions. If face-to-face reviews are required, they should be conducted individually for each supplier. The company should send written notification by email, followed up by a telephone call, requesting a presentation and listing the questions to be answered. It should be communicated that all data presented will be considered as part of the supplier's proposal and used in the evaluation, and that no discussion of bid prices will be permitted.

Each supplier should choose a spokesperson, and bring with them appropriate product experts or delivery personnel to address specific aspects of the proposal. The ideal format is to allow suppliers an initial hour for a prepared talk, with a visual presentation. Suppliers should provide hard copy handouts to the company participants with one soft copy also provided in a suitable medium. Suppliers will present a prepared talk addressing the questions submitted by the company, and questions or other interruptions should be kept to a minimum.

Following the formal presentation, the chairperson should lead the discussion, using the questions previously submitted by the evaluation committee and allowing other questions to be addressed. The evaluation team must refrain from making remarks that could indicate an opinion or evaluation of the proposal. The discussion should continue until all questions have been covered.

On a cautionary note, the interactive nature of a face-to-face conference can produce greater insight to proposed solutions, and the exposure to supplier personnel adds insight to subjective strength elements. A the same time, it can be so tempting for your staff to follow a course of seeing merit in a particular supplier's solution that you want to alter the requirements to accommodate that solution. If you value the integrity of your contracting processes, do not do so. If the desire to alter requirements is so compelling in meeting company objectives, then prepare an RFP modification with those changed requirements and provide them to all still-qualifying suppliers at the same time.

At your company's option, the supplier may submit any additional data desired within 24 hours from the close of the business day on which face-to-face reviews are held. At this point, the evaluation team's preliminary review and analysis has been completed, so the final scoring and selection can be done at the conclusion of the oral reviews.

It is worth noting that with the improvements in technology and the global nature of business a face-to-face meeting can be effectively achieved using virtual conferencing capability. The suitability of this approach will depend upon the nature of the project and the individuals' comfort and experience with using such technology.

Executive overview and supplier selection

To obtain executive consent to proceed, the supplier selection process culminates in a review report to appropriate company executives by the evaluation committee chairperson, based on the final scores, proposal summaries from the committees and rationale supplied on the evaluation sheets.

In preparing the evaluation team's report to the executive sponsor, remember that the sponsor is often involved in a variety of projects from a high level perspective and may need to be re-introduced to your project in the overview. You should state the basic objectives of the project, as well as the proposed scope of the project so the executive sponsor will understand the potential impact the project.

The briefing should address final scores, highlights of proposals, proposed technical implementation, staffing plans, cost and schedule. Be sure to report any findings from the evaluation process that might inform the sponsor's ultimate decision to proceed.

The report should include the results of the selection process, as well as evidence that demonstrates the recommended supplier has the technical competence, financial resources, and people resources to deliver the project or product successfully. It is important to include:

- A statement of the level of confidence in the proposed supplier schedules
- A statement of the standards for measuring the supplier's performance against established checkpoints.

On receipt of a 'consent to proceed' from company executives, the selection will be considered final, pending any negotiations identified as necessary in the consent to proceed.

12.5 Contract negotiations

The selected supplier and the corporate sourcing negotiation team will negotiate any open issues and pricing, if needed. It's wise not to notify unsuccessful suppliers until after negotiations have progressed. This allows you to keep other options as 'Alternatives to a Negotiated Agreement'. Some contracting experts recommend negotiating with the best two qualifying finalists in parallel to provide your company with maximum leverage and a more readily implemented alternative if unexpected barriers occur in negotiating with the first-place supplier.

Negotiations approaches, tools and techniques are covered thoroughly in the Negotiation phase section of this book.

12.6 Notifying unsuccessful suppliers

After the selection is made, and before notifying the suppliers, appropriate company executives should be given an executive summary of the project for use in the event that an unsuccessful supplier makes an unannounced challenge.

After selecting the winning RFP and completing negotiations, the unsuccessful suppliers should be notified by telephone and in writing that their bids were not selected. The strong points of their proposals should be reviewed and an explanation of how they might improve their future proposals should be offered. A short letter is normally sent to all unsuccessful suppliers after the contract is awarded, thanking them for their proposals.

Debriefing unsuccessful suppliers

A debriefing should be offered to the unsuccessful suppliers. Attendance should be limited to two to three people from your company and from the unsuccessful supplier. No evaluation scores or other bid responses should be discussed. The unsuccessful supplier must be convinced that the evaluation was objective and equitable and that their proposal was understood and considered in full.

CHAPTER 13

The influence of laws on the bid process

13.1 Introduction

This chapter explores a range of international laws and their effects on the bid process.

Key topics that are covered include:
- International legal variations
- UN Convention on Contracts for the International Sale of Goods (UNCISG)
- Offer and acceptance
- Closing the deal
- Dispute resolution

13.2 Basic principles

Most of your bids may be domestic in terms of content and jurisdiction. In this case, you have two immediate things to consider:
- Do you understand how your domestic laws affect bidding? For example, what constitutes a binding offer and acceptance? Must an offer be in writing to result in a binding commitment? Are there particular laws that you need to exclude at this phase?
- Has the customer included specific terms in this bid, or made compliance/acceptance a condition of bidding (in this or any price communication)?

The terms and conditions of the eventual contract are too important to be left to chance – and you don't want to find your negotiating position compromised by a lack of clarity or openness during the Bid phase. The Sales department would often prefer to leave things vague, especially if there is potential bad news or disagreement. This is not a good business tactic, nor is it safe. Now is the time to recognize and evaluate likely areas of conflict and to raise them and your proposed alternates/solutions.

13.3 The influence of laws: international summary

This section considers how things are affected if there is an international dimension to your bid.

The world divides into a series of legal codes and traditions that have significant impact upon the process that must be followed to establish a legally enforceable agreement – or to avoid a legal dispute. For simplicity, these are typically classified into contrasts between common law, Islamic law, civil law, etc. But in truth, while such generalizations are helpful, it is essential to ensure that you understand national or regional variations in detail. For example, while the US, UK, Australia and Hong Kong share a common law basis, interpretation and trade bloc influences cause growing disparities.

By contrast, the law governing the sale of services in the US is common law, which is developed from court decisions and varies more widely from state to state or country to country. Most standard service terms and conditions, in addition to covering issues not relevant to the sale of products/systems, also take the differences among the laws of the various states or countries into consideration.

It is also important to emphasize that this chapter relates to commercial contracts only and not to public or governmental procurement, which are driven by their own specific rules and practices.

During the bid process, best practice companies try to establish which laws and which contract terms will apply if they succeed in winning the bid. Often, it is of equal or greater importance to determine which laws or terms will not apply. Failure to be clear will typically lead to unintended and perhaps costly consequences.

The rules will vary by jurisdiction but you cannot, for example, assume that silence over the terms in the customer's Request for Information (RFI) or Request for Proposal (RFP) indicates that this is simply a topic for future discussion. Local legal principles or statute law may impose specific terms unless they are specifically excluded. Typically such provisions will be unfavorable to the seller.

For example, if you are trading goods in the US, the terms of the Uniform Commercial Code (UCC) will automatically apply. In areas such as liabilities, indemnities, warranties, payment terms, entirety of contract, you may be unhappy with the results. Similarly, if you are trading internationally, there is a high probability that your transaction will fall under the provisions of the United Nations Convention on Contracts for the International Sale of Goods (UNCISG).

With the continued introduction and take-up of technology by organizations and their staff across the business world, the risk profiles for bidding and contracting keep expanding. Most, if not all, legal systems are ill-equipped to manage international trading relationships. Arguments over governing law and jurisdiction are common, with courts being weighted against foreign litigants. The growing trade relationships between nation states require thought and consideration when defining the methodology of bidding and subsequently contracting. There is no single unique framework for international trade and international contracting. States that have signed international conventions are regulated by such conventions and agreements on a case-by-case basis and modified for the specific characteristics of any contractual relationship. In all situations such contractual relationships should be in writing.

When submitting a bid to a request for tender or some other form of contracting you must be alert to the intention of relevant parties that governs a specific relationship. When a bid is submitted (offer) and the other party accepts, the two parties give their voluntary consent to become bound to what is written in a contract and are obliged to fulfill the obligation as if it were a law. However, in some jurisdictions the behavior of the parties may give rise to a binding contract, even in the bid process.

In international trade the bidding parties need to be fully aware of the law that governs the process and the potential future signed contract. There are many issues to be understood and recognized in international trading and international legal variations, including such law as foreign corrupt practices law including:

- US – Foreign Corrupt Practices Act of 1977 (FCPA)
- UK – Bribery Act 2010
- Australia – Criminal Code Amendment (Bribery of Foreign Public Officials) Act 1999
- African Union Convention on Preventing and Combating Corruption- 2003.

Issues that may affect your ability to trade and operate internationally and affect the bidding process include:

- Differences between legal systems
- The question of which laws will apply in disputes
- Patent registration
- Extra-territoriality of overseas legislation
- Product liability
- Health and safety regulations
- Import / export regulations
- Competition law, including relationships with third party representatives
- Requirements for licenses, local content, joint ventures etc.

Before you negotiate an international sales contract or complete an international tender, review the following and determine your organization's position on each:

- Defining key terms (e.g. Incoterms 2000, which are the standard trade definitions most commonly used in international contracts)
- Limiting agreement to the contract
- Describing the goods
- Contents of the payment clause
- The passing of title / rights of repossession
- Trade terms (shipping terms, as with Incoterms 2000)
- *Force majeure*
- Dispute resolution
- Applicable law and jurisdiction
- Fees and charges – including what you are responsible for and what your contracting partner is responsible for
- Currency

Your company needs to ensure that it has checked the credentials of overseas partners and buyers/sellers.

The moment the parties agree an international commercial offer, both parties are expressing their agreement to that set out in the offer. In many countries the offer is as valid as a signed contract and therefore it is important that it is prepared correctly. Make sure that the offer you send (your bid) contains all information relevant to the commercial relationship. It is recommended that the offer contains as a minimum:

- Clear and complete information, without unnecessary formalities.
- Reflection of the intention of the parties involved to be bound by its obligations.
- Firm and definitive statements, without reservations, only exceptions.
- Validity period. If there is no validity period, then validity should be indefinite or infinite.

If your organization is accepting the offer, the written response should be an unequivocal declaration indicating the acceptance of the offer. If the answer to the offer contains substantial amendments, the offer is considered to be rejected.

Table 13.1 lists the basic elements to be considered as a minimum in any international contract, no matter what the jurisdiction. These are the fundamental elements to an international contract that should form part of your bidding response.

Elements	Description	Remember
Seller and buyer	Identification and tax details	Full details of the company and contact. It important to verify if the person who signs the contract has the power to do so. That is, if the person is a legal representative of the company. If the person is delegated by the manager or administrator of the company you should assure yourself of this fact by asking the legal representatives for verification and including this as an appendix to the contract.
Product	Detailed description, composition, functionality, etymologic denomination	Use the description appearing on the labels or user manuals. It is recommended to include customs nomenclature. Indicate that it observes the legislation of the country applicable to the product.
Amounts	Item, number of items, weight, volume, dimensions	The measurement unit must correspond to those used by the receiving party of the offer. Take into account the differences in the use of measurements between one country and another.
Price	Unit price, total price, payment currency	Clearly indicate the currency being used in the financial transaction. It is recommended to indicate the price in numbers and words with the currency beside it using the ISO 4217 three letter code. Tax treatment should also be identified, including whether any grossing up for any withholding tax.
Payment conditions	Check, transfer, letter of credit. Duration of credit, for example 30 days.	Indicate, if necessary, the name of the bank and account number. For installments or credit payments, respect the customs of the destination country.
Guarantees	Certificates and standardization. After sales service	Special reference to the ISO standard, certificate of origin and the standardization required in the country of the buyer.
Dispatching conditions	Means of transport. Container and packaging	List the number of boxes and number of items per box.
Delivery	Delivery date and location	Depends on Incoterm being used or that agreed in the contract. It is recommended to fix delivery conditions with an Incoterm for wider acceptance in international trade.
Validity	Date, validity period of the offer	Indicate the full date, day, month, and year of the validity (start and end date) of the offer.
Legal aspects	Applicable law, court having jurisdiction, arbitration clause, responsibility of the seller and limits of responsibility	Should indicate the applicable law to resolve disputes arising between the parties. Indicate the court and the country having jurisdiction to resolve the dispute. The arbitration clause can be included in the contract or agreed later. Responsibility of the seller, for example in the case of a delay in delivery and the limits of this Responsibility

Table 13.1   Basic elements of an international contract

Care should be taken in structuring cross-border deals. Poorly structured deals can be costly for both the company and its customers. Awareness of the principal tax traps will enable you to properly structure deals to minimize unnecessary tax costs and increase profits, for instance in some jurisdictions the location of where the contract is signed determines whether it is treated as a local or offshore.

Suggested actions that mitigate international cross-border risk:
- Local contracting for cross-border projects.
- Master Agreement with locally executed transaction documents.
- Staff secondments.
- Use of appropriate Human Resources (HR) programs to take advantage of tax issues.
- If inter company – proper application of transfer pricing policy.

Suggested contracting structures used to mitigate risk include:
- Local-to-local contracts
- Company entity with local presence to local customer
- Global contracts
- Master contract with local transaction documents
- Assignment model
- Subcontracting model
- Consolidated statement facility

Suggested local contracting:
- Customer contracts are signed by the local company legal entities and the local customer legal entities in the country where the services are supplied.
- Services are performed and invoiced locally with no centralized, cross-border management.
- Revenue is recorded locally and taxes are reported and paid locally.

Suggested master contract with local transaction documents:
- A Master Agreement between the lead company and the lead customer company is executed to establish the overall terms and conditions under which the local contracts will follow.
- The local contracts will be concluded between the local company and the local customer and will incorporate the terms of the Master Agreement.

Suggested subcontracting model:
- A single global contract is signed by the lead company and customer legal entities.
- Lead legal entity subcontracts with the local company affiliate for the performance of remote services to the local customer affiliate.
- The subcontracted entity will bill the lead entity via the inter-company billing system.

- The use of the subcontracting model requires tax sign-off to ensure that indirect and withholding taxes are properly considered.

Suggested assignment model:
- A single global contract is effected between the lead company and customer legal entities. The contract must contain a provision allowing assignment.
- The lead company and customer assign their rights and obligations for provision and receipt of remote services to the local company/local customer affiliate, respectively.
- The effective result is local contracts with locally issued invoices in the local currency with local payment.

Indirect taxes:
- Value-added Tax (VAT) and Goods & Services Tax (GST) are the most common type of indirect taxes.
- In Asia Pacific, tax rates range from 5 percent (Singapore) to 17 percent (PRC).
- VAT/GST systems allow a tax credit against taxes billed for taxes that have been paid. Such taxes are neutral.
- When services performed locally are billed locally to a locally tax registered customer, input credits make VAT/GST merely a timing issue.
- When locally provided services are billed cross-border, the VAT/GST becomes an unrecoverable cost. The customer ultimately pays for this as a direct unrecoverable cost or as part of the company's cost of services (built into the price).

When withholding tax (WHT), customer contracts involving cross-border payments consideration should be given to include a provision that allows the company to 'gross up' the invoice amount to account for the WHT amount keeping the company whole from a cash perspective. The impact on the customer relationship and the competitive position need to be taken into account as grossing up inflates the price paid and, in most cases, the WHT can be reclaimed under tax treaties.

13.4 The influence of laws: UNCISG

Because there are so many variations in national laws relating to the sale of goods, the United Nations has developed a set of rules governing international sales. This is referred to as the UN Convention on Contracts for the International Sale of Goods.

After decades of effort, the United Nations Commission on International Trade Law (UNCITRAL) promoted the adoption of the UN Convention on Contracts for the International Sale of Goods (CISG). At the time of writing the CISG applies to seventy-six nations, including most of the major trading nations.

Business people and legal representatives involved in international trade have to be aware of a vitally important aspect of the CISG: unless the parties specifically indicate that CISG does not apply, the CISG will be the governing law pertaining to all commercial contracts for the sale of goods between parties having their places of business in different countries which have adopted the CISG.

For example, if the parties do not agree to the contrary, a commercial sales agreement between a business in Monrovia, for example, and one in Toronto, (both Liberia and Canada having adopted the CISG), will automatically be subject to its provisions. However, if the parties to a sales contract wish to be bound by some other law, such as the UCC or Ontario sales law, they may opt out of the CISG by specifying that the other law will apply, as well as stating that the CISG will not apply, in cases of dispute.

The CISG is based partly on the common law tradition, but is also influenced by civil law and socialist law. Under common law, for example, a valid contract is an agreement which contains the following elements:
- It is entered into by mutual assent;
- It is supported by sufficient consideration;
- The parties have the legal capacity to enter into a contract
- There is no illegal purpose.

If any of these elements are missing there is, generally, a void contract.

The CISG, however, governs only the formation of the contract of sale and the rights and obligations of the seller and buyer arising from such a contract. The CISG is not directly concerned with the validity of the contract, where a person is induced into a contract by fraud, where a person does not have capacity to enter a contract, or where domestic law prohibits the sale of goods specified in the contract.

Offer and acceptance
Contracts can also be formed by an exchange of purchase orders that are accepted or confirmed through the exchange of forms containing conflicting small print terms. This happens quite frequently between parties in an international transaction. Under the CISG, an acceptance that contains modifications operates as a rejection of the offer, and constitutes a counter-offer, unless the modifications do not materially alter the terms of the offer and are not unacceptable to the offeror. If the offeror does not object verbally without undue delay, then the contract terms become those of the offer, as modified by the acceptance.

This means that the small print terms of an acceptance or order confirmation are binding unless promptly objected to, or unless they constitute material changes to the offer, or purchase order, with respect to price, quality or dispute resolution.

This is known as the 'battle of the forms' under both common and civil law.

The CISG states that an offer is accepted only at the moment it is received. The CISG also limits a party's ability to withdraw an irrevocable offer. Under the UCC, irrevocable offers can generally be revoked if they have not yet been accepted.

There is no contract until the offeree accepts an offer. Acceptance under the CISG may take the form of any statement or action on the part of the offeree that suggests an intention to be bound to the contract. However, under common law, the mode of acceptance must be one that is specified by the offeror, and if not specified, must be of a mode that is appropriate under the circumstances.

Fundamental breach

The CISG preserves the buyer's right to sue for breach of contract. However, the right to 'avoid' or terminate the contract and reject the goods is quite limited. The buyer may reject goods and require delivery of substitute goods if the contract has been 'fundamentally breached'. The result must be of such a contractual detriment to the buyer as to substantially deprive the buyer of the goods that were expected under the contract. In general, however, the CISG allows the seller who fails to perform on time, or who delivers nonconforming goods, to correct the performance as long as it does not cause the buyer an unreasonable delay or inconvenience. In addition, the buyer can also avoid the contract if, after notifying the seller to perform the contract within a reasonable time, the seller refuses to do so. This is a novel remedy in common law.

The CISG also gives the seller protection against the potential financial failure of the buyer. The seller may, by sending appropriate notice, suspend delivery or prevent the release of goods if it becomes apparent that the buyer may not have the ability to pay for the merchandise. The seller must continue with delivery if the buyer then provides adequate assurance of payment.

Under the CISG, contracts may be proven by any form, including use of the testimony of a witness or with parol evidence. (The parol evidence rule, in common law, prevents a party to a written contract from presenting evidence that contradicts or adds to the written terms of a contract that appears to be whole.) Also, formation of a contract under the CISG does not require the presence of consideration, as is the case in common law jurisdictions. Finally, the CISG eliminates the 'mirror image' rule of contract formation. Under the CISG, acceptances containing immaterial additional or alternate terms can still form a contract.

The CISG promotes freedom of contract over the regulation of private international behavior. It allows businesspersons to operate more efficiently in the growing international marketplace by replacing potentially litigious legal regimes, such as the UCC, with a set of laws that allows for self-regulation.

The following is the list of countries that have ratified or accepted the CISG Convention at the time of writing (Table 13.2).

Albania	Gabon	Peru
Argentina	Georgia	Poland
Armenia	Germany	Republic of Korea
Australia	Greece	Republic of Moldova
Austria	Guinea	Romania
Belarus	Honduras	Russian Federation
Belgium	Hungary	Serbia
Bosnia and Herzegovina	Iceland Iraq	Singapore
Bulgaria	Israel	Slovakia
Burundi	Italy	Slovenia
Canada	Japan	Spain
Chile	Kyrgyzstan	St. Vincent and the
China	Latvia	Grenadines
Colombia	Lebanon	Sweden
Croatia	Lesotho	Switzerland
Cuba	Liberia	Syrian Arab Republic
Cyprus	Lithuania	The former Yugoslav
Czech Republic	Luxembourg	Republic of Macedonia
Denmark	Mauritania	Turkey
Dominican Republic	Mexico	Uganda
Ecuador	Mongolia	Ukraine
Egypt	Montenegro	United States of America
El Salvador	Netherlands	Uruguay
Estonia	New Zealand	Uzbekistan
Finland	Norway	Zambia
France	Paraguay	

Table 13.2   Countries that have ratified or accepted the CISG Convention

The growth of such universal or consolidated standards continues, although slowly. There is growing consensus at both international and regional levels over standards for services, software, intellectual property rights, and in key areas like competition law, which can have a dramatic impact on what you bid and how you bid it. The issue of competition law in particular has a major effect on how a bid can be shaped and the nature of the business terms and conditions that are proposed.

These initiatives and their current state are covered in detail in the chapters on contract development and drafting.

UNCISG and UCC are similar but...

It is not possible in this chapter to compare and contrast the impacts of law on the bid process in every jurisdiction. We can only pick illustrative examples that demonstrate why this is important and may assist you in asking the right questions. For this purpose, we have selected from the UNCISG and the UCC.

The UN Convention on Contracts is similar to the Uniform Commercial Code (UCC), which provides the rules that govern interstate commerce in the US, but has many important differences. Among the differences:

- The UCC requires all contracts of more than $500 to be in writing. The UN Convention requires no writing in order for the agreement to be an enforceable contract.
- In the UCC, an acceptance of an offer containing non-material different terms and conditions still operates as an effective acceptance. Under the UN Convention, most non-conforming acceptances (having different or additional terms) will automatically be considered counter-offers.
- All terms relating to price, payment, quality and quantity of goods, place and time of delivery, liability and dispute resolution are deemed to be material terms. Therefore, a contract will not exist until agreement is reached on all material terms.
- Under the UCC, it is presumed that the offer is not firm (may be revoked, taken back) unless it is specifically stated that it is irrevocable. Under the convention, stating a time limit in which the offer must be accepted creates a firm or irrevocable offer.

Example: A seller submits a price quotation to a customer for 30 steel machine parts, giving a 60-day period in which the offer has to be accepted. Before 30 days is up, the currency fluctuation in the seller's country makes the offer unprofitable. The seller might like to withdraw the offer, but under the convention, if the customer orders within the 60 days, the seller must provide the steel machine parts at the quoted price.

UNCISG applies across countries

The UN convention applies to sales transactions between convention countries where there is no choice of governing law agreed to by the parties and even where there is a choice of law specified, it applies unless it is specifically excluded in writing. It does not apply where the entire transaction takes place within one country (e.g. China) and there is no involvement of a second country (e.g. Lesotho.) The convention is based on common law contracting concepts and tries to treat both the buyer and seller fairly. With a few exceptions, the parties are allowed to modify by contract any specific provisions that the convention would otherwise provide.

They cannot change the law to provide for something that would violate any other laws, either local, state, provincial or national. They cannot contractually avoid certain liability such as product liability or liability for death or personal injury, although they can provide limits on either party's contractual liability to the other party.

European Union (EU) law

Under European Union (EU) law parties are free to enter into a contract and to determine its contents, subject to the requirements of good faith and fair dealing, and the mandatory rules established by a set of Principles set out in *The Principles of European Contract Law 1998, Parts I and II.*

Either of the contracting parties may exclude the application of any of the Principles or derogate from or vary the Principles' effects. Article 1.103 allows for the parties to choose to have their contract governed by the Principles, with the effect that national mandatory rules are not applicable and that the effect should nevertheless be given to those mandatory rules of national, and international law which, according to the relevant rules of private international law, are applicable irrespective of the law governing the contract.

Under EU law the intention of a party to be legally bound by contract is to be determined from the party's statements or conduct as they were reasonably understood by the other party. EU law also states that if one of the parties refuses to conclude a contract unless the parties have agreed on some specific matter, there is no contract unless agreement on that matter has been reached. Contrary to contract law in common law countries, EU law states that contract terms which have not been individually negotiated may be invoked against a party who did not know of them only if the party invoking them took reasonable steps to bring them to the other party's attention before or when the contract was concluded. Such terms are not brought appropriately to a party's attention by a mere reference to them in a contract document, even if that party signs the document. This is an important point when preparing offers and looking at acceptance.

A promise which is intended to be legally binding without acceptance is binding.

In EU law a proposal amounts to an offer if:
- It is intended to result in a contract if the other party accepts it.
- It contains sufficiently definite terms to form a contract.

A proposal to supply goods or services at stated prices made by a professional supplier in a public advertisement or a catalog or by a display of goods is presumed to be an offer to sell or supply at that price until the stock of goods (or the supplier's capacity to supply the service) is exhausted.

Be aware that any form of statement or conduct by the offeree is an acceptance if it indicates assent to the offer; silence or inactivity does not in itself amount to acceptance. A reply that gives a definite assent to an offer operates as an acceptance even if it states or implies additional or different terms, provided these do not materially alter the terms of the offer. The additional or different terms then become part of the contract. However, such a reply will be treated as a rejection of the offer if:
- The offer expressly limits acceptance to the terms of the offer; or
- The offeror objects to the additional or different terms without delay; or
- The offeree makes its acceptance conditional upon the offeror's assent to the additional or different terms, and the assent does not reach the offeree within a reasonable time.

What do you need to find out?

Most statutory codes tend to be favorable to buyers, and there are a number of aspects where a seller may not like the result the law allows. In those cases, the seller may attempt to create terms and conditions that change the result to one more favorable to itself – but in some jurisdictions that may not be possible.

When you are preparing or considering a bid, you need to ask a range of questions, such as:

- Which terms are controlled by law and which are left to negotiation?
- If you are proposing your own standard terms, are the terms of your agreement valid in the country where the work is to be performed?
- Will the law protect your interests beyond the terms of the contract, and to what extent?
- What liabilities or other penalties might you incur under the law because of the other party's actions or inactions?
- What liability may be imposed for non-performance?
- What legal remedies or procedures are available to enforce the contract terms?

Many business transactions take place outside the bid and proposal process. In most cases, when only one country is involved, the local law where the transaction takes place will apply unless the parties agree otherwise. It is important to be aware of the laws that affect the formation of a contract and the obligations to which you may be committing your company.

13.5 **Offer and acceptance**

This section explains what sets contractual arrangements apart from other arrangements that do not attract legal consequences.

Remember that the rules about contract formation differ between common law jurisdictions and civil law jurisdictions; this section concentrates on common law. Contract law was established when there was a concern for certainty and a reasonable degree of precision so that business people knew where they stood in their entrepreneurial activities. Rules were set that are precise but the consequence is that it is often difficult to fit the precise model to what people actually do. Analyzing these situations in terms of offer and acceptance is sometimes very artificial.

The requirements for formation of a contract are agreement and consideration. There is a third element, namely, intention to create legal relations; this third element is rarely a problem.

Before looking more generally at offer and acceptance, it is important to emphasize that this is an area where the parties often try to play games. In many jurisdictions, the question of who made the offer and who gave acceptance is material in determining the levels of liability in any subsequent dispute. Sophisticated sellers will attempt to position their final signatures as acceptance of the customer's offer to buy or acquire the good or services. This allows them to take the position that the buyer is responsible for the selection/use of the product or service and was relying on their own professional judgment, rather than that of the seller.

What constitutes an offer?

Once you have made an offer you are immediately vulnerable to being bound by a contract because of someone else's action. As the famous American contract textbook writer Corbin has noted, an offer confers a power on the offeree. It confers a power on another to bind you in contract. Offers can be oral or inferred from one's prior conduct. When you respond, you are making an offer for acceptance. Beware of 'marketing-speak'. The basic test is: is it complete so that merely saying "I accept" is sufficient to constitute a contract?

Acceptance

Acceptance typically can come in one of three types:

1. Express – a direct and absolute outward manifestation of agreement, such as, "I accept your offer."
2. Implied – the acts of the parties show that the offer has been accepted, such as when both parties to a contract begin to perform the terms of the contract.
3. Conditional – acceptance is conditional on the happening of something, such as, "I accept your offer so long as you trim my tree in the next two days." By its terms, a conditional acceptance is a counter-offer.

Acceptance is the moment of contract. Acceptance determines when a contract comes into being. In some cases it may also be necessary to determine where a contract comes into being. The place of acceptance may answer this. Acceptance is the difference between contract and no contract. There are some precise rules that reflect the assumptions underlying the mechanistic model of offer and acceptance.

An acceptance must be in response to an offer – you cannot accept if you did not know of the offer.

However, to protect both buyer and seller, if an offer is intended it should always be in writing.

- Detail the scope of work (products, services, obligations) that the seller proposes to undertake for the price stated (if the offer is a fixed price). If not a fixed price, specify the unit price (for example, price per one or 100 items, price per hour of construction work or troubleshooting)

- Put in the technical, financial, scheduling and other assumptions on which the offer or proposal is based, so if they change, there is a basis for price changes.

Examples:
- Any required modifications to standard equipment to meet customer specifications
- The assumed value of the applicable currency and how variations will be handled
- The tasks that must be completed by the customer in order to enable the seller to deliver and/or install (import permits, Letter of Credit, other permits, security arrangements etc.)
- The dates by which the customer must be ready to accept delivery and/or installation
- The customer's acceptance of the seller's standard terms for warranty, liability and any other cost affecting terms
- Include an expiry date on the offer or proposal. You cannot be sure that the conditions on which the offer is based will remain stable for any greater length of time. Consider whether you want a right for earlier withdrawal of the offer and how this would be executed.
- If the seller has a general or standard agreement in effect with this customer covering the offered products or services, then refer to the terms of that contract. If there is no existing agreement, attach a copy of your company's standard terms and conditions of sale, unless you plan to accept the buyer's terms (or this is a condition of bidding).
- If additional terms will require negotiation, include a statement that the offer is conditional upon the seller and the customer reaching mutual agreement all other terms and conditions of contract.
- If this is a new customer or new product offering, be careful about agreeing to terms and conditions provided by the customer. Your contract manager or lawyer, in connection with making an offer, should review these for acceptability and counter proposals.
- Remember that under the UN Convention, if the terms of the customer's acceptance of the offer are different from the terms contained in the offer, you probably don't legally have a 'done deal' until both parties agree on all significant terms. However, be aware that under the laws of some countries you may have incurred significant obligations.
- Offers should not be made on major projects involving engineering, installation and other services without consulting all involved groups for their concurrence.

13.6 Conditional offers and revocation of offers

Most offers by their very nature are conditional. Offers can be conditional upon various factors as discussed previously. If any conditions are included, make sure they are clearly stated. Offers may be:
- Conditional on acceptance of the seller's standard terms and conditions
- Conditional on mutual agreement on additional terms and conditions

- Conditional on acceptance by the customer within a specified period of time
- Conditional on the price of materials at the time of contract.
- Conditional on the value of the applicable currency
- Conditional on government or other approvals being obtained within a specified period.
- Conditional on customer agreement to perform certain undertakings

Revoking an offer is somewhat more complicated. In accordance with the UN Convention, an offer is presumed to be firm if it includes an expiry date. Under the UCC, it is presumed to be revocable unless it is specifically stated that it is irrevocable. Under English law, the seller can revoke before the offer expires, if notice is given. It is important to include an expiry date to avoid having an open-ended offer.

Under the UN Convention, an offer can be revoked before it is actually received by the customer, but once it is received, it is up to the customer to accept it, reject it or accept it with additional or different conditions. If the conditions are different in the customer's acceptance, the seller then has to decide if they want to accept the changes.

If the seller forgets to put in important conditions, such as those discussed above, it will probably not be on solid ground legally to revoke the offer, even before the customer's acceptance. This highlights the importance of checking all the details and conditions before tendering an offer, counter-offer or acceptance.

Termination of an offer
Five different ways to terminate an offer are outlined below:
- The offeror may revoke or withdraw the offer. This is not possible if the offeror has, for a consideration, promised not to withdraw the offer for a certain time. This is called an option.
- The offer may simply lapse, either because the offeror makes it clear that it will lapse after a certain time or because it has become stale.
- It is possible to stipulate in the offer that it will come to an end if a certain event happens or does not happen – condition precedent.
- The offer may lapse on the death of the offeror.
- The offer may die if it is rejected by the offeree, for example when the offeree makes a counter-offer.

Intellectual property and competition/anti-trust law
Competition laws make certain practices illegal that are deemed to be anti-competitive and hurt businesses or consumers or both, or generally to violate standards of ethical behavior. In the US these are referred to as anti-trust laws, as they were originally enacted to counter the behavior of what were then called business trusts and now known as cartels. Other countries use the term 'competition law'; for example the EU has provisions under the

Treaty of Rome to maintain fair competition, as does Australia under its Trade Practices Act 1974.

Competition policy is entering a new age. Interest in competition laws has increased worldwide – watch for changes in legislation in the countries with which you are dealing.

Intellectual Property Rights (IPR)

In many organizations Intellectual Property Rights (IPR) is the lifeblood of the business. It is that intellectual property (IP) that your sales team sells to customers. It is therefore very important that during any negotiations, and especially in the bidding phase, that no member of your team inadvertently gives away ownership of IP. A slip of the tongue confirmed in writing by an astute party can end up with them having the license to your important IP and you may have to get permission from them to use it.

IPR is a complex area and not necessarily understood by individuals negotiating a contract. What may appear to be reasonable, for instance providing IPR ownership because one party had the original idea or because the customer is 'paying for it' may either overstate the contribution of the party who will own the IPR or significantly under value the contribution of the party who will not have ownership.

The key point to note here is that all care needs to be taken in the Negotiation phase. A lawyer or contract manager must review all written correspondence before release to the other party.

13.7 Problems with preliminary arrangements

Preliminary arrangements can take many forms. From the time the initial customer contact is made until the moment a contract is actually signed by both parties, there are many different preparatory or preliminary arrangements that take place.

These can be:
- Oral discussions or agreements
- Exchanges of information
- Price estimates
- Exchanges of letters, telexes
- Formal handshakes
- Memorandums of Understanding/Letters of Intent

People often assume that the parties involved in preliminary discussions are free to discuss possibilities and do not have to worry that their actions, written communications or phone calls may have legal consequences. Most people know that they are contractually bound (obliged to perform under the law or pay damages) once a contract is signed. Many of us do not realize, however, that such obligations can take effect in pre-contract situations. Let's take a look at some of the phases of the talks and negotiations between suppliers and customers where some form of contractual liability can arise.

Be aware that one or both parties (but more normally the buyer) may seek to incorporate all bid-related documents and conversations into any eventual contract. Hence it is critical that all dialog and communications are carefully monitored to ensure that they do not contain unauthorized or unachievable commitments.

Initial contacts

In the first phase, where general ideas are being discussed, there is usually no particular legal relationship between the parties. As the discussions and contacts continue, there can be obligations placed upon one or both of the parties.

A non-disclosure agreement is often introduced to cover exploratory talks. This may require all parties or only one to protect any information disclosed to the other. In entering such an agreement, it is important to consider whether the nature of the disclosure might pose a later threat or limitation on action – for example are you developing a product or service that may include similar ideas or know-how? In some circumstances, the appropriate step may be to warn the other side that you cannot accept a non-disclosure commitment.

Continued contacts

At the point where the parties are interested in pursuing the deal, technical and commercial conditions are discussed and information is provided or withheld. Some problems can arise during this period:

- There may be errors in the information provided. The customer may take some action based upon information that proves to be incorrect.
- The supplier might inadvertently make an offer, or the customer may think the supplier has made an offer. The supplier might not be able to follow through with the entire offer, or with some details of the offer.
- Either party may have no real intention of entering into a contract on the project or with this other party. Perhaps a party lacks the proper approvals to proceed. However, if one party relies upon the other party's representations and forgoes some other prospects, a binding legal obligation may arise, regardless of a party's actual intent.

It is important when having these preliminary discussions to be honest about your intentions, your authority or lack of authority, and the fact that these are exploratory discussions only. Let the other party know that you do not wish to incur obligations on behalf of either the customer or the supplier at this point in time.

13.8 Closing the deal

At this phase, which may occur before or after the supplier has submitted their proposal, the main points of the transaction have been discussed. There are many documents that have passed between the parties. The consequences that can be attached to the negotiations increase. Pulling out may no longer be an option without significant financial penalty.

Types of agreements or stipulations that are sometimes made during this phase either orally or in writing include:
- Intention to conclude a contract subject to agreement on terms and conditions
- Agreement to continue negotiations in good faith
- No negotiations with third parties during a given period
- Start of development or manufacturing with/without reasonable reimbursement of costs

Every person involved in a deal leading to a contract plays a part in the negotiation – either wittingly or unwittingly – and has the ability to help or hinder the negotiation and in turn close the deal or not. It is important to consciously recognize and plan for these negotiations, as you can be assured that the other party will do so.

The chapters on negotiation go into detail about the importance of planning and choreography. It is important that you give early thought to the structure of the deal and how the terms and conditions and structure will affect the price and negotiation. Any prices provided should be subject to a set of terms and conditions. This ensures that any changes to the terms and conditions can be linked to a change in price. Some items to consider are:
- The duration of the contract
- Whether it will be international or domestic
- Whether the other party is involved or seeking a joint venture
- Whether the deal involves the performance of business operations that may be subject to government regulation (e.g. banking, trading securities, telecommunications, etc.) Or government contracting where compliance with particular regulations may apply or involve the need for security clearances
- Whether the other party is interested in an alternative payment structure (e.g. a benefit based contracting approach, contra contracting)
- Whether either party is relying upon a subcontractor to perform any material portion of the contract and flow down of terms and conditions.

It is tempting to defer the discussion of difficult issues until final contract negotiation. This may prove short-sighted and lead to an inefficient use of resources. It is often better early in the engagement to address tough issues such as: requests for a joint venture; alternative price structure; termination charges; liability, IPR etc. If there is an issue that is a 'deal killer', it is an advantage to recognize this early, disengage, and redeploy the resources to another opportunity.

Some of the factors that influence the consequences of a preliminary agreement are outlined below.

Degree of detail

The more detail about price, work and performance terms, the more likely it will be held to be an enforceable contract.

Escape clause

You might put in the document a well-formulated possibility of pulling out of the deal without liability on either party. This may be sufficient in some countries, but not in others. Certain civil law countries subscribe to the doctrine of 'culpa in contrahendo' a Latin phrase meaning fault in conclusion of a contract, in other words pre-contractual liability.

This doctrine requires the parties to continue to bargain in good faith and provides for recovery of damages against the party whose conduct prevented the formation of a contract. Brazilian and Guatemalan laws have such a concept. In the Netherlands, courts are inclined to examine reasonable legal consequences in light of the social position of the parties, their mutual relationship.

Authorizations

If the Memorandum Of Understanding (MOU) or Letter of Intent authorizes one or the other of the parties to take some action, (e.g. order materials and supplies, obtain government approvals), it is more likely to be considered binding.

Complexity

The more complex the entire transaction, the less readily a Letter of Intent will be considered to be a binding contract on the parties conduct before, during or after negotiations.

Other considerations: Has a party started work? Did that party have a purchase order? Is it possible to reverse actions? Has any money been spent?

13.9 Pre-contractual negotiations

In pre-contractual negotiations, both parties must be aware of and consider each other's legitimate interests. As negotiations progress, this obligation increases. Each party in the pre-contractual phase should bear its own costs and risks and should not assume obligations or liability toward the other party in the event that negotiations are discontinued. In the event of careless or negligent dealing, the following types of problems may occur.

- Inappropriate use may be made of technical information / intellectual property acquired by either party during negotiations.
- If your prospects of concluding the contract were nil before the talks started, and negotiations were entered into anyway, this could be construed as forcing down the price of a competitor, or acquiring technical information.
- If negotiations are broken off without reasonable cause, the other party may have a claim for necessary costs in full expectation of forming a contract.
- One or the other party's representatives may not really have the authority to commit to the project, causing false expectations and possible damages. Under the law, such a person may be held to have "apparent authority" to bind his or her corporation despite the lack of actual authority.
- Positions taken during interim negotiations may prejudice positions the supplier may later want to take in the final contract arrangement, resulting in a compromised agreement

Using Letters of Intent

It is during this last phase of negotiations that documents entitled Memorandum of Understanding or Letter of Intent or similar titles are frequently used. These types of preliminary agreements, before an actual contract, do have a place in business, but only under very controlled circumstances. A great deal of obligation and liability can arise with their use.

The Letter of Intent, any letter expressing the intent to take or forgo some action, is probably the most dangerous written form a contract can take. In a business obsessed with customers and speed, where customers come to you with contracts that they assert must be completed almost instantaneously, the Letter of Intent has become a popular 'convenience' measure.

There is often a great deal of confusion as to whether a Letter of Intent is legally binding or not.

If a Letter of Intent or Memorandum of Understanding must be used it is vital that there is a clause that clearly indicates whether or not the document will be legally binding. If it is not legally binding it is usually prudent to indicate that the document will not be legally binding but that the Confidentiality clause will be binding .

The best alternative is not to create a Letter of Intent in the first place, but instead to insist upon a contract that contains all the elements and protections your company needs. In situations where a Letter of Intent is absolutely mandatory (there should be very few of these situations), the letter should be drafted to reflect no more commitment than you intend to include in the final agreement, should contain a limit of expenditure, should include or incorporate by reference your company's 'boilerplate' information, and should contain a clear 'drop-dead' date, at which time unless replaced by a contract, the Letter of Intent will expire. It should also include a clear understanding of what will happen if the Letter of Intent is not implemented.

Laws that govern the contract

This final section discusses choice of law and the use of Alternative Dispute Resolution (ADR). This section is repeated in the contract development chapter. It is included here because of the importance of considering such provisions in any pre-contract arrangement, such as formal bid documents or a Letter of Intent. Failure to be clear about the way disputes will be resolved – even at this early stage – may have dramatic consequences.

Both parties to a contract have to agree on the laws that will govern interpretation of the contract. Since contract law differs from one country to another, the choice of law provision can have a significant impact if either party ever finds the need to involve the court system. It is obviously hoped that there will be no need to resort to the courts, but many things can go wrong in a contract. Among the potential problems that could lead to litigation:

- One of the parties fails to fulfill its obligations, causing the other party to lose time, customers, and profits.
- The contract isn't entirely clear on what was included in the deal.
- There is disagreement as to ownership or right to use technical information
- Someone claims infringement of a patent, copyright or trademark
- The product doesn't work as the customer expected it to
- The customer doesn't pay

Let's look again at some simple examples of the impact of this choice. In the US, the law of whatever state is designated in the contract will be the controlling law. Generally sellers prefer to use their own law and customers prefer theirs. Many companies avoid use of the state of Louisiana since it is a civil code state and does not fully subscribe to the UCC. The particular law is significant because:

- Some states give very different interpretations to commonly used terms such as 'best efforts'
- Software laws can vary significantly from one state to another
- In the US, there is very specific language that must be used in the contract in order to require that disputes are resolved in the courts of a particular state.

In other countries, where the deal is executed entirely within one country, the law of that country will apply. In the international sales arena, most sellers and buyers wish to use the laws of their own countries. As previously discussed, since many countries are party to the UN Convention on Contracts for the International sale of Goods, that law will apply to any deal between two convention party countries unless it is specifically excluded. In choosing the law of a particular country it is important to ascertain the following:

- Is the law reasonable and understood by your company's lawyers and does it adequately protect your concerns?
- Do you have access to good legal advice within the country of choice?
- Will the expenses incurred by your legal staff and other involved parties be reasonable?
- Are the courts reliable and predictable in terms of outcome, or are they subject to local powers or influences that may prejudice a fair result?

Where the other side insists on the use of their own law, you should only agree to this after full risk assessment and formal acceptance by the approved internal authority (typically General Counsel). In particular, you must have undertaken detailed study of the potential impact of the customer's law regarding liability, warranty, protection of proprietary information, payment and creditor rights. Of particular concern to many companies are provisions relating to intellectual property (Patents, Trademarks and Copyrights, Use of Information, Software Licenses) and export control.

13.10 Arbitration and alternative dispute resolution

Many countries are reluctant to spell out all the specific remedies for problems in advance of the problem occurring and prefer to work out a resolution after the problem occurs, drawing on 'the spirit' of the contract, as opposed to common law reliance on the specific written word. It is for this reason that dispute resolution procedures agreeable to both parties in the contractual arrangement should be established in the beginning of the commercial negotiation. A dispute resolution procedure will only work if it is fair to all parties. To obtain fairness, the best time is at the beginning of the arrangement when expectations will be high and disputes are a secondary issue. Waiting to do so until a dispute actually arises is usually too late.

One technique, used primarily in the US construction industry, is to nominate a 'respected adviser', who has no formal mediation role but is an expert respected by both parties who is paid a small amount to read and understand the agreement. In the event that the parties subsequently reach an impasse on some issue, this adviser is requested to undertake a review and recommend a resolution. In the experience of the industry, this has proved very successful, with the parties in a high proportion of cases accepting the recommendation without the need for the prolonged and costly resort to formal mediation or other dispute resolution methods.

Frequently, the parties to an international contract may agree that traditional litigation using the courts may be too slow, costly and divisive to resolve their disputes. It may also put one of the parties at unacceptable risk of local prejudice against a foreign entity. They may instead agree to use arbitration.

What is the advantage of arbitration or mediation over using the courts? In general you will still need to use lawyers and a support staff and you need to pay for the cost of arbitration, whereas the state usually provides a judge at no cost to the parties. So cost has not proven to be a consistently good reason for arbitration and increasingly time is also not a factor. Advantages of arbitration may include:

- Limitation on discovery (asking for and obtaining documents from the opposing party)
- Earlier resolution of dispute in some arbitration systems
- Parties have greater control over the decision making process
- Arbitration decisions are subject to little, if any, court review (unless fall-back is provided in the contract)
- Confidentiality

When the dispute resolution procedure is written into a contract, a lawyer should be involved in determination of the appropriate language. Here are some reasons why this is so important.

Example: A US company enters into a joint venture with a Chinese organization. They agree to arbitration of disputes in Beijing. Here are some likely consequences:

- The arbitrators will be chosen from a panel of the Beijing Arbitration Institution
- Only Chinese lawyers will be able to argue the case, even for the US company
- The party losing the arbitration will have no review by the courts in China.

Understandably, a Chinese company would be just as reluctant to submit to arbitration in the US.

The path to dispute resolution is littered with many carcasses. Disputes can escalate out of control and take many forms. A dispute can be between buyer and seller, partners, bidding team members, head contractor and sub contractor. It starts with a disagreement, and then becomes a formal issue; the issue escalates and turns into a dispute.

Generally speaking, a process needs to be instigated to achieve dispute resolution. There are a number of processes and organizations geared to dispute resolution, but from experience many failures occur due to the lack of experienced problem breakthrough practitioners. Disputes have a significant cost impact to an organization, so resolution in a timely and effective manner is of the highest importance. Many organizations protect their customer satisfaction ethos and in a dispute this drives behavior and actions of certain staff that affects the ability to resolve when things move towards a dispute. A contract manager must work above all this and work through and resolve the issue. When issues drag out and become emotion-driven, they grow in size and cost impact and become more complex to resolve – intervention is needed. Intervention by a contract manager with expertise in rapid turnaround to resolution can – and often does – achieve resolution with improved customer satisfaction.

A key to successful dispute resolution is to discover the drivers and costs in the issue. Many disputes stem from different interpretations and create such statements as "You got it wrong," "We have a bad contract – e.g. white space clause" or "This would affect our profitability".

Determine who the key players are – that is, those personnel who are the key drivers behind the issue / dispute. Uncover the 'real' motivations behind each player – such clarity goes a long way to determining the resolution approach. Be sure to discover the real cost to your organization associated with the issue / dispute – often the 'real' cost is low, this also helps set the resolution approach.

Key objective 1: Seek clarity about what is driving the dispute and what the real cost will be to your organization.

The first priority is to establish a problem baseline. Create an 'Issues Cloud' to identify the issues. These are likely to include some or all of the issues below:
- Relationship breakdown
- Multiplicity of issues
- Embedded positions
- Adversarial environment
- Worn out arguments
- Status = Stalemate
- High stakes for both parties
- Company burning
- High costs

What are the business impacts and is there an urgent desire to resolve the dispute

What is the contract manager's view of the facts? Are we well positioned or not? Typical key factors in a dispute that is not resolved include:
- No compelling event for the customer to resolve (the less affected the less their desire to resolve)
- Your company is unable to mitigate its losses for fear of triggering termination for breach of contract

- Time pressure on your company's side – you have reached a must-resolve point with your company executive/s

The contract manager must establish clarity and take the emotion out of the dispute. A suggested roadmap for the contract management practitioner is outlined below:
- Separate the issues and build a 'history map' for each issue (who is driving data, correspondence, emails, minutes of meetings, Bid phase data etc.)
- Group the issues, e.g. 'cost impact versus no cost impact', 'scope versus non scope', 'scope groupings' etc
- Prepare an outline map of the situation and show both parties the positions and gaps between positions. The gaps become the focus of resolution negotiation
- Review with appropriate executives, propose observations and recommendations for a resolution strategy.

Key objective 2: Unravel the cloudiness, bring order and gather relevant data in a format that will assist the process of determining a resolution strategy.

All disputes can be resolved. The first point of call is to create the will to resolve, not only within your organization but also with the other party's organization. This can be achieved by working through the following objectives:
- Objective 1 – create a compelling event for the parties to want to resolve
- Objective 2 – be clear and assertive when seeking supporting data
- Objective 3 – crystallize strengths and weaknesses in your argument
- Objective 4 – gain support for resolution approach from your executive/s
- Objective 5 – be ready for the setbacks – be confident of your approach
- Objective 6 – act decisively and quickly to circumstances – don't procrastinate – and do persuade your executives to act in a decisive manner also.

Key objective 3: Create a situation that will open the door for a negotiated resolution.

Important points to keep in mind:
- The first notice of dispute is important. Be crystal clear in describing the issues, accurately describe the parties' respective positions and the gaps
- Attach a summary of the dispute case in issue breakdown format; ensure your arguments have been adequately tested and well supported, be compelling with your case structure, depth of argument and supporting data
- Resist any attempts to extend the resolution / escalation timeframes at the start
- Document and lock in key outcomes, actions and agreements achieved
- Be on the lookout for any 'Way Out' opportunities a party may offer
- Work hard to keep all players focused on key issues; avoid distractive arguments, respond to confrontational behaviors by restating the facts

- Keep your management well briefed and keep your team in 'sync' – this is one of the most important aspects of the process
- Keeping the team in 'sync' has one major challenge – that is, managing the difference between the internal 'Us' versus 'Them' views of formal disputes, especially if your lawyers are involved.

The legal view of the dispute is correctly a strict interpretation and will more often than not return a cautious view about your position, which makes it difficult for senior management to gain confidence about the outcome.

The contract manager view must be a broader commercial view and one that is less concerned about how successful you would be if the matter went to court.

Where you have done your homework carefully, you must be willing to put a higher degree of confidence in a favorable outcome for the company.

If you are the contract manager leading the dispute resolution team, always be ready for new information that will rock the foundations of your arguments – you will find in most cases that the new information is either irrelevant or can be turned to support your case. Be ready for what appears to be a change of heart from senior management, usually manifested as 'drop the case' or a 'significantly favorable settlement' to the other party.

The bottom line on the dispute resolution process

Create an opportunity to position both parties to achieve a settlement of the issues in the dispute. Don't be devoted to your desired outcome – a settlement is what you are ultimately trying to achieve.

There are many organizations throughout the trading world that offer dispute resolution services and advice; some of them are discussed here. Contract managers should be aware of what is available if a dispute arises.

- Dispute settlement is regarded by the World Trade Organization (WTO) as the central pillar of the multilateral trading system, and as the organization's 'unique contribution to the stability of the global economy'. More contracting parties now look at alternate dispute mechanisms to resolve issues. Arbitrators, conciliators and mediators are increasingly attracting international recognition for their skills in the resolution of commercial disputes both on and off-shore.
- The Australian International Arbitration Act 1974 has been developed to ensure that it is consistent with the 2006 amendments to the Model Law on Arbitration of the UNCITRAL Working Group II (Arbitration).

- The Asia Pacific Regional Arbitration Group ('APRAG') grown to 30 members is a regional federation of arbitration associations, which aims to improve standards and knowledge of international arbitration and will make submissions on behalf of the region to national and international organizations.
- ICSID (World Bank) is an autonomous international institution established under the Convention on the Settlement of Investment Disputes between States and Nationals of Other States (the ICSID or the Washington Convention) with over one hundred and forty member States. The Convention sets out ICSID's mandate, organization and core functions. The primary purpose of ICSID is to provide facilities for conciliation and arbitration of international investment disputes.
- The ICC (International Chamber of Commerce) is the voice of world business championing the global economy as a force for economic growth, job creation and prosperity. Because national economies are now so closely interwoven, government decisions have far stronger international repercussions than in the past. ICC activities cover a broad spectrum, from arbitration and dispute resolution to making the case for open trade and the market economy system, business self-regulation, fighting corruption or combating commercial crime. The ICC has direct access to national governments all over the world through its national committees. The organization's Paris-based international secretariat feeds business views into intergovernmental organizations on issues that directly affect business operations.
- The Permanent Court of Arbitration (The PCA) was established by the 1899 Convention for the Pacific Settlement of International Disputes, concluded at The Hague during the first Hague Peace Conference. The 1899 Convention was revised in 1907 at the second Hague Peace Conference.

Often companies will negotiate a compromise by agreeing beforehand to arbitrate in a neutral country under the rules of its arbitration institution. There are many institutions throughout the world, which handle national or international arbitration and have developed procedural rules to take care of most situations that may develop. Some of these institutions are:

- American Arbitration Association
- International Chamber of Commerce
- Asia/Pacific Center for Resolution of International Business Disputes
- London Court of International Arbitration
- Central American Arbitration Association
- Center for Dispute Resolution (CEDR)

You can use an international arbitration association only if the contracting entities are from two different countries. In some countries, law establishes the arbitration process.

Although arbitration is sometimes preferable to litigation, arbitration of a complex international dispute can be costly, involving teams of experts and lawyers and charges for the arbitrators. These costs can often be avoided by settlement procedures prior to arbitration.

Frequently contractual provisions for arbitration provide that the parties must first try mediation. A professional mediator or experienced third party neutral engages the parties in a negotiation process to facilitate settlement. Often the appearance of a neutral party in the case makes settlement possible and avoids the need for arbitration.

Alternative dispute resolution provisions can take the form of a required series of negotiations designed to settle the problem. These negotiations would begin at the technical level, then proceed to contract administrators and then go to high level executives. Most often, these are the steps that would take place in any event, whether or not they were listed in the contract. At the end of the series of negotiation steps, if a settlement was not reached, a professional mediator could then intervene.

Because disputes involving companies having different cultural norms and different legal processes can be so complex, often these disputes can be best resolved by providing up front, in the agreement for a multi-step dispute resolution process.

- The arbitration procedure should indicate the number of arbitrators, typically one or three, and the procedure for their appointment.
- Special qualifications of the arbitrator(s) can be part of the agreement, including nationality, language ability, technical or legal training and specialized experience, such as in the field of telecommunications.
- The place of arbitration should be designated and can be different from that of the administrating institution.
- The arbitration provision can be written to cover only specified disputes, such as breach of warranty, or to cover everything except certain issues. For example, a company holding a European patent would not want the validity of the patent to be determined by arbitration.
- The language in which the arbitration will be conducted
- The parties to the contract and their lawyers will have to decide on the arbitration clause based on the particular circumstances involved.

Alternative dispute resolution (ADR)

An alternative dispute resolution (ADR) is generally classified into at least five types: negotiation, mediation, collaborative law, arbitration and conciliation. ADR can be used alongside existing legal systems such as Sharia Courts within common law jurisdictions such as the UK.

ADR traditions vary somewhat by country and culture. ADR is of two historic types, methods for resolving disputes outside of the official judicial mechanisms and, informal methods attached to official judicial mechanisms. There are in addition free-standing and/ or independent methods, such as mediation programs and ombudsman offices within organizations.

Dispute resolution in international deals including the bidding process can be very complex and exhausting and also costly. ADR methodology provides an alternate to the legal court systems. ADR can include informal tribunals, informal mediative processes, formal tribunals and formal mediative processes. The major differences between formal and informal processes are (a) a court procedure and (b) the possession or lack of a formal structure for the application of the procedure. Calling upon an organizational ombudsman's office is never a formal procedure.

It is important to realize that conflict resolution is one major goal of all the ADR processes. If a process leads to resolution, it is a dispute resolution process.

13.11 Local law: civil code versus common law

In common law, 'conflict of laws' includes choice of law, choice of jurisdiction and recognition of foreign judgments. In civil law, the appropriate translation is 'private international law' because conflict of laws merely governs choice of law rules.

While private international law dates back to Roman times, common law 'conflict of laws' rules are relatively new, because the procedural requirement of service used to be sufficient to limit the jurisdiction of the court to domestic conflicts.

Civil law, being essentially substantive instead of adjectival, puts more emphasis on its choice of law rules, while common law, being essentially procedural, focuses on the rules of jurisdiction. The common law objective contract theory dictates that contractual promises are interpreted according to the reasonable expectation of the promisee (an objective standard). Civil law, which is based on the autonomy of free will, requires actual consent (a subjective standard), but presumptions of fact are available to the trial judge.

Common law is more adversarial, while civil law is more inquisitorial, when it comes to proving the substance of a foreign law, a question of fact arising in a choice of law or recognition of foreign law situation. With common law, foreign law is proven by the testimony of qualified expert witnesses, who are summoned to court, and subject to examination as to both their qualifications as experts and their knowledge and interpretation of the foreign law in question. In civil law jurisdictions, on the other hand, foreign laws need usually to be proven only by the production of a certificate, prepared by a diplomat of the relevant State or an expert in the foreign law concerned, who, however, is not called to testify as a witness at trial.

One of the areas in which growth of a modern civil law is most visible is in international commercial arbitration. With each passing year, there is an ever-increasing volume of reported arbitral awards (particularly in civil law jurisdictions, as well as in the US), and arbitrators are tending more and more to refer to previous awards rendered in similar cases, thus gradually developing a system of arbitral precedent. International commercial arbitration is also greatly aided by major international Conventions such as the New York Convention 1958 and the 1985 UNCITRAL Model Law on International Commercial Arbitration. Legislation based on the Model Law is now in force in such jurisdictions as Australia, Bulgaria, Canada, Cyprus, Hong Kong, Nigeria, Peru, Scotland and Tunisia, as well as in several US states.

CHAPTER 14

Costs identification

14.1 Cost overview

This chapter provides insights into cost identification issues that are important for a contracts professional to appreciate. Whereas some contracts professionals are also directly involved in finance, accounting or pricing issues, many are not and this chapter will provide key knowledge in the following areas:

- Tax and inter-company considerations in defining structure and decision processes
- Fundamentals of finance and accounting
- Costing and pricing the bid
- Price versus cost of relationship

Initial cost identification should be part of the cost/benefit analysis included in the business case and considered as part of the initial approval process prior to development of the Request for Proposal (RFP). Additional rounds of cost identification at key milestones in the bidding and contracting process will validate the assumptions made initially, and address any issues or options that have come out of the RFx (Request for Information – RFI, RFP or Request for Quotation – RFQ) process. Of course, the ultimate financial outcome will depend upon effectiveness of negotiations and post-award management.

Total cost

Total Cost of Ownership (TCO) attempts to identify all costs over the useful life of the asset. The TCO calculations can include the obvious: purchase cost, implementation costs, maintenance, and support costs. Thorough cost of ownership analysis embodies a 'cradle to grave' view of costs: from resources required to develop the business case, draft the RFP and manage the bid process, through to decommissioning and disposal of the asset.

TCO can include calculations for the cost of capital, as well as address factors for risk or experience. However, it does not address alignment with strategy, or the desirability of an investment. Performed thoroughly, TCO should provide valuable understanding of the magnitude of the investment.

14.2　Activity-Based Costing

Activity-Based Costing (ABC) provides an understanding of the true and complete cost of an activity by allocating overheads to products and services, moving overhead into direct cost based on an appropriate allocation of the overhead in relation to the proportion relevant to the specific product or service. TCO models are useful for evaluating an investment, but fall short when called upon for complex analysis. For example, TCO can estimate the cost of upgrading computer equipment in a manufacturing center or entering into an agreement to outsource capability.

Activity-Based Costing provides a process view across several investments, and gives insight into pricing and profitability. Activity-Based Costing in our manufacturing example would be used to evaluate the costs of all design activities and their contribution to the Cost Of Goods Sold (COGS). For example, if a company provides a standardized product, it is relatively easy to add all the costs associated with designing and manufacturing the product. But what if a customer wants a change from the normal product in its standard form, a different color, or different materials?

Activity-Based Costing provides insight into the costs associated with incremental design, testing and manufacturing. What will it cost to maintain separate inventories and raw materials? What are the additional labeling requirements? What are the regulatory and environmental impacts of the change? Once the full range of costs is understood, how will this be reflected in the contract with the customer – as an initial lump sum payment, or will the costs be recovered in per-unit price increases with minimum purchase guarantees?

By looking at complete process costs, Activity-Based Costing can become the foundation for a selecting a supplier. The knowledge of process costs also provide a better understanding of cost structures and is therefore a source of information to support risk analysis, contract development and negotiations planning.

Activity-Based Costing is a more sophisticated approach to identify costings enabling, amongst other benefits, a more analytical approach to setting prices. It is, however, more resource intensive and costly to implement and maintain.

14.3　Tax consequences

Cost identification should include consideration of tax consequences, because this can represent real savings or costs to a company. However, the ultimate realization of those savings or costs is dependent upon other activities and the company's overall tax status.

Therefore, statements of tax impact need to be clearly separated from the fundamental cost/benefit analysis.

Depreciation allows companies to write-off the pro-rated value of the asset over each year of the asset's useful life, which is regulated by taxing authorities and generally accepted accounting principles to be three years, five years, or some other time span, depending upon the type of the asset.

The write-offs allow companies to deduct the depreciation amount to reflect lower earnings, without affecting cash flows. The amount of the depreciation deduction and ultimate tax savings will depend on the company's overall profit picture.

Because the ultimate impact is dependent upon other factors, depreciation is often eliminated from cost/benefit analysis.

Other tax benefits include tax credits that are driven by the governing tax authority's policy. For example, local taxing authorities can provide tax incentives for investment in locations designated as free enterprise zones to drive economic revitalization. Other tax credits can reflect environmental initiatives. How these credits are realized depend greatly on the specific provisions and the company's over-all tax status, so again, these may be excluded from consideration in the business case. On the other hand, an investment can present tax liabilities, such as sales tax or ongoing property and use taxes. These taxes need to be considered as costs in the cost/benefit analysis and the aggregation of costs related to the investment.

14.4 Allocations

How allocations are treated depends upon who is doing the cost analysis. There is greatly differing relevance at the corporate and business unit levels. Business units need to consider allocations as a part of their cost structure, whether or not the allocations represent true costs.

Most allocations are somewhat arbitrary, yet directly reflect in the operating units' profitability reports. However, at the corporate level, true costs alone will impact the parent company's bottom line. While allocations will impact reported costs at the business unit level, they usually have no impact in the overall cost structure.

As a result, consideration of allocations can influence decisions such that they support a business unit, but are contrary to the corporation's best interests. The cost-benefit analysis should show outcomes with and without allocations so the best decision can be made.

14.5   Opportunity costs

Opportunity costs represent the potential impact of options not chosen when an investment decision is made. By selecting a project or a supplier, a company chooses to focus its resources on a specific path. In some cases, there is no value in considering the cost of not making another investment. In other cases, the investment can mean real sacrifice in other areas for the company. If access to capital is limited, the impact can be large.

Opportunity costs usually represent soft, less-quantifiable costs, and can only be based on forecasting and analysis. Before final supplier selection, opportunity costs should be explored and validated. Exploring the alternatives to the procurement choice fulfils governance requirements.

14.6   Cost of poor quality

In some cases, companies will make cost-cutting decisions during the procurement process that increase risk and expose to alternative costs. The potential costs associated with such risk exposure can be documented as part of risk analysis.

For example, a company may decide to reduce its investment in training on a new IT system in favor of having employees learn on the job. The decision makers must balance the time and cost associated with developing and implementing a training program with the costs that will be associated with users diminished productivity due to lack of training.

As opportunity costs, costs of poor quality are hard to quantify and difficult to predict. However, they are an important component of the cost framework.

14.7   IT systems costs

Let's take a look at an example of cost identification with respect to a hypothetical investment in an IT system, since IT investments present a significant degree of complexity in technical and non-technical areas. The costs can be expressed in terms of:
- Direct versus indirect costs
- Initial versus ongoing costs
- Hardware, software and infrastructure costs
- Personnel costs (for users and support personnel)
- Other costs associated with the investment

14.8 Hardware costs

In most cases, hardware is essentially a commodity item, in the sense that it is relatively easy to specify. Many companies have enterprise relationships with manufacturers, so sourcing may be as simple as placing the order. However, hardware related to a specific project may have unique requirements, and may even indicate sourcing outside pre-existing enterprise agreements, particularly for larger servers or specialized equipment.

Other project-specific hardware may include desktop workstations, laptops and portable, wireless devices. Hardware set-up, including development environments, can add significantly to hardware costs.

Indirect costs include acquisition and installation costs, which may be significant if specialized environments are required, such as 24×7 power back-ups, special routing equipment, etc. Finally, there may be necessary upgrades to existing equipment to support initial or future incremental volume or performance requirements.

14.9 Software costs

Software related to project becomes more complex. Some software companies require companies to purchase licenses for developers, even if they are employed by independent consultants working off-site. There may be fees paid to outside software developers for custom applications. Some applications may require integration software, database software, reporting software, quality assurance software, Extraction, Translation and Load (or ETL) software – the list can be endless.

These costs may vary depending upon supplier selection, so thorough disclosure in the RFx process is important.

14.10 Infrastructure costs

Infrastructure costs are generally incorporated in allocations or use-based fee system within corporations. However, infrastructure improvements directly related to the project such as increased bandwidth, new directory systems or infrastructure upgrades may be fully charged to the project. Corporate help desk support is usually figured as an allocation; however there may be a specific charge for training help desk personnel on any new, custom-developed applications.

14.11 Personnel costs

Personnel costs are often the most underestimated since it is hard to track staff who are not directly involved with development. Other personnel costs include infrastructure and support staff, business personnel who participate in requirements definition, evaluation, testing and data reconciliation, and user time allocated to training and learning the new application. In addition to productivity lost to learning, workflow backlogs and bugs in the new application compound the costs.

14.12 Other costs

Other costs directly attributable to the project include the full range of contracting activities: requirements definition, business case justification, RFx, negotiations, and project management.

Communications, change management and other support costs to drive acceptance and adoption should be considered direct costs attributable to the project. Cost calculations should also consider performance measurement, accounting, taxes and costs associated with retiring legacy systems.

14.13 Consensus on approach

It is critically important to be thorough and accurate with your approach to cost identification. Reliable estimates are fundamental to the budgeting process, and are more likely to win approval for additional funding as the projects are upgraded and expanded.

Reliable cost identification also allows more accurate allocations and better budgeting for future projects.

14.14 Credibility of assumptions

Accurate cost identification relies on solid assumptions: are there cultural and language issues that need to be addressed? Are users ready to adopt a new system? Are resources available to adequately define the requirements, validate data migration and test the system?

On the technical side, is system capacity and compatibility sufficient, have business processes been fully defined, has there been clarification and harmonization of change requests?

The best approach is to eliminate assumptions through research, analysis and proactive management.

14.15 Risk assessment

While the majority of cost components can be identified, there is always opportunity for unanticipated challenges. Part of cost identification includes risk analysis. Through use of knowledge management and performance measurement programs, contracting professionals can anticipate risks and identify cost scenarios associate with those risks. They are also able to minimize those risks through detailed requirements sessions, investment in risk mitigation technologies and other governance programs.

CHAPTER 15

Opportunity evaluation

15.1 Introduction

This chapter builds on Chapter 10: *Request for Proposal preparation and content* which explained how to manage the evaluation process as a buyer and develop, upfront, the criteria by which a successful bid response would be reviewed. This chapter expands on that topic from the supplier perspective and reviews the process by which a supplier understands the opportunities ahead and can successfully prepare the proposal response. It is important that both the buy- and sell-side contract management professionals understand the different motivating factors behind each process.

This chapter covers the evaluation of an opportunity to determine whether it fits into your strategic plan and whether the risks balance the benefits before making an offer or providing a quote in response to a customer Request for Proposal (RFP). The chapter will focus on specific bids or proposals, rather than generic market or market segment opportunities.

There are eight key elements that the contract management professional, whether buy-side or sell-side, needs to understand:
- Involvement
- Preparation planning
- Evaluating the scope
- Assessing the risk
- Avoiding reference pitfalls
- Evaluating the relationship
- Judging customer sophistication
- Evaluating future opportunity

15.2 Involvement

As discussed in previous chapters, the contract management team must be integral to the evaluation process from the earliest possible moment, usually the account planning and opportunity identification stages. This is essential to ensure that the terms of the proposed commitment and subsequent offer have been reviewed from all possible angles and that a balanced proposition is evaluated and presented to the customer. This will give the contracts professional the best chance of applying innovative thought to the process, proactively driving best value and contributing game-changing propositions.

In some organizations, the contracts professional can be reluctant to engage much resource in what they see as 'speculative' activity; they have too many 'live' bids to handle already. That is a bad mistake. Firstly, it sends a negative message to Sales, so next time they may not come. Second, it reinforces one of the biggest problems faced by most contracts groups – that is, the problem of being involved too late, when many of the terms have been set and when their role is trying to extricate the company from ill-considered commitments, or when the only thing left to be discussed is the 'boilerplate' – liabilities, indemnities, etc.

Lesson number one is – become involved as early as possible. It will make your job easier and much more fun. Welcome and encourage Sales engagement even if the opportunity is still a twinkle in their eye. Not only does it mean you can shape the direction and many of the terms, but you may even spot break-through ideas that shape a new offering. By the time there is a formal proposal in front of the customer, breakthrough ideas and innovative thinking that can shape the direction and flexibility in a new offering are often impossible.

In evaluating opportunities you should immediately be looking for two things. One, is there a chance to steer or guide the bid or the terms that will be sought? Second, is there evidence that a competitor has already done this, or that the bid is being 'angled' towards a definite winner? Just because someone else is in the driving seat does not mean that you should definitely 'no bid', but it is one of the early elements that must be explored and, based on the evaluation of your chances to re-shape the terms, it may determine how much effort and resource the opportunity really merits.

Of course, your ability to determine whether a competitor has influenced the opportunity depends in part on your competitive intelligence – how much do you know about competitive offerings or the terms on which they typically operate? Without this, you start off in the dark.

15.3 **Preparation**

Planning

An example of setting the requirements is found in the automotive industry; some years ago many suppliers struggled to win business, often finding their offerings and terms out of step with the industry.

What was happening was that the industry leader – Mercedes, at that time – was working with the buying community to define standards and terms. This ability to set industry standards is something that all suppliers strive to achieve. In technology, it was a role that IBM achieved for some years. In aerospace, it was Boeing. But such positions are hard to sustain – and growing buyer sophistication has resulted in a much more level playing field.

The thing that distinguishes these leaders, even today, is strategy and planning; they put competition on the defensive because they are better prepared. Whether through better market understanding or through more careful opportunity assessment and selection, they ensure their product or service offerings are aligned with customer needs. We have talked in earlier chapters about the ways that this market alignment is achieved, but of course no one has perfect alignment so the opportunity evaluation process is always important.

At heart, opportunity evaluation is about determining whether or not pursuing this opportunity represents a worthwhile investment of resources; and if it does, what is it going to take to win? Reaching that conclusion depends on a coherent process and effective teamwork that brings together the right range of skills and knowledge.

Of course, there is an alternative. Some companies just mindlessly pursue any and every opportunity that comes their way. Most of those companies go out of business.

Early involvement is only worthwhile if it is going to lead to effective cooperation and planning. Building a team environment is critical if we are ever going to get past the common perceptions that Sales are just cowboys, trying to get round the system, and that Contracts are just risk- averse bureaucrats who always slow things down.

So make sure you become actively involved and identify areas where you will accept ownership. Although precise roles and responsibilities vary by company, in our view the contracts role should embrace all aspects of the contract. That is the only way to ensure that all terms hang together and that risks and opportunities have been carefully assessed and balanced. It is also the way to gain status and credibility with other functions and departments.

One of the key benefits that flows from developing team strategy is that disagreements – and there will be many of those – are kept internal. You will have worked through the issues and options before you get in front of the customer. Let's look at an example of what can happen when this team approach to early opportunity assessment does not occur – and when internal groups try to take short cuts.

Company J

In this case study, the customer – we will call them Company H – was accustomed to buying products and components that it would then integrate as finished products or systems in its own advanced consolidation centers. Not unnaturally, they assumed this approach when they were looking to deploy a multi-supplier hardware and software solution that would be installed in its operating subsidiaries worldwide.

The Sales team in the preferred hardware supplier – we will call them Company J – was well aware of this project from its inception. They had done a good job of positioning the technical specifications in a way that favored their company. The customer issued a Request for Information (RFI), to which Sales responded without significant contract review; they had decided the requirements could be met using relatively standard terms and conditions. Even when the customer warned them that the indicative prices 'must be cut by at least 20 percent', Sales did not see this as a situation where the Contracts organization would bring any value. They focused their efforts on Finance, who eventually told them they should discuss the situation with Contracts 'because of its international dimensions'.

In their enthusiasm to win, Sales had overlooked or ignored a number of key issues. These included the fact that the products being shipped would not conform in all cases to local standards, resulting in problems with service and parts support, both during and after warranty. In some cases, there might be issues with country acceptance requirements. In others, the shipping in of product would certainly damage relationships with local agents or resellers, who would certainly refuse to provide support unless compensated.

Having grasped these potential problems, Sales then approached the Contracts group requesting 'a set of terms that would support this sale to the customer in the US, but guaranteeing warranty and service support in each country of final installation'. They also advised that such a guarantee could not be accompanied by any sort of price increase or separate charge.

The contracts team in Company J took a little time to understand the background. They avoided the temptation to berate Sales for involving them so late, or being so naïve. They avoided the temptation to simply insist on explaining the company's standard approach to such business. And they avoided the temptation to escalate (which may well have been a mistake and is one that many Contracts groups fail to do often or early enough – you only have to do this successfully once or twice and the message soon gets through).

Having understood the background, the Contracts team saw two scenarios that might represent 'win-win' alternatives. Both involved Company J taking the formal role of integrator under the contract (immediately seen by Sales as 'too fundamental a change').

Option 1 would have Company J undertake integration at its facilities in each country (or, where these did not exist, at a regional center). This would have the advantage that products would be configured to local specifications and standards, and the deal could be engineered to ensure support by local subsidiaries, agents or resellers. Title to products would pass only when installed, which would have dramatic impacts on cost through reducing taxes, duties and shipping costs. Overall, the project cost was estimated to reduce by up to 30 percent following this approach.

Unfortunately, they soon discovered that this approach would not gain customer acceptance because of sensitive security issues. The customer was not prepared to allow certain of the software products or final integration to pass outside its direct control.

But that left option 2, which although a little more complicated that option 1 retained many of its benefits. Under this plan, Company J would contract to deliver the integrated solution in each location, but would then appoint the customer (Company H) as its subcontractor to perform the actual integration and distribution services. That way, title would not pass until installed and the products could be shipped at normal transfer prices. Local subsidiaries / agents could once again be involved and have revenue flows that would incentivize their cooperation and support.

Although under this option – compared to the approach advocated by Sales – there would be delay in receiving revenue, this would be more than offset by the elimination of need for the substantial discount requested by the customer. It would also address the service and warranty issues that Sales had ignored and that would obviously be a major post-installation dispute with the customer unless addressed.

This attractive solution had two problems. The first was Sales. The Account Team liked the approach they had worked on with the customer's technical and product groups because it brought early revenue and ensured they did not have to share commission with overseas units or third party representatives. They said that re-opening discussion at this stage with such a fundamental change would be impossible and would probably result in the business being lost.

They escalated to their own top management and gained support from the Vice-Principal of Worldwide Sales, plus the affected Product Division General Manager. (Contracts was not alerted to either meeting and simply received the resulting instructions to 'find a way to fix this – fast'.)

The second problem was that the solution did not readily address local price variations, and this was further complicated by the customer wish to be billed and to pay centrally through its US headquarters. While these issues could be addressed, there was not time to handle them before the bid deadline.

The Contracts group now faced a problem that is classic to many of them – they had become involved too late; they had worked hard to formulate possible alternatives; they had not immediately escalated to ensure their issues and concerns were heard and supported by Sales.

Now they found themselves sandwiched between powerful interest groups both internally and at the customer, who believed they had a solution and saw Contracts simply as an obstacle, creating unnecessary delay.

So Sales pushed ahead and decided they would simply use standard contracts; they assured the customer that incremental services equivalent to the required discount would be provided at no charge. By that method, they avoided further internal review. But in the end, the Procurement and Legal review at Company H resulted in some leading questions. It became quite obvious that the agreements and commitments being proposed left some gaping holes when it came to local support. Company J appeared to be inept – and, to cut a long story short, a competitor won the business.

Requirements

In that example, it seems that the customer staff were also not well integrated. This is a common problem – and it is important that contracts groups open good lines of communication with their counterparts in the customer organization as early as possible. As our example showed, in today's increasingly complex world, it is not enough to have good communications on the technical specifications; we must also engage early to define the business terms that will best meet the customer requirement.

As a point of interest, Procurement and Legal in customer organizations also often feel excluded until too late in the game. They also often feel that Sales is trying to by-pass them until they can be steamrollered into agreement. So there is ample opportunity to develop direct relationships.

Have you ever received an RFP and found it confusing? Did it ever seem like two or even more different people had written it? You probably won't be surprised to learn that most RFPs are written by committee. That's why requirements are sometimes confusing or contradictory.

Another reason is that some customers believe that they should ask for anything they could think of and see which supplier will be willing to offer the most.

This may well be a valid way for the customer to proceed but it does give you a challenge. What do you really have to bid on? How do you find out? This is where your knowledge of the customer really pays off.

You can approach any contacts you have within the customer's organization and validate what has been asked. Remarkably few bidders take advantage of this. Not only are few questions asked but also they are not asked often enough. If questions are asked at all, there is usually only one round of questions. Once a set of answers is published by the customer, you – and in fact all of the bidders – need to ask the inevitable further questions that are needed to further clarify the answers.

Sadly, most RFPs are inadequate in their explanation of what is sought. Whenever there are several rounds of well-asked questions the customer invariably finds out that they missed something important in the requirements or in the description and the RFP needs to be significantly clarified.

Determining and testing flexibility

A corollary of validating the stated requirements is that we may determine that there is flexibility in the requirements or stated terms. This is a mistake one of the contributors to this book made early in his career in the aerospace industry. It was clear that the bid had been 'written' by one of his competitors. It was known that there was only one company in the market that could conform to the specifications. So the decision was made to 'no-bid' and work on our relationships to have the opportunity to properly influence the next bid.

Imagine the dismay when the winner was announced – and it wasn't the company that 'wrote' the bid. It was another competitor who actually had an inferior offering to the contributor's company. They used all of their contacts in the customer organization to find other things that were of interest than what was in the bid.

Of course, these days you do need to be wary about bid rules and not 'bucking the system' – but again, if you are involved early, this is often an entirely acceptable approach.

15.4 **Evaluating the scope**

A bid should be viewed as an opportunity to position and offer to sell your products or services to a customer or group of customers who have a requirement for what you do and create a compelling reason to buy at a price and on terms and conditions that will deliver the business objectives of the company such as revenue, contribution, earnings, and cash flow.

The decision matrix on opportunity scope begins with the strategic investment decision you make in the cost to bring the product or service to market and if this cost is worth the risk of competing for specific variable opportunities. This question of Return on Investment – or ROI – is attracting growing interest. It has tight linkages to the contract commitments, yet in most companies the assessment of ROI and its subsequent performance is a relatively weak discipline. In some sectors – such as construction – it is notoriously inaccurate. Few companies have reliable or practical methods that establish the data needed to determine opportunity ROI and in part that is because there is no effective costing of active term alternatives. Hence, as contract options are reviewed or discussed, there is frequently little attention paid to the cost impacts.

You may actually want to dissect the opportunity and list all of its requirements under the classic criteria of time, quality and cost. Then you will be able to clearly see which criteria may be able to be traded off for others. One way to keep the workload down is to get the electronic soft copy from the customer, then cut and paste the various topics in the three columns of a table.

Of these three criteria, time is probably the easiest to understand. It is about deadlines and whether or not they can be met. But although easy to understand, it is also an area of high risk, since there are many factors that can influence your ability to meet target dates.

Resources take a variety of forms and all of them represent money. You have finite assets – there deployment on this opportunity means they will not be deployed elsewhere. That is why evaluation is so critical. You may be using plant or equipment; you may be using human resources or skills. The questions are whether they are available at the time and in the quantity you need – or can they perhaps be acquired from someone else? In any case, resources come with a price tag: they cost money.

Finally, quality is about the standards of performance that you can achieve. Quality criteria are expressed in specifications, service levels or performance undertakings. Can you meet – or exceed – the standards required by this opportunity?

The interesting point with these variables is that you can generally improve any two of them, at the expense of the third. For example, maybe you can improve the schedule and raise the quality, but only at the expense of additional resources.

In assessing the opportunity, you should be trying to establish:
a) Which of the criteria matters most to the customer (time or quality)?
b) Are the commitments they seek truly a 'bottom-line', or are they a 'wish list'? Is this enquiry trying to establish viable suppliers, or are they really testing to find 'best in class'?

As you move forward with internal and customer discussions, it is important to explain your flexibility in terms of the trade-offs that will then ensue. Try to avoid positioning things as impossible to achieve; work instead to explain the consequences of achieving them. That gives others the chance to contribute ideas or creative solutions that you may simply have missed. Use every interaction with the customer to ask questions to both fill knowledge gaps and also sensitivity test their view of specific aspects of their requirements.

During the course of the sales process, new ideas and issues may emerge that change the shape of the deal, risks may be traded between the parties and the evaluation must remain the checkpoint against which all deal trades are evaluated. A risk factor can be applied where additional items are offered such as extended warranties, longer-term guarantees, payment terms and shorter lead times. All concessions have a financial or risk impact and these should be evaluated against a benchmark to ensure that commitments are not over-extended beyond the normal distribution for a specific customer segment. The contract management team should own the formal offer and be accountable for assessing whether a term is within the evaluation scope before committing the offer to the customer.

That is why it is important for the contracts professional to become familiar with financial and project management techniques, so that the relevant factors are included in the proposal and the commercial terms and also to support improved engagement between these key functional areas in the business.

Looking at the opportunity requirements, a valuable technique is to see the customer view. Step back and ask yourself why they are making that particular demand and always seek to understand why a specific requirement is important to them. Refer back to the options evaluation matrix in Chapter 10: *Request for Proposal preparation and content* to understand how the customer will potentially develop their business requirements analysis as it applies to the RFP. The more you understand about the customer's decision-making process, the more it will enhance your opportunity to secure the business from a competitor that only seeks to sell what it has to offer.

Such an analysis has many potential benefits. One is that it may direct you to specific high quality open questions that you now want to ask and creates a more positive, solution-seeking environment within the team. Insights gained from this exchange are all the more valuable because the customer gave you the answers and any ideas for added–value solutions or competitive differentiation can be linked directly to the customer

This analysis may also help you estimate the customer's priorities and weightings – or to confirm why they selected the things they did. From there, you can begin to identify where your capabilities meet or fail to meet the requirements – and how serious the gap may be, or whether the fact that you actually have capabilities that exceed customer expectations may be a source of advantage. Do not restrict your thinking and assume that you must close all the gaps. It may be possible to subcontract or partner with another more capable partner to deliver specific customer objectives and lock out competition at the same time.

At this stage, opportunity evaluation teams can often fall into the trap of focusing only on those gaps where they have a shortfall in capability. That is a serious omission. Having too sophisticated a capability can also be a problem because it often means you will have higher prices. For example, if the customer wants only 96 percent availability, but you offer 98 percent as standard, does that mean a lower performing and lower priced competitor might win?

In assessing the opportunity, you should be trying to establish:
- Which of the criteria matters most to the customer (cost, time or quality)?
- Are the commitments being sought truly a 'bottom-line', or are they a 'wish list'? Is this enquiry trying to establish viable suppliers, or are they really testing to find 'best in class'?

As you move forward with internal and customer discussions, it is important to explain your flexibility in terms of the trade-offs that will then ensue. Try to avoid positioning things as impossible to achieve; work instead to explain the consequences of achieving them. That gives others the chance to contribute ideas or creative solutions that you may simply have missed.

Service levels

Service levels can be expressed in a number of different ways: time to repair, up-time, time to answer a call, response time, average cost to fix, throughput, mean-time-between-failure, etc. The things they have in common are:
- They generally cost money
- The customer may or may not want that level of service
- They can conflict with each other and with quality criteria

The challenge is the same. Making sure that: a) you truly understand the service level criteria and b) if necessary, challenge whether the service level is appropriate.

We will talk later about the concept of determining whether you will be contracting for Things or Outcomes. For now, it is important to note that if you will be contracting for Outcomes, the onus is on you to really understand what the service levels are because you and you alone will be saddled with the cost of meeting them.

Determine skills inventory gap

Under the general heading of Resources we may need to consider whether we have the skills necessary to meet the requirements. This is particularly true of Services bids. The task here is a relatively simple one. Analyze the bid for the skills that are needed to meet the customer's requirements. List them. Then put the names of the people who will be available to perform the tasks against them.

If there are any gaps, research whether you have the skills somewhere else in the organization and, if not, whether you can acquire them on the outside. Calculate the cost of acquiring these skills and add them to your total cost thus determining the skills inventory gap and its cost.

Financial impact

Now that we have clarified a number of areas that can affect cost we are finally ready to analyze the financial impact. One of the most obvious financial areas to analyze is the profitability of the deal. This will probably be performed by the Finance member on your team. It is useful to look at this area both in the traditional business case fashion as well as looking at other factors.

The risk you assume in selling a product or undertaking a project should be assessed. It may be big enough that you may not even want to respond. Or you may want to ignore portions of the bid. However, most likely, the risk can usually be covered by other measure such as insurance, over-specifying a product, performance bonds, etc. Once again, this usually translates itself into additional cost, which can be used in the financial analysis.

No financial analysis would be complete without analyzing the effect of competition. This is why we emphasize so much the need for a team analysis. A financial person may well make all of their calculations based on the factors we have already mentioned. They may conclude that this translates into a certain needed price. However, the salesperson may know what the competitor is willing to do and whether the price is likely to win the bid or not. An engineer may determine that the product plan assumed that we would make a large sale to this customer and if we do not the cost will not be absorbed over the remaining anticipated sales. The final decision on what to bid will have to be made taking into account all of these factors and really needs to be a team decision.

15.5 **Assessing the risk**

Your team needs to list the gaps and set a timetable for their evaluation. You will be looking at each of them in the context of time, resource, quality and scope. Then you must size up the risk associated with each gap, from both an internal and customer perspective. Again, remember you must look at both the shortfalls and the areas where you exceed requirements.

A robust risk evaluation will consider the consequences if something occurs. A good place to being is by asking: "If this occurs, then…." (and state the consequence). From this you can begin to assess the likelihood and impact if the risk occurred. If the risk was proven to be significant enough that it would become an issue if no intervention was applied, then a mitigation plan or alternative approaches would be agreed and the timing of implementation.

Of course, where possible you will also be considering this in the context of known competitive capabilities and their likely reactions to the opportunity.

It would not be possible to list out a comprehensive set of risks that an organization could encounter. For the sake of brevity, we will concentrate on six key risks and discuss other risks in subsequent chapters. The most common forms of risks are:

- Liability
- Non-performance (types of remedies/damages)
- Regulatory compliance
- Enterprise risk (reputation risk)
- Consequences of failure (and loss)
- Non-response

Liability

When looking at all the different ways a supplier may become liable it can be frightening. There are physical third party liability risks where employees or products could cause physical damage to a customer, their customers, and the general public and so on. Liability also includes the possibility of consequential damages where the failure of your offering may cause your customer substantial loss.

Many RFPs now contain language that will hold the supplier legally responsible to the terms of the bid response even before contract negotiation. It is essential that your commercial team reviews the bid response, preferably on a standard pre-agreed precedent proposal format that does not require extensive legal review before bid. Any alterations to the precedent form contain non-evaluated risks and should be considered by the relevant subject matter experts before bid submission. There are many legal issues around bid validity. These should be carefully reviewed in your own areas of jurisdiction and any necessary internal approvals obtained to ensure that your bids are valid, capable of acceptance and, if accepted, the nature of commitment made before signature of the contract itself.

In jurisdictions where this is possible, some suppliers have responded by striking out the language that would hold them legally responsible before a contract is enacted. Customers usually view this tactic as evasive, believing that the supplier at best lacks confidence in its offering and at worst is not telling the truth.

Non-performance (types of remedies/damages)

The risk of non-performance is usually anticipated in an RFP and subsequent contractual agreement. This is usually expressed in the warranties, service levels, remedies and damages section of an RFP. They are properly called remedies. Sometimes you will hear or see them referred to as 'penalties'. This terminology is problematic, as courts of law are reluctant to entertain the concept of one party penalizing another as part of a commercial relationship.

Typically if you fail to perform according to an agreed level you will be asked to make some kind reparation or restitution. You will probably be given a certain period of time to 'cure' the situation – that is, either fix the problem or make the restitution.

This can be expressed as paying a non-performance fee, providing more resources, providing a higher specification product, additional services, etc. These can generally be accommodated in your response by assessing the likelihood of failure and the cost of making the reparation.

However, what you may sometimes see is a remedy of a different type – a non-financial remedy. There was a case where a government RFP required the winning bidder to guarantee that failure of their equipment would not result in the serious injury or death of the crew. If a crewmember died, the president of the supplier was required to visit the family of the deceased, attend the funeral and write a public advertisement that their equipment was responsible for the death. Your team will probably need to assess this kind of risk in non-financial, goodwill terms.

Regulatory compliance

There is a growing worldwide trend towards increased governance regulation. In the US, certain provisions or protections are increasingly being sought at early phases of supplier qualification. It is equally certain that, as a supplier, you need to be sure that the customer's demands will not cause issues with compliance. This can be on a host of potential issues, depending on the geographic scope of the opportunity. For example, in their ignorance, a customer may be demanding terms that contravene European competition laws, or data protection regulations. Or they may be looking for risk provisions that would cause serious concerns with the need to report under the US Securities and Exchange Commission (SEC) regulations, or payment terms that create conflicts with revenue recognition requirements.

As a contracts expert, you must be alert to all these things – and you may have to educate both the account team and the customer partnering with your legal colleagues as appropriate. With the recent increased focus on this area your company may also have a Governance Officer who you can consult.

Enterprise risk (reputation risk)

While enterprise risk may not be directly contained in an RFP it is there nonetheless. What will be the consequences to your company's reputation if your product is not adequate for the task? How influential is your customer in the industry? Is there a possibility that your customer may misuse the product? And in responding, what terms might enhance or damage your reputation?

Remember, there are no secure 'secrets'; don't believe that you can make deals behind the scenes with a specific customer and that this will not reach the attention of others.

On the other hand, if this is a leading-edge opportunity and your company does not win what might that say about the quality or innovation of your business? How might that affect future standing and competitiveness?

Consequences of failure (and loss)

Closely related to enterprise risk is the risk of failure. If your offering fails totally, what are the consequences? Are they just financial? Reputation? Will it affect other product plans? Or maybe will it help you in some way through the lessons learned?

Non-response

It may be that after assessing the risks, evaluating the opportunity or calculating the bid effort you decide that you do not wish to bid. This can be perfectly reasonable and acceptable. However, before you do, ask yourselves certain questions:
- What will be the impact on our customer relationship of no-bid?
- What will be the marketplace perception of our no-bid?
- In what way will we communicate our decision?

It is always possible that there may be an alternative way of answering the bid such as a sub-set, a short form or a different proposal. Be careful not to inadvertently reduce opportunities for future business.

Non-response is rarely a good thing (unless you are truly not in that business or none of the bidders respond). Even an unlikely bid, depending on the competitive circumstances, can be rewarded with very lucrative business.

Assessing the risk – SWOT

Now that we understand the bewildering array of risks that we are facing, what do we do about them? How do we assess their likelihood of occurrence and true impact?

One tried and true method of making a risk assessment is using the SWOT technique. The acronym stands for Strengths, Weaknesses, Opportunities and Threats and an example is detailed below (Table 15.1).

Category	Strategy	Strengths	Weaknesses	Opportunities	Threats
Liability	Minimize liability.	RFP does not have clear liability provisions spelled out.	RFP demands that we carry liability insurance in excess of our current policy limits	We can present our standard terms and conditions with our approved liability limits	Our competition routinely accepts these liability insurance limits and fails to implement them when they are awarded.
Performance	Ensure we are able to meet all the performance criteria	We meet nearly all the hardware performance criteria. We have a proven track record of meeting the service levels in most of the services requested. (List)	To meet all the hardware performance criteria we have to over-spec items and raise cost. To provide all the services we will have to subcontract / assign portions of the services. (List)	Some of the subcontracted services will be at a very advantageous cost which will raise the profitability of the business.	Some of our competitors are able to offer a one-stop solution.
Compliance	Ensure we are able to meet all compliance criteria	Our investment in Sarbanes-Oxley compliant software is by far the greatest in the industry.	All of our engineers specialized in compliance software are assigned to other projects.	We can offer additional compliance consulting services to the client either as a value-add proposition or as an additional revenue stream opportunity	We have been cited by the SEC (US Securities and Exchange Commission) of being in violation of minor reporting regulations. This might be perceived negatively by the client.
etc., etc. ...	...	...	...	...	...

Table 15.1   Example SWOT analysis

Looking at the chart, we see that the team has grouped the risks into categories Liability, Performance and Compliance in the leftmost column. The column headings have the SWOT categories listed.

We will start by looking at the first line, Liability. Under Strengths the team has noted that the RFP has not spelled out clearly any liability provisions. This is a good thing. We can ensure that our offer contains our standard limits on liability. However, under weaknesses we see that the customer does expect us to carry more liability insurance than we have. This can be remedied by obtaining more coverage.

However, while the lack of liability provision provides us the opportunity to name our own terms, we see a competitive threat. We know that they will agree to terms that they have no intention to honor. So our bid team has to make a decision how much of the cost to absorb. Additionally the team determines how best to communicate to the client:

- That we honor our commitments
- They should protect themselves by requiring evidence of compliance from their suppliers.

This analysis can be extended to the other areas of risk.

Risk mitigation

The following is an example risk mitigation process.

Encourage all members of your team to participate in the risk identification activity. Ask them to identify all concerns and issues whether they consider them risks or not.

Once identified the risks can be analyzed using the SWOT method described earlier.

The next step in the process is to plan the actions to be taken. While they may not be incorporated into the RFP response itself, document contingency plans for:

- Product design or process changes required
- Any negative consequences you are prepared to accept
- Any plans you have to study the risk further.

Once the plan is crafted, a tracking methodology needs to be detailed to clearly identify who will track what, when (or how frequently) and how it will be tracked and reported.

The next step is to plan for control. This is generally classified as project management. We need to identify who the project management will be and, as much as possible, how the project and any deviations will be controlled.

After completing the previous steps, their outputs must be communicated. This should be approached both before and after the response to the RFP. Seek the input and approval of anybody within the organization affected by this project.

15.6 Avoiding reference pitfalls

Few RFPs are issued without a requirement for you to provide references. If you do not have them it can be a challenge. Even if you do have an extensive list, you need to give careful consideration as to who to give out as references.

A little preparation can make a big difference. For example a current customer, who had acquired exactly what was being asked for in the RFP, reported to the buyer that they had done business with us before and were happy with us, but had never bought the product in question from us. What do you think that did for our credibility with the prospect? How did that happen?

Consider the following three factors:
- Reference relevance
- Reference strength
- Reference age

Sometimes you will be faced with a situation where you simply do not have a reference to a customer that has acquired the specific product or service in the RFP. In those cases your only option may be to give references to satisfied customers and acknowledge that you do not have references on that specific product or service. However, generally you need to give references that are relevant for what is sought in the RFP.

The problem in the example seems to have been one of an irrelevant reference. However, it was more indicative of 'reference strength'. There was a lack of recognition that the product the buyer was asking about was the same as the product they had previously bought. To avoid this, talk to the reference customer first.

In many organizations, sales departments maintain a ready reference list of customers who have consented to have their names used as a reference without being asked first. As seen in the example, this can be dangerous. Check with the customer every time; it is not just a common courtesy to ask for permission. This has several advantages. You can determine whether the contact details are still correct and even if they still work at the company. You may find out that there are still some lingering issues with the customer. Ensure that the reference knows who may be contacting them and what they are looking for. And of course, there are never too many reasons to have another talk with your customers.

In the example the product had been acquired some time before as part of a large complex deal. The transaction had happened too long ago; it was a small detail for the customer. Similarly, customers may want to find suppliers who have supplied the product or service recently. Obviously, you will have much to gain if you can provide them with good recent references. If you do not, consider using a past customer that is currently considering the same product, as an influential reference. This works well for yet to be installed products. Happy customers may be very happy to 'sell' to your prospect on why they are considering your new product.

15.7 Evaluating the relationship

How you respond to an RFP and how you evaluate the opportunity needs to be done in the context of your relationship with the customer or prospect. Have you done business with them before? Do they value you or not? Do you understand how they will decide the winning bid?

This is a very good time to take a hard look at what you really know about the customer. RFPs sometimes will indicate how the decision on the winning bid will be made. Sometimes they don't. Even when they do, experience has shown that unexpected things happen and a decision is made in a different way. Government departments and public institutions often have published rules by which the bids will be assessed. Anybody who has made bids in this sector will tell you that despite the rules the decisions seem to have been made in a different way.

There is no substitute to knowing your customer. The more you know about how the decisions will be made, who the decision maker is or are, what the underlying struggles between various interest groups are, the better you can craft a response that is likely to win. This is probably the biggest responsibility of the sales team. However everyone involved can contribute. There are three steps to making this successful:
- Understand the organization: With a little bit of effort the organizational structure of a company can usually be found out. You can often get printed organization charts from customers just by asking. They are sometimes published in business publications, found in databases such as Lexis-Nexis and even by searching the web. Knowing who reports to whom and who really issued the RFP can be tremendously useful.
- Know the decision structure: this is even more useful than the organization structure but is sometimes more difficult to obtain. Sometimes one person will make the decision. In large organizations, there may be several people involved in making the decision with some wielding more influence than others. It is extremely useful to have a good understanding of this.

- Use contacts and relationships: how do you obtain all this? Sales people on your team are going to have the primary responsibility to make contacts with customer personnel and establish good relationships. However, *anybody* in your organization can contribute. Perhaps you have a good friend in the customer's building. Your engineers may be making regular visits to the customer for service and gain a good understanding of what happens inside the organization. Your Accounts Receivable clerk may gather interesting information in their contacts with their Accounts Payable.

Figure 15.1 illustrates a technique that can be used to harness this valuable information.

	Servers	LAN	ERP	Middle-ware	Help Desk
Amanda Smith	☒	☑	☒	☑	☑
Charlie Whelan	☒	☒	☒	☒	☒
Leticia Gonzalez	☒	☒	☒	☑	☒
David Connelly	☒	☒	☒	☑	☑
Terry Davis	☑	☑	☒	☑	☒
Rita Melon	☑	☑	☑	☑	☑
Radesh Sinivasi	☒	☒	☑	☑	☒
Lee Thornbury	☑	☒	☑	☑	☒

Figure 15.1   Evaluating the relationship

This figure shows samples of different sales initiatives your company might be working on. It might be an upgrade to some server, selling some new modules to an enterprise resource planning (ERP) program, justifying the outsourcing of the customer's help desk. Of course, it could equally be the sale of aero engines, supply of spare parts and provision of maintenance services.

Down the side, list the names of all the main decision-makers and influencers within the customer. Then make an assessment of where each one of these people stands with respect to each project. Be careful to restrict your comments only to your perception of their amenability to the project, alliance to your company and whether their role will have influence in the process and if there are some reputation gaps that need to be addressed with this individual. It is completely inappropriate to make judgments about any individual. A good test will be if you would be willing to share your analysis with the customer and seek their insight from your initial thoughts. The titles Support, Opponent or Follower allow you to quickly see where to focus your team's resources to help influence the decision favorable to your organization.

Then focus your team on how to harness continued support from those in favor of the project and agree how to best understand the underlying tensions or issues of those that may not be as supportive and to help with more information, or at the very least ensure that any potentially negative influence is addressed. The managing director may have been a former employee of a competitor and may be subconsciously aligned to the way they work. Know these things and seek to find measures of mutual evaluation that will eliminate potential favoritism in the process. Make an assessment of who on the team has the most rapport or influence with the individuals concerned. Then develop action plans accordingly.

Remember, if your mission is simply to influence an individual, they will feel it. It may not help the bond of trust between you, as they may feel they are being used or manipulated just because they have a favorable disposition to your product or service. Best practice companies seek to continually understand and assess whether they can bridge any gaps, having understood the requirements of the customer.

Research by Vantage Partners has shown the importance of having an established relationship with the customer. If you have no history of bidding or winning business, the chances of success are less than 10 percent and you may wish to prioritize your time and resources accordingly. On the other hand, if you do not bid, you have not even started the process of building credibility for the future. Therefore establishing the strategic importance of the bid is critical.

15.8 Judging customer sophistication

One of the aspects of assessing the customer is by understanding how sophisticated they are in creating and evaluating RFPs. The degree of sophistication may well determine how much detail and commitment you need to provide in your response. It will also give you a good indication of what direction the negotiation is likely to take following the RFP submission.

There are several different ways of accomplishing this. The first is by analyzing the contents of the RFP itself. Most RFPs have several things in common: they state what the customer wants and they often omit *how* they want it. Sometimes they describe why. A list of requirements is given. Instructions are often issued on how to respond to the RFP.

The more sophisticated customers will show it by the completeness of each of these items. Their list of requirements will be detailed and show that they have a good understanding of the product or service they is looking for. The instructions will be detailed. Milestones for the RFP process will be given. The administrative questions that you are likely to have will have been anticipated and answered. You will be given precise instructions on how you can ask questions, who you may and may not contact and how answers will be provided – usually publicly to all bidders.

One indicator of sophistication is poorly understood by both the selling side and the buy side during the RFP process. Most people recognize that following a successful bid a contract will be executed between both parties. One of the decisions that has to be made in drafting a contract is: "Did you contract for a Thing or an Outcome?" A Thing is a product or a service with certain specifications. If the product was delivered according to the specifications and it does not do what the customer wants it to do, that is not the responsibility of the supplier.

In contrast, contracts for Outcomes describe what the end-result should be for the customer. The supplier then has sole responsibility to do whatever it takes to meet that end result. This is illustrated with a simple example below.

Some US Federal Government departments would award contracts for lawn maintenance via bids. They were used to contract for 'Things'. They now contract for 'Outcomes' (they call it 'Performance Based Contracting'.) They used to specify that the winner would be the company that would charge the least for mowing the lawns twice a week, water it daily, with a crew of five people, spray with fertilizer once a quarter, etc., etc., detailing all the activities they could think of. During the spring and fall the grass would grow rapidly and sometimes overgrow while, during the summer, crews would dutifully mow a lawn twice a week that hadn't grown at all. Now the contracts specify that the grass should be green at all times and of a length between 1.5" to 2.5". How often it is mowed, fertilized, watered, etc. is the responsibility of the contractor.

Sophistication will also be evident in the amount of commitment demanded upfront in the form of 'representation reliance'. Does the RFP already have terms and conditions to which they expect you to agree if you win? They might even incorporate the full contract they expect you sign in the RFP.

Look for other forms of language on 'representation reliance'. For instance they may ask you to sign that they can rely on your representation that you are experts. You may or may not know that this is extremely binding. If there is a dispute and you go to litigation the courts will treat you as 'experts' and hold you to much higher standard of conduct than normal, they way they treat doctors and lawyers. It is extremely difficult to plead ignorance in such cases and damages awarded by the courts tend to higher – even devastating.

Other language may get you to accept that all the contents of your proposal can be incorporated in the final agreement without further negotiation. They may even ask that the proposal has to be signed by the same person who will sign the contract. You will want to make sure that you word the proposal extremely carefully, with full legal review, under these circumstances.

These are some of the indicators of the sophistication of a customer that can be found in the actual RFP:

- Gather customer intelligence: another way of judging customer sophistication is by using what you know about them. Use all the resources you have at your disposal in understanding what depths the customer will go to when evaluating your proposal and negotiating the contract.
- Use your questioning opportunities to clarify the expectations of the customer. This is an opportunity to ask any sensible questions, including those that will reveal to you how sophisticated the customer is in the bid process.
- Understand the customer contracting organization: many large corporations do not have professional buying contract managers. Look for indications of sophistication in the structure of their purchasing and contracting organization. Indicators to look for:
  - Do they just have one purchasing department? Or do they have separate sourcing and procurement departments?
  - Do they have an additional Supplier Management function?

One of the terms to look for is 'Strategic Sourcing'. This probably indicates that they have adopted methodologies that are stringent in the way that they select and manage suppliers.

Typically if there is a separate sourcing department, their chief mission will be to negotiate the deal with you. The administration will be carried out through the Purchasing or Procurement function. If there is a Supplier Management function their responsibility will be to measure and track the performance of suppliers. They will be insisting on the collection of remedies and also ranking suppliers against each other to determine which ones most benefit the customer.

15.9 Evaluating future opportunity

Finally, before you feel ready to answer the RFP, this is a good time to reflect upon future opportunities. There are two reasons for this. One is that future opportunities may influence how you want to respond to the bid. The other is that this bid may contain opportunities to sell more now.

For example, following award a customer reported that they had chosen a bidder who was not the least expensive. The bid made them look at services they had never considered or realized that they would need. They felt that the bidder had a really good grasp of their true requirements and would be the better supplier to help them meet their future goals.

Such an opportunity may be contained right in the RFP. The customer may put in indicators of what their follow-on requirements are. They may even ask for any other ideas the bidder has. Your bid team should carefully examine these opportunities and decide how much you want to factor them into your response.

Even though the bid may not request it, you may have additional products or services that the customer could use. You may even have a different approach that the customer has not considered. However, if you do have a different approach, even one that is better than what the customer has asked, do your best to respond to the RFP exactly as asked. Your customer may not recognize the superiority of your approach and disqualify you without any further explanation.

Consider incorporating an addendum to the proposal as a way of giving the customer an additional option. Ask about the likelihood of future business, formally through the questioning procedures in the bid process. You can also find out by using the customer contacts and relationships we discussed. You can ask what the future business would look like. You can suggest what it could look like.

Once you get the feel for it you can also ask whether the customer is prepared to commit to the future business if you win the bid.

CHAPTER 16

Proposal preparation

16.1 Introduction

The objective of this chapter is to prepare contracts practitioners to deliver against increasing management expectations for value added and integrated involvement in a formalized Request for Proposal (RFP) response process.

This chapter aims to provide information, tools, techniques, case studies and best practice on the range of proposal preparation activities including:
- Identifying the customer requirements
- Evaluating the customer's buying criteria
- Risk assessing the response, Statement of Work (SOW), Service Level Agreements (SLA) and Terms and Conditions

This will enable you to:
- Manage the contracts element of the proposal development process
- Avoid common mistakes in communicating with the customer during an RFP
- Look for issues in the Terms and Conditions (Ts & Cs) that may require adjustment
- Find opportunities to innovate within the boundaries of your evaluation in order to present a winning proposal

16.2 Is it worth bidding? The four critical questions

- Does the customer understand the product or service?
- Does the customer have a driving need for the product or service?
- Has the customer designated the resources needed to buy?
- What happens if we decide not to bid?

Establishing the seriousness and readiness of the customer to buy is the most valuable skill that the sales team provides. These basic questions establish the customer's readiness to make a buy decision and lay the groundwork for an effective sales strategy.

However, the experience and motivations of the sales team should be evaluated. Sales personnel are notoriously optimistic and inclined to position every opportunity as 'strategic'. Is this a real prospect, or is the sales representative desperate? It is entirely appropriate for you to ask questions and ensure that the bid represents correct use of company resources.

Does the customer understand the product or service?

Educating the customer may be the main purpose of the proposal. If the customer is starting from a position of complete knowledge, their buy decision will be made quickly based on a few key variables. If the customer is starting from complete ignorance, or if the product or service is new, then the buying process will be much longer. The RFP response must cover much more ground. The RFP will reflect the customer's level of knowledge about the marketplace, available products and services and how they are sold. It may be necessary to introduce new concepts so that the customer can evaluate and understand the bidders value statements.

Introducing new concepts should be done early in the response document and repeated in each major section so that all response reviewers are informed buyers. Even if the bidder's offer is very different from the structure of the RFP some comparison should be made within the response. This section should show how the bidder's unique way of providing the product or service compares with the traditional method laid out in the RFP document.

For example, if a customer is asking for an enterprise resource planning (ERP) software package and the bidder is providing a value added application service model, the response should lay out the total expected costs associated with both methods of buying access to the application. Please bear in mind that your primary role is to get as close to what the customer wants as possible, so be careful not to confuse the customer with a very different proposal that may encourage them to accept a competitor's bid.

If the relationship with the customer is very good it may be worth investigating alternative approaches such as unsolicited proposals, sales-led demonstrations or product trials. These approaches to steering the customer to a different type of purchase do not work well unless the customer is willing to take chances. One technique that does work well is to clarify with the customer what their top 10 requirements are for a winning proposal and how they will evaluate whether you have met their criteria. This will give you a better understanding of the customer's evaluation process and give you a good baseline to rank your chances against those of your competitors. Your campaign action plan then becomes a more organic process where the sales and commercial teams modify their approach, seek to close any capability gaps and perhaps innovate around the requirements to give you a competitive advantage.

Does the customer have a driving need for the product or service?

Establishing the driving need helps puts a value on the product or service offered, but mostly it will determine lead time to decision and therefore which live sales prospect has best chance of conversion to revenue in the shortest period of time. In turn this drives where the concentrated sales focus should be to enable you to close the deal before the competition does.

If you are spending time in the midst of a proposal preparation understanding how your product will solve a problem, increase access to a market, or reduce costs, your competition may already be ahead of you. Competitive intelligence and segmentation done in advance of a live deal will give you campaign advantage; do your research upfront, know your customers and know how to position your offer to best meet the customer's needs. The campaign time should be best used to keep you in front, to innovate around key requirements and capabilities and to maintain positive focus.

Has the customer designated the resources needed to buy?

Establishing the buyer's budget sets the expectation range for the order quantity and potentially offering price. Understanding the budget expectation also establishes very clearly how well the customer understands the market and has assessed its needs. Where the buyer has not designated funds for the procurement, proceed with caution. An RFP without funding is a fishing expedition. The best way to do this is to establish the order process following selection and how the procurement will be executed in practice. Say that this will give you the requisite lead time to speculatively book inventory to the sales lead but have enough time to turn the tap off if the bid is not successful. If you operate a lean process, you should be able to convert a sales win into a deliverable in a short time frame. Use this inventory question to establish if there really is a budget, a lead time and a guaranteed order following sale.

What happens if you decide not to bid?

In the case that your company decides not to bid, you must be very clear about the reasons why you are not bidding; the customer should be advised of this at every level and all levels where there are relationships with the customer (buyers, and influencers). The message should be clear, focused, and consistent across the entire company. It must be positive and convey both respectful interest in the customer and the relationship that you enjoy, a clear intention to continue to do business with the customer and a very specific bounded reason why the current RFP is outside your current investment parameters, evaluation scope. Keep the reason non-personal, factual and business evaluation focused.

By doing this, your company maintains its integrity to always be honest with the customer, keeps the customer relationship intact, prevents the competition from planting issues with decision makers such as implied lack of commitment or doubt about your ability to deliver and it might just reveal whether the customer has simply asked for too high a specification at too low a price and is willing to re-establish some of their requirement criteria in order to maintain two or more players in the marketplace. Customers prefer to have competition for their business as much as you enjoy beating the competition. A monopoly supply or a high profile supplier is bad news for a customer as their leverage is reduced. If you are having a no-bid conversation, be prepared for the customer to re-establish their criteria and be prepared to state the circumstances under which you would be prepared to bid and test where the gap is. You will not only establish your competitor threshold but your customer's least acceptable buying position.

16.3 Understanding the customer

- Why are they inviting bids?
- Who will be making the buy decision?

While you will clearly have asked these questions in earlier phases of the bid process, you must return to them now to confirm the strength of your company's relationship with the customer and the appropriate tone and methodology for the response. Bidding from a position of knowledge and realism strongly improves the win rate of deals. In a perfect world, the customer's RFP document will spell out or imply answers to these questions. In most cases, however, having insight into the politics, organizational impacts and the personalities making the buy decision clarifies and gives context to the RFP and your response.

Why are they inviting bids?

Few customers are going to state publicly that they lack a key product, capability or function, yet of course that is why they are making this acquisition. Indeed, bidders are well advised to remember the old saying, "if you can't say something nice, say nothing at all". This means that significant effort will be required to subtly turn an obvious customer need into a positive statement of opportunity. Also, bidders must recognize that the days are long gone where suppliers could communicate, "You need our product or service because you don't have the skills to understand it".

When answering "Why are they inviting bids?" look for indications that the customer is unhappy with the current incumbent, has a new business model, or is entering a new market. From a contracts perspective these situations spell out how flexible the customer may be in accepting new terms and conditions, adopting a SOW (Statement of Work) or a new SLA (Service Level Agreement).

As you consider your planned proposal, remember that it must address the situation and relationship as perceived by the customer – not as you would like them to perceive it. For example, if they view this as a commodity acquisition, you should not respond as you would for a strategic partnership. Don't let your desired status drive the response. The response must gain customer buy-in before trying to reset the buying criteria.

Who will be making the buying decision?

When answering "Who will be making the buy decision?" look beyond the levels of signature authority. Your sales team should be able to describe and name key influencers, enablers and barriers. The strengths of these various stakeholders have marked impact on the response. For example, your sales team may determine that the customer's contracts team is a key enabler of the decision. This greatly increases the visibility and value-add of an integrated approach to the RFP response where the sales and commercial team innovate together. If a customer engineering team is driving the decision, your integrated bid team should include a technical expert to balance the customer decision making process. This integrated approach will give you 360 degree capability to manage customer requirements during the process.

16.4 Understanding the customer – buying criteria

- Win themes
- Stated buying criteria
- Unstated buying criteria
- Making comparisons
- Hot buttons

Successful sales strategies find a win/win between the customer's buying criteria and their company's capability to deliver as close to those criteria as possible. These win/win positions are win themes. These themes are then woven into all applicable parts of the response and repeated in the Executive Summary. These themes create a clear memorable message that the reviewers retain throughout the evaluation process.

Understanding the customer's stated and unstated buying criteria is one of the most important activities of the response team. Generally the RFP documents state that low cost, compliance, and ease of use are the main points that must be satisfied. In addition to this there are generally large amounts of qualifying data to be provided, especially for high technology and outsourcing buys.

The sales team, working with information on previous purchases with the customer, can tune in on areas where the customer will be particularly sensitive.

One unstated criterion is often that the successful bidder provides the product or service in a manner that is familiar to the users, keeping their learning curve as short as possible. Bidders should make every effort to provide resources for user communication and training so that the buyer does not see the offer as another problem to be dealt with after the approval process is over.

For example, Flybe, a European independent regional airline, makes buying decisions to outsource any of its airport ground handling operations to a third party on the assurance that fee paying passengers "don't see the join".

Most buyers today are sophisticated enough to look carefully at responses with unusually low price points; however it never hurts to show how your offer provides a price advantage. For example, the RFP may ask for a year-by-year price schedule. If your price includes start-up costs in year 1 and handoff costs in year 4, be sure to point this out so that the buyer can differentiate it from less complete offers. Contracts resources can provide tremendous value add by helping to create an 'apples to apples' comparison based on all the cost related contractual elements.

If the customer has specific areas of interest or past memories of failure, these are called 'hot buttons'. Make a list of issues that raise a strong emotional response within the customer's organization. Be sure to tread carefully in responding to these areas. For example, if the customer has just missed a major delivery date due to components from an overseas supplier not being available as promised, they will be unimpressed by a bidder who 'shops the global market for the lowest commodity cost'.

16.5 Understanding the competition

- Who is the incumbent supplier (if any)?
- Who are the competitors?
- Beyond market segmentation

The most important competitive analysis will focus on the current supplier or incumbent. This existing relationship puts the RFP in context, showing the customer's preferences and buying criteria.

These data points paint the background picture against which the RFP is set. For example, if the customer brings in a new senior executive from a top tier supplier, it may be an indication of readiness to change.

In order that your team doesn't miss any potential competitors, look beyond your own market segmentation and think about what other markets the customer may be part of. Looking at the customer within its group of related markets allows a bidder to see the customer as competitors will. This larger analysis may broaden the list of potential competitors.

For example, your chemicals customer may be a competitor's agribusiness customer – different market segments, but the same RFP. Your company may not be aware that these agribusiness suppliers are now able to compete with you in your market segment – for example John Deere makes tractors and provides health care management services, and Norsk Hydro produces oil, manufactures aluminium auto parts and farms salmon. Your customer's needs and history are known by all of its suppliers, not just those in your company's area of expertise.

16.6 Reviewing and assessing risks

- Risk Review
- Strategy

Making a bid/no bid decision is generally done by a review board to ensure that the risks and rewards of the deal are understood before submitting a proposal. As difficult as it may be to say "No" to a customer, it may be preferable to spending time and money on an offering that your company can't deliver, where margins are unacceptably low or where there is no realistic chance of winning. Contracts personnel add value to this decision by summarizing the risk in a concise Risk Review.

In summarizing the Risk Review, focus only on those elements that will make or break the deal, such as requirements leading to large contingency funds, unlimited liability, unacceptable service penalties, or acceptance of risk over which your company has no control. 'Unknowns' can be the riskiest elements; contract personnel should be on the lookout for missing information, attachments, information to be provided later, and items deferred to the negotiation stage.

Customers sometimes use layers of requirements (circulars or other separate documents) as a barrier to entry for new suppliers. Gaining access to these existing standards and requirements may make the difference between being the successful bidder and having a bid rejected. All risk items noted in the RFP should be logged as part of the contracts process, and become part of the handoff documents from sales to operations, and should be used during negotiations.

Although noting the risks is important, finding a way to mitigate these risks while submitting a responsive bid is the key to a winning strategy. The strategy for winning a particular deal often hinges on your company's ability to handle specific risks better than its competitors. For example a global multinational is better able to handle currency risk for international deals than a small domestic supplier, while a smaller player may be more willing to implement changes to its operational processes for just one customer.

Contracts personnel are ideally positioned to find creative ways to mitigate risks, through alternate language, careful demarcation of responsibilities, or identification of expert suppliers. Additionally, post-award contracts personnel offer access to the corporate history of how the company solved these problems in the past, and what was learned. This is not the time for "Yes but" or "I told you so;" this is the time for "Yes, and" thinking. While often exhausting, proposal exercises are powerful vehicles to extend the contracts team's network, gain access to decision makers, and take a role in operational success.

Bidding is a demonstration of competence, and should have the same level of prioritization as product delivery.

16.7   Working with the pursuit team

- Sales versus Operations
- Iterations of the document

In working with both sales and operations resources, contracts personnel should be aware of drivers and blind spots created by the very different way these organizations are rewarded. While sales teams drive to have happy long-term customer relationships, their immediate reward depends on getting to the customer's shortlist. As a result, sales teams may de-emphasize unknowns, choosing to 'get a foot in the door'.

Operations (often called Account Leaders in service oriented businesses) are responsible for the success of the resulting contract. As a result, they tend to drive for repeatable tried and true solutions. They also strive to keep any unknowns carefully outside their scope of responsibility.

Careful documentation of risk mitigation details is required when working out creative solutions between sales and operations teams. While many items can be negotiated after submission, these should be kept to a minimum and should not include items that will substantially change how a product or service is delivered. For example, the decision to use subcontractors should be made before writing any response.

Responding to an RFP is usually an iterative process, captured in versions by documentation management. This role organizes inputs from writers, technical experts, and other resources assigned to respond to specific RFP sections. The documentation manager is driven by the need for completeness, assembling the jigsaw puzzle of data into a coherent response in the customer's format.

Early versions of the RFP response tend to be filled with 'boilerplate' responses from past RFPs. These are then refined, edited and checked against the other elements of the deal. In providing inputs to the document manager, contracts personnel can work from a library of past responses to similar requirements, which are then organized according to the RFP and edited for accuracy against the actual RFP language.

16.8 Responding to the RFP documents

- Compliance matrix
- Review of SOW and SLA

Responding to the RFP generally involves filling out a compliance matrix, a table showing RFP items where the bidder complies/agrees and where the bidder is non-compliant/disagrees.

Customers can be very emphatic in their insistence that all respondents are completely compliant with their RFP statements, with dire consequences for those companies offering alternate language, or indicating non-acceptance of their statements. This leaves the contracts team to be both creative and defensive in finding a way to be agreeable without accepting unreasonable risk.

In addition to being compliant to what the RFP explicitly states, customers often request that bidders submit a separate SOW in which the bidder lays out which products or services will be provided, and how they will be delivered and managed throughout the lifecycle of the contract. Further, a qualitative document or SLA is also requested to delineate what constitutes an acceptable level of service for each of the products and service offerings in various situations that may arise during the course of delivery. Indeed, experienced bidders usually develop SOW and SLA documents even if the customer does not request them. This ensures that solution and costing efforts are working to the same metrics.

In reviewing the SOW and SLAs developed by the Pursuit Team, contracts personnel should focus on any escalation, service penalty, service rewards, or payment impacts implied by the customer. Additionally any areas of delivery where the customer is leaving responsibility with the bidder but withholding control of items affecting delivery success should raise concerns for the contracts and operations teams. Based on the bidder's standard operating functions, contracts personnel can work with operations teams in 'what if' exercises to ensure that the impacts of various possible delivery scenarios are understood, documented, and added to contingency funds where necessary.

16.9   Responding to the RFP documents

- Review of terms and conditions
- Risk Mitigation Strategy

Review of the offered terms and conditions is not always possible during the bidding process, as some customers omit them from the RFP. Despite this, contracts personnel should make every effort to become familiar with the customer's preferred terms and conditions. One generalization that customers object to in bidders' terms and conditions is a tendency towards passive rather than active clauses. While leaving the responsibility for taking action to the customer eliminates risk, it undermines the relationship. Instead, propose that unexpected issues are reviewed by a governance committee, which meets regularly to determine what actions – if any – are necessary by both parties.

Review of the terms and conditions is also complicated by a tendency on both sides to re-use documents that have not been updated to represent the current scenario in the RFP. While it would be easy to respond to such an outdated document with phrases such as 'to be determined during negotiation' advanced bidders use this as an opportunity to propose language that is both appropriate to the current product and service set, as well as aligned with their winning strategy.

Knowing the elements of the win strategy allows contracts personnel to tailor a risk mitigation strategy that emphasizes the company's strengths and minimizes exposure of weaknesses. For example, if the bidder is using an industry leader as a partner for service delivery, this minimizes the delivery risk and at the same time reinforces the value of the product or service provided to the customer. The contracts responses should reflect this strategy by focusing on the strength of the relationship with the partner, how that partnership will be governed, and how the bidder will communicate needed information between the customer and the partner.

A Risk Mitigation Strategy is developed through the various iterations of solutions tested and adopted for the RFP response. The Risk Mitigation Strategy must reflect the win strategy in addressing each of the items logged as a risk. Contracts personnel can simplify the strategy by looking for groups and patterns of risk that can be linked to key items in the solution. Creative solutions that mitigate groups of risk without materially affecting a compliant solution will be of great interest to the pursuit team. By communicating these solutions with the groups creating the response (before and during the Green Team exercise, described in detail below), the contracts team can remove roadblocks, reduce costs, and improve the deliverability of the end solution.

An example of this approach:

A pattern of risk to do with delivery and installation is identified in the RFP. The Risk Mitigation Strategy might be for the bidder to partner with an industry leader in these areas. This reduces the risk to both customer and bidder, and the increased cost is accepted as a part of meeting targets established by the customer.

In the same RFP, the bidder is aware of significant failures in the customer's ability to pay on time, based on an inefficient material or contracted deliverable receipt system. The Risk Mitigation Strategy counters this with a simple statement requesting that the customer indicates acceptance of a deliverable at an early stage before implementation in their operational structure. This significantly reduces liability while allowing the engineering solution to meet deadlines and stay on budget.

16.10 Characteristics of successful bidders

The following characteristics separate consistently successful bidders from the rest of the pack.

Successful bidders:
- Maintain strong relationships with the customer on multiple levels
- Understand the RFP requirements, impacts, and history
- Write responses tailored to the customer's decision process
- Leverage their relationships to influence and anticipate the RFP
- Articulate the close fit of their products and services to the RFP
- Offer strong financial incentives to the customer beyond lowest cost
- Package products and services so that they are easy to buy
- Demonstrate their strong competitive position with clear value statements
- Create offerings that they have tested and confirmed as deliverable by the budget holder and which result in quantified and manageable operational risk
- Integrate future account leaders, contract managers, the service delivery team and relevant technical experts into the bid response team at the very beginning of the sales process
- Demonstrate courage by no-bidding RFPs that are unreasonable, unprofitable or do not fit the bidder's strategic product and service plan

16.11 Customer contact

- Bidders' Conference
- 'Purdah' – customer-requested non-contact

In addition to writing deadlines, the calendar developed by the bid team may show the date of the Bidders' Conference (usually given in the customer's covering letter for the RFP, or instructions to bidders).

Careful preparation of questions for the Bidders' Conference should be coordinated through the sales lead or the Customer Account Leader. Questions submitted to the customer generally are circulated to all the bidders and can be a window into the competitive landscape, indicating who is struggling with the requirements, who is mystified, and who has inside information.

Customers often fail to anticipate the volume and detail of questions that will be asked by potential bidders. This results in long delays in answering these questions. Customers can compound the confusion caused by a questions process by refusing to extend due dates for submission of bids. In many cases, customers demand that bids are sent in, even though questions have not yet been answered. If this is the case, any RFP responses in these areas should include language that allows for changes later based on the answers to these questions.

As a general rule the fewer questions asked the better. However, due to limitations on access to the customer, this may be the only opportunity to clarify critical points that may drive the solution.

This limiting of access to the customer during the bid process is sometimes called 'Purdah' after the custom of separating special classes of people with a screen. The theory is that unlimited access between bidders and customer staff during the bid process can create problems in at least two ways. First, it creates the potential for bidders submitting proposals based on different representations by the customer. This can be a serious problem if the contract is later subject to litigation. Second, it creates the possibility that bidders will believe the RFP process is 'fixed', damaging the customer's reputation for integrity.

These risks must be offset against the real possibility that bidders have a better way of doing the work covered by an RFP. There are many circumstances where customers failed to listen to bidders during the proposal process and spent millions of dollars more on the acquisition than they needed to.

Even in US public sector procurement, this balance between protection and listening is recognized. In the Federal Acquisition Regulation (FAR), part 15 specifies the allowable kinds of contact allowed between the release of an RFP and receipt of bids. This is balanced against the ethics and transparency required in FAR part 3.

On the commercial side, 'limits on communication during the bid process' is often spelled out in the RFP. It should never be assumed that the customer will consider informal meetings during the Bid phase. However, significant opportunity can be missed if bidders fail to ask informal questions, and fail to participate in public forums to discuss questions and set out deadlines. Certainly, communication that is not specifically prohibited should be pursued as part of the data gathering needed to set bid strategy, but expect that anything sent to the customer will become visible to all the competitors.

In a closed bid situation where communication is limited, it is therefore vitally important to have built and established a solid relationship with your customers well in advance of any major procurement activities. The value of having a trusted relationship where the customer has advance knowledge of your capability to deliver, your pedigree of performance and your fair and honest approach to unforeseen issues will be a key in the evaluation process. A great price but no customer confidence will not win a bid. A good price and high confidence has a higher evaluation weighting.

16.12 Green Team review

- Green Team inputs
- Green Team process
- Green Team outcomes

While there is not always time or need in every response exercise for a Green Team review, the concept of a no-holds-barred brainstorming session can offer a lot of value. A Green Team meeting supports knowledge management efforts, and allows access to the collective knowledge of the larger organization. This enables the pursuit team to gain an outside perspective on removing roadblocks, filling in missing information and finding new areas of advantage.

Green Team members are selected from outside the pursuit team, representing various areas of the organization. They are selected for their ability to work in a creative environment and to propose 'out of the box' ideas. They bring their expertise, networks, and organizational knowledge to bear on the problems and solutions proposed by the pursuit team.

The Green Team process is a focused, short, and highly creative work session. It begins with an opportunity overview and summary presentation by the pursuit team, followed by a guided idea session by the Green Team members. This session should be moderated by a skilled facilitator to ensure that it is short, focused, and respectful to the members' ideas and suggestions.

Outputs of the session include: solutions to known problems, red flags for issues the pursuit team did not anticipate, workarounds and action items that address issues raised. Careful documentation of the outputs allows the pursuit team to quickly act and resolve issues that will affect the win-ability of the response.

16.13 Red Team review

- Red Team process
- Role playing
- Contract language

The Red Team performs an independent review and assessment from the customer's perspective, based on the completed RFP. The session should include an assessment of pricing wherever possible. The Red Team process is further described in Chapter 11: *Responding to an RFI or RFP*.

This process of review and response can be enhanced through role-playing activities. Selecting Red Team members who have not participated in the writing or development of the response can be difficult. Senior managers rarely have extensive time available for an all-day review. This means that Red Team sessions are often good visibility and training grounds for next-in-line managers, as well as other high quality staff who need to gain experience. As a last resort, some companies use outside consultants to support Red Team reviews. While this practice is common, it can present risks in that outsiders may not know the internal politics and drivers faced by the pursuit team.

Red Teams are a great opportunity for contracts professionals to sharpen drafting skills in a positive manner. Often wording in the contract area will appear to be correct and appropriate to the bidder's team, but will sound insulting, legally detailed or arrogant from the buyer's perspective. The Red Team can identify these types of statements and suggest subtle changes that will correct the tone, enhance the winning prospect and yet preserve the meaning and any necessary risk caveats of the bidder's responses. The challenge for contracts professionals is to fully embrace the constructive environment and learn how to draft appropriate bid language that protects the company from undue and un-quantified risk but is also clear, easy to read, customer-friendly and designed to win.

16.14 The Executive Summary

- Elements of persuasion – win themes
- Emotional argument – addressing fear, uncertainty and doubt
- Intellectual argument – logic and elegance
- Social argument – win/win

Writing the Executive Summary is a fine art, integrating sales strategy, competitive intelligence, and knowledge of customer 'hot buttons'. The best summaries are calls to action, pulling together the three classic types of arguments (emotional, intellectual, and social) to influence the buyer.

Leaving out one of the points will leave the buyer hanging. These documents can be quite short and succinct, or 10 page 'eye poppers' with color graphics and complex charts.

Writing the Executive Summary is usually left until the last week; however, the key strategy decisions that frame the Executive Summary (low bid, compliant response, creative financing) are made at the earliest part of the process. This can be a time for creativity, insight, and raw emotion. The Executive Summary is seen as the only part of the entire response where the bidder knows the customer is listening and can actually address an individual.

A classic summary employs emotional arguments by demonstrating the bidders understanding of why the customer is going out to bid. It also addresses any fears the customer may have about buying from the bidder. A deft writer guides the reader to an awareness of the weaknesses in the competitor's products by enhancing the qualities of their own compared to the customer's needs and raises doubts about the status quo so that the reader is motivated to look for something better.

In the next section the writer logically lays out the bidder's strengths, competitive differentiators and innovations, establishing the qualifications of the company in light of the competition. This is best done elegantly, with a minimum of overstatement and without making negative statements about specific competitors.

In the final section the writer shows the reader why choosing their solution is a sustainable solution and a long-term win/win scenario.

This argument is based on insight, 'gut feel' and competitive intelligence. The Executive Summary often takes the form of a letter signed by the writer or a top-level company official.

While sales teams may be hard-wired to reinforce selling in the executive summary, the commercial team who are more adept at complex drafting should be integral to the entire proposal construct so that the messages are consistent throughout and the subtleties required in the Executive Summary are presented in the best possible light. This is the one great opportunity for the contracts and commercial team, so show off their creative flair. Often, senior executives remember the Executive Summary for years after contract award. Contracts professionals should also ensure that the Executive Summary dovetails with contractual and operational commitments made in the deal. For example, the Executive

Summary may lay out a year-on-year efficiency gain; be sure the risk mitigation strategy has taken this into account.

16.15 Bid submission

- Delivery and acceptance
- Oral presentations
- Backchannel communications

The RFP often states explicitly how the response should be delivered to the customer, when, where, in what type of packaging, on what types of media, and how many copies. It is rare that the buyer actually physically accepts the response documents; however, if this is the case the bidder should be prepared by assigning the sales lead or account leader to be present at handoff. At a minimum, someone at the customer site should sign for the response package, so that there is a record of delivery.

Following the RFP response deadline, the customer may establish a time for oral presentations by the bidders. Often presentations are limited to a short list of potential winners. This is the time to pull out the stops and make a splash. Buyers who have waded through volumes of dry technical responses and tangled compliance statements are ready for a little razzle-dazzle.

Depending on the forum offered and any limitations set by the customer, the bidder should develop a flowing multimedia presentation that sums up the advantages of their solution and builds a positive picture of the future working relationship. The selected account team should be present with high-level company executives and board members with links to the customer.

Following the submission of the bid, communications with the customer are generally less limited. Any backchannel communication should be carefully coordinated through the sales team to reinforce the key messages and pick up on any customer concerns. This channel is found in formal situations such as golf games, and less formal lunch meetings, alumni events, social groups and hobby groups.

The backchannel is a great voice to use in preparing the oral presentation. One channel that can be less certain is the buyer. It is not unusual for the buyer to indicate dissatisfaction with the response, especially price. They may well be using the same pressure with all the bidders, hoping for one of them to make a better offer. This can be a negotiating tactic, or a simple lack of information.

16.16 Negotiations and pricing

- Changes to risk-reward equation
- Changes to scope
- Changes to pricing
- Lowball offers and evasive pricing
- Deal killers

The negotiation section of this book provides a comprehensive guide to negotiations. It is, however, important to bear in mind a number of key points while preparing the proposal.

During the Negotiation phase, the winning company can expect that the customer will try to eliminate any element of risk and retain every possible price advantage. The negotiators on both sides should be familiar with the details of the requirements. Negotiators for the supplier should also be aware of the risk mitigation plan, and areas of operations and delivery that might be affected during the negotiation phase. For example, giving the customer packaging options such as plain boxes without the supplier's logo, seems like a cost-free concession; however the shipping manager may have no way to stock, supply and accurately ship non-standard packages, adding difficulty and cost to the sale. Any change to that requires the suppler to add complexity to the delivery or accept risk will ultimately affect the expected rewards of winning the business. Enough of these changes can unbalance the risk-reward equation because the business becomes unprofitable. Naturally this is also true where the seller has responded with their standard practices in anticipation that the buyer will change.

Contracts teams would be well advised to know the RFP response thoroughly in regards to scope: small changes to the extent of work, geographical coverage, timelines, or delivery volumes can have an inordinately large impact on costs. While expanding the scope of a deal is generally good, expanding it into unexpected directions can overwhelm delivery teams and introduce huge overhead expenses. Customers often try to limit implementation risk by paring down the scope into smaller bite-sized pieces. It is vital that negotiators have understanding of start-up and overhead costs so that any changes to the rollout scope can be accurately priced.

Similarly, most customers will expect to negotiate price points in very fine detail. Knowing true overhead expenses, logistical costs and margin expectations in detail will allow the contract negotiation to progress more quickly. Another element for consideration is the bill-to-book cycle.

Depending on the industry, customers may expect a percentage discount if payment is made within a specified window following acceptance. In other industries, customers may expect the supplier to smooth out any commodities cost variations over multiple delivery cycles.

For any international deals where the supplier and the customer use different currencies careful consideration should be made with regards to which party accepts the risk of fluctuations in the valuations of the currencies with respect to one another.

Be aware of regulatory issues, laws affecting trade across boundaries and the impact of changes in small details that could have an impact on price, liability or other operational performance considerations.

Lowball offers can be a tool for establishing a new supplier with the market; the supplier decides to 'buy the business' or sell below cost in order to win. The danger to the buyer is that this may create a supplier who is unable to deliver long-term and at the same time, weaken the ability of other suppliers to stay in business. Low-balling can be used in conjunction with other bids to the same customer, as a way of enticing the customer by expanding the scope of the deal. It can also be seen as a way to move the detailed delivery negotiations off into the future so that the customer is locked in. In this case the supplier may expect to 'do well on the changes' or add higher margin business after winning a low margin deal.

In some industries, especially in new economic areas, customers are not aware of all the costs of doing business and can fall prey to evasive pricing strategies. These happen when the bidder leaves out important cost elements necessary for the customer to begin using the product or service – for example, telecom line termination costs. While generally the customer is at risk, suppliers who do not lay out such costs in their responses may find themselves out of pocket.

Which side bears these costs depends on the wording of the final contract.

Deal killers during negotiation are many. For example:
- Unbalanced currency risk
- Unreasonable demands for quality specifications outside of industry norms
- Delivery dates that are out of line with acceptance timelines
- Unreasonable termination provisions
- Limitations on hiring and selecting staff
- Onerous service penalties

What constitutes a demand by the customer that cannot be borne by the seller varies with each deal. A general guideline is to consider each request within the context of the risk mitigation strategy, comparing the needed changes to any offered rewards to ensure that the risk reward equation stays balanced.

16.17 **Relationship selling**

- Timeline for becoming the incumbent
- Influencing the RFP
- Knowing the competitive landscape
- Anticipating objections

In relationship selling the bidder develops extensive contacts and deep awareness of the customer's long-term goals and needs. Rather than visiting once a year to check on expected order quantities the seller becomes involved with long-term strategy and even goal setting.

Working with the customer to remove business roadblocks, the seller becomes a key to the customer's long-term success. This type of selling can be much more profitable because the seller is aware of the customer's needs well before an RFP is issued. It also takes much more time and effort on the seller's part – two years or more in the case of a large global services outsourcing. The buying cycle for complex projects can be somewhat shortened by providing the customer access to the right experts, information, forums and demonstrations early in the cycle.

By following the work with the customer over several years, the contracts team is uniquely positioned to provide continuity in developing the ongoing relationship. By maintaining notes, records and agreed contracts, the team has access to the customer's preferred buying habits, ability to accept risk, and desired terms.

Using this technique the seller may become the 'go to' party for the customer with respect to specifying exactly what it wants to buy. This allows the seller to influence either tacitly or directly what is written in the RFP. In some cases the seller is asked to write the RFP based on their product and service set. This may or may not limit the buyer's choices. At the very least it gives the seller more time to prepare and shape a response.

Influencing the RFP can be as subtle as circulating technical white papers through professional forums. The influence can also be overt, such as allowing the seller to issue the RFP under the name of a joint venture with the buyer.

In relationship selling evaluation of the competitive landscape takes on a more forward-looking aspect. The seller looks for competitors, not for today's needs but for the needs the customer will have in the future. Using a longer term outlook often leads to the realization that a competitor will become a valued partner, or even a valued customer. Such 'co-opetition' is becoming more widespread due to globalization and increased specialization by suppliers. From the contracts team's viewpoint, negotiations with suppliers take on added importance. The other company may be a competitor, partner, and customer all at the same time. Arrogance in any level of these negotiations could limit the types of business that the seller can win in the future.

Contracts teams can expedite the negotiation and deal-making cycles by anticipating the other parties' objections to contractual elements. Based on previous experience, the contracts group can offer acceptable alternatives. They can also re-direct the discussions toward win/win scenarios rather than 'dog fights'. The contracts team brings expertise in multiple levels of negotiation, awareness of business risk and awareness of business trends to the development of winning deals. This enables the contracts team to add value, reduce risk, and remove obstacles for customers, partners and suppliers.

CHAPTER 17

Evaluating the proposal

17.1 Overview

As mentioned in Chapter 11: *Request for Proposal management* the supplier selection process uses the evaluation criteria developed in parallel to drafting the RFP. This chapter covers:

- The process for establishing an evaluation framework
- Criteria relevant to products versus services versus. solutions evaluations
- Tangible, easily measurable criteria versus intangible criteria
- And other evaluation techniques worthy of consideration
- How to establish metrics that reflect evaluation criteria
- Ensuring balanced application / objectivity
- Managing expectations
- Gaining consensus on the process and the outcome

17.2 The evaluation framework

Companies are presented with an array of sourcing options. How do you decide among them? How do you achieve consensus or buy-in? What are the relevant evaluation criteria?

- Return on Investment (ROI)
- Cost
- Control
- Risk
- Longevity

Once a preliminary cost/benefit analysis has indicated a 'go' decision, and as the sourcing options are being explored, the project team should be establishing its evaluation criteria.

These criteria can include elements that are specific to the project, as well as corporate elements that are applied across all projects.

Goals of the evaluation process

A robust evaluation process fulfils several critical needs. It will

- Help define the range of options to be considered
- Provide the basis for selecting among competing sourcing options
- Allows objective evaluation of unconventional options
- Provide the foundation for ongoing performance measurement.

The process will even be a potential basis for terminating a relationship or evaluating changing suppliers

Additional benefits of an effective evaluation process include

- Promoting buy-in to evaluation outcome
- Promoting alignment with company mission
- Minimizing risk
- Speeding the evaluation process

Evaluation process

The first step is to develop an organizational evaluation model and process. This should ideally be at the enterprise level to assure consistency and buy-in to the evaluation outcome across all stakeholder groups. Such an organizational model must be supported, if not driven, by senior executives. The model should tie directly to enterprise or business unit strategy. This can be simplified if the organization has already established a broad strategic or performance measurement methodology, such as balanced scorecard. Those driving the enterprise evaluation model should facilitate discussion on high-level evaluation criteria, as well as on the scoring process. Experience has proven that for the model to be effective, the process must include broad stakeholder representation.

An enterprise model will work for strategic acquisitions, but will not have sufficient granularity for most evaluations. The project team must then develop a tailored set of criteria for each acquisition project. The enterprise model will serve as the framework for the project-specific evaluation model – defining the guiding elements that assure alignment with mission and strategy. At the project level, team leaders must facilitate discussion on specific criteria and scoring approach, again including all stakeholders in the discussion.

If there is no enterprise model, then the project leader must include executive leadership to sanction the evaluation process. Lack of an enterprise model also opens the risk that separate project-specific models will reflect differing organizational perspectives, and thus not harmonize in support of strategy.

Once the model is established, it's appropriate to communicate criteria with candidates so that they can respond directly. Of course, it is essential to support evaluation with Due Diligence.

The approach to scoring should be established at the same time the team is developing the evaluation criteria. We will review this in detail in later chapters.

Challenges

Selecting evaluation criteria is not as simple as it may seem. Unless a project impacts only a very small group of stakeholders, disagreement on the criteria is almost a given.

Once final, negotiated agreement on the criteria is reached, a new round of discussions will emerge on the weighting of the criteria to determine which should be given the highest consideration in evaluating sourcing options. In some cases, criteria will conflict.

Agreeing on criteria

Initially, agreeing on specific criteria is a challenge, especially when a project touches many groups or functions within a corporation. There are several approaches to move quickly to consensus. Companies that have built high-level strategically aligned evaluation frameworks find they are a safe and sometimes mandatory starting point. Such a framework provides strong boundaries for the definition process, minimizing time-consuming debate.

Where there is no such framework, it is important to be as inclusive as possible during the facilitated discussions. This is critical to driving buy-in. Once the broad list of criteria is defined, the team's business analysts can work on categorizing the criteria, eliminating redundancies and establish the scoring approach.

Ultimately, agreeing on criteria is simpler than agreeing on a supplier. Inevitably, detailed criteria choices will differ from business unit to business unit, function to function. It is also important to have the ability to change criteria and adapt to a specific decision.

Weighting evaluation criteria

Developing a broad range of criteria is essential for buy-in and unbiased scoring. In some cases, differing stakeholder groups will insist upon specific criteria or specific wording, resulting in two versions of the same criterion. Closely aligned or redundant criteria will bias the importance of those criteria. Weighting the individual criteria will:
- Reduce bias caused by redundancy
- Elevate the influence of the most important criteria, and
- Enable buy-in to the model by allowing and compensating for individual preferences

Weighting the high-level categories of criteria will allow the project leader to emphasize the most critical elements. For example, corporate policy may be to assure that strategic priorities do not take a back seat to technology considerations. Weighting the high-level categories accordingly will provide appropriate factoring and ample evidence of strategic focus.

Conflicting criteria

Inevitably, there will be conflicting criteria. In some cases, this will reflect the needs or interests of one stakeholder group vs. another's. It may reflect the common dilemma of embracing the corporate standard or approved supplier versus pursuing a 'best-of-breed' alternative.

A common rule in software development is that you can choose any two of the Speed – Quality – Cost priorities. A supplier can deliver quickly, at low cost, sacrificing features or quality. If the focus is on quality, then costs will necessarily increase, and so forth.

Ultimately, the resolution to these conflicts rests in building a balanced set of accepted criteria and following the outcome of the scoring.

Best alternative

Let's look ahead to the possibility that there is no suitable solution. While this will become evident in the bid phase, it's important for the project team to anticipate this and develop a solution within the evaluation framework. The evaluation criteria will direct the range of alternatives.

If technology factors are the problem, then the team may want to expand the range of possible solutions. If cost is the issue, then a renewed cost/benefit analysis and additional funding may be in order.

Supplier compatibility issues may indicate a need for a short-term commitment, with viable options for transition to another supplier at a later date. Lack of strength is strategic areas may lead to settling or abandoning the project altogether. This sort of exit strategy is a critical component of a credible evaluation framework.

Lessons learned – case study

If we look at case studies of organizations that have experimented with evaluation frameworks, we see outcomes that range from unqualified success, to unrealized expectations, to complete write-off.

- In one case study, a New York-based music industry technology organization was under pressure from executive leadership for higher ROI and greater project success rates. One of the contributing factors for this scrutiny was poor supplier performance. Accordingly, the Chief Information Officer (CIO) developed an evaluation model and scored the options.

Stakeholders rejected the outcome and model since they had not participated in building model. The attempt, while well motivated, was ill-conceived, and ultimately contributed to the search for a new CIO.

- In another case, an insurance industry technology organization developed a model in close collaboration with its stakeholders, but scored the options alone.

Some stakeholder groups claimed that the IT organization was ill-equipped to handle the scoring of business issues. While not a direct consequence, the implemented solutions have achieved low adoption rates, with users pursuing workarounds, or where possible, using the legacy system.

In order to avert future criticism, the IT organization plans to include stakeholder representatives during scoring as part of the reengineered evaluation framework.

The lesson learned: buy-in from ownership of the model and the related processes are critical success factors.

17.3 Primary categories

Tailor criteria to acquisition

There is a broad set of standardized criteria to assure strategic alignment and speed process – generally the enterprise level evaluation model. However, there are several criteria categories that are unique to the type of acquisition, whether they are products, services, outsourcing or even corporate acquisitions.

Products

Products can be considered to be any standard or customized item, of any value, any size, virtual or physical. These include software solutions, office equipment, inventory, sub-assemblies – really, anything that can be delivered.

Product-related issues include functional alignment with the requirements, compatibility with other products, and ongoing supplier support for product. Criteria typically include such categories as functional capability, Total Cost of Ownership (TCO), supplier longevity, risk, time and cost to implement and product reliability.

Services

Services criteria categories can include SLA, ability to accept and meet milestones, liability, terms and conditions, and negotiation approach. Services are often bundled with products – so in many situations, product and service criteria will apply.

Outsourcing

Outsourcing criteria add dimensions of corporate compatibility, full service versus selective or partial fulfillment, loss of control of the outsourced service, security, and ownership of resources, processes, data or other intellectual property.

Other acquisitions

Other acquisitions require specialized evaluation criteria. These acquisitions may include strategic partnerships, tactical partnerships, and corporate acquisitions. The criteria can include such hard-to-measure dimensions as the value of brand, organization and process, as well as the customer base.

17.4   Product evaluation criteria

As we look at product acquisitions, we see many dimensions beyond what they will do and what they will cost. Features are unique to each acquisition. The functional evaluation criteria should be driven entirely by the requirements; they will encompass technical, cultural and business elements, and are evaluated in terms of the degree to which the product addresses each element. In evaluating the products, it is unlikely that there will be a perfect match. The degree of customization will affect other factors such as cost and risk.

Time and cost

On those products that require substantial planning and implementation effort, time and cost to implement is a primary consideration. The initial purchase cost can be quickly eclipsed by consulting fees, construction costs, implementation support, taxes – or tax credits – productivity loss during implementation, and the costs of decommissioning or disposal of the old solution.

There are typically hidden or unexpected costs, including service disruption, costs associated with change control, relationship management and communications with stakeholders. Performing an effective financial evaluation is possible only after anticipating and calculating all the implementation costs. A product that carries a low purchase price may in fact be more expensive that other alternatives.

Total Cost of Ownership

Another financial metric used extensively with information technology purchases is Total Cost of Ownership, or TCO, over the life of the asset. For evaluation, these are broken down into short- term, medium-term and, depending upon the product's service life, long-term costs. The short- term costs can include license costs, hardware costs, consulting, training, internal resources and expenditures required for tangential property, plan and equipment such as controlled environments for hardware, special tools, or additional spare parts inventory. In the short term, opportunity costs associated with the inability to pursue other options should be considered.

Mid-term costs include ongoing administration, the potential impact on other licenses and agreements, and the effect on human resource staffing. Long-term costs include costs associated with upgrades, the cost of migration and retirement of the asset.

Supplier longevity

One of the great fears is whether the supplier will be in business long enough to support the product through its useful life. Technology companies appear to be the most volatile. Criteria include the company's share price performance, such as the three-year market capitalization trend, analyst consensus on the company's outlook, profitability and growth.

Supplier longevity does not necessarily predict product longevity. Suppliers often have clear product strategies, and it is important to be aware of these. They may plan to upgrade within a few months of your purchase, drop support for a version, or even retire a product altogether in favor of more successful product lines. Criteria that can guide your evaluation include the product's market share, share trend, and availability of consulting support. Independent Solution Supplier (ISV) support refers to the number of third party products that support or can be added on. Typically, products with longer life expectations will reflect more interfacing third party products.

Risk

Risk can include many categories, including technical, strategic and financial risk. Technical risk can reflect scalability, security, the ability to integrate the product with your processes, and the availability of internal or external resources to implement and support the product.

Strategic risk reflects dimensions of suitability, alignment with strategy, global compatibility and opportunity risk. An example of a poor strategic fit would be a global company's purchase of software that would not support multiple languages, or electing to establish a relationship with a supplier that had no plans to build production capacity in locations that are targeted for growth.

Financial risk includes inevitable unexpected or hidden costs that surface after the decision. Another risk is poor adoption rates or long learning curves that impair productivity and may severely affect return on investment.

Reliability

Reliability can have a profound impact on ROI. The costs associated with unreliable products include more that the cost of repairs and maintenance, and the simple cost of lost productivity. In complex assembly environments, process start-up can include lengthy set-up procedures and environmental preparation. In these circumstances, small equipment reliability issues can cut production in half, killing profitability. Software failures can alienate users and have long-term productivity impacts. Workarounds while systems are down create time-consuming work backlogs and introduce increased possibility for error.

Reliability evaluation criteria can include availability of solutions to address reliability, as well as the reliability performance of the product itself. Some solutions criteria include availability of system redundancy, back-up capability and basic system architecture. Popular performance criteria include Mean Time Between Failure (MTBF), uptime measured as a percentage of total operating time, cost performance and user satisfaction.

Solution evaluation criteria

In our discussion of evaluation criteria, we will combine services and solutions to include delivery of professional services, hiring contract workers, contracting turnkey solutions and all levels of outsourcing. Many of the product criteria may apply, especially the financial elements. However, there are many additional dimensions.

At the very least are the terms and conditions of the contract, and the degree to which they meet the buyers needs and compare to competitive proposals. With business process outsourcing, there are more complex liability and responsibility issues, as well as SLAs. To some degree, particularly in strategic partnerships, even the negotiations approach should be considered as an important evaluation criterion, since the approach may well provide insight into the tone of the potential relationship.

Responsibility and liability

Responsibility addresses who performs the primary delivery activities, as well as those activities that support delivery of services. These can include project management, performance measurement and other forms of support such as training. All elements are critical to the success of delivered services. However, suppliers will have relative strengths and weaknesses in these areas, which will impact at a minimum the additional costs required to adequately perform these activities. In the worst case, these services, poorly performed, will derail the project. Evaluation criteria would include the scope of these support services, as well as the supplier's ability to effectively perform these tasks.

Liability goes a step further and requires the supplier to assume responsibility for performance. Evaluation criteria include the degree to which suppliers will guarantee adoption rates, ROI, on-time delivery, successful integration with other systems, etc. Elements may include business interruption, and the remedies may be legal and financial. It may be that, depending upon the project, no suppliers are willing to assume liability. In some cases, willingness may indicate confidence in their ability to execute, or pricing to reflect the risk of financial penalties. Such terms are common in construction projects where delays can have huge financial ramifications.

Service levels

While the service level expectations may be specified in the requirements, providers will be likely to respond with varying levels of capability and cost. Service level evaluation criteria can include flexibility (or the degree to which levels can be negotiated from the supplier's standards), volume, availability, skill levels and response times.

Availability can have many meanings. Availability of systems is often expressed in terms of historical uptime as a percentage of full-time. Help desk availability is expressed as 24×7 or 7am to 7pm Monday through Saturday. With respect to delivery of consulting services, availability often refers to access to key engagement personnel or relevant subject matter experts.

Response times can be hierarchical, with critical issues specifying a 30-minute or faster response, and less urgent complaints allowing up to a day or more.

Ability to meet service level expectations may be a critical component of your evaluation. Proposed service levels in excess of your needs may indicate an opportunity to negotiate lower costs for services.

Terms and conditions

Evaluation criteria should include contract terms and conditions items such as
- Clarity and scope of services and deliverables
- Change control procedures and responsibilities
- Delivery, inspection, acceptance and rejection processes
- Quality and approach to project management
- Contract administration provisions
- Payment milestones and terms
- Provisions for termination of the agreement and its implications

Negotiations approach

A company's stated approach to negotiations can be a valuable evaluation criterion. A 'positional' approach is one of adopting a position and aiming to negotiate an agreement as close to that position as possible. This allows for only limited and very predictable negotiating, and in many instances, it degenerates into a 'battle of wills'.

Conversely, a principled approach to negotiations considers each party's perceptions and seeks to make negotiation proposals consistent with the other party's interests. Suppliers that employ a principled approach to negotiations are potentially more disposed to working through issues after the contract award, which can lead to a greater likelihood of success. Negotiations approaches are discussed in detail in Chapters 24 through 27.

17.5   Intangible criteria

Many projects and relationships depend for success on intangible factors that rely on organizational culture and behavior. It is important that these are included in evaluation criteria and evidence is sought to substantiate supplier claims. It is of course equally important for the supplier to consider these aspect sin assessing the opportunity since customer behavior will have a major impact on costs and results. Intangible criteria include:

- Reliability / honesty
- Resources (skills, allocation)
- Connections / networks (e.g. with key sub-contractors)
- Flexibility
- Understanding
- Suitability
- Reference quality

Because there may not be standards or metrics for these criteria, performance against them is relative. The answers may become apparent early in discussions. It is also acceptable to ask potential suppliers to respond to these specific issues.

Apply quantitative scoring to qualitative criteria by defining scales, such as '1' equates with no understanding of our industry or company, a '5' might indicate experience with the industry, but not our company or business unit, and '10' would indicate substantial experience or even an existing, effective relationship.

Reliability / honesty

Trust is typically built over time, based on levels of reliability and honesty (making realistic promises, keeping to them, exceeding expectations. There can be solid guides to evaluating trust. Is there an existing relationship with the supplier? If so, how have they performed against their claims? Will the supplier go the extra mile to meet your needs? What experience have other customers had? Is there evidence of claims or disputes?

A supplier's openness to sharing processes demonstrates trust, as does providing access to information. Trust is built when both parties do Due Diligence early on in the contracting relationship and work together to find solutions to complex issues.

Resources

Resource depth and quality are measurable, but determining the impact on the project may be difficult. Companies may like to keep much of that information private. Criteria can include the depth of 'bench' in terms of personnel with the skills relevant to your specific need. Does the supplier have the manufacturing capacity to fulfill your current requirements as well as your anticipated needs based upon your plans for growth?

Staff attrition / retention rates are important indicators of stability or growth. Clues can come from job postings, newsgroups or other back-door approaches. Will subcontractors be used on a project? Ask those competing to disclose subcontractor relationships and the controls that are in place to assure continuity and quality.

Connections/networks

In today's networked world, the ability of a potential supplier to make sustainable relationships with others in the industry and beyond is a core source of advantage. It is through those relationships that they may bring you added value or innovation. Evidence that they reach out to, or attract, respected partners and sub-contractors represents a good sign for their overall collaborative behavior and ethical standards, as well as representing potential value in its own right.

Flexibility

Flexibility can be addressed in terms of a supplier's willingness to be flexible with respect to their standard specifications, terms and conditions. This flexibility may carry a price – but it is important to set expectations early on.

You should also enquire about experience handling mid-course corrections, and what implications, beyond change control procedures, such changes will have. A large part of a final project budget can be changes from the original design.

Your own honesty with regard to the likelihood of change is also important. Markets may be volatile and it is often tempting to paint an optimistic picture of requirement volumes or timing, in order to negotiate a more favorable deal. But if you know there is a significant possibility of changes that could adversely affect the value of this contract, then your behavior is unethical and you can hardly complain if suppliers respond in kind. Truth and honesty is a two-way process.

Understanding

Does the supplier understand your business? What is their industry focus? Do they have experience with your company? How well do they understand the current project under evaluation?

Has the supplier demonstrated a desire to understand? Have you done enough to enable that understanding? Demonstrated understanding and success in similar projects in similar industries is a good predictor of success, and should weigh significantly in your evaluation.

On the other hand, do they bring valuable insights from other industries or geographies – perhaps in future markets, or equipped with ideas from outside your industry that could be a source of competitive difference? Simply replicating what your competitors are doing may not be the aim of the contract.

Suitability

Suitability refers to 'fit' on many levels – cultural compatibility, business processes and methodologies, consciousness regarding controls and confidentiality. Incompatibility can lead to problems – do not expect your culture or processes to change the supplier's approach to business, nor can you expect their operational excellence to rub off on your organization, unless that is part of the contract deliverables.

References

References are often the most important source of information regarding intangible evaluation criteria. Ask reference customers for information about trust, understanding and flexibility. Also ask references to validate responses to other, more tangible and measurable criteria. Reference responses are often given insufficient weighting.

Develop a reference questionnaire, and ask questions regarding all key evaluation criteria. Then factor the references' responses into the evaluation.

Also make use of the internet – there can be a wealth of information available that offers insights to strategic direction, market reputation and performance, staff turnover and ethical practices and standards. There are even research companies that can offer reports into many of these areas.

17.6 Other evaluation components

What-if scenarios

Other evaluation techniques can be used in conjunction with a formal evaluation matrix. What-if scenarios allow you to explore suppliers' reactions to unplanned situations, such as increased throughput, or accelerated implementation requirements. Develop multiple possible scenarios and ask candidates to outline responses to each.

Trial project or purchase

If a new, high-scoring supplier is being considered, or an existing supplier is being asked to deliver products or services outside their demonstrated area of proficiency, you may want to explore a trial project. The trial should be a low-risk purchase or engagement, and be engineered to test all dimensions of the envisioned relationship.

Red Flags

It is good to keep an eye out for issues or concerns that fall outside the standard evaluation criteria – the Red Flags. Though they may not be deal breakers, they should prompt questions and Due Diligence. Some of these issues include:

- **Hesitance to provide references**: Some companies hesitate to supply references for fear of overtaxing them. It is acceptable for them to ask that references are not to be contacted until the supplier is either a finalist, or has been selected pending favorable reference reports.

- **Heavily front-loaded payment terms**: If a company insists on high pre-payments, cash flow may be an issue. Further inquiry is recommended.

- **Recurring problems**: Ask references what problems they have had. If the same issue surfaces in more that one relationship, assume it will be an issue with you.

- **Lack of standard or appropriate contract provisions**: Suppliers that have not developed their own standard terms and conditions are likely to be less mature with respect to a given product or service. This should stimulate further discussion.

- **'Bait and switch'**: Companies that swap products, parts or resources may have credibility issues, or inventory or personnel problem. Either way, any deviation from expectations should be explored and resolved quickly.

- **Erratic or negative stock value patterns**: market capitalization is a sensitive barometer of corporate wellbeing – perhaps over-sensitive. Don't hesitate to ask senior management why the stock is erratic or underperforming; it may signal the possibility for stronger negotiations, or a warning to steer clear altogether.

17.7 Implementing the evaluation framework

Supplier selection assumes that the evaluation team will be using the evaluation framework that was established before drafting the RFP. In some cases, the responses to the RFP may uncover issues that were not adequately addressed in the original framework, and the team will need to decide what changes or additions need to be made. However, if the business need and requirements were on target, changes to the evaluation framework should not be necessary. If changes are required, all stakeholders should be made aware of the change as early as possible, and all those who worked directly on the original framework should have a hand in the modification. Failure to thoroughly communicate any changes before scoring will compromise the integrity and buy-in to the outcome.

The process for applying the evaluation criteria starts with assembling the evaluation team to score the responses to the RFP, and continues through publishing the outcome to stakeholders as appropriate. Once the winner, or group of finalists, has been selected the process moves on to drafting agreements.

Who should participate?

The evaluation process can be highly biased, and even the perception of bias can undermine efforts to achieve a broadly accepted solution. Just as with drafting of the business case, definition of requirements and development of the evaluation framework, scoring the responses needs to be an inclusive activity. Be sure to include all key stakeholders' representatives.

Bringing the scoring team together in a face-to-face session is the ideal approach; however, some proxy scoring may be necessary. The challenge is that scoring requires consistency in understanding and evaluating the criteria, and is a time consuming process.

Coordinating the evaluations is challenging, so it is important to balance broad representation with practical size. One approach to managing the process is to use webcasts and web-based polling technology to aggregate scores from multiple stakeholders. This allows interactive communication with the group, and automatic aggregation of the scores.

Team scoring

To assure broadest acceptance of the evaluation outcome, all team members must score each of the procurement options. However, it is not practical to have each member score all categories of criteria. Instead, have team members focus on their area of knowledge or expertise. Business representatives should score criteria such as Urgency and Alignment with Mission. IT scores Technology Readiness, and HR would be likely to score Cultural Readiness unless stakeholders are customers, in which case the sales group might better understand cultural issues.

The model should allow recording of each team member's score to allow review and discussion, and to support audit of questionable results. When it is not possible to bring people face-to-face, or to employ Web technology to run scoring sessions, the evaluation team leader must make provisions for asynchronous scoring. This can be done by sending the scoring model to remote members of the scoring team with detailed instructions, and asking the members to score according to the scoring guide for each factor. When team members cannot participate in a session, they should be asked to provide notes explaining each score, in case there are discrepancies in scoring that need to be reconciled.

Common definitions

To be effective, there needs to be a common understanding of the evaluation process and the evaluation criteria, down to the level of each factor and the meaning of each score in the scoring scale. These definitions must be established at the time the evaluation framework is created, and communicated to the team members at the time of scoring. One approach is to have the facilitators review terms, issues and scoring approach for each factor and validate that there is common understanding before scoring.

For example, in evaluating a knowledge management solution offering's capability with respect to imaging, the facilitator would read the requirement from the requirement definition document. It might read as follows: "ABC company has 350,000 standard report forms that need to be referenced as part of the audit process. Since the quantitative information is already in the database, the proposed knowledge management system need only reference the paper documents, allowing access to an electronic view when desired. The system will need to allow for image capture (scanning) and retrieval, both from the electronic record and from an advanced search capability that allows a minimum of three category selections (case number, date and name)." After confirming understanding of the requirement, the facilitator should review the scoring approach:

1 = Has no provision for imaging
2 = Is able to link to external imaging systems
3 = Has integrated basic imaging capability
4 = Has full linkages to sophisticated external imaging capability
5 = Has own, fully integrated imaging capability with ability to integrate enterprise taxonomy

At this point, the team is prepared to score the solutions after each bidder's capability is reviewed. It may be necessary for the facilitator to review the responses to the RFP with the team as part of the scoring process.

Reconciling differences

Even after careful review of each of the criteria and factors, there will be variations in the scores. The model should average the scores for each factor to minimize the effect of variation, excluding a value when a team member abstains from scoring rather than assigning an arbitrary value.

Generally, variations are insignificant. When there are wide variations, it is important to review the scores for the factor with the team members. Widely varying scores can be due to misunderstanding of terms, criteria or scoring convention, or bias caused by differing views or philosophy towards the investment. In those cases where scoring is done asynchronously by proxy, scoring notes should provide insight into the cause.

While some teams discard high and low scores to resolve discrepancies, it is a good idea to discuss extreme variations. Differing scores may indicate hidden issues that need to be addressed. Such discussions can lead to improving the proposed solution or resolve cultural or business process differences.

Exploring alternative views

Occasionally there will be a clear winner from the evaluation framework that scores highly with respect to each of the evaluation criteria. More frequently, options will have varying strengths. While the weighting of the primary criteria should point to a winner, it is important to review the winners by each category. Sorting the results by a specific factor may present results that differ from the overall score, prompting discussion among the scoring team, and if necessary, the business sponsors.

Reporting outcome

It is important to remember that the evaluation framework is a tool to support decision-making, and its output is not a binding decision. Once a consensus has been reached by the scoring team, the recommendation should be communicated in confidence to stakeholders for comment before drafting the agreement and entering into negotiations. The evaluation outcome will have varying impact on different stakeholders, so be sure that they are aware of the business issues, and the evaluation process, and have a chance to comment.

Remember that the evaluation outcome may not reflect the final decision, which is dependent on the ability to achieve a negotiated agreement.

17.8   Alternative approaches

Up to this point, we have described a robust evaluation process. It may be that some evaluations require less process integrity. For example, decisions among 'apples to apples' alternatives may eliminate cultural and other variables. However, decisions are rarely as simple as they seem.

Some of the cautions include the notion that cost is not a predictor of value. Seemingly low cost options may actually cost far more after wrestling with issues of quality, functionality or user bias against the low cost solution.

Also, pursuing easy targets may provide quick wins, but distract from critical, more strategic opportunities and solutions. Concerns over cost of evaluation should not compromise the integrity of the evaluation process.

Cycle evaluation

Some very complex projects may require a more segmented approach to evaluation. Detailed requirements gathering can be costly and time-consuming, so some organizations perform business justification and high-level decision-making early on in the selection process. This model provides for an initial round of evaluation to weed out competing approaches to the project. Once a top two or three options are selected, the company can invest in detailed requirements based upon the viable candidates. This affords greater confidence in the solution since the second evaluation reflects a greater degree of analysis and cost identification.

Financial review

What happens if responses to the RFP are at variance with the original specifications or cost estimates? Perhaps the originally envisioned solution is not technically feasible. Perhaps the solution is far more complex and costly. If no proposals are acceptable, or if worthwhile alternatives are proposed, the business case needs to be re-examined.

Parallel negotiations

If there is more than one potential alternative, you may decide not to make a selection and instead negotiate with multiple suppliers. Many companies have a policy of routinely conducting negotiations with the top two solutions providers. This reduces the risk of delay if negotiations stall or fall through with a single provider, and provides a viable alternative to either solution, increasing negotiations power.

You can reserve the right to make a selection from the best negotiated outcome, after terms for the agreements are defined. It may be necessary to re-apply the evaluation model if acceptable terms are achieved with more than one supplier.

Political environment

In some circumstances additional 'political' or 'soft' factors might come into play and affect a structured, analytical evaluation. This may be unavoidable in some circumstances but the contracts professional needs to ensure that their process and contributions to the process are rigorous and fair to ensure that any subsequent accusations of favoritism have no foundation. In highly political environments, consideration should be given to solutions like anonymized data to minimize the possibility of interference.

17.9 Factors for success

Using a clearly defined evaluation process eliminates much of the bias and contention around the selection of a supplier. However, to be successful, it is essential that there is agreement on the model, as well as a common understanding of requirements, process, terms and scoring.

Thorough research into the sourcing options is important to support accurate scoring.

Performance measurement

Adoption of performance measurement programs has been growing, especially since the enhancement of audit requirements and introduction of legislation such as Sarbanes Oxley. There should be a strong correlation among the business case, project requirements, the evaluation criteria and the ongoing performance measurement system. If the evaluation model has been complete and effective, it should become the foundation for ongoing performance measurement for the investment. Is it achieving its financial and functional objectives? Have the specific evaluation factors been realized, or have specific functions or overall capability fallen short of claims?

The evaluation framework is also a starting point for Due Diligence to validate information in the suppliers' proposals. Use the primary criteria and specific factors to develop a reference check questionnaire. The answers will inform issues in negotiation, provide a sound basis for risk analysis and management, and guide post-award contract management.

17.10 Summary

In summary, buy-in to the process is essential, from developing the evaluation model, to scoring the options. This can be achieved by leveraging communications channels to assure common understanding and acceptance of evaluation model. Be sure there is broad stakeholder representation throughout the evaluation process.

As discussed, you may want to keep your options open up to achievement of a negotiated agreement.

Finally, use the evaluation criteria as the basis for ongoing performance measurement to assure fulfillment of the original business case.

DEVELOPMENT PHASE

Contract and relationship types

Contract terms and conditions

Technology contract terms and conditions

Term linkages, managing cost and risk

Statement of Work and Service Level Agreement production

Drafting guidelines

CHAPTER 18

Contract and relationship types

18.1 Introduction

Business relationships take many forms. Before appropriate terms can be established, it is critical to determine the type of relationship that will best fit the capabilities and goals of the parties involved.

This chapter describes the major contractual relationship types, when they should be used and some of the primary issues, with advice on how to address them in the contract.

After reading this chapter you will be able to understand:
- The primary types of contracts in use for purchasing products and services.
- The key differences between solution and turnkey contracts.
- The challenges of outsourcing contracts.
- The risks inherent to these contracts.
- How contract terms can mitigate the risks in different contract and relationship types.

We will be looking at the major features of contracts for purchasing products and services and some of the typical areas of concern and discussion in those contracts. One of the biggest issues is who will set the base for the contract, creating the potential for the 'battle of the forms'.

18.2 The importance of relationships

With the dramatic increase in outsourcing since the late 1990s it is now commonplace for contracts to be five, ten or even twenty years in duration. It is entirely possible on long term contracts that items will come into scope in future years that will not have been contemplated or the technology even invented when the contract is signed.

While contracts should provide the structure and govern the trading relationship of the two parties who have entered into it, all contracts are created and managed by people. Regular governance and dialogue is key and a robust process for resolving any disputes will help to fix issues before they have a detrimental effect on how the parties see each other. Continuity of key personnel provides both parties with a level of assurance and is a critical success factor. Key personnel sections in contracts can be used to list the key roles, usually focused on seeking the customer's approval and providing a suitable alternative if the supplier wishes to change the person occupying such a position.

When constructing a contract it is essential that prior thought is given to how the parties will interact. The agreement could take the shape of a 'master and servant' relationship or be more collaborative. It depends on what products or services are being provided. If the contract penalizes the supplier heavily every time it fails to deliver then it is unlikely the supplier will risk using new technologies or processes, which stifles innovation. Conversely, if the contract does not incentivize the right behaviors, suppliers may lose focus and shift their attention to other, more profitable contracts. The nature of the contract and industry sector coupled with the impact of failure should be the sole factor dictating the approach to be taken.

Outsourcing has also seen a rise in multi-supplier subcontracting, where the customer has different suppliers providing different services, all of whom need to interact and work together. IT contracts commonly adopt this model, where you can have one supplier providing the IT hardware such as desktops and servers, another will be responsible for the networks and a different supplier will be the application developer. Frequently the suppliers in a multi-supplier model will be competitors and getting them to collaborate for the benefit of the customer can be a significant challenge. Customers should take care not to leave any gaps in responsibility between where the role of one supplier finishes and another starts. When something goes wrong the customer does not want to be in a position where the suppliers are all blaming each other and not fixing the problem. At the same time the customer should avoid overlapping responsibilities and liabilities as this can increase the cost or encourage a supplier to look for business elsewhere.

Larger, high-value contracts, particularly those with a public sector customer, can often seek fairly onerous rights on the supplier's own supply chain. Customers frequently want to approve subcontractors who provide a high percentage of the overall solution; they may want the ability to terminate a subcontractor for a change in control in its ownership or even reach through the prime contractor and take over the day-to-day running of the subcontractor. If such clauses are incorporated into contracts it is imperative that the contract deals with the consequences of what happens in the event that this clause comes into effect. Of course, such obligations will need to be incorporated into the contract between the prime contractor and subcontractor.

There are several critical success factors to a contract. Certainty of scope, service levels and payment terms are obvious candidates. However, an often overlooked area, where significant added value can be gained at no extra cost, is the importance of good relationships between the trading partners, as they are collaborating together to achieve a common goal.

18.3 Primary types of contracts used

Contracts assume great significance in business-to-business relationships. They are a means of assigning risks and responsibilities to the parties and provide a description of, and discipline to, the relationship. In the supply of services, the contract frequently represents the only tangible definition of what will be delivered and establishes important procedures for the delivery of services. Contracts also answer the questions 'who', 'what', 'when' and 'where', as well as 'what if'. 'What if' questions are raised while drafting or negotiating the contract to proactively identify risks, the associated consequences (positive or negative) if they occur and suitable mitigation plans.

In this chapter, we will examine a variety of contractual relationships for purchasing products and services that are common to businesses and focus on some of the key terms and areas for review related to each of them:

- Products and services contracts
- Solutions contracts
- Turnkey contracts
- Outsourcing

Responsibility and ownership for these contract and relationship types varies significantly between, and often within, companies, especially in areas like subcontracting, distribution or 'alliances'. However, organization matters far less than procedural clarity and accountability – and weaknesses in these are among the most frequent causes of failed relationships or lost opportunities.

18.4 Product and services contracts

Contracts provide considerable flexibility for the parties to agree to terms suitable for their purpose. However, it is important to understand the role of statutory terms that apply to the agreement, supplementary terms that cannot be excluded by agreement, construed terms that can be excluded only by express or specific language and any 'gap fillers' that will be applied in interpreting the agreement. In most jurisdictions, certain principles will apply unless specifically agreed otherwise. In many countries there are statutory terms.

In the US, for example, the Uniform Commercial Code (UCC) has been enacted. It covers the sales of goods (products in our terminology) and has had a significant influence on services contracts. In some cases, there are limits to what you can change. Like most countries, Germany has limits on what the parties can agree regarding product warranties; the EU has provisions on data protection. In international trade, the UNCISG will apply unless specifically excluded.

Contracts for the sale or purchase of products usually have simpler concerns than those for services, or for products and services together. Contract terms will differ depending on whether it is perceived as a one-time sale or an ongoing relationship. Major corporations often compete to impose their standard terms – in which case a 'battle of the forms' can ensue. This is discussed further in Chapter 21: *Terms linkages*.

In the case of ongoing product acquisition, the parties may agree to changes and modifications to the agreement, and there may be more flexibility over which party's standard form is used as the base for negotiation. Changes and modification to the agreement may expose parties to new risks and these risks need to be understood and managed in the negotiations. Ongoing agreements may take the form of a commitment contract or an 'as ordered' contract with each purchase order provided to the seller on the agreed-upon purchase order form. They may provide flexibility in the type or amount of goods shipped to accommodate future conditions.

Product and price

Do you need a contract? That varies by jurisdiction, but generally, a contract is recommended to limit potential disputes or manage the consequences of various risks that may materialize. In an agreement to purchase products, there are several essential terms to include:

- A clear and definite description of the type, quantity and quality of the goods
- A specified total price or a price given per unit or by weight or other measurement
- Whether or not prices can be adjusted (up or down) based on circumstances within or beyond the seller's control, such as general price movements, technology changes or the cost of raw materials.
- An indication of whether other costs, such as delivery charges, taxes and duties, especially when dealing internationally, will be charged separately from the price
- Letters of credit or other payment assurances
- The method and terms of payment and invoicing as well as reference to the currency and/or exchange rate to be used
- Rights or obligations to upgrade products over time, or as a result of new product introductions
- Delivery and title terms
- Terms associated with revenue recognition, such as ability to reject and acceptance

Delivery terms

Ensure that the delivery terms are clear and suit the business purpose:

- It must be clear whether delivery and acceptance occur together.
- Delivery terms should provide for a specific shipping date or a means of determining the date.
- Delivery terms may allow for delays related to circumstances beyond either party's control, or for other specified circumstances. For delay within the supplier's control, the contract should address whether there are consequences (e.g. penalties) for such delays. Your business objectives, and whether alternative sources of supply exist, will determine if a penalty is warranted to incentivize the supplier to minimize the possibilities of delays.
- When or where the title transfers from the seller to the buyer. Who has the risk of loss while the product is in transit?
- Who provides insurance coverage during transportation, and what happens if the product is damaged or lost?
- Ensure that packaging, production and transportation arrangements are completed in the time allowed in the contract.

Incoterms reliably address most of the issues here in international trade although care must be taken to use an Incoterm appropriate to the mode of transportation.

Warranty and performance issues

Understand and set boundaries around warranty and performance:

- Are the goods being sold 'as is' or does the sale include a warranty?
- Are the goods new, or qualified as new for tax purposes due to the inclusion of a limited percentage of recycled components or simply warranted to perform as new?
- Is the seller obliged to maintain or service the goods after delivery?
- Does the buyer have the right to return the goods? At whose expense?
- Can the buyer pass on the warranty to others? If so, what provisions must be incorporated into their agreement?
- What obligations are there to provide upgrades, improvements, new function or features during the warranty period? In addition, what are the customer's / end-user's obligations to accept / install these upgrades etc.?
- What is being specifically warranted (parts, labor) and to what level (e.g. specific performance standards, guaranteed availability levels, or simply 'merchantable quality')?
- What warranty has been implied? Take care over what is written or said about the product. Marketing can create implied warranties.
- What are the remedies available to the buyer; what types of warranty service are offered (e.g. on-site, consignment stock, mail-in)? What are the service hours and turnaround times being committed?
- In what circumstances is the warranty negated or voided?

- What about other warranties or representations? For example statements about business capabilities or honesty and validity of statements of risk, which link to issue of fundamental breach.
- Warranty period for the products supplied – in doing so there needs to be an awareness that different countries may have different minimum warranty periods governed by local law.

Intellectual property issues

Intellectual property (IP) includes inventions, patents, computer programs, product and service names, technical and business information, logos, artwork, geographic indication of source, industrial design, etc. Protecting intellectual property is very difficult and is often a sensitive topic. Losing control or infringement of their intellectual property can place a business at risk. Intellectual property litigation can be a very long and complex process with little certainty of the eventual outcome.

Why share intellectual property? You may want to develop a joint venture where it is necessary to share information to move forward. You may have a third party run a 'blind' test market for you to understand marketability; or you might be considering extending your business through the development of products for which royalties are received, or cross-licensing arrangements. Licensing permits a company to recover some of its development cost.

There are benefits and dangers in sharing intellectual property; it is important to ensure that the terms match the objective and realize the benefits while managing the risks. Some examples of intellectual property issues to consider are:

- Is the buyer prohibited from altering labels, packaging and other materials connected with the goods?
- If software or code is embedded in the product, are there restrictions on its replication, reverse engineering, etc.?
- Are there specific terms that the buyer is required to 'pass through' to their customers or other end users to protect your intellectual property?
- Does the product include another party's intellectual property or code (a supplier of licensor)? How must this be communicated and protected?
- Are there rules established to control advertising, marketing promotions etc to assure that your name and reputation will be protected?
- Are your company's name and trade secrets protected?
- Who owns newly developed intellectual property or how is ownership determined?
- What rights are granted to non-owner contributors?

It is important to understand that there are differences between patents, copyrights and trademarks and the protections offered to them under the laws of various governments.

Remedies and termination

As Robert Burns said, "The best laid plans of mice and men often go awry." Accordingly, significant attention should be devoted to the "what if" questions referred to earlier- that is, what will happen if specific risks materialize.

Termination and remedies are often discussed together since there are typically remedies invoked when terminating for cause. It is important to understand that remedies are also appropriate in other situations, such as if a product or service is not accepted. In general, remedies should be included in the contract for those situations that will have significant consequences if they occur and/or for situations that are likely to occur. Detailed guidance on remedies of this nature is beyond the scope of this book given the need to ensure they are tailored to the particular circumstances and legal jurisdiction. It is, however, important to consider remedies that provide practical support in encouraging performance and providing solutions to problems caused. These could include:

- Liquidated damages
- Re-work and re-testing within specified periods
- The ability to take over work
- The provision of additional resource in the form of people, products or services to mitigate any operational issues

Termination provisions are significant and warrant far more attention then they typically receive. It is important to think through every situation in which each party will have the right to terminate the contract. What are the implications for each party if that situation occurs and the contract is terminated? While it is important to consider termination scenarios in detail, it is also true that contracts are rarely actually terminated as the cost to both parties will be in most cases quite high. Termination is therefore usually the last resort. The practical relevance however can be higher than the actual probability of termination as it can be used as a negotiating chip or tool to exert pressure on the other party in cases where termination could be an option under the contract terms.

Termination provisions are often divided into termination for cause and termination for convenience. Termination for convenience essentially allows a party to terminate a contract simply because it no longer suits their purposes. Generally, the buyer will not allow the seller to terminate for convenience. Buyers generally insist that only they are allowed to terminate for convenience. The key negotiating points for these are the amount of notice provided if the buyer terminates for convenience and details around unwinding the contract. The key issue in most negotiations on termination clauses is the question of compensation. Regarding termination for convenience, the supplier is usually looking to recover all of their cost and as much actual or anticipated profit as possible. The buyer, on the other hand, is interested to protect their interest and minimize risk in cases of termination for default by the supplier.

With termination for cause, let us start with provisions that allow the seller to terminate. Generally, the buyer insists that these are as few as possible. *Force majeure* events that make normal performance impossible and termination for bankruptcy or non-payment may be allowed in the contract. If there are specific circumstances outside the seller's control that will make it impossible to perform, you will want to negotiate termination provisions to address those situations. Sellers in a standardized services environment may also have rights to terminate in end-of-life situations where support parts are no longer available or where software is not being kept up to date by the buyer with revision levels and bug fixes.

On the buyer's side, there often is a longer list of events that allow the buyer to terminate the contract. These revolve around failure by the supplier to perform, bankruptcy or change of control of the supplier, and other situations that comprise a material default from the perspective of the buyer. The buyer team will want to carefully consider all scenarios that will lead them to want to terminate the agreement and ensure that these are addressed in the contract.

The termination provisions should provide specific remedies to the buyer if terminating for cause. Generally, these include 'cover costs' – that is, compensating the buyer for any direct costs they may incur in contracting for completion of the services with an alternative supplier. The buyer may also wish to include liquidated damages or specific performance obligations, depending on their objectives. Some things to consider when drafting or negotiating these provisions include:

- What remedies are available to either party in the event that things go wrong? Are these remedies adequate and realistic in the context of the consequences and the alternatives available? This is a fundamental area of any agreement.
- What termination rights do the parties have and with what consequences or obligations? (Notice, cause, financial etc.)
- Are damage awards limited by individual incident or are they cumulative?

This complex area is explored in more detail in the next chapter: *Contract terms and conditions overview*

Customs clearance (import or export contracts)

Import/export contracts present their own challenges relating to local customs regulations. Customs clearance issues may be invisible to the customer if they contract with a local supplier who then manages all the importation issues. In projects where products are bought from an offshore company and local services from the same supplier's local entity, care needs to be taken to ensure that the two arrangements are seamless and there are not unexpected gaps in importation arrangements that the customer has to scramble to fill.

Some of the details to be worked out include:

- Which party is required to pay export or import duties, taxes and charges?
- Is the seller required to provide clearance documentation?
- Who is responsible for obtaining licenses or permits for exporting or importing the goods?

Again Incoterms is a useful tool to reliably address these issues.

18.5 Contracts for services

Service contracts can take many shapes and cover a multitude of items such as office cleaning, website support to consultancy services. A contract for the supply of services is required when engaging professional advice and guidance from a consultant or a labor force. Most suppliers will have their own terms and conditions; however, many sophisticated customers now have their own forms of contracts for services. Clearly, from a customer perspective, if you are managing numerous support contracts, it would be easier to have a portfolio of contracts that was as standard as possible. This would allow the contract managers to familiarize themselves with the agreement and avoid managing numerous suppliers each with difference terms and conditions.

These contracts can be relatively brief and should cover who is providing the services and their manager in the supplier organization. The scope of the services to be provided and the timescale in which they are required also needs to be included. It is important that the rates the supplier can charge are stated and how these charges come into effect (e.g. what constitutes a day when services are provided on a day rate). Termination, intellectual property rights (IPR) and limits of liability will also be referred to and the contract needs to include the requisite payment terms.

A contract for services may include products, in which case the same issues as previously discussed will arise. Some of the specific items to consider are discussed in greater detail below.

Scope of work to be performed

Who is responsible for defining and writing this key section of the contract? Will the buyer be providing the specifications for the work to be performed or the seller? Typically people who are not contract experts, such as technical managers, are the ones who write most scopes of work. This is an area of high risk as poor drafting causes many problems and disputes. They may override key terms or accept obligations inadvertently.

It is essential to be clear on the scope of work, particularly (for the seller) where the contract is fixed price, or (for the buyer) time and materials. For standardized services such as product maintenance or software updating there are typically published data sheets from the seller to describe deliverables and windows of service. For more customized professional services then a specific Statement of Work (SOW) will ensure that everything is quantified or qualified with milestones for when the major deliverables will be done. You may also want to specify the specific resources, skills needed, or process for things to be done. In professional services contracts it is usual to ask for personal profiles and case studies to demonstrate the individual's previous experience.

The contract should refer to both the project upon which the services will be provided and also the nature of the services the supplier will provide. It is important that the contract allows for change to the scope to be agreed and explain the process for introducing and managing change. If the supplier has quoted on a fixed price basis, it is essential that the scope is very clearly set out in the contract.

This subject is discussed further in Chapter 22: *Statement of Work and Service Level Agreement production.*

Development, design, installation and testing

Determine and specify how much control the buyer and seller have over engineering or development, design, installation and testing. Does the buyer have the right to request changes, to inspect, to direct the supplier's performance or outright reject it? Does the customer organization have dependencies and deliverables it must provide to enable the supplier to fulfill its obligations? In most contracts, the seller wants to retain control, unless the seller is being paid on an hourly basis, in which case it is not as significant. If the buyer exercises extensive control, it will affect topics such as acceptance testing, warranties and overall product liability.

Giving the buyer greater rights throughout development and delivery may generate cost risks; change management and control then becomes a key issue, but it may make their ability to reject the solution or claim non-compliance more difficult. The later in the project lifecycle a change is introduced the more it will cost and the greater impact it will have on timescales.

The contract needs to consider the use of third parties, such as subcontractors or teaming partners, in the performance of services or obligations. Does the seller have the right to use third parties; does the buyer have any right of veto; what are the possible performance impacts? Modern contracts are seeking powers for the customer to approve the appointment and termination of key subcontractors; some go as far as providing the customer the right to terminate if there is a change in control in the ownership of a key supplier. If the customer is seeking such powers, it is essential that the contract specifies what triggers this right. It would be uneconomical and introduce an unnecessary level of governance if the customer wanted the right to approve all suppliers. A more practical stance could apply to subcontractors who are providing a significant amount of the prime contractor's overall solution, e.g. more than 10 percent of the total contract value.

In construction and engineering contracts how will changes in any site conditions be handled? If this will involve delays or revised specifications, are methods for handling such change built into the contract?

Excusable delays and recoverable damages

As things may not go according to plan, the contract should make provision for excusable delays or recoverable damages for late delivery. Ensure that there are linkages between any damages recoverable under the contract and cause of delay. These terms can be used as positive or negative incentive. Consider what will be included under excusable delays.

Delays caused by buyer actions or inaction should excuse the seller from late performance. For example, if you do not provide a blueprint when scheduled, the contractor may not be able to build the product required on time. Their lateness is directly related to your actions.

Have a plan for the consequences of delay and by what procedures they will be handled and communicated.

It is not possible to predict every possible issue that will arise during the term of a contract. It is common for contracts to include a *force majeure* provision. *Force majeure* can be translated as a 'superior force' or 'act of God'. When incorporated into a contract it usually provides that if a party does not perform an obligation under the contract (for example, provision of services) for reasons outside that party's control (such as a natural disaster or the outbreak of war), the other party will not make that party liable for non-performance.

However, it is fundamental to understand there is no hard and fast rule about what constitutes *force majeure*. If a party is relying on a *force majeure* event to gain relief under a contract it will typically be for something fundamental. To prevent a completely unnecessary conversation, and more than likely a dispute, it is essential that the meaning of what constitutes a *force majeure* event is fully defined in the contract.

For example if work on a building site had to stop due to heavy snowfall that delayed progress by one week could the contractor claim *force majeure* as grounds for an extension of time? If it snowed in the UK in August then probably yes, but if it was in the middle of winter one suspects not. However, the contract would need to have 'exceptionally adverse weather conditions' as one of the *force majeure* events that provided relief. If the contract made no mention of this, then the parties would end up arguing the point, which could have a detrimental effect on their overall relationship.

Of course it is essential to document and monitor all milestones and deliverables, whether on time or delayed. The contract also needs to deal with what happens to any payments associated with milestones. Usually the payment is postponed until the milestone is successfully achieved; however this can be problematic if the customer has caused the reason for the milestone to be missed. Like all things in contracts, if this scenario is not discussed in the contract, the parties will have differing views if a delay caused by a customer occurs.

Limitation of liability

Buyers and sellers will have different views on liability. Striking a balance can be a challenge. Suppliers will take a view that risks should be shared, whereas the buyer would prefer the deal to be risk-free. Each has legitimate concerns and they need to be balanced with the degree of caution each should reasonably take. For example, sellers should be obligated not to misrepresent the capabilities of their service; it is not unreasonable to expect they should be penalized for dishonesty, lack of integrity or lack of care in understanding the buyer's needs.

On the other hand, the buyer also has some responsibility in this – they must analyze and describe their requirements sufficiently to enable a reasonable assessment of service suitability. They must also be honest and realistic about their business capabilities to absorb or handle the product or service. And they must recognize that if they wish to hold the supplier absolutely to their commitments, it is only reasonable for a similar expectation from the other side – and similar consequences if they fail.

One major issue here is the level of impact – for either side – if the deal goes wrong or performance does not meet expected standards. The consequences – and hence the risks – vary dramatically and are not necessarily directly related to the cost of the product.

Sellers performing services will wish to accept liability only for actions under their direct control and the liability should generally be limited to direct damages, no greater than the amount the buyer has paid for the performance of the contract. There are, however, certain instances where a supplier should entertain greater exposure where their failure to perform exposes the customer in areas like confidentiality or data protection. These need to be carefully considered and managed with insurance cover being an option for consideration.

The buyer may want to recover other forms of (consequential) loss and may want 'per incident' compensation. It is important to consider the likelihood of an event occurring and the scale of its impacts.

If the contract is too punitive or seeks a high limit of liability it is likely the supplier will not trial any innovation that could ultimately be of benefit to the customer for fear of a failure, which could have serious financial consequence on the supplier.

Suppliers should not be liable if any losses are due to the provision of false, misleading or incomplete information or documentation or due to the acts or omissions of any person other than the supplier. The contract should also state the aggregate liability, whether to the customer or any third party, of whatever nature, whether in contract, tort (a breach of duty not covered by a contract) or otherwise, of the supplier for any losses whatsoever and howsoever caused arising in any way connected with the project. The actual limit of liability should be clearly stated in the contract.

We need to consider the scale of impact. Limitation of liability is sometimes used as an incentive. It isn't. Try to focus on the areas that will increase the likelihood of success. Keep pushing the question – why is this so important? Can the issues be addressed through alternative approach?

Let's look at an example. Following the Bridgestone tire fiasco, Ford Motor Company decided to require all suppliers to accept unlimited liability provisions. Was this a reasonable approach? Are there better alternatives? What might suppliers do when faced by a situation like this?

What advice would you give management if your company wanted to pursue this type of approach?

Also it is important to remember that nothing in the contract can have the effect of restricting the supplier's liability in respect of any kind of loss, damage or liability that cannot or must not be excluded or limited under law.

This subject is discussed further in the next chapter: *Contract terms and conditions* overview

Milestones and method of payment

In a services contract it can be useful to set down milestones for payment, for example, upon contract signature, upon delivery of project plans, and after testing. When doing so it is essential that the milestone acceptance criteria are clear, unambiguous and objective. Suppliers should challenge wording such as 'to the reasonable satisfaction of the customer' and opt for drafting such as 'the milestone will have been met if there are less than two severity level 2 faults'.

Ideally, services should be based on an hourly or daily rate, but this is often difficult to agree, as customers will typically want a fixed price for cost certainty. Customers must appreciate that a fixed price contract means the price is only fixed in terms of the agreed scope that it is based on. If a fixed price was agreed to build a house and then the customer wanted to add another floor to the building this would be outside the original scope and the additional work would attract an additional charge. For a supplier to enter into a fixed price contract it would almost certainly include an allowance of risk and contingency; this could result in the customer paying more than it would have done in a time and materials engagement, which is low risk to the supplier. The role of the contract manager is key in fixed price arrangements. Customers must ensure that the channel for asking the supplier to undertake additional work is managed and governed so as to ensure that numerous departments in the customer organization are not requesting additional work outside the budget holder's knowledge.

In either product or service contracts, the method and timing of payments is of great importance. The seller is not the buyer's bank although some customers look to their suppliers either to effectively achieve zero cost financing or to bring in a third party finance house on preferential terms. In most projects, stage payments are important to cover costs already incurred and also to indicate commitment and good faith. Without stage payments the seller is at great risk. Any payment mechanism associated with the provision of services must be aligned to the contractual terms and conditions. It would be unfair on a long-term Public Private Partnership (3P) contract if the supplier has invested significant capital over a period of a number of months or even years, for the contract to be abandoned due to a *force majeure* event occurring before the supplier has had the opportunity to recover its investment.

There has been a rise in 'no win no fee' arrangements where the supplier does not charge for its services and only gets paid in the event of a successful outcome for the customer. This is common in the area of contractual claims. However, most customers think they are in an advantageous position when getting suppliers to agree to such arrangements, when the reality is the supplier may seek up to 50 percent of the recovered amount to pay for its time and the risk involved. It can be assumed that suppliers in this situation only take on such work if they felt that there was a good opportunity to succeed.

18.6 Solutions contracts

The drive for differentiation and value-add has caused many suppliers to accept greater performance responsibilities by aggregating products and services into 'solutions'. In part, this can also be an answer to growing pressure on high-risk terms.

Essentially a 'solution' implies a much higher standard than a 'package.' Solutions carry substantial responsibilities for performance, both interoperability of components, and suitability for the customer's (or end-users) intended use. Moving to selling solutions is something that many suppliers seek to do, as products become commodities. Buyers, who are often understandably cynical because of how sales departments misuse the term, often meet this with skepticism.

It is important to distinguish a true 'solution', which implies a readiness by the seller to stand behind the performance of their product and service package, versus simple 'bundling' where a seller is normally trying to mask pricing or charging and generally does not increase their performance commitments. In the case of bundling, the individual components typically retain their own performance standards and warranties – so there is no shift of risk.

'Solutions contracts' differ from other types of arrangements because the buyer is relying on the supplier's expertise to determine the package of products, services, engineering, design, and consulting necessary to solve a business issue or problem.

Examples of solutions arrangements include, but are not limited to the following:
• Systems or network integration and management
• Managing and optimizing customer resources, facilities or networks
• Implementation and operations – for example, marketing, billing, distribution or inventory management systems

This movement towards 'solutions' has spread from the IT sector into other industries, in part because it is seen as an effective way to reduce buyer risks, but also because it can substantially reduce their costs of managing multiple supplier relationships. For the suppliers, it is a means to differentiate and thereby avoid or delay 'commoditization' and the associated downward spiral on price and risk terms.

Issues in solutions contracts

In many other types of arrangements, the buyer specifies what types of products and services are needed. In solutions contracts the buyer may only specify the problem needing resolution and relies totally on the supplier for its resolution. The supplier must provide the complete specifications for the work to be done. A key issue here is that the supplier is representing that it has the technical know-how and expertise necessary to ensure performance. Assuming this to be true (and such claims should always be tested), things often go wrong because of the buyer's operational environment. Solutions contracts require much more effective 'teaming' and information flows between buyer and seller organizations; unfortunately, those charged with negotiating or drafting the agreement often lack detailed understanding of the business and technical requirements and capabilities.

The degree of risk in such arrangements depends in large part on the amount of customization that is required; it is in the interests of both parties to replicate previously successful 'solutions'.

However, for the buyer, this may fail to yield the performance or benefits they were seeking – especially if one of their drivers is some form of competitive advantage or differentiation.

A significant source of risk in such contracts is the dependency that frequently exists on the use of third party products or services. The need for accurate depiction of requirements, the negotiation of supporting contracts and the management of the ensuing relationships are all frequent areas for failure.

Are solutions the same as a 'turnkey' contract?

'Solutions' refers to a technical solution. The term does imply that once implemented it will work in the customer's environment and that it will provide the results for which the solution was developed. With solutions, a supplier may have the same risk of implied warranty of a fitness for a certain purpose as with turnkey projects. However, while 'turnkey contracts' refer to a project as a 'standalone project' (for example, a turnkey contract to build an airport), a 'solution contract' may just be the provision of a solution for a specific part within a project.

A solution can be the basis of a turnkey project. It can also be part of a turnkey contract. IT manufacturers have tended to use the term 'solution' to mean that the supplier provides the customer with a technical solution using the supplier's technology, which they will then integrate, deliver and install. Historically, the resulting contracts made little or no commitment to the interoperability of the component parts (e.g. hardware or software) and prices were based on the individual unit price lists – sometimes not even consolidated under a single invoice. The companies sold solutions, but delivered piece parts. Project management can be with the customer or a third party.

For a buyer, it is essential to understand what commitments are being made in terms of performance and interoperability. A true 'solutions' contract will establish clear liability on the supplier to ensure an effective solution; against this, the supplier must obviously be able to rely on accurate and timely information from the buyer about the business environment and conditions within which the solution will operate.

18.7 Outsourcing

The practice of outsourcing many functions or activities that had previously been performed internally by a company became very common in the 1990s, especially in the US and parts of Western Europe.

Unlike procuring a supplier or subcontractor for a specific project, outsourcing gives the day-to-day operational control of a function or service to a specialist supplier who will be responsible for the provision of that service for a number of years.

It is common for the staff of the customer who previously provided the service in-house to be transferred to become permanent employees of the outsourcing organization. In such circumstances the employment rights and benefits of each member of staff would also transfer across to the outsourcer. In the UK for example there is legislation in the form of the Transfer of Undertakings (Protection of Employment) Regulations 1981 (TUPE) to protect affected employees' rights. The regulations preserve employees' terms and conditions when a business or undertaking, or part of one, is transferred to a new employer. Any provision of any agreement (whether a contract of employment or not) is void so far as it would exclude or limit the rights granted under the TUPE Regulations.

Business process outsourcing (BPO) could mean that functions or departments such as Human Resources, Training, Help Desk and Accounts and Finance move to an external service provider. Building maintenance and facilities management is another common example. In the technology sector areas such as application development, operation and maintenance of systems and networks and help desks may be outsourced.

Many companies are refocusing their efforts on the areas where they have the greatest skills (their 'core competencies') and outsourcing other functions. Large organizations may simply acquire the needed areas of skill by purchasing other companies, particularly to support market or product development/diversification. Even areas like the development of new distribution programs (for example, through resellers or agents) are a form of outsourcing, since the alternative is to further develop in-house resources or capabilities. This is now translating into the mass market with branding such as Apple's 'Designed by Apple in California, Assembled in China'.

Outsourcing is transcending its traditional IT and data processing boundaries. The growth rate of business process outsourcing has outstripped that in the IT arena. There has been significant growth in such areas as logistics, human resources, building facilities management and back-office accounting services.

The concepts of outsourcing have been tested and proven in the IT arena and now are being widely adopted in non-IT areas – often by the same companies that have proven them in the IT arena. New suppliers, however, are stepping into the business process outsourcing arena and relatively low cost countries like India and the Philippines developing businesses that sell directly into the global marketplace.

There is starting to be a significant amount of standardization in specific service segments, such as data-centers, desktop, telecommunications and server management as these sectors become mature. Along with that standardization, specialist companies are emerging, pushing their expertise in areas like desktop. It also means many buyers have started to treat outsourcing as a commodity. Outsourcing contracts should focus on 'what' the deliverable or service should be and not 'how' the supplier achieves this goal. Wherever possible, suppliers should have the freedom to decide on how they achieve the outcome. This allows the supplier to leverage global assets and existing technologies, which should have a direct benefit to the customer in terms of lead times, reliability and overall cost. An example could be a call-center provider, where before outsourcing a customer would need to have its own dedicated call-center, premises and staff. An outsourcer may have a call-center that could serve numerous customers at the same time, bringing considerable benefits and economies of scale.

There are obvious areas such as security, disaster recover and business continuity management where the customer will want to mandate certain approaches and methodologies, especially in multi-supplier environments. However, by constraining the supplier's solution the customer should expect to pay more for such areas of service.

Industry consolidation has continued and new providers keep entering the market. Traditional product suppliers transform to become providers of managed services. Countries that were originally noted as being the source of low cost labor are now generating major outsourcing providers who compete with the early industry giants.

However, offshore suppliers raise a host of control and communication issues that can only partly be addressed through the contract. Many buyers have decided that, rather than confront these directly, they will use more established suppliers, but insist that they gain the price advantages of lower labor costs, thereby forcing all major suppliers to develop overseas subsidiaries or alliances where appropriate work can be undertaken (e.g. software development, claim processing, call-centers).

Another trend in outsourcing has been the increase in multi-supplier models, where the customer could outsource several functions to a number of different suppliers. It is key for customers, when adopting such an approach, to ensure there are no gaps or overlaps in the scope of what each of the providers is delivering.

Standardization helps drive strong price competition and higher quality service levels. This makes outsourcing a more affordable approach even for small and medium size companies. Major suppliers such as IBM, HP and CSC remain essential for the 'mega-deal', especially in government and in industries that are restructuring, such as telecommunications, utilities and banking. In such deals, only those with significant funds and a wide risk portfolio can absorb the costs of bidding and the risks associated with performance.

Why do companies outsource?

A company must first understand its reason for outsourcing. Is it just a financial driver or is the company seeking more? Is it to manage technology transformation, or to achieve much broader business or even industry-affecting transformation? Is it to move a problem area out (explicitly or covertly) so that someone else has the problem to fix? Once a company understands its objectives, it is in a much better position to choose a partner and, critically, to specify the key benefits it is seeking. It is important that a company's goals and culture are compatible with the capabilities and culture of the company with which it is forming a long-term relationship. The right partner should be selected based on complex goals.

When a decision is made to outsource, procurement departments may rush (or be pushed) to a Request For Proposal (RFP) that senior stakeholders may demand (who are keen for progress after making the strategic decision), as opposed to creating an environment that will lead to success.

From the perspective of the purchaser, the critical success factors for outsourcing are:
- Knowing the resources they are using and their cost and performance before signing a deal
- Measurement of the outsourcer in cost, performance and business contribution
- Determining how to add value to the outsourcing process
- Knowing the strategic direction they will be taking and building incentives for the outsourcer to follow the strategic direction,
- Establishing ongoing performance benchmarks
- Building in contractual flexibility

What should be outsourced?

Outsourcing has existed in some forms for many years. For example, corporations have used service providers in areas like catering, security and cleaning; these are important but in no sense 'mission critical' activities. The real shift began only in the 1980s when companies began to look at high risk-high investment areas of real strategic importance and recognized that outsourcing could offer improvements and address issues of affordability. IT was the lead area in global outsourcing – traditionally companies found the return on investment on IT expenditure disappointing, there were concerns about the levels of resource and expenditure required and many companies felt that IT was an area best left to global experts.

In principle, outsourcing should occur any time that the financial and strategic advantages outweigh the disadvantages. However, it is rarely simple to assess or measure the overall advantages and disadvantages. The costs and benefits are often hidden until after the decision has been made.

Changing business conditions can rapidly alter the rationale or economics. For example, in 1998 – 2000 many corporations moved to offshore application development, in part because of potential cost reductions, but primarily because of the dramatic shortages of skilled local staff. By the end of 2001, with the collapse of the internet 'bubble' and the threats of international terrorism, the environment looked very different and companies faced political and labor backlashes for their 'unpatriotic' attitude in giving work and jobs to companies overseas. (Incidentally at this stage many failed to achieve the expected cost benefits either and found they were having real difficulties in managing their offshore relationships). In areas like outsourcing, inter-company benchmarking and open discussion with other (non-competitive) organizations can be critical to success and a well-informed decision.

With increased experience, the offshore trend has stabilized and continues to grow. Contract development and management remain critical competencies – and many companies now turn to third party experts for assistance.

The advantages an outsourcer may bring are:
- Opportunities to leverage scale
- Opportunities to leverage capabilities
- Opportunities to reduce risks / manage complex relationships
- Source of investment
- Source of ideas
- Source of energy

These benefits, theoretically, result in improved performance and greater vision at a reduced or essentially similar cost. The disadvantages that some have experienced in practice are legendary:
- Loss of control – for example, of IT direction
- Increased costs
- Lack of flexibility in addressing change in the business
- Dissatisfied customers
- Extensive disputes and lengthy resolution processes
- Inadequate change mechanisms, including transition rules
- Need to adjust to regulatory changes
- Loss of data and in-house skills (limiting options for an alternative approach),
- Lack of suitable remedy in the event of failure

While a well-drafted contract, effective negotiation and committed contract management cannot eliminate the opportunities for failure, they can certainly reduce its consequences and assist in the likelihood of success.

Outsourcing contracts introduce a range of specific terms and issues. These include topics or areas such as:

- Labor laws
- Intellectual property and data ownership
- Procedural and other company 'know-how'
- Change management – long term
- Transition – cooperation will be required between competitors
- Governance, escalation procedures
- Dispute management and resolution
- Management and use of third parties / subcontractors
- Data protection / privacy laws
- Security, maintenance of records
- Compliance with government regulations in all countries of operation

The 'mega deal'

Some of the contracts customers are seeking are too big even for giant global corporations. This could be due to the diverse nature of services, the capital requirement or even the need to apportion and manage risk appropriately.

Customers may seek expressions of interest from consortia where two large companies (the Tier One providers) would form a Joint Venture company, potentially incorporating several smaller, specialist companies (the Tier Two providers). There is usually a lead Tier One provider and the contract with the customer will require either provider to take over the running and responsibility of the contract on its own if the other provider fails.

18.8 Turnkey contracts

The term 'turnkey' in business terminology means that the buyer needs only to turn the 'key' to the system and it will work. Integral parts of a contract to buy a turnkey system of any type are the terms and conditions for the acceptance of the system and when/how payments will be made. The contract must define what it means for the system to work, and what is expected of the system, so that the buyer can accept the system and the supplier can be paid/recognize revenue. Defining acceptance and associated milestones is a critical task for such contracts.

A law dictionary defines 'turnkey' as: "A term used to designate those contracts in which the contractor agrees to complete work of building and installation to point of readiness for use. In the oil industry it means a contract where the driller of an oil well undertakes to provide everything and does all work required to complete the well, place it on production and turn it over ready to turn the key and start oil running into tanks. "

For IT companies, a turnkey project might include network planning and design, detailed engineering, procurement of equipment and software, installation, network integration and network interfacing, project management, the provision of civil engineering (if required), testing of the network and handing over of the network to the owner/customer 'ready for commercial use'. The network as delivered must meet the specifications and parameters as described in the contract.

Although the term is widely used, there is rarely a 100 percent turnkey contract. In most cases, suppliers are also asked to provide some work outside the turnkey scope that creates additional interdependencies and interfaces, or the buyer provides some of the scope on which the supplier continues to build.

Why would a buyer want a turnkey contract?

A primary attraction of the turnkey contract for the buyer is the ability of the customer to consolidate and transfer risk from itself onto the supplier. The relative infrequency with which such major projects are undertaken, and the inexperience of the buyer's staff, means that in theory the supplier should be able to perform the project at lower cost and with reduced chance of failure. Under the turnkey approach, many of the major management responsibilities of the customer are transferred to the turnkey contractor.

A turnkey contract involves the activities of design, fabrication, installation, construction and testing of the systems components; project management for the systems components; program and systems integration management; design oversight services for any civil engineering, inclusive of the design management and design support during construction. All these are effectively transferred to the turnkey contractor, who will have responsibility for managing those activities and ensuring that budgeting, scheduling and system performance specifications are met.

In addition to relieving the customer of a number of management-related risks and responsibilities, the turnkey contract provides the customer with single point responsibility. Increase in costs, errors or misjudgments in design, coordination and management of subcontractors etc. are entirely at the risk of the turnkey contractor.

What are the legal implications of the term 'turnkey'?

The use of the term 'turnkey' under English law implies that the supplier gives a warranty that the deliverable is fit for the purpose it is intended to be used for by the owner. It may mean that interfacing with third party networks is a responsibility of the supplier, even if it is not stipulated in the scope of work as a supplier deliverable. The reason for this is that the system to be delivered will not work properly without those interfaces and the owner cannot use it for the intended purpose. Case law in the US indicates that the term 'turnkey' creates a warranty that the system will work as an integrated whole, with consequences for the supplier if it does not.

In civil code countries the supplier may also end up with responsibilities that go beyond the Scope of Work (SOW) as defined, to the extent that they will be expected to deliver a working system that meets the expectations of the customer. The consequence for the supplier is that they (not the customer) have to ensure clear and exclusive definitions for system acceptance and performance requirements.

Issues of importance in turnkey contracts

Scope of Work (SOW)

It is essential in turnkey contracts that the SOW and the responsibilities of both parties are described in detail. Since the seller is typically deemed to be the more competent party, it is especially important in the event of litigation that buyer responsibilities are clearly stated; lack of clarity will rebound on the seller. However, as always, this may be affected by whoever 'owns the paper'. Deliverables that are the responsibility of the customer should be listed (e.g. site selection, site acquisition etc.) The agreement should specify the consequences of either party not meeting deadlines for deliverables, especially if delay has economic impact on one party that far outweighs the effects on the other party.

The SOW should clearly list the assumptions on which the system planning/design and the deliverables are based (including the time schedules). In the event that one or more assumptions turn out to be false the agreement should specify the consequences (price adjustment, adjustment of time schedules, etc.).

Quite often the system design and planning are not yet finalized at the time of closing. It even happens that detailed site surveys have not been carried out yet. The system design, the quantity of equipment to be installed and the deliverables and services described and quantified in the SOW are only estimates. If that is the case, the contract should stipulate this and it should contain an objective procedure for determining the final system design and deliverables. The absence of such a procedure may result in an increased risk for the supplier.

System design

If the supplier in a turnkey contract has system design responsibility, it should ensure that even in the design review process the responsibility for the system design stays with the supplier. In the event of a dispute between the owner and the supplier on design issues, the supplier's opinion should prevail, as it will be held responsible in the end for the quality and performance of the system to be delivered.

Change management process

Change requests from the owner/customer that include a request to change the design may lead to a shifting of design responsibility (liability) from the supplier to the owner/customer.

The agreement should specify how changes will be agreed between the supplier and the owner and what the consequences may be, evaluated using risk assessment methodology. One aspect of change management is to be aware of what rules have been established in the main agreement, particularly when it comes to precedence of the documents. While many agreements include the ability to create changes to include additional and new work, whether such an additional document can overwrite the terms and conditions of the original must be clear. If the terms and conditions of the original agreement do not match the new work scope, the main agreement will have to be changed as well as creating the additional scope.

Compensation

There are three basic compensation schemes that are used for design-build contracts and are appropriate for a 'turnkey' contract: Cost-plus-fixed-fee, Firm Fixed Price, and Cost-plus-fixed-fee/lump-sum. Critical timing concerns can be accommodated by the addition of bonus terms for meeting or exceeding time frames. These are discussed in more detail in Chapter 21: *Term linkages: managing cost and risk.*

18.9 Summary

In this chapter, we have discussed contracts where something is being supplied or acquired and the key issues and challenges associated with them. With any contract, it is critical that each party identifies its risks and that those risks are appropriately considered and addressed in choosing the contract and relationship types and negotiations of the terms.

If two contracting parties spend sufficient time in shaping the deal and establishing the most appropriate relationship and governance structure the project is likely to perform better than adopting a relationship framework that is either too harsh and punitive of failure or the opposite and too favorable to the supplier with little or no incentive to perform.

CHAPTER 19

Contract terms and conditions overview

19.1 Overview

This chapter explains the basic contractual terms that should be addressed in all types of procurement contracts as well as specific terms that should be   considered in more detail depending on the type of procurement. This chapter provides a practical overview of contract terms and Chapter 20: *Technology contract terms and conditions* provides complementary detail. It is, of course, important to recognize that the legal fabric changes through new law, court decisions and individual jurisdictions; where would a book for contracts professionals be without a good liability disclaimer!

19.2 Start right

It is essential to understand the legal aspects of the formation of a valid contract, as otherwise the contracts may be void with no legal validity from the beginning or voidable even though in the past the customer and supplier have purchased and sold goods without any legal problems. This basic understanding is particularly important as commercial contracts are usually of high contract value for both customer and supplier.

Invalid and unenforceable contracts cannot be enforced and confer no rights on either customer or supplier. Legality and enforceability issues go to the root of the formation of a contract, when a matter goes before a court of law for implementing contract terms – such as payment to the supplier or delay to buyer due to non-performance by the supplier.

It is recommended that every company should arrange for its contracts professionals to undergo relevant legal training by local commercial/business lawyers familiar with the customer's business. If the company has a well established procurement department, there should be a complete legal audit of the department and regular assessment of the legal compliance of all procurement contracts. This will help the company to be legally safe before the court of law in the event of contract disputes initiated by the supplier. In particular, the company's lawyer will be able to get the best legal remedy for the customer's company from the court because of proper legal compliance and audit.

By understanding some of the following defenses the contracts professional will be aware of what could go wrong if the contract is void or voidable because of ignorance of the legal principles behind valid contracts.

- That the defendant (supplier) did not enter into the agreement.
- A or B was not the agent of the defendant (supplier) (if alleged by the plaintiff/customer).
- The plaintiff has not performed the following conditions—(Conditions).
- The defendant did not—(alleged acts of part performance).
- The agreement is uncertain in the following respects—(State them).
- The plaintiff has been guilty of delay.
- The plaintiff has been guilty of fraud (or misrepresentation).
- The agreement was entered into by mistake.
- The agreement was rescinded under Conditions of Sale, No. …….. (or by mutual agreement).

19.3   Purchase contracts and why they matter

Purchase contracts contain basic parts: defining what you want to buy, a price for the purchase, and how you determine you have received what you have ordered. It should be simple, but if you look behind pages and pages of 'boilerplate', you will often find these basics are not there, or are unclear.

Ensure that these critical aspects are clearly defined in your contract. That is, a person with no knowledge of the transaction should be able to pick up the contract, read it, and understand those basic parts.

If there are cross-border transactions, procurement personnel will need some basic understanding of the contract laws of countries with which the company regularly does business. The rules by which many contracts are governed are provided in specialized commercial laws that deal with particular subjects. Most countries, for example, have laws that deal directly with sale of goods, lease transactions and trade practices. For example, most US states have adopted Article 2 of the Uniform Commercial Code (UCC), which regulates contracts for the sale of goods. There are also many Acts around the world that deal with specific types of transactions and businesses. For example, the UK has the Sale of Goods Act 1979, which governs the contracts between suppliers and buyers. Contracts in India are governed by legislation such as Indian Contract Act, 1872, and Sale of Goods Act, 1930.

19.4 Areas that the contract should address

The elements included in a contract for the provision of goods or services depend on what is being procured, the associated risks, and the contract value. The larger the amount of money, the larger the business exposure; but risk is directly related to the impact of the service or product being supplied and purchased. For example, security and confidentiality become more important when the supplier is processing or handling the customer's internal data and end-customer data, if this is different.

The basic and fundamental contracting terms/concepts in contracts depend, to a certain degree, on the legal jurisdiction. They commonly include:
- Proposal/offer
- Promise
- Promisor/offeror
- Promisee/offeree
- Consideration (in common law countries)
- Competency of parties
- Lawful object
- Valid contract
- Void contract
- Voidable contract
- Communication of proposals
- Acceptance of proposals
- Revocation of proposals

Proposal or offer: When one person signifies to another their willingness to do or to abstain from doing something, with a view to obtaining the assent of the other to such act or abstinence, they are said to make a proposal or offer. A proposal, when accepted, becomes a promise. The person making the proposal is called the 'promisor', and the person accepting the proposal is called 'promisee'. A proposal/offer cannot take effect so as to create a binding contract, unless and until it has been brought to the knowledge of the person to whom it is made.

Communication of an offer or proposal: The communication of a proposal is complete when it comes to the knowledge of the person to whom it is made.

Acceptance of the proposal: When the person to whom the proposal is made signifies their assent to it, the proposal is said to be accepted. When a proposal is accepted it becomes a promise.

Communication of acceptance: The communication of an acceptance is complete when the promisee's acceptance comes to the knowledge of the promisor or should reasonably be expected to come to the promissor's knowledge. Note that an offer can only be accepted by the offeree- that is, the person to whom the offer is made.

Revocation of proposals and acceptance: The laws surrounding revoking proposals and acceptance vary across jurisdictions and also depend upon the specifics of how a proposal was sought and made in the first place. In many countries, in the absence of any specific agreement between the parties, a proposal may be revoked at any time before the communication of its acceptance is completed by the proposer, but not afterwards. An acceptance may be revoked at any time before the communication of the acceptance is completed by the acceptor, but not afterwards.

Agreement: Agreement is reached when offer and acceptance match, sometimes referred to as a 'meeting of minds'. An agreement enforceable by law is a contract. A contract is unenforceable if one or more of the conditions below is not met.

- Competency and capacity of the parties to enter into contract (parties should be of legal age – that is, not a minor, of sound mind, should not be disqualified by law, and should have the authority or be reasonably expected to have the authority to enter into a contract)
- Free consent of parties (there should not be any elements of coercion, undue influence, fraud, misrepresentation, mistake between parties)
- Lawfulness of consideration
- Lawfulness of object
- The contract should not be expressly declared to be void

Consideration: A consideration is made by the offeree in return for the offerer executing their promise (which might be doing something or refraining from doing something). The consideration must have some value that can be quantified objectively, usually money. In common law countries the contract is unenforceable if there is no consideration, because there is no reciprocity of benefits: one party has given nothing in return for what he or she has received. Note that inadequate consideration is not grounds for voiding the contract. In civil law countries consideration is not an essential element in forming a contract.

Lawfulness of object: The consideration or object of an agreement is lawful, unless it is forbidden by law or is of such a nature that if permitted, it would defeat the provisions of any law, or is fraudulent or involves or implies injury to the fraudulent property of another or the court regards it as immoral or opposed to public policy. In each of these cases the consideration or object of an agreement is said to be unlawful.

Changes in terms of a concluded contract: No variation in the terms of a concluded contract can be made without the consent of both the parties. While granting extensions or making any other variation, the consent of the supplier must be taken. While extensions are to be granted on an application of the supplier, the letter and spirit of the application should be kept in view in fixing a time for delivery.

Discharge of contracts: A contract is discharged or the parties are normally freed from the obligation of a contract by due performance of the terms of the contract. A contract may also be discharged:

- By mutual agreement. If neither party has performed the contract, no consideration is required for the release. If a party has performed a part of the contract and has undergone expenses in arranging to fulfill the contract it is necessary for the parties to agree to a reasonable value of the work done as consideration for the value.
- By breach. In case a party to a contract breaks some stipulation in the contract which goes to the root of the transaction, or destroys the foundation of the contract or prevents substantial performance of the contract, it discharges the innocent party to proceed further with the performance and entitles them to a right of action for damages and to enforce the remedies for such breach as provided in the contract itself. A breach of contract may, however, be waived.
- By refusal of a party to perform. On a promisor's refusal to perform the contract even before performance is due, the promisee may at their option treat the refusal as an immediate breach, putting an end to the contract for the future. In such a case the promisee has a right of immediate action for damages.
- In a contract where there are reciprocal promises. If one party to the contract prevents the other party from performing the contract, the contract may be put to an end by the party that was prevented from performing and the contract is thereby discharged.

19.5 Types of contract and some issues

Generally speaking, contracts for the supply of products and/or services can be subdivided into three basic categories:
- Purchases
- Leases
- Services

Procurement contracts are contracts of sale where an offer to buy or sell goods is made by acceptance of the offer and where the supplier transfers, or agrees to transfer, the property in goods to the buyer, for a money consideration called the price. The definition of the term 'goods' may vary according to the law enacted for the territory. For example in India 'goods' as defined under the Sale of Goods Act, 1930, means every kind of moveable property other than actionable claims and money; and includes stock and shares, growing crops, grass, and things attached to or forming part of the land, which are agreed to be severed before sale or under the contract of sale.

Goods may be specific, unascertained or future goods. 'Specific goods' means goods identified and agreed upon at the time a contract of sale is made. 'Future goods' means goods to be manufactured or produced or acquired by the supplier after the making of the contract of sale.

The goods are said to be in a 'deliverable state' when they are in such state that the buyer would be bound to take delivery of them under the contract. The 'delivery' means voluntary transfer of possession from one person to another.

The 'documents of title' are regarded in law as equal to goods for the purpose of transfer of property in the goods. They can be transferred from one person to another in the same way as goods. The documents of title of goods are used in the ordinary course of business as proof of possession or control of goods, or authorizing or purporting to authorize, either by endorsement or by delivery, the possessor of the documents to transfer or receive the goods represented in the documents.

Note that the contracts for the sale of goods are not the same as contracts for work and materials for intangible goods such as software. The distinguishing factor being the principle transferring property. In a purchase, you are acquiring rights to the item, essentially transferring title of that item from someone else to you. Software purchases are a special case: You are actually purchasing a lease to use the software, but rarely have any direct rights to the underlying software. This can be an important distinction, depending on how you intend to use the software. Computer hardware purchases can have many restrictions on use and relocation even with a purchase (e.g., export control laws restrict your ability to resell or transport certain items outside the US). IT contracts usually require coordination with your technical department to confirm specifications and requirements – and technology changes so quickly that specifications can age rapidly and be out of date. So, liaison with your IT counterparts will be valuable.

19.6 Separating business and legal terms

It is important point to organize your review and negotiation time and develop a good working relationship with your corporate law, business and technology departments. Depending on your procedures, few terms in a contract merit legal review once the master/ standard contract (containing your approved legal terms) is established.

For example, the purchase price for the goods, provided the price is reasonable and not subject to special conditions or further bids, generally does not directly interest the legal department. That is, no legal issues generally arise concerning whether you pay $10,000 for a piece of software or $10,599. Similarly, whether you have a 5 percent cap on annual maintenance or a 6 percent cap is a business term and not a legal term (how the cap is described in the contract is a different matter).

By separating the terms of legal interest from those with purely financial or operational significance, you should be able to speed up your negotiations by running parallel processes:
- Legal reviews for any changed legal terms
- Contracts professional reviews for all other terms

Contracts professionals play a key role in ensuring that these two strands are synchronized so that any accommodation in one area is factored into decision making appropriately in the wider context, say the cost of insuring an onerous legal term.

Standard forms of contracts should be used wherever possible and the terms of contract must be precise, definite and without any ambiguities. Once you have a standard contract (Master Agreement) in place, you will spend most of your time working with your business and technology partners to clearly identify the purchase needs and the business and technical parameters that should be negotiated into the contract on behalf of your company. A collaborative and proactive relationship with the three parties; legal, business and operations will help to shorten your negotiation cycles and keep delays to a minimum.

Be aware that a 'one size fits all' approach will not work. You will need to have Standard Forms Contracts for your major areas of acquisition; however, it is unlikely that terms which are appropriate to obtain oil leases or machine parts for example will serve to purchase technology. It may be necessary to work from a supplier's standard agreement to address more specialized purchases outside of your core business knowledge. This can be addressed by working with your legal and business teams to identify core requirements and concerns and build those in or carve them out of the supplier's standard offering.

19.7 Key elements in contracts

This section addresses the core of commercial contracts, the focus of risk management and the most frequently negotiated terms identified in IACCM's global surveys. Although some of these elements are legal in nature, they affect the business relationship with your supplier and can greatly limit your company's exposure in unforeseen circumstances.

Definitions

Any word or phrase that has a particular meaning in the context of the contract (sometimes referred to as a 'term of art') should be defined. Here are some general terms that usually need clear definitions:

- Customer (are you extending the contract to all of your subsidiaries?)
- Confidential information (what is included and excluded)
- Parties (should be defined to be clear if you mean both supplier and customer or others)
- Precedence (if you have schedules, attachments or other references, you need to define the order of precedence in case there are any conflicts (generally, the order is the Master Agreement, schedules, attachments, supplier's response to the Request for Proposals (RFP), the RFP, then supplier's literature as supplied – please adjust for your particular contract)
- Price (to define what you owe)
- Program, product, software (are these all the same, or are there differences that you need to define?)
- Schedule (if you're going to put purchase terms in a schedule, you should define 'schedule')
- Subsidiaries/affiliates (when either company changes you know who is included in the contract)
- Supplier (who is the supplier; does it include the supplier's subsidiaries?)
- Term and termination (how long the contract is in force, how it can end and what happens when it ends)

An in-depth understanding of your contract will determine which terms need further consideration.

Limitations of liability

Liabilities are an important part of managing business risk between partners. Often, both parties will mutually exclude or limit certain liabilities to reduce unintended risk. Liability clauses in contracts can state the maximum damages either party is responsible for breaches of the contract.

It is important that the contract reflects the relative risk of damage for a breach. For example, a part may be relatively inexpensive but its failure can result in much larger damages (e.g., car tires). Suppliers will try to limit their liability in such circumstances, but this should be avoided (the supplier should have reasonable levels of insurance protection). The outcome of negotiations on limitation of liabilities may affect the purchase price of a product. Liquidated damages are often used to assess reasonable damages in circumstances where calculating the exact damage may be difficult after-the-fact, and are often used to compensate for late deliveries.

Warranty

A detailed warranty clause should be incorporated in every contract, requiring the supplier to, without charge, repair or rectify defective goods or to replace such goods with similar goods free from defect. Any goods repaired or replaced by the supplier are normally delivered at the customer's premises without costs to the customer.

Warranty terms that are incomplete or not fully understood invite disputes between the customer and the supplier. For example, cases have been observed where the installation of the equipment is included in the scope of contracts but the standard warranty clause of '15 months from the date of shipment/dispatch or 12 months from the date of delivery, whichever is earlier' is also incorporated in the contract. If there is a delay in installation of the equipment, the warranty expires even before the installation of the equipment or sometimes only a very short period of warranty is available. In installation/commissioning contracts, it is best practice to trigger the warranty period from the date of acceptance.

Some suppliers offer no warranties at all and paid maintenance starts upon delivery. Customers need to assess whether this is appropriate for expensive, mission-critical purchases, especially of software or IT products as it weakens the ability to reject once the maintenance starts. This should be a practical consideration rather than a philosophical or belief system debate. Consideration also needs to be given the any minimum warranty period required by local law.

Customers and suppliers may need to reach agreement in relation to goods accepted by the customer that prove to be deficient during the warranty period. In most circumstances both parties should accept the solution for the supplier to repair or replace. There will, however, be some circumstances where the fault cannot be resolved. In anticipating this scenario, the parties need to consider the degree of likelihood, whether this can be decreased or mitigated by the acceptance regime or whether some further contractual remedy is necessary.

Software is an intangible product – you can't directly inspect it or its performance; so software purchases require additional scrutiny. Where custom software developed for your environment is sold, the supplier should warrant its right to license (that it has clear title to the software), that the customer has the right to use the software unencumbered, that it will conform to specified requirements or, if none, to advertised/represented attributes, that it won't adversely affect the customer's systems (compatibility), and that you know what the supplier will do if their software is non-conforming. The standard right should be to have an unlimited ability to use the software in the last licensed format to allow for access to historical data. Where off-the-shelf software is sold you will not receive warranties that are so robust but the software should be warranted to substantially conform to its published specifications. Be aware that no software will be warranted to operate uninterrupted or error free.

Suppliers often include third party or open-source software within their own software. You need to ensure that the supplier warrants all the software on the same basis and they have the right to incorporate such software. Open-source software is frequently not warranted and will require the customer to understand the nature of the license and its application to the customer's environment.

The Warranty clause may further outline standard of work, fitness for purpose and freedom from errors and defects. These are fertile grounds for disagreement between customer and supplier and subsequent dispute if agreed as the terminology is so wide that it can be interpreted in different ways. A practical, rather than an ideologically driven approach will yield the most appropriate results. It should, however, be noted that software will not be warranted as error free given its nature but bug fixes should be provided under warranty services and in post warranty support agreements.

Intellectual Property Rights

Where custom deliverables or software are sold then it may be appropriate for the Intellectual Property clause in the contract to state that:

- The ownership of all copyrights, trademarks, patents and other proprietary rights in any and all creative works, research data and reports, writings, sound recordings, pictorial reproductions, drawings, film and video recordings, and other graphical representations, and work of any similar nature (whether or not eligible for copyright, trademark, or patent protection) arising as a result of the supplier performing hereunder (collectively known as 'Works') shall vest with the customer.
- The supplier expressly agrees hereunder that this Agreement is a 'work for hire' contract and that neither the supplier nor its employees/ agents shall have any control or ownership in any form or manner whatsoever in the title, copyright or other proprietary rights to the Works. All such title and rights shall vest in customer, free of any encumbrances, licenses, conditions or qualification.
- The supplier and each of its employee/agent performing hereunder hereby agree that they irrevocably assign to the customer all their rights in any Works developed by them in the course of performance under the agreement with the customer and during the term of the agreement with the customer. The supplier agrees that they will assist the customer or its assigns, in securing any protection that the customer deems fit, including registration as copyright, trademark and patent, for such Works in [country] or any other country, at the cost of the customer.
- The supplier hereby declares that, the agreement with the customer shall be sufficient to show their irrevocable intent to assign their rights in the Works to the customer and copies of the agreement shall be sufficient to declare to any one such intent. The supplier hereby waives any right to be stated as the author or any other rights flowing from the Berne Convention. The customer may make any changes, modifications, additions etc., to the Works.

- The supplier hereby undertakes not to use intellectual property of any third party, without valid permissions from such third party, in the performance of any services under any Purchase Order issued hereunder. The supplier shall inform the customer in writing about the use of any third party's intellectual property by the supplier. The supplier shall indemnify and hold the customer harmless from any action by any third party for damages or injunction, for the violation of such third party's intellectual property rights, by the use of the Works, including costs and lawyers' fees.
- The supplier and/or its employees/ agents shall not, for any reason whatsoever, use any Works, either wholly or in part, without the prior written permission of the customer. The supplier agrees that it shall not use any name, mark, logo or design associated with the customer for any purpose whatsoever without the prior written approval of the customer.

When purchasing standardized services such as break-fix maintenance or off-the-shelf products then it is not reasonable to assume a Work for Hire position. In such cases it is reasonable to assume that the supplier will need to own the intellectual property brought to the table along with any enhancements to their intellectual property developed in the course of delivering your services.

Confidential information/data protection

Confidentiality is sometimes an afterthought, but should be a priority at the start of the dialogue between customer and supplier. A non-disclosure agreement (NDA) is just one part of a comprehensive confidentiality program and not a substitute. Be careful if the other party is handling your data, and especially careful if the data includes financial or personal health information or goes cross border, since data protection regulations apply. The confidentiality provisions in the final agreement may complement or override existing NDAs, depending on the nature of the arrangements.

There should be a provision in the customer-supplier agreement as follows:
- The supplier agrees that any information received by the supplier during the course of the supplier's performance under the agreement, which concerns the personal, financial or other affairs of the customer, its officers, employees or agents shall be kept in full confidence and shall not be revealed to any other person, firm, organization or other entity.
- The supplier further agrees that it will use such confidential/ proprietary information solely for the purposes of the agreement and for no other reason whatsoever without the prior written permission of the customer.
- The supplier shall indemnify the customer for all liabilities, costs and expenses, including lost profits which the customer may incur as a result of the supplier and/or supplier's employees / agents breaching the Confidentiality clause. Such clause should survive the expiration/ termination of the agreement.

Delivery and acceptance

It is essential to address delivery and acceptance early in the process to ensure clarity and avoid disputes between the parties to the contract at a critical time in the contract implementation. The customer needs to know when and where they will receive the deliverables under the contract and how they will establish they meet the requirements of the contract. In turn this enables the supplier to know when they have done what is required of them, when all or a major part of the payment will be triggered and when revenue may be recognized.

Delivery period

The period for delivery of the ordered goods and completion of any related service(s) such as installation and commissioning of the equipment, operators' training, etc. must be properly specified in the contract with definite dates. In truly time critical contracts it may be appropriate to have time deemed to be the essence of the contract. The real test of this is whether the deliverable can or will be used by the customer if the supplier is late.

Terms of delivery

The terms of delivery are decided depending on the nature of goods to be purchased, transportation facility available, location of the customer or user, location of the prospective supplier(s) etc. Terms of delivery determine the delivery point of the ordered goods from where the customer is to receive or collect the goods. Terms of delivery have direct bearing on the quoted prices. Delivery dates in contracts should incorporate standard and commonly used terms of delivery. For transportation of goods from foreign countries, the customer and supplier should use the International Commercial Terms (Incoterms) evolved by International Chamber of Commerce (ICC), Paris.

It is critical to address delivery and acceptance criteria early in the process, especially with customized software. The contract managers need to be part of the project team to understand the timing and impact of a lack of delivery. This understanding, coupled with clear and concise specifications/requirements are essential for robust clauses. Many contracts do a poor job of thoroughly describing what is being delivered and upon what conditions the customer will accept those deliverables. This invites disputes between customer and supplier.

The following documents are needed for clearance/receipt of domestic and imported goods. The supplier must send all the relevant dispatch documents well in advance to the customer to enable the customer to clear or receive (as the case may be) the goods in terms of the contract. The required instructions for this purpose are incorporated in the contract.

The usual documents involved for this purpose are as follows:

- For domestic goods: within the agreed time of dispatch, the supplier must notify the customer/customer, consignee, (others concerned), the complete details of dispatch and also supply the following documents (or as instructed in the contract):
  - Supplier/supplier's invoice indicating, among other things, the description and specification of the goods, quantity, unit price, total value
  - Packing list
  - Certificate of country of origin
  - Insurance certificate
  - Consignment note
  - Manufacturer's guarantee certificate and in-house inspection certificate
  - Inspection certificate issued by the customer's inspector

  Any other document(s) as and if required in terms of the contract.
- For imported goods: within the agreed time of dispatch, the supplier must notify the customer/customer, consignee, (others concerned), the complete details of dispatch and also supply the following documents (or as instructed in the contract):
  - Supplier's invoice giving full details of the goods including quantity, value, etc.
  - Packing list
  - Certificate of country of origin
  - Manufacturer's guarantee and inspection certificate
  - Inspection certificate issued by the customer's inspector
  - Insurance certificate
  - Name of the vessel/carrier
  - Bill of lading/airway bill
  - Port of loading
  - Date of shipment
  - Port of discharge and expected date of arrival of goods
  - Any other document(s) as and if required in terms of the contract

Normally no extensions of the scheduled delivery or completion dates should be granted to the supplier by the customer. The exceptions are where events constituting *force majeure*, as provided in the contract, have occurred or the terms and conditions include such a provision for other reasons. Extensions as provided in the contract may be allowed through formal amendments to the contract, duly signed by the parties to the contract. Liquidated damages for defaults on the part of the supplier are frequently agreed in contracts as a way of compensating the customer and limiting the supplier's liability.

The customer may also negotiate the following remedies for supplier non-performance:

- Extend the delivery with imposing of liquidated damages and other denial clauses
- Forfeit any performance security

- Cancel the contract
- Impose other available sanctions/penalties

Definition of what is being delivered

A large number of contracts fail to adequately specify what is being delivered. In an IACCM survey, over 85 percent rated improved requirements definition as critical towards improving their company's contract performance. Work with your technical counterparts. Get the documentation for the product (especially important for software). Acceptance is usually tied to conformance with the published documentation and not whether you like the product.

In some circumstance is may be possible to obtain a trial of the product for free or a nominal amount. This can be useful in helping to define what needs to be delivered by hands-on experience. It is, however, important to understand the basis for the trial as it might result in an automatic purchase if the trial period isn't kept to or it might overly influence the individuals using the product.

Termination

Before discussing termination of purchase contracts, these are some operational and legal steps that a customer needs to take:

- Performance notice. A situation may arise where the supply/services has not been completed within the stipulated period due to negligence /fault of the supplier. However, the supplier has not made any request for extension of delivery period but the contracted goods/services are still required by the customer, who does not want to cancel the contract at this stage. In such a case, a Performance Notice (also known as Notice-cum-Extension Letter) may be issued to the supplier by suitably extending the delivery date and by imposing liquidated damages with denial clauses etc.
- Correspondence with the supplier after breach of contract. The customer or its authorized representative must not enter into correspondence after expiry of the delivery date stipulated in the contract because such a correspondence will make the contract alive. This situation will not allow the customer to cancel the contract straight away without first serving a Performance Notice to the supplier. However, even after expiry of the delivery period of the contract, the customer may obtain information about past supplies etc. from the supplier. At the same time the customer must make it clear to the supplier that requesting such information is not intended to keep the contract alive, does not amount to waiving the breach, and is without prejudice to the rights and remedies available to the customer under the terms of the contract.

Termination is often overlooked in contracts, rarely enforced but useful to focus minds and absolutely critical if something goes extremely wrong. *Convenience* termination is when either party decides they no longer want to provide some service or delivery. This can have huge negative consequences, so it must be carefully considered and addressed in the contract. Generally, suppliers should not be allowed to terminate for convenience. *For Cause* termination is when one party breaches or threatens to breach the agreement and may be accompanied with a notice and cure period. Note that some breaches by their nature cannot be cured in a reasonable time period. *Force majeure* concerns excusing performance for conditions outside of either party's control (acts of God, flood, fire). However, certain suppliers might be expected to perform even during such events (e.g., disaster recovery providers).

Cancellation of contract for default

The customer may, without prejudice to any other remedy for breach of contract, by written notice of default sent to the supplier, terminate the contract in whole or in part:

- If the supplier fails to deliver any or all of the goods within the time period(s) specified in the contract, or any extension thereof granted by the customer; or
- If the supplier fails to perform any other obligation under the contract within the period specified in the contract or any extension thereof granted by the customer.

In the event the customer terminates the contract in whole or in part; the customer may take recourse to any one or more of the following actions.

- The Performance Security is to be forfeited.
- The customer may procure, upon such terms and in such manner as it deems appropriate, goods similar to those undelivered, and the supplier is liable for all available actions against it in terms of the contract.
- However, the supplier must continue to perform the contract to the extent not terminated.

Before canceling the contract and taking further action, it may be desirable to obtain legal advice from the Legal Department of the customer.

Termination of contract for insolvency:

If the supplier becomes bankrupt or otherwise insolvent, the customer may, at any time, terminate the contract, by giving written notice to the supplier, without compensation to the supplier provided that such termination will not prejudice or affect any right of action or remedy which have accrued or will accrue later to the customer.

Termination of contract for convenience:

After placement of contract, there may be some unforeseen situation compelling the customer to cancel the contract. In such a case, the customer sends a suitable notice to the supplier for cancellation of the contract, in whole or in part, for its (customer's) convenience, among other things, indicating the date with effect from which the termination is to become effective. Depending on the circumstances, the customer organization may have to compensate the supplier on mutually agreed terms for terminating the contract.

The customer could consider the following issues when incorporating termination clauses in contracts for suppliers:

- Violation and failure to abide by any terms and condition.
- Making any false representation/declaration to the customer.
- Supplying goods of inferior quality or un-inspected goods.
- Rendering services (including after sales services and maintenance services) of inferior quality than the contracted ones.
- Failure to execute a contract or fails to execute it satisfactorily.
- The required technical / operational staff or equipment are no longer available with the company or there is a change in its production/service line affecting its performance adversely.
- Declared bankrupt or insolvent.
- Adopting unethical business practices.

Payment and invoicing terms

Payment and invoicing terms need to be specific and comprehensive. Customers should ensure they understand the requirements of their accounts payable colleagues. Suppliers should ensure that they are able to invoice in the manner specified in the contract.

In general, payment should be linked to delivery or performance of services. Milestone payments require very clear acceptance criteria. Especially in large complex purchase arrangements, a good description of payment terms will prevent misunderstandings.

The clauses on payment should clearly state that the customer must pay the supplier the price for the supplies/services indicated in the relevant purchase order issued by the customer, if the supplier has satisfactorily delivered the supplies or performed the services in accordance with the requirements of the contract.

The supplier must invoice the customer for the price stated in the purchase order, for the supplies delivered and services performed. The customer makes all payments to the supplier as stated in the supplier's invoice. The supplier is solely responsible for paying any and all costs, expenses, fees and taxes that are related in any way and manner to the fulfillment of the suppliers obligations flowing from the agreement with the customer, incurred by the supplier and/or its employees before, during and after the term of the agreement with the customer, which the customer has not expressly agreed to bear. Reimbursement of any costs or expenses agreed to by the customer is normally up to the maximum amount, if any, as stated in the relevant purchase order. Invoices for expenses must contain detailed itemizations and be accompanied with bills, invoices, or other documentation showing proof of payment.

The customer, at their discretion, may withhold the whole or part of any payments to the supplier, relating to any purchase order issued, to such extent as may be necessary to protect the customer from loss due to, but not limited to, the following causes:
- Defective work not corrected within the time period specified by the customer.
- Damage to personnel or property of the customer or third party caused by act, omission or negligence of the supplier, or its agents or employees.
- The breach of any of the provisions of the agreement with the customer by the supplier.
- Failure of the supplier to perform the work in a timely fashion to meet the completion date/s specified in the relevant purchase order.

Clauses such as this one should be incorporated into the contract so that if there is any defect in the work or breach of any of the terms of the agreement with the customer by the supplier, including failure of the supplier to perform in a timely fashion, the customer may approach any other party to perform the work which the supplier was to perform and the supplier shall indemnify the customer against all costs and expenses incurred by the customer as a result of the party performing such work.

Documents for payment

The documents required from the supplier for release of payment by the customer must be clearly specified in the contract. The paying authority also has to verify the documents received from the supplier, with corresponding stipulations made in the contract, before releasing payment. The important documents that the supplier might have to provide in order to claim payment are:
- Original invoice
- Packing list
- Certificate of country of origin of the goods to be given by the supplier or a recognized Chamber of Commerce or other agency designated by the customer for this purpose
- Certificate of pre-dispatch inspection by the customer's representative if appropriate
- Manufacturer's test certificate
- Certificate of insurance
- Bill of lading/airway bill/rail receipt or any other dispatch document
- Confirmation that the product is new, un-used and also meets any other relevant contractual requirements

When claiming payment, the supplier also has to certify in their invoice that the payment being claimed is strictly within the terms of the contract and all the obligations on the part of the supplier for claiming this payment have been fulfilled as required under the contract.

19.8 Summary

While contracts can become extremely complex, remember that the three fundamental parts, defining what you want to buy, the agreed price, and your acceptance criteria, are all too often poorly articulated and misaligned. To be effective, the contract should thoroughly address the basic business, contractual and technical elements of the purchase. While weak requirements definition is the most cited area of failure, all three elements should be detailed and comprehensive.

Also keep in mind the nature of the product, service or project being contracted for. It is unrealistic to expect customized provisions in relation to off-the shelf purchase that you will need in a customized solution environment. You will just prolong negotiations unreasonably if you attempt to treat all situations with the same level of expectation for all scenarios.

CHAPTER 20

Technology contract terms and conditions

20.1 Introduction

This chapter builds on the previous chapter, *Contract terms and conditions overview*. It discusses specific terms and issues relating to technology products and services, from both the buy side and the supply side.

This chapter provides insights into the contractual challenges in a market segment whose issues and techniques increasingly touch business activities in all other market segments and focuses on the following areas:
- Scope of the contract
- License types
- Ownership of Intellectual Property Rights (IPR)
- Maintenance services
- Hardware contracts
- Service contracts

20.2 A specialized discipline

Legal terms and conditions specific to IT have evolved relatively recently and are still undergoing transformation. Recent laws such as The Uniform Computer Information Transactions Act (UCITA)[4] have been written to create a clear and uniform set of rules to govern such areas as software licensing, online access, and other transactions in computer information. On a worldwide level, there are substantial and on going discussions within the Hague Convention regarding software rights and protections.

---

4 Approved by NCCUSL in 2003) (http://www.nccusl.org/update/)

Efforts by the World Trade Organization to impose a more consistent and predictable regime of protection for intellectual property rights have particular significance in an area like software, where copying and replication are so easy. And major trade blocs such as the European Union have enacted relevant legislation that creates local definition, especially in areas such as customer rights to modification and ownership of derivative works.

Most important is the concept of licensing, where a supplier retains ownership of the software code but allows its use under certain conditions described in the licensing terms. The licensing terms become paramount to describe how you can use the software and under what conditions.

UCITA

In particular, UCITA attempts to clarify and/or codify rules regarding fair use, reverse engineering, consumer protection, warranties, shrink-wrap licenses, and their duration and license transferability. UCITA generally approves the validity of software licenses, including shrink-wrap and browse-wrap agreements, as long as the user is given an opportunity to return the goods (at the seller's expense) if the license terms are found to be unacceptable.

UCITA was drafted by the National Council of Commissioners on Uniform State Laws to resolve the inadequacy of the Uniform Commercial Code[5], which only addresses the requirements of contracts for sale of tangible goods, not the sale of intangible goods such as computer services. UCITA has been enacted in Virginia and Maryland and has become a hot topic of debate in other states as to whether it balances the rights of the customer and supplier.

In the US, it is uncommon to see restrictions on decompilation and/or reverse engineering included among the proposed contract terms. Decompilation is the reverse process of compilation – that is, creating high-level language code from machine/assembly language code. Converting source code into object code is called 'compilation', and converting object code into source code is called 'decompilation' or 'reverse engineering'. Compilation is technically easy; decompilation, however, is technically very much more difficult. Reverse engineering had its origins in the analysis of hardware for commercial or military advantage. The purpose is to deduce design decisions from end products with little or no additional knowledge about the procedures involved in the original production. The same techniques are currently used for software systems to replace incorrect, incomplete, or otherwise unavailable documentation. Both compilation and decompilation are regarded by the law as 'copying'. A license is required before the purchaser is allowed to compile, decompile, or reverse engineer software in which the supplier holds the rights.

---

5 First published in 1952. (www.law.cornell.edu/ucc/ucc.table.html)

However, a limited exception to this is provided by the so-called 'decompilation right'. This is an exception to copyright that makes it lawful, under certain limited circumstances, for anyone to decompile a program in order to create another, independent program that is interoperable with it (that is, can be used together with it). The question of using decompilation or reverse engineering will arise where the original source code is kept secret. It may then be necessary to decompile an operating system in order to understand how it works, so that a user may then write a program that runs on that operating system; or to decompile a business rival's word processor so that a user can understand how it stores documents in files, so that they can enable their competing word processor to read those files. Because owners of copyrighted software do not want others decompiling and using their software, contracts often include a clause that forbids the de-compilation of the one party's object code into source code by the other party. Where decompilation is performed in order to discover the internal code, it is illegal. However, decompilation is commonly allowed in order to achieve interoperability of software programs by use of the "clean room" process. In practice, therefore, only a well-resourced business will be able to take advantage of the decompilation right. In any case, it is best to contact a legal advisor on the proper rights and process. Note that in contracts involving the US federal government, reverse engineering is usually expressly prohibited.

European Union

Within the European Union (EU), the EU Directive (91//EEC of 14 May 1991 applies. In the UK, the Copyright Designs and Patents Act 1988 was amended by the Copyright (Computer Programs) Regulations 1992[6]. These Regulations were replaced by the consolidated Directive 2009/24/EC, which came into effect on 25 May 2009. The Directive confirms the legal protection of computer programs. It provides that computer programs and any associated design material will be protected as literary works in accordance with the Berne Convention for the Protection of Literary and Artistic Works. The Berne Convention is an international agreement was agreed in Berne Switzerland in 1886 and established the harmonization of copyright amongst signatories, the agreement. This meant that copyright under the Berne Convention became an automatic right without the need for formal registration. However, when the US joined the Convention in 1988, under 17 USC 412 (US Code), statutory damages are only available for works that have been registered with the Copyright Office before infringement, or within three months of publication.

Before the introduction of the EU Directive, the UK's Copyright, Designs and Patents Act 1988 (as amended) (CDPA 1988) had made provision for the protection of copyright in computer programs as a 'literary work'. The EU Directive harmonized the laws of the EU

---

6   See http://tinyurl.com/35xf4tx for further details.

relating to the protection of computer programs and includes matters for which the CDPA 1988 made no specific provision.

The EU Directive was implemented by the Copyright (Computer Programs) Regulations 1992. Section 50A (2) of the 1992 Regulations defined a '**lawful user**' as a "*user of a computer program if (whether under a license to do any acts restricted by the copyright in the program or otherwise), he/she has a right to use the program.*"

In particular the 1992 Regulations:
- Introduced modifications to the definition of literary work by including preparatory design material (Regulation 3)
- Modified the meaning of adaptation and translation in relation to computer programs (Regulation 5)
- Modified the meaning of 'issues to the public of copies' and 'infringing copy' so as to strengthen the distribution rights of copyright owners in the UK subject to exhaustion of rights inside the EU (Regulations 4 and 6)
- Removed certain acts relating to computer programs from the general application of the Fair Dealing provision in Section 29 (Regulation 7)
- Introduced new sections 50a, 50b and 50c into the CDPA 1988 (Regulation 8) containing specific exceptions to the exclusive rights of the copyright owner in favor of a lawful user:
- Permitted the making of a back-up copy (new section 50a(1))
- Defined a lawful user (new section 50a(2))
- Permitted limited decompilation of a computer program (new section 50b(1)) subject to compliance with certain conditions (new section 50b(2) and (3))
- Permitted restricted amounts of copying and adapting for lawful use, including for error correction (except where otherwise provided for) (new section 50c)
- Introduced an amendment to Section 296 extending the category of persons against whom remedies may be sought under that section in respect of dealing in devices designed to circumvent copy-protection for the purpose of making infringing copies (Regulation 10)
- Introduced a new section 296a, which renders void any term in an agreement which seeks to prohibit or restrict the doing of any of the acts permitted under Sections 50a and 50b or the use of any device or means to observe the functioning of a computer program (Regulation 11)

New Section 296A of the CDPA 1988 permits a lawful user to:
- (b) where the conditions in section 50B(2) are met, the decompiling of the program; or
- (c) the use of any device or means to observe, study or test the functioning of the program in order to understand the ideas and principles which underlie any element of the program."

This does not however permit the lawful user to use the underlying ideas and principles to be copied directly unless the 'clean room' technique discussed above is employed.

The computer program may also be de-compiled if this is necessary to ensure it operates with another computer program or device, but the results of the decompilation[7] may not be used for any other purpose without infringing the copyright in the computer program. It is also common practice where one of the parties is a signatory of the United Nations Convention on Contracts for the International Sales of Goods 1980[8] for the Convention to be excluded in UK software contracts as the UK is not a signatory.

Within this highly specialized area is the concept of licensing, where the supplier (usually the owner of the software program) retains ownership of the software program but allows its use under certain conditions described in the software contract and which is described below. The licensing terms become paramount to describe how the customer (or lawful user) may use the software program and under what conditions.

20.3 Definitions

It is standard practice for practitioners to include definitions in contracts (whether software or hardware contract) whether term of art or not, to avoid any risk of misinterpretation in the future and this is highlighted in Chapter 19: *Contract terms and conditions overview*. Technology contracts are especially susceptible to misinterpretation when the terms of how the technology may be used and by whom are defined by other common terms.

Table 20.1 below shows some key terms that often appear in software contracts (these are in addition to the terms already mentioned in Chapter 19: *Contract terms and Conditions Overview*.

---

7   Decompilation means taking the language of the original software program and changing it into a
    language that can be better understood.
8   See http://tinyurl.com/2kfxgrfor further details.

Definition	Comment	Example of Definition
"Effective Date" or "Commencement Date"	This is usually the date when the contract starts. Some contracts refer to a "Go Live Date" as the date when live use of the software will commence.	"Effective Date" shall mean 3 May 2012.
"Authorized User"	There should be a clear definition of who is considered a user of the software. These individuals are defined usually defined as "Authorized User". This may have been identified in the parties section or in the charges schedule. The definition of user will be important from a maintenance perspective so that only those users who have been identified have access to the software support and maintenance services.	"Authorized Users" shall mean those Employees, agents, authorized contractors or authorized subcontractors of the Licensee who are identified in Schedule [X].
"Employee"	Those employees who are licensed to use the software as specified in the contract. It will be for the licensee to identify, part-time employees and contractor employees who will need to use the software. The licensee must ensure that any subcontractor who is providing services to it and who need access to the software is identified as an authorized user.	"Employee" shall mean those full-time employees, part-time employees and/or contractors who are entitled to use the Software.
"Hardware"	This is a straightforward definition. It is common for all types of equipment or hardware to be specifically itemized by type and serial number in a specific schedule. It is important to identify the specific hardware items for ownership as well as support purposes and for the parties to determine what happens to the hardware on contract termination.	"Hardware" means the specified computer hardware or equipment which is situated at the site on which in conjunction with the Software is licensed to operate together with the specific name and release version of the operating system software as stated in Schedule [X].

Definition	Comment	Example of Definition
"Maintenance Services"	This category will require two separate definitions (hardware maintenance services and software maintenance services). These two definitions should then refer to two separate schedules that set out in detail what will be provided by the provider as maintenance services. it should also address whether this will include new releases etc.	"Maintenance Services" shall mean the Software Maintenance Services as described in Schedule [X] and the Hardware Maintenance Services as described in Schedule [X].
"Major Release"	This is one or more versions of the software that may contain new functionality and are usually designated by the use of a numerical identifier (e.g. version 1.0 to version 2.0). Major releases usually consolidate all previous versions of the software program.	"Major Release" means a conversion to a new version of the software which will include new functionality (e.g. version 1.0 to version 2.0).
"Minor Release"	This is a new version of the software that may contain significant functionality and is usually designated by the use of a numerical identifier (e.g. version version1.1. to version 1.2). Minor releases will usually consolidate all previous releases.	"Minor Release" means a conversion to a new version of the software which will include significant functionality (e.g. from version 1.1 to version 1.2).
"Patch"	This is a piece of object code that is usually integrated into an executable software program to fix a software program bug.	"Patch" means software provided by the supplier to resolve a specific reported software program bug relating to the software.
"Service Pack"	A service pack is a software package that contains several updates for the software program. Individual updates are typically called patches. When the supplier has developed several updates to a software program, then the supplier may release all the patches together in a service pack.	"Service Pack" means a version of the software which consolidates all previous patches. Under some circumstances, this may include minor functional enhancements.

Definition	Comment	Example of Definition
"Software"	This is usually the supplier's proprietary application which is licensed to the customer. The application software may be identified by name or version number in the definition. This is distinguished from third party software which is licensed by the supplier to the customer in accordance with the terms of the third party licensors.	"Software" means the supplier's proprietary software set out in Schedule [X] or in the order form.
"Site"	This is the location where the software or hardware is physically located or where the location where the software may be accessed by the authorized users as specified in the software license.	"Site" means the premises owned by the licensee where the software will be located and where the software is licensed to be used.
"Third Party Software"	This is usually software which the supplier will use as part of an integrated software solution to be provided to the customer. The use of such third party owned software will be subject to the terms and conditions imposed on the supplier by the third party licensors. Third party software may include open source software, freeware or shareware software. Unless consent is received from the third party licensor. It is usually expected that the supplier will pass through the third party licensor's terms and conditions to the customer either by way of the contract, read-me disclaimer or shrink-wrap or click-wrap license.	"Third Party Software" means the third party software set out in Schedule [X] or in the order form which is owned by the third party licensors set out in Schedule [X] or in the order form and which is sub-licensed to the customer in accordance with this agreement.
Update	A new version of the software including new functionality or capacity.	
Upgrade	Software provided to fix bugs, make small corrections, provide update changes but essentially no material changes to the software release.	
"Workaround"	This is a procedure or a temporary fix that bypasses a problem and allows a customer to continue working until a permanent solution can be provided.	"Workaround" means a method of avoiding an incident or problem either by a temporary fix or by a technique in order that the Licensee is able to continue to use the Software.

Table 20.1   Key terms in software contracts

It is important to note that definitions will need to be adapted to suit the particular requirements of the proposed contract. Only an in-depth analysis of the proposed contract and/or market will determine which terms need inclusion and further consideration by the parties at the drafting and Negotiation phase.

20.4 Scope of Use

Scope of Use is at the core of the software licensing terms and conditions. Software companies will be reluctant to give the customer unlimited use of their software without charging licensing fees since their core business revenue is licensing fees (and, indirectly, maintenance fees based on a percentage of licensing fees are important sources of revenue and control for them). How use is granted is one key element that directly affects the price of the deal.

The Scope of Use or License Grant describes the ways in which customers can use the software, for what purposes, and who can use it. Be aware of granting and/or receiving rights to use the software in derivative works, in resales and re-licensing if the customer intends to build extensions to the software or have the software undergo customization. This may require the customer to work with its technical counterparts and legal experts to craft terms and conditions that allow the customer the flexibility to perform such work while retaining ownership (usually a desired goal) of the new code. This often results in intense negotiations with the supplier.

Where either the supplier or the customer use 'free' or open source software (either as a stand-alone product or embedded in another software tool), it is very important to review the license terms. Even though the software will not require a royalty or license fee for use, there are often restrictions on how the software can be used or transferred to others' use. Review the terms carefully and any restrictions should be clearly set out in the contract for the other party to understand how he software may be used.

Most contract managers develop, or request technical leads to develop, an inventory of software provided to the other party and software provided from the other party. Along with the list of products, the rights of use should be developed and reviewed periodically by the contract manager and technical leads to ensure that (a) no infringement is occurring; (b) no rights have been lost due to lack of notification to the other party; and (c) return of software is completed upon termination of the contract.

Training and awareness of the rights held by the customer under a contract should be undertaken for the customer's developers and managers. Thus, if and when new software is developed, employees will be expected to notify the contract management team of the addition to the inventory. Depending on the customer's policies, contract managers may be required to report such new software to the legal department at corporate headquarters to determine whether a patent should be obtained.

20.5 License types

The license type and the license term is also at the core of the software licensing terms and conditions. A software contract will specify the license type and license term, which will describe how the software can be used by the authorized users and for how long. The type of license will also determine the license fees and also determine the cost of future fees for additional access. Both customers and suppliers will be keen to ensure that the license type and term is appropriate for the specific project and the license fee paid.

The two most common license types are shown in Table 20.2.

License Type	Scope of Rights	Example Clause
Perpetual license (usually described as an unlimited limited license in US software contracts)	The customer will have the right to use the software beyond the duration of the software contract. There may be restrictions in the software contract on the operation of this license. For example, whether the perpetual license will terminate when the maintenance services contract terminates or whether it is subject to the standard termination clause in the software contract. "The word 'perpetual' can carry different shades of meaning. It can, for example, mean 'never ending' (in the sense of incapable of being brought to an end) or it can mean 'operating without limit of time. Therefore, when the Defendant terminated the Support Agreement, it also terminated the license for it to use the Mill Master software." BMS Computer Solutions Ltd v AB Agri Ltd [2010] EWHC 464 (Ch) (10 March 2010) – [9] The customer will expect to pay a one-off license fee at the start of the software contract and not for each year of the software contract.	"Subject always to Clause [X] (Termination) and following delivery of the software, the supplier in consideration of the payment of the license fee grants to the customer a personal non-exclusive, non- transferable perpetual license to use the software at the site on the applicable hardware subject to following restrictions:.."

| Term license (usually described as a limited license in US software contracts) | The customer will have the right to use the software for the duration of the software contract. There may be restrictions in the software contract on the operation of this license.

The supplier may expect the customer to pay annual license fees in advance of the start of each contract term or as a one-off license for the entire contract period in advance. | "Subject always to Clause [X] (Termination) and following delivery of the software, the supplier in consideration of the payment of the license fee grants to the customer a personal non-exclusive, non-transferable license to use the software for the license term at the site on the applicable hardware subject to following restrictions:.." |

Table 20.2 Common license types

The type of license will require an evaluation of the customer's business strategy, needs and Total Cost of Ownership (TCO). Aligned to the software's TCO will be the payment terms, which may be variable in an attempt to relate software cost to the value that the customer gets from the software. The premise is that the larger a customer gets in some dimension, the more valuable the software and therefore the more they should pay. In theory, this allows smaller payments when a company is small, and larger ones as they grow and become more successful. In some contracts, non-tiered software pricing means that customers pay a flat rate for the software regardless of their size.

Popular tiered pricing models include usage payment terms, which are based upon the number of the times the software is accessed or the volume of processing, the number of employees, central processing unit (CPU) capacity and the number of location(s). To determine the best approach, the supplier will need to ensure that it has assessed and segmented its target markets and the approach being followed by the competition. In recent times, with the advent of software as a service model, the pay as you use (PAY GO) payment model has gained in popularity.

To avoid major arguments during the relationship, it is important to define what is meant by perpetual or term license and to identify the license restrictions and to ensure that contract terms and conditions specify the expectations of both customer and supplier.

There are also other license arrangements such as:
• Shared licenses – this may arise where there is joint ownership of the intellectual property rights in the commissioned or bespoke work. The parties may agree that one party owns the full rights in the commissioned work but the other party is granted a unlimited license to further develop and enhance the commissioned work without permission from the party that owned the original copy.

---

9 See http://tinyurl.com/34ckwwy for further details.

- Third party license rights – whereby the subcontractors or agents of the customer will have access to the software provided confidentiality agreements are put in place and the software is not licensed to competitors of the supplier.
- Short evaluation licenses – where software is evaluated for 30 to 90 days without the payment of a license fee.
- Click-wrap or shrink-wrap licenses – these are more common where off the shelf software is provided rather than where bespoke or commissioned software is provided.
- Freeware or open source licenses – this is an inexpensive way to obtain robust software but the supplier will need to ensure that the specific requirements of each software license has been fulfilled so that the supplier's proprietary software does not itself become "open source". In addition, the supplier must pass on to the customer the open source software or freeware terms and conditions in the contract.

20.6   Assignment and rights to use

Continuing with the theme of usage rights, the parties will need to have addressed future uses and changing circumstances in the contract. Most companies change their structure. Between spin-offs, divestitures, and acquisitions, the corporate landscape can change dramatically. Try to foresee possible activities to protect both customer and supplier's commercial requirements by crafting terms and conditions that address these situations. The supplier will need to anticipate the demands from the customer to protect their rights of continued use. Statements should be included in the intellectual property section of the contract addressing the proper usages and rights of licensed software or software sub-licensed from other parties. This should include any embedded software.

Sometimes the customer may want to outsource the use of the software to a third-party service provider or allow contractors to use the software on their behalf by including rights to do this in the contract. The supplier will need to consider the position and rights that it wants to take in such a situation. Suppliers of software may think very carefully before allowing access to key intellectual property, especially if access is provided to competitors and there is a risk of endangering the supplier's position in the marketplace by making the software available to third parties. The supplier will need to decide how much control it will have over the way in which the customer's subcontractors will have access to the software.

Many suppliers resist sub-licensing and some charge a fee to authorize the transfer to new sub-licensees. They also limit the support rights for services by these subcontractors unless payment is received from the customer. The supplier's preference will be for the customer to be liable for breach of contract if the customer's subcontractor fails to follow the contract in terms of acceptable software uses. The customer may be successful in attempting to get the subcontractor to enter into a direct contractual relationship with the supplier instead.

Assignment of rights to use of the software, in situations where ownership of a party changes or ceases to exist, must also be carefully analyzed before acceptance by the contract. Such an assignment means that software or other valuable intellectual property is subject to use by future and unknown successors to the existing co-party. The supplier may need to consider use of a restricting clause prohibiting assignment of such intellectual property to known competitors. Parties may also voluntarily enter into a three party novation agreement whereby the existing contract is transferred to the new contractor who is acting on behalf of the customer, with the supplier's consent.

20.7 License versus ownership

A license is generally just a right to use a product or service. However, customers may want to embed a product into their own product or service, and then grant certain rights to their customers.

Customers may also seek to add functionality or to pay for customization/development. Ownership of modifications and derivatives is frequently contentious – and also often affects the supplier's warranties and indemnities (for example against third party claims). Customers may demand sole ownership, joint ownership, rights to exploit or rights to prevent licensing to others. If they have invested in or paid for these modifications, they may be concerned about protecting their use or to recover the cost of their 'invention'.

Supplier contract managers should ask themselves the question, "Is this software important to my company, or is it unique to the customer's business?" If the answer is yes for the latter situation, there is less value in fighting over the ownership of the software and in the interest of the relationship, more value in finding an accommodation with the customer. If the software is important to the supplier, restrictions on the use of the software, higher fees, or sole ownership may be the proper solution.

As already mentioned in the context of software, the issue of ownership of the intellectual property rights in a work product is critical and frequently contentious in a services contract. The customer will often demand ownership, typically by defining the output as 'work made for hire'. In some cases, this is a legitimate requirement – for example, where the customer has provided the design or original ideas. In others, there may be a legitimate concern, such as maintaining competitive advantage or protecting confidentiality and sometimes it is completely unreasonable, but ownership is stipulated in the customer's standard terms and conditions. In all of these instances, the supplier will need to decide on a commercial basis whether the customer should own the intellectual property rights in the work product.

The supplier may want to protect their ideas, methods and intellectual property in order to maintain the competitive edge. The supplier may not want to relinquish rights and will rarely want to share ownership rights – that is, joint ownership of the intellectual property rights. Joint ownership will hamper both parties' ability to use the work product without consultation and, from a commercial perspective, it is invariably impractical. So negotiation is frequently valid and there are many ways that the rights and interests of both parties can be adequately protected. These include options such as licensing, ownership of derivative works, non-compete or limitation on sales provisions, or joint development and exploitation.

From the customer's perspective, the concept of 'work made for hire' is critical in any services contract where the customer is contracting for a customized or bespoke product (e.g., a new computer program, a marketing campaign, advertisement, creation of a new product to sell). Unless the services contract specifically assigns ownership of the intellectual property rights in the work product to the customer, then the first owner of the work product will be the supplier. Therefore, it is critical from the customer's perspective that they should seek to include protections to prevent the supplier from claiming ownership or even joint ownership of a work product in the services contract before services begin. In addition, if the work product is being assigned to the customer, then the supplier should provide appropriate intellectual property rights to indemnify the customer if the supplier used freelance contractors to create the work product and to confirm that the intellectual property rights of any third party were not infringed during the creation of the work product.

If the work involves customized aspects that would be of great value to the customer's competitors, then the customer may seek to either prohibit such sales or to require a certain period of exclusivity. However, it may be more appropriate where the customer is unable to exploit or maintain the work product (software product) for the supplier to exploit the product commercially and to establish a larger customer base so that there is adequate support and maintenance services as well as future product releases.

Example:
A market research and data company worked with four customers, the leading adult beverage companies in their categories, to develop an account trade classification and unique location numbering methodology, which would become the industry standard. In this case, all five companies worked collaboratively to develop a better way to identify accounts and track them. The customers had exclusive use of the process that they helped to create, for a year after implementation, and then the supplier was free to sell to their competitors.

20.8 Audits and compliance

It is common for software contracts to contain an audit clause to enable the supplier to audit the customer's use of the software in order to confirm compliance with the contractual terms and conditions. Generally, customers will allow annual audits with reasonable notice and scope and provided there are strong confidentiality provisions in place. The supplier will typically agree to pay for the cost of the audit themselves unless they find substantial non-compliance. Dependent on the contract terms, the customer may agree to run usage reports and/or deliver lists of user IDs/names in lieu of on-site audits.

Software owners are treating non-compliance more seriously, as are their trade groups (the BSA (Business Software Alliance)[10] and SIAA (Software & Information Industry Association[11], for example). PC software can be monitored by various PC survey products; companies such as Microsoft and their VARs (value-added resellers) have programs to track software usage and whether such usage was compatible with the terms of the software license. The customer may also want to have audit rights to enable it to ensure that that the maintenance services and any associated service levels are being performed to the standard stated in the contract. In certain contracts such as public sector contracts, the customer may require additional audit rights relating to the processing of data or the assets stored by the supplier as part of the service provision.

Example clause:
The customer shall have the right to audit the supplier's compliance with this Agreement on giving seven days' written notice to the supplier. At the customer's option, this audit may cover documents only or may include on-site audit, subject to the customer notifying the supplier of the identity of any on-site auditors and giving confirmation that any external auditors have entered into appropriate confidentiality agreement.

20.9 Software maintenance services

Software maintenance services can be services delivered as part of an original contract and can continue to be a delivery requirement after the rest of the contract is complete and has terminated. Within any service contract, there is usually a section addressing on-going software maintenance during the life of the contract and another section addressing any maintenance of software services where the contract has terminated. The parties should also address the situation where the supplier becomes insolvent, in which software source code escrow arrangements will become important. With these arrangements, a copy of the

---

10 See http://tinyurl.com/nsua2w for further details.

11 See http://www.siia.net for further details.

supplier's source code is kept by a trusted third party to ensure access to the source code if the supplier becomes unable for any reason to support their software.

Other than the purchase price, maintenance pricing will be likely to have the largest impact upon the Total Cost of Ownership (TCO) of the software. Maintenance pricing, terms and conditions will often be a separate section in a large procurement contract. Maintenance terms should include what kind of maintenance will be provided by the supplier and under what circumstances.

Maintenance costs can be calculated in many ways. Frequently they are a percentage of the discounted purchase price plus any subsequent software license purchases. The customer will need to be very aware of unregulated future maintenance pricing or any pricing based upon factors beyond the customer's control and will need to include "caps" on maintenance fee upgrades. All contracts should have some kind of maintenance cap or a formula to limit onerous price increases.

The price of maintenance is increasingly negotiable. While the major suppliers have traditionally resisted flexibility, they are now prepared to vary the percentage charge. The typical range is currently 15-20 percent.

Other than the costs, there are several other policy decisions that need to be made and about which customers may be concerned. First there is the question of support and how it will be delivered. Software maintenance generally includes telephone support assistance by the supplier, electronic self-help (usually via their website), and perhaps even on-site visits for more serious issues. Be sure the terms define service levels and set expectations for the maintenance program.

For most suppliers maintenance begins when the warranty period ends (usually 30 to 90 days after delivery or acceptance). Increasingly large customers may have a policy about when maintenance should start and end, and may demand the ability to 'synchronize' the maintenance term with their own internal calendar, or to be synchronized with other product schedules, especially if the software is part of an integrated solution.

The customer will also need to be clear in the contract about definition of maintenance release or fix, new versions and upgrades and whether charges apply. Policies on upgrades vary significantly between suppliers and have created customer concerns. For example, Software suppliers often rename products and merge products together. If the supplier does this, the customer will need to consider whether it will be penalized, lose maintenance coverage or be forced to buy new or different products unexpectedly. The customer should also ask whether it will be required to stay current or within a limited number of releases by taking upgrades in order to continue receiving maintenance protection and whether it will be entitled to obtain longer periods of usage for a particular version. For example, the customer may be willing to accept maintenance coverage for the latest two major releases, but agree to not being supported for releases older than that.

Finally, the customer will need to consider the terms in conjunction with the supplier's marketing messages. Suppliers often represent the value their product will bring, in particular the savings and efficiencies. To the extent that this is true, it creates a dependency on the part of the customer. For example, the customer's ability to recreate manual processes will be lost if it reduces headcount or eliminates specific groups after implementing new software. Such a powerful marketing message should cause the customer to understand the risks that are created by its dependency on the supplier's software. The customer should scrutinize the terms and conditions to ensure it is protected – security of access, quality and timeliness of support, avoidance or unpredictable increases in fees or charges. In addition, the customer should use the contract to ensure that the supplier is incentivized to perform by the prospect of liquidated damages in the event of failure or to make cost savings for the customer by sharing the benefits of the savings with the supplier. It is essential to have studied the supplier's terms and ensure that the customer is equipped with answers to the questions and concerns that it will legitimately have during the procurement discussions.

20.10 Hardware contracts: overview

Hardware may be acquired by the customer in a variety of ways: purchase, rental or lease. The customer's rights relating to the hardware will be determined by the nature of the contractual relationship. For example, a hardware rental agreement may contain an option for the customer to purchase the hardware at the end of the rental period at a discount and for most customers, this form of hardware contract has the potential to prevent future obsolescence and to save money as there will be no upfront capital expenditure.

Generally, many of the principles that apply to software contracts also apply to hardware; the importance of definitions, delivery and acceptance obligations, environment and interoperability issues, right to relocate hardware, the obligations to provide support and export regulations. In the UK, the customer will need to consider the requirements of the Export Control Act 2002[12] and in the US, any export controls imposed by the US Department of Commerce[13] .

Hardware requirements can include performance specifications, usually to meet or exceed certain standards, which can be built in to acceptance tests if important to the customer.

12 See http://tinyurl.com/38k4two and http://www.bis.gov.uk/exportcontrol
13 See http://www.bis.doc.gov/ for further details.

More complex hardware items such as servers and storage units will need to be evaluated in conjunction with both the customer and supplier's specific technical requirements during acceptance testing to ensure that a successful installation has taken place.

The parties will also need to consider disposal costs of hardware or other equipment, which may have environmental issues covered, for instance in Europe by the EU's *Waste Electrical and Electronic Equipment* (WEEE) Directive, and possible data security concerns. Embedded software (such as firmware or any other operating system software) in hardware will need to be reviewed so that appropriate licenses have been secured in the hardware contract. Furthermore, access to confidential information and data security issues during the installation of the hardware should be reviewed so that there are no security lapses.

The parties should also consider whether the hardware contract should contain business continuity and/or disaster recovery provisions in complex hardware contracts where the supplier will be providing ongoing maintenance services and where the hardware is not located in customer's premises.

20.11 **Performance**

Hardware technical specifications involving processor speed, or disk rotational capabilities related to data throughput, may or may not be important to a particular deal. If the customer is purchasing a software product based on a need for increased performance, then they should develop acceptance criteria based on that business objective. This is an aspect of contracting and negotiation that underlies much contention. The supplier is likely to represent that their product will be well suited to the customer's need in the sales proposal but may try to eliminate such representations in its contracts in respect of performance warranties or performance criteria.

The supplier will point to the fact that many performance factors are outside its control and depend on related actions (or inactions) by the customer or other parties. Specific performance commitments represent substantially greater risk. The customer should ensure that the supplier is equipped to undertake such commitments, thus protecting their customer's required performance requirements and thereby gaining a significant competitive advantage. Hardware specifications may also be important in order to synchronize with the equipment to be provided by the customer. If this is the case, the supplier will need to ensure that the contract is conditional on the customer providing equipment that meets these specifications so that the supplier is not in default.

Ultimately where the customer is purchasing hardware to solve a business problem, it is essential to define any acceptance of such hardware by the customer in terms of solving that business problem. The customer will need to check whether the supplier is prepared to contractually accept this responsibility, provided the solution is within the supplier's control and the resolution of the problem is directly addressed by the contract. Otherwise, and more typically, performance acceptance is based on meeting the supplier's published specification for the hardware purchased by the customer.

20.12 Support and maintenance services

A typical support and maintenance services contract may contain the following obligations:
- First line support such as help desk facilities
- Second line support such as response and resolution times
- Support for firmware or operating software embedded in the hardware
- Provision of spares
- Provision of upgrades
- Anti-virus support
- Remote access facilities outside support hours cover
- Escalation procedures
- Out of scope services

In a rental or lease arrangement the customer will want to understand a supplier's approach to its product and technology lifecycle. Given today's rapid change and development, the customer may be concerned whether the supplier will address this through new product introductions that may rapidly put the customer on outdated technology or through a coherent upgrade policy. The degree to which the upgrade policy forces the customer to adopt each upgrade or to enable selective application may have significant implications for the customer's business.

Issues of cost and functionality may require the customer to plan and control adoption of any such upgrades especially where these impacts extend to the way that the customer interfaces or provides services. The supplier may typically want the customer to upgrade regularly to stay within a certain period of time and the customer will want to consider obtaining availability of certain upgrades for a period of time at a specified price. It is also important to identify exactly what has changed in terms of functionality and interoperability in order to plan and cost-out the upgrade. The hardware services contract should specify who, or what level, in the customer's organization is authorized to approve upgrades and the installation of them.

The maintenance services contract should be based on historical data for failures, breakdown, redundant features, and criticality of process. For response timing, identify the proximity of the supplier's parts depot or expert locations to the customer's location(s), since response time based on criticality is a key feature of a maintenance service contract.

In complex high value contracts, support services (whether this is for software or hardware) may be typically set out in a document described as a Service Level Agreement (SLA) . Naturally an SLA will contain service levels (sometimes called key performance indicators) which are an integral part of creating good service contracts (especially where the supplier is performing a particular business process). Drafting and negotiating specific terms in the SLAs requires deep cooperation between the technical staff and the business process owners. Monitoring the service levels takes time and effort and there is no point in preparing SLAs that will never be monitored by the customer. During the drafting and negotiating stage, it is important to clearly define terms such as up-time, reliability, responsiveness, testing time, time for turnaround of test, and time to fix a problem. From a customer's perspective, statistics provided by the supplier should be independently audited or measured by the customer's contract manager.

In complex contracts, it is common to see service credits for failing to meet service levels and incentives (such as service debits) for exceeding service levels. Such performance incentives will ensure a successful outcome to the contract or provide a dispute resolution solution without actually terminating the contract.

From a legal perspective, it is important to ensure that the service credits are a genuine pre-estimate of loss and not a penalty. Service credits likewise with liquidated damages may be considered to be unenforceable under UK law.[14] From a supplier's point of view, the supplier will try to ensure that service credits are sole and exclusive remedy for the supplier's failure to achieve the service levels. From a customer's perspective, the customer will try to ensure that while service credits may be limited to a capped amount that the customer is still entitled to use the overall liability cap specified in the contract to recover additional damages and that service credits are not the sole and exclusive remedy.

---

14 See Dunlop Pneumatic Tyre Co Ltd v New Garage & Motor Co Ltd [1914] UKHL 1 (01 July 1914).

1.1 In respect of Service Credits, the supplier's liability shall be limited in each Contract Year to £[xxxxx] [the greater of £[xxxxx] (subject to indexation) or [xx] percent of the annual Charges].

1.2 Subject to the annual Service Credit limit in Clause 1.1, where applicable the supplier shall automatically credit the customer with Service Credits in accordance with Schedule [X] (Charges and Invoicing). Service Credits shall be shown as a deduction from the amount due from the customer to the supplier in the next invoice then due to be issued under this Agreement. If no invoice is due to be issued then the supplier shall issue a credit note against the previous invoice and the amount for the Service Credits shall be repayable by the supplier as a debt within [10] Working Days of issue.

1.3 Where Service Credits are provided as a remedy for Service Failure in respect of the relevant Services it shall be the customer's exclusive financial remedy except where:
- the aggregate number of Service Failures (whether the Service Failure relates to the same or to different parts of the Services) exceeds [specify a pre-specified number] over a period of [three] consecutive months;
- any Service Failure that exceeds the Service Threshold;
- the failure to perform the Services in accordance with the Service Levels has arisen due to [theft, gross negligence, fraud, or willful default]; or
- the customer is otherwise entitled to or does terminate this Agreement for the supplier's Default pursuant to Clauses [X] and [X] (Termination for Cause).

1.4 Where Service Credits are not provided as a remedy for a Service Failure and the supplier has failed to address such a Service Failure to the reasonable satisfaction of the customer, then the customer may, on written notice to the supplier, withhold a proportionate amount of the Service Charges for those Services until such time as the relevant [Service Failure is remedied][Services are restored]. [Provided that the relevant [Service Failure is remedied][Services are restored], the customer shall resume payment of the relevant part of the Service Charges, including payment of the amount retained.]

1.5 Not more than [insert frequency] during the Term, the customer may, on at least three months written notice, change the Service Credits applicable to one or more Service Levels provided that:
- the principal purpose of this change is to reflect changes in the customer's business requirements and priorities, or to reflect changing industry standards;
- the change is not specifically intended to penalize the supplier for poor performance in relation to any particular Service Levels; and
- there is no increase in the total value of Service Credits potentially payable.

Table 20.3   Service Credits clause (pro-customer)

1.1 If the Service Level falls below the [quarterly] target of [98 percent] for the online availability for the Software, a Service Credit of [1 percent] of the [Quarterly Service Fee] for each full percentage point by which the resultant availability falls below the [quarterly] target of [98 percent] will be allocated to the customer as its sole and exclusive remedy.

1.2 A Service Credit will take the form of agreed additional services to the value of the Service Credit. These services will be provided in the form and at a time agreed by the parties.

1.3 The above measurement will take place for each complete [quarter] and will commence on the first day of the third complete [quarter] following [the acceptance of the Software].

1.4 The total aggregate value of all Service Credits in any one quarter relating to the Software shall not exceed [10 percent] of the [Quarterly Service Fee].

1.5 The parties acknowledge and agree that the Service Credits payable under this Clause 1 shall be in full and final settlement of the supplier's liability for failure to achieve the Service Levels. Such Service Credits are accepted by the parties as being genuine pre-estimates of the losses likely to be suffered by the customer.

1.6 The supplier's failure or non-performance of its obligations under this Agreement shall be excused and the supplier shall have no obligation to pay Service Credits under this Clause 1 or have any other liability in respect thereof to the extent that such non-performance results directly or foreseeably from a failure to by the customer to meet any of its obligations under this Agreement.

Table 20.4   Service Credits clause (pro-supplier)

20.13 Upgrades

Customers will want to understand their supplier's approaches to product and technology life cycle. Given today's rapid change and development, they will be concerned over whether suppliers address this through new product introductions that may rapidly put them on outdated technology, or through a coherent upgrade policy. The degree to which that policy forces them to adopt each upgrade or enables selective application may have significant implications to their business. Issues of cost and functionality will cause them to want to plan and control adoption – especially where these impacts extend to the way they interface or provide services to their markets or customers.

As a supplier, if you want customers to upgrade regularly to stay within a release window, you will want to consider offering availability of certain upgrades for a period of time at a specified price. It is also important to identify exactly what has changed in terms of functionality and interoperability in order for the customer to plan and cost-out the upgrade.

The contract should specify who, or what level, in the customer's organization is authorized to approve upgrades and the installation of them. This is especially true when it involves any parameter associated with increased software (e.g., MIPS, processors/engines) or other costs.

Don't forget about disposal costs of hardware or other equipment, which may have environmental issues and possible data security concerns. Who will be responsible for them?

20.14 Compatibility

Compatibility needs to be defined for each environment, by the customer and the supplier. Historically, suppliers have sought to move responsibility to the customer through 'selection and use' criteria. However sophisticated customers are reluctant to accept this transfer of risk and take the view that the supplier should have the technical skills to determine and commit to interoperability. Compatibility is usually most critical with a networked component (router, hub, switch, server).

The customer must understand the target environment and structure its acceptance tests where compatibility will be an issue. The customer will need to ask what protections are provided by the supplier for product upgrade compatibility, especially the software built into the network equipment. In some cases, the supplier does not provide the compatible software or hardware add-ons, but rather will rely on business relationships with third parties to determine and/or supply particular parts. If this is the custom of the selected supplier, the supplier will need to make sure that the customer is made aware of such relationships in the contract.

In some cases, third party suppliers provide discounts in the fees they charge the seller that are then passed on to the customer. In other cases, the reselling may involve costs to the customer that are greater than if they bought the equipment or software themselves. If a third party seller is involved, customers are encouraged to request an estimate of the costs before committing to the contract.

20.15 Services contracts: overview

A company typically enters into service contracts to augment its own capabilities; for example to procure skills either difficult to develop internally, too expensive to develop in the needed timeframe to meet a critical need where time is of the essence, or to provide a skill, functionality, or operation missing in the current environment.

The provision of consultancy services is aligned to the provision of software and hardware, whether on a short-term or long-term basis. Consultancy services will vary from contract to contract but may broadly cover implementation or installation services or additional services required for the specific project. Such service procurement may involve the procurement of an individual contractor (whether software developers, software programmers or project manager) for a task or to perform a particular process, operation, or defined activity. For example, it may be necessary to procure skills either difficult to develop internally, too expensive to develop in the needed time-frame to meet a critical need where time is of the essence, or to provide a skill, functionality, or operation missing in the current environment. Often an individual contractor from a supplier organization may only be effective if integrated into the customer organization's processes and procedures and will operate as a seamless extension of the relevant organization with little or no distinction between the relevant organization's employees and the individual contractor. There are many opportunities for the supplier to add value to customer organizations without adding headcount, but to achieve this added value it is critical to understand the customer's business goals and objectives.

Unlike products, there is no tangible deliverable in many services agreements, so performance characteristics tied directly to specific goals are important and should act as a driver for the definition of clear roles and responsibilities for both parties. The issue of roles and responsibilities is often inadequately addressed. Obtaining clarity indicates that the parties have properly considered and analyzed the actions or processes required for success. It also protects the parties, reducing their risks and the likelihood of disputes. Without clarity, the probability of confusion, delay and cost overruns are substantially increased.

In dealing with service contracts, often the schedules will set out:
- The responsibilities of the consultant
- The functional responsibilities for each customer's employees
- The required education and skills sets for the consultant (s)

20.16 Statements of Work (SOWs) and milestones

Management of service contracts via the terms and conditions in the service contract is very important to prevent future disputes and misunderstandings. The 'deliverables' going to the customer must be set out in specific and detailed terms and should be set out in a document usually described as a Statement of Work (SOW) or a Work Package.

Complex managed service contracts may include an overarching master services agreement with clearly defined SOWs, milestones, and performance metrics. It is not mandatory to have either milestones or the performance metrics, but they will make the contract easier to manage from both parties' perspective. Governance, change control procedures, escalation points and reporting requirements should also be clearly defined in the SOW.

In contracts where delivery of services involve access to and processing of customer data that is confidential, it is a good practice to include an analysis in the SOW of what data is accessed or transformed, the amount of data, and the level of confidentiality of the data. By following this procedure, both the supplier and the customer are aware of the likelihood for breach of confidentiality and can ensure that data privacy and security are maintained. This process is especially important where records are of a medical, financial, or government classified nature.

Good project management includes monitoring the project to ensure delivery against the SOW. Thus, the more guidance it provides, the greater the chances of successful completion. Clarity in these areas also assists greatly in identifying when change is needed, and in avoiding or speeding resolution of disputes.

Customers will often seek a 'knowledge transfer' from the supplier to enable their staff to eventually perform the functions themselves. The necessary steps might be detailed in the SOW. Good communication between the supplier and customer project and/or contract managers is critical to seamless project quality and knowledge transfer and they are assisted greatly by clarity and thoroughness in the original contract documentation.

For more detailed discussion and guidance on Statement of Works, please see Chapter 22: *Statement of Work and Service Level Agreement production.*

20.17 Termination

Many contracts ultimately fail because there is no clear language describing what occurs at the contract's end. The issues this creates are in no sense unique to technology contracts, but there are aspects of IT that have made them occur with greater frequency. In particular, the relative newness of most IT products and software makes it harder to predict results. This increases the likelihood of disputes about performance and the relative contributions of the parties to whatever results were achieved. These factors must be adequately considered in setting terms in such areas as payment, acceptance, and termination.

The most common areas for terminating the contract are:
- 'For Cause' termination: this means that either party has breached the contract in a way that cannot be cured. In such cases, the party breaching has a much greater duty to make restitution. Critical contact links are the definition of what represents 'cause'

or, more pertinently, a 'fundamental breach'. The second link relates to the contractual consequences remedies that arise.

- 'For Convenience' termination: this occurs at the option of either party, usually with some minimum notice. Typically, a customer does not wish to allow a supplier to terminate for convenience; it is certainly essential to assess the consequences it might have and protect against them. From a supplier's perspective, termination for convenience will be unwelcome from a revenue recognition perspective.

The severity of impact depends on factors like contract duration, the extent to which resources were committed, the payment terms and obligations for early termination. The customer will need to consider what the effect of termination will be on their business and processes and whether there will be a downstream impact on future business.

Overall the impact of termination is likely to be greatest if the products being produced are highly customized and therefore offer little chance of use or a long ramp-up time for another supplier to step in and continue development. However, suppliers may actively seek termination for convenience provisions if this is a new technology or a new application where results are unpredictable. In such situations, the right to walk away with limited financial consequences is very attractive to them.

The final point on termination is to be aware of its potential use as a lever for renegotiation. If the customer is able to threaten a supplier with transfer of the services to a competitor, this becomes a powerful weapon to drive down prices or extract expensive concessions. However the customer will need to be certain that it is not tied into the supplier's product and can terminate the contract without disrupting its business operations. Suppliers will negotiate wording to defend themselves from such situations by having fixed term contracts, to ensure that their products continue to dominate the market, and that they continue to provide value for money and innovative services.

The question of what happens to payments for partial work product upon termination needs to be made on a contract-by-contract basis. Generally, a customer will want any termination for cause to result in forfeiture of any payments paid in advance in addition to other contract liabilities such as damages where the supplier is in breach of contract. The supplier may well resist where the customer has received a benefit from its services before termination.

Terminations for convenience by the customer generally require payment to the supplier for any 'winding down' activities plus possible liquidated damages for the early stoppage of the services. The supplier will need to ensure that rights of the customer to suspend work cannot be used as a *de facto* termination of the contract without the associated payment liabilities.

Upon termination, a customer may require transition assistance to allow another supplier to continue to perform the service. This may include:

- Transfer of data – transfer of customer-owned data to the customer or another organization
- Staff transfer – the supplier's staff are transferred to the customer. The transfer of staff is regulated by the Transfer of Undertakings (Protection of Employment) Regulations 2006 (TUPE) in the UK and is a complex area where specialist employment law advice should be sought
- Knowledge transfer – the supplier's staff must train the customer's staff to use the product where the product is owned by the customer
- Transfer of partially completed product including potential designs or drawings – this may be contentious to the supplier if original source code is required to transferred unless the customer owns the intellectual property rights in the partially completed product.

A termination clause must also consider and address rights or obligations to continued performance during the transfer period from one supplier to another; for example, in respect of services for work completed, or transfers of data or knowledge to support mission critical operations and for instance, the impact on a customer's business where the supplier is capable of switching off access to a vital software product.

Each of these requirements may have severe implications to the supplier regarding their competitiveness and market reputation. They represent extreme risks to a supplier and therefore will be resisted or, if unavoidable, the possibility that they could occur will need to be minimized.

20.18 Summary

Technology procurement contracting presents a higher level of complexity than most other types due to issues of privacy and security, intellectual property rights, the technical interdependency of systems, the array of term and condition options, and the fact that most key business processes are highly dependent upon technology. The relative unpredictability of installed performance is also greater than in most other industries – and the method and techniques of measurement are less mature or defined.

This results in two major areas of concern for the customer:

- How predictable and well controlled are the costs associated with this procurement?
- How confident can the customer be that the results achieved will be at or above the levels set out in their requirements? As part of this calculation, the customer must also

consider the realities of legal recourse and the extent to which the supplier has a vested interest in the outcome.

The customers and suppliers who can work together to achieve the greatest assurance in these two areas will emerge as consistent winners.

CHAPTER 21

Term linkages, managing cost and risk

21.1 Overview

This purpose of this chapter is to provide information about best practice processes, methods, tools and techniques on how to develop intelligent, business goal focused agreements that find the right balance between risks and costs and business opportunities. This chapter challenges the reader to look objectively at terms and conditions to seek the best deal from a win-win perspective and covers:

- Contract structure
- Active terms (terms that affect cost)
- Passive terms (terms that affect risk)
- How they relate; key inter-linkages between terms
- Opportunities to share cost and risk reduction through creative contracting
- Pricing arrangements

After reading this chapter you will be able to:

- Recognize the need to analyze the downstream effects of term choices and risk strategies
- Understand the balance between cost and terms
- Examine each side's goals and term options objectively
- Validate your objectives against term options to ensure they make business sense
- Align your objectives with the other parties to reach synergy
- Create options and alternative terms for effective cost, risk and opportunity management

21.2 The challenges of term linkages, managing cost and risk

Contracts are necessary, so what are your goals? From a subjective point of view you want to minimize your risks and costs and maximize your profits. But so does the other party. The goal is to find the right balance:

- You want to minimize the degree to which terms and conditions get in the way of your business objectives without negating the issue of establishing an acceptable business risk profile.
- You want to create focus on the right things to minimize the time spent on negotiations.
- You want to ensure that the internal process is lean and easy to use, has the lowest possible cost, and presents the least chance of mistakes and omissions.
- You want to ensure that a governance process is in place so that change is managed effectively and control is maintained to achieve the expected results.

21.3 Contract structure

Contract structure must be appropriate to the nature and the value of the relationship being formed; contracting is not a one-size-fits-all activity. You will also want to maximize the efficiency of your contracting activities. Contract structure should have some common legal elements for all contracts and solution-specific elements depending on what is being bought/sold. For example, the contract structure for selling an item or commodity (e.g. raw materials, computer hardware, gadget) would be very different from the contract structure for a complex services arrangement (e.g. software development or a business or IT outsourcing arrangement). In the latter contracts, there will be more emphasis on warranties, Intellectual Property (IP), security, and service levels than with the commodity type contract. A click-through process may work for commodity-based (simple and repeatable) contractual relationships, but for complex customized service contracts like business process outsourcing, IT or business transformation) a more flexible and interactive contracting method will be preferable.

You might use a combination of methods to get to your final agreement - using a click-through approach to get through the minutia efficiently in order to get to terms that have to be discussed and agreed. This enables you to focus on the important topics.

Inefficient methods cost time, money, increased negotiation and potential risk through lack of clarity.

Case study – your company
While reading this chapter, keep in mind the different relationships that your company manages. You must be able to overlook the entire portfolio of contracts. Consider the following list of questions:
- Approximately how many different contracts do you have?
- Approximately how many variations in contract structure?
- Approximately how many different terms and conditions are there?
- What items are considered when reviewing a proposed change?
- What is the exact cycle time for agreeing contracts?

- What is the frequency of each term variation? Which terms?
- Do you examine each side's goals and term options objectively when considering variation of terms?
- Do you have a strategy to align your objectives with the other parties to reach synergy?

21.4 Negotiated terms

Each year IACCM undertakes an analysis of the terms that are most frequently negotiated. This is based upon member surveys; the replies represent a wide range of industries and several thousand contracts professionals and other related professionals. These terms are important because they reflect where the market stands in its perspectives on risk and cost. Most negotiation is about re-balancing business risk and cost – so each time you negotiate or amend a term, you are potentially changing the risks and costs to your company. At the same time, you may be affecting your attractiveness as a supplier or customer.

IACCM in recent years has also asked its members what they would like to focus on in order to reach more business success. The 2011 results are shown in Table 21.1 below.

	The terms that are negotiated with greatest frequency	Terms which would be more productive in supporting successful relationships
1	Limitation of Liability	Scope and Goals
2	Indemnification	Change Management
3	Price/Charge/Price Changes	Communications and Reporting
4	Intellectual Property	Responsibilities of the Parties
5	Confidential Information/Data Protection	Service Levels and Warranties
6	Payment	Price/Charge/Price Changes
7	Service Levevls and Warranties	Limitation of Liability
8	Delivery/Acceptance	Delivery/Acceptance
9	Liquidated Damages	Dispute Resolution
10	Warranty	Indemnification
11	Insurance	Payment
12	Scope and Goals	Audits/Benchmarking
13	Service Withdrawal or Termination	Information Access and Management
14	Applicable law/Jurisdiction	Intellectual Property
15	Responsibilities of the Parties	Business Continuity / Disaster Recovery
16	Invoices / Late Payment	Confidential Information / Data Protection
17	Change Management	Applicable law / Jurisdiction
18	Performance Bonds / Guarantees / Undertakings	Liquidated Damages
19	Dispute Resolution	Service Withdrawal or Termination
20	Audits / Bechmaking	Entirety of Agreement

Table 21.1   Commonly negotiated terms

As the most negotiated terms list illustrates, the top priorities are strongly weighted towards costs and risk containment clauses. But is this strategy always the right one from a business goal and win-win perspective? The terms in the right column represent the terms negotiators believe will yield more productive results and perhaps indicate a paradigm shift in term linkages and how we construct agreements and apportion costs and risks.

21.5   Active versus passive terms

An active term requires a process or resources for its implementation or management. Terms that fit this description would include procurement procedures, audit obligations, invoicing and payment, including review procedures.

A passive term limits or controls the consequences if something goes wrong, but is typically irrelevant if things go well. Terms that might fit in this category would include Limits of Liability, Dispute Resolution Procedures, Early Termination Provisions .

Some terms - for example warranties – contain both active and passive elements. In this example, a warranty defines the scope of responsibility or liability (passive), but may also set a period of time limit, specific levels of service or actions that will be taken to ensure compliance (active).

21.6   Terms Audit

A Terms Audit needs to ensure that terms align with:
- Business objectives
- Market or business needs and priorities
- Resource capabilities and commitments
- Business processes (and opportunities for their improvement)
- Risk assumptions

If terms are aligned with these factors and steps taken to ensure continued alignment over time, then contractual and business risks are minimized.

This is a critical activity throughout the product or service lifecycle. We will look at some examples later in this chapter.

Questions to consider during the Terms Audit are listed below. How you answer each of them will affect the way that you develop terms.

- What are the strategic drivers and goals for our business?
- What are the strategic drivers and goals for our business partners?
- What additional goals (if any) apply to our group?
- For each contract term, have we identified what strategic goal(s) it supports?
- When it comes to negotiation and contract management, where do we spend our time today?
- Which specific terms and conditions or contract types do we spend time on?
- Does time spent support the goals?
- What are the gaps that need to be addressed?

For example, does your company focus on price to the exclusion of cost? Could the cost of business be reduced to give greater benefit?

The outcome of a Terms Audit may be more limited in public or government markets, given the frequent inflexibility of the buyer. This should not, however, be used as a reason not to assess and understand the approach to terms and conditions so as to assess the appropriate focus, strategy and tactics.

21.7 Term analysis

The terms of a contract can have a significant impact on the cost of a contract or the risk involved. Terms that you or your contracting partners have embedded in standard 'boilerplate' clauses in contracts can have severe effects on your business if they are not reviewed and analyzed.

Don't accept lack of clarity or definition in reviewing and defining the requirements for the project. Understand clearly the business objectives and the long-term goals. This means that you must identify the key internal stakeholders and where necessary validate assumptions directly with them.

Two things tend to happen with terms:
- They are not updated to reflect changes in business circumstances or market conditions.
- They are frequently based on assumptions of probability or best practice that are not tested.

Since few organizations have any methodical system to check or validate the use or effectiveness of terms, most organizations go on reusing the same ones time after time. Changing the term is often difficult because of the approval process it involves (passive) or because of the resources and process implications (active). However, organizations should look holistically at the product and the market when developing their product marketing campaigns, or at the business requirements when making an acquisition. Review of terms should be an on-going process with the legal department to make sure they are still relevant to the business, competitive in the marketplace and within the range of acceptable risk tolerance of the company.

As an illustration, let's look at a data storage supplier. Their systems are nearing commodity status and therefore the competitive challenge focuses on just a few characteristics: price, delivery, uptime commitments, response time, and overall data storage and retrieval quality. But in fact not all the supplier's customers are identical and market segmentation may offer opportunities to differentiate through higher value terms. This segmentation will reveal the need to look at utilization of the product and avoid a one-size-fits-all approach.

For example, one sales representative has two prospective customers: one is a stock exchange and the other is a large corporation that needs to produce internal financial reports. Each customer is looking at exactly the same hardware. If a standard approach is taken, neither customer may be happy, since they both have different needs.

The stock exchange is looking for a highly reliable, always available, system, with protection against interruption or data loss. Any downtime or irregularities will have a severe impact on their business and trades.

On the other hand, the corporation is mainly concerned about data integrity and retrieval by their existing reporting tools. Any system outage will be an impediment to reporting, but not to business continuity.

Each system is necessary and will result in a sale for the supplier, but as we can see the goals for each customer organization are different and thus should generate different terms and conditions for the contracts for its acquisition. It will affect pricing, support, service levels, warranties – a wide range of terms, but will make absolutely no difference to the core product.

Be imaginative when reviewing terms and conditions to reduce overall performance costs and to align with business requirements. Is there a better way to handle a concern? Look at the term from as many points of perspective as possible. Remember that if you can see ways to drive down the supplier's cost, this can be traded for a price or term concession. If you can find a way to reduce the buyer's risks or offer something of unique value, this may expand the deal and generate competitive advantage.

Identify where you and the other party agree, and where the requirements coincide with your respective capabilities and strengths. To achieve further success, focus your efforts on driving out the number of the mismatches or areas of weakness and focus on gaining strength on those areas that coincide with each party's respective needs and requirements.

21.8 Shifts have impact

Skilled contract developers recognize that seemingly innocent terms can have huge impacts on the long-term costs and risks of a project or relationship.

Best practice companies review their contract templates on a regular basis to anticipate shifts in market conditions or reflect business conditions. Is a term past its prime? A term that once worked for you may now be working against you.

There are a variety of shifts that can affect negotiations including business, market, economic, and political, and regulatory matters. For example, from a customer perspective, a fixed price (without any inflation price indices) might be highly desirable at a time of general price inflation; but it may represent a real exposure in a market or industry where prices are potentially going to fall. From a supplier's perspective, just the opposite desirability exists. A compromise position that can be offered is to share the risk of future inflation risk between customer and supplier.

A different illustration is the shift that has resulted from concerns about corporate governance. More companies are concerned about insurance issues and suppliers are increasingly nervous about unquantifiable liability exposure. Revenue recognition rules have similarly raised the importance of the payment terms and provisions around acceptance or rights of rejection and return.

A current issue that IT suppliers are wrestling with is the provision of providing a high limit of liability for breach of security relating to personal information or confidential information where the customer has control and influence over the degree of security requirements.

21.9 Paradigm shifts

A change in business environment may require a paradigm shift[15]. The way you have done something in the past may not be the best way to do it in the future, and recognizing the differences is key. The term shouldn't be the issue; the business objective is what matters.

Let's look at an example where the customer's business need is to manage risk. A shift occurs because changing business requirements require you to look for a new supplier and the existing supplier may not be able to meet the new requirements.

---

15 A change in the basic assumptions, or paradigms, within the ruling theory of science (according to Thomas Kuhn: *The Structure of Scientific Revolutions* 1962),

The customer organization is in discussions with a potential supplier and has a particular contracting paradigm based on past experiences with similar suppliers. Due to past circumstances and events the organization has developed specific terms in order to manage risk. These terms are now embedded in its standard contract and experience has shown that this approach works well.

Now the negotiations with the potential new supplier have stalled because these terms are sticking points. Even though the supplier's product fulfills the customer's new need, and everything else is acceptable, neither side wants to budge and the negotiations are in jeopardy. What often happens in situations like these is that no one discusses why a particular term is in a contract and what it represents; what the business reason behind it is.

By sticking with the existing paradigm of managing risk through specific terms, you will have a hard time coming to a win-win solution. Consider stepping back, identifying and analyzing the issue and the business need. You may recognize that the offending term(s) serve the wrong purpose. If risk management is the issue, approach your partner and discuss whether there may be alternative ways of managing project risk. You may find that a fresh approach frees the discussions to find better ways of doing business together that are mutually beneficial.

An example might be a 'Most Favored Customer' clause. While examining the contract, you wonder if what you are signing today will be competitive tomorrow. Your concern is responsible and legitimate. You are also concerned to show those business units that will be implementing the contract that you have protected their interests. You know that Most Favored Customer is not an effective tool and will be resisted by a supplier. So maybe you start adding clauses of your own: for example, exit clauses, limited price increases or defined price decreases based on volume or over time. You start thinking about re-bidding the contract regularly to ensure a competitive price, although signing up to a longer term or a committed volume agreement can often result in achieving more attractive prices from suppliers.

First, make sure that the arrangement really requires a clause of this type. Then take a fresh look at the terms and see if there isn't a creative way to reappraise the price of a product without having to go through the time, trouble and expense of a complete re-bidding process. Is there a way to make the price fluctuate with the market? Can you link the price to a price index? What else might you do to address this? Other alternatives include a benchmarking provision or competitive market test provisions or a sharing of future inflation risk between customer and supplier.

Second, how can the customer demonstrate to a supplier that it is in their interests to find a solution to the customer concerns? Solutions here might include having the supplier pay for regular third party audits, or alternatively you could make the requirement for a creative solution part of your Request for Proposals (RFP) process. The supplier may want to comply if in return they obtain a longer-term business transaction. Make it part of the competitive bid process and you might be surprised by the creative solutions that are generated – as opposed to the negative reaction a Most Favored Customer clause is likely to generate. As part of the RFP process, require each supplier to respond to the RFP as written but in addition to the 'answer the mail' response, allow the suppliers to propose alternative solutions to the business requirements. The customer will then have compliant responses as well as some creative supplier approaches and ideas to consider.

Look for approaches that build cooperation and consensus rather than confrontation or compromise. Try to look at win-win situations where the models you used before are reversed to drive out more value.

Let's look at an example. Imagine that you are a company that needs to outsource some services. Outsourcing deals often focus on price and deliverables, not overall business goals and results. Try to ask the outsource provider to look at how it can best apply processes, technologies and capabilities that will drive value to you. The business goals could be to reduce costs, improve services or win new markets. Ask the outsourcing provider to deliver those specific results and shift the risk for reaching this success to the outsource provider. Now, you need to give something in exchange for this risk taken by the outsourcing provider. You must therefore allow the outsource provider to earn additional profit for achieving this incremental value, and this profit must be above and beyond industry average profits for their service area. In addition you must commit yourself to provide a certain level of business for the outsource provider, e.g. a long-term contract. This new technique - called Vested Outsourcing - is a way to create true business values in the contract and creates a win-win situation.

21.10 Legitimate terms that miss the point

Most Favored Customer clauses are just one example of clauses or terms that fail to deliver against real objectives. Too often contracts are written to specify how something will be done, rather than what the goal is. That often stifles creativity and causes contention; it usually results in the goal being missed.

The way that certain Statements of Work (SOWs) or Service Level Agreements (SLAs) are described provides some classic examples. Let's look at this clause for instance:

"Grass will be cut every Wednesday during the months of April through October and treated with Famous Lawn fertilizer and weed killer every fourth cut."

What are the goals here? Why may they not be exactly met? What could be done instead?

It might be raining on a Wednesday or a drought exists and the grass has died back. Famous Lawn fertilizer brand may not be available or a cheaper equivalent is available. So your approach led to an inefficient service and did not incentivize improvement in performance or cost. Try to create a clause that focuses on your real business goals - to maintain a beautiful lawn - and build in a benchmark clause, if needed.

Now let's apply this thinking to a warranty clause example: You offer a one-year warranty, that states 'repair or replace', and as policy you mostly repair. Competitors have increased their warranty to two years. Your product managers want to introduce a three year warranty in order to differentiate your product.

Your research shows that:
- Costs are forecast to be low because most corporate users dispose of the product after two years and the warranty is non-transferable.
- Longer warranty periods are mostly being offered and valued in a consumer market, while your customers are mostly corporations.
- Most product failures are initial product failures occurring in the first 30 days and 80 per cent of ongoing claims are associated with the same product.
- Customers are dissatisfied with 'repaired'. They want and believe they are entitled to new products.

What would you do? One answer would be to develop the right for initial failures returned within 30 days to be automatically replaced with new products. Replacing with new products would actually be a greater and more valuable differentiator to your customers, as well as providing your company with a cheaper method to manage.

21.11 Performance cost of the deal

The objective of any negotiation is to get the best deal. Part of the cost figure is the performance of the contract. Sometimes we insert terms or insist on terms that drive up cost and aren't in balance with what we really want. Always consider value and cost in the context of needs and intended use over the term of the agreement (Total Cost of Ownership - TCO).

For example, don't make assumptions about the most effective delivery model, especially in complex or multi-location deals. Make sure you have understood the business capabilities of the customer, the supplier, and third parties to ensure different cost models can be explored. Who can manage shipping and delivery at the lowest cost? Where should integration take place? Who is best positioned to provide relevant skill requirements?

21.12 **Acceptance provisions**

Acceptance provisions are usually based on past experiences and are written accordingly. An alternative approach is to involve the supplier in the development of acceptance provisions that suit both companies. Put the delivery of acceptance criteria in the Request for Information (RFI) and emphasize the need for creative approaches to effective acceptance criteria. Encourage creativity and innovation from your suppliers – it will generate new ideas that may represent the latest best practice. As a supplier, take every opportunity to persuade customers of your commitment to true win-win terms – creative solutions that reduce the mutual risks of failure.

21.13 **Preferences – supplier versus buyer**

Sometime we have legitimate and ostensibly reasonable issues, but they can be very difficult for the other side to manage. We need to differentiate and understand what is required versus what is merely desired.

For example, some jurisdictions have revenue recognition regulations that affect payments and the timing for which a supplier may 'book' the revenue as earnings. The pressure to show revenue will affect the way the supplier wants to get paid.

Maybe as a buyer you would like a 30-day right of return. But cancellation rights like this keep a supplier from booking the revenue for 30 days. Maybe they can accept this situation if you ask them in October, at the start of a financial quarter. But they will have much more of a problem in December, when it will hit quarter and/or year-end results. You may be able to use this to your advantage – in October they may accept your demand; in December they may offer other concessions to have you drop that request. As a supplier, you may steal an advantage over your competitors by having thought about this in advance. The key is to be flexible enough to find solutions that work for both parties.

21.14 **Multi-country projects**

Contracting for the rollout of a replicated deal across multiple locations and multiple countries will have plenty of challenges and opportunities. There is significant complexity around structure and content. Look at the big picture and develop the best model for achieving the business objectives.

One major issue is knowing what you need to know and finding the information. You are challenged with analyzing the data to come up with a cost-effective and workable solution.

For example, a global supply and distribution business goal is to supply product as quickly, efficiently and cheaply as possible. The resulting plan may look very different in the US from the same plan in Europe, Russia, or Asia. Even states within regions may have to have different elements that effectively deal with local conditions. In this example, one size will definitely not fit all, and will cost you dearly if you try to force it. Conditions and needs in your own location are likely to vary significantly - you need to understand and categorize these variations to develop a logical and cost effective solution that matches your needs and supplier's capabilities.

SLAs provide an example. Paying for 24X7 service on a piece of equipment that is non-critical and infrequently used will not make sense. In remote areas it may be impossible for the supplier. Review the business need and risk and determine the acceptable level of coverage for each location or equipment type. State that to the supplier and see if they or a subcontracted third party can comply. Multiple levels of support for a variety of conditions may be the best and most cost efficient way to deliver service. A variety of definitions and conditions can be developed to express the true support needs of each business type. The end result is to fit the service to the business needs.

21.15 Contract pricing arrangements

Research shows that performance-based contracting might be superior to traditional pricing and contracting models, yielding not only lower costs and higher margins, but also acting as an incentive to innovation (IACCM Research Highlights, 2010). However, traditional pricing models have great importance in many contracts. We will now explore the direct linkages via contract pricing arrangements; some of them link to performance-based contracting. Here is a list of arrangements:

- Firm fixed price
- Fixed price with economic price adjustment
- Fixed price incentive
- Firm fixed price, level of effort
- Time and materials (cost reimbursement)
- Cost sharing
- Cost plus fixed fee
- Cost plus incentive fee
- Cost plus award fee
- Time and materials and labor-hour

Firm fixed price

Firm fixed price contracts require the delivery of specified products and/or services at a price fixed at the time of contract award with limited rights of price or service adjustment.

It is appropriate for use when fair and reasonable prices can be established at the time of award, definite design or performance specifications are available, products are off-the-shelf or modified commercial products or services for which predictable and competitive prices can be offered, and any performance uncertainties can be identified and reasonable costs estimated in advance. Any fixed price service or product contract should include measurable service levels for the supplier to meet. The potential advantages for the customer are that it places total responsibility and risk on the supplier. The disadvantages for the supplier are that it lacks flexibility in pricing and performance but an advantage is that it does provide a predictable revenue stream over time. A well-documented contract change control and governance process needs to be part of the final agreement to accommodate changes in services after the contract award.

For many customers this is the preferred type of contract and the most commonly used, requiring the least amount of contract administration on the part of the customer, while pushing the risk of performance and cost over-runs onto the supplier. However, if the supplier can produce the product or service at a lower cost than forecast in the sale model, then the supplier has an advantage. It is important to pay close attention to change provisions and mechanisms under such agreements. Buyers should make enquiries about the supplier's history and organization in managing changes. Sophisticated suppliers commit to a fixed price and then drive their profit in the change process.

An effective 'Sweep' clause can be used to make sure that changes required in the normal course of delivering the services are not abused by the supplier. The intention of a Sweep clause is to make sure the customer did not miss something that the supplier would claim was not in scope, then demand additional compensations to perform the work that was implied. A balanced Sweep clause is one that includes services related to the RFP services that were being provided by the previous supplier just before contract signing. On the same point, an overly broad Sweep clause creates additional unknowns and risk to the supplier. The intent is a way to capture depth of the requirements rather than expanding or broadening them.

Fixed price with economic price adjustment

Fixed price with economic price adjustment contracts are used where the market for a particular supply or service is especially volatile or the contract is of such length that inflation of costs is inevitable, and the customer needs a contract for a term greater than just an initial quantity purchase. It is possible to use a contract type that allows for adjustment in prices based on changes in market conditions. Although the contract contains initial firm fixed prices, the prices are adjusted accordingly during the performance period based on the changes in an independent pricing index. The consumer price index or other commodity price indices that are not controlled by the supplier can be used. The contract must contain a clause explaining how the price adjustment will be made, identifying which price index is to be used, the frequency of adjustment, sharing of inflation risk, and any overall ceiling or floor price.

Fixed price incentive

Fixed price incentive contracts provide incentives for efficiency in performance by offering high profit for outstanding performance, modest profit for average performance, low profit or loss for below average performance. The contract contains a price ceiling, a target cost, a target profit, and a formula for adjusting the profit based on performance, e.g. by using benchmarks. It is appropriate for use when cost incentives will be likely to result in savings and better performance than a firm fixed price contract. An alternative to the target profit, for those suppliers who do not want to expose their cost of delivery, is to provide service levels with incentives. The supplier is incentivized to out-perform and is rewarded with additional price and has a disincentive to under-perform because they would incur service level credits. This approach is quite common in business process outsourcing.

Achievable incentives must be identified and criteria established for evaluation of performance to determine if the incentives are met. The incentives must be objective.

The advantage of this contract type is that it causes the supplier to be more efficient, as profit (or price) is tied directly to performance. The disadvantage lies in the difficulty of evaluating performance. This contract type should not be used unless it is determined to be the least costly type, and other types are impractical. Sometimes performance and delivery incentives are added to the basic cost incentives in this type of contract. The key is to establish service levels and incentives that are objective, measurable and directly related to business value.

Firm fixed price, level of effort

A firm fixed price, level of effort contract is useful in some cases to cover professional services. It provides a specific number of hours for a stated period of time at a fixed price. It describes the scope of work in general terms and often includes specifics related to the types of skills the supplier personnel should possess. The supplier is normally required to submit reports showing the results achieved with the level of effort, and payment is based on effort expended effort rather than fixed deliverables or end results.

This contract type may be appropriate when the work cannot be fully defined in advance but the level of effort can be identified.

The contract may call for a specific project to be completed, or the customer may be buying the required services over a given period of time. The advantages to the customer are that the supplier must perform without an increase in the price and level of effort. This type of contract can be used in situations where a cost reimbursement contract would otherwise be necessary. The disadvantage is that there is no guarantee that the desired results will be achieved.

The limitations on using this type of contract are that it should only be used when the work cannot be clearly defined. The level of effort must be identified with reasonable assurances that the desired results cannot be achieved by fewer labor hours. Level of effort contracts have a heavy contract administration burden on the customer to assure that the supplier makes the best possible effort to achieve the desired result. In this type of contract the customer is purchasing expertise priced by an hourly rate rather than an end result.

Time and materials (labor rates)

Time and materials contracts have an estimated cost ceiling (a not-to-exceed price) that is negotiated at the time of award, which caps the price for the services to be delivered. Supplier profit is generally built into the supplier labor rate. Labor rates should be market-competitive for the skill set and geography of origin. Discounts for the labor rates should be negotiated for any long-term engagements (more than three to six months). Time and material contracts are frequently used for the purchase of labor resource with no defined end-item deliverable (sometimes called 'staff augmentation') and also may be used when a fixed price contract is not practical, due to the magnitude of performance uncertainties. Contracts with nonprofit organizations are generally performed on this basis.

The advantage of this contract is that it is economical if the supplier is efficient and conscientious in performance. The disadvantages are that it has a heavy contract administration burden, requiring surveillance by technical personnel to assure against supplier inefficiency and waste, and there is little incentive for the supplier to reduce costs.

Benefit/cost sharing

A benefit/cost sharing contract is similar to the time and materials type, except that it provides for sharing of costs between the customer and the supplier, rather than full reimbursement of cost. The parties agree to a sharing ratio at the time of award, illustrated by buyers share then sellers share. For example, there might be a 60/40 sharing ratio, where the customer has 60 percent of the cost/risk and the supplier has 40 percent of the cost/risk.

Use this type of contract when there is a high probability that the supplier will realize substantial commercial benefits as a result of receiving the work. An example would be development of a new product or system for a customer that could then be sold on the open market by the supplier. In this case the customer should negotiate a perpetual, royalty-free right to use the developed work product, while the supplier would be likely to receive the intellectual property rights associated with the developed work product. This would enable the supplier to market the resultant product or a derivative of the same in the commercial market place.

The advantage is the mutual benefit to the supplier and the customer, but the disadvantages are that there is little incentive to control costs and there is a heavy contract administration burden to ensure that costs are efficiently used. The contract must contain a ceiling amount and the supplier should be able to show conclusive evidence of anticipated commercial benefits to the customer. This type of contract is rarely used because of its complexity and difficulty to manage.

Cost plus fixed fee

Cost plus fixed fee contracts are among the least preferred contract types by a customer because they place total responsibility for contract performance on the customer. However, in some cases their use is necessary because to use any other type of contract would cause the supplier to charge excessively high prices due to its need to cover the risks associated with the uncertainties involved. Cost plus fixed fee contracts have an estimated cost and fixed fee (profit, stated in a specific money amount) negotiated at the time of award, and costs are reimbursed up to the estimated cost and the specified fee is paid. The fee is normally stated as a percentage of the costs and it may only change when the customer directs a change in the work to be performed. This contract is appropriate for use only when no other type of contract will work, such as when there is a high degree of uncertainty surrounding technical and cost factors.

The advantage of a cost plus fixed fee contract is that it enables work to be performed with only a general scope and indefinite specifications, where the exact nature or extent of the required work is unknown. The disadvantages to the customer are that it provides minimum incentive for efficient cost control, there is a heavy contract administration burden, and the fee is paid without risk to the supplier. As with all cost reimbursement contracts, the supplier is only required to exert commercially reasonable efforts to perform required work unless otherwise agreed, e.g. best endeavors or similar concepts.

There are two forms of cost plus fixed fee contracts. In the first type the scope of work must have a definite goal or target, and an end product to be delivered. The second type has a scope of work stated in general terms and requires the supplier to deliver a specified number of hours of effort for a specific period; and no end product is required to be delivered. The completion form requires that the supplier completes and delivers an end product before any payment on the entire fixed fee can be made.

Cost plus incentive fee

Cost plus incentive fee contracts are appropriate when a fixed price incentive contract is not possible because of the technical and cost uncertainties. Performance objectives are known and confidence in achieving those objectives is high. A formula that will provide for performance incentives can be negotiated.

The following are negotiated at the time of award: target costs, target fee (profit), Minimum and maximum fees, and a fee adjustment formula. There may be delivery or performance or cost incentives, either individually or in combination. The formula is applied and adjusted upon completion of the work, within the maximum and minimum fee limits. Fees are increased from the target fee if there is a cost under-run and decreased for a cost overrun.

The advantage to the customer of this type of contract is that it encourages economical and effective performance when a cost reimbursement contract is necessary. The disadvantage is there is a heavy contract administration burden in monitoring the attainment of the various incentives.

Cost plus award fee

Cost plus award fee contracts combine the elements of the cost plus fixed fee and cost plus incentive by providing an estimated total cost (costs are reimbursed), a minimum fee, and an award fee based on the quality of the supplier's performance. Criteria are established measuring the supplier's performance and evaluated periodically throughout the contract for the purpose of determining any award fee due the supplier. The award fee decision is not subject to the filing of a claim by the supplier. It is a unilateral decision of the customer that is not subject to further review.

Typically this contract is used where the measurement of activity can only be subjective, as objective standards are not available. Milestones, targets or goals are not identifiable.

The advantage of this contract is that it provides more incentive for supplier efficiency than a cost plus fixed fee contract. The disadvantage is that it requires significant resources for contract administration, as a fee determination panel must be established and constant monitoring of the contract is necessary to ensure that the award fee accurately rewards actual performance. In addition, meaningful criteria for assessing supplier effort must be developed, and award fee decisions must be timely to affect any desired changes in the quality of support effort. New contracting models use intermediaries who measure performance and award fees according to industry standards (benchmarking).

Time and materials and labor-hour

A time and materials contract provides for payment of direct labor-hours at fixed rates and material at cost, no fee or profit for materials. The hourly rates are 'loaded' rates that include all indirect costs and profits. The contract contains a price ceiling that the supplier may only exceed at its own risk. The labor-hour contract is a time and materials contract in which there is payment only for actual labor hours. These contracts are not preferred by customers in most cases, due to their lack of incentives for controlling costs and hours expended. They may be appropriate when it is not possible at the time of award to estimate the cost of a project with any degree of confidence, or the nature of the work is known but not the amount of time required.

The advantage is that either of these contracts may fulfill a special need that no other contract type can achieve. The disadvantage is that the technical personnel must perform extensive surveillance of the supplier to preclude inefficiency or waste since there is no positive profit incentive for the supplier. These types of contracts may be needed for maintenance or repair services under emergency conditions. The contract may be structured like an indefinite quantity contract and issuing delivery orders may obligate funds, or the contract may simply obligate funds for the ceiling amount.

21.16 **Summary**

Conflict on terms and conditions should ring warning bells. No best practice business will have conflict over terms and conditions without awareness that it is happening and why. Unmanaged and uncontrolled conflict creates friction in business relationships that diverts resource, increases emotional levels (in a bad way), and ultimately leads to irreparable damage in business relationships and results.

Contracts professionals' goals should be:
- To use the technology, tools and skills to create relationships and environments where issues are discussed.
- To avoid poorly thought through or irrelevant conditions.
- To strive for discussions on real business needs: cooperation versus confrontation.
- To create solutions through cooperation and mutual benefit.

If all parties are openly and honestly trying to serve the business needs and objectives surrounding the project, the best results will emerge. Deal components should optimize performance of both parties and inspire all to do their best.

CHAPTER 22

Statement of Work and Service Level Agreement production

22.1 Introduction

This chapter addresses the cornerstones of contract creation and development, the Statement of Work (SOW) and Service Level Agreement (SLA) documents and covers:

- When they are needed
- What they should contain
- The importance of clearly defined requirements for each kind of document
- The level of detail required for various types of SOWs and SLAs
- The importance of having in place a change management process to maintain the flexibility often needed to complete the tasks

22.2 What is an SOW?

An SOW is a document describing the essential and technical requirements for items, materials, or services, including the standards that will be used to determine whether the requirements have been met.

The SOW is generally an exhibit to a Master Agreement. This Master Agreement states the general terms and conditions that apply to any work being performed. If special terms and conditions are needed for a particular work engagement, they should be stated in the SOW and identified as taking precedence over the Master Agreement in an Order of Precedence clause in the Master Agreement.

An SOW should identify measurable or verifiable performance and acceptance criteria; such criteria minimize any uncertainty about whether work has been satisfactorily completed.

Generally, the SOW is to be used when requesting customized or project-specific jobs. The SOW describes the project, including the tasks required to complete the project as well as any other applicable terms. Each task will have individual written completion criteria, as appropriate. A typical SOW will set out an estimated schedule for the project, which may be specified in phases or tasks, along with negotiated pricing and payment schedules. The project will begin on the start date specified in the SOW and will end on satisfaction of the completion criteria set out in the SOW. In more complex projects the SOW can be restricted to the technical description of the required deliverables with the other aspects, such as price, payment and timing, contained in other parts of the contract documents.

A Statement of Work may be simple or complex, flexible or definitive, depending on what it describes. It can be as simple as a 'brand name or equal' description, or as complex as the specific requirements for a software development, an outsourced business process, or a new building. Regardless of the complexity of the requirement, all SOWs should include the following critical elements:

- All tasks to be performed
- All deliverables
- The price
- Project specifications
- The completion/ acceptance requirements
- Any assumptions

22.3   Why is an SOW required?

A good SOW is like any other piece of expository writing in that it must be well organized. It must educate those who read it by moving from things generally understood to the exceptional items, from the commonly known to the highly specialized.

It is as important to the supplier as it is to the customer that the agreement for work performed is formalized in a legally binding document. Within the document it is imperative that control mechanisms such as acceptance criteria or service levels are documented to ensure successful completion of the project.

The SOW generally represents a working document that will be used by many different parties to oversee and manage the deal. Clarity, simplicity and thoroughness are key attributes to minimize confusion and dispute and to provide a good baseline for assessment of change.

22.4   Basic process for developing an SOW

The creation of an SOW should begin by gathering the business needs and goals, functional and technical requirements. Next, the project should be assigned a timeline from start-up to completion, to determine if it can be completed within an acceptable time frame. All the deliverables should be determined and listed along with their schedule of completion. Each deliverable should have a specific definition of what it is, constitutes completion and makes them acceptable.

Finally, the payment for the deliverables should be tied directly to their acceptance. However, in certain circumstances it will be appropriate to agree to advance payments or stage payments that are linked to agreed periods, achievements or milestones, or that recognize the scale of start-up expense for the supplier.

The six steps in the basic SOW process are described below. They are:
1. Gather functional/technical requirements
2. Define overall project timeline (plan)
3. Deliverable/checkpoint schedules
4. Quality management
5. Completion/acceptance criteria
6. Compensation and payment schedule

1. Gather functional/technical requirements

The functional and technical requirements need to clearly address the business objective. One way to ensure that is to hold Requirements Gathering Sessions. These should be held with all interested parties, including users and experts, to gather the requirements. Detailed functional and technical requirements from initiation to completion of the SOW are necessary if the supplier is expected to hold to and be measured on financial, schedule and performance criteria.

The SOW should plainly state what is wanted, not how the work is to be done. Wherever possible suppliers should be encouraged to determine the best method of performing the work to achieve the results required within the specified functional/technical framework. When necessary, specifications and standards may be defined; however, these should not be unnecessarily restrictive. If the SOW does specify 'how' work is to be done, it should require commercial items or best practice wherever possible. The SOW must provide a detailed description of the product to be provided, service to be performed or system to be developed relative to desired output and performance.

Sometimes, to avoid misunderstandings, it is equally important to explicitly determine what not to do or what is excluded from the SOW. A RACI chart is also a practical and important summary to quickly identify each party's obligation and validate them through the contract creation process.

2. Define overall project timeline (plan)

If a schedule will be involved, a detailed written Project Plan should be developed before beginning the project. The plan must identify each task and deliverable, from beginning to end of the project, along with all associated dependencies. Ensure that the people who will be performing the tasks or scheduling experts have developed the time estimates, and that they are not someone's off-the-cuff guess. Upon acceptance of the project plan and schedule, it establishes a base timeline, which may be used for performance measurements. Once the project begins, the supplier and customer project teams will monitor the plan to avoid conditions arising that could jeopardize the project.

3. Deliverable/checkpoint schedules

The deliverables must be measurable and quantifiable items that can be identified in the various stages of the work product detailed in the SOW. Figure 22.1 provides sample deliverables associated with an SOW.

SOW Process Example of Deliverables / Checkpoints

This is an exhibit from an actual SOW. *The supplier is contractually bound to start the project on December 12, 2003 and end on April 3, 2004. The Change Management Process will document deviations to the project schedule, checkpoints or functionality of the project.*

Figure 22.1   Sample deliverables associated with an SOW

4. Quality management

To meet best practice the supplier's quality control and quality assurance procedures must ensure that:

- Deliverables meet requirements
- Deliverables are executed within the agreed time frame
- Deliverables shall have no known defects
- Deliverables are maintainable and can be enhanced to meet anticipated changes
- Deviations from the supplier's organizational standards and procedures are approved, in writing, before the implementation of such deviations or changes have no effect on the cost, quality or time-scales of the contract and there is no effect on form, fit or function of the product / service
- Quality control standards used by the supplier's employees result in the desired quality level in project deliverables
- Project management and control procedures and standards are being followed
- Project statistics are collected for improvement in the process and also for use as the historical basis for enhancing the accuracy of future estimates

5. Completion / acceptance criteria

It is critical to define the completion criteria for each project and how they will be used to measure the acceptability of each deliverable. These agreed-to criteria detail both parties' obligations relative to the performance of the deliverables.

The criteria are measuring tools so both parties will know when a deliverable is acceptable. Once the supplier specifies that a deliverable is complete, acceptance testing should begin. The deliverable will be accepted or rejected according to predefined, and mutually approved, procedures and criteria detailed in the SOW.

The supplier will want to ensure that this is conducted on a timely basis, using objective criteria, qualified personnel and under conditions that fairly represent operational conditions. The customer will similarly want the test conditions to provide an accurate set of results that are likely to be replicated in normal operations. The SOW needs to specify rights and obligations in the event of partial acceptance or rejection.

Completion will occur when you have accepted all test cases and deliverables, and all supplier responsibilities have been closed through sign-off, and final billing has been submitted and paid.

Completion and acceptance criteria are also important to determine when the deliverable's warranty period, if applicable, starts.

6. Compensation and payment schedule

Invoices and payments in the amounts identified in the SOW will be payable when a deliverable or milestone is completed and accepted according to the SOW acceptance criteria and documented to the supplier according to those criteria. Final payment will not normally be made until the entire project has been accepted in writing, and may be subject to retention amounts for some period of trouble-free operation, or compliance with defined service levels. Retention is especially likely if this project is one component of a larger contract – whether or not being fulfilled by the same supplier. It may be used as a performance incentive or to encourage cooperation. The supplier, however, may require full or substantial payment in the event that the customer uses the deliverables before granting acceptance.

SOW process consideration: change management

When either party identifies a required change, that change must be validated. It is important that any changes to the project that affect the terms of the SOW are managed through a formal Change Management process. It must be determined whether the change requested is already included in the SOW, or is a new item that will need to be added. The cost and schedule impact must be determined before initiating any change to the SOW. If both parties agree that the change is necessary, and accept the cost and schedule impacts, then the change should be documented and added to the SOW in the form of a formal amendment.

Change management is covered in detail in Chapter 32: *Change control and management.*

22.5   How do SOWs and SLAs relate?

An SOW contains a description of the products or services that will be provided. An SLA defines the level of support under which services are provided to ensure that the SOW is achieved on time. In order to understand what is included within the SLA, let us examine some possible candidates for SLAs.

As a way for keeping current the major enterprise resource planning (ERP) systems or new development for these systems, many companies are outsourcing their ERP systems or help desk responsibilities. The most common candidates for outsourcing today are Human Resources (HR), Finance, program management, software development and help desk.

The SLA is a comprehensive tool to monitor and manage supplier performance for the provision or receipt of the services provided. The SLA typically identifies the fixed measurements for the delivery of the services and spells out measurements for performance and consequences for failure. In addition, both parties must clearly understand their respective roles and responsibilities.

In an outsourcing environment, SLAs are intended to encourage supplier performance to achieve a level of overall service that meets or exceeds the level of quality that existed for the same services before execution of the Master Agreement, and at a significantly lower cost. In other words, the supplier's quality should be equal to or greater than your internal service levels and the costs should be equal to or less than existing costs for those services, whether currently provided by internal or external resources.

The sharing of risk is always of concern to both parties. The supplier in most cases would be happy to provide a straightforward Time and Materials agreement in which the services are provided and the hours billed. The customer would like to have a fixed price to work with and wants to put the burden on the supplier to provide the appropriate services without having to manage the numbers of individuals. Service levels are a mechanism for measurement that provides a comfort level to the customer that they will get the services required for their business and to the supplier that they are no longer required to provide headcounts and staffing levels. The challenge is that there is always a desire by the customer to know where the initial pricing came from, which invariably leads to a headcount discussion. This comes into play later when service levels are being met, and the individuals who support them are seen to be involved in providing other services.

There may be situations where either:
- Current service levels and cost are unknown and have not been monitored
- This is a new service or function that was not previously performed

In such circumstances, it is important to undertake tests or benchmarks that provide some reasonable base against which performance expectations can be set and measured.

The customer will want to fully understand the cost of receiving services and the basis for the calculation of those costs. Further, the SLAs are intended to keep pace with improvements in industry standards for quality and efficiency over time, with all SLA changes agreed to between the parties. An SLA may set either specific improvement targets over time, or criteria against which review and change will occur. Although this may seem burdensome to a supplier, there are some real benefits to be gained by defining improvement criteria. One is that it reduces the competitive threat of regular re-bidding, or more attractive offers during the terms of the agreement. Another is that it lessens the likelihood and costs of handling unplanned change requests and disputes from a dissatisfied customer.

The SLA can be part of the SOW, or written as a separate agreement. If the SLA is a specific section in the SOW, the general terms and conditions of the Master Agreement and any special terms in the SOW apply with the special terms taking precedence over the Master Agreement. It is important to ensure, regardless of where the terms are situated, that there is a section dedicated solely to the SLA's terms and conditions. If written as a separate agreement, all terms and conditions normally found in your Services Agreement should be made part of the SLA.

The quality of the SLA is important. It must be complete, comprehensive and accurate in its coverage. It is essential that both parties understand and agree to their obligations described in the SLA.

22.6 Service Level Agreement (SLA)

An SLA specifies in detail the support the supplier will provide to the customer. It may also set limits or conditions on performance based on customer or third party obligations.

It must include:
- Levels of required performance
- Consequences for failure to reach or maintain these levels

- Descriptions of the parties' roles and responsibilities in achieving the performance levels

Consideration should also be given to including consequences in the event that the service levels are exceeded. Section 21.8 below goes into more detail about the content of the SLA.

22.7 IACCM outsourcing survey

IACCM recently ran a survey on outsourcing to identify the 'pain points'. The respondents were contract and sourcing managers from cross-industry backgrounds and currently involved in outsourcing deals.

The survey results indicate that developing outsourcing SLAs is a concern in sourcing deals to more than 75 percent of participants. They indicated the need for training or more information in establishing SLAs and metrics. Since poorly written service agreements are clearly such a concern, it is not surprising that performance monitoring and disputes are two of the top three concerns about outsourcing.

If you are entering into an outsourcing deal, the business requirements must be clearly understood and articulated in order to write workable SLAs. Take the time upfront to ensure that the business goals are adequately reflected and that the selected measurements are unambiguous and will accurately demonstrate the nature and cause of any problems or shortfalls.

22.8 What is included in an SLA?

The purpose of the SLA is to describe the service level models that monitor and manage performance of the supplier. Customers will want the SLA to continuously measure and report the supplier's performance. You may mutually agree on a ramp-up period before actual measurement of a service level, to enable a period when expectations will not be disappointed and problems can be ironed out.

Some examples of typical metrics, measurements and performance tracking are:
- Number of pieces
- Run rates
- Uptime
- Response or problem resolution time
- Project actual turn-around time versus estimated turn-around time
- Defect rates and resolution

- User satisfaction
- Cost per transaction or time period

Best practice metrics include:
- Pro-active problem resolution
- Time to fix
- Dispute frequency

Before execution of the Master Agreement, all parties agree to the SLA's performance requirements, performance periods, and reporting requirements. The SLA should include specific performance metrics against which you can evaluate the service provided. A good SLA agreement will specify when, by who and how requirements are monitored to verify that SLA requirements are being met. Increasingly, monitoring is online and real time – periodic reports are too limited in their application and do not support pre-emptive problem resolution and another growing trend is the use of third party specialists to monitor performance.

SLA components example: scorecard

A scorecard is one method for the customer and supplier to measure progress. The service level scorecard summarizes the supplier's performance with an agreed scoring matrix. If there is a target range, or a threshold must be met before a category can be scored, ensure that is understood.

On a periodic basis, each service level metric is scored, whether or not the target level is achieved. Achieved targets will receive a score equal to the agreed upon scoring matrix, which in our example is 1. Missed targets will receive a score of 0. The scores are added together under the weighted system to determine the final or reporting score.

It is recommended that both sides sit down together to determine what will be measured, who and how it is to be measured and how it is to be scored based on the business requirements. We recommend using the SMART method for defining performance objectives. (Specific, Measurable, Relevant, Time bound.) The scores, method of recording and reporting must be clear and acceptable to both parties before scoring begins.

As we have discussed with other items, have a change process in place in case what you think is important to measure turns out to be the wrong thing. Both sides will want to ensure that the business goals are being met. If a system of metrics has missed the mark, they can all be achieved while the business goal is missed – threatening the longer-term interests of both parties.

For example, if you have outsourced a help desk and framed the metrics around speed of response and call time, you may find that calls are answered quickly and cleared quickly, but the problem is not resolved resulting in call-backs. In this case the targets are hit, but the business need of resolving issues efficiently is missed.

SLA components example: direct metrics

A direct metric is the single lowest level metric that will measure the supplier's performance, where the supplier has the direct responsibility for the performance of the project. A simple example of a direct metric is hours worked; say you are building something and the supplier is billing by the hour for people. So the direct metric is actual hours worked, and the analysis is hours worked versus hours estimated or budgeted.

In a simple example, there is a metric that measures work completed and compares it to the budgeted work hours. This example includes a metric result with a 0 tolerance. That is, actual hours to complete the project should not be more than the estimated hours; when the actual is divided by the budget the total should be 1.0 or lower. The project will be considered on budget if completed within budgeted hours.

In our example, there were 40 budgeted hours to complete the project and the supplier's actual time to complete the project was 42 hours. Using the formula, the project-on-budget result is 1.05 and is unacceptable because the criterion is 1.0 or lower.

Hours worked is an overly simple measurement, since there is nothing stating what was worked on or accomplished. It is a valid measurement and typically used for billing purposes, but a poor indicator of project success. Let's just take this example for instance, if during that time frame the supplier was to build 12 units in a 40 hour week and they completed 13 in 42 hours, they would have failed one metric and surpassed another.

Other direct measurements are pieces made, length of item produced, volume filled, etc. Direct metrics have their place in contracts and projects, but ensure that the metrics you choose to measure success use are meaningful.

SLA components example: defect rates

The defect rate is a measure that applies to the supplier's responsibility to produce acceptable goods or services. The principal intent of the defect rate is to assure that you are receiving a level of quality equal to or better than agreed.

To demonstrate defect rates we'll use piecework as an example. Piecework defect rates pertain to requests from customer to supplier to manufacture or produce individual pieces, whether that is a module of programming code, calls to a help desk, spool of cable, bottle caps, gadgets, chips, processors, etc. The key is that for X number of pieces delivered the number of defects will be less than Y; where y divided by x results in a percentage indicating the defect rate. Whatever that percentage or defect rate is will typically be set to meet or beat industry or regulatory standards.

For example, you are running a bottling operation and fill 10,000 bottles per day for your customer. Your bottle cap provider is supposed to match your run rate by delivering 10,000 caps per day, and have a defect rate of less than one percent, or no more than 100 bad caps.

If you were measuring software development or installation, the total number of defects is the total of all programming errors or bugs in a particular module. In this instance, they may be further broken down into classifications. For example, 0 critical or work stopping defects will be allowed.

SLA components example: staffing

A staffing metric is used to track supplier performance in providing requested resources within expected timeframes or for stated durations.

Staff delivery rate will be based on the number of business days between the date you present a request for supplier personnel and the time a suitable candidate provided by the supplier is available to begin work. To meet this metric, the supplier must provide a resume accurately describing the candidate in no less than X business days (here the number of days is negotiated) before the desired start time for the candidate, and must deliver the candidate to start work on the date required. You also agree to the number of days allowed to review each resume. To be suitable, a candidate must have the skills described by the job qualifications section of the personnel request.

Both sides will have negotiated in advance the lead times by skill level; the more rare or in demand a skill, the longer the lead-time required to bring in the right person. The skill level criteria will be an exhibit to the SLA or SOW and lists all skill levels that may be required and the lead-time and rate for each skill level.

SLA component example: supplier satisfaction survey

Sometimes the only way to measure a supplier's performance is to survey the customer base; the frequency of this should be determined in the SLA. In these instances a formalized satisfaction survey should be used. Online surveys are easy, fast and inexpensive. Of course care must be used to create metrics that make sense and have relevance, and the questions must reflect the criteria. You can always do a small sample survey and then poll the participants individually to get feedback on your effort, to see if you are getting across what you want to communicate and getting back responses that are useful.

Be aware that surveys can be manipulated to almost guarantee the results that the survey writer wants, so ensure that whoever is conducting the survey does it as objectively as possible. If possible, both parties to the contract should have a say in the survey questions and answer choices.

Always include a box for comments to pick up those valuable nuggets of information that people want to communicate. Sometimes the best suggestions for a resolution come from those surveyed. Professional marketers use surveys as a means to ask better questions later. An online survey can be followed up with a more personal interview style survey if greater depth of understanding is required.

The example questions below reflect satisfaction surveys to determine service level attainment. Both parties must define and agree to performance factors stated in the SLA and found in the survey. Performance factors can be rated to meet your needs, for example:
- 5 for outstanding
- 4 is very good
- 3 is satisfactory
- 2 is unsatisfactory
- 1 is poor

Define each rating explaining what that rating means. For example:
- Outstanding: outstanding performance sustained over rating period.
- Unsatisfactory: meets or is below minimum quality requirements.
- Poor: unacceptable performance consistently below minimum quality requirements.

Both parties establish a formal plan to improve the specific quality measurements when unsatisfactory results occur, and timeframes in which those improvements will be accomplished. Obviously, further opportunities are jeopardized by marginal performance, and the contract itself may be in jeopardy of being breached.

Both parties will have to agree what levels of service and satisfaction are acceptable, and if the aggregate of all performance factors needs to be equal to or greater than a satisfactory rating. If an individual performance factor is unsatisfactory or worse, specific criteria should be in place to address that failure. A supplier overall rating of unsatisfactory or worse will constitute a service level failure. How you will address that should be included in the contract.

22.9 **Other SLA considerations**

Finding the balance between what the customer desires and the risk level the supplier is comfortable with agreeing to takes considerable discussion.

No supplier is going to sign up to provide a service at a 100 percent availability without a price that provides for multiple redundancy and a lot of back-up personnel. The customer will drop the percentage in order to pay a reasonable price. But the parties have to balance the cost and percentage while taking into consideration the unit of measurement. A 95 percent percentage may seem very reasonable at first sight, but if the quantity being measured is small, a single failure may result in missing the service level. This has the effect of making the SLA 100 percent availability. One possible solution to this dilemma is an agreement that no single failure will result in a service level failure.

SLA credits

Providing a clearly defined set of service levels is the first step in the agreement, but without consequences there is little value. When reaching the agreement on these consequences, some of the areas to take into consideration are:

- The customer wants the services, not the money.
- The SLA consequences provide an incentive to provide the services and improve their efficiency, not a penalty for failure.
- The ability for the supplier to 'earn back' a credit due to the customer provides additional incentives to correct problem areas.
- The supplier will be more likely to accept the SLA credits if there is a cap on the maximum penalty.
- The ability to adjust the credit mechanism on a regular basis to reflect issues and changes in focus is a benefit to the customer. This also requires that sufficient notice is given to the supplier so their focus can be adjusted appropriately.
- Trading monetary credits for additional services
- Providing bonuses if the supplier exceeds the specified service levels. This re-enforces a positive relationship but needs to be underpinned by real value being delivered through over-performance.

Statement of Objectives (SOO)

There is a growing use in US federal contracting of Statements of Objectives (SOO). The customer includes in the RFP an SOO containing the desired ultimate purpose, end objectives or transformation attributes of a project. The installation environment and any relevant constraints are also described, but there is no effort to attempt a description of the specific work to be performed in achieving the objectives stated in the SOO. The suppliers are instructed to interpret the SOO and describe their solution(s) in a Performance Work Statement (PWS) when they submit their bids. Through a 'best value' evaluation process, the optimum combination of solution excellence and business features (cost, schedule, performance history, etc.) leads to a selection for contracting, in which the winning PWS becomes the contract SOW.

Continuous improvement

Service levels evolve over time. If the supplier is achieving every SLA without any issues, the incentive is of little value. For those SLAs that are being consistently met, the agreement can include an automatic improvement clause. These are usually re-leveled on an annual basis based on the previous 12 months of measurement. The basic improvement is often described in terms of a percentage of the difference between the existing SLA and 100 percent. An adjustment should also take the actual achieved SLA levels into consideration. This can provide protection to both parties in avoiding excessive changes upward or resetting the SLA at a level that is still effective.

22.10 Summary

In summary, the following information is applicable to the overall SLA metric process.
- A scorecard is created by summarizing all reported metrics.
- The customer and supplier develop and agree SOW, budgets and delivery schedules.
- During the SLA set-up period, determine which applications are within the scope of the SLA. If there is a ramp-up period, or delay until full measurement begins, that must be explicitly stated.
- Determine who in each of the parties will be responsible for managing and administering the SLA metrics process. This includes managing and performing the planning, tracking/collecting, reporting and reviewing of all metrics on a periodic basis. In the event of a failure of any metric, each party should be notified in writing immediately. The supplier will be provided a reasonable opportunity to review the details of metric failures and propose corrections.
- There are a number of reasons why the metrics may fail that are beyond the control of a supplier. Any failures attributable to such events or actions should be excluded from all SLA metric calculations. Some examples of these discrete, identifiable event(s) or action(s) include network problems in networks provided by customer, hardware issues in the customer's hardware, the customer's downtime not caused by the supplier, availability of customer's personnel, other third party interaction, etc. Have provisions for such unforeseen instances.
- On a periodic basis, the customer and supplier will review the SLA results. Changes to the SLA require agreement and must follow the process of your change management program.
- The dispute resolution process applies in the event of a dispute between the parties.

CHAPTER 23

Drafting guidelines

23.1 Introduction

This chapter provides information, tools, techniques, and best practice on a range of contract drafting activities including:

- Identifying our role in contract development. What are the facts of this particular transaction or relationship; how do the facts of this situation differ from previous examples? What areas of contract will the issues or facts affect?
- Whose law will control the contract and will it affect the drafting and implementation of the contract?
- Examining contract language to see if it is clear and concise. How can the language be improved? Can everyone read the contract and agree to what it means?

After completing this chapter, you should be able to:

- Understand drafting principles and rules
- Think holistically about the drafting process and results
- Identify opportunities for improvements in our contracts

23.2 Clarity

The primary factor that makes quality of drafting critical is clarity. This is not just with respect to legal concerns, but more importantly it is to reduce the chances of dispute or disagreement throughout the life of the contract.

Lack of clarity causes confusion and with confusion comes higher cost of performance, potential damage to relationships and – at its worst – damage to a company's image with the other party, or to the public or to other customers.

Good drafting demands clarity and in achieving this, it acts as discipline not only between the primary parties, but also with other stakeholders, internal and external.

In reality, most of us do not regularly write agreements in their entirety. It is more usual to be producing amendments to specific clauses, or producing attachments such as Statements of Work (SOWs) or Service Level Agreements (SLAs). The principles covered in this chapter apply to any form of document that is part of or associated with the contract, such as the specification, SOW, or other contract documents.

23.3 Contracting transformation

The focus of contracting has transformed from specific requirements to a strategic view of the business plan and the marketplace. Understanding critical trends in the market will be crucial to keeping up with an ever-changing business environment. Product lifecycles are decreasing rapidly through technological improvements, and what once took years or months can now be done in days or weeks. The new business model will use technology-enabled systems that are driven by flexible business rules, rules that encourage contracting professionals to be innovative and use good business judgment.

A driver of the transformation is technology. Traditionally contracts were always in paper form, as physical entities. In the contracting world today we are moving towards the question of 'paper or electronic?'

The environment for contract drafting, submitting proposals, and procurement has changed and will not be restricted to paper. The design of these documents will be non-traditional in whole or part. Design and order of contracts for an e-business or web-based business environment is considerably different than for traditional business and print copies. 'Click through' agreements and clauses are changing the paradigms of contract and transaction structure.

For example, 'click through' clauses that are frontloaded into many websites today address the repetitive legal aspects before any real transaction is conducted. Consider how these types of changes can affect the way we contract.

There is an increasing trend to contract via an online auction process in which customers set up the terms and conditions applicable to the future contract and require the suppliers who wish to bid to agree to these conditions. Suppliers then compete in the auction to be awarded for the project in a real-time process to determine who will be finally awarded the project. Once the project is awarded to one of the suppliers, the final price plus the conditions previously agreed by all of them constitute the final agreement for the transaction. Such auctions raise interesting challenges to the extent that it is feasible for a supplier to seek to vary the stated terms and conditions. This will depend on the nature of the work being auctioned and the relationship between the customer and the supplier.

One caveat: since the e-business world is in its infancy compared to traditional tangible paper, we will have to stay current with the legality and enforceability of electronic agreements. There could be a lot more turmoil in the e-business environment as it matures, compared to the relatively static world of paper contracts.

As you consider the rest of this chapter, consider how the contract terms will be delivered. If you are working in an electronic environment, your views on drafting should be different from those of someone who is still working in a paper-based environment. For those in a paper-based environment is there an opportunity to embrace technology?

23.4 The contract document

When you have analyzed the business deal and identified your priorities, it is time to set the deal down in writing or an electronic format. The main purpose of any contract is to describe the transaction in a way that reflects the understanding of the parties. It is the 'rules of the game' document.

During negotiation, the contract draft compels the parties to focus on the major issues and forces a systematic review of those issues, a sort of 'reality check'. It also forces the parties to address and resolve difficult issues before problems concerning those issues arise. After negotiation, it provides an evidence base in dispute resolution, or informal settlement proceedings, making clear to the parties what their intended result should be. The more complete the agreement, the less possibility of a dispute over a problem.

However, your contract serves another very important purpose, that of answering questions. These are not just the questions beginning "Who, What, Where, When, etc." but also "What if…?"

- What if the product is defective and the customer can't use it?
- What if the customer needs to make changes in a construction project mid-stream?
- What if new intellectual property is developed and to whom does it belong?
- What if the customer declares bankruptcy and your company has provided them with equipment or materials?
- What if you sign a contract under duress?
- What if the parties have a dispute?

As the list above shows, a contract also provides answers to questions and remedies for problems and risks that arise during its performance and, sometimes, long after. If a contract is well drafted, it should provide answers and remedies for most problems and risks that may arise in the transaction it covers. Many organizations develop a living play-book that describes the elements that should be present on each contract type, as well as listing fall-back provisions, highlighting risks with each choice made and providing a step-by-step guided approach to developing the right contract for the particular business scenario. It is important to keep such a play-book updated to reflect changes in laws, processes, lessons learned from other contracts and also business strategy and perspectives.

If the contract has been drafted well, you should be able to find an answer for almost every situation. It may not always be the answer you desire, but if negotiations were done properly customers and suppliers will at least have been forewarned about the possibility of the negative result. If the contract is incomplete (or worse yet, if it doesn't even exist), you will be forced to look at other evidence, such as letters, oral testimony, or custom in the industry, most of which may be less beneficial, inappropriate or irrelevant. It is very important to remember that the contract is created to address all the events or risks that you don't anticipate and provides clarity on the outcome for each specific scenario.

23.5 **Why a written contract?**

It is rare for sellers who understand the risks to deliberately opt out of having a written agreement with a customer. Most sales employees understand the value of having a written document describing the business deal so that clear evidence of the deal and its terms is available if a dispute arises. However, many salespeople do not realize that they may accidentally make an oral contract, without understanding that their actions have now committed the seller to a deal that contains no protections for the seller. Many people have the mistaken impression that the only way to create a contract is to generate a multi-page document with a large number of terms and conditions and official signature lines for the parties. Nothing could be further from the truth.

A contract is simply a promise between parties. Basically, the following has to be identifiable: the parties, what is being sold and bought, and when (approximately) the transaction will occur. The written contract has to be signed or agreed to via e-signature process by both parties to make it legally binding. E-commerce has changed everything. The internet allows for speedier transactions, operating in a paperless, faceless global village with its unique problems, fraud and security risks and strengths.

The question of "why a written contract?" does not occur in some jurisdictions. For instance, Russian businessmen will not expect that it is possible to conclude contracts other than in writing or with a signature because this is required under Russian law for most contracts; they will not assume that other law can apply and allow for oral contracts. In other jurisdictions the business culture may not be so clear.

The US's Universal Commercial Code (UCC) does not even require that the parties establish a price, filling in that blank with the fair market value of the goods or service at the time of contracting. The promise could be written on a paper napkin, a scrap of paper, or the wall in someone's office, and if the items listed above were included, that scrap of paper, paper napkin, or wall could be admissible as evidence, and the contract could possibly be enforced against the objecting party.

Worse than this scenario, however, is that sometimes even a written statement is not required. A conversation over dinner or at a sales meeting with the customer could, if the subjects above are discussed and agreed to, be enforceable as well. The Statute of Frauds, which is in effect in most US jurisdictions, might provide a defense in that it states that contracts valued over five hundred dollars ($500) must be in writing to be enforceable, but the parties' statements or actions with regard to the transaction may often negate that defense. Many countries do not even require that contracts are in writing. The bottom line is "Understand that oral contracts are relatively simple to create and take pains to avoid their creation!"

What are the problems associated with an oral contract? As a film producer famously said, it "isn't worth the paper it's written on". The main problem is proving the basis of the deal, because the understandings of the parties are not clearly defined anywhere. Instead, vague, poorly defined statements that can be construed in several different ways are often the only determinants of the deal with clear statements usually presented only for issues not in dispute. Oral contracts also have large gaps in coverage on a number of issues. These gaps will be filled in by the UCC, the UN Convention or common or civil law, but the answers that the applicable law provides are often not the answers that we want.

Unfortunately, not everyone understands the concept of oral contracts. You can provide a great benefit to your internal business partners if you learn that someone has made an oral contract by insisting on following up with a written agreement, and using your company's standard terms and conditions to the extent possible. This may be able to undo at least some of the damage and should, at least, result in clarity as to what was actually agreed. You may not, however, be able to get as good a deal as you would have otherwise, since the other party will have little incentive to negotiate with you after you have already committed to do business with them.

23.6   What form should be used?

A contract can take many forms. Among these are purchase orders, letters of intent, letters of agreement, and even term sheets and SOWs if the right elements are included. We tend to use the word 'contract' to describe only a particular type of formal agreement, but the critical factor is not the type of writing, or whether writing exists at all, but the extent and intent of a party's promise.

The main benefit of a well-written contract is its entirety and clarity. You may not need much to make a contract, but 'short and sweet' will generally result in a bad contract. If you leave resolution of issues to law found outside the contract (UCC, the UN convention and common or civil law), you risk that the law's result will be other than you intended. What type of 'contract' should you use to describe your deal? There is no simple answer to this question, but your chief consideration should be:

> *"Will the document I am using be sufficient to describe the transaction completely and provide my company with the protection it needs?"*

A standalone purchase order from a customer is sometimes sufficient if it is for a one-time product order only and is also used for ongoing product purchases, as long as it references a General Purchase Agreement (GPA) that has been previously negotiated. Many companies will go through considerable effort to get a GPA or Master Services Agreement (MSA) in place that is extensive and structured in such a way that subsequent work can be undertaken by means of securing an SOW or Service Order. The intent behind this mechanism is to allow expedient processing of subsequent work and the SOW would simply contain the scope of work and other defined parameters while relying on the MSA or GPA to govern the relationship.

Some companies have a form called a Service Order which would be applicable to a one- time service arrangement or applied against a General Agreement or MSA with the customer. Where there are specific terms applicable to different products or services offered by a company, such as differing warranties or maintenance terms, a standard 'boilerplate' agreement covering a particular product or service may be used. One thing to keep in mind is that clauses can always be added to purchase orders, either mechanically or by attachment.

23.7   Rules of contract interpretation

The general rules of contract interpretation as employed by most US courts provide insight into the kinds of issues that frequently arise.
- Words are to be given their plain and normal meaning, except where prior usage may vary the normal meaning of the word.

- Technical words are to be given their technical meaning.
- Where possible, words will be given the meaning that best represents the intentions of the parties. Every part of a contract is to be interpreted, if possible, so as to carry out its general purpose. The circumstances under which the contract was made should also be shown.

When drafting a contract, the writer should ask such simple questions such as these:
- What am I trying to convey?
- Could it be interpreted in more than one way?
- How could I say it better?
- If someone unfamiliar with the contract were to read it, would their understanding match mine?

Rules of contract interpretation – common law countries
In common law countries there are three additional rules:
- The court fills in missing terms. If parties have agreed to all the material (important) terms of a contract but have neglected to settle some details, the court will fill in the details that are reasonable under the circumstances.
- Ambiguities are construed against the drafter. If a written contract is ambiguous, the court will use the interpretation that is less beneficial to the drafter of the document.
- Parol Evidence Rule[16]. Courts will not allow the introduction of extrinsic evidence other than the written contract to alter the terms of the contract

These rules do not generally exist in civil law countries. Many civil courts will even accept oral contract amendments or other prior written memoranda contrary to the Parol Evidence Rule.

23.8 Other contract interpretation guidelines

Some other interpretation guidelines to consider while drafting are:
- Words prevail over figures in the event of conflicts. For example, 'three' spelled out, versus the number 3.
- Specific and exact terms prevail over general 'boilerplate' language.
- Prior course of dealings may be considered to provide meaning to a term in dispute.
- Order of precedence clauses will be respected (in common law countries)

---

16 The Parol Evidence Rule is a substantive common law rule in contract cases that prevents a party to a written contract from presenting evidence that contradicts or adds to the written terms of the contract that appears to be whole.

23.9   Background to contract drafting

Why is contract drafting such a challenge, and why are so many contracts written poorly? It is relevant to note that lawyers assert the contract must be both clear, especially in avoiding ambiguity, and in accordance with appropriate legal conventions. Lawyers therefore have a significant role in contract drafting. The dilemma is that most lawyers and contract drafters are not generally trained in the art or science of contract writing. Contract drafting remains largely driven by the legal community, because the fallback role of the contract is to support litigation. Practically, however, contracts professionals should play a strong and leading role in drafting because:

- First, legal convention is not always an appropriate limitation.
- Second, it could contribute to lack of clarity. If we subscribe to the premise that contracts should be living documents and business tools, resorting to legal terminology may not help.
- Third, there are typically many sections of a complex contract that may have been written with little or no involvement by trained lawyers – areas like SOWs or SLAs are typical examples. This can create exposure and possible conflicts.

The basic premise of this chapter is the assumption that the contract represents an important tool for ensuring clarity of the transaction and relationship, and that the contract is an essential vehicle for communication between the parties to the agreement. The contracts professional is best placed to facilitate this through a combination of legal understanding and business operational perspective. This can avoid the situation where a legally sound document does not address the real business issues or local dimensions.

Because commercial contracting is relatively new to Russia, standard contracts common in other jurisdictions are frequently used without them being adapted to the local drafting culture and needs. For instance, in the insurance market, the use of standard contracts common for the London market creates a very substantial degree of confusion because Russian insurance legislation requires different terminology. The effort to create a local standard derivatives contract for instance has lead to a very complicated document because the continental models have not been taken into account. The software market has, for a long time, used license agreements which under local law raise a number of questions and issues.

Although the lawyer is a major stakeholder and could even be the ultimate owner of contract drafting, no individual should perform this role in isolation. The contracts professional should ensure that the relevant internal business stakeholders and other functional experts contribute and collaboration in the drafting, since all parties are going to have to live with the results.

23.10 **Drafting best practice**

To minimize disputes over legal jargon, best practice companies today perform contract drafting as a team effort. This ensures clarity in terms of business intent and ease of understanding. Business leaders do not generally use the language of legal jargon. A team effort is therefore more holistic and requires that the team review the entire contract; this ensures consistency of language, form and content. Lessons from these contracts are replicated across contracts over time, as companies build databases that collect experiences and lessons learned, to create best practice.

Consider that during the life of an outsourcing relationship, hundreds of people may need to understand and manage the relationship in accordance with the contract terms. Ease of understanding and clarity of intent are fundamental requirements. To achieve such goals, best practice corporations are adopting 'plain language' approaches to their contracts and agreements – and thereby enabling them to be used as vehicles for communication rather than a source of obscurity, which can result from too much legal jargon.

In summary, we must create an environment where the chances of confusion, failure and/or dispute are minimized.

23.11 **Before you start**

Before you start, you must understand the business needs and goals. Begin with the end in mind.

Next, make sure that you understand the environments in which this contract will be used and delivered.
- What are the norms for this party or market?
- Do they have any effect on what you are trying to produce or the way that you are proposing to do it?
- Does the structure or delivery mechanism change any of the terms?
- Is there an existing or 'sanctioned' template in hard copy format or kept in the electronic contract repository you should be using to ensure that the best practice your company has developed is fully used?
- Will you be drafting an agreement with various options to select from that range from low-to-high risk?

Remember that the higher the degree of fairness in the agreement provisions, the quicker it will be to finalize it, thereby reducing the cycle time. As well, consider building a living play-book to help govern a consistent and effective approach to contract drafting.

23.12 Drafting a complete agreement

The basic premise for all contract drafts should be that the contract should provide a clear, concise allocation of the risks between the respective parties. Such risk allocation should include a consideration of each risk that the parties might experience. All contracts should be created by using an appropriate contract checklist, which ensures that each contract risk is considered and adequately addressed.

When creating an entire agreement, you should draw on precedent – other similar forms of agreement or appropriate standards or model clauses, such as a corporate template library. Good business practice dictates that you minimize the number of variants, since this might inadvertently incorporate risks that previous samples have excluded. It is also confusing and potentially costly to the business to manage multiple variations of clauses that have the same or similar intent.

If there are no existing templates for what you are drafting, it may be valuable to draft your document in the form of a template and generalize where appropriate, so that it can be re-used later to create a similar type of agreement.

23.13 Amendments and attachments

When drafting amendments or attachments to complete or add to an existing agreement, it is essential that you scrutinize the structure, style and content of the original agreement.

Some considerations for review:

- Ensure consistent structure and terminology. If the agreement refers to 'Attachments', do not start calling these items 'Supplements' or 'Exhibits'. If this is an 'umbrella' or 'blanket' relationship agreement covering a range of products or services over time, be clear about what you are amending or supplementing – for example, is it the entire agreement and does it affect all future transactions and orders, or is it specific to one particular order or product / service type?
- Use definitions. Be aware of existing defined terms and use those same definitions throughout the document or amendments. Make sure you state the precise meaning of the definition and assure that use is consistent. For example, if the term 'Customer Enterprise' is defined as "all legal entities that are more than 50 percent owned by the customer or its parent company", then you must be cautious with use of words like 'customer' or 'enterprise'. With this example, each time you use the term 'customer', it may not include other legal entities; the word 'enterprise' therefore could create confusion. You may also need to clarify if 'Customer Enterprise' would automatically include any new parent company, if there was a change of ownership.

- Maintain words and drafting principles. Do not introduce new words or drafting principles that could cause either confusion or complexity. Even though a word may not be a defined term, you should use the same words to describe the same object or intent. For example, a reference in the original agreement to 'personnel provided by supplier', should be followed by use of the same wording. If you do intend something else, consider a switch to words like 'supplier's staff' to provide a deliberate difference. Similarly, if throughout the original agreement, notice periods are defined by a number of days (e.g. "will give 30 days written notice"), do not switch to different and confusing concepts – such as "shall give one month's notice" or "shall give 20 business days notice". The intent may be similar, but the variation becomes confusing both in terms of interpretation and in terms of possible administrative (system) consequences.

Administrative and system considerations

Whenever drafting a contract or individual contract terms we must be conscious of the administrative and system capabilities of the parties. Any term that requires an action needs resources of some sort for its implementation and / or management. What you write may make perfect sense, be entirely clear in its intent and completely reasonable from a legal perspective; however, someone must assure that it is feasible. Other questions you may want to address include:

- Is it the most cost-effective solution? Will special treatment be required?
- Does it represent a level of complexity or variation from norms or standards that will increase the possibility of non-compliance or failure?
- Do prices include or exclude taxes or shipping charges?
- Is the policy the same for all products or services, in all geographies or to all customer sets?
- Is the currency clear? (A major multinational US company agreed a contract in New Zealand with prices detailed in dollars but did not clarify that there were meant to be US dollars. The New Zealand customer did not realize that this was an error and required to pay in New Zealand dollars leaving the US company with an expensive lesson learned).

This is an aspect of drafting that is frequently overlooked, especially by lawyers who may not be familiar with the business processes, systems capabilities or general business policies.

As an example of this principle, what are the standard policies regarding payment terms – 15 days, 30 days, 45 days? What is the standard trigger for payment becoming due – upon shipment, upon receipt, upon acceptance, receipt of invoice?

These are fundamental issues when it comes to the cost of running a business; systems will have been programmed assuming certain principles. Any variation to those principles not only costs more because of the need for reprogramming or manual handling, but it also increases the chances of non-compliance or error. Therefore, they must be considered in drafting of contracts.

It should be apparent that clauses failing to establish clarity or failing to reflect company policy open the door to significant impacts on cost, invite disputes, damage relationships and can jeopardize business. The people who are drafting the contract must have enough understanding of the business processes to be able to ask relevant questions, adequately address the issues or close potential loopholes.

23.14 Drafting techniques

In all contract drafting activities, you must continually ask whether the language clearly, directly and completely states the agreement.

The following are some suggestions:
- Write in the present tense.
- Write in the active voice: Ask who is obligated to do something or to refrain from doing something. For example, do not say, "authorization will be granted by buyer" – Say, "The buyer will grant authorization."
- Avoid wordiness and delete unnecessary language. Don't say, "In consideration of the mutual promises herein contained, the buyer agrees to pay the seller 4 dollars per item. Say "The buyer shall pay 4 dollars per item"
- Draft in gender-neutral language. For example, "The buyer has the option…" rather than "The buyer may exercise her authorization…"

23.15 Contract terminology

Draft your words with care and be consistent in your use of words. Do not change a word unless you wish to change the meaning and conversely, always change the word you use when you wish to change the meaning. Let's take the word 'Execution'. In English this word means putting someone to death. As used in contracts, it could mean contract performance or it could mean contract signing. The word 'Prepare' might mean to get ready to do something or it might mean to actually do it. 'Turnkey' can have many different interpretations as we have seen in the Contract Types chapter, and should not be used in a contract unless clearly defined. Some words have different meanings in different languages.

Make sure you validate your choices and show understanding if there is apparent confusion.

Time
Be careful with references to time and dates. Not everyone operates in the same time zone, calendar, or date format. Agreeing to a delivery on 9/7 might mean receiving the goods on the 9th of July or September 7.

When asking for delivery on specific dates, review the actual day/date to ensure that you are not inadvertently hitting a weekend, holiday or other date that will result in schedule conflicts or unnecessary costs. A day that has no specific meaning to you may be a holiday in another region. Or a plant may have a scheduled shutdown the same week you expect a product to ship.

A contract many say "within 9 months of contract execution", but you cannot be sure when the contract will be 'executed' because the time of execution could be any time between the date the first party signs until receipt of the contract signed by all required signatories. It is better to tie the time element to a specific date, such as the effective date of the contract when it stated in the contract or to a specific event such as 30 days after receipt of the customer's purchase order by the supplier.

Language of obligation, authorization and conditions precedent

The language of obligation, authorization and conditions precedent must be used precisely. Let's look at *Shall* and *Will*.

- Use 'shall' to state an obligation or duty. Avoid using 'shall' to describe events that will occur in the future. If your writing is in the present tense, 'shall' can be reserved for obligations. For example, *The buyer shall deliver to the seller a listing of all embedded switching equipment at least 20 days prior to the seller's undertaking of site selection.* Traditionally the word 'shall' has been used to denote obligations; don't say, "In the event that one of the parties to this agreement shall be in default…" Say "If one party or the other defaults on this agreement".

- 'Will' can be used as an alternative to 'shall', but use one or the other; don't use both to mean obligation. If you need to refer to an event that will happen in the future, use 'will' instead of 'shall'.

Some leading US experts suggest avoiding the use of 'shall' completely. Because of inconsistent findings in US courts, the word 'shall' has become potentially risky.

Now let's look at *Must* and *May*.

Use 'may' to designate a right or privilege, with no obligation. As in: *The seller may elect to do acceptance testing at a remote site in lieu of testing at the buyer's premises.*

Use 'must' to designate a requirement prior to a party taking further action. For example: *The buyer must submit a notice of deficiency to the seller within 10 days of the completion of testing.*

Without such notice, the system will be deemed accepted by the seller. In this case the buyer has a duty to submit the deficiency notice and if he/she doesn't notify the seller he/she will be precluded from claiming a deficiency later.

Once you have drafted an item, consider whether you have used a term that requires greater specificity. Predict whether the term might cause problems in the future. This can be complicated by the norms in drafting. It is typical for Russian contracts to list the obligations of the parties. For instance, Article 3 of a purchase and sales contract would frequently stipulate that the seller is obliged to provide the goods and Article 4 would include a statement that the purchaser is obliged to pay the purchase price. This structure is probably due do Soviet tradition, where it was important that the state bodies quickly identified the obligations they were taking on. It does not encourage clarity about the sanctions for violation of any of the duties.

When you have stated an obligation, ask, "What happens if the obligor doesn't do it? "Ensure the answer is an appropriate consequence with recourse that supports the contract objective, providing a reasonable level of compensation.

Additional documents – schedules and attachments

If additional documents need to be incorporated into the contract and are too large to be physically incorporated, be sure that they are referenced by a unique document number and date.

Also check for inconsistencies between the main contract and any incorporated documents. If there are inconsistencies and they cannot be reconciled, be sure to include an "Order of Precedence" clause.

Very often for long-term or major contracts the standard 'boilerplate' clauses are included as the main body of the contract, and the specific details of the agreement - description of goods and services, price, delivery terms, invoicing terms etc. - are included as schedules or attachments to the main contract. This allows for changing of individual schedules without modifying the entire contract. It is important that all schedules or attachments are referenced in the main body of the contract. This can be done by adding a clause that states *"This contract includes the following schedules"*: and then list them, such as:

- Schedule A – Statement of Work
- Schedule B – Pricing Agreement
- Schedule C – Payment Terms
- Schedule D – Delivery Terms

Cross-check the agreement for internal references. Make sure the references are consistent and accurate. For example, "see exhibit C." Ensure that exhibit C actually exists, and is what you mean to be referencing.

Terms and conditions

A *term* is a part of the contract that addresses a specific subject. Contract clauses contain terms.

A *condition* is a phrase that either activates or suspends a term. A condition that activates a term is called a condition precedent. A condition that suspends a term is called a condition subsequent.

Excellence at drafting is about not just being a good author, with word and language skills, but also about being a good detective. It demands the ability to analyze a situation, understand salient facts that surround it and ask a whole series of 'what if?' questions that ensure the parties have a common understanding both now, and as their relationship progresses. The 'what ifs' are an attempt to protect your agreement and understanding against the range of uncertainties and changes that will inevitably occur during the life of an agreement, things like new people, new organizations, perhaps new ownership, changing business and economic conditions, changing regulatory environment and new competitors.

23.16 **Writing style**

This section will review some of the common elements of style where a little change can go a long way towards clearer communication. We'll review:
- Connecting and working words
- Compound prepositions
- Superfluous word clusters
- Redundant jargon
- Punctuation
- Presentation

Connecting and working words

A working word is an integral part of the idea being communicated. A connecting word is one that makes it easier to read. A 'rule of thumb' is: connecting words should not exceed working words.

For example: *In the event that there is a waiver of the indemnity provision by the Supplier, a letter confirming the waiver must be produced by the Supplier for the purpose of inspection by the Customer.*

This is hard to understand because there are more connecting words than working words.

Let's try: *If the Supplier waives indemnity provision, the Supplier must confirm this to the Customer.*

A simple edit creates a statement that is clearer and easier to understand.

Compound prepositions

Avoid compound prepositions and simplify the language. Let's look at these examples.

- Don't *use by reason of* – when *because* will do.
- Don't *use by virtue of* – when *by/under* will do.
- Don't *use for the purpose of* – when *to* will do.
- Don't use *in relation to* – when *about* or *concerning* will do.
- Don't use *inasmuch as* – when *since* will do.
- Don't use *in accordance with* – when *by or under* will do.
- Don't use *prior to* – when *before* will do.
- Don't use *with reference to* – when *about* or *concerning* will do.
- Don't use *on the basis of* – when *by* or *from* will do.

There are many more where these came from. Identify them and simplify when you can.

Superfluous word clusters

Again in an attempt to simplify and clarify, eliminate superfluous word clusters when you see them. Here are some examples:
- *In some instances* – can be simply stated as *sometimes*
- *Until such time as* – can be simply stated as *until*
- *In the event that* – can be simply stated as *if*
- *Insofar as* – just omit it completely or rewrite the sentence

Again, there are many more where these came from. Eliminate them on sight.

Here's another tip that may help you with your editorial duties. 'Which', 'who' and 'that' often indicate an opportunity to reduce words or clarify.

Redundant jargon

Moving on to just plain redundant and repetitive language, look at this list:
- Null and void
- By this act and deed
- All goods and chattels
- Hereby sell and convey
- Repair and make good
- Settle and compromise
- By this Will and Testament

The words in each pair mean the same thing. Pick one and use it. There is no benefit in redundancy.

Verbs

Use base verbs rather than derivative nouns and adjectives to get your point across. Let's review these examples; once again we are using the 'less is more' approach.

- Instead of *make a complaint* – use *complain*
- Instead of *draw conclusions* – use *conclude*
- Instead of *make a decision* – use *decide*
- Instead of *make payment* – use *pay*
- Instead of *take action* – use *act*

Punctuation

Punctuation is very important in clear writing. Punctuation is the guide that lets the mind separate thoughts and ideas. Poor punctuation will lead to poor communication. For example:

> That that is is that that is not is not

It is difficult to discern its meaning, until punctuation is inserted:

> That, that is, is. That, that is not, is not.

Presentation

Presentation is another visual element that can make your point clearer. Well thought out presentation can help you to make your documents and contracts clearer and easier to follow. If they are easier to follow while reading, they will be easier to follow during execution. In this case there really is a link between form and function.

If you are presenting the contract in an electronic media, the look and feel of the delivery tool will be different from paper, but the same idea applies. Ease of reading and comprehension is key.

Non-native speakers, when drafting, particularly suffer from not complying with these recommendations. They firstly feel their vocabulary is insufficient, whereas they would have produced a better draft if they had limited their vocabulary. Secondly, because they have a system of putting together their thoughts that relates back to legal, business, and technical terminology and *colloquialisms* that may be unknown to the other side, the effort for review and negotiation increases considerably. Finally, if they do not understand the stylistic issues alluded to, they will frequently be frustrated in the review process.

23.17 Tools

There are a variety of tools at your disposal when drafting a contract, some of which we have discussed already. The following are some more tools for you to explore; this list is certainly not complete, but provides a starting point. Use any tool appropriate that will make drafting and implementing a contract more efficient and productive.

Contracting software

As technology improves, the process of drafting and delivering contracts will continue to evolve. Drafting differences can be costly and risky, with a greater degree of error. There are numerous tools available that will allow you to continually improve your templates, thereby streamlining your contract drafting and finalization lifecycle. If you are going to be generating a large volume of contracts and don't already have an automated system, you should consider investing in one. There are models offered in both Software-as-a-Service (SaaS) form and those that are installed within your network and infrastructure. A simple search of 'contract management software' on the internet will give you with some examples to look at. Reports from leading analysts and associations (e.g. AMR/Gartner, Forrester Research, Aberdeen Group and IACCM) will also yield similar results.

Contracting is changing from drafting individual contracts to mass-produced agreements that have minimal changes for greater efficiency in production, execution and management. We have also entered a world where electronic signatures are becoming more and more acceptable, which alters the drafting of the contract to take specific provisions for electronic signature into account.

For example, a service contract and hardware deal, although recognized as different and used for two different suppliers, are actually different versions of the same contract. Tracking and management becomes a much simpler process.

Drafting database

The language used in describing the agreements reached during negotiations is critical and can determine the success or failure of a contract. Thus, the art of drafting the contract document is in many ways as important as the art of negotiating the agreement itself.

Drafting differences can be costly and risky, with a greater degree of error. The science of contract management can complement the art of contract drafting by providing relevant samples of previously approved contract text. A good contract repository effectively stores contracts both as unified documents and also as individual clauses. Thus, when the drafting team is in the process of drafting a contract they can use the contract management system to identify where to find typical contract clauses to fit their needs, text that has been successfully employed in previous agreements. This will speed up the contract creation process and reduce the risks associated with starting over each time a new contract needs to be drafted.

When drafting the library clauses or templates, it is important to use an object-oriented approach where you try to make each clause/section generic so that it can be used in as many agreements as possible without alteration. This will lower your maintenance burden significantly; in global organizations it will also help reduce language translation costs.

You will need to use certain data management skills in order to effectively create and manipulate a contract repository. The investment in acquiring these skills will be more than paid back by the increased efficiency and accuracy associated with leveraging existing and effective contract language.

One thing you must consider when developing or using a drafting database is the maintenance of the database. In order to maintain a best practice database you need to rate the entries and delete or mark the poorer examples. You do not want to develop a large database of slightly different terms and conditions when one can be reused. The 'garbage-in garbage-out' principle applies. There are a number of tools available that enable organizations to manage their templates and library clauses. It may be worthwhile to invest in a tool of this type, which can also help you in managing the entire contract lifecycle.

Checklists

One important tool in the contract manager's toolkit is a checklist. Checklists are a low-technology solution, but they are effective in managing the drafting of a contract. You can use checklists to ensure that all elements of a contract have been covered sufficiently, or all attachments have been created and appended.

Checklists are also a good way to manage drafting and implementation when you do not have direct control over the entire process.

23.18 Summary

It is not easy to draft a document that describes the transaction in a way that reflects the understanding of all parties involved. The tools and ideas provided in this chapter will assist the process of clearly and effectively communicating the business goals and objectives in a contractual relationship and ensuring they are documented both as evidence if there is a subsequent dispute and as a working tool to support the contract implementation.

Some points to remember:

- How will your contract be delivered – on paper or via an electronic medium?
- Be aware of the contract interpretation guidelines that will affect the implementation of your contract.
- Investigate and understand the controlling laws and how they will affect your contract.
- Strive for clear, concise language, which will aid in the implementation later, not hinder it.
- Remember the differences between the language of obligation, authorization and conditions precedent.
- If you use industry- or area-specific terminology, make sure it is defined clearly.

NEGOTIATION PHASE

Negotiations overview and objectives

Approaches to negotiation

Negotiation styles

Negotiation techniques

Tactics, tricks and lessons learned

CHAPTER 24

Approaches to negotiations – framing, strategy and goals

24.1 Negotiations overview

Negotiation is a business topic that attracts extensive writing, yet relatively few works are especially memorable or widely referenced.

The Harvard Negotiations Project has probably been the most influential source of thinking in the field of negotiation, with *Getting To Yes*[17] perhaps the most quoted book on this topic. It introduced important concepts such as distinguishing 'positional' from 'principled' negotiation, as well as the oft-cited 'BATNA' (Best Alternative To A Negotiated Agreement).

But it is more than 20 years since *Getting To Yes* was first published and much has changed over that time. So while its underlying concepts remain useful, they are increasingly challenged by the realities of today's negotiating practices.

Cooperation and negotiation

The ability to cooperate is one of the distinguishing features of the human species – and is quite obviously fundamental to trading relationships. Stemming from this, 'collaboration' is a key management theme at present, with many believing that increased cooperation is needed to make sense of our complex world. Yet collaboration is dismissed by many managers, who feel that attempts to collaborate are not reciprocated. Buyers, in particular, suggest that suppliers 'take advantage' of customers who act fairly. This mentality certainly dominates business negotiations. Year after year, IACCM's research of the 'most frequently negotiated terms' reveals unrelenting focus on risk allocation and 'penalties', even though negotiators acknowledge that other terms (for example, change management, scope and

---

17 Ury, William. *Getting Past No: Negotiating Your way From Confrontation to Cooperation*. New York: Bantam, 1993

goals, communications and reporting) should take priority. Both sides blame the other for this impasse; there is a feeling by each side that it would be more collaborative if it were not for the other.

Recent scientific research has shown that humans are right to trust cooperation – that it is based on a strong instinct for optimized economic benefit. Reporting on work undertaken at the University of California, The Economist observed "An open hand makes evolutionary as well as moral sense" – in other words, trust pays dividends. It is in that case ironic if the cynicism of the average negotiator is standing in the way of greater trust and therefore of improved economic outcomes.

The real world of the negotiator

Many of us who are engaged in business-to-business negotiations would probably question this research. In the real world, cooperation is frequently notable for its absence. Negotiations are driven by relative power – both internal (between functions) and external.

It is extremely unlikely that we can turn all negotiations into a collaborative experience. Indeed, in many cases the scale of potential economic return would not make the effort worthwhile. There will always be 'positional' negotiators and our skill must be to determine whether it is worth the effort to try to reform them, or whether to accept the risks that are inherent in their approach, or to do business elsewhere.

These negotiation chapters are designed to assist overall understanding of negotiation and to offer practical hints and tips in reaching better and more sustainable agreements. They encourage a collaborative approach because the evidence points to the fact that collaboration is more likely to yield higher benefits to both parties. And when we say 'collaborative, it is important to emphasize that collaboration does not mean abdication, it does not mean lack of rigor, it does not mean failure to monitor or verify. In fact, truly collaborative trading relationships will frequently require more planned meetings, more shared information, more structured changes or amendments than the adversarial, penalty-based approach that is the typical outcome from 'positional' negotiations. The big difference is that time is spent on alternative – and more productive – topics, geared towards a successful outcome, rather than allocating blame for disappointing results.

A changed – and still changing – environment

In commenting earlier on *Getting To Yes*, we observed that there have been many changes over the past 20 years and that these have substantially altered the context within which negotiation occurs. Without doubt, the most fundamental of these is our networked world. The advent of the internet has steadily transformed the environment for negotiators. *Getting To Yes* was written before e-auctions, before e-commerce, before contract management software. It was written at a time when risk management as a formal discipline was in its infancy; when 'outsourcing' had not been invented; when there were many fewer lawyers; and when international contracting took a very different – and less regular – form. Commoditization, category management and compliance were non-existent concepts; it was still usual for business to be done on either the supplier's standard terms, or for there to be no formal contract.

The impacts of these changes include the fact that, in many parts of the world, most negotiation today is virtual, no longer face-to-face. Standard terms and conditions are far more prolific, especially for Procurement, and these have led to increasing 'battles of the forms' which often seem to preclude logic or business judgment. Negotiation has often become a matter of battling to secure functional positions, sometimes at the expense of business interests – fighting for terms that are mandated by Legal, Finance, Operations or other powerful internal functions. Indeed, for many, the internal negotiation is often more complex and time-consuming than the external negotiation.

The overall complexity of reaching consensus on a negotiating position and the physical remoteness of many of the parties was not something that was envisaged in *Getting to Yes*. Yet this is the reality for many negotiators today.

A further challenge is the increasingly cross-cultural nature of negotiation – and the fact that the purpose, timing and extent of implied commitment are seen in very different ways. In some cultures, negotiation creates finality, a binding agreement. In others, it generates a framework, non-binding in its nature, but rather establishing principles that are relevant at the time they are agreed. In some cultures, 'a contract' is the normal output from a negotiation; in others, 'a contract' is deemed either irrelevant, or perhaps even insulting (by its implication of a lack of trust).

Getting To Yes also did not distinguish transactional negotiation from relational negotiation – yet there are marked differences. And while 'transactional' tends to be associated with 'positional' (and 'relational' with 'principled') this is not universally true. For example, in many commodity markets where supply is constrained, suppliers impose long-term relational contracts on their customers. In some markets, business only happens when there is a pre-established relationship; in others, there may only be transactions, or they may be a necessary pre-cursor to 'a relationship'.

Throughout this book, we have sought to equip the negotiator with a wider sense of awareness, a readiness to ask questions, a willingness to listen and observe. Without these qualities, in today's complex, inter-connected business environment, we cannot act collaboratively. We can only be 'positional' negotiators protecting rules and boundaries.

24.2 Introduction to framing, strategy and goals

This chapter gives an overview of the aspects that best practice negotiators address to ensure the interaction with the other parties is as successful as possible. Before a negotiation begins there are several steps that should be completed. Understanding these steps can help prepare for a successful negotiation and eliminate some of the confusion that often stalls negotiations. This chapter provides a best practice understanding of the following key elements:

- Framing
- Goals
- Developing a negotiation strategy
- Planning and tactics
- Tools for establishing a negotiations foundation

24.3 Framing

Framing is how we see the world. It results from both (a) how the world really is and (b) the nature of the person who perceives it. People can perceive the same object - or any other item in the world - very differently and are often not aware of the particular frames they use. They are driven by many factors, in particular their 'human needs' that we will explore in some detail later. These human needs are themselves programmed by the business, industry, culture or social environment in which they operate.

Framing in negotiation is about organizing, shaping and focusing the negotiation situation. Framing is a perceptual process where we are trying to make sense of complex situations, in ways that are meaningful to us, so that we can respond properly. Perceptions can be affected by personal factors such as experience, motivation and emotions, but also by contextual elements. The perceptual process can vary between an automatic unconscious process and a more controlled deliberate process. The perception of social processes especially implies a more conscious deliberation to frame the situation. The knowledge of the perceptual process (see Figure 24.1) is helpful when entering a negotiation situation if the negotiator is able to build an appropriate frame. Research has shown that the presentation of information can have a critical effect on how decisions are made under situations of uncertainty. An example from Bazerman (2001)[18] displays the potential in framing.

---

18 Bazerman, M.H. (2001): Judgment in Managerial Decision Making. New York: John Wiley & Sons; Lewicki, R.J., Saunders, D.M., Bruce, B. & Minton, J.W. (2003): Essentials of Negotiation. London: McGraw Hill

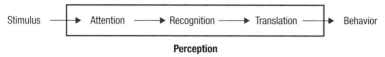

Figure 24.1:   The perceptual process

For example, a large car manufacturer has recently been hit with a number of economic difficulties, and it appears as if three plants need to be closed and 6,000 employees laid off. The vice president of production has been exploring alternative ways to avoid this crisis. She has developed two plans:

- Plan A: This plan will save one of the three plants and 2,000 jobs.
- Plan B: This plan has one-third probability of saving all three plants and all 6,000 jobs, but has a two-third probability of saving no plants and no jobs.

Another way of presenting the plans could be:

- Plan C: This plan will result in the loss of two of the three plants and 4,000 jobs.
- Plan D: This plan has a two-thirds probability of resulting in the loss of all three plants and all 6,000 jobs, but has a one-third probability of losing no plants and no jobs.

The facts in the two sets of alternative plans are identical, but the information is framed differently. The first situation has a positive framing, 'a sure gain,' and in situations like this the majority has a tendency to be risk-averse and will go for plan A. The other situation has a negative framing, 'a sure loss', and this will trigger our tendency to be risk seeking in a way that we will go for alternative D, a possible chance of losing all jobs.

As framing represents the strategic part of communication, it is important to analyze the situation to find the important issue, and work out how best to frame and present the information. In negotiation both parties have frames; if the frames match, the parties are likely to focus on common issues and if the frames do not match the communication can be difficult. If one party has preferences about issues to be covered or outcomes to be achieved they should work to ensure that the preferred frame is being accepted by the other party. As negotiations evolve you should also be aware that the perception of a situation may change, or that new perspectives are brought into the negotiations. This re-framing may be intentional or it may emerge from the conversations. The important thing is to think through the whole negotiation process, from both parties' perspectives as far as possible, so that re-framing initiatives can be managed properly.

Researchers estimate what our frames are by observing our communications in negotiations. We can identify people's frames by noticing how they act – particularly their oral behavior – and by asking them questions for which the answers provide insights about how they frame issues. The following seven types of frames are the most common:

- Substantive

- Loss-gain
- Characterization
- Outcome
- Aspiration
- Process
- Evidentiary

Substantive:
- What the conflict is about
- Focused on a key issue or concern, e.g., price, or payment terms.

Loss-gain:
- How the parties view the risks associated with particular outcomes
- Focused on the risks associated with any negotiated commitment.

Characterization:
- How the party views the other's framing, strategy and goals
- Focused on what the parties think of each other.

Outcome:
- What predispositions the party has to achieving a specific result or outcome from the negotiation
- Focused on getting a particular outcome above all else.

Aspiration:
- What predispositions the party has toward satisfying a broader set of interests or needs in negotiation
- The aspirant tries to assure that his or her basic needs and interests are met

Process:
- How the parties will go about resolving their dispute
- Focused less on specific negotiation issues than on who is at the table, how the deliberations will proceed, what rules are explicitly and implicitly being followed throughout the negotiation, and if it is fair.

Evidentiary:
- Facts and supporting evidence that parties present to support data or "evidence" that argues for or against a particular outcome or loss - gain frame
- Parties with this frame are focused on the evidence that is offered to support or refute positions.

When working on the framing issue, it is helpful for the negotiators to raise some basic questions for themselves:

- What is the purpose of the communication?
- What do we want the other party to think, feel, or do?
- How will the message affect the other party?

24.4 Goals

In the same way that a football team defines its objectives before starting a game, the negotiation team must define the goals it wants to achieve.

A good place to start the planning process for the upcoming negotiations is to look into the organization's overall goals. These overall goals should function as guidelines for the process of developing specific goals for the coming negotiations. Goals should be specific and realistic targets, compared to wishes that could be hopes or fantasies. In the process of developing goals it might be clear that some goals can be achieved through a single negotiation session, and more complex goals can only be achieved through a series of meetings where things can develop incrementally.

In particular, negotiators need to understand:

- The goals they want to achieve: as sometimes not everything goes perfectly as initially planned, the team should plan for:
  - Primary goals ("what do we want to achieve if all goes well?"),
  - Secondary goals ("what do we aim for if there is a problem along the path?"). These are sometimes called "concession goals".
  - And potentially for mitigation goals ("in case all goes wrong, what do we expect?"). Sometimes called "walk-away" or "fallback strategy", it can be useful at this stage to explore this path as it will set up your bottom-line expectations and identify the reasons why you could get there.
- The priorities among those goals,
- The potential for packaging goals together, and
- The possible trade-offs among goals.

For both the priorities and the potential for packaging, it is very important that you identify both the variables that drive your business perspective and the ones that drive the other side's analysis and position.

This is why framing is essential. Frames and goals sometimes evolve together. Goals are not just what we wish for, but realistic wants. They generate issues and the issues generated can usually be linked with the issues of the other party. This allows trade-offs between the parties.

Goals should be established using the following rules to enable them to drive a successful negotiation:

- Goals should be realistic. Goals that are not achievable or too ambitious at a given stage of the negotiations can only lead to frustration. That is why your goals must be reasonably limited in the sense that you should believe that the other party is (1) able and (2) willing to accommodate to achieve them;
- Goals should be measurable. They may be tangible (price, volume, delivery date, damage limitations) or intangible (relationship, image, reputation of the negotiators), but in all cases, you should be able to define a way to measure them.
- Goals should be defined in time. Your goals may (and certainly will) vary depending on the stages of the negotiation process you are in. Some goals are very short term (e.g., get an indication of a budget or a win price)
- Goals should represent an effort from both parties. Negotiation is about doing business, hence at the core of buying and selling. Offering standard solutions may be suitable for standard situations if they truly exist in your marketplace but complex contracting requires contract professionals to add-value and create solutions that deliver for all parties to the negotiated agreement. Whichever side of the table you're on, you must convince the other side of the potential interest a proposed solution may have for them, and obtain something in return to demonstrate that you have succeeded in convincing them.
- Goals must be directly related to your company's business interests. For example, if the buyer is interested in establishing a quick and reliable chat function as part of its customer service program, then all of the negotiation team's goals must directly relate to both quickness and reliability. Therefore, your team should not compromise reliability during the negotiation process.

When setting your goals during the different negotiation phases, you must keep this in mind: each goal must represent somehow a step forward towards a successful conclusion.

24.5 Strategy

After deciding on goals, the next step is to develop a strategy for the negotiations. Strategy is the overall plan on how to achieve the goals of the organization. A negotiation strategy should be a plan, which specifies the choices a negotiator will make in every probable situation. Your strategy is intended to integrate your goals, targets and actions into a cohesive whole.

When negotiating, negotiators usually vary between concern for our own goals, and concern for those of the other party. Therefore in selecting a strategy you need to answer two questions: (a) how concerned are we about the substantive outcome at stake and (b) how concerned are we about the relationship aspects at stake? Tactics are detailed plans of action identified to support the strategy. A random selection of tactics, especially hardball negotiation tactics, does not constitute a negotiation strategy. Your strategy drives your choice in tactics.

Goals and frames affect our strategy. A good strategy takes into account four elements:
- Strategy is a matter of choice – it is not forced upon us.
- Strategy must acknowledge the chance element of negotiation.
- Strategy deals with interdependence – the fact that the goals of each require the cooperation of the other.
- Strategy must deal with the fact of our incomplete knowledge of the other party's interests, needs, and strengths.

Normally when deciding upon a strategy, an organization has a unilateral approach, everything considered, pursuing its own goals and focusing on their own outcome. In negotiation it is necessary to consider the other party's interests or motivations because the main foundation for negotiations is mutual dependence.

It is important to balance the substantive outcome and the relational outcome of the negotiations. The balance that is chosen affects the negotiation style and approach. The difficult part can be to decide on the relational outcome; what type of relationship you want with the other company, , the level of commitment (yours and theirs), the level of interdependence, the level of open and free communication, and so on. In the deliberation of the relationship issues, it is wise to review the history of the relationship, and if it is not an ongoing relationship, the extent of the relationship your company will need to reach its goals.

The alternative strategies that can be developed on the basis of the relational and the substantive outcome dimensions are presented in Figure 24.2.

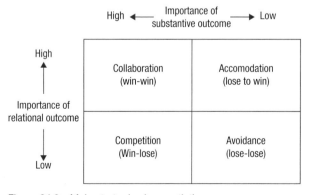

Figure 24.2   Main strategies in negotiation

Four strategies or styles are noted above. Each has its advantages and disadvantages. No one strategy will be appropriate for all negotiation situations. Throughout this chapter and the chapters that follow, we'll focus your attention on the two prevalent strategies: collaborative and competitive.

Choosing your strategy

When analyzing strategies you must answer two questions.

1. How important is the relationship to your company's overall goals for this deal.
2. How important are the substantive issues to your company's overall goals for this deal.

If both a good relationship and the substantive outcome are of great importance, then a collaborative (integrative) strategy is appropriate. If the substantive outcome is more important than a good relationship, a competitive (distributive) strategy might be appropriate. Accommodation as a strategy can be chosen if the relationship far outweighs the substantive outcome. If neither the relationship nor the substantive outcome is of importance, you should avoid becoming involved in negotiation.

Competitive strategy

The competitive strategy is by far the most widely recognized strategy. More books and articles have been written supporting this strategy than any other negotiation strategy. It is so ingrained in the western cultures' psyche that it is hard to imagine another negotiation strategy. Much of what follows in this and the subsequent chapters supports a competitive strategy.

The hallmark of the competitive strategy is the premise that in order to win the other side must lose. When people are asked what it means to negotiate, most answer "to get a good deal for me or my company." Implicit in their response is the fact that a good deal for them is a less than good deal for their counterparty. But there is another, albeit less dominant, strategy.

Collaborative strategy

This strategy has gained wider acceptance as companies enter into increasingly interdependent relationships. When customers and suppliers enter into multiyear alliances, strategic partnerships or outsourcing agreements, the relationship becomes as important, if not more important, as the substantive issues.

In the past, some negotiators have viewed collaborative strategies as weak or soft: the fear being loss of control and excessive vulnerability. Negotiators who know only the competitive strategy risk damaging an interdependent deal. By their nature, alliances, strategic partnerships and outsourcing arrangements require a softer approach that ensures trust, mutuality of outcomes and long-term stability. Hardball tactics, normally associated with the competitive strategy, can undermine trust, pit one party's gain against another's loss and threaten instability as customers and suppliers terminate "bad" deals so they can enter into "better" deals.

The pure strategies have been presented above, but in real-life situations it can be necessary to mix strategies into what we can call a compromising strategy. There can be elements in the negotiations that are suitable for collaboration, other parts where a competitive approach is better and yet other parts where an accommodating approach is wise. The choice of the strategic approach depends, of course, on the negotiator's ability to analyze the whole negotiation situation.

24.6 Stages of negotiation

Studies of negotiation behavior have identified predictable stages through which most negotiations pass. These four stages are:
- Stage 1: Orientation and positioning
- Stage 2: Argument, compromise and search for alternative solutions
- Stage 3: Emergence and crisis
- Stage 4: Agreement or final breakdown.

Stage 1: Orientation and positioning
One of the key factors of success is to agree with the counterparty how the respective teams will work together. This includes who within each party will participate in the negotiations, how these will move forward and when they should come to a positive conclusion.

Define the working relationship
- How: usually the team need to assess together the needs, the expectations, and the solutions proposed. This usually implies setting up workshops, writing down, sharing and reviewing the minutes of those meetings, establishing and following up a list of questions and issues with the corresponding actions plan.
- Who: there are various layers of people within each party. In order to have an efficient working relationship, it has been proven useful to write down who, among all the people identified in the decision tree, will participate in the various meetings. If we go back to the Framing phase, we need to check that our negotiation teams are aligned with the other party's decision tree, and that no one is left uninformed along the negotiation path.

There is no single formula for team composition and structure. Best practice negotiations recognize this; do not try to impose a standard approach but do ensure the inclusion of standard elements:

- Involvement of operational personnel to ensure the negotiations are firmly connected to business needs and expectations
- Involvement of commercial contract experts, lawyers and finance personnel whether in the teams that execute the negotiation plan or support and contribute to the plan
- A process for resolving open issues including appropriate escalation paths
- The joint management of the negotiation to ensure it stays on track and focused on a successful business outcome

Negotiate and agree on the agenda
Another key factor of success is to plan each of the required meetings and position the milestones in support of any significant dates or required events. Both parties should agree to the planning, commit the necessary resources to be available, monitor the progress and raise alerts if necessary.

As this exercise will include positioning the resources identified earlier and taking into account the time constraints, this is a way of identifying and agreeing on those work-streams that can progress in parallel.

Initial negotiating positions
It can be difficult to assess what your initial position should be. It is worth bearing in mind that studies analyzing competitive strategies, such as Jeanette Nyden's *Negotiation Rules!*, show that the first party to establish their position more greatly influences the final outcome of the negotiations by anchoring the discussions around the opening position. Negotiators using a competitive strategy will seek to establish the best position for his company, regardless of their counterparty's reaction.

When choosing a collaborative strategy, the challenge is to establish the range where you should be: establishing a zone within which both parties can reach agreement and avoiding a situation where the other party will consider there is no likelihood of ever reaching agreement or the opening position offers no counterparty of any change in subsequent discussion.

One way of establishing this range is to assess the following:
- Information about the market price – what is being paid and by whom
- Assess any unique or different aspects about this particular project along as many axes as you can in terms of scope, service, quantity...
- What alternatives do the parties have (if any)?
- What are the parties' expectations? (Bigger quantity? More service? Lower costs? Other?)

- What are the parties' stakes in this negotiation That is, what happens if the negotiation fails? To the people who are negotiating (personal stakes)? To the companies negotiating (corporate stakes)?).

It is unlikely that you will have completely perfect knowledge of the various dimensions that will drive the negotiation decision-making. It is important to understand the information gaps and assess how best to fill them either by research or by asking the other party – this latter approach will need to be timed, choreographed and validated in order to obtain meaningful information rather than a refusal to respond or an answer that is skewed to drive any subsequent negotiations in a particular direction.

Once you have done this assessment, both through the pre-negotiation steps and then during the initial discussions, you can have a better view of what the project is reasonably worth, how it is likely to be perceived by the other party and where an opening offer should be positioned in terms of the other party's objectives, choices and to drive the right value for your own side.

But before releasing anything, you need to take into account other dimensions of the puzzle: the different variables in your proposal. There are four kinds:
- The ones important to you as they drive your costs/benefits ('driving variables'). You get those by a thorough financial analysis of your proposal.
- The ones that may look very attractive to the other party, but either do not represent a high value or a high cost to you ('attractive variables'). You get those by listening actively and patiently to your counterparty and asking the right questions at the right time in a structured way.
- Tangible benefits – those readily quantifiable in financial terms.
- Non-tangible benefits – those not so readily quantifiable but which may still add value for the other or both, such as being a launch partner of a new technology.

Once you have identified the variables, you will need to anticipate what the future scenarios and possible trade-offs could be, keeping as many attractive variables as you can while knowing that these should be traded against elements that are highly valuable to you.

Stage 2: Argument, compromise and search for alternative solutions

Once the positioning has been set and the initial negotiations have taken place to evaluate the respective positions, it is now time to work on how to converge on an agreement.

This means refining your supporting points and information to find the best way to present them. Not only are you trying to be persuasive, you are also trying to gauge your counterparty's ability to meet your needs, wants and concerns. In turn, your counterpart will be trying to persuade you too.

Looking for alternative solutions and seeking compromise

Sharing the business case (both the presentation and the financial model) will be the first step in your negotiations. The output of these first meetings will tell you which areas of your proposal should be refined. You will now have to find alternative solutions for the next round. This has to be done jointly (e.g. through joint workshops), exploring with both teams which elements of your proposal can be redefined: it could be in your product/ service description, in the pricing, in the SLAs but also in some more peripheral elements of your proposal.

There are two important points at this stage:

1. Whatever alternative solutions you may come up with, make sure that your counterparty's operations teams fully endorse them before presenting them in the next negotiation round. Otherwise it may backfire during the negotiation round, leaving you with no solution.
2. This exercise is about making concessions, but remember this is true on both sides.

Too often we tend to focus only on what we should give away rather than what we should trade for (and too often we just look at the price). This is more about relative importance of giveaways (perception vs. materiality): what we could trade for might not be of much value to us, but could be of very high value for your counterparty, and similarly you may ask in return for something which may not be of great value for them but is very valuable to you (this leads to what is sometimes called the 'win-win' trading).

Stage 3: Emergence and crisis

Trying to converge

After having explored the different alternatives, the parties are working on converging into some sort of 'final stance':

- On one hand, your counterparty now has a better view of what your positions are, where you have shown some willingness to compromise and what are your more difficult points;
- On the other hand, you have a clearer view of what the counterparty may ask you as a 'final effort'.

Bear in mind that neither of the positions are actually 'final'. These are just set to check whether convergence can be achieved by the parties who are engaged day-to-day in the negotiation process.

As we have seen in the previous chapters, there are many decision layers at stake above the one you are engaged with. Each of these layers may potentially come back to you with an additional requirement, which implies that more efforts will be required by both parties later on during the final agreement process. It is important to keep this in mind and avoid being in a deadlock situation tomorrow because of poor (or too optimistic) anticipation.

Pressure for agreement

At this point in the negotiation process, after having explored many paths, you may want to conclude as quickly as possible. But your counterparty is in exactly the same situation: their management has set goals, which themselves are defined in time, and now the deadline is approaching. Pressure is building up on both sides. Your team is getting tired of all the workshops, negotiation rounds, re-pricing exercises. Bear in mind that your counterparty's team is in exactly the same state.

While you are wondering when this is going to end, your counterparty is entering a phase where they are doubting their choices: "Have we chosen the right suppliers/partners? Is the service model that we designed or that we have been proposed the correct one for our organization? Do they serve the objectives that have been set for us? What are the risks for taking such or such decision? What are the risks of not taking any decision?" These are all the questions that may pop up in your counterparty's head. All the risks are not yet fully identified and evaluated, and especially because it is still unclear, it is being magnified.

This is the phase where you need to anticipate the crisis and its outcome, and one of the best known ways to do that is to reassure your counterparty on their choices.

You will need to spend much more time than before working closely with them, at all levels of management, and accompany them in the comparative assessment of their alternatives, in the risk evaluations and in building mitigation strategies.

By creating this increased intimacy, you will be able to check their full understanding of your proposal and get a better understanding of their SWOTs (strengths, weaknesses, opportunities and threats).

One approach that has been proven successful is to understand who in your counterparty's operational team is your highest level sponsor (typically one level below the negotiation leader). You should increase contact with this sponsor and proof-test your ideas. Note that you may find more than one sponsor; in this case you should work with each of them separately.

This should help you to present a revised summary of your proposal to your counterparty, putting forward its most valuable elements as perceived by your counterparty, reassure him on the risks and your ability to manage the mitigation strategies decided earlier and magnifying your competitors' weaknesses (if known). If you have successfully managed to convince your sponsor earlier, he/she will be your best advocate during the negotiation.

Crisis occurs

Sometimes and despite all the points above, your counterparty retains their doubts and the crisis occurs:

- Your whole business case is questioned.
- Your counterparty is threatening to break up the negotiations with you.
- Their expectations are suddenly restated at a higher level.
- They suddenly understand that they are about to commit and are afraid of making any commitments.
- Their management has changed their minds about some essential element of the deal and told the negotiation team to start over.

This situation should be handled carefully if you want to keep the negotiations on track. Often, with a renewed effort at understanding the underlying reasons for the crisis, an impasse can be avoided.

- Listen to what your counterparty has to say.
- Ask questions (to be sure you have understood what they have said).
- Reformulate and agree on a common understanding.
- Isolate each outstanding issue.
- Get partial agreement on each issue.

And on top of that, you must pay particular attention to all non-verbal messages and signals that may be sent during face-to-face negotiation sessions.

Then your next step is to work on each issue and come back to your counterparty with a set of satisfactory answers.

Stage 4: Agreement or final breakdown

This is the most difficult time in the negotiation: you believe you have given all that you could and nevertheless your counterparty is not satisfied. It seems to you that you cannot do more, whether financially or technically, but if you really want to win this deal you will need to find a way out of this deadlock.

The first step is to think back to Stages 2 and 3: what are your counterparty's stakes? What are the elements that are most valuable to them in your proposal? What convinced them to continue negotiating with you after the first rounds of discussion? What happens if no positive outcome is found? What are the concerns that have been expressed during the crisis phase? What conditional agreements have you obtained?

The second step should be a brainstorming within your team: how should you address each of those concerns and come up with a new proposal that could be a decisive move forward? What concessions will you have to make? Which ones are within your current mandate and which ones require a new signed-off mandate?

Finally, think of what can be traded in exchange for the concessions you are going to make. At this stage, do not hesitate to put out those concessions that you know are most costly to your counterparty, hence showing that you are really making a major final effort and that each party has to make its part of the way to reach a positive outcome.

Most of the time at this stage of the negotiation, provided that you have found ways of waiving all other objections, what is needed is financial creativity: ways to spread costs over a period of time, financing solutions, discounts in the form of loyalty schemes or any other solution that makes your proposal more attractive from a purely financial point of view.

In all cases, remember this is your final proposal. Make sure on your side that you have done everything you could; but also make sure that you share with your counterparty that you cannot go beyond this final proposal.

Deadlock or basic agreement occurs

Once you have decided on how to present the results of your brainstorming, it is time to go back to the negotiation table and present your final proposal.

The outcome is straightforward:

- Either you come to a basic agreement and you agree with your counterparty on a period of exclusivity during which you will work on developing and structuring the main contractual terms;
- Or it turns out that what you have come up with proves to be insufficient and this is the end of the story. (Remember you have stated that you could not go beyond all your last concessions.)

Agreement structuring

In the event you have agreed to pursue your discussions, it is now time to structure the whole deal. You should keep in mind at this stage that the negotiation is not totally over, as your counterparty may come up with some last minutes 'nibbles' that they will request to include. This is why you should have a list of additional items that you desire in the agreement (such as longer term, additional scope, more flexibility, less onerous SLAs) in case such requests pop up in the discussions (remember that you have listed those in the steps above).

Wrapping up

The last and final stage is to write down the actual contractual terms, making sure that they truly reflect everything that has been conceded before. This is actually a very important phase as either party may forget what the other party has previously agreed during the numerous negotiation rounds.

Please note that some cultures require explicit closing rituals; if you fail to observe those, you might jeopardize the entire transaction.

24.7 Leveraging your experience

One of the key attributes that commercial contract professionals bring to their organization is the ability to leverage experience. It is, therefore, worth considering these four stages in terms of a other negotiations with which you or your team have been involved. Remember those cases and consider what these questions make you think about.

What factors speed up or slow down the stages?
Speed up: this could be the end of existing contract, reversibility clause, pressure from the counterparty's management for cost-cutting. What have you experienced?
Slow down: incorrect assumptions about the decision tree, lobbying from competitors or another external party. Any other factor you can think of?

How can the third (crisis) stage be managed?
Anticipate, prepare alternatives, be reassuring. What else?

What management styles appear to be more or less effective?
As it depends on the other party's behavior style, present examples of matching behaviors that are favorable to a positive conclusion, and examples of antagonistic behaviors, which lead to bigger conflicts.

24.8 Planning and tactics

Preparation and planning are fundamental to negotiation – and lack of adequate preparation is without question one of the primary reasons why negotiations fail, or fail to realize optimum results. Without these, 'good' deals can emerge, but more by luck than judgment and certainly not on a consistent basis. Consider the following questions:
- Goals - what do you (they) really want to accomplish?
- Issues - what issues arise because of those goals?
- Bargaining zone - What are your (their) range of acceptable agreements?
- Arguments and evidence - What arguments can you (they) offer in support of trades, and what evidence will back them up?
- Trades - what are you (they) prepared to trade, and in exchange for what?

Before you begin, personal honesty is also critical. How good is the other negotiator? How good are you? Should someone else be leading this deal? If you expect a losing proposition, chances are you will be right! At a more general level, you should have established a mentor in preparation for when things get tough.

Many negotiation experts agree that a linear planning process is appropriate.
The more issues you have, the more there is to trade. The downside is that with lots of issues negotiations can be lengthy.

- The bargaining zone represents the area across which you will negotiate on any given issue.
- Arguments and evidence are the tools used to win on the issues.
- Trades are what will yield the elements that for you constitute a win.

Getting prepared

It is good practice to use some form of negotiation planner to provide a simple, organized way to address the key requirements in planning. You should follow your own internal planning guides as appropriate.

Goals generate issues, and as the negotiation develops and new issues arise, they must be examined to determine if they really fit with the negotiator's goals.

You must estimate the goals and issues of the other party, which should be indicated from the Statement of Work (SOW) or pre-negotiation meetings.

It is important to understand to the best of your ability the frames of those on the other side. You will acquire more knowledge of them as the negotiation progresses.
- Establish your objectives
- Establish your tactics
- Question your assumptions
- Rehearse

Bargaining zone

A bargaining zone is created when an upper and a lower limit are set. This is also called the Zone of Agreement or Zone of Probable Agreement. Figure 24.3 sets out this concept below. The Zone of Agreement is the area between two extreme positions, or walk away points. One the one hand, the buyer will have their walk away point, which is the upper limit of the zone. Everything beyond this upper limit is out of range and no deal will be reached. At the other end is the seller's lowest limit or walk away point. Any number below the seller's walk away point will kill the deal. Technically, the area in the middle is the Zone of Agreement.

In reality though, there are Discomfort Zones. These are areas below the buyer's upper range but the buyer feels that they are paying too much. These buyers will feel discomfort and may seek to prematurely re-negotiate the deal to get a better price. Just above the seller's lowest limit is their Discomfort Zone. Sellers in this area feel that they are losing money on the deal and may cut corners to regain lost ground.

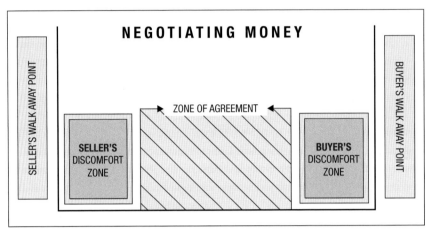

Figure 24.3   Negotiating money

Best Alternative to Negotiated Agreement (BATNA)

BATNA is your *'best alternative to a negotiated agreement'*. It is the course of action your company will take if it is unable to reach an agreement with its counterparty. A BATNA must get your company at least substantially the same, if not better, results, than the anticipated agreement would get your company.

Most negotiators mistake and misuse BATNAs during the course of the negotiation process. A BATNA is not some pie-in-the-sky dream of what *could* be. It is a realistic and viable option that will allow your company to reach its goals. Buyers make the mistake of thinking that all suppliers are alike, and therefore, use a supplier's competitor as a BATNA. However, all suppliers are not created equal. We know of one circumstance where the buyer walked away from a deal with one supplier and entered into a deal with another supplier who was unable to meet the buyer's increasing demand for product. In that case, the alternative supplier did not provide a true best alternative because it failed to meet demand, placing the company in a perilous position with its customers.

Sellers, on the other hand, underestimate a buyer's BATNAs, or in the worst case scenario, are in denial that the buyer has any BATNA at all. That kind of poor analysis leads to arrogance and lost deals for good reason.

Your BATNA is your fallback position if a 'meeting of minds' cannot be achieved. It could include (1) maintaining the 'status quo', such as keeping a function in-house rather than outsourcing it, or (2) it could mean re-deploying resources to another opportunity. The point is that a final agreement should represent value to both parties better than any other alternative.

Figure 24.4 illustrates how one might plot out the opening position relative to one's BATNA.

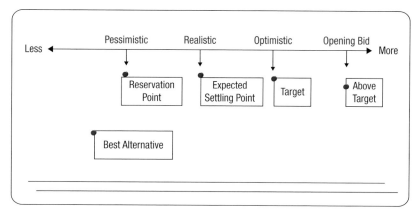

Figure 24.4   Bargaining zone

Trade-offs

A trade-off is a mutual exchange of value between parties. A concession is usually a unilateral gift to one party that is not reciprocated by the demanding party. Because issues are often linked, e.g., delivery date and payment date, trade-offs offer opportunities to meet needs while exchanging value. The more collaborative your strategy the more you must think in terms of trade-offs rather than demand concessions.

When using a competitive negotiation strategy, trade that which is of lower value to you for that which is of higher value to you. Your counterparty will do the same for themselves. Find those elements that are of high value to the counterparty but of lower cost to you to find 'win-win' trade-offs. When using a collaborative strategy, it is wise to make trades that are of mutual value to both parties. Not only will this engender trust, it will actually get your company a better deal in the long run.

Estimate what trades the other side will accept, based upon your knowledge of how similar negotiations went – either with that company or with others who are comparable in that industry. As the negotiation develops, you will be able to approximately determine the bargaining zone of the other side.

Arguments

You should have an argument ready for any item that you think you might trade for. Your arguments should justify what you are asking for. They should be based on precedent wherever possible – from past negotiations with the same customer or publicly available industry information. Fairness arguments should state the criterion of fairness you are using and why it should apply.

Always consider evidence that does not support your argument, and be prepared to deal with it.

The point of the planner is not to fill in every blank before the negotiation begins: that is unrealistic. Fill in as much as you can, based on (1) what you know and (2) what you can make a reasonable estimate on. Then, as the negotiation proceeds, fill in more blanks and change those already filled in as new information becomes available. Save the planner as a reference for future negotiations -in the same industry or with the same people.

24.9 Tools for establishing a negotiation foundation

There are four basic areas to consider when using tools to establish a negotiation foundation:
- Managing information
- Negotiations checklist
- Business intelligence tools
- Knowledge management tools

Managing information

We are surprised by the continuing lack of data that most negotiators have at their disposal. Most negotiators recognize that information is power. But in a competitive negotiation environment, negotiators will withhold information and use it only to strengthen their position. On the other hand, collaborative negotiators will use information to strengthen the overall outcome of the agreement. For example, a collaborative negotiator will share baseline assumptions in order to establish fair and meaningful key performance indicators (KPIs).

Information flow and knowledge management are sources of weakness in most negotiations because people withhold critical information or fail to interpret important information accurately. In general, negotiators assume the other side has much greater knowledge than is in fact the case. When both parties make this assumption, the deal is off to a bad start.

In the coming years, contract management software is likely to transform this situation, but today there is remarkably little internal collection and exchange of data – and even less from the outside. Despite electronic enhancements, negotiators must still accurately interpret data and share all relevant data.

Recent IACCM surveys have indicated the following sources are used when developing and gathering information for negotiations with the percentage frequency shown:

- Formal feedback/recording process - 42 percent
- External sources – internet, law firms - 37 percent
- Surveys, focus groups etc. - 12 percent
- Competitive research - 8 percent
- New employee interviews - 6 percent

The key to a successful outcome of a negotiation is to be knowledgeable about (1) what you want, (2) a clear rationale on why you want what you want (so that you can defend and persuade the other side of your position), (3) information to support that your request is within industry and market standards, and (4) you have developed alternative compromise positions that still meet the general desires. One essential element is to know your information and objectives before the negotiations begin.

Business intelligence

Business intelligence leverages quantitative data that is often extracted from enterprise business systems. This might include:
- Detailed financial information
- Budgeting and forecasting
- Business process data
- Needs assessments

The outcomes allow:
- Knowing about the history and forecasts to predict multiple complex scenarios
- Leveraging fact-based decision-making

Knowledge management

Knowledge management leverages qualitative data and information that is captured and stored in the business' knowledge systems or retrieved from third party resources. Such information might include:
- Best practice or lessons learned
- Competitive assessments
- Risk assessments
- Cost models
- 'What-if' simulation analysis models
- Past pricing or contract information

- Tools and templates
- Governance and internal processes/approvals

One important source of information that is often overlooked is interviewing subject matter experts in your own organization. These are the people who have intimate knowledge of certain subject areas. These experts should not be overlooked or undervalued as a source of information in preparing for negotiations. Going one step further, these experts can be selectively brought into negotiations during certain aspects to add credibility to your own arguments or to use as further leverage.

The outcomes allow:
- Use of enterprise 'body of knowledge' to strengthen your position
- Facilitating real-time and asynchronous collaboration with those outside the negotiating team
- Bringing facts to bear during the negotiations

Contract management software

Contract management software allows companies to add speed and integrity to the contract development process. However, it does not substitute for planning and strategic activities. Some of the benefits derived from contract management software include:
- Reducing contract development time. The ability to build contracts automatically based on pre-approved templates with prescribed criteria. This can be used for commodity type products and services; however for more complex product or services (customized products or services or IT and business process outsourcing), the automation benefit is somewhat diluted as these contract types do lend themselves to automatic contract builds.
- Achieving higher levels of quality and consistency
- Storage, archive and query ability of all contracts. Repository and query ability varies by contract management software. It is best to establish an organization's requirements for contract storage and retrieving.
- Creation of a knowledge based repository. This can be valuable when there is a need to search for rationale or example contract provisions that may have been used for similar contracting situations.

24.10 Summary

In this chapter the focus has been on planning for negotiations where the main elements have been framing, and goal setting and strategizing. Through the subjects that have been discussed, we have given a broad picture of the complexity of negotiation planning, when it comes to both the psychological and instrumental part of the planning.

Key issues to think about throughout negotiations:
- The benefits of working on the framing of the negotiations
- The purpose of goals in negotiations
- The importance of the main strategic approach to the negotiations
- How to anticipate the different phases of the negotiation and mitigate the risk.

Remember this is all about trading (i.e. making concessions on both sides), but in a structured, proactive, well-thought through process and not in a chaotic, empathic and reactive way.

And above all, always keep in mind what you want to achieve during each stage of the negotiation process.

CHAPTER 25

Negotiation styles – positional versus principled negotiations

25.1 Introduction

Negotiation style has a major effect on the outcome of the negotiation. This chapter describes the alternatives and outcomes that different styles typically produce. Each of the two styles outlined below correlate to a strategy. You must pick the appropriate style and strategy pair. If you pick one strategy and not the corresponding style, you are sending mixed messages that are sure to delay if not derail the process.

Your decision on negotiation style must be driven not only on your own goals but also by your strategy. Your counterpart will also choose their style and strategy. If the two parties choose conflicting styles and strategies, one of you must change your strategy and style.

In this chapter, we'll describe how to use different styles and discuss the benefits and risks associated with them. By the end of this chapter you should be able to assess when to use the different approaches, how to identify the style other negotiators are using and how to use tactics and approaches that counter those tactics or bring them around to your preferred approach. You will be able to:

- Understand and use different negotiation styles
- Understand and recognize positional negotiation
- Understand the advantages and disadvantages of positional negotiations
- Understand principled negotiation
- Understand the risks and opportunities of alternative approaches.

25.2 Perspective and precedent

Negotiation must be viewed in the context of a wider process. That means negotiations are always affected by the perceptions or beliefs the parties bring to the table. These include fundamental issues such as past relationships, respective views of strength, beliefs about competitors or alternatives, precedent, history or market perception.

Culture also plays an important part. The negotiation will also be affected by views of 'fairness' and the degree of planning and coordination undertaken by the parties. Often companies overlook the fact that 'negotiations' extend from inception of a potential relationship through to its eventual conclusion; during this time, there may be hundreds of individual negotiated events, internal and external, that contribute to the eventual outcome – successful or unsuccessful. Like any series of events, individual elements may be deemed a success, but they do not guarantee ultimate satisfaction or 'victory'.

25.3 Negotiation options: positional versus principled

The two core approaches to negotiation are commonly called *positional* and *principled*. Essentially positional negotiation correlates to the competitive negotiation strategy. Because the competitive strategy seeks to gain at your counterpart's expense and the positional style seeks to limit discussion, they usually go together. The positional style tends to lead to what are termed win-lose results, as opposed to the collaborative style of a principled approach and its results, which tend to be termed win-win.

Principled negotiation is employed when you are serious about finding a mutually acceptable solution, and therefore, correlates to the collaborative negotiation strategy. We're going to explore the characteristics of each of these styles in more detail later.

Most negotiators have a natural preference for one approach or the other, but experienced negotiators need to be able to use both. You should understand and practice both styles; you also need to find methods to understand and establish the preferred styles of the members of your negotiation team. You need to be able to use and protect against those members' preferences during the negotiation.

In general, for example, functional specialists from areas such as Finance or Legal are perhaps narrower in their outlook. They tend to be more likely to have positional attitudes, and show less interest in the validity of the views or arguments of the other side, or indeed of their own team members. This can be an asset when deployed effectively. And, it can ruin deals when deployed as a thoughtless hardball tactic. If you fear that a subject matter expert may disrupt the deal flow, talk to them about the value to the company if the deal is won and the loss and lack of viable alternatives if the deal is derailed. Regardless of these experts' narrow focus, no one wants to intentionally kill a good deal and leave their company vulnerable in the market.

You must select your style to accord with your objectives, your strategy, and of course you must have established a planned and consistent approach throughout your team. It does not mean that you will all follow the same approach all of the time; it simply means that variations, changes and inconsistencies must be planned.

Finally, you must have researched and planned for the style of the other side, and the individual members of their team.

25.4 Factors that influence your choice

There are three factors that influence your choice of negotiation style. The same factors will play with the other side, so you will need to go through these factors not only from your team's perspective, but from the other team's perspective as well.

Authority

One of the most powerful factors is *authority*; do you have the people on your team who are authorized to make commitments on all areas of the contract and agreement? Does the other side have those? If not, you are going to find areas that are constrained where inevitably the negotiation is going to be more positional in its approach. If you have the authorized parties on board, then it can become more principled.

You have to decide whether this matters so as to determine whether you insist on the right experts or authorized individuals from their side being on their team and, equally, who you want on your team. Is this a deliberate elimination or is it something that you wish to include?

Relative power

The same applies when you look at things like relative power and the beliefs the parties have over their power and influence over the negotiation. Do you consider yourselves to be the dominant party or do you see the other side as the dominant party? How do you think they see this? It will have a major influence on the style and approach that they adopt.

Relationship

How important is the customer-supplier relationship to the overall success of your company? If the relationship is critical to your success, such as in the case of business alliances, strategic partnerships or outsourcing arrangements, both parties' styles will need to be more principled.

25.5   Positional versus principled negotiation

A positional approach involves a person adopting a position and aiming to negotiate an agreement as close to that position as possible, without even exploring alternative outcomes or paying real attention to the other side. It is a style that allows for only limited and fairly predictable negotiating. In many instances it degenerates into a 'battle of wills', each party wondering who is going to' give in' first.

People adopting a positional style will assume that only one party can emerge from the negotiation a clear winner. This is often termed the 'win-lose' approach.

The principled approach, on the other hand, has a different set of primary assumptions. These are that the parties share some common interests, that the outcome will be improved if there is full discussion of each participant's perspectives and interests, and that we live in an integrated and complex world where our problems can be best resolved through an application of intelligence and creativity. The expectation is to arrive at a situation where both parties benefit: a 'win-win' approach.

25.6   Characteristics of positional negotiating

At its heart, positional negotiation tends to arise because one party determines that they are not prepared to take any significant risk. This may be driven by the fact that they have particular power in the negotiation, that the choices for the other side are rather limited or alternatively if it's a buying situation that there are extensive alternative choices and therefore they don't particularly need this specific supplier.

On the other hand, it can be driven by a highly uncertain highly risky deal, where neither party comes feeling confident that they understand the risk or that they can contain the risk and therefore wishing to try and push as much of that risk as possible onto the other side.

While this approach is more typically connected to buyers, and specifically to lower level buyers driven by things like one dimensional performance measurements, such as cost savings, or a culture of "we know what's right" or a perspective that "the supplier is the enemy", it typically also represents a lack of authority and this can apply on both sides. Either party coming to a negotiation and - for example - insisting on their terms and conditions is probably not empowered to negotiate those terms and conditions to any meaningful degree.

This is very typical in areas like the technology industry and many of the other suppliers you deal with on a day-to-day basis. In these situations the sales representatives were taught that negotiation was objection handling and that they had to resort to hidden figures somewhere in the background at corporate headquarters, if they wanted to get variations to the terms. This is a classic example of positional negotiation, of avoidance and evasion.

You have to understand the impact of such an approach on the likely outcome. You have to assess the areas of the deal where you may be taking a positional approach, and ensure that this is truly going to be working towards your advantage.

25.7 Characteristics of principled negotiation

Principled negotiation will be prevalent in many of the deals that you are working on, so although elements may be positional, overall you want to get to a much better understanding of the shared opportunities and risks that prevail. This means that you have to be much more open and collaborative in your approach and your style. You have to be serious about unearthing the interests of the other side and you have to have done good groundwork in understanding your own internal interests and how they can best be met. You have to be ready to explore alternatives and options. Overall success in a principled negotiation will be defined in the relationship that results, not the specific contract terms that are signed. You have to remember in this context that contract signature is just a milestone; it isn't an end point.

25.8 Recognizing positional negotiation

These items apply to a positional negotiation:
- Extreme opening demands
- Threats, tension, pressure
- Stretching of the facts
- Stick to positions, focus on rights, create obstacles
- Being tight-lipped, evasive
- Want to outdo, out-maneuver the other side
- Want clear victory (win-lose result)

Bottom line: positional negotiation is manipulative. It is designed to intimidate the other party so that they lose confidence in their own case and accept the other side's demands. The approach is often characterized by the ploys or tricks and tactics discussed in Chapter 27: *Tactics, tricks and lessons learned*. It also reflects the issue of power, not always an abusive power, *but sometimes a calculated approach to mask or overcome weakness.*

Some examples:

- Extreme opening positions: People adopt extreme positions because they achieve more favorable settlements on the range of issues that they set as their goals. Since virtually all settlements include some level of compromise, they frequently end up somewhere in the middle. A high or low start point will generally create a more favorable result. Our case studies and research certainly bear this out.
- Focus on rights: The negotiator will often focus on rights to justify their positions. Repeated reference to the legal / moral / economic 'right,' or to some aspect of the history of relationship between the parties, to make the other party(ies) accept it. This will be particularly effective if it is difficult for the other side to establish the alternative facts.
- Aggression: In a 'battle of wills', social niceties may be dispensed with. The style of a positional negotiator is often very aggressive and may include threats or the inclusion of an environment where there is a high degree of tension or pressure. Personal attacks directed at the other negotiators may sometimes be viewed as justified and will be the case, particularly in some cultures.
- Evasion and creation of obstacles: These are amongst the tricks you will encounter. You will have to test out whether you consider particular techniques and tactics to be principled and acceptable as negotiation forms.

Examples like these will arise when the party has no real intention of negotiating or plans to do so on a very limited agenda. The obstacles they create can include things like the denial of authority, or the introduction of delays so they can avoid items that don't suit their immediate agenda, in the hope that you'll run out of time and that executive pressure will force you to move on to items that they are more comfortable addressing.

25.9 Advantages and disadvantages of positional negotiating

The advantages of positional negotiating include:

- **Time**: It can result in a more rapid conclusion. If all parties involved are being positional then the negotiation may soon break down, or the weaker party may concede. Alternatively, once the parties recognize that they are all adopting the same approach, the negotiation may move on to the concession giving stage and thereafter settlement.
- **Uncomplicated**: It is uncomplicated in its approach. It does not require much preparation time or resource. Indeed positional negotiation may, unfortunately, simply reflect a lack of planning or lack of senior management commitment to the deal or relationship. If that's the case, it's important to understand it. It's a weakness if it applies to your side and may be a lack of commitment if it's the other side. Once into the negotiation, in an

uncomplicated environment like this, the ground rules become easy to understand, for example an extreme opening position will lead either to an acceptable compromise or to a breakdown of the negotiation.

- **Favors the powerful**: Positional approaches tend to favor the powerful. If there is a marked power imbalance between the negotiating parties, the powerful party will often achieve what they want by being positional. And if you have no intention of compromising, what is the point of wasting everyone's time by implying there's flexibility?

- **Inexpensive**: Since this style is often linked to limited or no planning, the amount of time and the involvement of skilled resources are both minimized. So potentially this is a much less expensive way, in terms of time and cost.

Disadvantages include:

- **Damages relationships**: Positional negotiating tends to damage relationships. Although the relative power of the parties may mask this, the weaker party will always be looking for alternatives and opportunities for escape. Customers may not be able to take action in the short run but may leap on opportunities. The same applies with suppliers – they inevitably feel less loyalty and concern for a customer who has consistently forced them to accept 'unreasonable' or onerous levels of risk or especially aggressive terms. And may, therefore, not provide the hoped for levels of support to address a problem of the customer's making.

- **Inflexibility**: A positional approach does not lead to creative or alternatively potentially superior solutions because the parties are focused on staying as close as possible to their opening positions. So it never opens up to a wider discussion with a chance to create incremental value. Arguments over price are particularly likely to get stuck this way, when perhaps a focus on cost of ownership or cost of supply might reveal greater value alternatives that lead to a mutually beneficial solution.

- **Failure rate**: The failure rate of positional negotiating is also higher – both during and after negotiation. If the product or service is complex or the deal innately high risk, the probability that implementation will fail is substantially greater. This is because risks are not adequately explored and therefore mitigation is never enabled, since this form of negotiation is about superficial risk shuffling or avoidance.

- **Achieves unsatisfactory / inefficient agreement**: Even when the relationship or contract does not fail, the arbitrary, unplanned nature of the agreement rarely optimizes the potential benefits for either party. And the style of negotiation often creates an environment of continuing dishonesty and unwillingness to raise uncomfortable issues, especially by the 'losing' party. So this can result very often in unsatisfactory change procedures and extensive disputes during implementation. There is a tendency to fight on every issue and there's a failure to identify or forecast problems before they occur.

What you save in time at the front end will more than cancelled out by extra time in management and implementation.

- **Causes loss of focus**: Positional negotiating is rarely stimulating, especially for the less powerful side, and skilled resources are therefore rarely attracted to such negotiations. Reducing a loss is not as heroic as gaining a win. This attitude is dangerous, because deals like this, if they are going to be made, truly merit attention from some of your best people because these are the situations that are going to make tomorrow's disputes, law suits and claims.

You have to think carefully about this list and decide in the deals that you are undertaking which style is going to be more appropriate, or which set of styles and combination of approaches; what the mix is that needs to be made, depending upon what area and aspect of the deal you currently talk through.

25.10 Advantages and disadvantages of principled negotiating

Advantages include:

- **Builds trust**: The principled approach engenders trust. Using this approach, both negotiation teams are focused on the issues and concerns before them, and are not posturing for advantage. Open and honest communication usually leads to more open and honest communication. Positional negotiation often stifles communication leading to countless misunderstandings.
- **Maintains relationships**: Not surprisingly the principled approach helps us in maintaining relationships. It is unlikely to provoke the aggression that is often the result of positional negotiating. Since the emphasis of the parties is on a mutually beneficial agreement, there is a reduced need for competitiveness and the parties are typically going to end up on good terms with each other, thus setting the foundation for a positive relationship.
- **Achieves satisfactory / efficient agreements**: Since the parties have not limited themselves to the narrow confines of who is right to prevail, the agreement can meet as many of the parties' needs as they have been prepared to reveal. So it can achieve a much more efficient and satisfactory agreement.
- **Flexibility**: Principled negotiation also allows flexibility over what and who is included in the negotiation. As particular interests or the need for specific expertise becomes apparent, other individuals or players can be brought into the negotiations. Newly disclosed interests may result in the negotiation going into areas that weren't even anticipated beforehand.

- **Achieves agreements**: The characteristics of principled negotiation should result in agreement more often than not. This style does allow for at least partial agreement, whereas positional negotiation tends to be complete failure or complete success. Partial agreement will often stand a good chance of subsequently leading to a wider agreement on everything, or a decision to narrow the overall scope of the deal and negotiation to something that is in mutual interest, and to handle other pieces of it through another approach.
- **Redresses power imbalances**: Principled negotiation can redress power imbalances. It can establish alternative routes or solutions that can change the power balance. It can create a greater interdependency, for example with a supplier it can generate a source of differentiation or competitive advantage that didn't previously exist. The challenge here is to develop a significantly compelling value statement that the more powerful party is enticed to engage and to some extent give up that power.
- **Stimulating**: Principled negotiation is more stimulating; it doesn't have the predictability associated with the positional approach. The parties have scope for achieving comprehensive satisfying agreements, but of course that won't occur unless both parties are prepared to commit open-minded creative professionals to the process; individuals who view winning as something that occurs for both sides and is measured over time.

There are, however, disadvantages.
- **Time**: This type of negotiating can prolong the process. The ultimate result often justifies the time spent, but not always. Some people simply don't know how to work collaboratively, and meetings can drag on without ever reaching an agreement.
- **Complexity**: In some respects principled negotiating is also far more complex and demanding than its positional counterpart. More effort is going to be required by both parties, preparing for and during the negotiation. Different skills are needed. The negotiation team will have to draw on a range of in-depth knowledge during the process.
- **Cost**: Principled negotiation tends to be more costly. The additional hours for discussion, research add substantially to the overall costs, but the real issue is the impact on quality and the opportunity of the resulting deal. For many suppliers, bid costs of up to or exceeding a million dollars in an outsourcing environment are not uncommon, so they should be deciding whether this is a worthwhile investment to be making.
- **False comfort**: In developing a comfortable supportive style of negotiation, there is a risk that the parties convince themselves that the mutual interests are going to be enough to overcome potential risks or obstacles. So retaining objectivity in principled negotiation is essential. Don't let the quality of the relationship overwhelm your judgment. You have to remember the negotiators themselves may not be directly involved in many stages of the implementation. So the feelings of confidence and rapport that they have created may not be shared once you are back to the implementation phase in your organization.

25.11 Non-negotiable issues

Most large corporations mandate a positional style for certain areas of the contract. Obviously you must be aware of where those restrictions come from and you must comply with them. If they need to be challenged, that is certainly within your remit and authority to do so, but this has to be an internal discussion - not one with the negotiating partner.

The restrictions that are created may be due to regulatory conditions, for example laws relating to bribery and corruption, or around the need to protect core assets, for example licenses or patents. These terms are essentially non-negotiable and the size of the list varies, both by country and by industry. For some industries, such as financial services, telecommunications, aerospace, the levels of regulation are substantial and therefore reduce or eliminate negotiability in significant areas of the contract. In countries such as Germany or Portugal, statute law is much more pervasive than in common law countries such as the US and the UK. In countries such as these, large areas of the contract are unaffected by negotiation, since if local law is the basis of the contract the statutory provisions will prevail.

The recent issues around corporate governance have added to the list of contract clauses either directly affected by legislation or that have become the subject of more rigorous internal policies.

Examples of these are the payment provisions effected by revenue recognition rules, and the legal liability clauses where Sarbanes-Oxley may demand management disclosure.

It is critical that you understand these, not only in the context of your own company, but also of the party with which you are negotiating. It is pointless to drive demands for negotiation in areas that are quite clearly outside the power of the negotiators to grant or discuss.

The differences in negotiation tradition existing around the world

Negotiation and contract management tradition and experience vary significantly between countries. Unlike the US, where most things are negotiable, and the power of negotiators to drive changes is therefore extensive, countries with a large body of statutory law limit change and therefore formal negotiation styles are different. In common law countries the specific terms and wording of the deal are viewed as critical and they absorb many hours of negotiation. In the US especially this tendency has been reinforced by the influence of lawyers. The typical US company employs many more lawyers than their international counterparts. In civil law countries the spirit of the agreement is what matters.

How is that translated? In common law countries a confrontational and uncompromising style involving legal experts was at least typical in the past. In other countries the terms of the agreement tend to attract far less confrontation and legal involvement. It's more normal for an understanding to evolve between the business people and for its documentation to be far less formal. This is important because it drives the style and expectations of the parties. In many companies negotiators outside the legal department don't have authority to negotiate core contract terms. By definition, therefore, you are forced to be positional in handling those terms.

Your strategy has to focus on the areas where you have some authority or negotiability. What about the other side? Will they accept this agenda? Will they take a similar approach to core terms or are they prepared to focus on areas where you have flexibility? The answer to this is going to vary. If you are confronting some major corporations you can be certain there will be conflict and you will need a clear plan and strategy for handling it. If you are working with small suppliers or customers they may recognize there is no point in tackling the legal 'boilerplate', and indeed they are unable to afford the associated costs. So they are going to place all their resources and emphasis on the other areas of the contract or deal. They are going to look for ways to work around the terms and conditions that you are imposing.

25.12 Countering the positional negotiator

How do you go about countering a positional negotiator? First, you have to hope that it isn't a surprise. If the other side has adopted a positional approach and you weren't expecting it, the chances are that you haven't done your homework well enough and that you will be unprepared for major areas of this negotiation. So we recommend that you want to halt the negotiation as quickly as possible, that you get together with your team and that you delay long enough to make sure that you have a strategy to handle this particular event, whether or not that takes minutes or days.

You should think through two or three very sound reasons why a positional approach will work to their disadvantage. Are there are compelling reasons why they should change their style? Work with those two or three reasons – not just everything you can think of – and test them first for their persuasiveness with colleagues or mentors within your own organization. You need to try to quantify the benefits that will be achieved by switching approach. If you believe the opposing negotiation team will be unmoved, because they lack the vision, or lack the authority, you may decide to reach higher in the organization before the negotiation starts. That way, if your arguments are compelling, you may generate senior management interest without appearing to undermine or demean the other side's negotiating team, and therefore will have reset the rules and the playing field before you begin.

Do you have reason to believe the negotiation is not reflecting corporate or management policy on their side? You should establish the likely approach based on factors such as other negotiations with their company, patterns in their industry, or stated policy positions by their executives. If these give you grounds to undermine or challenge the positional approach they have adopted, you should have planned ways to introduce these. Your aim in such situations should be to create doubt, uncertainty and discord in the other team based either on the unreasonableness of their approach, or a fear that they may not in fact get support from their management.

Learn from children. One of the techniques that young children use to great effect with their parents is to consistently and continually ask questions, and push for more and more justifications. In forcing you to give more answers and more justifications they wait until you come up with the weakest, then they pounce. Their style and their technique is to make you look ridiculous or to undermine your position and your credibility. They make your position appear untenable.

There are two important points here, If you are acting in a positional form, make sure that you have decided what your two or three key reasons are, justifications for that position, and stick to them. Do not be tempted to expand your reasons and your list just because the other side keeps pushing and pushing as if you are being unreasonable. Always remember that is a tactic that you can use with them. Once they have revealed a weak reason and you have undermined their rational, that's when you start to push for compromise and concessions.

Use logic to sell your ideas or alternatives. People don't like to appear irrational or unfair. So consistently blocking against very reasonable and logical arguments makes people feel uncomfortable. If they appear illogical, if they really can't cope with the arguments that you are presenting it is probable that someone else is pulling their strings. It's usually an indication that you are negotiating with the wrong person. This means that you have a choice: you can either accept their position with whatever small compromise you can extract, or try to move to whoever in the organization is really in control.

Finally, listen and learn. A positional negotiator is generally somebody who can be pushed in terms of their comments or in terms of their further illustrations of why it is that they are taking their particular position. You know that many times they too are uncomfortable with that. Under pressure they will often start to resort to anger or bluster to justify their particular position or to try and force things to move on. All of these tactics present opportunities. The opportunity for you is to listen; you will discover many more things about their interests and their justifications that may create an opening for you to counter and suggest alternatives that have real value to them in areas that they and perhaps you have not originally considered. At that point you can begin to propose some trades and begin to address some of the concessions that you have been looking to obtain.

25.13 Is principled negotiation worthwhile?

All of this discussion assumes that collaborative discussion and principled negotiation is worthwhile and leads to superior results. In an IACCM/Vantage Partners study, few (if any) of the participants saw any downside to collaborative negotiations. The majority in almost every area recognized some benefits, and at least 20 percent in every area reported significantly higher returns through using collaborative or principled practices.

Issues in principled negotiations

If you have decided that principled negotiation is your preferred route, it won't necessarily be all smooth sailing. If the other party is more powerful it will be essential that you have tools and techniques to encourage and persuade them of a need to move to a more principled approach.

The most obvious tactic is to discuss both parties' best alternatives to negotiated agreement (BATNAs). If you are a buyer your BATNA might have more immediate meaning, since you usually have alternative suppliers to choose from. Suppliers also have alternatives in the face of unreasonable positional negotiators. Suppliers often have many opportunities and can (and will) put resources into deals that will get them the best result. If neither party has a viable alternative to negotiating with one another, both parties must discuss the "consequences of no agreement".

Specialist advisers encourage negotiators to analyze the consequences of no agreement. Both parties look at the impact of no agreement. In an outsourcing arrangement that can be very substantial. Helping people to focus on the costs of not reaching an agreement can really concentrate minds and make them realize there is a substantial benefit in yielding to a particular demand or request that you actually have, which can include a more collaborative approach.

Watch out for wolves in sheep's clothing. There are negotiators who intentionally choose to start talks with an air of collaboration, just to lull the other side into a vulnerable position. These same negotiators then turn positional, taking their counterparts by surprise. Negotiators who choose this path are betting that their counterpart will concede. Make sure you are not using a principled approach if you aren't seriously intending to make meaningful trades through the negotiation process. That misleads the other side and misleads and frustrates your own team. It may also force your counterparty to walk away, for good.

Finally, what if the other side won't play or is using tricks or ploys to try to sabotage the form of the negotiation? As a principled negotiator you should be insisting on negotiation in a way that's acceptable. The principled negotiator can ask about the other side's concerns, you should show that you understand those concerns, and having done that you should ask for mutual recognition of all concerns. Show that there is respect within the negotiation and that there is an opportunity to table the set of issues that you feel need to be discussed.

If you can establish the exploration of all of those interests, then you are often able to create an environment where the positional negotiator is at least open to some level of brainstorming of options and thinking in terms of objective criteria under which decisions can then be made.

This can, of course, prove rather theoretical in the context of many positional negotiations; it's only going to work if you can establish interest on the other side and where they have the power and ability necessary to make the switch in behavior.

Addressing issues in principled negotiations

One of the methods that has been observed as most effective in addressing the positional negotiator is what is known as 'matching, pacing, leading and modeling'. One thing that's for sure is that if you have a positional negotiator, simply challenging and threatening them right from the beginning is not going to be effective. They will become more entrenched in their position, more dogmatic and less open to change. So it's critical that you give them an opportunity to let off steam. If they have emotions they want to get out, if they have facts that they want to lay on the table, however biased those may be, whatever their positions may be or their justifications, sit back and listen. Try to encourage more and more conversation out of them. Certainly, if they start from a position of anger it's very difficult for someone to sustain that anger over time if they are getting no real response.

As you sit through it, you are going to pick up many useful and interesting pieces of information. And steadily you are going to be able to start intervening, but not with anything that contradicts or challenges their particular position, but rather perhaps, a few proposals that you feel begin to meet or match some of the issues that they have raised or some clarifying questions that are going to further help you with developing your negotiation position and strategy.

In that environment it is unusual for any negotiator not to become steadily more open to the leads that you are providing, and to move to a position of much greater cooperation and a productive means of negotiation.

25.14 Summary

We have already discussed some examples of ways that you can drive behavior and how you need to understand the various needs of all other parties in the negotiation. In this concluding section we summarize those needs and see how they play in terms of driving negotiation behaviors.

- Security and stability needs: it is important to try as much as possible to be like your opposite number. People tend to be more influenced by people who are like them and have similar priorities or have shown an empathy in sharing those priorities.
- Social needs: you need to demonstrate respect for the other side and earn it from them. People tend to want to do business with people they like or respect and who in turn, like and respect them.
- Esteem: the other side has to do a good job too; they like to do a good job for their bosses and the company. If you undermine them they are going to be much less committed to the deal or structuring a deal. It's much more tempting for them to walk away and give reasons why they cannot reach an agreement, than to with someone that has challenged their specific esteem.
- Be considerate and thoughtful: do your research on the other side for personal likes and dislikes. People generally want to do deals with people they can trust and who are professional.
- Respond to basic human needs: try to introduce some level of pleasure into the negotiation process. That's obviously a culturally sensitive issue as to what is appropriate, but people like things to be interesting and they like to be entertained. Don't bore them and don't overwhelm them.
- Finally, wherever possible let the other side believe they are in control and that it is actually you who's helping them meet their objectives.

Consider all these factors and how they play in terms of your response and your attitudes, the things that are likely to encourage you to reach an agreement, to be more flexible, and to want to do a deal with the other side. Then employ those tactics and techniques in your own negotiation styles.

CHAPTER 26
Negotiating techniques

26.1 Introduction

Effective analysis and planning enable a successful negotiated outcome. This chapter provides best practice insights into the following key negotiation techniques:

- Issues of relative power
- Opening the negotiation
- Principles for assembling the team
- Managing the team
- Maintaining consensus
- Handling changes or conflict

26.2 Preparation

The single most prevalent cause of failure of negotiations is lack of adequate preparation. This is often because the negotiator or the wider team contributing to the negotiations have not had adequate training in the many components of negotiating preparation or perceive there is no time to plan. As Malhotra and Bazerman of the Harvard Business School observe "The problem is usually not *faulty* preparation, but a *lack* of preparation altogether!"

One of the major challenges encountered in most organizations is coordination of internal resources to agree on a negotiation strategy and plan. Varying functions and individuals have conflicting perspectives, motivations and interests. Success depends on understanding these, and working to constructively overcome the internal obstacles. The internal negotiation can actually be more complex due to the lack of motivation or willingness by key stakeholders to cooperate.

All too often negotiations and schedules can go off-track because one or both sides have come inadequately prepared for discussions. For example, a subject matter expert did not read the other party's detailed revisions to a draft contract and is hesitant to agree to any revision. He or she sits through the entire discussion refusing to be drawn into any substantive discussion.

Or because their schedules did not coordinate, the legal, commercial and financial departments did not have an opportunity to review the agreed commercial term sheet. So the other side receives a contract form that does not reflect discussions between these groups, although the other side may consider it to be the complete version from your side.

These mishaps happen all too often between companies that are doing business for the first time and especially ones that reach out across continents. There are few agreed protocols, the pace of business in each company varies, and quite often people speaking the same language mean different things. Be sure to gauge the cultural and linguistic differences, and be sure that your legal counsel and other experts who contribute to the negotiations but may not be at the negotiating table are advised as well.

Reading

Typically, negotiations are preceded by, revolve around, and conclude with documentation. The importance of reading with care and well in advance of a scheduled discussion cannot be adequately stressed. From a negotiation perspective, a careful read usually arms the negotiator with insights into the other side's thinking process. Analyzing the manner in which a proposal or provision has been articulated in writing allows the negotiator to extrapolate one or more potential "where they are coming from" positions. These are hypotheses on why the other side wants what they have asked for or what they have proposed.

To summarize, reading should generate a list of questions for which a skilled negotiator should get answers during the course of discussions with the other party

Persuasion

If negotiation is defined as the process by which parties come to agreement, the key technique becomes persuasion. To achieve your goals you must understand relative strengths and weaknesses and have an appreciation of theories of human motivation. This understanding and appreciation are as critical to marshalling your own side as they are for the other party

Since the various stakeholders may differ in their perspective of what is a priority, persuading others in the organization to work cooperatively is often a challenge. Many contract managers observe that either they are not involved in the team to their full capacity or that they are brought in too late in the process. However, involving the key personnel at the right time is critical to effective negotiation preparation and planning.

Based on the needs outlined above, we can conclude that there could be approaches we take, or reactions we have, which may be counter-productive in gaining acceptance for our perspective and influencing the outcome.

We should always strive to rise above personal feelings or self-esteem issues; therefore, it might be useful to consider the approaches that could elicit negative reactions and why this might be. We could then be more persuasive in our approach to the other stakeholders.

Motivation

Motivation is a critical element of negotiation – it is defined as the inclination to do or not to do something. People generally want to achieve balance – which is why they might react negatively if they feel pressured to move on something, or if they feel the proposition they are being asked to accept is fundamentally unfair. There are positive and negative factors in all things that motivate us and they operate in combination with most business transactions. Better and lasting results are generally achieved through positive motivational influences.

Understanding responsibility

In any complex contracting process, answers to the multitude of questions are obtained from many sources. The negotiation team leader should gather the facts and information and develop appropriate strategy and tactics. While other participants may have access to some of the facts and have strong positions based on their perspective, it is ultimately the responsibility of the team leader to make decisions – and to be accountable for them.

Consider the negotiations that occur within your company. Who typically controls:
- Strategy?
- Information gathering and sharing?
- The agenda?
- The negotiation process?

Going beyond this – and testing your responses – who is truly accountable for the outcome of the negotiation? Also consider that if there is accountability, what are the metrics used to gauge success or failure, when are these measurements made, and who makes them? The fact is that in many organizations, there is no clear responsibility for the negotiated outcome; 'good' and bad results are often based on primitive 'scorecard' metrics, or on a more general feeling of whether we "won".

Division of responsibility

An IACCM benchmarking study aggregated responses from sales and procurement contracts professionals, representing over 100 companies, ranging from small and mid-sized organizations to some of the world's largest. When assessing how negotiation responsibilities are allocated, contracts professionals generally control setting strategy and leading the negotiations team, with other groups having scattered responsibility for these elements. Responsibility on the sales side is more evenly split between the contracts department and the business unit or sales department for the establishment of price targets.

Less than half of these contracts professionals are responsible for negotiation of all contract terms. Responsibility is generally shared based upon what group has authority for a particular term. It is essential to understand whether we are leaders or influencers and behave accordingly. Let's take one of these areas – the question of team make-up. This is often contentious. Some people are anxious to be included – maybe for entirely legitimate reasons, but also sometimes because of power or control issues. Others who maybe should be there may not want to attend, viewing themselves as too busy to allocate the time. This will require that the negotiating team leader "negotiates" with stakeholders to obtain the "right" people for the negotiation team and might involve the contracts professional negotiating to be involved.

Individual and group preparation

Both the individuals and the team must be properly prepared for any negotiation. Companies that achieve their negotiation goals typically have a strong culture of building a consensus-based approach towards negotiation strategy. Consensus is a process of consulting key stakeholders, gathering views and attempting to arrive at a decision that all or most of the stakeholders would agree with. This may require some or all stakeholders to "compromise" with their original goals but is likely to result in a position that more closely represents the best interests of the organization.

Before negotiators take their seats, the stakeholders within an organization must spend time collectively answering several questions. We suggest that you first look at your own organization and team, before turning your attention to your counterparty. One of the major problems we encounter in most organizations is the difficulty of coordinating internal resources to reach an agreed negotiation strategy and plan. Functions and individuals have conflicting motivations and interests. Success depends on not only understanding these, but working to overcome the obstacles in a positive way.

Us	Them
What are our priorities?	What are their priorities?
Who are all of our stakeholders?	Who are all of their stakeholders?
Are there internal conflicts regarding motivations, goals and points of view?	Are they facing internal conflicts regarding motivations, goals, and points of view?
When and how will we involve subject matter experts, like lawyers?	When and how will they involve subject matter experts, like lawyers?
What information will we share, when and with whom?	What information will they share, when and with whom?
What is our history with them?	What do we know about how they perceive us and their work with us?

Table 26.1   Factors influencing negotiation strategy and plan

Introducing experts

Subject matter experts can be deployed very effectively in negotiations but care should be taken in introducing them in to the negotiation process. Some of the factors that must be considered by the negotiation team leader include:

- In-depth knowledge results in reduced risk in area of expertise; however, the expert may be hard to control. In fact, some experts, like lawyers, may have their own agenda. It is wise to synchronize the lead negotiator's agenda with all subject matter experts' agendas.
- They can provide technical information to establish a firm position on behalf of your organization; ideally, without compromising your relationship with the counterparty. But they can be 'parochial' due to lack of knowledge/authority in other areas being negotiated.
- They can align with the experts of counterparty; however, they must buy in to the organization's negotiation strategy and tactics. Otherwise they could jeopardize other aspects of the deal, or the total deal.
- They may bring information or knowledge that supports your position in other areas of the deal; however, this can sometimes add to complexity and duration.
- They may speed the process by facilitating direct communication with counterparty experts.

26.3   **Negotiation power**

Negotiation power can be defined as the ability of the negotiator to influence the behavior of another. Commentators have observed a variety of attributes of negotiation power that should be considered:

- It is relative between the parties;
- It changes over time;
- It is always limited;
- It can be either real or apparent;

- The exercise of negotiation power has both benefits and costs;
- It can include the ability to punish or reward;
- It is enhanced by facts (e.g. legal, regulatory, official statistics), personal knowledge, skill, resources and hard work;
- It can be directly related to the ability to endure uncertainty (potential risk);
- It is usually enhanced by a good relationship with the counterparty;
- It must be considered in establishment of the party's BATNA (best alternative to a negotiated agreement) and can be affected by changing the alternative;
- It exists to the extent that it is accepted by the other party

Measuring power

A useful measure of power in negotiation is the amount of cooperation that one side needs from the counterparty. This is illustrated in Figure 26.1 The lines intersecting the two power axes represent the respective needs for cooperation of the negotiating parties. The party represented by the vertical axis – because it requires more cooperation – has less power than the other side.

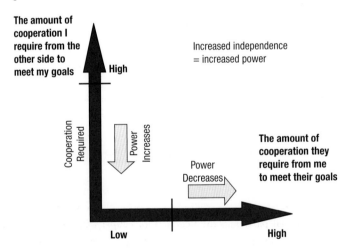

Figure 26.1   Measuring power

If the counterparty recognizes that you need their cooperation, they have power. This could lead your counterparty to choose a competitive strategy and positional style. If your counterparty needs your cooperation, you have power. You may then likewise choose a competitive strategy and positional style. In a balanced power situation, both companies ought to choose a collaborative strategy and principled style. Since neither party needs the other party's cooperation more than the other, competitive tactics will quickly undermine any potential deal.

In a competitive negotiation situation, to attempt to equalize power, the side with less power has two choices, represented by the black arrows:

1. They can lessen their own need for cooperation, e.g., by establishing a better Best Alternative To Negotiated Agreement (BATNA) – represented by the downward arrow.
2. They can assert that the counterparty is really more dependent than they realize, e.g., by showing that only they can provide what the counterparty wants – represented by the horizontal arrow.

In a collaborative situation, power may still wax and wane over the course of the discussions. To stay collaborative, negotiators must resist the urge to take advantage of shifts in power. Seizing opportunities to exert power will create a negative feedback loop and force your counterparty to seek similar opportunities. Interdependent parties who use competitive tactics will sacrifice trust, efficiency and total deal value.

Sources of power

Within all negotiations, information is probably the most common source of power. Competitive negotiators *withhold* information to gain leverage, while collaborative negotiators *share* information to gain leverage. In both circumstances, the negotiator is using information as a form of power.

Power derived from expertise is a special form of information power. It requires selective use of very specific or technical information. Another source of power is the capacity to provide or withhold resources. Resources include money, supplies, manpower, time, equipment, and critical services. For example, a large company with the capacity to buy large quantities has a form of power which it might use to extract price concessions from a supplier.

Finally, an overlooked source of power is personal integrity. Successful negotiators are trusted and respected by all parties to the negotiation. People with integrity are able to reason with people who are unreasonable and influence decision makers to see things from their point of view. Unfortunately, some negotiators use tactics such as Good Cop/Bad Cop routines that erode trust and respect. They are sacrificing their personal source of power.

26.4 **Abuse of power**

Where there is access to power, there can be abuse of power. The professional negotiator should recognize that the use of power has ramifications; therefore, power should be used wisely. The shift of power to the other party over a period of time must be carefully considered. At times, the appearance of shifting power can give an advantage in the negotiation; if you concede on two or three small items, you may then leverage for a larger item that is necessary to meeting your case.

There is considerable interest in establishing ethical standards and maintaining personal discipline in reaction to potentially unethical negotiating behaviors. While ethical standards will continue to be debated, some professional negotiators and researchers have attempted to list some potentially unethical behaviors or 'dirty tricks'. Such a list includes:

- Lying and exaggeration
- Bluffs and threats
- Intentional stalling to gain advantage
- Non-disclosure of material facts
- Last minute add-ons
- Obscurantist behavior about facts or precedents

26.5 Opening offers

Two vital and interrelated questions for negotiators are:

- Who should make the first offer?
- What form should the first offer take?

For negotiators in a commercial context, the questions are slightly different:

- How do we structure the offer?
- How do we present elements on which we cannot agree?

This is why most 'opening offers' in a commercial negotiation take the form of a response to a Request for Proposals (RFP) or a presentation describing the offer. Some requests are very complicated, with hundreds of items and requiring exhibits in the response. Others are very simple, but can be complex because they are so high-level and general. The seller may not want to offer too much in response, but offer enough for the buyer to have sufficient information on which to make a decision. Similarly, if you are the buyer, you want your request to be broad enough to allow the seller to present ideas you may not have considered, but specific enough to be sure the response includes the key elements you are seeking to receive.

Three openings

Many negotiators try to avoid making the first offer, or begin or respond with exaggerated offers or positions. What form should the first offer take? Three common ways that negotiations are opened are:

- 'Soft' high (the maximalist opening), claim to be soft and yet open; set an extreme target in the hope that the other side will quickly move to a point within the bargaining zone

- Firm reasonable (the 'equitable' opening), claim to be firm and that the opening offer is an equitable i.e. 'fair' offer
- Problem solving, suggest that the negotiation is to solve a common problem via objective assessment

As a rule, negotiators should not make an opening offer when:
- You (buyer or seller) don't understand the market for the product or service. For buyers, this happens when a company first begins to purchase what had been done or made internally. For sellers, this happens when it is invited to enter a new market by a buyer or it voluntarily widens its target market.
- You don't understand the bargaining range for the product or service. We discussed bargaining ranges in Section 23.7. Without understanding the bargaining range one party is likely to establish a price that is too far from the middle. In those situations, one party usually walks away because it thinks the gap is too great.
- Your company doesn't have accurate internal financial or production data. Without accurate data, companies under-buy or overpay. Unfortunately, rather than recognizing the problem as a data or information issue, the parties blame each other for underperforming or price gauging.

Opening tactics

Of course, each opening has advantages and disadvantages and is appropriate in differing situations. It is essential that skilled negotiators:
- Know how to open by any one of these three methods, appropriately adapted to the situation at hand.
- Even though they may have a preferred style, are able to use all three openings with confidence.
- Practice in damage-free simulations using alternative methods, assessing probable roadblocks/results
- Establish through understanding of the other party which of the three forms of opening is likely to be most effective. In some situations, this may not become apparent until the negotiation is under way. The opening may be dictated by a third party, such as an outside negotiator or bid manager.
- Be able to articulate clearly and concisely the well-known advantages and disadvantages of each form of opening.

Openly or by known coded messages, negotiators normally identify to the other side which of the three openings appears to have been used. For example, negotiators use a number of codes to indicate a soft high opening when proposing a settlement of disagreement:
- "On the current facts, we would be prepared to settle for..."
- "Our client is claiming ..."

Each of these invites a counter that may establish different facts or considerations – thereby also revealing some of the other side's thinking and rationale.

Whichever route you choose, use logic to sell your ideas. Logic is seductive – people don't really want to appear irrational or unfair.

When making a presentation to a buyer, the seller should determine whether to begin with facts about their company or move direction into an outline of the issue and how the seller proposes to solve the buyer's need.

26.6 Physical/logistical considerations

Creating an environment conducive to a negotiated agreement is important to all negotiations. Consider the counter-situation when the environment, either by design or lack of thought, is not conducive to agreement the result can be less than desirable. An urban legend circulates about a specific large corporation who forces its vendors' negotiators to sit in stark hallways on hard, metal chairs. Then the corporation's representatives usher the vendors' negotiators into stark rooms, to sit on hard, metal chairs. The legend tells us that this tactic speeds the negotiation process and gets the corporation better financial results. Speed and discomfort may lead to less than optimal financial results. Dutch psychologist Carsten de Brue has shown that negotiators under time pressures rely on stereotypes and make cognitive short cuts.

Regardless of your chosen strategy (competitive or collaborative) consider the following factors when creating an appropriate environment:

- Ensure the room is arranged so that no one's chair is at the head of the table, unless a facilitator or arbitrator is employed.
- Don't have anyone sit or stand in front of the door (appears as a barrier to exit)
- If in doubt, dress conservatively and appropriately for the culture..
- Use a low, moderate tone of voice; have someone assess your use of tones – avoid abrasive, impatient or condescending tones. Also avoid being too strident or loud, or trying to out-shout the other side, especially on points of debate.
- Make sure the room is comfortable – sufficient space, seating; not too warm, cold, noisy or drafty.
- Try to have the parties sit together, facing the 'issues' in the form of a whiteboard, chart etc., rather than facing each other. Objectify the issue and separate it from the participants.
- If you do have a room set up with facing tables, try to mix up the seating, instead of having each party sit on one side. That looks like opposing teams. If you need rationales, ask all persons of a particular discipline to sit in a particular area.

- Have water available in the room or conveniently located. Make sure that everybody knows where they can get a beverage and where the restrooms are located, if the markings are not obvious. This allows people to attend personal needs discreetly and without disrupting the discussion.
- Establish some regular timing for "convenience breaks" or "bio-breaks" but be prepared to be flexible if the discussion is going well, or if a break appears necessary to defuse tense or potentially antagonistic discussions.

The choice of venue can make a crucial difference to the manner in which negotiations are conducted. Most commercial contracts negotiations tend to be held at the offices of one of the parties, usually the buyer. A neutral location, such as a conference center or hotel meeting room, can put the parties on equal footing. Alternatively, if one party has multiple locations, a conference room in a building other than the usual office building might be an option. It has the advantage of minimizing the possibility of interruptions from colleagues and other staff members.

Buyers tend to call suppliers in to their offices. This is time and cost efficient from their perspective but misses an opportunity to experience the supplier's environment, which may reveal aspects about the supplier not evident from a meeting away from their premises.

You can take advantage of natural breaks in the negotiation, such as a meal break or an overnight break, to convene with the persons on your side and discuss any of the above questions. It is very important to discuss the negotiation between days of a multi-day negotiation to assist your standing, review any agreements or other accomplishments, reorder 'wish lists', reassess the values you have placed on certain items and that you believe the other side has placed on items, and to plan the tactics for the next session.

26.7 **Connecting with the other side**

Face-to-face

Face-to-face negotiations provide the optimal opportunity to achieve mutual agreement. Studies show that face-to-face negotiation reach an agreement more than 80 percent of the time. Most of us can easily read others' visual, auditory and kinesthetic cues. We may also be able to sense the attitudes or concerns of the people in the room. However, the cost to bring people together can be prohibitive. Sometimes a long single-day negotiation is considered of value when the only cost is transportation and the gains are substantial. Other times a multi-day negotiation is best served by having everybody in one location to continue ongoing discussions.

The other advantage of face-to-face negotiations is the lack of distractions from telephones, computers, colleagues, and other outside forces. You do need to agree that communications devices will be in the 'off' mode and checked only on breaks. Sometimes, especially at an early stage, all electronic devices may be banned in favor of paper and pens, to further encourage interactions. At a later stage, someone may connect a computer to an overhead projector for real time drafting or review of supplementary documents or proposal materials. Some groups like to begin with a presentation of their expected goals or the bid offer, or their experience and other information. Just be sure that you don't prepare such an extensive presentation that the real goal of the meeting is lost. Also, do not put things into the presentation that would lock you into a term that you otherwise would hope to negotiate.

When choosing a collaborative strategy and a principled style, plan on significantly more face-to-face communication, than in other circumstances. Collaboration is more successful when people are able to professionally bond and establish trust. Most people understand that establishing a professional bond or a trusting relationship depends on interpersonal interaction.

Telephone

The telephone supports auditory communication; however, it masks visual and kinesthetic cues. In telephone negotiations people feel remote and may take positions – particularly aggressive ones – that they would not generally take in person.

There are also potential security risks with telephone negotiations. For example, you might not be aware of all the people on the other side, because you cannot see them. It is easier to have side discussions while on the telephone because of mute buttons and the lack of ability to see the others.

In addition, it can be harder to understand proposed changes to the text, unless the telephone conference is run in conjunction with a web-meeting or other visual review of changes.

Video conference

Although better than the telephone or internet because body language can be read, video conferencing fails to provide subtle cues, since our view is limited to the direction or focus of the camera. For example, the camera may be focused on one or two people, and others seems to be disembodied voices. Or the camera may be focused on a whiteboard or other visual support, and everybody is a voice unless they are writing on the whiteboard. It is worth noting that video conferencing technology is developing quickly to providing a richer more natural experience.

Electronic (email, web-meetings, and shared folders)

The computer removes all sensory communication, leaving only words. All context and subtext is lost. It is therefore not a desirable format for serious and complex negotiations. In fact, studies show that email-only negotiations have the highest failure rate: nearly 50 percent of email-only negotiations fail to reach an agreement. That is like flipping a coin! In addition, significant security issues exist with internet negotiations.

Tools such as video conferencing, web-conferencing, telephone and internet communications, such as programs to easily share information, can be effective cost and time savers. These tools should only be used once relationships have been established in face-to-face encounters. The trust that develops in early face-to-face meetings can carry over to other media for more routine discussions. If relationships deteriorate during the negotiations, it may become necessary to bring the parties together again to re-establish appropriate relationships.

In today's economic environment – global markets , constraints on travel, reduced staffing levels, and abbreviated response times – we must adjust to a variety of negotiating formats. It is imperative that we adjust to the varying forms of communication. We must adjust our message; we must test feelings or thoughts in new ways; we must find approaches that build rapport and relationship without necessarily involving physical contact.

One key to this is to assure personality continues to be apparent; when we are not in a room together, we should not let introductions, social niceties or manners disappear. While we may be employing technology, we are still human beings – not computers! Be sure the neither side loses sight of this.

Generational differences

It is worth noting that the generations who have no experience of work without the internet, email, instant messaging, mobile telephony, social networking view communication in a different way from older workers who are not as familiar or confortable with new electronic forms of communication. This provides opportunities for considerable learning but also frustration as company policies and attitudes of senior personnel may not be supportive of innovative use of technology.

It is worth noting that younger workers don't completely understand the ramifications of electronic communication. We've found that younger workers are unaware of the fact that email communication is a formal business communication, and can create a binding contract. When negotiators are too casual in their communication, dismissive or unprofessional in relating to their counterparty, the relationship suffers. But when a worker sends an email telling the other party to disregard a provision of a written contract because "it doesn't apply here" that worker may be modifying the contract and binding their company to that statement.

It is important to educate all negotiators about the appropriate use of email. Negotiators should understand the ramifications of speaking without authority in email and the professional tone they ought to adopt when negotiating contracts.

26.8 What happens if there is no agreement?

Viable alternatives to an agreement

If you go into a negotiation without any backup plan, *and* you get to the point where you're unable to reach an agreement that satisfies your interests, what happens?

If you have nowhere to turn, you keep negotiating until you reach agreement—any agreement. This is where bad deals are made. Viable alternatives prevent bad deals. We suggest you ask yourself these three questions to help you determine your if you have any viable alternatives:

- What can I (my company) do all by myself (itself) to pursue my (our) interests or goals? For example, a buyer may choose to keep a service in-house rather than outsourcing it. If the service provider cannot offer a better solution and price than the in-house service, the buyer has a viable alternative.
- What can I say to the other party to help them understand and respect my interests? An extreme example might be to go on strike. Usually, we recommend a more measured approach, like explaining issues using other words in a face-to-face meeting.
- How can I bring a third party into the situation to further my interests (such as a mediator, or subject matter expert). For example, a buyer and supplier who were stalled about the price of raw materials brought in an expert to explain the fluctuating price of the commodity. That explanation helped both companies reach mutually beneficial pricing model.

Value opportunities and trades

As a result of the value opportunity analysis, the parties may emerge with a very different view of their respective power or influence over the negotiated outcome. They may also find previously unspotted opportunities to add value - for example, by packaging additional elements or guarantees into the deal that respond to an identified area of need or weakness.

For instance, a supplier might have the following thoughts:

In my analysis, I've come to realize that the time-frames sought by the buyer will be severely threatened if these negotiations break down. Rather than just exploit this by holding out on other issues, I may be able to turn this into a trade. Since I know that my company can meet the time-frames, I will emphasize our strengths by offering some sort of delivery guarantee. In return, I will ask for a trade from the buyer in another area of the agreement.

In this example, we see an opportunity being used as a trade for something else of value. Additionally, these trades add, rather than diminish, value.

Making a 'No Agreement' analysis

Recent research[19] suggests that in addition to considering your alternatives, and value opportunities, another – and often more revealing – analysis is to simultaneously consider the consequences if no agreement is reached. In the example above, if the supplier were to use timing against the buyer, it is possible that the negotiations would break down entirely.

In a 'no agreement' analysis you should ask yourself, what would they lose; what would they have to do as a result; and what would the consequences of this be. Examine each question in terms of:

- Costs (price, resources, cash flow)
- Benefits
- Time or speed implications
- Additional or changed risks
- Resource or skill implications
- Credibility, image (of the business or individuals)

You would also need to ask yourself these same questions to get a clear and unbiased picture. In this business-to-business environment, it is rare that there is not an alternative supplier or an alternative customer, so this assessment of the effects of not reaching agreement is much more meaningful. It should of course take account of both the positives and negatives for each side.

Planning your alternatives

When developing your negotiation strategy, take some time to create the four following items:

- Estimate your 'cost of no agreement'
- Estimate their 'cost of no agreement'
- Define the areas where you can trade
- Define the areas where you think they may want to trade

The 'cost of no agreement' means what you will gain or lose, and what the other side will lose or gain, if you fail to reach an agreement. This could differ depending upon whether the agreement is reached in a short timeframe, or whether the negotiation drags on for six months or longer. It can also affect some of your decisions whether to concede on points –

---

19 Think!Inc

is there a time at which failing to reach agreement is more costly than conceding on terms that previously were sacrosanct?

When you meet with the other side, have a plan that will enable you to test your assumptions to these four items, as well as the "Wants" and interests from above. Listen, ask questions, obtain information, and then review the lists for both sides to validate your calculations and assumptions. You may find that some items you had thought important to the other side are not issues at all, or that the value is different from what you expected. You may also find that there are items you had not considered that appear to have substantial value to the other side and need to be added to one of the lists.

Following that meeting or discussion, determine areas where you can 'create value' for both sides. Where can you propose trades, create package options that improve on the 'cost of no agreement', design 'win-win' options, and otherwise establish some of the negotiating points that you need to use going forward. Is there anything to which you can agree immediately, gaining negotiation points? Is there anything you can see as an obvious trade-off to propose to the other side?

You may want to consider packaging your solution in several different ways. Offer different solutions depending upon which model the other side deems more critical. In the example above, the trade-off was money versus time. The overall deal may be equivalent, but those points trade against each other and let the sides determine which is more important. If you propose multiple scenarios to the other side and they say "no" to all of them, ask which they like least. That way, you start to understand the different values they place on the potential trade items, and can focus on the areas you have discovered are most important.

Ask whether there is something that can be changed in one of the scenarios to make it more appealing, and see whether that leads to a trade-off to which your side is willing to agree,

Avoid getting stuck into negotiation on a single item. That can put undue value on that item, while leaving too many others open to interpretation. You should always try to maintain your flexibility by having a multi-item package to negotiate. If the other side appears stuck on a single item, suggest that it is 'parked' while other items are discussed. To acknowledge the importance to the other side and keep from losing sight of it, you can write the topic on a piece of paper and post it on a wall, where it will be easier to find once the other items are negotiated. Sometimes the solution to the other items presents a solution to the 'parked' one as well.

26.9 Technological challenges

The traditional 'set piece' negotiation where participants sit in the same room and work through the issues is now the exception rather than the norm. The changing geographic scope of business, technological innovation and ever increasing work pressures mean that the bulk of negotiation is performed virtually using conference calls, webcasts, and email. The tightening of travel budgets because of the challenging economic environment has accelerated this trend to virtual negotiations.

But how prepared for this are we really? We read of financial traders who make errors using their electronic systems, like the UBS trader who made a US$31Bn mistake in February 2009. A somewhat noticeable amount. What mistakes do we make in our automated and non-automated systems and at what threshold do they become visible? Certainly at US$31Bn but that is a somewhat extreme amount.

The reality is that our preparation for the virtual world is largely personal and historic. Looking at the negotiation programs that are commercially available, the underpinning assumption for the vast majority is that the negotiation will take place face-to-face. The work and surveys being carried out by IACCM's Negotiation Community of Interest confirms the view that not only is the perception of a negotiation's characteristics is outmoded this is combined with negotiation being addressed as a personal development matter rather than a company-wide capability within a company-wide negotiation process.

So what to do? The ideal is, of course, being in a position to initiate or lead corporate-wide initiatives to meet the critical challenges for your company. You, however, may not be in such a position or realize that embedding change can take appreciable time.

Establishing a replicable process

Ideally this is company-wide. It is also feasible to achieve appreciable operational efficiencies and greater negotiated value by establishing a consistent process simply within the commercial function and using it to manage the other stakeholders and the overall negotiation process. Individuals can also apply this very effectively to their personal workload although this, of course, has far less impact for the overall business.

Significant benefits can be realized regardless of the size and resource available to an organization. Changing the way in which negotiations are planned and executed by instituting a strategic approach is an option available to all commercial professionals now and can be addressed in a focused manner or across a company.

Using collaborative tools

There are a number of proprietary software tools available to support collaboration. They tend, however, to address individual elements of the range of activities necessary to establish and manage collaborative relationships effectively. Innovative technology is available that addresses negotiation within the overall collaborative endeavor and provides the capability to support strategic relationships in a more productive manner.

Tools can be leveraged to enable better business results. It is, however, important to provide a warning. Using the wrong tools can damage outcomes. For instance, treating every negotiation as collaborative is as risky as using e-auction tools for all procurement categories. Despite technological advances, humans must analyze the entire situation and choose the right technology to fit the circumstance.

Increasing skills and capabilities

There are a multitude of negotiation skills companies who can provide useful individual tactical capability. Far fewer organizations provide strategic insight and capability. Appreciable benefit can be achieved by tapping into the thinking of the strategic approach and even more so if you engage with them directly. The IACCM Negotiation Community of Interest provides an excellent focal point for driving this learning.

Coaching

In the absence of any negotiation coaching practice where you work, institute one. Engage with fellow negotiation professionals to seek and offer coaching. Care, of course, needs to be taken about using your personal network outside of your company but this can be beneficial if you are able to ensure that confidential and commercial sensitivities are not compromised.

Rehearsals

Instituting negotiation rehearsals for those key negotiations whether they be virtual or face-to-face can provide deep insights both into the business issues that need to be addressed and also individual/team capability. The simplest form is practicing your negotiation opening in the privacy of your home or office. In its fullest form, replicating the negotiation environment, dynamics and players to carry out a complete 'mock' negotiation. Anywhere on the line between these two points will be a wise investment of time and energy.

Technological challenges

Every now and then a new technological application pierces the consciousness and enters the public's consciousness. Twitter achieved this in January 2009 due to the posting of the first picture of US Airways Flight 1549 on the Hudson River. Suddenly there are references to Twitter across the media with articles on the people who use it (Barack Obama, Stephen Fry, Britney Spears to name just three). Many of us would have heard of it before the ill-fated flight from La Guardia airport but who of us has consciously determined whether it can be used beneficially for our business, profession or career? Who remembers Twitter being a discussion point at IACCM Americas Conference in 2008?

There is no doubt that technology has had, and will have, a huge impact on how we live and work. The key personal development issue is whether it is something that will happen to us or something that we embrace and use to our advantage.

With so much going on in the technology world the key is awareness of what is out there enabling an assessment of what may be relevant or adaptable. To help with this, the following are a list of ten technologies that have been identified as adding much to personal productivity. Some are relevant on a personal level rather for a team or organization. All, however, show what is possible and should stimulate thought as to what you can use for your benefit.

Things	http://www.culturedcode.com/things/
Evernote	http://www.evernote.com/
Squarespace	http://www.squarespace.com/
Dropbox	http://www.getdropbox.com/
TweetDeck	http://www.tweetdeck.com/
Googledocs	http://www.docs.google.com
RTM	http://www.rememberthemilk.com/
Xobni	http://www.xobni.com/
KallOut	http://www.kallout.com/
OneNote	http://office.microsoft.com/en-us/onenote/

There are also a number of technology thought leaders and observers who blog (and tweet) frequently and regularly. Shortcuts to finding them include Techmeme (http://www.techmeme.com/), TechCrunch (http://www.techcrunch.com/) or Alltop's ego portal (http://egos.alltop.com/).

Personal organizational development challenges

In demanding times, it is easy to feel too challenged to address personal development. Survival can sometimes seem like the overwhelming priority. The reality is, however, that focusing on personal development is the best way of addressing and surpassing this priority. Investing in the future, whether done through sponsorship from your company or self-initiated and self-funded, will pay dividends.

The key is establishing an appropriate framework to enable what actions will help most – buying that book, listening to a podcast, attending an IACCM Ask The Expert call or attending a workshop. The authors of this guide suggest the following five key elements that can be adapted for organizational or individual use:

1. Objective - crystallizing what you want your organization to achieve or what you want to achieve
2. Development requirements - what are you going to invest in to do your job now, to meet your objectives and, often overlooked, what do you enjoy?
3. Competencies –a clear understanding of your existing and future state competencies
4. Development resources - what resources can you access? Some may be free or little cost, like most IACCM events, podcasts, books, and magazines.
5. Attainment targets - how do you know you've got where you want to go?

CHAPTER 27

Tactics, tricks and lessons learned

27.1   Introduction

The preceding Negotiation phase chapters highlight the best practice of addressing negotiation as a strategic process rather than a tactical activity. This is important in achieving consistently excellent negotiation outcomes as it avoids relying too much upon the individual capabilities of the people involved as well as on luck and timing. It is, however, important to recognize that the best strategy can be frustrated by poor implementation.

This chapter addresses the following key best practice in negotiation tactics:
- How to handle the 'last gap'
- The five key areas of successful (or failed) negotiations
- How to recognize common ploys (what to watch out for, how to counter and when to use these ploys)
- Have a clear understanding of ethical versus unethical behavior and understand the primary causes of failed negotiations
- Apply scientific research to give you the best chance of success

27.2   The last gap

What is the last gap in a negotiation? It is the last step necessary to reach an agreement between the negotiating parties. In competitive negotiations, often that last gap or last increment emerges after long and exhausting negotiations that have led to agreement on all issues but one. For example, that one issue may be: "How to cross the difference between $600,000 or $1 million in the parties' 'final offers?"

Most negotiators and business people can relate horror stories about becoming stuck on the last issue of a lengthy negotiation and not always finding a mutually beneficial resolution.

An extreme example occurred in the Philippines where a local billionaire business magnate used a hardball negotiation tactic. The magnate decided to manually revise the terms of a partnership agreement with an overseas multi-national by increasing the amount of money to be paid by his prospective partner at the agreement signing ceremony. The prospective partner had flown in their CEO and had not anticipated such a situation. The CEO responded that the last minute manual change to the agreement was not the way the CEO would do business. Further, it destroyed the mutually beneficial partnership. The CEO left the signing ceremony to go straight to the airport to fly out, never to return. The tactic did not achieve its intended purpose.

The importance of the last gap

Why does the last increment or last issue assume such importance and so often –at least anecdotally - provide a stumbling block to a negotiated settlement? There are a number of possible explanations:

- The last dance - final loss of the conflict or the relationship
- Unfinished emotional business
- The last straw - "I have given up so much already"
- Sense of having been tricked
- Skilled helpers attempt to prove 'worth'
- Recriminations for lost time and money

The last dance

Negotiations have often been compared to a dance, where one or both parties circle one another, reluctant to end the process. The most clinging form of this last dance has been described as *'negative intimacy'* [20] "This occurs where one or both parties are finding meaning to life by being a martyr, or by being in constant conflict. A settlement represents loss of meaning. Thus the last gap will never be crossed but will be preserved. Even if the other party concedes the last gap, the 'negatively intimate' negotiator will create a new last gap - known as an 'add on' [21]In scenes reminiscent of the Colombo TV detective character there is "just one more thing".

Unfinished emotional business

The last gap may represent unfinished emotional issues between the individuals involved and this prevents commercial reality or common sense from prevailing. The dominant method of negotiation in Western cultures has traditionally been positional bargaining. Each party makes an extreme claim and - by gradual increments - moves towards a

---

20 I. Ricci *Mum's House, Dad's House* New York: Macmillan, 1980

21 *Examples:.* W Ury, *Getting Past No* (London: Century, 1991))". (The Last Gap (Gasp) in Negotiations. Why is it Important ? How can it be Crossed? by Professor John H Wade, Bond University, Gold Coast, Queensland, Australia)

resolution point somewhere between those extremes. Repeat players such as corporations are experienced in playing this game. However, one-off or less experienced negotiators tend to go through disappointment and anger as they see their original claim whittled away by one concession after another. This is particularly so where they believe that their original offer was reasonable, or at least not unrealistic. And sometimes, as they draw to the end, they start to focus on how the result will look with their superiors or colleagues; indeed, a reaction is sometimes the result of an internal review, which concluded they had to go back on certain issues.

At the end of several rounds of mutual concessions, both (now angry) negotiators may have a strong sense that each has conceded so much already that they have 'lost' – and cannot accept losing yet again on the last issue. Accordingly, each disappointed disputant digs in and insists that the other concede on the last issue.

The last straw

Some negotiators feel this final impasse is the last straw. They have been steamrollered all day and now they are putting up a stop sign to preserve their integrity. A dramatic walkout may also be staged or threatened. The walkout relieves the pressure of the negotiation room, avoids the last concession, demonstrates to all how intensive the pain is, and may inflict some pain on the other side for his or her 'unreasonableness'.

Negotiators should be able to anticipate the walkout, and normally have a variety of strategies ready to prevent or delay its occurrence. This is because a walkout enables each side to characterize the other as unreasonable - one for unreasonably causing the termination of the meeting, the other for immaturely exiting. Each party is stereotyped, and a new cause for a relationship conflict is founded. Additionally, after a walkout, it is difficult to muster enthusiasm, cash and timetables for another face-to-face meeting. Strategies to avoid the last gap, including preventing walkouts, will be discussed shortly.

Sense of having been tricked

Some negotiators sense that they have been tricked when the negotiations reach the last gap, and someone predictably suggests 'splitting the difference'. This is because they believe that their first offer was reasonable, whereas the other party's first offer was wildly exaggerated. The standard process of incremental concessions has left the range of offers biased towards the exaggerated opening offer.

The person who perceives that he or she opened reasonably will often be fuming for being punished for his or her reasonable behavior. This pattern of behavior of course encourages some experienced negotiators to avoid opening with reasonable offers. Even more experienced negotiators will tend to discuss how negotiations should open – 'firm reasonable' or 'soft high' - before the process starts.

Negotiator's need to prove worth

The last gap is sometimes a sticking point as the negotiators want to win that gap both to establish their skill and, if they are independent skilled contractors, to further justify their fees.

Customers will face triple disappointment if they lose their expected outcome, lose the last gap, and then have to pay incremental fees to outside consultants (such as lawyers and accountants) from their diminished share. Lawyers understand the marketing need to justify their fees and to support disenchanted clients who will be their main source of publicity for future clients. Therefore some lawyers may feel the need to negotiate long and aggressively on the last gap.

Recriminations for lost time and money

Reaching the last gap sometimes brings home a depressing reality to one or all the negotiating parties. They are about to settle for a deal that was offered and rejected previously, with nothing to show for the extra tension, absences from work, uncertainty and costs – not to mention the possible loss of face with peers and management. This often results in angry statements, particularly by less experienced negotiators, and can make navigating the last gap a tense passage of blame and defense, both within and across negotiating teams.

Reopening the negotiation

Another variant, not truly a last gap but certainly as frustrating, is where one or other party seeks to revisit one or several items in an apparently 'closed' negotiation. This typically happens because there has been some form of internal review, which may relate to factors such as changed business circumstances or the original negotiators operating outside their boundaries of their mandate or knowledge.

Such situations are not uncommon in major corporations, especially in complex deals. Not only does this create a complex internal negotiation to drive an agreed approach back to the other side, it obviously causes distress or anger for the other party. Often, the party seeking to reopen the discussions will introduce a new negotiator.

In such circumstances, it is critical that the initiating party has planned and rehearsed their approach. This must include minimizing the issues to those that are truly important and trying to express each of these in terms that illustrate to the other side what it stands to lose without agreed changes. In the end, the original negotiator will inevitably lose some face – but it is not in your interests typically to discredit any individual. Greatest focus must be on the 'sales' message of why the overall package now being proposed is also beneficial to the other side.

Can the last gap be avoided?

Are there any strategies to avoid the last gap in negotiations or is it inevitable?

The most obvious way to avoid or at least limit the impact of the last gap is simply by being aware – and ensuring others in your team are aware – of its likelihood. This awareness will ensure you remain in control and reduce the sense of panic or anger, which you, or fellow team members, might otherwise feel and which can easily result in bad decisions.

The first two of the following tactics work best when you and your counterparty are using competitive negotiation strategies. The last two tactics work best when you and your counterparty are using collaborative strategies.

Keep something in reserve

Prepare for the gap discussion by having something ready to give. Reflecting standard negotiation principles, the 'something' should be of high value to the offeree, but of lower value to the offeror. Identifying these extras requires that you have undertaken a search for the interests, needs and goals of the other side.

Maximized opening offer

Some negotiators say: "Open high, as it is easy to give up something; but very difficult to take back". This approach often leaves some margin for final concessions around the last gap. However, it can cause deadlock or even termination early in the negotiation. Used against an experienced negotiator or client, the maximized claim is usually readily identified, named and ignored. So if using this approach, it is critical to ensure a 'soft' position to allow withdrawal / change without compromising credibility.

Problem-solving opening approach

Another preventative strategy is to open communications in a problem-solving style. For example, "We have the following five goals". "My client has the following three concerns …"; "This is our understanding of your requirements"; "We are willing to discuss possible options or solutions but would first like you to set out your general or specific concerns and goals"; "Can you provide us with the following information and documents so that we can ensure our best offer".

The Alternative Dispute Resolution (ADR) industry suggests that a helpful problem-solving approach will dispense with positional bargaining and the last gap. This is not entirely correct. Even a packaged and linked multi-issue offer eventually becomes specific in its terms, and at that point there may be a last gap. Therefore, you may have to rely on the last tactic to help you close the gap.

Saving face

It is safe to say that most Westerners vastly underestimate the human need to save face. Many Asian cultures recognize the need to allow people to save face in order to move forward. We found that some last gap situations can be solved with some attention to how the proposed solution can help you and your counterpart save face.

Saving face means that a person will save his/her self-respect from ridicule, whether in the minds of others or in their own judgment. "But face is much more than ego. It is shorthand for people's self-worth, their dignity, their sense of honor, their wish to act consistently with their principles and past statements – plus, of course, their desire to look good to others."[1] Allow people the room to find a reasonable way to explain why they appear to be 'backing down', 'changing course' or 'giving you a special deal'.

27.3 How to cross the last gap in negotiations

In some business environments the last gap is anticipated and there are, for instance in Japan, closing rituals that need to be respected and followed. Even in the Philippine last gap disaster example mentioned at the beginning of this chapter, the overseas company had not done their Due Diligence as it was well known that the Philippine business magnate would behave in the manner they experienced.

Apart from leveraging local business culture or anticipating the last gap, what strategies are available to cross this hurdle in negotiations? Firstly, it is crucial to realize that there are often many solutions and there still is opportunity to identify the most acceptable of these; so avoid a dramatic and premature walkout before all the options have been considered.

There are many options for closing the last gap:
- Talk/try to convince
- Split the difference
- Expand the pie by subdividing the last gap
- Expand the pie by an add-on offer "What if I moved on"
- Refer to a third party umpire
- Chance by flipping coin or drawing from a hat (if the outcome really doesn't much matter to you)
- Transfer the last gap to a third party
- Conditional offers and placating incremental fears –"What if I could convince our side to...? How would you respond?"
- Pause and speak to others, obtain advice
- Pause and schedule time for a specific offer

Try to convince

A common response in competitive negotiations is for one or both negotiators to re-hash old arguments in an attempt to convince the other party to give in. Typical examples include:

- "I have given up so much in these negotiations; now it's your turn"
- A long list of the merits of the speaker's claims, and the weaknesses of the other side
- An angry speech about how the listener's first offer was outrageous, so he or she should make the last incremental concession "to be fair"
- A lengthy speech about the cost of litigation, the costs already incurred and the likelihood of settlement at the door of the court
- A detailed historical version of the concessions made to date in the negotiation leading to the predictable conclusion that it is the listener's turn to be reasonable and make the last concession
- A short but angry speech with express or implied threats about walking out, stonewalling, escalating etc.
- A combination of some or all of these speeches

Such approaches rarely appear to be directly successful in crossing the last gap. The listeners may become inflamed to hear such a one-sided presentation so late in the day, and deliver a counter speech. The speaker may back himself or herself into a positional corner. Nevertheless, used with judgment, some degree of managed speech making at the last gap can be effective if, for example:

- It is in extreme contrast to behavior exhibited at all earlier stages of the negotiation
- It is based on indisputable fact
- Your aim is to test the seriousness of the other side
- You know that the other side is weak or lacks overall support for their position (e.g. team is not unanimous or their senior management takes a different view)

Collaborative negotiators use an alternative approach. They stress to the listener that each party has a mutual aim, goal, or set of objectives. They stress that by staying on course, both parties will arrive at a win-win situation. Finally, a collaborative negotiator will provide the listener with her interpretation of her issues and your suggestions for solving these issues.

Splitting the difference

This method is commonly suggested where the last gap consists of money or other divisible items. It has the merit of simplicity – that both parties 'lose' equally and that it is culturally commonplace. However, given the complex psychological dynamics surrounding the last gap, splitting the difference may be seen as too quick, part of an orchestrated plan of attack, or involving another painful loss. And it may also be completely illogical.

Expanding the pie by sub-dividing the last gap

The last increment can sometimes be divided in ways apart from an equal split by dividing the time of use or time of payment. For example:

- The last $10,000 can be paid over time in installments
- The last $100,000 can be paid at a later date with accrued interest

Expanding the pie by an add-on offer

You can attempt to overcome an impasse by re-opening a decided issue, or adding another issue to the negotiating table, like the customer agreeing to be a reference site for the supplier or the supplier agreeing that the customer will be a launch partner.

In this way, you seek to prevent the last issue from being the last. It is not always easy to re-open or to discover extra value to place on the bargaining table. One of the clear benefits of questioning and listening skills is that a negotiator can develop ideas on the needs, concerns and interests of the other party and save items for introduction if required. Some negotiators begin bargaining with a positional style. When an impasse is reached, they switch (or have a fellow negotiator switch) to an interest-based problem-solving approach.

Refer to a third party umpire

The last item can be resolved by:

- Agreeing to refer the whole dispute to an arbitrator or mediator;
- Agreeing to refer just the issue of crossing the last gap to an arbitrator or mediator

In mediation, the disputants may request that a trusted mediator makes a recommendation or a binding decision on how the impasse should be resolved.

Arbitration uses several alternative approaches to bring parties to a resolution. These include:

- Baseball arbitration (both parties submit a figure to the arbitrator who can only choose one of the submitted figures)
- Night baseball arbitration (both parties submit secret and sealed offers; the arbitrator makes a decision and opens the sealed offers; the offer closest to the arbitrator's decision is binding)
- High-low arbitration (parties agreed to the range of outcomes; the arbitrator can only decide within that range)
- Scope arbitration (the arbitrator is only authorized to decide upon a range of outcomes divided by, say, 15 percent; parties agree to settle within that range)
- On-the-papers arbitration (a cheap and quick decision-making process where there are no oral presentations).

Chance

Chance provides an important option for deciding who gets the last gap. One option is flipping a coin:

- It's cheap and fast
- Involves an equal chance of winning or losing
- Avoids loss of face by being beaten by other, more personal strategies
- Is so abhorrent to some risk-averse disputants that they return to the remaining list of options with enthusiasm!

Drawing from a range of solutions

This is an alternative version of chance that avoids the all-or-nothing result of flipping a coin. Several solutions are written out on slips of paper, placed in a hat, and the one drawn out prevails. For example if the last increment is $20,000, then ten slips of paper can be placed in a hat beginning with $2,000 and ending with $20,000 with gaps of $2,000 written on each slip of paper. The drawer receives whatever number is on the drawn piece of paper; the residue of the last gap goes to the other disputant. Of course this method can be extended to a range of more complicated alternative solutions.

Transfer the last gap to a third party

This option involves both parties agreeing to transfer the last gap to pay the fees of skilled helpers such as lawyers or mediators, or to pay for renovating a business before a sale. Such transfers to third parties may have the clear benefits of mutually avoiding a loss, and of wedding a third party to the solution chosen.

Conditional offers and placating the incremental fear

Where a pattern of incremental bargaining has been established, each disputant will usually be concerned about the consequences of initiating any offer across the last gap. Why? Because any offer is likely to be whittled away by an incremental counter offer. For example, if the last gap between A and B is $20,000, and A offers to split the difference ($10,000 to A), how is B likely to respond? B is likely to respond, split the difference again –only $5,000 to A. Thus there is a reluctance to make the first move, and the impasse remains intact. Some negotiators make exploratory conditional offers in an attempt to avoid incremental counter-offers. This works best if there are at least two negotiators on each negotiating team.

- Negotiator 1: "What if I could persuade my team to make a split-the-difference offer. Would you guarantee that you wouldn't try to cut down our offer?"
- Opposing negotiator: "Let us talk about this in private for a moment. We'll be right back."

A negotiator attempting to discover the other side's willingness to settle for a hypothetical offer can manipulate this option. However, the other side's response is also conditional ("if your client makes that offer") and can be withdrawn.

Pause and speak to others

The intensity of a negotiation or mediation session means that it is easy to become weary, to lose perspective and to make 'a mountain out of a molehill'. Additionally, some people are cautious and are accustomed to reflecting upon options available before making a commitment. It is a helpful strategy to suggest a break to consider one or more written options, with a clear appointment to resume negotiations, and with encouragement for each disputant to speak to specified trusted third parties. Where a mediator is being used, it is often helpful for all disputants to make contact during the break to clarify, brainstorm and hypothesize on negotiation dynamics (for example, "What will be the likely response if I make this offer"?).

Pause and schedule time for a specific offer

As a variation on the previous procedure, the parties can actually draft a precise or general form of offer before the break is taken. This may, for example, represent "splitting the difference" which is too difficult to swallow during the negotiations. A time and place is then agreed to accept or reject the offer and, if necessary, to return to the negotiation/mediation table. This procedure gives a concrete proposal, reduces the fear of incremental haggling during the break, provides a deadline, and allows the parties to return to the negotiation table knowing what has been decided.

27.4   Competitive tricks and ploys

Tactics are a means to an end. Tactics, when used appropriately, get you closer to your goals. Bad tactics are those that get you further from your goals. Good tactics get you closer to your goals. Neutral tactics could go either way depending on the circumstances. When choosing tactics we suggest that you have a goal in mind and select the tactic that will get you closer to your goal.

In particularly contentious negotiations, parties will use tricks or ploys in an attempt to gain an advantage. Tactics may be unethical. Often the receiving party will perceive them as unfair. Whether unethical or not, tactics that create a perception of unfairness are disruptive to the negotiation process. Such tactics may include 'good guy/bad guy' routines, uncomfortable seating, and appeals to senior management.

Deception is not a tactic; it is deception and must be avoided, even when choosing a competitive strategy. Parties may deceive their counterparty about the facts, their authority, or their intentions. The best way to protect against deception is to seek verification of the other side's claims. It may help to ask them for further clarification of a claim, or to put the claim in writing. However, in doing this it is very important not to be seen as calling the other party a liar; that is, making a personal attack.

Some people believe that even if you cannot trust the other party, you can still negotiate with them. If you fall into that camp, have your facts ready and confirm everything in writing. If you cannot confirm something, ask to confer, or reconvene until you can to ensure that the facts are accurate.

If the other party has represented themselves as the decision-maker and after an agreement has been reached advises you they "have to get it approved", let them be aware that the agreement is no longer binding. Both sides can now make alterations as needed. If the other negotiator does not have the authority to agree to the deal, there is no deal. Put this in writing, immediately.

Psychological warfare

When the tricky party uses a stressful environment, the principled party should identify the problematic element and suggest a more comfortable or fair change.

Another trick by experienced negotiators is to read your notes upside down. This can be countered if you use notes by printing in a smaller font size where you can still read but the other party will find it difficult to read from other side of the table.

Subtle personal attacks can be made less effective simply be recognizing them for what they are.

Explicitly identifying them to the offending party will often put an end to such attacks.

Threats are a way to apply psychological pressure. The principled negotiator should ignore them where possible, or undertake principled negotiations on the use of threats in the proceedings.

Psychological games - individual attacks

If someone employs the tactic of attacking you or causing you discomfort – your immediate reaction is to conclude the negotiation as soon as possible. In fact, it may cause you to give in, just to get out of there. Confident, skilled negotiators do not allow this to happen.

In some jurisdictions companies record (video and sound) the negotiations and review the proceedings to determine any weaknesses in the other side. They may also set up a room that is uncomfortable – seating arrangements, sun shining in your eyes after lunch. If you believe this is the case you should immediately request a change. Either another chair, or change rooms. If they refuse, tell them that the conditions are not satisfactory (not a personal attack, "You made me sit with the sun in my eyes!") and we will have to meet at a different time or place to be able to have any chance at success.

If it is a personal affront, for example "Are you qualified to be here?", or "You look ill. Are you feeling OK?" recognize the attack. Bringing it up "You know my qualifications, so can we proceed?", or "I've never felt better, but thanks for your concern" is the way to alert the other party you know the game. Most of the time, it stops this from further recurrence.

Using threats is a frequently used tactic to acquire concessions. Statements like, "I'll move all my business" are common to try to use perceived power to get what they want.

Time tactics are also used as a ploy to get concessions. If you have flown from another state or country to negotiate the deal always keep your flight details confidential. When you are asked "What day does your flight home go?" always answer "Oh, I have an open ticket and am here to conclude the negotiation! Thanks for asking."

Many negotiators, when attacked or placed in uncomfortable situations tend to overlook them and try to move on. This is the result the tactical negotiator needs.

The last class of trick tactics is positional pressure tactics which attempt to structure negotiations so that only one side can make concessions. The tricky side may refuse to negotiate, hoping to use their entry into negotiations as a bargaining chip, or they may open with extreme demands. The principled negotiator should recognize this as a bargaining tactic, and look into their interests in refusing to negotiate.

They may escalate their demands for every concession they make. The principled negotiator should explicitly identify this tactic to the participants, and give the parties a chance to consider whether they want to continue negotiations under such conditions.

Parties may try to make irrevocable commitments to certain positions, or to make take-it-or-leave- it offers. The principled party may decline to recognize the commitment or the finality of the offer, instead treating them as proposals or expressed interests. Insist that any proposals be evaluated on their merits, and don't hesitate to point out unacceptable behaviors.

Positional power

This is very common when negotiators start negotiating to save the relationship instead of trying to reach an agreement. Positional power is employed by negotiators who are trying to position the other party into negotiating with themselves. They place the other party into a position where they are the ones making all the concessions.

Take a recess, caucus, reconvene. If it's a "take or leave it" deal, let it alone.

- A walkout: a gambit to get you to concede something to get them to return to the table. Wait them out. If there are issues, they can be handled in due course in the negotiation.
- Nibblers: they return after the deal has been concluded asking for a small concession. It can be because they "forgot" something, or "something changed, can you help us out?"

The best way to reply to this is to say, "If we are going to reopen the contract, then it will be satisfactory to reopen the entire contract for further considerations. We would like a few small changes, ourselves." Usually, this stops the tactic.

Tricks of the trade

Even when both parties commit and agree to writing there are still tricks and ploys to be wary of.

The following are some dangerous words and phrases which, when included in a proposal, can result in misinterpretations, misunderstandings, and unintended expectations on one or both parties. Proposals should not contain words or phrases that imply something that will not or cannot be provided.

Words that imply guarantee or warranty
- Complete
- Insure, ensure, assure
- Meet future business needs
- Increase competitiveness

Words with legal implications
- Partner, partnership, alliance
- Guarantee

Words that imply perfection
- Unique
- Any, all, every, none
- Always, never
- Uniquely qualified

Superlatives
- Minimum, maximum, best, optimum
- Lowest, highest, greatest, latest, earliest

Phrases that are open ended or vague
- Includes
- For example, e.g., etc...
- But not limited to

This list is not exhaustive but gives you an idea of what to look out for during the bidding, negotiation and eventually the formal contract phase, especially if you do not have auditing/drafting control.

In many instances the parties negotiating a deal are not the ones who will manage or provide the services when the contract is signed. The deal-makers move on to the next deal and leave the results of their negotiation for others to interpret And may not be concerned about any emotional fallout from the manner of the negotiations and the subsequent negative consequences during the contract implementation period.

How to deal with tricks and ploys

There is no denying that it's much easier to reach optimal negotiation outcomes when you and your counterpart do trust each other. But what can you do if you don't trust the person with whom you're negotiating? Here are a few tips to keep in mind:

- *Be aware.* Understanding that negotiations may not be carried out in a straightforward manner and being alive to possible approaches enables a state of readiness to deal with the situation however difficult or challenging.
- *Check your own assumptions.* First, make sure your assumption that they're not trustworthy is based on hard evidence/data, and if it's not, be open to changing your perception of them. Try talking with someone else who may be able to help you see things from a more neutral point of view. But if there are good reasons not to trust your counterpart, then you must seriously consider whether you want to do a deal at all. It won't get any better and your counterpart won't become trustworthy overnight. *Verify their standards.* Don't just take their word for it! Ask them to provide objective evidence/data to back up the options/information they're putting forward. And, do your own research to verify information that's critical to the deal.
- *Ensure all commitments are extremely clear and operational.* One way to do this is to set very clear milestones, so you can actively monitor whether they're fulfilling the commitments they've made to you. Consider also including clear incentives for performance (e.g. discounts for early payment).
- *Keep your alternatives in mind.* At the end of the day, if you don't feel you can trust them to uphold their end of the deal, you may decide the safest choice for you is to consider your alternatives. So never lose sight of what you can do away from the negotiating table to meet your interests on your own!

Never give something away for free. Always obtain something in exchange that is of high value to you.

These are just several of the tactics used by negotiators. When faced with tricks and tactics, it is vital to remember some key points:

- If you prepare and plan your negotiations, you will be more equipped to deal with tactics. You will always know where you are going, where you are in the process, and will know what you can do if negotiations are unsuccessful.
- The objective of the negotiator is to obtain, efficiently, an agreement that is fair to both sides. It is customary for both parties to want to keep the relationship intact.
- Remember you can only correct and control the situation, not the other person. Your focus has to be on the problem and the process and definitely *not* the other person.
- A negotiator may not only require negotiating the issue, but also the ground rules of the negotiation process. Set the ground rules up front.
- Recognize when a tactic is being employed. Address the tactic with the other party. Do not personalize it ("You are lying to me!").
- Always have sufficient confidence to stop proceedings if they are not going well. This can be via a discussion group, or even rescheduling for another day or venue.
- Always know what you will do if an agreement cannot be realized. Having that knowledge can and will prevent you from proceeding in a negotiation where tactics are muddying the issue. Know where you are in relation to what you will do if negotiations are unsuccessful, throughout the negotiation process. Do not allow the use of tactics cause an agreement to be worse that what could have been done on your own.

Most of us have to negotiate on a regular basis for goods and services we require in our lives. Not all enjoy the process, and many do not because they are not equipped to handle the use of tactics in the negotiation process. Understanding tactics and how to deal with them, coupled with more detailed and focused planning of negotiations will give negotiators better outcomes for both sides. This gives the negotiator the confidence to do what is necessary to alter the process so it will work, rather than focusing on the behavior of the other side. Last, when tactical negotiators learn how their tactics can be neutralized, they stop using them and begin to get better results.

27.5 **Another perspective**

Negotiation can be defined as the process by which parties come to terms on a particular matter in which they have corresponding or complementary desires. Selling, buying and negotiating are about getting others to agree to your ideas and the key word here is persuasion. To achieve your goals you must have understood your relative strengths and weaknesses, and those of your opponent, and have an appreciation of theories of human motivation. As we have illustrated, this understanding and appreciation matters as much in marshalling your own side as it does the other side. Indeed, the internal negotiation can be more complex due to the lack of willingness by your key players to cooperate.

Motivation is therefore a key element in negotiation – that is, the inclination to do or not to do something. People generally want to achieve balance – which is why they react badly if they feel pressured to move on something they regard as unnecessary or undesirable; or if they feel the proposition they are being asked to accept is fundamentally unfair. There are positive and negative factors in all things that motivate us and in most business deals, they operate in combination. In general, better and lasting results are achieved through positive motivational influences.

Remember the core human needs that drive motivation and how they can be used to achieve your goals.

27.6 **Summary**

Overall, the key rules for negotiation are:
- Be prepared, do your research on the other side
- Know your strengths and weaknesses
- Determine firm goals (top, bottom, target) before you enter the negotiation
- Ensure all team goals are known and compatible
- Don't deviate from your goals; and make sure the team has adopted and sticks with them
- Trade concessions, never give something for nothing
- Don't start trading until you have sold the basic deal; make sure you have 'sold' your proposal in general terms

Without first selling the deal you have nothing to negotiate; you cannot finalize something that is as yet not fully desired, or where the desires are in fact different. Use logic to sell your ideas. Be ready to walk away from bad deals.

If the negotiation stalls or gets stuck, resell the deal. Understand that each party may have a different point of view. Go back to basics, to be sure they recall what is at stake. Restate features and benefits of your proposal / achieved in the negotiation to date. Specify and ensure understanding of the objection, then find out what you have to do to address these issues. Offer conditional compromise ("if I can get you X, will this be OK?". Offer a collateral benefit that appears to provide more than you are getting in return. Be ready to move to the 'lost sale' approach – "It's a pity we couldn't agree, can we spend a few minutes just looking at how this might have been avoided?" – and then see if this provides an opening to identify the real objection and resell.

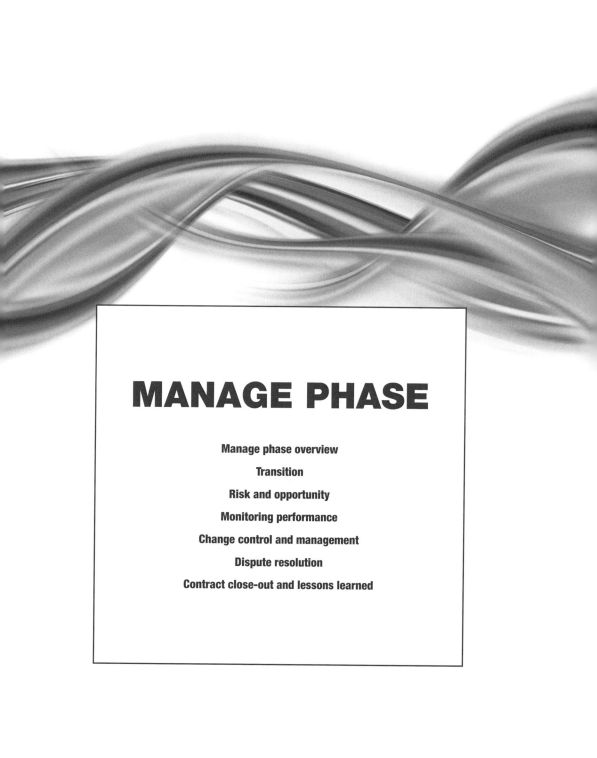

MANAGE PHASE

Manage phase overview

Transition

Risk and opportunity

Monitoring performance

Change control and management

Dispute resolution

Contract close-out and lessons learned

CHAPTER 28

Manage phase overview

28.1 Introduction

This chapter provides an overview of the key elements of the Manage phase of commercial contract activities. The underlying best practice is that regardless of a contract professional's scope of responsibility, whether it finishes or starts at contract signature or covers the entire contract lifecycle, the Manage phase delivers the business outcomes for all parties involved and may impact, positively or negatively, business opportunities in the future.

Leading corporations have increasingly recognized the importance of improving their post-signature contract management capabilities. This area has changed dramatically as the 21st century has progressed, with that change most marked amongst leading suppliers where the status of post-award contract managers has grown, to a point where salary levels are frequently equivalent to those of the negotiators and dealmakers.

The change has not been so marked among the buyer community. Too often, post-award contract management is undefined and not viewed as any sort of specialist activity or meriting specific training. However, dealing with your customers or suppliers, you will increasingly require a highly trained contract management specialist. Gone are the days when low-level contract administrators simply oversaw key milestones and monitored delivery or invoice status. You are now up against a team of skilled negotiators who are proficient in the latest techniques to ensure contract growth and margin retention. If you aren't prepared, they will take every advantage they can.

For example, one leading outsourcer identified cost reductions and revenue improvements of more than 5 million US dollars for every additional contract management expert they introduced. Another leader in this field has recruited and trained more than 800 contract management professionals in the last three years, all with average salaries over US$100,000. These organizations recognized the business need and opportunity.

Contract professionals, therefore, need to understand the key elements that contribute to making the Manage phase as successful as possible to inform and shape their activities both before and after contract signature. This section of this book covers:

- Manage phase overview
- Transition to implementation
- Risk and opportunity
- Monitoring performance, tools and techniques
- Dispute handling and resolution
- Contract close-out and lessons learned

28.2 Manage phase overview

If the principal goal of pre-signature contract negotiation is to establish an agreement to which both parties are committed, capable of performing and that meets their business objectives and goals, then the principal objective of post signature contract management is to ensure that each party performs according to their obligations and, in more complex contracts, recognizes the need for change. In the Negotiation phase parties often spend extensive time and money in debating "what happens when it goes wrong" clauses and provisions, like indemnification, liability limitations and termination. These are very contentious areas, which sometimes masks the fact that the interests of both parties are to ensure the contract will lead to expected or successful outcomes. Over-emphasis on containing or avoiding possible risk by omitting statements from the contract can result in incomplete contracts and vaguely drafted language that does not clearly express responsibilities or performance commitments.

So, behind our relatively simple definition of the role of post award contract management lies a range of tasks and considerations which are relatively consistent in what needs to be done but are massively variable in terms of the related workload and complexity. Agreements for customized products and services are the most complex because of the lack of standard specifications and benchmarks. To achieve our definition there is need for detailed analysis, disciplined communication, rigorous monitoring, managed change, consistent documentation and mutually agreed goals. All of these are underpinned by coherent and planned processes.

The key objectives of contract managers include the following:
- Transition to implementation
  - Promote awareness
  - Enhance visibility
  - Internalize stakeholder goals

- Risk and opportunity
  Identify and manage risks
  increase revenue/reduce cost
- Monitoring performance, tools and techniques
  - Enforce terms of performance
  - Ensure compliance
  - Optimize efficiency
  - Manage relationships
  - Maintain and retain the contract records
  - Management reporting
- Change control
  - Document changes
- Dispute handling and resolution
  - Manage and resolve contract issues
- Contract close-out and lessons learned
  - Leverage knowledge

Transition to implementation

Promote awareness

Often the people performing a contract have little or no knowledge of the terms of the contract they are performing. Nor do they realize that work is actively being monitored for fulfillment of contractual obligations. It is advisable for the contract manager to convey important information about the fundamental contract terms and requirements to the project team members and stakeholders. This can be accomplished through a contract overview presentation or training tailored to the various groups supporting the project. The awareness training should include such topics as scope, deliverables, confidentiality, intellectual property and data protection requirements, limitations and restrictions (e.g., key personnel, subcontracted supplier or third party approvals, locations of performance, etc.) cost controls, and relevant processes (e.g., contract change control, communication protocol, charging mechanisms, etc.). The contract manager should deliver periodic updates to address any changes to the contract or implementing processes and to reinforce the importance of contract compliance.

Enhance visibility

Further visibility of the active role of contract management is accomplished by making copies of contract documents available either electronically or physically, abstracting contracts and pulling out data elements for reference, and participation by contract managers in project meetings and management reviews. The contract manager should be the central and initial point of contact for all contract interpretation issues and compliance concerns.

Internalize stakeholder goals

For any contract there is a business case in some form that was presented and accepted during the Initiate phase. The business case for what eventually becomes a contract contains the goals of the organization and the stakeholders who championed the work. By working to achieve stakeholder goals through contract management objectives, and identifying how contract modifications may affect the underlying business case, the contract manager will add the most value to the organization. How well contract management objectives are aligned with strategic and business goals in negotiation and drafting of the contract, though, will in part determine the contract manager's added value.

Risk and opportunity

Identify, understand and manage risk

All companies seek to anticipate risks, so that they can be selective in their acceptance and effective in their management. To the extent that some risks cannot readily be anticipated, they endeavor to develop early warning systems and robust mechanisms for containment. But these methods largely focus on risks of things going wrong, ranging from natural disasters through market failures, to new regulations or shortages of supply.

There is of course another category of risk - and that is the failure to spot or exploit opportunities. This is the field of innovation and change, and covers new markets, new customers, new products or services, new routes to market or new business capabilities. A truly mature risk management regime is of course one that addresses all three categories.

Increase revenue/reduce cost

Contract managers for both customers and suppliers occupy a central place in transactions from which they have visibility of the entire contract. Further, it is the contract that legally defines the transaction, both its parameters and its inner workings. Supplier contract managers, for example, increase revenue by recognizing tasked work that is outside of scope. Conversely, customer contract managers can reduce costs by identifying when work is being done that is not required and by adhering to terms that adjust pricing.

Monitoring performance, tools and techniques

Enforce terms of performance

Performance under a contract may deviate from the terms and conditions of the contract for both innocent reasons and for reasons of moral hazard[22]. Techniques that contract

---

22 The risk that the presence of a contract will affect the behavior of one or more parties. For example, people with insurance may take greater risks than they would do without it because they know they are protected

managers use to maintain fulfillment of contract terms include the following:

- Acceptance tests and acceptance-like reviews of key working documents and periodic status reviews.
- Measurement of key attributes of performance.
- Audit of compliance with deliverables and obligations set out in the contract.
- Requests for assurance from the other party that terms will be complied with in the future.
- Notices of material breach of terms with a period for cure of the alleged non-performance.
- Stopping work orders and suspension of future tasking until of the causes of non-performance have been determined.

Ensure compliance

Besides terms of performance, there are laws, regulations, policies and industry standards, both specified in the contract and existing outside the contract, with which work and payment must comply. Contract managers must receive regular legal briefings on existing and new laws, etc., and how they affect current 'live' contracts. Requiring documentation and auditing work are the two most common methods of ensuring compliance.

Optimize efficiency

The essential purpose of contracts is to structure transactions and lend confidence to the parties that the transaction will be conducted without conducting additional transaction costs. Contract managers have a duty to minimize transaction costs. Automation of contracting processes is one way. Bundling requirements into fewer tasks is another. Business improvement methods such as lean manufacturing and total quality management can also be applied to the contracting process itself.

Manage relationships

In recent years a school of thought has emerged that says post-signature contract management should be less about enforcing terms and conditions and more about working with the other party, often called 'relationship management'. An example of relationship management is the eSourcing Capability Model for Services (eSCM) set of models developed by Carnegie Mellon University's spin-off organization IT Services Qualification Center (ITsqc). In cases where the product or service is too complex to be captured in contract language or where assumptions and requirements are subject to change, contract managers may be called on to play a greater role in management decision making.

Management reporting and records retention

Contract management is responsible for ensuring that contract terms and conditions are being fulfilled, including any reports and reporting activities that are specified in the contract. Ensuring the reporting required by the contract is available means that contract managers must task the other party to provide information about the contract; it also means that contract managers must understand their own organization's reporting requirements and ensure that procedures are in place for the required reporting and its retention. Because they are responsible for interpreting and understanding the contract, it is incumbent on contract managers to review the contents of both incoming and outgoing information for timeliness, sufficiency, and compliance with contractually prescribed formats and to verify that that reports are being sent to the right recipient according to the contract and are being retained according to the contract and company policy

For reports that contain proprietary and confidential information, contract managers are responsible for ensuring use of proper notices, means of delivery, distribution only to authorized persons, and other protections against misappropriation or loss of rights. Confidentiality clauses may require that proprietary and confidential information is returned or destroyed, and that information provided at management meetings is declared proprietary and confidential.

Contract managers may also take other reporting roles. Contract management often has ownership of central contract document repository systems in which all other information generated under the contract is stored. Reporting of financial data about the contract such as spend analysis and revenue recognition may also fall under the contract manager role.

Exception management is a method used to streamline the size and volume of reports. In exception management, only deviations from expected or required results are reported. Using performance measurement data as an example, in an exception management approach the contract manager would only create reports in instances where supplier performance had failed.

Change control

Document changes
Changes to the initial agreement arc common. Often the engagement between customers and suppliers expands in some areas and contracts or ends in others. The contract manager's objective is to capture any changes to the agreement in the written contract by means of change orders, written amendments, or additional work orders.

Dispute handling and resolution

Manage and resolve contract issues
Dispute resolution is a formal process for resolving disputes about performance of the contract or about actions taken or claims made relating to the terms and conditions of the contract. The governance terms and conditions typically contain detail on issue escalation and dispute resolution procedures. It is the contract manager's responsibility to be familiar

with the issue escalation and dispute resolution procedures in the contract and ensure that the parties are following those established guidelines whenever appropriate. Terms and conditions for dispute handling and resolution commonly include an established escalation path and timescales for resolution at each step of the process, with notice requirements, and prescribe the forum in which the parties are required to take disputes that cannot be resolved within the boundaries of the contract's established escalation process.

Contract close-out and lessons learned

As defined by the US Department of Defense Acquisition University, close-out confirms that the contract is officially terminated by performance and that there are no uncompleted legal obligations of either the customer or the supplier. 'Termination by performance' means that all contractual obligations are discharged because they are fully executed (or substantial or partial performance has been accepted in lieu, as in the case of de-scoping a contract) – there is nothing left undone.

Close-out assures that the correct payment is made to the supplier, the correct deliverables are received by the customer stakeholders, and administrative and fiscal obligations have been performed including disposition of property and assets. Ascertaining proper delivery and payment is easier in contracts with fixed prices because the price is fixed, the final invoice is usually received promptly, and the goods or services are identifiable and accepted. Delivery and payment are more complex in cost-type contracts. In a cost-type contract, indirect rates might have to be audited.

Close-out might appear simple at first, but some common complications arise. In government contracting, for example, if a contract's funds are depleted, financial approval must be obtained for the deficit. By the same token, a contract's unused funds must be identified and de-obligated in the budget. If the supplier has been overpaid, the customer needs to recoup those payments. Besides under-funding and over-funding issues, other obligations need to be resolved. Subcontracts should be settled by the supplier, although the supplier's obligation to the customer to do so will vary depending on the contractual arrangement. Customer-provided property and classified data issues need to be resolved as well. Additionally, patents, royalties, and other administrative obligations in the contract might exist and need to be addressed.

Once the contract manager has determined that all contract obligations and required administrative actions have been fully and satisfactorily accomplished, and no outstanding disputes or legal actions under the contract exist, they can obtain a mutual waiver or release of claims that binds the parties to their mutual agreement that the contract has been fulfilled and is terminated by completion.

In commercial contracting, close-out tasks that must be managed by the contract manager often include providing or receiving notice of termination or non-renewal in accordance with the terms of the contract, raising visibility among the delivery team and stakeholders about the contract provisions that govern termination. In outsourcing contracts it is common that a termination assistance services scope of work must be agreed upon and managed. Contract close-out activities also involve confirming the completion of all applicable contract deliverables, providing notification to subcontracted suppliers, delivery centers and/or landlords for any leased facilities, reconciling outstanding invoices and completing financial transactions, facilitating the return of property to its appropriate owner upon contract completion, addressing the disposition of software licenses and associated ongoing maintenance obligations, managing intellectual property and adhering to internal processes for data privacy and records retention.

28.3 Contract management activities

Many contract management activities tend to be administrative and repetitive in nature. However, even the most mundane and bureaucratic contract management activities can enable proactive problem identification and make a difference between realizing expectations and moving into dispute.

Sources of contract management activities

Contract management activities come from several sources.

The first and primary source of contract management is the administrative terms of the contract itself. Administrative terms that typically appear in the contract can include acceptance testing, service level measurement, invoicing and payment, proof of insurance and financial responsibility, human capital management, property management, legal notices and others. These activities are enforceable under the contract, though in and of themselves they may not rise to the level of materiality. In some instances, the contract manager may need to set up administrative processes for these contractual obligations. Other activities such as invoice approvals, signature approval levels and facility security procedures internal to an organization are usually not specifically addressed in contracts.

Contract management activities may already exist outside the contract as standard operating procedures of one or both of the parties. Existing contract management procedures for contract management may be considered best practice by the contract management function. Conflicts can arise between administrative activities described in contracts and existing practices if drafting does not account for them.

Activities for managing contracts are imposed by third parties, namely regulatory agencies. External activities exist regardless of contract terms and can even supersede contracts. Sarbanes Oxley reporting of financial data from contracts in the US is an example of an extra-contractual process for which contract managers may bear responsibility. In these circumstances, contract managers must obtain legal advice on how to comply with these mandates.

Before we move into the detail, let's take a moment to overview the role and activities covered by contract management in the post award phase. Your personal role may vary, as will the level of authority you have. These will depend on issues such as seniority, the specific nature of the contract, its coverage and the importance of particular tasks or issues. It is essential that you understand your specific role and authority in relation to all other team members and stakeholders. If you are the only or most senior contract manager this includes the need to ensure that others in the contract management team have a clear understanding of their role and their levels of authority.

The initial set-up phase is when contract analysis is occurring; when meetings internally and with other parties to the contract are focused on ensuring common goals and identifying potential risks; when you are building and executing a communications plan and a resource plan; and when you are establishing standard forms reports, tools and processes. The lead contract manager and project manager are responsible for ensuring all this is done and that it is adequately communicated. Individual members of the extended contract management team are responsible for making sure that they have understood their role, that they have the skills, knowledge or tools required to perform and they have asked questions in areas of doubt or highlighted issues.

As you move from set-up to steady state management, the contract management activities should become more administrative in nature. In a well managed project, they will focus on monitoring performance and handling contractually required activities such as invoicing, payment management, cost recording, participating in reviews or maintaining data and documentation records. However, although this may be mundane, the work is critically important. It is in this phase that contract management can enable proactive problem identification, when communication capture can be critical to continued control. It is in this phase that discipline makes a difference between realizing expectations and moving into dispute. And it is at this stage that those organizations that are not following best practice tend to take their eye off the ball; they allow the tasks to be handled by low level administrators, who focus on compliance rather than proactive opportunity management.

In any long-term deal, steady state is just a momentary condition. Throughout the lifetime of the contract there will be change and contract management has a key role to play in this. Not only do they provide much of the background documentation to support or respond to a request, they also manage the associated negotiation and revised contract terms. Any change will reactivate many of the set-up processes. Indeed, significant changes can drive high levels of activity almost to the point of new contract start-up. Contract managers must ensure that requested changes are assessed, properly accepted or rejected, recorded and communicated, along with their impacts on price, scope, deliverables and/or timing.

The third key area for contract management relates to claims and disputes. The contract manager will be involved in initiation or receipt depending on which party is originating. In respect of the contract, you must take the lead in rapidly resolving any open issues or areas of doubt. The role will typically include analysis, evaluation and proposing resolutions, drawing on many of the records that the contract management team has built and maintained, in addition to the supervision of the relevant clauses and provisions from the original agreement and any modifications that have already been made.

Contract management will generally be involved in resolution, sometimes controlling the decision, but in many cases where there is severe disagreement, most likely in an advisory capacity. However contract managers need to understand the options that are open and the routes that could be followed in resolving the dispute.

Finally contract management has a lead role in contract close-out. Again the activities around termination or transition are going to involve many other functions, but contract managers are key in oversight, communication, associated documentation and ensuring compliance. We must always complete our records, document any continuing obligations and capture the final lessons learned for input to any similar future negotiations or relationship.

28.4 Contract management software

No chapter on contract management would be complete without mention of the growing range of contract management software. Contract management software is most valuable in large organizations with large spend or revenues, a high number of transactions and many trading partners. Recording and communication are keys to our effectiveness and professionalism. Obtaining the right documents fast, knowing all the key milestones and actions required, recording decisions, changes and lessons learned are all critical to contract management functional performance.

Contract management software systems can take the form of subscriptions to Software-as-a-Service (SaaS) products. Enterprise-wide contract management systems run on private networks within an organization and across all departments. Electronic data interface systems interface customer organizations with suppliers. Features of contract management software include contract creation, clause libraries, automatic workflows that forward documents for approvals to specific individuals in an approval chain, and 'tickler' features such as automatic alerts of important dates. Other features include dashboards that use graphics to present performance data such as service levels. Online analytical processing capabilities collect and process aggregate data across multiple contracts.

Contract management software can be beneficial in several ways.

Simplification and doing more with less

Contract management software simplifies the Implementation and Management phase. Contracts are developed using the software, which automatically captures all relevant terms and milestones in digital format and distributes the data within the organization according to sharing rules. Or data elements in the contracts can be manually entered into the software using a data coding system. Digital copies of contract documents can also be viewed by stakeholders. Ongoing contract management outputs such as change orders and status reports are immediately and readily made available. By automating clerical tasks such as reporting, software eliminates time-consuming non-value adding activities and reduces contract action management cycle times, freeing contract managers to focus on performing tasks that deliver greater value.

Standardization

Closely related to the first attribute, contract management software drives the use of standardized templates for both contractual documents and associated reports.

Moving from individual memory to corporate memory

Contract management software gives visibility into both past and current transactions between parties. The contract manager can see what discussions are under way, how they are being settled, opportunities for offset or reasons to reject a settlement on the terms proposed. Some software products use discussion threads to build corporate memory and knowledge share about dealings with other parties to contracts. By warehousing data and creating transparency into overall relationships, contract management systems create intelligence that can be used to improve decision-making.

Controls and checkpoints

Contract management software controls and monitors internal processes, including the status of contract actions. Automation of processes improves compliance with policies and regulations. Automation also provides mapping that identifies bottlenecks and inefficiencies.

Use of software creates transparency into contract management activities and invites a collaborative, integrated team approach to contract management, not just with stakeholders but with other contracting parties and potentially even auditors and regulators. The days of contracts lying forgotten in dusty corner filing cabinets are long gone. In reality, the nature of contracts themselves is turning from that of a single static document containing terms and conditions towards that of structures for the gathering and sharing of information on performance of associated third party suppliers and partners.

Typically, contract management software should have these core capabilities:
- A centralized and searchable contract repository that can be searched by supplier, by service/supply, by timeframe etc and is easy to navigate
- Collaborative contract creation and workflow that allows multiple users to create, update and track the status of contracts
- A template repository of standard contracts and clauses
- Monitoring and alerting against milestones such as contract review dates, payment milestones and expiration alerts
- Reporting and analytical tools to enable analysis of key suppliers, spend etc
- Roles, permissions, and security
- Data import and export capabilities

An effective contract management system has a central database that provides visibility into contract spending, alerts as to contract status, secure access for collaboration, performance monitoring, and data import and export.

28.5 Contract management resource planning

Planning

The Program Management Institute, in its Program Management Body of Knowledge, divides planning for management into the following knowledge areas, each with its own inputs and outputs. Each of the areas as applied to contract management is described further below, on behalf of the customer and the supplier:
- Integration management planning
- Scope management planning
- Time management planning
- Cost management planning
- Quality management planning
- Human resources (HR) management planning
- Communications management planning
- Risk management planning
- Procurement management planning

Integration management planning

Subsequent to the handover meeting, the contract manager draws up a contract management charter that begins by citing authority to manage the contract. Authority to take ownership of the contract may be documented in corporate governance policy statements or it may come as a memorandum written specifically for the contract or it may only exist as an understood operating procedure. To establish authority, the contract manager may need to take additional actions to obtain buy-in from stakeholders and others in the organization who ostensibly have responsibilities under the contract.

The charter will also state the goals and objectives for the contract and for management of the contract. Based on reading and interpretation of the contract, the contract manager will have produced an abstract or briefing document that summarizes and distills the contract. At this point the contract manager will also have conducted a kickoff meeting or held discussions with stakeholders about their expectations. In the charter, the contract manager will (as appropriate) discuss any gaps between what was intended by negotiation teams in reaching agreement, the expectations or goals of stakeholders, and what can reasonably be interpreted in the contract document.

The contract manager also draws up a contract management plan. This plan gives an overview of the contract management activities required by the contract and how these activities will happen in coordination with each other. In writing the plan, the contract manager will need to review what coordinated activities are already in place, either in the form of corporate governance or past practices, and the coordinated activities that will need to be put in place. The plan will also identify the automated systems within the organization that will be required to support contract management activities and communications, and the tools, practices or professional third party expertise needed.

Contract management activities will require direction and management, as well as monitoring and control. A contract management plan lists and describes what activities are required by the contract (and other policies and regulations), how they will be accomplished, who in the organization is responsible for completing the activities, and how the activities will be monitored for completion.

Much of contract management planning resembles project management planning; however, unlike project planning, there should be limited need for configuration management or change control for contract management. Factors initiating configuration management include reallocation of contract management responsibilities due to personnel turnover or reengineering within the organization, automation of administrative activities, or changes in corporate governance and external regulation.

Note: to avoid confusion, change control for contract management planning is different from managing changes in the contract Statement of Work (SOW) or terms, which is one of the contract management activities.

Scope management planning

The contract management plan will define the scope of contract management. Scope for contract management is defined by the SOW being performed in the contract and how the contract allocates contract management responsibilities between the parties. In project management, scope may be defined in greater detail through development of a work breakdown structure (WBS). The WBS prepared for performing work can be used by contract managers to identify contract management activities in relation to the work. A WBS also identifies deliverables. In contract management, deliverables will usually be additional contract documents, contract performance measurements, risk monitoring, acceptances, results of audits and investigations, invoices, and notices.

Adherence of contract performance to scope is a contract management activity.

Time management planning

Contract management plans include estimates of the time needed to perform activities and estimates of resources. Time management analyzes the sequences and attributes of activities to determine how long activities will take and how much and what type of resources are required by the activities. Resources are estimated by listing activities, describing what is required to perform them, and locating resource availability within the contract management function and in other departments involved in contract management, including automated systems availability, functionality and user access.

Flagging poor contract performance or claiming breach of contract due to non-performance for reasons of inadequate resources are contract management activities.

Cost management planning

Contract management plans estimate the cost of the activities. Contract management is a type of cost called a transaction cost. For the supplier, depending on the type of pricing used in the contract, contract management may be an indirect cost that the supplier can charge to the customer, or it may be purely overhead. Estimating contract management costs requires Activity-Based Costing analysis using hourly rates or some other labor metric and the duration of activities calculated through time management. Customers may benchmark the total cost of contract management against total contract value to determine how reasonable the costs are.

Accounting for costs is a contract management activity.

Quality management planning

Measuring the quality of contract management should also be included in the plan. Quality of contract management is a matter of performance of contract management activities required by the contract as well as compliance with policies and regulations affected by contract management.

Measuring the quality of contract performance is a contract management activity.

HR management planning

Management of contract management personnel can also be addressed in the plan. Contract management is a skilled staff function requiring specialized skills, knowledge and capabilities of individual contract managers and the use of tools and practices. The human resources knowledge area includes assigning roles and responsibilities, both within the contract management function and outside the function, incorporating direction and management of personnel in the contract management plan, building competency, and measuring personal performance.

Consenting to supplier staff who will perform the contract and other decisions about contract performance are contract management activities.

Communications management planning

The contract management plan includes a communication plan. Communications in contract management closely resemble communications in project management. Planning communications begins with looking at what information is required by the contract together with the roles and responsibilities of those performing contract management activities and organization charts and office locations for personnel involved in contract management. The means of communications must also be decided on in planning. This requires looking at how often information needs to be updated (e.g., weekly reports), what communications methods are available, the capability of personnel to use the means of communication, and whether personnel are physically able to meet in person or are dispersed and must meet virtually (e.g., teleconferencing).

The communications plan supports the objectives of information distribution, performance reporting and stakeholder management.

Risk management planning

In addition to managing risks that arise from performance of the contract, contract managers can address risks caused by failures in the execution of contract management activities, the organization of contract management, contract management communications, resource and cost estimating, or other areas of contract management planning and operation. To manage contract risks the contract manager reviews the contract and project documents such as the WBS, the contract management plan and organization charters, operating procedures, corporate governance policies, availability of resources and communications, and other areas covered in the contract management plan to identify, assess and address risks. Examples of this type of risk management include: not documenting instances of poor contract performance, failure to respond to violations of standards and regulations governing the work, and delay in providing status reports to stakeholders.

Procurement management planning

Just as there are two types of risk management practiced by contract managers, so there are two types of procurement management. Procurement for the purposes of contract performance is subcontracting work to other suppliers. For contract management planning, procurement is acquisition of additional resources required to execute contract management, such as hiring a third party consultant to conduct a maturity assessment of the contract management function, or purchasing centralized document management software. These supplies to the contract management function represent additional contracts that must be managed.

Prioritization

After planning for contract management and settling on an organization of personnel inside and outside the contract management function, the contract manager will prioritize which activities and communications are most important to achieving goals and objectives. Prioritization will be driven by several factors:

- Performance of contract work and fulfillment of contract terms and conditions that might lead to material breach
- Mitigation of the largest negative risks to contract performance
- Compliance with governance policies and external standards and regulations
- Activities for which competency is weak or for which practices and tools are not available

28.6   Communication

We find that contract implementation is probably most endangered by poor communication. Sometimes key stakeholders don't even receive a copy of the contract. Or it is simply mailed out (email, physical mail, or however it is forwarded) with the belief that as long as everybody's got a copy, it's going to get properly implemented. Experienced contract managers know that short cuts in communication mean higher risks and more work later. To avoid this you need to make sure that you have undertaken an effective and constructive communication exercise.

Experienced and successful project managers will tell you "communication, communication, communication." But don't confuse communication with information. Communication means understanding the needs of the recipient and sending simple, targeted messages that explain what needs to be done, why and what value it brings. Try to communicate in the style of, and using terms that will be readily understood by, the recipient. Make it easy for the recipient.

We've already discussed undertaking proper analysis, about documentation and terminology and expression that will be easily understood. It's essential to bear in mind that this contract may be implemented across multiple cultures; if this is the case, many of the people who are receiving this information are not operating in the same native language as the contract. So the onus is upon the lead to make sure that you have understood what it is that needs to be communicated, whom it needs to be communicated to, and that it is expressed in terms that they will understand.

You must make the communication succinct enough that the recipients are reading the things that they really need to know as opposed to confusing them with documentation that has no relevance to the task you are asking them to perform.

You also need to be clear about what communication you expect back. What reports do you want? What systems or procedures must they use in order for you to be able to centralize documentation and information that you need to manage proper control? Don't leave such things unclear. Don't complain about the lack of information flowing back if you've never thought through the issue or the challenges of how and when it will be communicated.

You must highlight the specific high-risk or high priority areas and make sure that they receive particular attention. And finally, whether you're looking internally or externally, think about how you express your message in a way that incentivizes cooperation and compliance. There will be many people who, for whatever reason, don't agree with what's being implemented or don't understand why it's being implemented in a particular way. If we don't take the time and trouble to help them to understand and to give them the right incentives to conform to how we want to do it, then it is our own fault if the implementation starts to fail.

Communication: sales challenge

So that means you have some selling to do. This means that you have got to think creatively about the way that you communicate. And you have to work on methods and channels. For example, can you call a meeting or do you need to visit them individually? Does a stakeholder prefer phone calls or emails? And you must work out how to handle new team members and bring them up to date during the project.

You could be looking at a lot of stakeholders in complex deals. There are many examples where this may run into the thousands of people with some responsibility for the implementation to run smoothly. You may also be looking at organizational and geographic diversity. For example, there will be people in Finance who have one particular set of measurement systems and drivers; there will be people in project management; there will be people in procurement, information systems, and the business units. Each of them has different interests, and different perspectives.

There are multiple locations, some of which will feel friendly to what's going on, some of which may feel threatened. Their level of linguistic ability and skill may vary significantly.

There are many options on how to communicate and the environment should determine which combination to use. Are you going to do this through physical meetings? Are you going to do it by phone, webcast or email? Are you looking at pulling together a core, initial team and have them responsible for cascading it? If you are going to cascade, is that going to be on a by-region basis, by-country basis, or by business area or function?

Finally if you know that we're looking at a long-term relationship (that's anything more than three to four months) there are going to be changes in personnel throughout the lifetime of the contract. Your communication and your sales message are ongoing. You have to have good induction documentation, which means that individuals who are coming new to the project can pick up, understand and move into their role seamlessly, avoiding a lot of confusion or potential mistakes.

Communication: a shared activity

Remember you don't need to do everything yourself. Identify and use other resources who have an interest in the contract succeeding.

Many times people fall into the mistake of believing that because we work in the same organization that we're all on the same side. The truth is our management systems, our measurement systems and the various interests that we have around job security are not always in line. You need to have thought through the reality of the environment into which you are implementing. That means you need to have thought actively about who are your true allies. Who is, perhaps, indifferent? And who is actively opposed? And you need to have thought up a plan to make sure that you have aligned with your allies, motivated those that are indifferent and that you have overcome those who are opposed.

Among the allies there should be executive sponsors. How closely are they allied? How much do they care? Are there mechanisms that you can introduce that can make them care more? Are there ways that you can communicate to gain executive buy-in and sponsorship that will help you to overcome opposition or difficulties? You are looking for managers throughout the organization who have some vested interest in the success of this particular deal, or where you can create an environment where they have a vested interest in success.

You also need to think about the role that the other contracting parties can play. Many fail to develop synergies and to create a joint marketing and selling plan that makes best use of each other's resources. Creating joint materials can often be useful and ensure the consistency of the message.

The other parties have a very real vested interest in making sure that implementation is smooth. That significantly reduces their timeline, costs and reduces their risk of failure. So you should be exploiting that. You should be actively going to them and looking for specific activities they will undertake to help implementation. On the other hand, you have to remember that they have a vested interest in giving that communication a particular spin. They are trying to improve their profitability and they're also trying to create circumstances where, if things go wrong, they can point fingers at you and your people. So, find the right balance and make sure that you have not lost control over information or communication.

Communications: setting some rules

As we have discussed, a major root problem of unsuccessful projects is poor organizational structure. In such situations, team members may be unclear about their roles or their reporting lines; therefore you must fully define responsibilities and authorities.

Maintaining comprehensive records of communications and decisions is also critical. Memory and understanding of conversations or informal communications will differ. Research shows that within hours of a meeting, the participants will recall it so differently that you might not recognize it as the same meeting. Another survey has demonstrated that people will subconsciously fill in missing memories as they see fit. Don't rely on people's memories for your success.

In project management it's ideal to have a single point of contact between the parties for all correspondence and for both parties to understand this and to make it work. However, in practice this can be difficult, especially in large projects, so ensure interface control measures are in place to effectively communicate. As a contract manager, you need to be sure that you're aware of all communications that relate to contract terms, performance or change.

Uniquely identify all correspondence with sequential numbering and require suppliers to do the same. This is an excellent and very effective tool to control correspondence and to avoid doubt or dispute over what the prevailing terms have now become. It also makes finding correspondence easier and removes any doubt over the current version.

Some organizations don't use a structured amendment or versioning process and this can result in extensive disputes.

You must keep complete structured project and contract files. A very common problem in projects is the inability to find key communications. Design a standard filing system where all projects documents are diligently filed, whether online or physical. Files must also be accessible to project team members – worldwide if necessary. Effective interface control and control of communication is one of the most simple, yet effective tools in controlling and managing a project. Getting these tools in place at the beginning of a project provides a firm foundation and will return a great deal of value throughout the project lifecycle.

Is there such a thing as informal communication in a contract relationship? Many people will use the term 'I say this informally,' but this can be very dangerous, and you must be careful how and what is communicated. Many projects founder on disputes that involve directions that were misunderstood, misrepresented or misapplied. In our normal lives, we know how often our memory of a conversation or of what we've said is diametrically different from what other parties record or claim to record. If something is important, it must be recorded and agreed to by joint sign-off. If it isn't important, then it probably shouldn't be said.

Correspondence between you and other parties must be clearly defined as project or contract communication. **Never** rely on verbal communication as the means of passing information or instructions between interfaces. **Always** follow up any verbal communication in writing.

28.7   Summary

In conclusion of this chapter, consider some of the aspects that are specific to a large complex organization. Your communication effectiveness, what you communicate, how you communicate, to whom you communicate, is going to be geared around a number of issues of organization and management system. In a complex environment, you make a mistake if you assume that everybody is on the same page, that they're all motivated by the same things. There are many vested interests around the organization in addition to the need to manage across cultural divides, linguistic divides and other variations of organizational interest.

So you, as a contract manager, must be familiar with the area in which you are operating and understand how to communicate in a way that responds to people's interests, needs and views. You must understand the structure of your organization. You must understand the impacts of measurement and motivation systems and organizational behavior. And in thinking about that, think not only of your own, but also the key players in the other organization. What are their measurements?

You must be able to think about and understand the differences of forms of contract or agreement, the legal and financial issues, the resistance you may face by people claiming that they're required to do things differently. You need to know enough to understand what is real and what is a an excuse, and suggest alternative approaches that will work

There are often important legal and tax implications, both benefits and limitations, which affect the way that you and your contract partners implement and manage the contract. You need to understand those. There is no point either in exposing your organization's structure or trying to force the other side to do things in a way that would expose their organizational and tax structure.

CHAPTER 29

Transition

29.1 Introduction

Contract signature represents a major milestone in the contracting lifecycle. Sales organizations celebrate the success of winning new business and purchasing organizations celebrate the money saved and other acquisition benefits of the deal. The celebrations, and sometimes bonuses triggered by contract signature, may, however, mask the challenges in implementing the contract to achieve the benefits anticipated at contract signature.

The much stated cliché is that the contract is put away in a drawer the moment it is signed and only looked at (if it can be found) in the event that something goes wrong. Whereas this is an overstatement of reality, the cliché does contain more than a grain of truth. A partner in a leading London based law firm observed that around half of his clients who requested assistance to re-negotiate an existing problematic contract came to him looking to obtain provisions already contained in the original contract.

The first step, therefore, to achieve the benefits anticipated at contract signature is not to put the contract away in a drawer but to ensure the effective transition from the Initiate, Bid, Development and Negotiation phase activities to those of the Manage phase and this chapter identifies the necessary steps and activities.

29.2 Contract management after signature

Let's look for a moment at some of the typical comments that arise related to contract implementation. The point here is that the contract is a fundamental reference document for all those who are needed to contribute to success, and that contribution includes the user groups. Your communication role should not only be ensuring roles and obligations have been defined, but also that expectations have been properly set. One of the most frequent issues between contract parties is that the supplier is trying to work to specific documented requirements and obligations, but in the customer organization, everything is being judged against expectations.

Now as a contract manager you're the bridge and therefore the potential fall guy for internal complaints and dissatisfaction.

Make sure you read and understand the contract. One way to ensure full understanding of obligations and sharing of risks with appropriate stakeholders is to develop a contract briefing document that summarizes the contract clauses, obligations, actions and rationale behind non- standard areas. This must identify who is responsible for doing what and can form the base of the communication plan. (Simply sending out hundreds of pages of contract documentation is often little better than not sending out the contract at all.) Your initial draft of the contract briefing document may well change as a result of the handover meeting, as you hear other viewpoints and expectations. Of course, the contract briefing documents must be readily accessible in electronic form to all with a need to know.

The contract handover meeting is key to managing risk. An effective handover meeting will reduce risk; a poorly executed handover will increase risk. Since people are the number one risk factor, involve the bid, negotiation and implementation teams to obtain a continuum. To drive involvement and interest consider a series of meetings or perhaps use webcasts to make certain that the handover is thorough and effective.

Many handover meetings degenerate into arguments over how well the deal was negotiated, or the wisdom of specific commitments. Such discussion is unproductive. Your task is to ensure the commitments, whether good or bad, are understood and that plans for their implementation and monitoring are developed. Highlight those that appear exposed; consider mitigation techniques, including possibilities for negotiation or change.

29.3 Contract analysis

Contract analysis is driven by the need to communicate the rights and duties and other content of the contract to the organization in order to:
- Guide the expectations of stakeholders who have an interest in contract performance
- Initiate and direct actions of organization personnel who will have responsibilities under the contract
- Enforce terms and conditions against other parties to the contract.

Dealing with disparities in stakeholder expectations
A recommended approach in contract analysis is to identify disparities between contract terms and conditions, the intent of organizations at the time of entering into negotiations, and stakeholder expectations. An example of this approach is shown in Figure 29.1.

Disparities arise between these three sets of understandings of the agreement underlying the contract because of the phases and different groups of participants in the contracting process. Negotiators start with business goals and objectives and risk assessments developed earlier in the Initiate phase. Through negotiations an agreement is reached that achieves some - but usually not all - of the goals and objectives. Negotiated agreements are then drafted into contracts. Contract drafting should capture the intent of the parties but does not always do so due to human error and the limits of communication. Contract managers take ownership of the management of contract documents; they understand the agreement through interpretation of terms and conditions. Contracts are intended to benefit stakeholders in the organization. Stakeholders think of contracts not as terms and conditions or as negotiated agreements but as expected outcomes that will serve their interests. These expectations originate at the beginning of the contracting cycle and may continue unmodified by the negotiations or the final contract. Further, expectations can vary from stakeholder to stakeholder depending on their own organizational interests.

Contract managers must obtain a holistic understanding of expectations based on goals and objectives and other factors, the intent behind negotiated agreements, a reasonable interpretation of the final contract, and the gaps between them. It then becomes the task of contract managers to educate stakeholders on the actual contents of the contract through development of the contract briefing document, and work to build consensus with stakeholders on what should be expected.

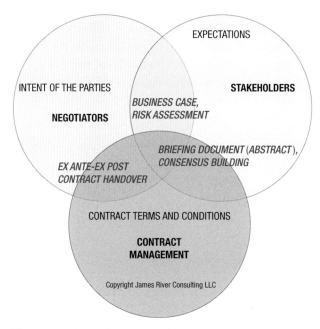

Figure 29.1   Intent-Expectations-Interpretation Analysis

Active and passive clauses analysis

Dividing contract terms into active and passive clauses is a technique for quickly determining what both contract managers and stakeholders who are part of the extended contract management team are expected to do, when they are expected to do it and how they must do it.

Active clauses are those that require processes and resources for their performance. They are things that must occur, whether it is a simple obligation such as raising an invoice or a contracts obligation such as ensuring the maintenance of, for example, confidentiality or nondisclosure provisions or others such as overall payment or change procedures.

Passive clauses are those that typically only come into effect in the event of something failing to occur or an occurrence that is contrary to the terms of the deal. The passive clauses, conversely, tend to be those that are handling failure or dispute. They are things like limitation of liability or the indemnity provisions, many areas of intellectual property, those that on a day-to-day basis do not actually take active management.

Ideally you should not have to work through a contract on a case-by case basis to identify active versus passive terminology. That's something that, in best practice corporations, has been done in advance, so that you're really just looking for the exceptions to the rule, the non-standard elements for specific negotiated areas or the incremental terms and conditions that are specific to this deal. The rest of it should have already been covered with standard practice and process to facilitate not only your analysis, but also its communication. That way, you concentrate on the things that need to be done differently rather than always 'reinventing the wheel' around the things that are or should be the same.

This approach supports the creation of standard guidance documents, which should be made available as a first level source of guidance or help to those affected by the contract.

29.4 What is 'the contract'?

Make sure you understand what constitutes 'the contract'. It is, of course, far more than a legal document or something stored by the legal department. The contract contains many legal terms and there are elements that you will only revert to if and when things start to go wrong, and even with the advice and leadership of in-house experts in the legal department. But it contains far more than that. Contracts have a range of business terms, attachments and specifications. They include a Statement of Work (SOW) and Service Level Agreements (SLAs). Often they incorporate bid documents, letters, change orders and specifications.

Anything that is referenced as part of the contract is part of the contract. And that often means a lot of documentation. So one of the first things you need to make sure you've done is to understand what exactly is the contract and what is being excluded.

Integration

Contracts can include many separate documents including a SOW, project plans, specifications, SLAs, operational level agreements, standard terms and conditions, bid and proposal documents, letters of intent and other negotiation documents, change orders and specifications. 'Integration' is the legal operation by which several documents or data sources that are otherwise independent are read together as a single contract. The legal process of forming an agreement through offer and acceptance is a different process from integration. Integration assumes the existence of a valid underlying agreement. Integration has to do with determining the entirety of a written contract.

Currently, many paper contracts reference internet URLs[23] presenting additional legal terms and conditions and other contract language. The combining of written paper contracts and digital documents that is now recognized in most countries internationally as having legal validity has resurrected questions that were thought to have been well settled in Anglo-American law. Regardless of the circumstances, as contracts become less monolithic in their construction, risks of clerical error, conflicts between terms, redundant contracts, moral hazard, and unauthorized amendment and renegotiation grow, requiring more contract administration.

In deciding whether a document, web page or other content are legally part of a contract, contract managers should ask a series of questions see (Figure 29.2).

29.5 **Analyzing and understanding terms and conditions**

Contract interpretation

How contracts are written can vary widely from contract to contract. Some documents are written in very legalistic language using Latin phrases and terms of art found in common law. Other contract documents are written in a plain style that avoids 'legalese'. Some knowledge of legal terminology is required to become fully competent to interpret contracts. Black's Law Dictionary is a well-known reference book in the US for looking up Anglo-American legal terms.

---

23 Uniform resource locator – the global address of documents and other resources on the World Wide Web

Q1:	Is the document/data identified within the contract? If so, is the ID unique or specific, e.g., title, description of contents?
Q2:	Does the contract state that the document/data is incorporated by reference and made part of the terms?
Q3:	Does the contract have an integration clause?
Q4:	Does the document/data content complete the contract?
Q5:	Do the document/data terms conflict with the contract?
Q6:	Is the document physically bound, e.g., stapled, or the data electronically linked, e.g., hyperlink, to the contract?
Q7:	Is the document/data dated and does the date predate or coincide with the date of the contract? Copyright James River Consulting LLC
Q8:	What is the source of the document/data? Was the document/data created within the ordinary course of business, e.g., sales quote?
Q9:	Was the document/data signed or otherwise show acceptance by one or both parties?
Q10:	Does anythig about the document/data suggest that it is marketing or otherwise not intended as contractual language?

Figure 29.2   Questions about whether content is legally part of a contract

The idea that contracts should only be interpreted by lawyers is completely irrational for a number of reasons, however. If ordinary people in an organization are unable to understand a contract, then the contract fails its essential purpose, which is to capture an agreement in writing.

In the Anglo-American legal tradition, rules apply to how contracts are read and understood. In the US the rules of interpretation are set out in the Restatement (Second) of Contracts, which is the premier treatise on contract law. The Restatement provides the following rules of interpretation paraphrased and summarized below:

- Ordinary meaning. Language is given its ordinary meaning in a country.
- Terms of art. Technical terms and words of art are given their technical meaning.
- Interpretation of the whole. A contract is interpreted as a whole and all of its constituent parts are read as belonging together.
- Manifest intent. Conduct of the parties after the contract is signed should determine if their interpretation is reasonable. Where intent is not clearly manifested, interpretation should account for all manifestations and the apparent purpose of the contract should be given great weight in determining intent.
- Specific over general. Specific provisions qualify general provisions where conflict exists.
- Construe against drafter. Interpretation that works against the party who drafted the contract language should be preferred over others.

- Original language over forms. Where there is conflict between preprinted contract terms and custom negotiated terms, the negotiated terms take effect.

Material breach terms

Some contract terms and conditions are more important than others. A supplier is only liable for breach of contract if it has materially failed to perform the contract. 'Material' means that if not performed, the other party will lose some or all of the value it sought in making the agreement. Terms that are material to the agreement usually appear in the statement of work or other description of the product or service being delivered, as well as in many 'boilerplate' contract clauses containing legal rights and duties that will diminish the benefit of the transaction, if not followed. Many of the administrative terms found in contracts that are important to contract managers in carrying out their responsibilities are not material to the underlying agreement. An opposing party that does not file reports on time may be frustrating to a contract manager but is probably not grounds for claiming contract breach.

Conditional terms

Sometimes all or part of contract performance is based on conditions, either 'precedent', 'concurrent', or 'subsequent'. 'Conditions precedent' are events of some kind that must take place before a party becomes obligated to perform, even though the party has already agreed to perform. 'Concurrent' conditions require the simultaneous exchange of performance by both parties. 'Subsequent', on the other hand, means that the obligation to perform will continue until some kind of event occurs, at which point the obligation will end. Determining when conditions precedent and subsequent take place is a question of fact, not a question of law. What defines the condition can be simple, such as delivery of cargo, or complex, such as price determined by market forces.

29.6   **Core contract elements analysis**

Contracts can be thought of as having four core elements:
- What is the contract about (scope)?
- Who does what according to the contract (roles and responsibilities)?
- How do we know the contract is working (service levels, measurements, milestones)?
- What happens if something happens or doesn't happen according to the contract (recourse, penalties)?

Scope is usually found in an SOW or description of work listed as a section in the main body of the contract or attached as a separate document.

The second area is that of roles and responsibilities. Who has promised to do what, to whom, for whom and when? The roles and responsibilities can be contained in many different places. There are likely to be sections that are specifically titled 'Roles and Responsibilities' but many of the others appear in areas such as the SOW. Again, you need to have summarized and understood in detail what the roles are. What are the responsibilities? What are you expected to do? What are they expected to do?

Then you move to an area that is essentially about whether or not you know the deal is working. Performance measurements may take the form of entirely separately signed contracts called SLAs that are incorporated into the main contract. Project milestones will be found in project planning documentation, which may or may not be incorporated into the contract, usually as part of the work statement.

Finally, there will be mechanisms that address what happens if the deal goes wrong. This includes the legal provisions related to rights of termination and other things such as indemnities, remedies and *force majeure*. But in addition to those provisions there are all sorts of control and reference mechanisms that occur in the contract, such as change management processes, or formal notification, which must be understood and followed. There are also very often financial consequences, such as liquidated damages or service credits that may apply in the event either party fails to meet its commitments. It is also a matter of capturing core objectives – for example, volumes, revenues, and performance descriptions.

If you're going to be effective in managing the contract you have to be able to live and breathe all of these things over the next few years. They are areas that you must have recorded and turned into language and terminology that you and others in your organization can understand. There is no substitute for the fact that you're going to have to read the contract. You're going to have to highlight and mark up those areas that are critical to the overall long-term running of the deal.

29.7 Setting priorities

Having completed your analysis of these active and passive terms, and put together your plan for their communication to the rest of the organization, you need to move into the question of prioritization. Focus on the things that represent risk to the project, its results or the team members, including you. What are the issues and who are the people who could derail you? What is the probability of that happening?

Areas that represent risk are the things that are new and different, the things that people are not familiar with and therefore either make mistakes or are resistant to because they don't agree. They simply believe that something else should be done or perhaps they don't understand what it is that's being requested of them.

There are other categories of high risk, for example things that are politically or organizationally sensitive. An outsourcing deal may be resisted because people feel threatened by a particular shift or change in the way that they work or who they work with.

There are deals or topics that are particularly high profile because of executive interest. You need to be conscious from a personal point of view and from an organizational point of view and make sure that such deals receive particular attention. Finally, there may be areas where you know there has historically been a problem with other implementations or with this particular contracting partner, where you will want to put in specific reporting mechanisms to monitor and ensure that things are running and their on track.

29.8 Transition meeting

The communication process is consistently identified as key to successful projects.

Communication must be rigorously executed and well planned. Have the other side present their communication plan to ensure alignment. Develop common tools and take advantage of web- based technology. Feel able to question the other side on specific skills, experience, and incentives that apply to their staff.

Long before the inaugural meeting, you will have been validating the contract management organization with your supplier. You will have checked to ensure they operate with handover meetings similar to the one that you've just conducted. This acts as the backdrop for you to have a joint project inauguration meeting. The key sub-element of the meeting is for the contract management team from both the supplier and the customer to come together, to ensure that there is clear agreement and understanding of the mechanisms you're going to use to share and exchange information and to undertake long-term contract management activities.

Handover of the contract represents the bridge between the pre-signature and post-signature contract management phases. The primary purpose of the handover meeting is to take ownership of the contract within the organization. In doing so, contract managers and those who preceded them in negotiations must engage in knowledge transfer of the challenges that were faced in reaching an agreement, the status of the relationship between parties in the wake of negotiations, and (as will be discussed later) an understanding of what those representing the organization in negotiations intended their agreement to accomplish. This is independent of the contract manager's interpretation of the contract on reading it later in the Analyzing and Understanding step.

The handover meeting should be structured in a way that helps to achieve the above purposes by following these practices:

- Have the meeting chaired by a positive facilitator who focuses on looking to the future
- Take an inclusive attitude towards negotiators when discussing management of contract performance
- Follow a meeting structure and agenda that doesn't waste peoples time or involve unnecessary participants
- Use group techniques that generate teamwork, consensus and enthusiasm

The agenda for the handover meeting should cover, at a minimum, the following items:

- Key contract terms and conditions
- Project deliverables
- Timescales for delivery and key milestones
- Project reporting requirements (and who receives reports) and validation that the reports will give early warning of non-compliance or exposures
- Budget and payment plans (cash flow forecasts and contingencies)
- Clarification of aspects of the contract or project requirements

The negotiation team members participating in the handover meeting may also be stakeholders and organization personnel who will work with the contract management function later in the Manage phase. If present, the handover meeting can also serve as the kickoff meeting for planning and organizing how contract management will be undertaken and how contract management communications will be established.

29.9 Transition and organization

Implementation and communication are the key topics covered in this chapter. Building close alignment, understanding roles and responsibilities and developing reports and communications are critical. There should be no confusion over the interfaces and the authority of each interface in making or agreeing decisions.

Implementation and communication process and policy is something that you should have designed generically for all of your contracts. However, in complex environments, there are likely to be some levels of customization required. In this chapter we discuss those changes in detail; they should be based upon the specifics of a particular contract.

Key outputs from handover and organization are:
- Identifying the people who are going to be closely involved and responsible for its implementation
- Design or formalization of the process, which includes the customization elements that there may be; for example, the creation of particular skills or a particular project office design
- The organization and responsibilities – how tasks will be divided to ensure smooth and consistent implementation
- Looking at the other party's overall organization of responsibilities and making sure that there is proper alignment of roles and activities
- Making sure that there is complete understanding in both organizations and agreement between those organizations over the specifications and delivery requirements of this particular deal

29.10 Transition - meeting goals

Contract managers are typically handling long and complex contracts. The negotiation team may have been split into several different groups, covering different elements of the deal. This is something you should remember when it comes to the handover meeting and organization plan.

You may similarly want to create some level of subdivision and not just a core team that's taking an overview of the entire deal and then bringing in some of the subgroups to work on the individual elements. Structure the meeting in a way that helps you avoid resistance. This is achieved by:
- A positive facilitator who focuses on success
- Inclusiveness
- A meeting structure and agenda that doesn't waste people's time or involve unnecessary participants
- Use of techniques that generate teamwork, consensus and enthusiasm – we will illustrate those with ideas in later sections of this chapter.

The agenda should cover, at a minimum, the following so you can gain agreement and common understanding of:
- Key contract points
- Project deliverables
- Timescales for delivery and key milestones
- Project reporting requirements (and who receives reports)
- Validation that the reports will give early warning of non-compliance or exposures
- Budget and payment plans (cash flow forecasts and contingencies)

- Any unclear aspects of the contract or project requirements
- Any actions on your company staff (roles and responsibilities)

Remember that one of your key tools for this meeting is the contract briefing document.

29.11 Summary

The contract will often be at a high level, and this is the time for detailed definition of specific approaches. It's important that you consider the use of systems and procedures. You may want to establish tools and metrics during the meeting that will improve the probability of success. How are you going to undertake data capture? How are you going to monitor performance?

It is particularly important to spend time looking at the risk areas - that is, the areas that are likely to lead to disputes, which you know to be potentially fraught with danger. Make sure that resources have been allocated into those areas and that you have thought in advance about the metrics that you're going to need to get early warning. Research shows that before the end of the first third of a project, and as early as one tenth of the way through, you can tell with relative accuracy whether it will run as planned or not. It also shows that in many cases, the warning signs are not identified or ignored, in the hope they will simply go away.

Finally, the role division within the overall project structure is the other area that must be absolutely clear. Roles and responsibilities have to be well defined so that there is no potential confusion, no overlap, and no gaps.

CHAPTER 30

Risk and opportunity

30.1 Introduction

The pre-contract signature activities should ensure a comprehensive assessment of the risk and opportunities associated with the contract that has just been signed. The nature of these activities may, however, mean the risk and opportunity assessment is implicit or buried within the contract documentation or associated internal business case or authorization papers. The assessment may also have been considered solely through the lens of contractual risk without considering wider practical implementation aspects. The contract liability provisions may, for example, be crystal clear but not reflect the real world practicalities of which party is best placed to manage the specific risks that could trigger these liabilities.

This chapter looks at how best to use the pre-contract signature risk and opportunity assessment and how to keep it live and relevant during the life of the contract.

30.2 Understanding risk and opportunity

The individual responsible for the commercial contractual aspects during the contract implementation may discover during the transition from pre-contract that the risk and opportunity assessment falls into one of the following categories:
- Full and comprehensive
- Partially complete
- Substantially incomplete or missing

The first step is to understand which category applies by understanding:
- The contract using the documentation input from the transition
- The practicalities involved by seeking input from the operational team responsible for the contract implementation

- The other parties whether they be your main counter-party (customer or supplier) or other players along the supply chain all the way from the very end-customer through to the lowest tier of subcontractor
- Experience from other similar contracts

Developing this understanding provides an assessment of any existing risk and opportunity register or similar documentation or database and triggers the development or creation of such register/document/database.

Risk and opportunity register

Risk registers catalog individual risks, give information about the threat they pose and how they are to be managed, and provide updates on the impact of the risk. A sample risk register is shown in Figure 30.1 below, which combines risk **identification** and risk **monitoring**.

As shown in Figure 30.2 (from the UK HM Treasury's *Orange Book*), risk management is iterative. Risks may dissipate in their impact or likelihood while new risks appear. Mitigation strategies that are proving ineffective are revisited.

Post-signature contract risk assessment and response

Contract managers must continue to identify risk through the life of the contract. This can be by personal involvement in meetings and also through:

- Project status and quality assurance reports. Much of mitigation has to do with monitoring work and looking for signs of the cause of risks. Project plans in Statements of Work (SOWs) usually include periodic reporting on project status. Project status information can be used to detect risks to cost and schedule objectives. Likewise, quality assurance programs in work statements produce reports that are useful to contract managers in monitoring risks.
- Customer inspections and industry certifications. Suppliers are often required by contract to offer evidence of customer licenses and approvals upon request. Contracts can also include clauses requiring the supplier's facilities and operations to receive certification of compliance with industry-wide quality, safety and security standards. Contract managers can prompt suppliers to manage risks that threaten compliance by requesting information generated by customer inspections and third party certifications. Contract managers may learn of deficiencies revealed in the licensing or certification process that present risks to contract performance.
- Proof of insurance. Suppliers are usually required to carry insurance coverage naming customers as additional insured parties and to provide proof upon request under insurance clauses. Often insurance companies, by the terms of the policy, require their primary insured party to perform risk management on an enterprise-wide basis to reduce the potential for claims. Contract managers for both customers and suppliers should be

Risk Identification Register								
As of _____ (Please give a specific date)								
Name of the Project _____ Project Number _____ Client _____								
Risk Item Number	Date Identified	Description of Risk	Probability of Risk	Total Cost Impact	Cost Impact Based on the Probability	Strategy for Mitigation	Schedule Impact	Current Status
			A (%)	B($)	C($)=A*B			

Project Manager _____ Date _____
Quality Assurance Manager _____ Date _____
Business Unit Manager _____ Date _____
Contracts Administrator _____ Date _____
Others_____ Date _____

Excerpted from RV Krishna, Contract Management (April, 2005, National Contract Management Association)

Risk Monitoring Report						
As of _____ (Please give a specific date)						
Name of the Project _____ Original Risk Item Number _____						
Revision Number _____ (A Revision Number must only be issued, if the risk status has changed from the original. This should be issued by the Quality Control Office.)						
Risk Item Number	Date Identified	Description of Risk	Probability of Risk	Total Cost Impact	Cost Impact Based on the Probability	Strategy for Mitigation

Project Manager _____ Date _____
Approved by the Quality Assurance Department _____ Date _____
Management Approval _____ Date _____

Figure 30.1   Sample risk register

aware of the risk management requirements of insurers. Proof of insurance language in contracts can be broadly interpreted to include disclosure of risk management activities.

- Change orders, work orders and clawbacks. Change management clauses provide a process to restate contract performance terms such as scope, requirements, places of performance, delivery dates, etc. Changes can mitigate risks simply by correcting clerical mistakes in the drafting of the contract or mis-stated administrative responsibilities.

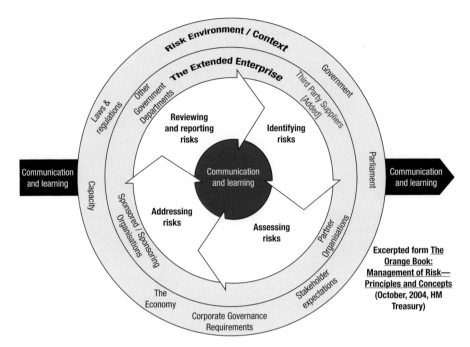

Figure 30.2   Risk management cycle

Risks of not achieving objectives because the customer's work requirements and specifications have changed, or the assumptions about business conditions and technical feasibility on which the parties negotiated the contract, can be addressed through change clauses. Similar to change orders, work tasking can be used to avoid risk by delaying or altogether avoiding risk sources. Clawbacks allow companies to unilaterally subtract pieces of work scope by taking them over themselves or recontracting them out to third party suppliers.

- Subcontracting. Both subcontracting of work and hiring of key management and technical personnel by the supplier are usually subject to the prior consent of the customer. Because these situations in reality amount to subcontracts involving the entire contracting process beginning with the Initiate phase, the contract manager can use contractual prior consent power to conduct risk identification and assessment in selecting subcontracting parties and defining and negotiating subcontract terms.

- Cure provisions. Acceptance clauses under a contract stipulate to terms giving the supplier an opportunity to cure deficiencies in work product. Cure provisions in acceptance clauses can be broadly interpreted by contract managers to also require a risk assessment by the supplier of the reasons for the defect and a response plan for managing against future occurrences.

- Customer direction and control. Liability of a supplier for the impact of risks (liabilities) that occur while performing work at the customer's direction is a gray area in contract relationships. It is not uncommon to see language in contracts, included by the supplier, relieving the supplier from liability for work directed by the customer. To reduce its own risks, the customer should engage in an assessment of risks before tasking the supplier.

- Indemnification clauses. Liability for damages to third parties and the legal costs associated with defense against third party law suits require contract managers for both parties to inform each other of potential risks leading to exercise of rights under an indemnification clause.
- Exchange rate clauses. Many approaches are taken by contracting parties in addressing the issue of inflation or deflation of pricing terms in contracts due to later variations in exchange rates between a customer and supplier in different countries with different currencies. Regardless of the approach taken, most payment terms allow room for contract managers to 'hedge' the risks of rate variations by timing payments. For example, customer contract managers may balance the risks of advance payments to a supplier with the chance of unfavorable dips in the value of the customer's currency.

30.3 Understanding and managing opportunity in contracts

Contract managers can look for opportunities to improve quality, performance, value for money, or other aspects of performance. Terms and conditions of the contract may or may not address continuous improvement or have commercial motives such as monetary incentives for seeking improvement incorporated in the contract. Where a transaction is not completely specified in a contract but rather leaves the parties to cooperate, part of the improvement process should be to aim for alignment of objectives, so that customer and supplier are working towards the same things, and both deriving benefits when they are realized.

The UK Office of Government Commerce (OGC) identifies the following contract management practices as ways to seek improvement:
- Incentives
- Continuous improvement
- Benefits based payments
- Added value

Incentives. Incentives are contract clauses intended to motivate the supplier to improve performance by offering the payment of premiums for meeting service levels and key performance indicators. The intended outcome of incentives is to increase value for money rather than cost savings as with penalties. In addition to contract clauses, contract managers can implement the following incentives post-signature:
- Guaranteed or fixed levels of capacity, allowing for more supplier capital investment planning
- Revenue sharing, profit sharing, or tariff reduction

- Commercial opportunities in related areas
- Opportunity for innovation.

Continuous improvement. Continuous improvement can take place in the performance of the contract, in the value for money received for products or services, in the supplier's operations as a whole, in the performance of the supplier's contract management team, or in the customer's own profit performance. Improvement does not equate to reduced costs alone at the expense of quality. Examples of continuous improvement include the following:

- Improved customer satisfaction as measured by independent surveys
- More efficient ways of providing the specified product or service
- Useful additions to the product or service
- Elimination of obsolete aspects of the product or service
- Use of new technologies
- Improvements in supplier or customer organization procedures or working practices
- Improvement in the interface between customer and supplier organizations.

Benefits based payments. Where the product or service is intended to support business change in the customer organization, payments should be linked as far as possible to customer objectives. Benefits based payments to suppliers are made dependent on the realization of benefits to the customer organization. The approach emphasizes collaboration on identifying opportunities, building a business case including calculating return on investment and articulating risks, and on program implementation. Payments are made for discrete work projects, reducing concerns about the guarantee of value for money over a period of time and attempting to predict future outcomes at the beginning of the contract.

Added value. Adding value means bringing something to a commercial transaction beyond what was originally envisaged in the contract. Added value can occur at three levels: new opportunities; innovation; and economy of scale or rationalization. Added value should be readily capable of identification through measurement against the contract.

Opportunity and risk management tool

A number of successful companies and organizations worldwide have found it useful to summarize all of their project-related opportunities and risks into a short, simple document, often just a few pages in length, called a project 'do-ability' analysis, which can be tailored and used by any organization to briefly summarize the opportunities and risks before or after an organization bids on said project. The project do-ability template in Figure 30.3 below was developed by Gregory A. Garrett, a member of the National Contract Management Association, as part of an opportunity and risk management methodology.

Project Do-ability Analysis

Project Manager Do-ability Assessment   Yes [   ]   No [   ]

Executive Summary

Project Name:

Customer:

Location(s):   Estimated Revenue in US $:

Start Date: Completion Date:

Prepared by: Phone #:

Fax: E-mail:

Excerpted from G Garrett, <u>Contract Management</u>, April 2005 (National Contract Management Association)

(1) Describe the project requirements/deliverables.

(2) Evaluate the project techniacal requirements, availability, and research and development.

(3) Evaluate the feasibility of the project schedule. (Attach milestone schedule.)

(4) Evaluate the reasonableness of the project financial commitments.
     (Attach the Project Business Case.)

(5) Conduct high-level risk assessment. Consider the following risks if appropriate:
     pricing, payment terms, acceptance, waaranty, liability, R&D, implementation, environmental, etc.
     (Attach the Risk Management Plan.)

(6) Describe significant assumptions implicit in the evaluation of the technical, schedule, and financial
     commitments.

(7) Assess the skills of the selected project team members (experience, education, training, professional
     certifications, strenghts, and weaknesses).

(8) Executive assessment of project:

     Do-able: Yes [   ]   No [   ]

Figure 30.3   Project 'do-ability' analysis

CHAPTER 31

Monitoring performance, tools and techniques

31.1 Introduction

The transition triggered by contract signature establishes roles and responsibilities, and processes and reviews are established. Areas of risk or uncertainty have been explored and are either resolved or the subject of ongoing review. So now, contract managers are monitoring and managing and that means a role to observe, supervise, review and maintain course. This will be done though specific measurement or testing; your goal is to maintain control and ensure that the project is moving at the anticipated speed and cost toward the accepted scope. The objective of good performance management is to ensure that a proactive governance model is implemented early on and there is effective use of metrics to determine potential issues going forward.

In many companies, performance management only becomes visible when things start to go wrong. It is then that poor or ineffective contract management is exposed and the following types of questions arise:

- Why didn't you warn us?
- Where are your records and correspondence so we can clearly illustrate that the other side is at fault?
- If the other side is not at fault, what were you doing?
- If the other side is at fault, shouldn't you have spotted it sooner and taken steps to avoid the problem?

But this view of performance management is focused solely on compliance and ignores improvements and growth opportunities – it is retroactive and reactive in design and nature.

Best practice contract management is more proactive and includes frequent progress reviews at all levels of management. Senior leadership expects their skilled contract management resources to:

- Clearly define and schedule reporting processes to accurately reflect progress, issues, contract growth, overruns, schedule slippage, and new exposures.
- Track data points methodically and exactly.
- Ensure there are mechanisms in place that provide early warning of downstream problems. (Remember that reliable warning signs can be seen in the data as early as the 10 percent mark.)
- Identify opportunities to improve results faster or cheaper, increase value or scope.
- Ensure all members of the contract implementation teams are aware of the aspects of the contract that are relevant for them.

In this chapter, we're going to explore the process and the practices that underpin all these items.

31.2 The contract management role

The role of the contract manager is to maintain contractual integrity and ensure that a specific project stays within the agreed contractual framework. This requires contract managers supporting business teams on the supplier side or on the customer side to increase business volumes, reduce costs and educate the respective teams in the commercial aspects of the project. Experience shows that many successful contract managers have some level of legal training along with business acumen, or have extensive experience as business professionals, paired with fundamental negotiating experience.

If contract management quality is high, there should be a successful implementation of processes encompassing the entire contract lifecycle within an organization. Once the role is well established, business surprises and contract disputes should occur with less frequency because quality processes include regular monitoring and recording of progress, especially around incidents that could affect performance and commercial results. Additional success factors are integration of contract managers as trusted business advisors in their own organization as well as regular and effective communication between the contract managers on both sides. A common goal, aside from a successful implementation, is to avoid unpleasant surprises.

There is no standard definition of contract management, neither does a uniform understanding of the contract management role exist. The responsibilities, skills, experience, and sourcing for the role are shaped by the organization and industry of the business. Depending upon the company, some of the activities described below might be executed by project office staff rather than the contract manager. It is, however, imperative that the contract manager ensures that the necessary activities are performed regardless as to whether he or she is actually performing them themselves.

At a recent conference, a project expert described the contract management role as falling into one of three categories:

- The administrator, who is concerned about monitoring milestones and compliance with the negotiated agreement from a contractual and commercial perspective and is driven by events
- The manager, who focuses primarily on the contributions of the relevant resources and achieving contract goals
- The entrepreneur, who is proactively looking to develop and help grow the opportunity provided by the project

Best practice contract management puts in place automated systems to address the administrative and much of the managerial dimensions to enable the right degree of focus on the more challenging managerial and entrepreneurial aspects.

Make sure that you have considered the scope of activities needed to be performed by contract management professionals and have a plan and process in place for each. It is important to clarify, document and communicate the objectives of the contract management team and distinguish these from the responsibilities and functions of other parts of the organization. The understanding of the role of the contract manager by the business, and with other internal groups with whom the contract manager interfaces, is a key factor in determining the success of the role. This should encompass not only the items to be performed but also the aspects that contract management will not discharge either because they are not relevant or someone else is responsible for them.

Contract management is undertaken because, without professional oversight, terms and conditions will often be ignored, the underlying intent is not achieved, or required updates and amendments are overlooked. In itself, that would imperil the project and probably the business cases of each party, but there's more to it than that. No contract or project plan is perfect and added to these imperfections, circumstances change, whether as a result of the business environment, requirements evolving or being better understood or a combination of any of these factors. This means there will be new risks and new opportunities. So you have to assume that during a contract's lifetime, there will be changes, disputes, claims and counterclaims, as well as exciting new opportunities to be explored and potentially developed.

The organizational objective is to achieve the original vision and goals at the very least and if possible exceed them. The chances of doing that are dramatically increased with a robust and certain base, maintained through the contract life, against which performance is assessed, changes are agreed and risks and rewards adjudicated. That base is primarily provided through the contract and the associated contract management processes. Remember a key goal in having a contract is to control risk; this is also a fundamental declared aim of project management. Ignoring or failing to update the contract introduces and fails to manage risks, potentially leading to negative commercial consequences.

31.3   Post award contract management activities

Schedule, Cost and Scope are the trinity of contract and project management. If one is changed, it is likely to affect at least one of the other two and this is considered further in Chapter 32: *Change control and management*. In this chapter the focus is on the following primary contract management duties:
- Schedule and performance management
- Quality control through managing the deliverable review and acceptance process in accordance with the contract.
- Data management and recording
- Invoicing and payment tracking
- Cost management and reporting
- Document management

Schedule and performance management

It will be important for all contracting parties to monitor and record compliance with roles and responsibilities, and to keep them aligned with the expected outcomes. Examples include:
- Due dates including dependencies, key assumptions and risk mitigations
- Customer/supplier supplied data or equipment
- Scheduled or required meetings or reviews
- Obligations to advise, inform or train others
- Obligations to have or provide facilities or specific operating conditions
- Obligations to provide updated lists of files, locations, users, interfaces, software licenses, etc.
- Obligations to invoice or pay
- Obligations relating to timeliness of deliverables review and acceptance timelines and procedures
- Obligations on meeting quality, service levels and other defined metrics

As there's always the risk of not meeting the expected outcomes, the provision of addressing performance problems and missed outcomes needs to be documented.

If these types of things were deemed important enough to document in the contract as responsibilities, someone considered they were critical to performance. Failure to monitor and report not only jeopardizes results, but also loses a potential lever in the event of claims or disputes. From a best practice viewpoint, technology lends itself to most effectively capturing and monitoring the list above, as well as reporting and escalating, will be key in ensuring performance against the contract and meeting the business objectives of the contracting parties. This has to be done after perusal of the contract and proper identification of all the notices, actions, risks, flow-downs and doubts or inconsistencies that might occur.

Monitoring schedules

Internal and external performance should be managed against a range of contract requirements and indicators, also known as key performance indicators (KPIs). KPIs are the predefined indicators that provide an accurate assessment of the status of the project. These can include milestones that can be scheduled dates or deliverables, specific responsibilities and agreed service level targets. The report structure will have been established in implementation and it should be real-time if possible, making use of web-based systems. There should also be quality controls making sure it is complete and accurate. For example, reporting should include spot checks or cross-reporting systems.

The reporting structure and process should be kept under review to ensure it is meeting its intended objectives and modify it if it isn't working or if there are new data needs. Management reports are fundamental to measuring, monitoring and controlling performance as well as the ability to identify problems and take early, pre-emptive action. The touchstone in assessing what data should be collected to ensure that it will help identify causes rather than symptoms, as it is causes that must be addressed when problems are detected. Otherwise, those problems and the associated disputes are likely to be overwhelming.

For instance, if a target date is expected to be missed or was missed and/or the deliverable was accepted on a later date, the schedule may now be recorded as changed by the other side. The missed date may have been deemed as revised because of the lack of compliance with the timeline and the acceptance of the deliverable, and future deliverable dates need to be changed to reflect the new schedule. So in this case, failure to monitor and report the slippage results in a new timeline for one party that may not be acceptable to the other party. But if the incident was not noted, or the deliverable review and acceptance processes and timelines written into the contract were ignored and more milestones went by, any recourse based on the initial slippage is severely weakened.

A deliverable that comes in late and misses its scheduled date should always be looked at closely. But deliverables or milestones that are achieved early should also be looked at closely. Missed dates could be good or bad for the project depending on the reasons behind the date change. For example, a switch in technology that will be more beneficial than the original specified could have caused the late date. Or poor planning and estimating could have been the cause for the early delivery and the schedule accuracy for the duration of the project is now in doubt.

All dates should be tracked and results communicated as they occur. If a date is missed, whether early or late, it is a point that should be discussed and resolved and downstream timelines re-evaluated and changed if needed. From a best practice standpoint, there are a number of leading project management tools available that can be used, in conjunction with team collaboration sites where real time updates are distributed, thereby ensuring all stakeholders are aware of the current status. Escalations should be built into the process with a clear path for resolution. In addition, each critical task should have a fallback provision on what happens if it doesn't get done on time (what are the impacts?) as well as any contingency actions. Thinking all of this through upfront will help mitigate the inherent risks and increase the chances of success.

Monitoring performance

Much of performance monitoring is communication, either to the contract manager or from the contract manager. The list of activities in this section is not exhaustive, given the variety of contracts and associated projects, but can be viewed as a core onto which contract specific actions can be added. One common theme throughout performance monitoring is communication. If you start with the end in mind, and communicate the goals of the contract, setting up the monitoring mechanisms to achieve those goals becomes easier.

A clear and unambiguous view of expectations between the contracting parties is critical, and should always be aligned with business requirements, which themselves change over time. Without this, you will move into uncertainty and dispute. This clarity gives you the ability to promptly recognize and respond to variations and mitigate or avoid cost overruns or delays. Remember that the contract briefing document, or a version of it, can be used to articulate clear expectations and to monitor and check for changed conditions.

Take a moment to think about your organization:
- What mechanisms are in place to monitor and track performance?
- Do they support the goals of your contracts?
- Do they allow for protection against changing requirements and their impact on the contract?
- Do they reveal opportunities or only problems?
- What might the organization do differently?

The best advice is to keep the number of metrics to be measured to a minimum number of relevant, performance indicative dimensions. Using this approach, it will not only be manageable, the organization will have clear data to make continuous improvements.

When monitoring performance, you can exploit quality variations in the organization's favor to achieve incremental benefits or budget savings by ensuring their retention. Sometimes good things happen unexpectedly and those achievements can be used as trade-offs later, or to set the new standard. For example, while developing and installing an order entry system for a company, the supplier's programmer put in additional features that were not in the specifications, but seemed obvious to them. It took very little time and did not affect the schedule. The supplier management was going to have the enhancements backed out but was persuaded not to do so. The contract manager was smart enough to maintain full records of this incident. The users were pleased with the results and later, when a requested feature could not be implemented, accepted the earlier features as a trade-off. Both sides won, and a possible dispute was avoided.

Performance management

Another area of performance management to consider and track is performance of the product or service itself. Part of performance management is to ensure that contractual obligations are being met. Some of the more difficult deliverable areas to measure and manage are:

- Obligations to advise, inform or train others
- Obligations to have or provide facilities or specific operating conditions
- Obligations to provide updated lists of files, locations, users, interfaces, software licenses, and documentation
- Obligations to be fulfilled by the other party

These obligations are even trickier to manage if they have not been clearly defined and documented, which is why it's very important to ensure requirements, deliverables, obligations, assumptions and dependencies are clearly documented and articulated.

For example, to what level are the trainees to be trained? Is it a one-size-fits-all program or customized? Is everyone supposed to perform at the same level or attain at least baseline knowledge? How do you measure and assure training performance or performance after training? Are there any pre-requisites for the trainees before they should attend the training?

An obligation to provide facilities or operating conditions is another difficult area that requires close examination. Perhaps the agreement calls for a development facility to be provided that reflects the location where the product or service will eventually be installed or performed. Since no two facilities are exactly the same, how do you determine if the development facility provided is compliant? Will the product or service developed elsewhere function as anticipated in the customer environment, and how do you ensure that before installation? Obviously the terms around performance should be in the contract, but it is the contract manager's job to ensure that performance expectations and obligations will be met, or request a formal change.

Another deliverable that can be a source for concern is data. There are many attributes to data. Let's look at a few.

First, let's imagine you are expecting data in a specific format and if the other side does not deliver in that format, the project suffers. The contract has simply specified that the data must be 'useable', but the supplier's definition of useable and yours do not align exactly. You must work with the supplier to align the data definition as you progress so that the business will be able to use the data as delivered. Obviously, the sooner a situation like this is identified the better, so early close monitoring and performance trials or pilots will be key to success.

As another data example, the supplier is responsible for transitioning a customer's data from the legacy format to the supplier system format during a system upgrade. But the customer fails to provide the data in a way that the supplier can use. Both parties must work to resolve the mismatch quickly in order to preserve the contract timeline and identify the consequences of the mismatch.

Finally, consider the installation of a complex system that will eventually be maintained in-house. All of the operational documentation should be accurate, including the list of all source code and files that are used to run the system. All of the details about how it all ties together with your legacy systems will also be important. A contract manager is unlikely to be able to verify the comprehensiveness of the documentation provided and will, therefore, need to ensure the operational team has mechanisms in place to perform this verification.

Risk and issue recording and resolution

It is worth remembering that the contract manager's role is not about being able to show what and how it was the fault of others that things went wrong, nor of masking reality and pretending that everything went right. The contract manager is successful if surprises and disputes are avoided.

Whenever your reports or analysis indicate that something is operating out of line, take it seriously. Don't simply wait to see whether it's repeated in a future month, since by then it may be too late to take effective corrective action. Capture it early and analyze the issue. If necessary, engage other team members and experts. Make issues visible and have proposed solutions at hand. Take appropriate action and ensure there's an interim report, to show whether this is an indicator of an ongoing problem or whether it was just an anomaly.

It's critical that contract risks and issues are identified early, that they're incorporated into action item lists, that there is ownership for their oversight and a potential resolution and (of course) that there is consideration early on whether and when escalation may be required.

Problem tracking can be as simple or as sophisticated as your organization's systems and culture will allow. Software packages are available that track issues by automatically issuing a number and providing preset fields to capture all of the relevant information, and provide workflow capability so that items can be assigned to individuals or groups to investigate or resolve. Or it can be a simple worksheet that has a numbering system and columns to capture the data necessary.

This is a list of typical data on a tracking form for contractual risks:
- Risk or Issue number
- Reported date
- Reported by
- Status (i.e.: Open, Closed, Hold, Pending, etc.)
- Risk or Issue Description (this can be two fields – one short and one long)
- Person Responsible (either owner of the issue, or owner of the resolution)
  - If a Risk, assessment of probability and impact
  - If an Issue, assessment of impact
- Subject Matter Experts required to contribute
- Other party's Person Responsible (if applicable)
- Other party's expected position (if applicable)
  - Status and next action required
- Resolution
- Resolution Date

It is best that the parties to the contract track risks and issues on the same forms and formats. This may not always be possible and in such situations where this can't be avoided, it is essential to establish a mechanism to cross-reference all parties' issues and periodically verify that each side has the same items captured. It will be up to the contract manager to determine if full list view-ability is open to the other side, since your issues such as internal financial impacts may be tracked in a form that is not relevant to the other party or inappropriate for them to see.

Another thing to remember is that contract risk and issue management responsibility has a tendency to bounce around. For example, the customer reports a bug in a program that is being installed. The supplier puts a patch on their site for the customer to download and install, and provides installation instructions. The responsibility has changed at least twice so far for this one problem. It could keep bouncing back and forth until the final fix is installed and proved to work. If sight is lost of who is responsible at any point in time, things may break down and turn into larger issues.

Again, make sure that problems are identified and addressed quickly and that the status of all open risks and issues, and who is responsible for their resolution, is known at all times.

Tracking deliverables and acceptance

Another critical topic in contract management is the subject of deliverables and their acceptance. The term 'deliverable' will be used in this chapter to cover both:

- Tasks to be completed or documents to be communicated not requiring any formal acceptance
- Deliverables which have to be checked for their compliance with specifications by the other party and if determined to be compliant, to be formally accepted.

Your job involves ensuring that the deliverable review and acceptance terms and conditions in the contract are correctly operated and consistently enforced, recording and monitoring the various schedule dates and milestones to ensure that when something is due that it has actually been completed and submitted. Best practice contract management will perform three additional key things:

- Determine exactly what should be monitored and how, what the contractual basis for that deliverable is and what the acceptance criteria are for that deliverable according to the contract, including the time allowed in the contract for its verification and approval by the other side
- Determine exactly who needs to be involved, which interaction is required in order to be confident that the goal will be achieved;
- Determine a fallback position or action plan for when a concern arises.

All of these will be driven by asking 'what if' questions and understanding the likely causes or reasons for failure. Additionally, watch out for changing conditions as these would trigger further 'what if' questions and preparation for their possible consequences.

Examples of changing conditions that might cause concern include:

- Negative financial results
- Shifts in market strategy or direction
- Volatile markets
- Mergers or acquisitions
- Changes in key management or personnel
- New competitors or product innovation

Acceptance is one of the most fundamental and potentially contentious issues a contract manager will face. In complex long-term agreements, acceptance will usually be attained at major milestones or intervals, with stage payments often linked to acceptance. In such cases, acceptance may simply mean testing or validating that development is on track, rather than physically transferring goods or product.

At each acceptance, the parties must have agreement on what was required, based on the specifications and requirements documented in the contract - or agreed additional aspects if not stated in sufficient detail yet. Does the product or service meet these requirements? Are the requirements accurately and unambiguously detailed in the contract? What seemed very clear at the time of negotiation and implementation is often less so by the time acceptance is upon you. And the accepting party may be facing changed circumstances that have altered their requirements or need.

If the circumstances have changed, the contract may allow for some of these changes or they may have to be negotiated as revisions. To eliminate the risk of a deliverable not being accepted, it's critical that the contract is kept current and modified by each party to reflect the updated requirements to meet the expectations of both parties.

Then there is the question of what constitutes acceptance and the consequences of non-acceptance. What must a supplier do to remedy shortcomings? What was agreed in the contract, what is the governing legal frame? What must the customer do if a product or service is fundamentally compliant? Is partial acceptance allowed? Should it be agreed via contract change? All of these issues should have been embedded in the contract or may be provided by the applicable legal framework. (See Chapter 19: *Terms and conditions overview* for more information, as well as Chapter 34: *Contract close-out and lessons learned* for discussion of final acceptance.)

It's incumbent on the contract manager to be familiar with all the elements of acceptance and to highlight issues. Whole teams of players and sponsors may have changed since the project began or the contract was signed. Even the current contract manager may be different from the original individual in the role. This is why comprehensive documentation of deliverable requirements, the deliverable review and acceptance process and well-structured databases are essential. It will still be your responsibility to sort out the key deliverables and acceptance criteria. If you find yourself in this type of situation, validate at every change of personnel what the acceptance criteria and delivery schedules are; and if documentation is unclear or lacking, insist on setting or obtaining clear written expectations.

When a specific acceptance is imminent, you must refresh your memory on the exact provisions and the content and expertise concerned. In addition to any specific performance criteria, you'll need to advise on what will constitute or drive acceptance. For documentation purposes, written communication is preferable, even if not explicitly foreseen by the contract.

- Is partial or deemed acceptance an option given by the contract or applicable law? If so, what does this mean in terms of payment, retention and supplier obligations?
- Does the contract require specific performance?
- Under what circumstances, if any, can a supplier refuse to make good on any defects or shortfalls?
- Are there criteria to apply to certain levels of deviation that lead to acceptance on provision of a specified amount of liquidated damages?
- Is there a warranty or fit-for-use clause that can alter acceptance?

Let's look at three of those areas in slightly more detail. First, let's explore acceptance by inaction, where failure to indicate rejection is deemed to be acceptance under the contract terms. This arrangement might sometimes be more favorable to suppliers than to customers. From a supplier's point of view, this is desirable since it places the onus firmly on the customer to ensure that the necessary reviews and approvals are undertaken and that communication occurs as required in the contract. From the customer's perspective, deemed acceptance can be desirable to compel organizational compliance and timeliness if deadlines are tight. Depending on the type of contract and scope, it might even be negative for the supplier if the interaction of the customer is not happening: it increases the risk of exponentially increasing impacts if the supplier continued without interaction.

Secondly, let's look at the area of partial acceptance. If the contract required specific performance and allowed partial acceptance, the supplier may accept a major risk. The supplier must provide precisely what it says in the contract, regardless of the cost or implications of achieving that particular series of performance parameters. It's something that most suppliers are going to resist during negotiations, but may be allowed in new development projects. Specific performance is something that is a very high-risk response for suppliers, particularly in a highly customized deal. If specific performance was accepted, you need to be driving the particular commitments and achievement of those goals.

Thirdly, acceptance of individual milestones may be a good option in complex projects, requiring huge pre-investment of the supplier and intense interaction by both supplier and customer to ensure alignment and to reach the agreed goals. Benefits are earlier payment pro-rata if agreed, linked to reaching milestones, with the customer having the opportunity and responsibility of influencing or correcting the progress of the project by accepting or not accepting a milestone.

Sometimes a contract will give latitude for improvements. For example, if development is extended over a long period of time and industry standards are changing fast, the contract may include some benchmarks that come into effect at the time of acceptance. Perhaps the solution will meet industry standards, or will represent a leadership role in industry standards. If that's the case, you need to ensure that those standards have been defined, are measurable and have been measured, and the relevant data has been collected and updated, so that you know precisely what you're looking for at the time of acceptance. Conversely, industry standards that are not clearly defined or linked to a certain date carry the commercial risk for the supplier that calculated effort may not be sufficient to meet industry standards that have changed in the course of the project.

If you are using industry standards, you must define what industry you are referring to, and ideally provide a list of companies that you will use as benchmarks. (Even better is to list those applicable standards from international organizations or standards bodies.) Will they only be customers of the supplier or customers of competitors as well? How will the data be gathered and validated?

Where and under what operating conditions acceptance will occur is also critical. Is it an operational period of, say, a week, a day, a month, or quarter, or year-end? Is it a requirement to fully operate in a specific customer's live business unit or only under optimal test conditions at the supplier's own site?

The duration of the test period, measurement criteria and methods that will be used must be noted and planned for. Overall this is a high-risk area for both parties. The supplier has significant costs and reputation at stake. The customer has a significant business requirement to meet and has similarly made a major investment in success.

One approach to obtaining acceptance is for the subject matter expert stakeholders or user groups themselves to develop and conduct final acceptance testing, under the guidance of the project team, using real live examples and work experience. This allows the end users to be included and feel ownership, paving the way for acceptance. It also lends credibility to the testing, as the product will perform the business function that it was intended to. However, there is a downside risk if you have not provided the subject matter experts with enough forewarning to prepare adequately, or training in the product, or support in developing a valid testing methodology.

Managing invoicing and payments

A subject that is very closely related to acceptance is invoice submission and payment. This is a critical issue for both parties in terms of timing, accuracy, frequency and amounts. In a project, the supplier, or customer, or both, could have significant financial commitments at stake. It is imperative that both sides are tracking the invoicing and payment process and results. Neither side should be ignoring their responsibilities in this area. Invoices should be prepared in accordance with applicable requirements in the contract, and payments made as agreed. Any dependencies on service levels, credits, or milestones should be clearly documented with minimal room for errors in interpretation.

In general, the customer wants to retain its money for as long as possible to limit its risk and maximize the incentive for supplier performance. This is accomplished by tying final or stage payments to acceptance. It may require the supplier to make a significant investment and finance a high-risk development, trusting that the customer will operate with complete honesty and integrity and not try to avoid eventual payment. For example, a payment dispute may arise because circumstances have changed, resulting in the customer using less volume than anticipated and agreed on; or due to a change in customer business needs, this particular application or solution is no longer really needed in their business at all. As long as the supplier is complying with the requirements and specifications in the contract and obtaining acceptance for each deliverable as required by the contract, the customer would not have any grounds to dispute the invoice and withhold payment.

The contract will specify the basic principles under which payment will occur, the high-level process of invoicing, the amounts to be charged, and the frequency or events that are going to trigger payments. Specific procedures should have been agreed in the contract implementation reviews, and it's these procedures that you are now managing. It's essential that the contract manager ensures compliance with whatever was agreed. Failure to pay creates a wide range of exposures including a reasonable basis for a supplier to cease or delay work. At the very least, it will create issues of trust and integrity that may damage the relationship.

Increasingly, especially in the US, supplier attitudes toward payment terms are driven by revenue recognition rules. They are reluctant to accept any conditionality or potential for retention or refund, since this affects their ability to book revenue. This is covered in more detail in Chapter 19: *Terms and conditions overview.*

Payment methods

There are four basic models for payment, ranging from payment in advance to payment on results. They can represent massive differences in terms of timing and risk. And as mentioned, in these days of revenue recognition regulations, they also have dramatic impacts on the supplier's ability to report revenue and profit.

Each payment method has its own complexities. Many contracts have a hybrid system, using some or all of the methods shown. This means that the risks can be shared and performance incentives remain in place. For example, payment on results often represents the supplier's profit and is based on usage rates or consistent performance against targets or goals. Some level of continuing payment is entirely consistent with stage payments or acceptance payments, and provides basic cost recovery.

Payment can be used as an incentive tool, in a 'carrot and stick' strategy. If getting paid is difficult, it is a major disincentive for the supplier, but having some retained payment, which drives good performance and cooperation is important to the customer. For example, if you were working under an installment plan, you would want to have prompt payments along the way as milestones are met and achieved, to keep the supplier interested in servicing you, and hold back final payment until your acceptance criteria have been met. How long retention occurs and the conditions for release will vary, but if there are long-term performance goals, it should incentivise the supplier in achieving these. The customer can also consider bonus payments as a possible incentive to have a supplier exceed expectations by either delivering early or achieving higher service levels.

Any conditionality that applies to payments requires specific consideration. Is there potential recourse where recovery of some or all of the payments made is possible, in which case the supplier cannot recognize the revenue? The issue of payment is a significant study area in its own right and is covered in detail in Chapter 19: *Terms and conditions overview*.

For the contract manager the key issue is to know exactly what terms and process have been established and then to ensure compliance. The major issues for contract managers are to make sure that stage payments, or payments on results, reflect milestones achieved or costs actually incurred and that invoices reflect work that was performed. The payments should also include any applicable non-performance offsets that are credited. Again, the better payment provisions are articulated in detail in the contract, the better the project will proceed. Communication is paramount, especially in this case, since payments are one of the key reasons for the work being performed in the first place. Specific attention should be given to any bank guarantee that may be provided as a condition of payment.

Measurement and valuation

In general, under payment management, customers will be responding to supplier invoices but there may be occasions when customers initiate payments without a discrete invoice. In addition to validating the fact that there has been an event that justifies payment, such as a service delivery or milestone achieved, you will need to ensure that the payment accurately reflects the value provided. Check that the project has progressed to a specified level or that services were delivered in the volume stated in the contract - not just that the date has passed.

If the contract is being performed on a time and materials basis and not tied to milestone events or completion of deliverables, the customer will need to check to ensure that the hours invoiced are accurate and that the rates being applied are consistent with what is allowable under the contract. In all circumstances, the customer should pay according to the provisions in the contract.

The contract may be established as a value management arrangement where the value of the work is only accepted at set points. Let's look at a simple example. A customer has contracted with a supplier for the painting of a new warehouse building and agrees to 25 percent payment on the start day, 25 percent upon completion of the interior painting expected to occur after one week, 25 percent payment upon completion of the exterior painting expected to be completed after two weeks, and the final 25 percent upon completion of inspection and sign-off by both parties.

The customer wouldn't send the painter a payment when 50 percent of the time has elapsed, because the relevant stage of work might not be complete. If it has rained for the entire period, it is highly unlikely that any exterior painting of the warehouse was accomplished. In this case half of the fees – the 25 percent for the exterior painting combined with the final 25 percent payment – is tied to satisfactory performance. As a customer or prime contractor, always make sure that final payment is adequate to incentivize timely performance or completion of the specified work by the supplier or the subcontractor.

While managing costs, be clear whether performance penalties can be retained from payments due such as service credits or liquidated damages. Analyze and understand the contract and process that was agreed to handle this. Be aware of the rules that apply in different regulatory environments, affecting payment rights and obligations. If you are managing the payment activity across national borders or overseeing remote staff with that responsibility, you need to question the enforceability of the contract terms or procedures in each jurisdiction. Be careful that you don't compromise your dispute or claim by failing to comply with invoicing or payment terms.

It is advisable for contract managers to be aware of the main challenges around payment and ensure that the invoicing and payment process that is implemented has minimized the likelihood and frequency of delay, disruption and dispute, and is simplified. This will help preclude the unnecessary absorption of resources and additional administrative effort that is manual and costly. Expect that issues will arise about the timeliness and accuracy of invoices, the verification of their receipt, content and processing for payment, the resolution of disputed payments, and service credits or retentions, and plan accordingly.

Cost management

Part of cost management is payment management, but cost management goes beyond that. Cost management starts before the contract is signed, in the Bid and Negotiation phases, and continues throughout the contract lifecycle. Cost management in the Manage phase revolves around the execution of the agreement and good project management.

Having or providing the right tools and resources for a particular assignment is a cost management activity. Load balancing and resource management is another tool. Managing to KPIs is also a cost management tool, as you maintain focus on the end result and avoid distractions. Having a robust system that enables easy budgeting and tracking is yet another cost management tool.

One of the best cost management tools available to you in the Manage phase is an effective contract change management process. If changes are not controlled and contract changes (including scope, schedule and pricing impacts) effectively documented and agreed to in a timely manner, costs will increase. (Chapter 32: *Change control and management* provides more information on this topic.)

Document management

Experience shows that formal communication between parties can be difficult, or can even lead to conflict. Reassuring statements of key personnel made towards the other party might be interpreted as binding confirmation and go beyond their original intention. Best practice recommends that there is a process to ensure involvement of the stakeholders before formal communication is provided. In this context the contract management team should cross-check contractual positions and current claims. All formal communication must be properly recorded and documented. Special attention should be given to the timely issue and recording of any notice requested in the contract.

Records and documentation

Filing of records in one place is critical to performance. Ideally this should be an electronic file that is simple to use and consistent in convention. Web-based or intranet systems can be effective repositories and there are a variety of tools available. How documents are saved, where they are saved, and the naming conventions used are very important. Others must be able to find the records they need with minimal effort. If the contract manager is not in control of entering all documents, ensure the system is understood and followed by other team members. It is customary for the contract manager to be responsible for retaining relevant contract documents and records and to ensure items are kept safely and securely, in accordance with operational, legal and tax retention requirements.

When negative performance or progress variations are identified, the contract manager should develop and agree on a plan for them to be remedied. The key aspect of this plan is a joint commitment to improve performance, or eliminate the variance. The plan should be monitored and measured for effectiveness. The ability to make progress may be jeopardized if the contracting parties don't agree on the facts and lack sufficient documentation.

A simple example would be a reservation system that fails regularly for extended periods of time, hampering its customer's business. The customer has decided to issue a claim for service credits based on the outage durations and the service cost. If either party does not have a reliable record of up-time, down-time and failures, it is clearly at a disadvantage in achieving reconciliation or filing or challenging a claim or dispute.

While differences of opinion are inevitable at times, you can reduce their frequency and severity considerably by having appropriate documentation in place. This is essential, as proof of intent, evidence of actual performance, agreement of changes or revisions, proof of current or past claims. Ultimately, if the contracting parties can't reach agreement, the accessibility of the contracting records and documentation will be fundamental to any arbitration, mediation or litigation. The contracting party without solid evidence and facts is exposed and at risk. It is the contract manager's job to build the files and maintain the records that constitute the evidence required.

Let's look at the elements needed.

The data file
Your documentary records should include:
- Request for Proposal (RFP), Request for Information (RFI) and all amendments
- Response(s) to RFPs and RFIs
- Contracts and agreements (including changes), often referred to as the 'contractual baseline'
  Selection criteria and rationale
- Progress reports
- Testing plans and results
- Acceptance criteria, metrics and letters.
- Copy of deliverables
  - Notices of deliverable submission
  - Notice of customer acceptance, comments and/or rejection of deliverables
- Payment authorizations
- User communications / complaints
- Contact / meeting summaries and minutes
- Action item / resolution list
  - Notices of any nature that are sent or received pursuant to the contract
- Dispute, claim records, change history and documentation
- Communications around contract change requests and variations to contract.

These are the documentary records that should be included in the contract management virtual file. The specific list may vary by the nature of the contract and in accordance with the organization's internal rules and policies. The contract should spell out what documents, agreements, appendices, and attachments constitute the contract.

Generally speaking, the customer organization typically wants to incorporate the supplier's response to the RFP into the contract. Suppliers tend to resist this approach for a variety of reasons, but a principal concern is that a proposal is often written as a sales document and not as a contract. It is important to know whether the proposal is or is not part of the contract. The proposal is a critical document and should be included in contract records, whether or not it is incorporated into the contract.

Throughout the lifetime of the contract, the contract manager should monitor and maintain records of progress reports, meeting minutes and other communications, particularly those between the contract or project managers for the contracting parties.

Building good documentation discipline is something that should be initiated from the outset. It is advisable for the contract manager to put an end to informal discussions for which no real record is maintained and to preclude the situation of the other party having a distinct advantage because they have access to contract records that your organization has not maintained. In the event of dispute, the party with the most comprehensive records typically prevails. This may seem simple and obvious but the number of organizations that fail to maintain full and accurate records is astoundingly high. In surveys, corporations admit that up to 10 percent of their contracts are lost and as many as 30 percent are hard to find.

31.4 Status reviews: internal

There will be a variety of formal reviews occurring over the lifetime of the project, and the frequency should be decided at the outset. Precisely what review sessions are held and which ones you are involved in will vary by the nature of the contract, the nature of the project manager and their particular approach and style. However, the contract manager needs to make sure that there are internal reviews on a regular basis. These will often be via conference calls, webcasts or other methods as well as physical reviews between some of the key stakeholders and the leaders of the different elements of the deal. At the very least, the contract manager should be having a monthly contract review; they should establish a schedule for this very early on in the project and ensure that it is maintained and followed.

The meeting schedule can drive the contract manager's reporting cycles and associated analysis. The contract manager should attend these meetings and ensure that those who are required to provide input - that is, those who have specific actions or responsibilities – are prepared. It is advisable for the contract manager to maintain the issues list and distribute it before the meeting for the project members to update and return, or at least, be prepared to discuss. Make sure the meetings are given priority and do not defer the meetings. Such behavior sends the negative message that these meetings are optional and monitoring performance is not important.

Of course, there must be focus on those items that are not going well and need corrective action. Give key indicators briefly, and then move to items under threat, actions planned or recommended. The contract manager should use the opportunity to review actions and get support or resources, or to identify need for help in planning actions, using these sessions to explore potential opportunities. Do not focus solely on the things that are going wrong; include time to identify things that are going right and things that could go even better.

Do not fall into the trap of waiting for a scheduled meeting to report critically bad news. If an off-schedule review is called for, then organize it. Remember people don't like surprises, especially unpleasant ones.

31.5 Status reviews: external

The contract manager must also organize and participate in regular reviews with other contracting parties. Like internal reviews, the style and approach to these will vary. It depends on the style of the project manager, or deal owner, what was agreed between the organizations and the severity of the issues to be addressed. There may be occasions when the contract manager wants to have specific reviews directly with the contract staff from the other party. There will be other occasions when this will be a sub- element of the overall project review meetings. Either way, the contract manager needs to make sure that their team is prepared and briefed and to have a very clear set of agenda items and opportunities to be discussed.

Unfortunately, it is easy for external reviews to slip due to internal pressures or to spend time on unnecessary items. Basic progress reporting should be automated. Review sessions should be structured and discuss:

- Out-of-line situations – that is, reporting on anything that is not progressing to plan (exception reporting)
- Concerns on items at risk and how they are to be fixed
- Changes and opportunities
- Issues for escalation
- What is going right and appreciated

As with any meeting, have an agenda that has been agreed before the meeting (to allow proper preparation), confirm who will attend, agree on any specific presentations or required reports/inputs in advance, and then follow it.

31.6 Typical issues and problems

Let's recap on some of the problems that are faced by most organizations and that affect their major contracts and projects. In any large complex corporation, especially one with multinational operations, such problems are inevitable. As a contracts professional, there are risk areas that the contract manager needs to have considered and planned for because they are issues of organization, management and process and therefore, in large part, something the contract manager can either control or manage. While technical issues are sometimes at the root of troubled projects, it is in fact more typically the business issues that cause significant problems or failure. This is true of customers and suppliers alike.

For example in a recent analysis one major supplier of complex services identified that more than 70 percent of claims and disputes could be tracked to issues with contract negotiation, implementation or associated management system and organizational conflicts. The types of issues we typically find are not really technical in nature. This is why the contract manager's business skills and awareness are critical and needed to undertake regular business assurance monitoring, covering the steps discussed in this chapter.

Although in this chapter there have been few direct references to subcontractors or partnering arrangements, the principles described apply equally to the management and control of such relationships. Multiple participants inevitably introduce greater complexity and risk of failure, together with the need for monitoring of back-to-back or complementary commitments and actions.

31.7 **Summary**

This section concludes with a reminder of the comments made in Chapter 28, *Manage phase overview*. Leading companies have made major investments in hiring and developing professional contract managers; they are mandating processes and building a global network, in terms of skills, software tools, communications and performance measurements and rewards.

Many supplier contract managers have direct incentives to grow the contract in terms of revenue and profit. It is a positive reflection on the contract manager to have the status and motivation to make decisions and care about customer satisfaction. It also implies that contract managers are poised to take advantage of any weaknesses, to protect their margins against customer claims and to resist unfavorable changes. Similarly, contract professionals in the customer company will be looking to minimize costs and extract maximum value, including avoidance of uplifts or additional charges.

The professional contract manager must discern and recognize the strength and commitment level of the other contracting party. If they have good contract management discipline, they will recognize the fact that they will be working to maximize their performance goals; if they have weak contract management discipline, there will be gaps. Some gaps may create risks in the project that could lead to project failure.

- The contract manager must maintain strong internal co-ordination and is encouraged to work closely with his/her contract management colleagues: Observe standard forms, processes and systems.
- Use the agreed tools and report accurately and on a timely basis.
- Report conversations, events, and communications in a comprehensive form.

These approaches will make the contract manager more valued, better informed and less absorbed by day-to-day problems, leading to best practice contract management that outpaces the performance levels in many other companies.

CHAPTER 32

Change control and management

32.1 Introduction

This chapter addresses the factors of change and will help you to understand how to assess, interpret and, if needed, control project changes and manage the implementation of agreed change or disagreed change that becomes a disputed change or more commonly known as a claim. It is presented in four sections:
- Understanding change, its effect and who may initiate it
- Designing and managing a change control process
- What is a contract claim?
- What to do when the parties to the contract do not want a change control process

32.2 The realities of change

There is a commonly held view in business that a contract should address every eventuality and document a clear, black and white, unchanging picture of the commercial relationship between the parties to the contract. Consequently change is often viewed as a problem and a failure. Experienced business people realize, however, that change is not about failure. In any complex situation or where a project extends over a long period of time, change is inevitable. Static conditions are very rare and may even indicate hidden risks. You should be worried if there isn't any change, since this would imply either weak controls, or lost opportunities or a highly regulated environment that limits choice and innovation. So within limits, change is inevitable and positive.

The major factors of change can be categorized as follows:
- Changing business needs – particularly prevalent in a medium to long-term contract
- Changing organization – the customer and/or supplier undergoes some form of restructuring whether due to merger, acquisition, new location or new products

- Technology shifts – technology develops continuously and it may be appropriate to leverage a particular development
- Organizational priorities change – the customer may consider other projects as being higher priority affecting key personnel, the money available or the timing
- New legislation or regulation – unavoidable external requirements over which no party to the contract has control
- Imperfect scope description – elements of the project's design and deliverables do not fully meet the defined need and require re-working.

This means that you will need a well-documented process under which changes will occur. It also means that a good understanding of the contract baseline is essential. If you do not understand the base, how do you know when it is changing?

Change is often a source of contention between parties, not least because it may negatively affect one or other of the parties. Regardless of the reason for the change, the quality of clear obligations and requirements, planning, implementation and the change process itself will be fully tested.

What is change?

When the contract is negotiated and signed, the complete requirements of the final contract documentation represents the agreed position between the parties – the customer and the supplier. Once the contract document is signed, any alterations, enhancements, deletions or substitutions are, therefore, changes.

The contract documentation naturally should include all obligations of the parties including requirements concerning program, technical specification, performance, and quality and applicable terms and conditions. It should also include a clear process for change management. Throughout the project delivery process changes will occur for one reason or another. The skill of the contract manager lies in having a comprehensive understanding of the contract and all of its obligations and requirements, together with being able to recognize changes and manage the change process throughout the lifecycle of the contract.

Change management reintroduces many of the skills and tactics of the original negotiation, with each side having different goals and objectives. For example, there may be concerns around financial consequences, timing or the possibility of trade-offs.

Examples of changes

When implementing the contract, consider the likely sources of change and monitor them. For example, will prices or charges potentially change and if so, what can cause this? Is user satisfaction important, or is there a volume or revenue commitment? Are markets volatile or is significant organizational change likely? Are there impending regulatory shifts? If you find that you are not on track, when might a change be necessary and what form might that take?

Your goal is to stay in control by preparing for change and avoiding surprises.

Let's look at some typical reasons for contract change:
- There may be errors or omissions in the contract documentation. While every effort is made to draft robust contract documentation, in large complex contracts errors or omissions can occur.
- The scope may change. Based on business needs either side may wish to increase, reduce or otherwise modify the scope of work to be carried out.
- There may be technical change. Either side may wish to change technical specifications. During a project of long duration, technology or service delivery capabilities or methods may alter significantly enough for one side or the other to request a change.
- One of the parties may invent something that changes the entire scope of the relationship and the method of delivery of its objectives.
- Timelines may change. The customer may wish to accelerate the project program, or the supplier may ask for more time to carry out their work or the customer may also postpone the start-up of the program or instruct a stop order for a temporary period.

Other parties may initiate a change, for example, the customer's customer, partners in a training agreement, major sub-suppliers.

Effect of change

A contract change generally has one or more of the following major impacts:
- Cost. The contract price may increase, decrease or remain unchanged. The change may, however affect the cost base of one or both parties to the contract either directly or indirectly.
- Program duration. This could decrease, or increase or remain unchanged.
- Supplier performance. This could improve or deteriorate. Key performance indicators (KPIs) and the results of monitoring the supplier performance to them may change. New KPIs may need to be established.
- Service Level Agreements (SLAs). These may not be met or could be alter ed to reflect changing customer requirements, so new SLAs may need to be established.
- Statement of Work (SOW). The SOW may need to be adjusted in terms of responsibilities, deliverables or milestones. If something happens that causes one of the parties to have to perform more work than originally planned or included in the original price structure, this would create a change to the scope of work that can be charged.

A change may also affect contract terms, intellectual property ownership or processes. In some cases it could even lead to a more innovative contract or partial or complete termination. For example, the prospect of a new design or technology being available could have a fundamental impact on the way a contract is delivered.

Even if it is agreed that a change has no visible effect on the contract terms it should still be recorded in accordance with the process; otherwise it might become a later source of dispute, or internal exposure - for example in an audit or executive review. These 'no impact' changes, when taken individually, may have no quantifiable impact, but taken in total they may actually accumulate to have a significant impact. Make sure your change control process reviews this type of change periodically to ensure you are not suffering cumulative effects, or failing your duty as a contract manager to ensure full recording and reporting.

Some companies adopt strict risk management principles to identify potential sources of changes that affect key deal components. Best practice anticipates change by proactive foresight of things that may happen and to ensure that your chosen interventions are timely, rather than allowing changes to become risks that turn into issues needing to be reactively managed.

Who can initiate change?

Some contracts detail restrictions to the ability to initiate change requests to specific aspects of the contract or to only one of the parties to the contract. More generally change requests may come from either side. The customer, or the supplier, or both, can initiate a contract change. The most important factor, however, is to understand who within either the customer's organization or the supplier's organization can initiate contract change or agree to contract change. You must ensure that the contract defines what form requests should take, where they should be sent, the process and authority by which they are reviewed and accepted or rejected, and the form that communication of the decision will take.

Usually the process and authorities will vary depending on the scope and consequences of the change. It is important to have these parameters clearly defined and communicated in both parties' organizations.

Include in the formal contract who has authority to initiate and agree to changes. If this clause is not in the contract, then make it absolutely clear in the project inaugural meeting, and record in writing which individuals have the authority. This may be in the form of a job title, rather than a specific name, as people change roles within organizations. At each project review meeting, there should be formal reporting on any change requests that were received outside the agreed process, and their status. Make note of the response and reiterate the change control process. Make notes of changes where there is a debate about whether the activity was included and of any interpretation issues relating to the SOW. There is a real risk that the change control process can be leveraged financially; this breaks down trust and confidence and leads to contention.

If contract changes can be requested by *anyone* within the customer's project team and implemented by *anyone* within the supplier's team, then project control and financial stability is lost. The most unsuccessful projects prove this.

32.3 Designing a change control procedure

You must have a standard change control procedure in place that defines how changes are to be managed throughout the project and contract lifecycles. The procedure should be simple and effective; it should identify the stages through which a requested change will pass.

Agree and communicate the change control process throughout your organization and make sure the other side does the same. Ensure everyone understands how the change control procedure works, what forms to use and what their individual responsibilities are in evaluating, managing and implementing change. Include executives who might either initiate or agree changes. It may be appropriate to ensure that all key stakeholders are completely accountable for major decisions and record that a strategic decision was made.

At the project inaugural meeting, explain how you intend to manage and control any changes that may arise. Gain the other side's agreement to abide by a company policy and not accept changes from anyone not on the authorized list.

Basis of decision

The decision whether to accept or reject a change should always be based on a number of rules. The fundamental logic should be:
- Is the change unavoidable (e.g. legislative changes, mergers, etc)?
  Or
- Does the change increase the overall benefit to the organization (taking into account any impact on the costs, benefits, timescales and risks)?
  And
- Is the project team able to make such a change?
  And
- Is the change best done now, or would it be more beneficial to defer it until the current work is complete?

Change control and management process

Looking in more detail at change management, it is a process that controls the development or evolution of a project. Changes will occur in all complex projects or relationships and result from a wide range of factors, many of which are outside the direct control of the project or contract manager. Unmanaged change and 'scope creep' represent a major threat to success.

A Change Control Board should be established to oversee the execution of each change and must have sufficient authority and resources available to make its work effective.

A change control process should be a documented process, such as the one outlined in Figure 32.1, recording:

- The change description
- Justification for the change
- Impact of the change
- Acceptance of the change
- Implementation of the change
- Verification of the change

Scope & Change Management

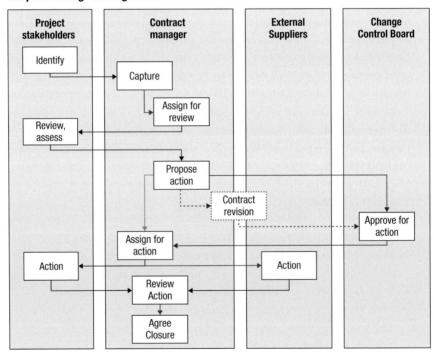

Figure 32.1   Change control process

This process can flow down from the organization's configuration management process. The process should ensure that traceability is always maintained by following a sound document naming convention, document numbering scheme, strict labeling and effective version control. The process should define a method and point in time when the document needs to be baselined. It should define the review and approval process of each change and format in which it is to be recorded. It is a good practice to keep a 'redline' copy of each version so that any changes can be clearly identified.

It is important that the process defines the responsibilities and corresponding authority empowered, considering the complexity and nature of the contract, needs of the contract lifecycle stage, the mapping between documents and clauses and the degree of verification required.

The initiator of the proposed change lists out the description of the change, the contract clause or item within the scope of the change, the interested parties to the change, the business case for the change, and criticality of the change. These are the inputs for an effective evaluation of the impact/consequences and thereafter making a decision whether to accept the proposed change or not. The initiator should bring together or coordinate among all the interested parties and facilitate evaluation of the consequences of the change.

The evaluation exercise should be based on the complexity of the contract and the criticality of the proposed change. It should consider the merits of the business case, the consequential risk, the impact on the schedule and cost. The exercise should consider some qualitative risk analysis methods according to the requirements of the interested parties. The risk score gives the owners of the activities a better decision-making ability.

Below is an example of how a risk analysis method can help in decision-making. Some threats during the change management stage of a contract lifecycle have been identified for illustration. The owners of the activity rate the factors influencing the threat on a scale of High=3, Medium=2 and Low=1. The overall score is the product of all the three factors. The organization can decide the threshold of the acceptable level. In this case a score 0-8 is Low, 9-17 is Medium and 18-27 is High.

- A threat is anything that can lead to loss or hardship to the organization
- Vulnerability is a weakness existing in the organization
- Probability is the chances (likelihood) of an event happening or materializing
- Impact is the effect on the organization

For this illustration there is a threat of SLA breach because of a proposed change to an SLA for service desk response times. Currently the SLA is for a response within four hours, with service credits for queries that are not responded to within that timeframe. The customer feels that a two-hour response time would be more appropriate, judging from customer satisfaction surveys with end-users. The current charge for responding to a query is $1.55, with service credits of $10.00.

Looking at the history of response times, the breakdown is as follows:
- 48 percent of email responses in less than 2 hours
- 26 percent of emails in 2-3 hours
- 24 percent of emails in 3-4 hours
- 2 percent of emails in over 4 hours

The supplier agrees to the change, if the charge for each query is increased to $1.75 and the service credits decreased to $6.00.

Alternatively, they have suggested a scenario where they would commit to an average response time of two hours, with a charge per query of $1.65 and a formula-based exception percentage with an exception rate of $7.00

The task for the customer organization is to assess the risk of breaching the SLA, based on the supplier's track record. They should work on the feasibility of reducing the score by putting in additional controls or transferring the risk. A root cause analysis (RCA) is a useful tool to look at. The initial risk scores need to be revisited after the controls have been identified. At first, these scores will be very subjective; you will notice that results become more reliable as the practice matures in the organization.

This kind of an analysis helps the decision maker to approve or reject a proposed change. If approved, the analysis clarifies understanding about:
- The risk that the organization is exposed to
- The controls that the organization can put in place to reduce the risk
- Whether the risk needs to be transferred to a third party
- What kind of internal approvals are needed at to document the management acceptance of the residual risk
- How to ensure compliance to the change approved

Not all of the evaluation of the change needs to be subjected to rigorous risk analysis. Seasoned professionals' experience, foresight and opinion are also reliable, but it is important to document how you have arrived at a particular conclusion and why a particular risk is taken.

The approver can be at different levels depending on the complexity and impact of the proposed change. The approver of the change should verify and satisfy that the proposed changes are necessary, the impact has been evaluated and its consequence is acceptable to the organization. The approver has to ensure the changes are properly documented and labeled; they should be satisfied with the planning of the implementation of the changes proposed and consider the opinions of all the interested parties. They should also ensure that all the interactive documents and clauses to proposed changes are identified and were within the scope of the impact and consequence analysis. This activity of change control and management feeds in to the overall management of the contract lifecycle.

The organization should consider including the contract change control and management process as an integral part of their mainstream audit program. The contract manager should ensure that a self-assessment of this process is carried out at defined intervals.

Management can define different metrics to measure the efficiency and effectiveness of this process, such as:

- Defining SLAs for each activity in this process
- Percentage of change requests initiated during the last 3 months within the SLA
- Percentage of change request closed during the last 3 months within the SLA
- Percentage of RCA completed during the last 3 months within the SLA
- Number of recommended controls during the last 3 months within the SLA
- Percentage of implementation of the recommended controls during the last 3 months within the SLA
- Percentage of completion of self-assessment of the process during the last 6 months within the SLA
- Percentage of closure of non-compliances found during self-assessment within 30 days of the self-assessment

A best practice indicator is the quality of your potential contracting partner's processes and resources that are used in managing change. This will have a significant impact on the relationship, efficiency and the success of the project. Poor quality should ring alarm bells; high quality should alert you to the need for matching capabilities, otherwise you will be at significant disadvantage in negotiating the consequences of change.

You should have a list of questions to ask about the change control process:

- Who is going to be responsible for receiving, reviewing and overseeing change requests?
- What processes do they use to monitor and oversee changes?
- What is the average cycle time for change requests to process and reach resolution for contracts or projects similar to this one?
- What is the organizational structure devoted to contract management?

Make your process easy: easy to find, easy to access and easy to monitor. Try to build in consistency and compatibility with the other side. For example, use the same data, terminology and electronic interchange. Have documents redlined to record amendments and progress, and use a change control sheet to track changes.

Finally, your contract should reflect any core principles of change control management that you consider critical to success. This should extend beyond simple forms and agreement of escalation procedures, which is where many of today's agreements stop. You may want to include service levels or performance metrics related to change management. Examples are cycle times for response and consequences of failure to respond in a timely fashion to change requests or to execute agreed changes. You should also consider what measurements are needed to monitor possible needs for change. These may not be formal service levels, but rather areas that could give you early warning of exposures. An example of this may be the accuracy or timeliness of price quotes or invoicing information provided.

Standard change control form

A very effective project management tool is to have a standard change control form. Put your forms and process online where people can access and review them. Make sure the review process is well defined and followed; an automated workflow system helps with this. Monitor the progress of any proposed change, and deal with them promptly before they become urgent or a crisis.

A typical change control form is less than two pages, and follows the key stages of change management:
1. Identification of proposed change
2. Evaluation of proposed change
3. Approval or rejection of change
4. Implementation of approved change
5. Verification of compliance with the approved change

Note that the phrase 'Proposed change' is used. Until the change is actually approved and implemented with a formal contract variation, it is not a change.

Consider also who has the best skill to effect the change, It may be that a change is needed but the party accountable for delivering it does not have the best expertise and would waste time and money effecting the change. It is possible in highly technical contracts for the subject matter expert to deliver the change for an agreed price.

The 'Identification of proposed change' section should include:
*   The unique proposed change reference number
*   The date the change is proposed
*   The source of the proposed change - the customer, the supplier, both the customer and the supplier, or some other party
*   The name of the person who initiated the proposed change
*   A comprehensive description of the proposed change.
*   All parties affected by the change and a brief summary of how they are affected.
*   Review or approval requirements to reach resolution.
*   The reference documents

The 'Evaluation of proposed change' section should include:
*   Expected cost or price implications of the proposed change
*   Contract implications
*   Program implications
*   Technical implications
*   Operational implications
*   Potential trade-off or negotiation items that could affect the outcome
*   Internal reviewers and approvals

Each evaluation should be performed by the people best able to carry out the evaluation, and always reporting to the Change Control Board as defined above. The Change Control Form should be signed and dated by them. This section should be reviewed by the contract manager, who includes an overall evaluation.

In evaluating the impact of the proposed change, consider the range of affected stakeholders and whether distributing the proposed change for their evaluation would be prudent. Many changes have an impact that is broader than expected, and often have to be revoked or further modified. However, best practice processes are designed to ensure front-end analysis is undertaken to restrict review and approval to those with a real need to know. Avoid "just in case" processes – they are inefficient, take too long and lead to inferior decisions. A reliable approach to use is the RACI model:

- **R** - Who is responsible for doing the work
- **A** - Who is accountable for approving and leading the work and owns the budget or the resources for the work
- **C** - Who needs to be consulted about the work as it may affect their work
- **I** - Who needs to be informed but has no veto, decision or direct impact

If these roles are agreed in advance, it eliminates the opportunity for non-contributing bystanders to express opinion and potentially take up time and effort diverting the course of the contract from the nominated decision makers.

The 'Implementation of proposed change' section should include:
- All decisions on actions related to the change
- The effect of change to the contract
- Signature and date by project manager or executive
- Authority to vary the contract (in case the contract does not state the representative from each party authorized to make contract changes).
- Reference to the original contract varied
- The variation number of the change

Change control tips
The following are tips for change control:
- Use online tools.
- Carry out the change control process promptly and make sure everyone works to the procedure.
- Keep back-up documentation and records, and make them easily accessible.
- Promulgate (communicate widely) the decisions in a timely fashion.
- Check the impact of changes on other programs so that if one project starts to veer off course, there is an opportunity to bring it back into alignment with other parallel projects.

- To vary the contract you will need to follow your company's standard procedures on creating contracts, and go through an internal review process before signing. The appropriate levels of approval will need to be obtained to vary the contract.
- A contract change could have a minor impact on the original formal contract or it could have a profound effect. One of the most frequent problems is that variations are agreed without checking for impact on other terms and a conflict of terms is created, which creates a loophole for non-performance and dispute. It is important to read and consider the whole contract and downstream effects when making variations.
- Ensure the change records all aspects of the changes to the contract. These should be drafted, discussed and agreed between the customer and the supplier and identify the specific change(s) in the contract wording to ensure there is always an up to date version of the contract avoiding the possible misunderstanding caused by having multiple documents with cross-referenced changes that might not be clear individually or collectively.
- Be sure to include in the wording of the change agreement: "all other terms and conditions remain unchanged". You are only varying a specific area of the contract.
- Keep your management and project team informed of ongoing change negotiations. Remember, no one likes surprises.
- When both parties sign the variation the contract is then formally varied.

Managing an effective change control process may seem like additional work, but it will actually reduce workload in resolving problems that would otherwise occur. It may also help to reduce the number of changes over time by eliminating illegal or unsound changes.

Recording contract changes

To record contract changes, simply call them change no 1, no 2, and so forth so they are uniquely identified to both parties.

It is a good project management practice to keep all documentation relating to the change in a file, or, if your company has them, in the virtual project team room. You will often need to refer to the change in the future, during acceptance or close-out.

Review the change at your project review meetings and report on it in the same way as the original contract.

32.4 **Contract claim**

The supplier can initiate a claim for a variety of reasons: the customer's failure to meet responsibilities, or having to do more work than agreed to, incurring more cost or having the program changed by the customer outside the formal change control process. At the monthly project review meeting always formally ask the supplier if there are any claims, and formally record the response in the notes of the meeting.

Similarly, the customer may initiate a claim if contract conditions have not been met. For example, service levels were not met or milestones were missed. It is similarly wise for the supplier to ask specifically at review meeting whether all aspects of the contract are progressing to the customer's satisfaction and to record the response in the meeting minutes.

With good change control procedures, followed by both parties, claims should not arise. However, they might occur if:

- Procedures were not followed
- A change was rejected
- A supplier carries out 'unauthorized work' such as may be asked for or instructed by someone who does not have the authority to request it
- The supplier raises an issue, which is not dealt with under the change control process
- The project is moving towards a dispute.

Claims should be seen as a red flag that all is not well.

Lessons learned

The claims process can be a function of the prevailing business culture. It can be ingrained in an industry, part of the norm in a country or a pattern of behavior with a particular customer or supplier, for instance clawing back concessions made during the contract negotiations. Make sure you have checked this and be prepared. If it is the norm for you, also consider the impact on the other side if you start initiating a claim.

For example, in civil engineering contracting culture, claims have been an inherent part of the project management process. Suppliers frequently try to raise a claim, often with the intent of increasing the contract price. Sometimes the claims are saved up until the end of the project where a claim settlement meeting is held to resolve them. This results in additional unforeseen cost for the customer, as well as damage to relationships, and can often lead to formal dispute and legal cases. Claims can form a very significant part of the project price.

In other industry sectors, for instance supermarkets, customers leverage their market power and seek out minor imperfections in produce supplied to them to justify withholding of payment to suppliers.

Anticipating claims

Claims can be anticipated by:

- Managing and understanding your contract.
- Embedding the right measurements that give early warning.
- High quality and continuous communication.

Use the formal project review meeting to fully review all issues; use the project plan to track progress, and explore root causes of lags or errors in activities performed. Formally ask the other side if they have any claims and/or any change requests that require action through the change control process. Record the responses in the meeting notes, and distribute them to the participants; follow the same procedure with all participants in the deal.

If something is not as it should be, don't assume it will be put right or believe the assurances of others that it is under control. Make sure it is formally discussed and documented. Formal documentation tends to force out the truth.

What to do with a claim

If you are faced with a claim, it may be appropriate for it to be managed as part of the change control process or this might not be the appropriate forum given the nature of the claim and it should be handled in a parallel process. It is important to determine the root cause to assess the validity of the claim. Once the root cause is established and the claim is determined to be valid, implement steps to avoid such claims in the future.

Process claims according to validity and correct procedures as defined in the change control process and as stipulated in the contract.

32.5 When parties do not want a change control and management process

Sometimes a customer or supplier may be reluctant to include a formal change control and management process in the contract. In most cases, this will come from the customer, who may be reluctant to set up such a process during the Negotiation phase of the contract. There may be a variety of different reasons, such as a perception of insecurity to be limited to performing changes in a certain way during contract execution, or the limitation to the right that the customer may want to have to make changes to certain clauses unilaterally. This will involve more complexity each time a new change is requested by the parties, as any change will have to be negotiated, documented and signed on a case-by-case basis and with no standard process.

However, the lack of a formal change control and management process in the contract does not mean that changes may not be tracked. Although a formal process to manage changes will not be included in the wording of the contract, the Change Control Board and the contract manager may continue tracking any changes that occur after the contract starts. In this situation it is even more important than when the process is included in the contract to ensure that whenever a change is requested by the customer, the Change Control Board and the contract manager are involved. The contract manager may then capture the information around the change proposed, at the same time that the Change Control Board oversees the execution of the related change.

On final agreement on the change, a Change Control and Management matrix may capture all the changes occurred since start of contract execution, while the recording of contract variations could be made as described above. This will record any changes agreed between the parties, both through formal documents signed by each of the parties' representatives, or through written acceptance (not necessarily the signature of a formal document by the two parties) of other minor changes affecting the scope of the agreement.

If there is no change control process in the contract, sharing of information around the agreed changes is essential. During the Project Meeting review or each time a new change is agreed (this will depend on the frequency of new changes agreed to the contract), the contract manager may send the customer a written update of the changes matrix, and request comments if there is any disagreement with any of the changes. This matrix may include simple headline information such as the date when each change has been agreed and became effective, a brief description of the change and a reference to the documentation and representatives who approved the change.

Through this process the parties will be aligned on all the changes agreed since the signature date of the contract, although there is no formal process agreed and included in the contract documentation.

32.6 Case studies

Excellent change control

An example of a project with good change control processes in place was the construction of the primary circuit for a commercial nuclear power plant. It was a project with a budget of £3 billion and duration of five years, and involved around 25 suppliers supplying diverse equipment and services.

The creation of the primary circuit was a project in its own right and formed the largest and most complex element of the whole power station.

The project scope covered the specification, engineering, procurement, installation and commissioning of the nuclear steam supply system and its overall project management. It included mechanical, electrical and chemical processing equipment and also the control systems. It was a very complex, advanced technology project with a tight construction program and with many interfaces between suppliers.

And it was a success, despite the complexity. This was predominantly due to:
- The expertise of its project and contract management team and their commitment to communication
- Robust contracts and specifications that were well documented and easily accessible
- Excellent project management procedures
- Good team relationships
- A robust change control procedure that was consistently followed
- Team incentives and commitment to succeed, rather than a blame culture

Changes were kept to a minimum by the precise and complete original specifications and contracts. Any unmanaged change could have caused serious project cost increases and serious program disruptions. A robust, but simple, change control procedure was in place and when any potential changes occurred they were managed very effectively. The team operated flexibly, committed to their joint success, rather than competing or drawing rigid demarcation lines over roles and responsibilities.

Weak change control

In a contrasting example, there was also a complex technology project, which required some creativity to produce new hardware, software and circuitry. Its goal was to design and manufacture a fixed and mobile telecommunications system forming an essential part of a larger infrastructure project with significant operational safety implications.

The contract was very onerous and reflected both the customer and ultimate customer's requirements, but with heavy penalties for failure. A high proportion of the time spent on contract negotiation focused on these penalties.

Although the project was complex, in terms of technical requirements from the customer, there were no formal interfaces among suppliers. One supplier was employed to design and manufacture the equipment and two key specialist sub-supplier manufacturers were carrying out the manufacturing.

The project is still ongoing and struggling with delivery over 12 months behind schedule. Overall, it is a classic example of poor project management, and in particular, weak change management. The expected outcome is a formal legal dispute between parties.

The project is a disaster for both the customer and the supplier due to several factors:

- The customer and supplier are very weak in overall project and contract management control. Neither party has good project or contract management procedures in place.
- The control specifications were poor, and the payment mechanisms were poorly defined.
- Poor team relationships and poor morale characterized the project almost from the start. The focus was on avoiding or apportioning the blame.
- Customer and supplier change control procedures were not aligned.
- The customer changed project managers three times, and the supplier changed project managers five times; there is no specified contract manager on either side.
- The supplier did not manage sub-suppliers effectively
- Throughout the project duration, few records of changes have been kept by either party.

32.7 **Summary**

- Change is inevitable. Be aware of and anticipate the major factors of change:
  - Changing business needs
  - Changing organization
  - Technology shifts
  - Organizational priorities change
  - New legislation or regulation
  - Imperfect scope description

- A structured and disciplined change control system will save time, effort and money and will protect all parties to an agreement
- It needs to be easy to use to avoid non-compliance
- Needs to be documented to understand the accumulation of change and any compound effect
- The flow of cost, risk and price needs to be clearly understood to avoid the change control process being used as a mechanism to leverage deal value
- Agree how incentives will stay aligned for the duration of the contract.

CHAPTER 33

Dispute handling and resolution

33.1 Introduction

This chapter explains:
- What constitutes a dispute
- The causes of disputes
- The importance of having a workable and agreed dispute resolution mechanism in a contract
- How to prevent or avoid a dispute

Dispute management and resolution is a complex process that draws on many of the skills and capabilities addressed in earlier chapters. For example, many of the attributes mentioned in the sections on negotiation will come into play in preparing for and managing a dispute. You must fully understand the 'frames' or perspectives of each side, decide your goals and objectives, marshal facts and information, and build a clear and agreed upon strategy.

The critical considerations and requirements to achieve a successful outcome are:
- Dispute resolution techniques and methods
- Dispute causes and resolutions
- Developing dispute resolution practices
- Elements of merit for claimable disputes
- Moving a dispute to a claim
- Defense against claims
- Understanding typical roles and scripts in claims issues
- Getting from a filed claim to settlement
- Selecting and implementing the appropriate dispute resolution techniques

The strength or weakness of your case will be decided by a wide variety of factors, including not only issues of relative power, but also many aspects of precedent, record keeping, and the appetite of each organization to prolong a potentially damaging dispute. It is essential that you understand your authority and the wishes of executive management in terms of settlement range and options.

Don't forget that the other side also needs to have prepared its supporting evidence, so establish early on whether they are truly equipped and authorized to reach agreement, or whether you are embarking on an exercise in frustration.

33.2   What is a dispute and what causes a dispute?

What is a dispute?

For our purposes, a dispute can be defined as an unresolved issue between contracting parties: the customer as the principal and the supplier as the provider of goods and services.

It is likely that any dispute can be tracked to one or more of the following causes:

Selection
- Inadequacies in Requests for Information (RFIs), Requests for Proposal (RFPs), and/or Requests for Quotation (RFQ), collectively known as RFx
- Inadequacies in Statement of Work (SOW)
- Incomplete assessment

Management
- Poor progress assessment to date
- Weak or inconsistent performance ownership (customer and/or supplier)
- Inadequate supplier management or customer relationship plan
- Change not controlled

Technical
- Isolated from project
- Technical exchanges missing or weak

Communication
- Incomplete
- Misdirected
- Absent

In many instances, a dispute occurs because the parties have different perceptions, inferences or beliefs in relation to the facts and circumstances. Parties rightly view their contractual entitlements and respective values as fundamental rights or obligations and when contractual provisions are unclear or ambiguous, the differences in the views creates 'interpretations' which in turn can cause the parties to shift from a harmonious relationship to a relationship which is in dispute. In some cases parties may not realize or agree that they are in fact in dispute.

In many publicly available forms of pre-printed contractual documents dispute recognition and resolution provisions offer contracting parties a default opportunity for the parties to notify each other when a dispute arises and then engaging in the process or processes identified to resolve the dispute within a reasonable period of time.

However, sometimes a contractual provision for dispute handling and resolution may not survive the period of the contract. For example, a dispute recognition provision may only offer the contracting parties the option of notifying the other contracting party of a dispute in relation to the quality and cost of the work performed up until the date of practical completion after which date the contract is effectively discharged and the dispute handling and resolution provisions for the warranty or defects liability period may be enshrined at law and not in contract.

The causes of disputes

The causes of disputes change with every contract and set of circumstances. In simple terms, the three underpinning causes of contractual dispute are:

- Ill-will between the contracting parties
- Miscommunication by poorly made and maintained contractual documentation including the content, construction, management and retrieval of contractual records and specifications
- Departure from agreed or reasonable processes, procedures or standards, in contract or at law

Generally, any dispute can be tracked to one or more of the causes outlined above – a failing in the requirements definition and selection process; poor management during the contracting or implementation phases; or misalignment of technical resources or communication.

It is easy to state that the main cause of contractual dispute is money. Money is only a way in which we value contractual entitlements. Certainly a contractual entitlement to claim for payment using money must precede the value otherwise the value would be applied without entitlement.

The most common subject in a dispute is money. The customer contract manager needs and wants to deliver the project and contract deliverables at the agreed price within the agreed time and to the agreed level of quality. The supplier needs and wants to be paid the contractual entitlements at the agreed values, which in turn deliver a return to the supplier's shareholders. A perceived, inferred, believed or a known departure or deviation from the financial expectations of the customer or the supplier can result in escalation to a dispute as well as influence its intensity and magnitude.

The intent and content of specifications are commonly disputed, particularly when the requirements are unclear and/or incomplete. Vague or poorly constructed, reviewed and published specifications can lead readers to wonder exactly what the customer has or had in mind at the time of forming the contract which in turn creates ample opportunity for a dispute. Conversely, if the supplier fails to clearly specify what is to be delivered, to what quality and by when, the customer is left to wonder what the supplier has or had in mind at the time of forming the contract, which once again establishes opportunity for ambiguity, misconception and assumption, all of which are intrinsic to the initiation and protraction of a dispute.

Payment for work done is a frequent cause of dispute. Depending on the payment mechanisms in the contract, the invoice may not match the customer's expectations and this may lead to payment being withheld either in full or in part. Evidently, money is central to issues in dispute, but it is not necessarily the cause. Different expectations can be compounded by variations, latent conditions or delays and their respective causes. To find the cause of the dispute, you need to ask yourself if your invoice reflects entitlements at an agreed or reasonable value and the evidence that supports the entitlement such as a written variation or change Order made in accordance with a contractual change control procedure.

A customer may withhold payment from a supplier because of organizational processing errors or inefficiencies, or quite simply not being able to pay. This is certainly a situation where a dispute is active.

Poor management of a contract and particularly the change control process can itself lead to a dispute. It is essential to manage change effectively and efficiently such that a genuine change or variation to the contract is acknowledged and accepted by the parties to prevent a dispute at a later date. This is especially important for post-contractual activities including correction of defects and return of retention monies or securities.

A dispute may create or be the consequence of a breach of contract by either party. Any breach of contractual provisions, which is not corrected in a timely manner after collecting the facts to determine the cause of the breach, can lead to rapid progression to a dispute, which may lead to precipitous action being taken by the parties and ultimately require resolution in a judicial forum unless otherwise stated in the contract.

A dispute may result from different expectations of the quality of the work performed by the supplier, who asserts that the goods and services provided meet the contract specifications or are to industry standards and therefore fit for the intended purpose. The customer may disagree with this assertion and this in turn may lead to the creation of a dispute.

The above is a non-exhaustive summary of the causes of contractual dispute. It is not intended to be a comprehensive list but to help you appreciate the diverse potential for dispute.

Importance of dispute recognition, management and resolution mechanisms

It is essential to have workable and agreed mechanisms for dispute recognition, management and resolution in the contract. To avoid contractual dispute you can start by recognizing where and when contractual conflict exists or might exist and then manage that so a dispute is prevented or at least resolved in line with the intentions of the contract. The most appropriate time to recognize and preferably avoid contractual conflict and dispute is before the start of the project delivery and the formation of a contract.

A specific interaction between the parties at the contract handover stage to identify the likely areas of contractual ambiguity and an undertaking to resolve any matters that arise is a useful step in creating and maintaining contractual harmony.

In addition to open and effective communication in all contractual dealings, the inclusion of express dispute recognition, management and resolution processes provisions improves the opportunity for the parties to bring forward their grievances early and in a factual manner. More detail on such provisions is presented later in this chapter.

How to prevent or avoid a dispute

The contract should contain all the information needed for a supplier to carry out their work, or at least inform them where to get it. If key information is missing or incorrect, then the supplier will claim that this has caused them delay or additional cost. If as project manager you disagree that the supplier has an entitlement to claim for delays, variations or additional costs, then a dispute is likely.

The contracting parties should continue to evaluate the potential for conflict and dispute throughout the life of the contract, and manage each occasion as well as contributing to the recording and reporting of any learning.

A contract which is formed at the contract negotiation stage on the basis of crystal clear and unambiguous entitlements and values, roles and responsibilities, contract purpose and information, performance requirements and contracting party interfaces is much less likely to experience contractual disharmony. The likelihood of conflict and dispute is significantly reduced, if not eliminated. Genuine effort in preparing contract specifications, information and requirements at the development stage delivers a tangible benefit to the negotiation stage.

33.3 Common operational disputes causing ongoing problems

Very few things in life ever run totally smoothly and this is also true in the management of projects and contracts. On a day-to-day basis it can be said that the level of contractual harmony or disharmony is directly linked to the extent of repetitive operational problems, which may be classed as disputes.

As a general rule, the contracting parties prefer not to progress to dispute and where contractual conflict is nil or negligible, the likelihood for dispute is non-existent or so slight that a state of contractual harmony is achieved.

Progression to dispute is certainly a journey to disrupted commercial relationships and the potential for the project and associated workload become dominated by disputes. It is necessary to recognize, manage and resolve these disputes before any escalation affects the individuals involved or the project overall. There is no doubt that the best way to manage disputes is to prevent them from happening in the first place.

Frequent and typical operational examples of disputes involve money-related issues, contract performance and information issues, change control, and of course, people issues.

Money and contractual performance

Referring to a recurring dispute catalyst, money, it is evident that on-going problems can transfer into operational disputes. Some examples include:

- A customer suspending the supplier from work due to slow progress and withholding payment while others to perform the work of the supplier with the intent of charging the work of others back to the supplier
- A supplier who is not compliant with the requirements of a Service Level Agreement (SLA) may have service credits imposed or liquidated damages applied by the customer, where such contractual provision exists
- A supplier accelerating work based on the apparent direction of a customer in order to meet the contractual milestones or date for practical completion and ultimately claiming for payment for extra resources required for the acceleration

To prevent or resolve money-related disputes, effective and efficient project management is of prime importance and this involves the comprehensive collection, collation, analysis and review of appropriate project performance data. In turn this management will remove or at least recognize the basis for protracted argument or dispute. If you can clearly prove whether or not the contractual performance requirements have been met, then you will be able to correct contractual departures and deviations before they become burdensome.

If contractual obligations are not met or provided then the withholding or deduction of monetary amounts is a simple mechanism for a contracting party to:
- Correct any or all damage flowing from the incomplete or inadequate performance
- Remedy the current situation to achieve or ensure future contractual compliance and performance

If everyone understands clearly what has been done and why, then escalation to dispute is less likely and in some cases not possible. Contract managers must be mindful of their own requirement to manage the contract and not necessarily the organization.

Information
Information is another aspect that can frequently lead parties into a dispute. The contract may or may not specify exactly what the supplier is required to provide and when. Customers, however, will expect comprehensive, robust information from the supplier, which meets the requirements as they see them. This disparity in expectations can lead to dispute and contracting parties rightfully expect accurate and useful information to flow between them in a timely manner.

For example, if one side requests a lot of extra information or detail the other side may object, since it is costing system and/or man-hours to prepare. To avoid this potential dispute area, make it very clear in the project inaugural meeting, and in regular contract or project review meetings, exactly what is expected from both sides, and gain commitment to provide it. The basis of this meeting should be to discuss and articulate contractual entitlements and their values.

If a contracting party repeatedly fails to provide project reports or performance information on time, not only are the objectives of the contract affected but you will be at a great disadvantage in managing your project. You will need to find out why it is happening and take appropriate action.

Change control
Chapter 32: *Change control and management* highlights the critical importance of managing change in preventing disputes. Implementing the best practice identified

and recognizing that contractual change affects contractual performance will reduce or eliminate contractual dispute.

People

Dealing with people always creates issues. For example, you might have a personality clash with a contracting party representative. It can happen, and sometimes it is simply the result of ill-will or bad 'chemistry' between you. There are a number of tools and methodologies, like Myers-Briggs Type Indicator or the Birkman Method, to help identify personality types and communication styles. Awareness of your own style and assessing those with whom you work can help overcome potential clashes, particularly if the individuals involved are from different extremes of the personality type spectrum.

Another common issue is where the contracting partner's representative or resources is performing inadequately. You depend on them a great deal to enable you to effectively carry out your role, however if someone is not able to understand requirements, or is not physically or mentally able to execute them, then you need to take appropriate action. You do not want your project to fail or be delayed because of incompetent or difficult individuals.

Carefully examine the contract regarding the appointment of personnel, as some provisions require the parties to approve appointees and their skill sets before an individual takes up a position. Some contracts will in fact enable the parties to remove those people whose skills sets are incorrect for the contract or simply because they are trouble makers not trouble shooters. If you are not getting satisfaction, escalate the problem quickly to senior management and ask for problem people to be removed from their role and replaced with more competent resources.

The request for and actual removal of people from a contract should not cause you any worry as long as the request is for a proper purpose and focused on the best interests of the contract and the project. When requesting a change of resource it is critically important to outline the contractual needs to enable the contracting parties to satisfy those needs. Be certain to present the facts only and leave emotive references aside.

33.4   What does the contract say about dispute resolution?

Where the contract provides

If the contract provides for dispute recognition, management and resolution then the parties are obliged to use those provisions to their full extent before seeking resolution outside the contract.

Where the contract does not provide

Where the contract does not expressly provide for dispute handling and resolution, without the employment of experienced, qualified and skilled practitioners, there can be a dispute about the way to handle and resolve a dispute. The parties need to reach some consensus in relation to handling and resolution of disputes. Otherwise there can be a complete breakdown or divergence in communications, which can have dire consequences on the contract and the related project. This is somewhat problematic if the parties are already in dispute. There may be little that they agree upon. In such cases the dispute handling and resolution process or mechanism may be decided by others, either by senior managers not involved on a day-to-day basis or by taking legal action. Neither route, of course, is particularly desirable.

Steps to take

Where the contract does not expressly provide for dispute handling and resolution, the following will guide you through to some conclusion.

First, obtain a clear understanding of the nature of the dispute. Understanding an issue requires listening first before you can receive, analyze, review and translate the nature of the dispute into your own language.

Understand each point of view even though you may not necessarily agree with it. The best way to tell if you do understand it is to put it into your own words and ask the other party if that is a correct articulation of the issue. Once you have agreement on what the issue is, you can move on to resolution.

The customer or the supplier may define the strategy for dispute resolution, as long as both sides agree and include appropriate clauses in the contract. Certainly, a well-articulated contract will include appropriate dispute handling and resolution provisions, which should be viewed as part of the actual contract management process. The processes and staging of dispute handling and resolution may not be the same in-contract as those in the pre-contract or post-contract stages.

Before contracting, always ask yourself how dispute resolution was addressed in your previous contracts and personal experience. Was it effective and successful? What worked and what didn't? How could it have been improved? Then construct contractual dispute handling and resolution provisions in line with that experience and the objectives of the current contract and project.

The contracting parties should contribute to the construction of dispute handling resolution clauses of the contract. Even though you may not have been involved in the design or negotiation of the contract, you will certainly be involved in the resolution of any disputes that may occur throughout the delivery. It is never too late to contribute; after reading and understanding the existing processes for handling and resolving any disputes, ensure that your contracting partner also understands how disputes are to be dealt with, and that your processes are in alignment with each other.

If you are faced with the situation where the contract does not provide in total or in part for the handling and resolution of disputes, the following non-exhaustive summary will assist you with proceeding to the next stage:

- Agree with your contracting partner on a dispute resolution plan at the outset
- Simply use your management skills to resolve the dispute at the operational level and within the general requirements of the contract between the parties and without external advice or assistance
- Ask the other party if they are prepared to go down the route of senior management escalation or facilitative negotiation processes such as conciliation or mediation to resolve the dispute
- Let the legal system resolve the dispute.

It is best to begin with the end in mind and to have a dispute handling and resolution process in place before there is a dispute irrespective of express or implied contractual provisions.

33.5 Possible consequences of a formal dispute

It is the role of the contract manager to look after the best interests of the company under the contract, to swiftly identify the root cause of the dispute and to secure the satisfactory resolution of the dispute to the contracting parties' satisfaction. The contract manager's motivation to manage or resolve conflict and contractual disputes will be governed by the impact of the dispute on the contract and any potential future business interests.

Regardless of any informal escalation of a dispute between the respective contracting parties, senior management will need to be aware of it and work with the contract manager to find a satisfactory resolution. Naturally, this may absorb a lot of management time, which may not have been allocated or budgeted for resolution of disputes in the original cost model. This could simply be additional man-hours relating to management of the dispute, mitigating the impact of the dispute on the relationship, solution finding or fighting the case through the courts. Failing to resolve disputes promptly can be very costly for all involved. As is common in most jurisdictions, the losing party will pay costs if the dispute goes to court.

If the resolution of a dispute goes as far as a court case or regulatory review, then even more of the contracting parties' time will be taken away from the day-to-day management and successful delivery of the contract. The full history of the dispute will need to be clearly documented, briefed to lawyers, and the strategies discussed at length. Those individuals closely involved in the dispute may be required to give evidence in court as witnesses.

A 2006 study from the Centre for Effective Dispute Resolution (CEDR) identified that conflict cost UK businesses around £33 billion a year; this was directly due to poor conflict management. The key conclusions identified in the study confirm that 80 percent of disputes have a significant impact on the smooth running of business and that managers may spend over 689 days of time trying to sort out any cases valued in excess of £1 million. This was a distraction that may prove too expensive to sustain over time as it is time taken away from their revenue or value creating main jobs. In contract, in-house teams spent on average 172 days on similarly valued cases. CEDR points out that whilst the in-house legal team may be paid to manage disputes, this is not the case with other managers.

There is also a personal dimension. Can the contract manager be damaged because of a dispute? That depends. Is the dispute situation a personal failure? Or are you doing your job properly and looking after the best interests of your company under the contract? Certainly no one ever wants to be personally involved in a dispute. It may bring you to the attention of your senior management for the wrong reasons and a spotlight will be on you to establish the cause and resolution of the dispute.

If you become embroiled in a dispute, it will detract your attention from day-to-day management of your contract. Something could go wrong due to lack of attention, and the project delivery could suffer. In fact, you could be led into another dispute situation. Depending on the size of the dispute, resolving it could affect the performance of your entire company.

The same applies to your contracting partner. You need them to be concentrating on the effective delivery of the contract. So if they are embroiled in a dispute with you or some other party, it is possible that performance will suffer and your contract requirements or expectations may not be met.

If the resolution of a dispute goes as far as a court case or regulatory review, then even more of your time will be taken away from the project. The full history of the dispute will need to be clearly documented, briefed to lawyers, and the strategies discussed at length. You may be called to give or defend evidence in court.

Litigation is expensive and the total cost in terms of money and man-hours could be very expensive to both parties regardless of who is the ultimate winner. The bottom line is to avoid disputes if at all possible, or resolve them as efficiently and effectively as possible.

33.6 How to avoid a dispute

As we have discussed, most disputes can be avoided. They may be a result of the following factors:

- Failure to deliver the project in accordance with the contract
- Poor contract or project management
- Lack of or poor communication
- Lack of risk management procedures
- Poorly drafted contract or no contract at all.

Disputes can sometimes occur through changes in business conditions beyond the control of the project team. Some examples could be a serious business downturn, regulatory or legal changes, new strategies, new products or lost customers.

One way to avoid disputes is to manage your contracts and projects effectively. It is recommended from time to time to undertake a risks audit, reviewing the contracts in existence, ensuring that lessons have been learnt from past disputes and that robust procedures are in place to mitigate any risk of future disputes. These procedures may include a review of the following:

- Has any work been undertaken without a contract being signed?
- Are standard terms and conditions correctly incorporated into contracts?
- Has training being provided to staff on the standard terms and conditions?
- Is there an effective dispute resolution procedure?
- Have you got appropriate insurance in place?

We have already discussed the need to have a robust contract in place, which carefully addresses all the delivery requirements and obligations of the parties. This is certainly the best way to minimize the probability of disputes occurring. However, once the contract is in place, it is important to manage your project in a way to avoid disputes and to be compliant with those terms and conditions. If there are amendments to the scope of the project, then these amendments should be recorded in writing and signed off by the parties.

We have also discussed tools and techniques to maintain control over the project and contract. These include having regular formal review meetings, change management, risk management and reporting and tracking all issues related to delivery. Such effective management will certainly help to minimize disputes, as well as help in resolving them at an early stage.

Anticipate potential disputes: do not merely manage your project on a day-to-day basis and deal with issues as they pop up. Plan ahead. Anticipate where a dispute could arise. Try to eliminate potential disputes before they even occur. The delivery of your project should be carefully planned, and that plan should be regularly monitored. At each review meeting actually ask your contracting partner if they have any views on anticipated disputes or areas of difficulty. Keep a record of the response in the meeting notes.

Resolve potential disputes at project or contract manager level before they escalate. You are managing the project and will have an operational working interface with your contracting representative. Always try to work closely with them; not just on a business basis but also on a personal basis, working together for the benefit of the project, since both parties want a mutually successful outcome to the project.

Resolve potential disputes quickly. If you see a dispute looming the best technique is to eliminate it before it occurs. It can be equally effective to resolve a potential dispute quickly. Do not ignore it and do not allow it to grow, as ignored issues tend to get larger in importance and urgency as they age. Use all your skills and understanding to clear away the seeds of a dispute. Get the issues out in the open. Force them to be discussed and maintain a risk register of any issues that are likely to cause potential disputes. Allocate owners to each risk to ensure that the potential risk is managed and not ignored or kept hidden from the senior management of both supplier and customer.

33.7 **Dispute handling and resolution: recovery**

As we have discussed, the fact that there is a dispute means that something has gone wrong. It is important that you have considered the entire set of options available to you and that you know which of them your organization is ready to support and which of them you are authorized to use or threaten. Potential options include:
- Increase emphasis on partner responsibilities for management
  - Additional contract management resources
  - On-site representation (skills appropriate to issue)
- Escalation
  - Review by their senior executives
  - Execute review
- De-scope or refine project
- Initiate second source effort (internal or alternative supplier)
- Terminate (in whole or part)

You will need to consider whether you need to reach agreement or whether you have alternatives to a negotiated settlement. This may dramatically alter the negotiating power of either party.

It is important to remember that your task will normally be to settle issues that have arisen as a result of dispute and to secure a satisfactory resolution – for example, compensation. Payment of compensation does not necessarily mean the end of the potential solution to the issue. You will also want to avoid repetition of similar problems in the future and circulate any lessons learned throughout your organization.

In general, you are going to want to implement change procedures that secure future performance by both organizations. Any such amendments to the delivery of the project should be recorded in writing and agreed by both parties. This in turn may lead to a set of more fundamental and potentially highly contentious solutions that ultimately may result in contract termination.

Certainly a major decision like termination of an existing project will need to be discussed and decided by the senior management team involved in the particular project together with the contracting party's in-house legal function. It may even be accompanied by legal action. However, in some circumstances you may suggest de-scoping or some similarly radical step to the project, if you realize there are commitments that cannot be met by either party. It is essential that you have considered and planned for all possible recovery options including any potential unbudgeted costs.

The options available may be frustrated by the need to consider the dispute resolution process and procedure set out in the contract before any attempt is made to resolve the dispute through the courts. If the contract contains a dispute resolution clause, then the contracting parties will need to follow the specific obligations set out in that clause before any other option is followed; failure to do so may result in costs being awarded against the non-compliant party.

Failure to consider or have suitable dispute resolution clauses may lead to the following situations:

- Requirement to follow an unsuitable dispute resolution process for the dispute in question
- A party many be denied a remedy unless and until a dispute resolution process has been followed;
- Costs being awarded against the party that has not followed the dispute resolution process.

Use of technical reports

In any contract, there is an element of technical expertise that ensures success in the project or works undertaken. When a dispute arises in relation to certain works, technical reports may be used to help a contracting party to better understand the technical aspects of the work. We will focus on technical report contents that discuss defective work as this is a reason frequently used for withholding payment in contractual disputes.

Technical reports do not always have to be written by a recognized expert in a field. They can be written by a competent and experienced practitioner who documents their experiences with a project, product or process, or all, in mind.

When any technical report is prepared, it should be written with the likely readers in mind and awareness that, once authors commit their work to print, many readers are likely to come into contact with the report who do not know the explicit details of the disputed issues. Those readers may include the customer, the supplier, a superintendent or even the judge of a court.

The general definition of a technical report is: *a focused representation of interpretations based on submitted, investigated, actual or likely calculations, facts, materials, measurements or other data or documents.*

A technical report may include a desktop review (no site visit), presentation of laboratory or other samples and related test results, site measurements and investigation or a combination of these.

A well written technical report will assist the parties in better understanding the issues in dispute but will not always address all issues or deliver a 'knock-out blow' and will convey detailed analysis and conclusive statements which enables an reader to make a decision about the issues.

Before commissioning a technical report, make a decision on what the dispute is about and map out the specific issues. Specific issues in relation to defective works are usually centered around:
- Designs
- Specifications and customer instructions
- Defective workmanship
- Extensions of time
- Variations to designs, specifications
- As-constructed conditions
- Retention monies and defects liability periods

Select an appropriately qualified, competent and experienced individual or organization to prepare, investigate, challenge, draft, review and publish the report.

Agree the terms, boundaries and time frame of the technical report with the author and convey the all of the disputed issues to them that they are to write about.

Select a suitable and preferably independent practitioner, professional, expert or other experienced, competent or qualified individual or team as the technical report author to report on the project, processes and products or all three. If the author has a relationship with one or more of the parties, then state what it is so that the reader can make their own decision as to the content and usefulness of the technical report. The key is to expose the root cause of defects and demonstrate how these causes have resulted in defective work and convince the reader how the disputed issues should be considered and resolved.

33.8   Resolution steps: from least to most complex

When a dispute does arise, there are a number of ways that it can ultimately be resolved. Here they are listed in terms of complexity, time required, third party involvement, and use of the legal system. The specific route to resolution will, of course, depend upon the contractual provisions and the management and choreography of those involved.

Negotiation – party-to-party negotiation to determine the root cause of the issues and the quantum of the losses involved to decide a sustainable outcome based on the interests of both parties.

If unsuccessful in negotiation then progress to mediation.

Mediation – using a third party neutral to guide the parties through a structured process to determine the most sustainable outcome in the interests of the parties and enabling the parties to decide the most appropriate future for their business relationship.

If unsuccessful in mediation then progress to arbitration.

Arbitration – using a third party neutral to hear the parties positions in an party agreed forum with a party appointed arbitrator, such that an award may be presented by the arbitrator after reasoned deliberation in accordance with the common law and the rules of natural justice. Depending on the terms of the contract and the applicable legal system the arbitral decision may be final and binding or subject to possible subsequent litigation.

If unsuccessful in arbitration, then progress to litigation.

Litigation – using a court of competent jurisdiction with a court appointed, judicially competent case manager to hear the evidence of the parties in an adversarial manner in accordance with the doctrine of precedent and the rules of natural justice, to hand down a final and binding determination, notwithstanding any rights to appeal.

Of course other forums and processes exist and these may include a combination of dispute resolution processes or mechanisms.

33.9 Solutions to disputes: negotiation

How you resolve a dispute depends on the nature of the dispute. The first thing to do is obtain a clear understanding of the nature and cause of the dispute, if known or identifiable. Understand each point of view and articulate the issues to gain agreement on understanding. By listening, acknowledging, reframing and summarizing the issues in dispute you can begin to understand the dispute and then progress to asking questions as to how the dispute is able to be resolved.

Beginning at the project or contract manager level it is sometimes best to start the exploration and articulation of the nature and causes of the dispute in a clinical manner. It is possible that just that process of looking at the dispute from different perspectives alters perceptions, inferences and beliefs enough for parties to progress down the path to resolution. You may find that all of the contracting parties have contributed to the dispute and this may make it simpler or sometimes more complex to reach a negotiated agreement.

When faced with a dispute always first try to resolve it at the operational level, subject to the personnel at that level having the requisite skill and will to resolve the dispute. Resolution of disputes at the most interactive levels of a contract makes sense, but sustainability of resolutions is critically dependent on those making the resolution having both the responsibility and authority to decide for their respective organizations.

Agreement between the contracting parties is critically important to the sustainability of any resolution. Since you have a working relationship with your contracting partner, it is important to know and help each other when handling and resolving a dispute. Make detailed notes of the background and history of the issue and any discussions or telephone calls or correspondence related to it. Discuss the dispute with your contracting partner at the regular project or contract review meetings and record results in the meeting notes.

Whether you wish to immediately escalate a dispute in your company or not, report on it in your regular monthly report and keep your management informed. Some contract conditions will include dispute escalation clauses that require disputes to be escalated to senior management of both companies as the next step in dispute resolution.

Where a contract does not specifically require this step, it is still a very effective process. The dispute may be escalated to your line management or even up to the executive group of the respective contracting parties. Your contract, for example, may be just one of several contracts between the organizations and there may even be some form of strategic alliance between them where neither organization desires escalation to a stage of more formal dispute resolution, so resolution by senior management is a distinct possibility.

An illustrative example is where a paper manufacturing company was implementing an order entry and planning system from a supplier who also supplied much of the measurement and control equipment at the facility. Since the equipment contracts were far more lucrative than the order entry system, the customer was able to use the weight of the entire plant to get the supplier to resolve disputes over system functionality. The senior supplier representative actually proposed this solution in order to protect the company's interest as a whole, to the delight of the system implementation team. Once both sides knew that any dispute had the potential to go to the 'top-level' immediately, things were less contentious.

We have discussed earlier the need to follow the contract wording on dispute resolution. This would have been agreed at the contract negotiation stage so both parties should understand how disputes are to be further escalated for resolution. You must understand and follow this agreed process, but as our example illustrates, circumstances change, be ready for that too.

Parties can and do settle their disputes, well before involving an external facilitator and the message for project and contract managers is to plan and plan well and when change occurs, plan again and in any event, plan for change.

Recognizing that party-to-party negotiation should always be the first step in dispute handling and resolution, escalation to senior management level and other forums is dependent on the sustainability of any process or resolution at the project level.

Although fairness is a notion that can be applied to all kinds of activities, its content will depend upon the context in which it is being used. The context and background are very important.

33.10 Solutions to disputes: mediation

Mediation is a structured process where the disputing parties are facilitated through negotiations to a sustainable resolution, by an impartial and disinterested facilitator irrespective of whether that resolution requires the parties to do something or nothing. It is up to the parties and not the mediator to decide how and when their dispute is resolved.

In mediation the representatives of the contracting parties are facilitated through a structured process such that the issues are drawn out at first, followed by discussion of the content of the issues and then working through the identified issues to explore options for resolution. On arriving at the point of option generation, the parties can elect to proceed to a sustainable resolution or to otherwise proceed with or without a negotiated agreement. In general terms, any agreement made by using a mediation process is confidential between the parties but not binding, as far as the law provides.

It is important to reiterate at this point that it is the parties who discuss the dispute and decide the matter between themselves. The mediator is there purely as a facilitator and cannot offer advice or attempt to impose a solution or judgment.

The experience, qualifications and skills of the mediator drives the process as the mediator is the master of the process but the servant of the parties. The mediator is responsible for exposing the disputed issues and preventing the parties from becoming or remaining deadlocked, so that a sustainable resolution is achieved.

As an Alternative Dispute Resolution (ADR) process, mediation has the advantage of offering a quicker and cost effective forum for the parties to settle their dispute in a less confrontational environment, all of which are significant advantages over the arbitration and litigation processes which are also available to the parties to settle a dispute.

Irrespective of parties entering into ADR forums for exposing the 'game plan' of the other party, it is a valuable process that can reduce the overall time and cost for dispute resolution.

33.11 Solutions to disputes: arbitration

Arbitration is a structured process that can be used by disputing parties to have their contractual issues heard in a quasi-judicial setting with the added benefit that the arbitrator is both procedurally competent and experienced in dispute resolution procedures and technically competent and experienced in the field of the disputed matter or issues.

The key to the selection and use of an arbitrator in a dispute resolution process is agreement between the disputing parties as to who will be the arbitrator. The nomination of an arbitrator can be at contract formation or at some point after.

Arbitration is subject to control of the courts but is not part of the actual judicial system. The arbitration hearing, the equivalent of a trial, is chaired by an arbitrator who is selected by both parties. In the event that the parties cannot agree on an arbitrator, an independent body may be used to select the actual arbitrator.

For contracts in an international environment it is usual to define the rules to be applied according to an international body or organization established in a 'neutral' country. For instance the Swiss rules of International Arbitration of the Swiss Chamber of Commerce is one frequently mentioned for this purpose.

Contracts commonly include a contractually binding arbitration clause stating the procedures to bring about the arbitration hearing and also naming an independent body or person who will select an arbitrator in the event of a dispute.

Traditionally, arbitration has been cheaper, quicker and less formal than litigation with the added advantage of being held and decided in private. Also if the dispute involves complex technical aspects then a specialist arbitrator with experience in the dispute issues can be appointed. Arbitration is not merely the production of a binding judgment for the parties to abide by its content but a reasoned award based on adversarial and inquisitorial techniques used to enable a technical assessment of the facts surrounding the dispute. In litigation a judge may have no experience in matters other than legal issues.

For an arbitration award to be valid and enforceable, the agreement must be in writing, and once in writing it is enforceable by the courts.

One of the main differences between arbitration in the UK and in continental Europe, is that in Europe the parties will usually specify that the decision of the arbitrator is final and cannot be subject to appeal. This makes arbitration advantageous in that the dispute is concluded in one hearing. In the UK, however, an appeal on the arbitrator's decision can be set aside on the grounds that it contains an error of law, and is subject to the appeal process of the superior courts in a jurisdiction using litigation.

33.12 Solutions to disputes: litigation

Unless an alternative means of resolving disputes is stated in the contract, litigation will is the default forum for the parties. Unfortunately, it can be the most expensive, complex and protracted of the available dispute resolution processes.

Many commercial contracts will state that the contract is subject to the laws of a specific country, or as in the US, a specific state. In international or inter-state contracts, it is obviously important to have carefully selected the country or state under whose legal system the contract is governed.

The primary disadvantages of litigation are cost, the length of time to reach a decision, the involvement of external providers such as lawyers to present submissions in a forum which is only interested in law and not the technical aspects of the dispute and the possibility of adverse publicity for the contracting parties before, during or after the publication of a judgment by a court.

The general steps in litigating are as follows:
1. The claimant (the plaintiff) instigates the proceedings.
2. The party against whom the claimant is acting, the defendant, has a period of time in which to admit the claim or contest it.
3. If a defense is involved, then directions will be issued to the parties as to exchange of documents.
4. The matter will then be set down for a trial date.

You must be aware that if a dispute progresses to mediation, arbitration or litigation there will be a very large amount of work for the contract manager, project manager and the project team to prepare detailed documentation and to study and record the complete dispute history for the forums and hearings.

If the dispute is subject to legal settlement you could still be required to give evidence in the legal proceedings even if you have changed employers.

33.13 Case study: an actual dispute and how it was resolved

The following example relates to a large rail project in the UK.

A contract for the construction of new railway track and refurbishment of existing railway track for a new Metro System in a major UK city deteriorated into dispute during its performance. The project was important and expensive and was apparent to the public.

The value of the overall Metro Project was many hundreds of millions of pounds, and was for the delivery of new trams and the construction of a complete new railway infrastructure on which to operate the trams. The overall Metro Project was a Private Finance Initiative (PFI) and therefore the customer only started earning revenue to recover the costs of financing the work on practical completion and commissioning of the system. Naturally, the system had to be able to operate and carry fare-paying passengers in order for the customer to receive the revenue.

The construction of the railway track was a project in its own right, and formed the largest and one of the most complex elements of the complete Metro System. It was completed over five years ago and has performed successfully since its commissioning, despite the contractual problems.

The project scope covered the design, materials procurement, and construction of the railway track, which ran both on ballast and in streets. It was complex in terms of planning to a tight construction program, but traditional in terms of the levels of technology. There were no interfaces between other suppliers but a great deal of careful co-ordination was needed, especially to construct in-street track.

One supplier was employed on the Track Project and carried out all the work with no subcontracting.

The contract was very onerous and prepared for the customer by a firm of major international construction lawyers.

The project was a disaster for both the customer and the supplier for a number of reasons:
- Both customer and supplier were weak in project management control – although not a contractual provision this certainly lead to contractual disharmony
- Neither party had good project management procedures in place
- The contract specifications were poorly written and presented
- Payment mechanisms were poorly defined
- There was poor project planning and co-ordination
- Team relationships were ineffective and poor morale developed
- Neither the customer nor the supplier had change control procedures in place
- The customer changed their project manager three times
- The supplier changed their project manager five times

Changes throughout the project were extensive and largely due to poor planning and poor co-ordination, by both the customer and the supplier. The supplier incurred many delays and significant extra costs. Specifications and customer requirements also constantly changed. In fact, the customer's basic design specifications were almost entirely rewritten.

Throughout the project duration, very few records of changes were kept by either party.

The outcome was a protracted litigious formal dispute and arbitration.

The project was eventually completed by the supplier. However, when it was nearing completion they informed the customer that they were making a commercial claim.

The customer initially rejected the claim, and, in accordance with the contract, the dispute went to arbitration after about eighteen months.

After careful, expensive, and time-consuming, preparation of evidentiary material by both parties, the arbitration hearing found in favor of the supplier and against the customer which resulted in an award of some 35 percent of the value of the original contract. The customer had to pay the amount awarded to the supplier as additional supplier costs and also had to pay the arbitration costs.

The supplier recovered their costs, although they made no profit on the awarded value.

The main reasons for the award against the customer were that the poorly constructed and managed contractual provisions created contractual disharmony and this led to dispute which was amplified by the ill-will and poor working relationship between the parties. Additionally, the contract had poorly defined payment terms and the supplier had clear evidence extra costs were incurred due to the activity, inactivity and conduct of the customer.

Effective and professional contract and project management procedures, and particularly change control procedures, would have produced an entirely different result.

33.14 **Summary**

Dispute resolution is heavily reliant on contracting parties being in tune with the practicalities of delivering the project or contract outputs as agreed.

The three underpinning causes of contractual dispute are:
• Ill-will between the contracting parties
• Miscommunication by poorly made and maintained contractual documentation including the content, construction, management and retrieval of contractual records and specifications; and
• Departure from agreed or reasonable processes, procedures or standards, in contract or at law.

A dispute may create or be the consequence of a breach of contract by either party.
The processes and staging of dispute handling and resolution may not be the same in-contract as those in the pre-contract or post-contract stages.

Before contracting, always ask yourself how dispute resolution was addressed in your previous contracts and personal experience.

Agree with your contracting partner on a dispute resolution plan at the outset or let the legal system resolve the dispute.

The contract manager's motivation to manage or resolve conflict and contractual disputes will be governed by the impact of the dispute on the contract and any potential future business interests.

One way to avoid disputes is to manage your contracts and projects effectively.

Resolve potential disputes at project or contract manager level before they escalate.

Recognize disputed issues early. Aim to resolve a dispute quickly based on the interests of the parties and the contract with a view to preventing the dispute from recurring, if possible.

How you resolve a dispute depends on the nature of the dispute. Some contract conditions will include dispute escalation clauses that require disputes to be escalated to senior management of both companies as the next step in dispute resolution.

Follow the contract wording in a dispute resolution provision.

CHAPTER 34

Contract close-out and lessons learned

34.1 Introduction

This chapter provides information, tools, techniques, and best practice on closing out the contract activities and quantifying lessons learned, including:

- Types of termination and close-out
- Impacts on required actions
- Termination of relationship versus project
- Continuing obligations
- Records and knowledge capture
- Sample forms

A contract may end for a variety of reasons, including routine expiry; voluntary termination by one or both parties; or disagreement. In this chapter we will look at the impact that different types of closure have on the actions that must be taken. We will briefly touch on the distinction between ending a relationship agreement and the completion or termination of a specific project. We will also discuss the different ways a relationship agreement can end – amicably, and otherwise.

Most contracts involve some level of continuing obligation even after they have been formally terminated. The degree of such obligation will vary significantly depending on the circumstances of the deal and the continuing significance of the product, service or its related items – for example, intellectual property or usage rights.

We will also highlight and provide samples of forms that can be used to support a successful and complete contact close-out. Finally, we will discuss the importance of capturing lessons learned.

This is a key best practice area: few organizations have succeeded in building a robust approach or systems to ensure past mistakes are not repeated and past successes are replicated. It is an area of growing focus, especially with the increasing mechanization of contract management through new software applications.

This chapter will enable you to:
- Smoothly manage the contract close-out process;
- Understand the contract close-out and continuing obligations process; and
- Capture and use lessons learned for future use

Any close-out or termination takes proper planning and preparation. A key goal of this chapter is to assist in ensuring all the necessary areas have been considered and the process is managed smoothly. Advanced planners consider the events that will lead to or be required by closure, and integrate them into the original contract documents. Planning ahead for closure makes the process easier when it occurs.

34.2 Types of termination or close-out

Often contracts come to a close quite naturally, because the contract term has expired or because final acceptance has occurred. Expiry can be by agreement or because one party overlooks an obligation to notify the other of renewal, and sometimes the services continue informally beyond this date until the passage of the expiry date is noticed. There are variants to both of these events that will be discussed further later in this chapter.

In addition to these natural and harmonious close-out situations, there is also the question of termination for cause or convenience. Although this may not be acrimonious or represent a breach (indeed the US Uniform Commercial Code defines termination as a legal ending to the contract where it has not been broken by either side), it is often the case that some level of dispute accompanies termination. This may delay the close-out process, or it may mean that there is litigation or quasi-litigation running in parallel to the close-out procedures.

34.3 Final acceptance

Final acceptance applies when the contract is a project with milestones to be met. The last milestone may be final acceptance, or there may be a review and final acceptance after the last milestone is reached. The contract should clearly state whether final acceptance is separate or included. An example of a separate final acceptance would be approval after inspection of the finished product or system. Sometimes after successful performance tests final acceptance is preceded by provisional acceptance, which sets the clock ticking for a period during which performance is monitored, in accordance with provisions in the contract, successful completion of which then triggers final acceptance.

The terms for final acceptance and the actions resulting from it should be clearly spelt out in the contract. In general, the Statement of Work (SOW), work order or specifications will be the key documents to determine whether obligations have been met by both customer and supplier, enabling contract close-out to proceed. If the final acceptance involves approvals or certain steps, language covering remediation and re-examination may be included. It is important to bear in mind that final acceptance documents need to be signed and formally issued both to ensure records are complete and, in some circumstances, to enable the supplier to present the documents to a bank or financial institution to release payment if financial instruments like letters of credit or financing are being used.

Final acceptance can occur at three distinct levels: unconditional acceptance, partial acceptance and total rejection.

An unconditional acceptance means the product or service has met the requirements detailed in the contract and there should now be a smooth transition to close-out.

Partial acceptance indicates that there will be multiple steps to closure. If acceptance is just partial, it can be because part of the product or service is accepted and, by definition, other parts are rejected; or because certain steps must be accepted before continuing to the next step. If the partial acceptance contains conditions, the supplier has some continuing obligations in terms of actions that must be taken to meet the contract requirements and terms. In this latter case, the contract will not be closed until such requirements have been met or the parties have agreed changes that amend the deliverables.

While not an acceptance, total rejection (instead of partial rejection, the other half of partial acceptance) can occur. In this scenario, the product or service has failed in some fundamental way to satisfy contracted standards. Such situations typically lead to disputes and claims, often initiated by both parties. It is obviously a failure in contract and project management processes if total rejection occurs, certainly if it is in any sense a surprise. But there have been instances where such rejection is relatively nebulous, where a customer is simply looking for excuses because of changed needs or circumstances, or revised requirements. It is experiences like this that have made suppliers extremely wary and insistent on clear acceptance criteria that leave little room for doubt or subjective interpretation

As final acceptance approaches, both sides must ensure they have reviewed and prepared all requirements, test procedures, documentation etc. to avoid delays and to protect their position at this critical phase. Sometimes a 'dry run' is held internally or with both parties to reveal potential issues that can be mediated before the final review.

34.4 Final acceptance: actions

Final acceptance will trigger a number of actions. Once the customer has confirmed that the product or service is deemed acceptable, the supplier will prepare and present the final payment request, if it is stated thus the terms of the contract that final payment is dependent upon final acceptance. In other situations, the customer needs only to sign a document indicating acceptance.

If the product purchase comes with ownership rights, the supplier will provide the appropriate title documents. If product ownership will remain with the supplier, licenses or use rights should be presented to the customer in order to use the product as agreed. These rights may be contained in the original agreement or may be a separate document.

For example, if a software company and your company (as a customer) worked together to develop a product, the software company will usually retain ownership of the product and the right to license the product to other companies. You may have negotiated that your company retains the right to use the product for a period of years upon completion of development and final acceptance. Your acceptance starts the license period countdown clock running.

In some instances the supplier may not be able to book the revenue on the project until the customer officially documents unconditional acceptance. The customer's acceptance in this case enables the supplier to fully recognize the revenue on their books. Sometimes the supplier will create a default condition that allows it to recognize the revenue if the customer delays acceptance. This prevents a personality clash from resulting in punitive action when there is no substantive basis to delay final acceptance.

In other instances the customer may have made the supplier purchase a bond or create an escrow account as an insurance policy that the product would work as expected. Now that the customer has formally accepted the product, the bond or escrow account can be closed, and the liability of the supplier removed.

Once final acceptance and payment have occurred, the customer needs to ensure that the supplier removes all liens and claims against its company regarding this product. All liens, claims or liabilities need to be officially resolved. For example, a lien may exist against hardware or other products to ensure payment for the goods, and otherwise the supplier can take back the goods for non-payment.

34.5 Expiry of term

A contract may expire naturally at the end of its stated term. This may be because the contract covers a service or product that the customer does not intend to continue using, or may have decided to replace. Or, the supplier has determined to stop producing the product or providing the service now that the term has ended. If your business requires the continuation of products or services, you need to be aware of the termination language in the contract and whether there is a deadline by which you need to notify the supplier of your intent to renew.

If you decide to continue the services or use of the product, you can simply replicate the existing contract, if it was satisfactory, with updated timings and pricings. You may decide that you want to change the terms of the agreement – for example, adding more options or upgrading the underlying hardware or other devices – and as the supplier for the new terms. You can also test the market by putting the contract out to a competitive bid, basically revisiting the Request for Proposal (RFP) or Request for Information (RFI) process. Or you may have gained the knowledge and skill to produce the product internally now, and thus need only a transition of the service from the outside supplier to you.

If you choose to take the service in-house, well before the termination date of the agreement you need to ask some questions, including:
- Are the internal resources in place to take over the responsibilities?
- Do they have what is needed to succeed?

However you choose to proceed, it is wise to have a succession plan in place before you need it, and revisit it regularly during your risk assessment or project review meetings. Especially if you are not continuing the agreement, you need to be prepared in case the supplier simply walks away on the final day and leaves you without information or support. You may also need a succession plan if you miss a deadline by which to advise the supplier of your intention to renew the agreement, or if the supplier declines to renew under new terms.

34.6 Termination

Termination implies that the relationship is ending before its natural, or originally anticipated, end date. This is not simply expiry of the agreement, but requires an affirmative action by one party. Termination may be for convenience, and the parties agree to part ways or end the contract mutually. For example, you have decided to pay off a loan early, since your research has shown that paying the early termination fees is more advantageous than maintaining the loan.

Of course, another reason for termination is Cause or Default, when one party may not be happy. For example, a supplier has continually failed to deliver critical parts to your organization on time, and in sufficient quantity for you to produce your product. Your customers are not happy, and threaten to buy from another company. For this reason, you may elect to terminate the agreement with your supplier and find another source of the parts to keep your customers happy. It would be a Default if the supplier had committed to provide the parts within a certain timeframe and failed to do so, or For Cause if the supplier's failure was causing harm because of your inability to meet customer orders.

The circumstances surrounding termination may significantly affect the way it is resolved and the problems encountered as the parties work towards resolution. It must be remembered that an acrimonious termination may be accompanied by threats of litigation or actual litigation. What is done, what is said, what transpires, what records are maintained or exchanged at this stage, may have critical impact on the outcome. Before moving to a termination, you may wish to consult with your company's executive team, financial office, risk assessment group, and legal department.

34.7 Expiry of term or termination: actions

As described above, there are significant variations in how expiry or terminations can occur and how they may progress, based on the circumstances involved and how the parties communicate. When drafting your contract, ensure that the expiry clause covers all known business requirements, reflects current business rules and processes, and projects the needs at the end of the term. When you reach an expiry or termination point, you should be prepared with a current understanding of business needs and appropriate plans to move forward.

The Termination for Convenience section should cover a broad range of circumstances, but no matter how creative you are, there still may be some exposure. Items to be considered are:

- The time required for notice (Thirty days? Ninety days? Six months? One year?)
- To whom should notice be sent? Just to the person in charge of the contract, or also to a corporate office or executive team member?
- What obligation would either side have upon the notice? Will there be a transition back to the customer/customer, or to a third party?
- What money will be paid in relation to work performed up to the termination date and in anticipation of the contract proceeding without such termination
- If the contract involves shipments of goods, what if a shipment is in process? Must it be accepted or can it be rejected – and who pays for reshipment?
- If subcontracts, licenses or other commercial agreements associated with the contract must be terminated early as a result, who pays the fees that may be charged?

When terminating a contract for convenience, how you proceed may determine the ongoing relationship with the other party and how future agreements are entered into, as well as being affected by concurrent agreements with the other side. An objective and convincing business case for terminating that agreement can preserve an ongoing relationship or keep the way open for future efforts.

Termination for Cause clauses in the contract will stipulate basic procedures and usually list the requirements that must be met before 'cause' is reached. For example, if you are terminating for a late delivery, the clause might require that deliveries are regularly late, or that the late delivery is more than a certain time period (two days? a week?) late. It may also include a remediation clause that lets the other side repair the damage within a certain time period, after which the notice of termination must be withdrawn.

The Termination for Cause language is a section where careful and thoughtful drafting will produce metrics that can be accepted by both sides. As noted above, when instigating the termination for cause, you may want to provide your legal team with all the necessary background information, and obtain their good guidance before proceeding. Real or implied litigation may result or be part of the exit strategy for you or the other party, and you should be ready for it before sending the termination notice. In some cases, having a list of actions that are considered a breach of the agreement and allowing mediation, with termination possible only after a series of breaches, may be one way to prepare for problems without risking litigation.

No matter what method is used for severing the contractual relationship, remember that key issues should be addressed, including:
- Obligations to pay, including for work performed previously or which may need to be performed as part of the termination activities
- Title and rights to goods and products produced in the course of the agreement
- Ownership of deliverables or work in progress
- Transfer of rights such as software licenses, designs, or rights of use
- Obligations to cooperate with the new supplier

For example, your contract with a supplier is expiring and the support of their product is now going to fall to your help-desk people. Have they agreed to a smooth transfer of documentation and knowledge to your internal employees? Have you mapped out a clear process and schedule to accomplish a smooth and successful transition? What fallbacks have you implemented to ensure that they keep up their side of the bargain? You might be holding final payment until the help desk successfully handles a certain number of calls, or has been error-free for a specified percentage of calls over a certain time period.

34.8 Close-out - key risks after the delivery of the contract

After the delivery of what was agreed upon it is helpful to have a formal close out and to identify key enduring terms, such as warranties, transition, insurance, confidentiality and intellectual property clauses that need to be complied with in the future.

Contract closeout is the process of administratively closing a contract after it is completed; including certifying that all services and deliverables are satisfactory and all costs have been settled.

The desired output of this stage is a completed formal close-out process. This includes:
- a determination whether a number of issues have been met, such as whether all deliverables have been met, payment made/received, whether enduring obligations/ rights have been listed etc (see below for a list of such issues); and
- the determination of 'lessons learned' so that these lessons can be used to reduce the incidence of similar mistakes reoccurring.

What is the key risk?

Contract management activities do not usually abruptly end when the services/goods have been delivered. There is a risk that a number of loose, but important, ends still need to be tied up, and the process which does this is called 'close out'.

It is a significant risk because the parties do not know what is left to be done.

Contract close-out is the most unheralded phase of the procurement process, yet, when performed efficiently and effectively, it can protect the purchaser's interests and free up significant dollars for current-year program priorities.

How to overcome this risk

To get the best out of the close-out process begin preparing for close-out well before contract completion. But first it is important to understand the two types of contract completion:
- *Physical completion*: Contracts are physically complete when contractors have rendered all services and the buyer has accepted all documents, materials, data, and other deliverables. But, often there are a number of issues still to complete.
- *Administrative completion*: Contracts are administratively complete when all administrative activities have been accomplished, releases executed, and final payment made. An incomplete contract file should not be closed: eg: the contract is in litigation/ under appeal or issues are still outstanding.

Close-out procedure: summary

You should have a defined close-out procedure that you follow for each contract. This should be stated in the contract and should be relevant to the goods or services contained in that contract. Some of the typical activities include:

- Verifying physical completion of contract items
- Confirming completion of other term and condition obligations
- Ensuring that continuing obligations are enabled
- Obtaining necessary forms, reports, and clearances
- Resolution of outstanding claims or disputes
- Making or receiving final payment(s)
- A final documenting of the lessons learned

The exact process that you follow will depend on your organizational requirements and contract structure. Whatever the process, ensure that all of the items that are required (which may not include all the ones on the above list, or may include additional items specific to your organization or the contract) have been reviewed and completed before the contract is considered officially closed. See the IACCM library for sample checklists for different relationship types.

34.9 **Continuing obligations**

Before termination, make a thorough review of the contract for areas where either side has ongoing responsibilities, such as protection of data or intellectual property, that may continue after the contract has ended.

Once you are no longer working closely with the other party, how do you protect your data or intellectual property? For example, the contract stipulated that upon completion or termination of the project that the proprietary data that you provided for development and testing purposes is removed from their systems and that any backup media be purged of the data. How will you ensure that it was actually done, or how will you obtain assurances to that effect? Sometimes the contract requires that physical copies be returned, and an affidavit that ephemeral copies (such as software) have been destroyed.

Or a different example: What if a supplier fails to produce the product that the customer designed and developed? If the customer terminates the production contract, what steps are being taken to ensure that all proprietary information, designs, specifications, etc. are returned from the supplier and will not fall into competitors' hands? The Intellectual Property and Confidential Information clauses of the contract should spell this out, and be executed at this time.

Royalties and license fees

Sometimes the end of a project for one group is the beginning of a project or task for a different functional area. Suppose your marketing team has just developed new brand licensing agreements with other suppliers, representing significant additional revenue for your company. As the contracts and marketing team disbands, happy in the knowledge that they have developed a successful brand, the accounting department must determine how they are going to collect and process (or calculate and pay) the license fees that will be generated.

In another example, after a product is accepted a warranty period may start. In some cases a warranty requires no commitment on the customer, but other times the warranty does require action or commitment on the customer's side. Customers should have a process in place so that the company does not invalidate the warranty. For example, a large piece of equipment is warranted against defects for five years as long as it is shut down and routine maintenance performed quarterly. Is that requirement communicated to the production managers, and do they have the machine scheduled for maintenance as required on their production schedules?

Software companies will often introduce product updates, upgrades, and new versions, requiring a company to keep up with its release and patch schedule, or to maintain a small difference parameter (usually called "n-1"), or the software company will not support the product. This may require a great deal of planning to effectively comply with, as user notifications and coordinated scheduling may be necessary to minimize the impact of a new release or patch on the workers. Many companies have lost the right to free upgrades because they have not followed the upgrade pattern or because they failed to pay an annual maintenance fee.

Record retention policies and procedures are governed not only by company policy, but by legal requirements. As a general guideline, financial and property records, supporting data, statistical records or any document relating to an agreement should be retained for a period of three years after submission of the final payment, or three years after disposition of the property, whichever is later. This also applies to subcontractors, who should be required to keep their records at least that long. Some customers may require that records are retained for a longer period, and you may need to highlight this to other departments or operating groups to ensure that they comply with a non-standard requirement.

However, there are exceptions to the above guideline. If any litigation, claim or audit is started before the three-year expiry period, as a rule the records must be retained until all litigation, claims or audit findings have been resolved. You must keep supporting documentation, including approvals to purchase and screening documents, as well as the main documents. Your legal department or risk assessment or audits group may instruct the groups as to special retention requirements when responding to audits or litigation.

34.10 Lessons learned

The contract manager has a duty to record and disseminate key aspects of contract performance. There are a few key questions to continually ask throughout the project and for which the answers should be recorded. What worked well? What didn't? What changes are recommended for next time? How might problems be avoided or resolved more quickly? What did we learn about this customer/supplier, industry, or type of project that might affect future terms and conditions?

As the project progresses, have a methodology to capture lessons as they occur. Encourage people to record their lessons and suggestions for future improvement. If you capture the information as the project progresses, you will capture more and better data than trying to mine people's memories after the fact. If the change is suggested to contract language, sometimes you can incorporate that into standard language templates so that it will be automatically used on future agreements.

A best practice is to gather the project team together for a final close-out and lessons learned and review session at the end of the project. You need to do this before the participants move on to other projects and are difficult to get together again, and while the activities are fresh in people's minds. You might find out what about the drafting and negotiation process worked well, and where they think something could be improved.

It can be difficult for a contracts person to do this, because your participation tends to occur at the beginning of the relationship, when the contract is drafted. If it is possible to remain in communication with the production teams or customer, or otherwise to review the contract's applicability and effect on a regular basis, you can try to do this. Some companies assign a contracts person to remain key to the contract, which means you will be contacted about extensions, amendments, and other changes. These could be opportune times to learn what is working well and what needs to change, and why.

One more key area regarding lessons learned is that they have to be filed in a manner that allows people easy access to them and are organized in a manner that provides value. Just dumping a bunch of ideas on a flip chart and filing it behind your door, or compiling a pile of text documents that are not classified in any manner are not effective ways to collect and pass on knowledge. A thoughtful and organized process will allow people to find the information they require and to use the lessons of past experience. There are many tools for this; find the one that works for your environment. Some use shared databases, or have periodic 'lessons learned' articles in newsletters or conference calls when these can be discussed. Other groups use discussion boards and email lists to raise issues and ask for suggestions to resolve them. If you think that something may be an effective method for your company and it is not in use, find out who to approach to suggest it.

34.11 Summary

A contract may end for a variety of reasons, including expiration of term, voluntary termination by one or both parties, or an unresolved dispute. Closures can be cumbersome and usually highlight the interfaces between contract managers and finance and legal as payment, financial instruments and claims may be involved. Some level of continuing obligation even after formal termination may need to be addressed.

The manner in which a contract ends is as important as to how it starts. The parties should have a defined close-out procedure that takes into consideration:

- Physical completion of contract items have been verified
- Obligations defined in the contract have been completed
- Continuing obligations are enabled
- Necessary forms, reports, and clearances have been obtained
- Final payment(s) have been made and accounts reconciled
- Lessons learned have been documented

Annex A Glossary

Acceptance criteria: these are the criteria to determine that the business objectives have been met, and that the requirements have been delivered.

Activity-Based Costing (ABC): provides an understanding of the true and complete cost of an activity by allocating overheads to products and services, moving overhead into direct cost based on an appropriate allocation of the overhead in relation to the proportion relevant to the specific product or service.

Alternative dispute resolution: ADR. It is generally classified into at least five types: negotiation, mediation, collaborative law, arbitration and conciliation. ADR is an alternative to a formal court hearing or litigation.

BATNA: 'best alternative to a negotiated agreement'

Battle of the forms: refers to the debate over whose form, contract, document, format, etc. that the contract will ultimately end up using. It comes from corporations pushing their form over the other sides, for various reasons.

Bid phase: the second phase in the contract management lifecycle. This phase explores the bidding and proposal activities undertaken by each party to determine the extent of the 'fit' between needs and capabilities. It examines the financial aspects of the proposed relationship and highlights the legal and regulatory issues surrounding bid and proposal activity.

Boilerplate: standard legal language (the small print) used by many companies, organizations or standard-setting bodies to simplify their contracting procedures. Boilerplate clauses are drawn from the long legal experience of large firms, and normally cannot be negotiated by the client or customer.

Break-even analysis: explores the return in terms of that point in time when revenues from the investment equal the amount of the investment. This is the break-even point.

Change control process: a change control process defines how changes are to be managed throughout the project and contract lifecycles. It should identify the stages through which a requested change will pass. It should document: the change description; justification for the change; impact of the change; acceptance of the change; implementation of the change; verification of the change.

Civil law: a system of laws based on written legal code that govern disputes between individuals. Civil law is applied to issues involving property and contracts, as opposed to criminal acts.

[Source: The American Heritage® Dictionary of Business Terms Copyright © 2010 by Houghton Mifflin Harcourt Publishing Company.]

Collaborative negotiation strategy: this strategy is based on a win-win premise and has gained wider acceptance as companies enter into increasingly interdependent relationships

Commercial management: 'commercial' is often used to describe activities that are non-technical and can therefore embrace areas such as sales, marketing and business operations. Our definition embraces only those areas that are of direct relevance to the structuring, content and performance of the contract. We see the role of a 'commercial manager' or of the 'commercial process' to ensure that all relevant stakeholder views have been incorporated and evaluated, to ensure that the needs (of the customer) and capabilities (of the supplier) have been aligned. In this sense, we view the contract as a tool to undertake and oversee 'commercial assurance' of a deal or relationship and this may be from either a customer or supplier perspective.

Common law: common law is a body of legal rules that have been made by judges as they issue rulings on cases, as opposed to rules and laws made by the legislature or in official statutes.

Competitive analysis: gaining an understanding of the competitive positioning of individual companies within the market.

Competitive negotiation strategy: the competitive strategy is based on the win-lose premise that in order to win the other side must lose.

Consortium: an alliance between companies by which, in tendering for a project, they make clear to the customer that it is their desire to work together, and that their tenders have been coordinated on that basis. A consortium has limited and entire scope, stands behind its own work and participants' work, has direct control of its own scope, and has less control over participants' scope.

Contract change: when the contract is negotiated and signed, the complete requirements of the final contract documentation represent the agreed position between the parties – the customer and the supplier. Once the contract document is signed, any alterations, enhancements, deletions or substitutions are, therefore, changes.

Contract close-out: the process that confirms the contract is officially terminated by performance and that there are no uncompleted legal obligations of either the customer or the supplier. Close-out assures that the correct payment is made to the supplier, the correct deliverables are received by the customer stakeholders, and administrative and fiscal obligations have been performed including disposition of property and assets.

Contract clause: a provision included in a written agreement or contract. A contract clause will address an aspect of the contract between parties, detailing the agreement to ensure all parties understand what is expected of the other.

Contract claim: a supplier can initiate a *contract claim* for a variety of reasons: the customer's failure to meet responsibilities, or having to do more work than agreed to, incurring more cost or having the program changed by the customer outside the formal change control process.

Contract management: the planning, monitoring and control of all aspects of the contract and the motivation of all those involved in it to achieve the contract objectives on time and to the specified cost, quality and performance..

Contract or Commercial Manager: the role assigned to contract management activities. These terms should be taken as indicating the performance of particular contract-related tasks, irrespective of who is actually performing them.

Contract owner: a specific individual – identified either by name or by title – who has ultimate responsibility to ensure the implementation and oversight of the contract and successful delivery of its expected deliverables or outcomes.

Contracting process: a high-performing business process through which successful contracts and trading relationships are formed and managed. Differences in the process will result from the types of contract or relationship that a business wishes to enable; for example, high volume commodities demand a fundamentally different model from complex services or major, long-term projects. The list of tasks remains consistent; the difference is over who performs those tasks, how they are performed, and the time it takes to reach completion.

Cost/benefit analysis: this analysis consists of three steps:
1. Calculate the investment cost
2. Project the savings or additional revenue
3. Determine return on investment (ROI) from the cash flows

Step 1, investment costs, can be thought of as the costs associated with completing the project. Step 2, expense savings, can be thought of as the day-to-day operational costs of the business function that is affected by the project. Expense savings are the benefit side of a cost / benefit analysis. Step 3, the ROI, shows whether the project is worthwhile given the projected expense savings.

CSF: Critical success factor

Deliverable: a specific and defined obligation within the contract to deliver a particular item, which may be tangible (e.g. a manual, a product), or intangible (e.g. an idea or a service). 'The Deliverables' lie at the heart of most contracts.

Development phase: the third phase in the contract management lifecycle. This phase is dedicated to the development of an appropriate form of contract and the considerations and issues that most frequently require attention. It provides a framework that should enable better understanding of the risks associated with the specific relationship that is being evaluated and also provides a base for negotiation planning.

Dispute: in contract management a dispute is an unresolved issue between contracting parties: the customer as the principal and the supplier as the provider of goods and services.

Dispute resolution: the method by which the parties to an agreement will reach resolution on disagreements. The dispute resolution process may involve a series of steps through which escalation of the dispute will occur. These may include internal forums (for example, executive management within each company) as well as external methods, such as Mediation, Arbitration or Litigation.

Due Diligence: generally, due diligence refers to the care a reasonable person should take before entering into an agreement or a transaction with another party.

e-auctions: electronic auctions (or reverse electronic auctions as they are sometimes called) are on-line auctions where selected bidders submit offers electronically against the purchaser's specification.

ERP: enterprise resource planning

Equity Joint Venture: an Equity Joint Venture entity has a separate identity and autonomy in pursuing strategic business opportunities. The investors typically have allocated degrees of:
- Ownership (this can vary from under 50 percent - non-controlling - to 70 percent or more - complete control)
- Operational responsibilities
- Financial risks and rewards

Final acceptance: applies when the contract is a project with milestones to be met. The last milestone may be final acceptance, or there may be a review and final acceptance after the last milestone is reached. It can occur at three distinct levels: unconditional acceptance, partial acceptance and total rejection.

Financial model: financial modeling usually refers to cash flow forecasting, which involves the creation of detailed models, which are used for strategic decision making.

Force majeure: can be translated as a 'superior force' or 'act of God'. When incorporated into a contract it usually provides that if a party does not perform an obligation under the contract (for example, provision of services) for reasons outside that party's control (such as a natural disaster or the outbreak of war), the other party will not make that party liable for non-performance.

Green Team review: the Green Team review enables the pursuit team to gain an outside perspective on removing roadblocks, filling in missing information and finding new areas of advantage. Green Team members are selected from outside the pursuit team, representing various areas of the organization. They are selected for their ability to work in a creative environment and to propose 'out of the box' ideas. They bring their expertise, networks, and organizational knowledge to bear on the problems and solutions proposed by the pursuit team. (See also *Red Team review.)*

Incoterms 2000: International Commercial Terms (Incoterms) evolved by International Chamber of Commerce (ICC), Paris. Incoterms 2000 are the standard trade definitions most commonly used in international contracts.

Initiate phase: the first phase in the contract management lifecycle. This phase is devoted to ensuring understanding of markets and their interaction with business needs and goals. It explains the importance of aligning these factors with contract structures, terms, policies and practices, to increase the probability of successful trading relationships and the overall efficiency of the contracting process. Without such alignment, contracts rapidly become viewed as an impediment to doing business.

IPR: Intellectual Property Rights

Intellectual property (IP): includes inventions, patents, computer programs, product and service names, technical and business information, logos, artwork, geographic indication of source, industrial design, etc.

Internal rate of return (IRR): an IRR calculation forecasts the rate of return offered by an investment project over its useful life and is sometimes called the *yield on project*. It is estimated by finding the discount rate that equates the present value of a project's cash outflow with the present value of its cash inflow. The calculation results in finding the discount rate that will cause the net present value of a project to be equal to zero.

ICCPM: International Centre for Complex Project Management

JAD: Joint Application Development

Joint venture: a cooperative business activity between two or more separate organizations for strategic purposes. These organizations can be privately owned companies, government agencies or other existing joint ventures. The joint venture may be implemented solely through contractual agreements to engage in cooperative or joint activities. In the marketing context, these are usually called 'Teaming Agreements' while in the development context they are more commonly termed 'Joint or Cooperative Development Agreements'. A true joint venture is implemented through a new entity in which a company and other parties make an equity (ownership right) investment.

KPI: key performance indicator

Last gap: in a negotiation the *last gap* is the last step necessary to reach an agreement between the negotiating parties.

Lessons learned: a process for capturing and documenting key questions to continually ask throughout the life of the contract and the answers, such as "What went well?" and "How could that aspect have been managed better?" An effective process will allow people to find the information they require and to use the lessons of past experience.

Letter of Intent: is generally an agreement to agree. It outlines the terms between parties who have not formalized an agreement into a contract. Letters of Intent are generally not binding and unenforceable; they should be used with caution. Such letters indicate an intention to do something at a later date.

Manage phase: the final phase in the contract management lifecycle. This phase examines the approaches needed to ensure successful implementation and management of the signed agreement. Many contracts span multiple years and it is frequently the case that they undergo major changes and, potentially, fundamental renegotiations. It is this phase that determines whether or not the results or outcomes envisaged at the time of contract signature are in fact achieved – or perhaps even exceeded.

Market segmentation: the process of splitting customers, or potential customers, in a market into different groups, or segments, within which customers will respond similarly to a marketing action. Market segmentation enables companies to target different categories of customers who perceive the full value of certain products and services differently from one another.

Master Agreement: is a contract reached between parties, in which the parties agree to most of the terms that will govern future transactions or future agreements. A master agreement permits the parties to quickly negotiate future transactions or agreements, because they can rely on the terms of the master agreement, so that the same terms need not be repetitively negotiated, and to negotiate only the deal-specific terms.

Memorandum Of Understanding (MOU): a written document executed by certain parties which establishes intentions, policies or procedures of mutual concern. It does not require either party to obligate funds and does not create a legally binding commitment.

Monte Carlo simulations: problem solving technique used to approximate the probability of certain outcomes by running multiple trial runs, called simulations, using random variables.

Negotiation phase: the fourth phase in the contract management lifecycle. This phase provides an in-depth guide to negotiation of a contract. It recognizes that a growing number of negotiations are today 'virtual', using technology as an alternative to face-to-face meetings. It also highlights many of the issues and challenges that contract negotiators tend to encounter, both within their own organization and with the behavior or attitudes of the other side.

NPV: Net Present Value: the difference between the present value of cash inflows and the present value of cash outflows. NPV is used in capital budgeting to analyze the profitability of an investment or project.

NDA: non-disclosure agreement. A signed formal agreement in which one party agrees to give a second party confidential information about its business or products and the second party agrees not to share this information with anyone else for a specified period of time.

Opportunity cost: represents the potential impact of options not chosen when an investment decision is made. Opportunity costs usually represent soft, less-quantifiable costs, and can only be based on forecasting and analysis.

Options evaluation: a method whereby the possible options generated by the team can be assessed to identify the option or group of options most likely to meet the business requirements.

Outcome: the term used to describe the totality of what the contract is set up to deliver. For example, this could be an installed computer system with trained staff to use it, backed up by new working practices and documentation; a refurbished and equipped building with all the staff moved in and working; or the provision of repair and maintenance services that ensure high levels of product or service availability, compliance with safety regulations and on-going cost reductions.

PLM: product lifecycle management

POC: (single) point of contact

Positional negotiation: the positional style tends to lead to what are termed win-lose results and correlates to a competitive negotiation strategy.

Prime contractor: has entire scope, stands behind its own work and subcontractors' work, has direct control of its own scope, and has contract control over subcontractors' scope.

Principled negotiation: the principled negotiation style leads to win-win results. It is employed when a negotiator is serious about finding a mutually acceptable solution and correlates to a collaborative negotiation strategy.

Procurement: the combined activities of acquiring services or goods, including ordering, arranging payment, obtaining transportation, inspection, storage, and disposal.
[Source: The American Heritage® Dictionary of Business Terms Copyright © 2010 by Houghton Mifflin Harcourt Publishing Company.]

Procurement contracts: contracts of sale where an offer to buy or sell goods is made by acceptance of the offer and where the supplier transfers, or agrees to transfer, the property in goods to the buyer, for a money consideration called the price. The definition of the term 'goods' may vary according to the law enacted for the territory.

Quick win: a cost reduction opportunity that can be fully implemented within twelve months and has no detrimental impact upon the medium and long-term strategies within the Commodity/Category plans.

RACI model: an approach for defining levels of stakeholder involvement, assessed as**:**
- **R** - Who is responsible
- **A** - Who is accountable
- **C** - Who needs to be consulted
- **I** - Who needs to be informed

Red Team review: the Red Team performs an independent review and assessment from the customer's perspective, based on the completed RFP. The Red Team comprises senior departmental managers who read the entire proposal or specific sections with the aim of ensuring the proposal complies with the requirements of the RFP, is clear and consistent and addresses the key win themes throughout, while identifying any risks to the supplier or the purchaser. (See also *Green Team review.*)

Request for Information: RFI: the customer has little information about the solution and needs to explore an idea or get information from suppliers about how they would solve the customer's needs.

Request for Proposal: RFP: used to solicit proposals from suppliers where the customer has strong and well thought out business requirements.

Request for Quotation: RFQ: the customer has precise information about purchase (usually a commodity item), there is little variation in the product and the customer is primarily interested in the best price on the best terms.

RGS: Requirements gathering session

ROI: Return on investment

RFx: [a combination of] any of the following – RFI, RFQ, RFP

Risk register: a risk register catalogs individual risks, gives information about the threat they pose and how they are to be managed, and provides updates on the impact of the risk.

Service Level Agreement (SLA) is a comprehensive tool [document] to monitor and manage supplier performance for the provision or receipt of the services provided. The SLA typically identifies the fixed measurements for the delivery of the services and spells out measurements for performance and consequences for failure. It must include:
- Levels of required performance
- Consequences for failure to reach or maintain these levels
- Descriptions of the parties' roles and responsibilities in achieving the performance levels

SMART objectives: Specific, Measurable, Actionable, Relevant and Time-bound

STEEP: Sociological, Technological, Economic, Environmental and Political factors

SOO: Statement of Objectives (SOO)

Statement of Work (SOW): is a document describing the essential and technical requirements for items, materials, or services, including the standards that will be used to determine whether the requirements have been met. A Statement of Work may be simple or complex, flexible or definitive, depending on what it describes

A **subcontractor** has limited scope, stands behind its own work, and has direct control of its own scope.

Sweep clause: the intention of a Sweep clause is to make sure the customer did not miss something that the supplier would claim was not in scope, then demand additional compensations to perform the work that was implied. A balanced Sweep clause is one that includes services related to the RFP services that were being provided by the previous supplier just before contract signing.

SWOT: Strengths, Weaknesses, Opportunities and Threats analysis

Termination: ending the contractual relationship before its natural, or originally anticipated, end date. Termination may be for convenience, where the parties agree to part ways or end the contract mutually; or for cause, where there is a breach of the agreement.

Terms and conditions: a *term* is a part of the contract that addresses a specific subject. Contract clauses contain terms. A *condition* is a phrase that either activates or suspends a term. A condition that activates a term is called a condition precedent. A condition that suspends a term is called a condition subsequent.

A *condition* is a phrase that either activates or suspends a term. A condition that activates a term is called a condition precedent. A condition that suspends a term is called a condition subsequent.

Terms Audit: a review of contract terms to ensure that terms align with business objectives, market or business needs and priorities, resource capabilities and commitments, business processes (and opportunities for their improvement), and risk assumptions

TCO: total cost of ownership. TCO calculations can include the obvious: purchase cost, implementation costs, maintenance and support costs. Thorough cost of ownership analysis embodies a cradle-to-grave view of costs: from resources required to develop the business case, draft the Request For Proposals (RFP) and manage the bid process, through to decommissioning and disposal of the asset.

TUPE: Transfer of Undertakings (Protection of Employment) Regulations 2006, which regulates the transfer of staff from one employer to another.

Turnkey project/contract: the term 'turnkey' in business terminology means that the buyer needs only to turn the 'key' to the system [or facility] and it will work. Integral parts of a contract to buy a turnkey system [or facility] of any type are the terms and conditions for the acceptance of the system [or facility] and when/how payments will be made. The contract must define what it means for the system [or facility] to work, and what is expected of the system [or facility], so that the buyer can accept the system [or facility] and the supplier can be paid/recognize revenue.

UCITA: Uniform Computer Information Transactions Act (US legislation).

UNCISG: UN Convention on Contracts for the International Sale of Goods. Applies when trading internationally - the CISG applies to seventy-six nations, including most of the major trading nations.

Underpinning contract: a contract with an external supplier covering delivery of goods or services that support the performance of the Master Agreement or contract.

UCC: Uniform Commercial Code. Applies when trading within the US.

Vested outsourcing: an outsourcing relationship where companies and service providers become vested in each other's success, creating a true win-win solution.

What-if scenarios: these allow the customer to explore suppliers' reactions to unplanned situations, such as increased throughput, or accelerated implementation requirements.

WTO: World Trade Organization

Annex B IACCM training

Training and certification

IACCM has developed the leading managed learning program for both procurement and sell-side commercial and contract managers. The professional development program is designed to meet the needs of large corporations and government agencies, small to medium enterprises (SMEs) and individuals. More than 4700 people are currently raising their skills and knowledge through IACCM's web-based, cost-effective programs. These programs address:

- **Skills Assessment:** Assessing skills against commercial competencies, identifying development needs against external benchmarks.
- **Managed Learning:** A flexible but structured web-based learning program, designed to educate practitioners in contract management throughout the contract lifecycle.
- **Certification:** An internationally recognized certification in contract and commercial management.

E-Learning Curriculum

The IACCM eLearning portal provides a range of learning modules and relevant resources specifically for contracting professionals.

These resources include links to a wealth of contract management information, tools and templates. IACCM has worked to define robust, web-based curricula supporting the entire contracting lifecycle and the skill and knowledge requirements for both the sales and procurement functions.

The Contract Management lifecycle extends from pre-bid activities, through bid processes, drafting, negotiations and post-award contract management, with modules covering all these areas, as well as topics which run right through the lifecycle, such as risk management and international contracting. Modules run an average of 30 minutes with audio and visuals, and provide up to two hours of instruction when combined with integrated reading materials, case studies and surveys.

IACCM offers programs to suit individuals and corporate teams, and strives to make the learning practical and applicable, through the use of message boards, webcasts and other interactions.

For more information please see www.iaccm.com

Index

A

Acceptance criteria 38, 39, 40, 44, 45, 46, 116,
 159, 179, 305, 328, 332, 334, 352, 373, 381,
 382, 383, 385, 548, 549, 553, 556
Activity-Based Costing 222, 510
ADR (Alternative Dispute Resolution) 210,
 217, 218, 483, 597

B

BATNA (Best Alternative To Negotiated
 Agreement) 417, 436, 437, 455, 464, 465
'Battle of the forms' 197, 293, 296
Bid phase 8, 133, 165, 189, 214, 265, 276, 519,
 554
Boilerplate 23, 57, 123, 130, 210, 261, 318, 367,
 400, 401, 408, 453
'Boilerplate' contract clauses 525
Break-even analysis 71

C

Change control 31, 34, 40, 46, 50, 51, 104, 115,
 130, 157, 278, 281, 283, 359, 386, 499, 502,
 509, 510, 542, 555, 561, 564, 565, 566, 568,
 569, 570, 571, 572, 573, 574, 575, 576, 577,
 582, 584, 585, 600, 601
CISG 195, 196, 197, 198
Civil law 190, 196, 197, 201, 208, 218, 219,
 320, 399, 400, 401, 452
Collaborative negotiation 444, 455

Commercial and contract managers 625
Commercial Management 6, 7
Common law 4, 190, 196, 197, 199, 200, 201,
 211, 217, 218, 319, 320, 401, 452, 453, 523,
 594
Competitive analysis 15, 23, 170, 258
Competitive negotiation 437, 438, 444, 465,
 479, 483, 485
Consortium 85, 90, 91, 92, 93, 94
Contract change 549, 555, 556, 563, 564, 565,
 568, 571, 572
Contract change control 375, 499
Contract claim 561, 572
Contract clause 409, 412, 452, 520, 535, 567
Contract close-out 498, 499, 503, 504, 506,
 549, 603, 604, 605, 610
Contracting process 2, 3, 4, 5, 7, 8, 26, 78, 175,
 186, 221, 461, 501, 521, 534
Contract management 1, 3, 6, 7, 8, 15, 18, 23,
 39, 103, 118, 127, 130, 149, 150, 163, 165,
 168, 173, 178, 182, 183, 184, 214, 229, 230,
 237, 312, 344, 367, 412, 418, 438, 440, 452,
 497, 498, 499, 500, 501, 502, 504, 505, 506,
 507, 508, 509, 510, 511, 512, 522, 527, 528,
 535, 536, 539, 540, 541, 542, 548, 555, 556,
 559, 560, 569, 576, 577, 587, 591, 604, 610,
 625
Contract manager 7, 18, 19, 23, 76, 87, 173,
 203, 205, 213, 214, 215, 250, 263, 301, 306,

328, 343, 344, 347, 354, 359, 413, 460, 497,
498, 499, 500, 501, 502, 503, 504, 505, 506,
507, 509, 510, 511, 512, 515, 516, 520, 521,
522, 523, 525, 527, 529, 532, 534, 535, 539,
540, 541, 544, 545, 546, 547, 548, 549, 552,
553, 554, 555, 556, 557, 558, 559, 560, 562,
564, 565, 568, 571, 575, 577, 581, 585, 588,
589, 591, 595, 596, 599, 602, 613, 614
Contract or Commercial Manager 7
Cost/benefit analysis 68, 74, 75, 76, 221, 223,
223, 276
CSFs (Critical Success Factors) 74, 170, 277,
294, 295, 311

D

Deliverable 46, 67, 103, 104, 106, 116, 117,
158, 159, 179, 180, 255, 263, 281, 284, 302,
304, 310, 314, 315, 322, 326, 328, 358, 371,
376, 377, 382, 383, 385, 499, 501, 503, 504,
506, 510, 528, 529, 542, 543, 545, 548, 549,
552, 553, 556, 562, 563, 581, 605, 609, 610,
616
Development phase 8, 291, 519
Dispute 6, 13, 14, 21, 23, 51, 61, 80, 92, 93,
125, 169, 190, 191, 196, 202, 210, 211, 212,
213, 214, 215, 216, 217, 218, 233, 249, 282,
294, 296, 301, 303, 312, 313, 315, 318, 325,
326, 328, 358, 359, 382, 387, 389, 394, 395,
397, 398, 399, 401, 403, 406, 413, 422, 449,
450, 486, 498, 499, 504, 505, 506, 515, 516,
522, 530, 540, 541, 543, 544, 545, 546, 552,
555, 556, 557, 559, 564, 572, 573, 576, 579,
580, 581, 582, 583, 584, 585, 586, 587, 588,
589, 590, 591, 592, 593, 594, 595, 596, 597,
598, 599, 600, 601, 602, 604, 605, 611, 614
Dispute resolution 96, 106, 189, 192, 196, 199,
211, 212, 213, 215, 216, 217, 218, 354, 366,
394, 397, 502, 503, 579, 586, 587, 588, 589,
590, 595, 596, 597, 598, 601, 602
Due Diligence 185, 275, 282, 284, 290, 484

E

E-auction 18, 418, 476
Equity Joint Ventures 97
ERP (enterprise resource planning) 70, 88,
158, 247, 254

F

Final acceptance 51, 154, 549, 551, 604, 605,
606
Financial model 78, 80, 81, 82, 154, 430
Force majeure 59, 192, 300, 303, 306, 329, 331,
526

G

Green Team 262, 265

I

ICCPM (International Centre for Complex
Project Management) 60
Incoterms 192, 297, 301, 328
Initiate phase 8, 11, 500, 519, 521, 534
IP (Intellectual Property) 15, 16, 17, 18, 65, 84,
95, 112, 113, 119, 122, 124, 155, 198, 204,
205, 209, 211, 278, 298, 313, 326, 327, 336,
346, 347, 348, 361, 364, 377, 397, 499, 504,
522, 563, 603, 610, 611
IPR (Intellectual Property Rights) 205, 301,
335
IRR (Internal Rate of Return) 73, 74, 75, 81,
208

J

JAD (Joint Application Development) 36
Joint venture 3, 85, 86, 94, 95, 96, 97, 191, 207,
212, 271, 298, 313
Joint venture consortium 27

K

KPIs (Key Performance Indicators) 84, 126,
354, 438, 535, 543, 554, 563

L

Last gap 479, 480, 481, 482, 483, 484, 485, 486, 487

Lessons learned 35, 119, 242, 276, 398, 403, 439, 447, 498, 499, 503, 506, 549, 573, 592, 603, 604, 610, 611, 613, 614

Letter of Intent 208, 209, 210

M

Manage phase 8, 497, 498, 519, 528, 555, 559

Market segmentation 15, 19, 20, 258, 368

Master agreement 58, 194, 323, 324, 381, 386, 387, 389

Memorandum Of Understanding 79, 208, 209

Monte Carlo simulation 69, 70, 71

N

NDA (non-disclosure agreement) 165, 167, 206, 327

Negotiation phase 8, 187, 205, 269, 343, 415, 479, 498, 519, 554, 574

NPV (net present value) 73, 74, 81

O

Opportunity costs 224, 279

Options evaluation 161, 162, 163, 237

Outcome 5, 8, 29, 30, 33, 35, 38, 39, 45, 48, 52, 53, 54, 67, 77, 79, 82, 84, 114, 119, 128, 130, 211, 214, 215, 221, 223, 238, 249, 265, 273, 274, 276, 277, 285, 286, 288, 289, 298, 306, 310, 324, 354, 362, 367, 398, 418, 421, 422, 424, 425, 426, 427, 428, 431, 432, 433, 438, 439, 440, 443, 444, 446, 447, 459, 472, 476, 479, 482, 484, 486, 492, 493, 497, 498, 521, 535, 536, 542, 570, 576, 579, 591, 594, 600, 608

Ownership of the contract 509, 527

P

PLM (product lifecycle management) 15, 24, 25

POC

POC (point of contact) 141, 142, 143

Positional negotiation 418

Prime contractor 85, 90, 91, 93, 95, 96, 294, 303, 554

Principled negotiation 417, 443, 444, 446, 447, 448, 450, 451, 455, 456, 489

Procurement 5, 6, 7, 25, 27, 30, 33, 51, 52, 56, 68, 79, 87, 107, 108, 111, 122, 135, 136, 137, 138, 141, 142, 143, 144, 145, 147, 150, 151, 159, 161, 165, 166, 190, 224, 234, 250, 255, 264, 265, 286, 311, 314, 318, 351, 358, 361, 366, 396, 419, 476, 508, 512, 514, 576, 600, 610, 625

Procurement contract 146, 317, 321, 350, 462

Q

Quick win 160, 161, 288

R

RACI 383, 571

Red Team 175, 266

Resolution 592

RFI (Requests For Information) 18, 107, 108, 109, 110, 111, 112, 113, 114, 115, 116, 117, 118, 119, 120, 135, 136, 137, 149, 150, 165, 166, 167, 169, 175, 178, 190, 221, 232, 266, 373, 556, 607

RFP (Request For Proposal) 18, 31, 46, 68, 75, 95, 107, 110, 111, 113, 114, 117, 119, 120, 135, 136, 137, 138, 139, 140, 141, 142, 143, 145, 146, 147, 149, 150, 151, 152, 153, 154, 155, 156, 157, 158, 159, 160, 161, 163, 165, 166, 167, 169, 171, 172, 173, 174, 175, 177, 178, 179, 180, 181, 182, 183, 184, 185, 186, 188, 190, 221, 229, 234, 235, 237, 240, 241, 242, 244, 245, 246, 248, 249, 250, 251, 253, 254, 255, 256, 257, 258, 259, 260, 261, 262, 263, 264, 266, 268, 269, 271, 273, 285, 287, 289, 311, 324, 371, 375, 393, 466, 556, 580, 607

RFQ (Requests For Quotation) 135, 136, 137, 138, 166, 221, 580

RFx 135, 137, 138, 140, 141, 142, 143, 147, 182, 183, 184, 221, 225, 226, 580

RGS (Requirements Gathering Session) 108, 110, 116

Risk register 79, 532, 591

ROI (Return on Investment) 31, 32, 42, 44, 69, 70, 149, 236, 273, 276, 279, 280

S

Sales consortium 85

SLA (Service Level Agreement) 43, 81, 103, 123, 157, 159, 180, 253, 256, 261, 277, 280, 354, 371, 374, 381, 387, 388, 389, 390, 391, 392, 393, 394, 396, 402, 430, 433, 522, 523, 526, 563, 567, 568, 569, 584

SMART objectives 104, 161, 162, 389

SOO (Statement of Objectives) 393

SOW (Statement of Work) 36, 96, 103, 130, 154, 158, 173, 178, 253, 256, 261, 302, 315, 358, 359, 371, 381, 382, 383, 384, 385, 386, 387, 391, 394, 396, 400, 402, 435, 510, 522, 523, 525, 526, 532, 563, 580, 605

STEEP (Sociological, Technological, Economic, Environmental and Political factors) 20, 21

Subcontractor 15, 55, 60, 85, 92, 93, 95, 96, 105, 170, 174, 207, 233, 260, 283, 294, 302, 303, 309, 313, 314, 340, 346, 532, 554, 559, 612

'Sweep' clause 375

SWOT (Strengths, Weaknesses, Opportunities and Threats) 20, 242, 243, 244, 431

T

TCO (Total Cost of Ownership) 68, 117, 221, 277, 278, 345, 350, 372

Termination 5, 19, 81, 82, 84, 90, 93, 96, 98, 99, 100, 128, 130, 139, 204, 208, 213, 270, 281, 299, 300, 301, 302, 324, 327, 330, 331, 332, 340, 343, 344, 345, 355, 359, 360, 361, 365, 366, 481, 483, 498, 503, 504, 506, 526, 564, 592, 603, 607, 608, 609, 611, 614

Terms and conditions 3, 13, 14, 15, 18, 24, 26, 27, 31, 42, 54, 59, 68, 78, 88, 96, 107, 109, 110, 113, 121, 125, 131, 137, 150, 154, 157, 160, 166, 173, 174, 181, 189, 190, 194, 198, 199, 201, 203, 207, 232, 235, 243, 249, 253, 256, 262, 277, 280, 281, 283, 285, 300, 301, 305, 306, 309, 313, 316, 317, 329, 335, 339, 342, 344, 345, 346, 347, 349, 350, 351, 358, 363, 364, 367, 368, 380, 381, 387, 396, 397, 398, 399, 409, 413, 419, 446, 453, 500, 501, 502, 503, 508, 512, 520, 521, 522, 523, 525, 528, 535, 541, 549, 552, 553, 562, 572, 590, 613

Terms audit 121, 123, 126, 127, 128, 129, 130, 131, 366, 367

TUPE 309, 361

Turnkey 87, 91, 280, 293, 295, 308, 313, 314, 315, 316, 406

U

UCC (Uniform Commercial Code) 190, 196, 197, 198, 199, 204, 210, 296, 318, 399, 400

UCITA (Uniform Computer Information Transactions Act) 335, 336

UNCISG (United Nations Convention on Contracts for the International Sale of Goods) 189, 190, 195, 198, 199, 296

V

Vested Outsourcing 371

W

What-if scenarios 284

WTO (World Trade Organization) 215

Other publications by Van Haren Publishing

Van Haren Publishing (VHP) specializes in titles on Best Practices, methods and standards within four domains:
- IT and IT Management
- Architecture (Enterprise and IT)
- Business Management and
- Project Management

Van Haren Publishing offers a wide collection of whitepapers, templates, free e-books, trainer materials etc. in the **Van Haren Publishing Knowledge Base**: www.vanharen.net for more details.

Van Haren Publishing is also publishing on behalf of leading organizations and companies: ASLBiSL Foundation, CA, Centre Henri Tudor, Gaming Works, IACCM, IAOP, IPMA-NL, ITSqc, NAF, Ngi, PMI-NL, PON, The Open Group, The SOX Institute.

Topics are (per domain):

IT and IT Management	Architecture (Enterprise and IT)	Project, Program and Risk Management
ABC of ICT	ArchiMate®	A4-Projectmanagement
ASL®	GEA®	ICB / NCB
CATS CM®	Novius Architectuur Methode	ISO 21500
CMMI®	TOGAF®	MINCE®
CoBIT		M_o_R®
e-CF	**Business Management**	MSP™
Frameworx	BiSL®	P3O®
ISO 17799	EFQM	*PMBOK® Guide*
ISO 27001/27002	eSCM	PRINCE2®
ISO 27002	IACCM	
ISO/IEC 20000	ISA-95	
ISPL	ISO 9000/9001	
IT Service CMM	OPBOK	
ITIL®	SAP	
MOF	SixSigma	
MSF	SOX	
SABSA	SqEME®	

For the latest information on VHP publications, visit our website: www.vanharen.net.